By Darrell McBreairty

Alcatraz Eel: The John Stadig Files (2005)
Allagash Summers: The Philip Calvin Hughey Sr. Photographs (2010)
At A'nt Ev's (1977)
Cancelled Dreams and Other Works (1987)
Cancelled Dreams (2014)
Conversations with A'nt Ev': An Oral History of the Allagash (1982)
Diaries (1978)
Lamentation in Two Parts (2000)
Seasons (2007, 2014)
The Passing of Martha O'Shea (2001, 2014)
Tommy (2014)
Voices (1979)

THE KELLYS OF KINGSCLEAR

Darrell McBreairty

Copyright © 2015 by Darrell McBreairty

Darrell McBreairty
33 Walker Brook Road
Allagash, Maine 04774
USA
dmcbreairty@yahoo.com

All Rights Reserved. No part of this book may be used or reproduced in any form or by any electronic or mechanical means including informational storage or retrieval systems without written permission from the author except in the case of brief quotations embodied in critical articles and reviews. All violations of copyrights will be pursued to the full extent of the law.

ISBN 0-9765743-3-0

Limited to a print run of one thousand copies.

McBreairty, Darrell 1949 —

The Land Grant Map (No. 125), included in the photographs and utilized for the cover, used with permission from the New Brunswick Department of Natural Resources, Fredericton, New Brunswick, Canada.

For Eva (Kelly) McBreairty, known as Aunt Ev' to everyone in Allagash, Maine. Her stories brought her family and community back to life for a child desperately in need of acceptance and unqualified love. Although I was not officially her grandson, she loved me very much. Without her, my life would have been very different, and my search for the history of our family back to Eastern Canada, Colonial America and Ireland would never have happened.

"It is funny, but it strikes me that a person without anecdotes that they nurse while they live, and that survive them, are more likely to be utterly lost not only to history but the family following them. Of course this is the fate of most souls, reducing entire lives, no matter how vivid and wonderful, to those sad black names on withering family trees, with half a date dangling after and a question mark."

Sebastian Barry: *The Secret Scripture* (New York, New York: Viking, 2008).

Research from a number of online sources establishes that the Kellys, Kelleys or O'Kellys of Uí Maine were the most important sept of the family in Ireland; although, the name originated independently as O'Kelly or Kelly in Counties Atrim, Derry, Galway, Laois, Meath, Roscommon, Sligo and Wicklow as well as MacKelly in Connaught Province. Ceallach was the ancestor of the various Kelly septs. The Kelly family motto "Turris Fortis Mihi Deus" translates as "God is a strong tower to me."

A table containing the Irish Birth Indexes of 1890, appearing in *Irish Genealogy: A Record Finder*, edited by Donal F. Begley, states that the Kelly name is found "in every County in Ireland — chiefly, however, in Dublin, Galway, Mayo, Roscommon, and Cork." (p. 215)

Wilbur C. Abbott (*New York in the American Revolution*) writes in regard to the Loyalists,

> The inexorable logic of events proved that they were wrong — for did they not lose the fight? Yet a more generous attitude might now be taken; for they, too, were Americans, and it would seem that they were surely as much entitled to that slender compliment of recollection as the leaders of the Confederacy. (p. 146)

Abbott continues,

> These "Tories" naturally incurred the bitter hatred of the revolutionary party while they were alive, and the vilification of patriot historians when they were dead, as traitors to their country. . . . It was *their* country, no less than that of their opponents; they wished to keep it what it was; and they conceived they had at least as great a right to take up arms to maintain the government as their antagonists had to take arms against it. (pp. 211-212)

PREFACE

The search for John Kelly began in my branch of the family with my Aunt Edith (McBreairty) Kelley (22 October 1923 – 14 April 2008), who wrote a few papers in high school on the Kelly family and started composing family charts from information she collected from her mother, Eunice (Kelly) McBreairty (10 August 1886 – 15 April 1975), as well as other elderly family members.

I am descendent from Thomas and Eunice (Kelly) McBreairty, whose daughter, Margaret "Maggie" (McBreairty) McBreairty Hughey (22 May 1906 – 29 October 1998), was the mother of my mother Hope Eileen (McBreairty) McBreairty (12 June 1932 – 19 December 2010). Eunice (Kelly) McBreairty was the daughter of Charles and Sarah Ann (Mullins) Kelly. Although I was born out of wedlock, I am also the grandson of Charles (31 July 1881 – 16 June 1960) and Stella (Sirois) (21 May 1888 – 29 November 1983) Kelly. Charles Kelly was the son of James and Josephine (Hunnewell) Kelly. So I am descendent from both James and Charles Kelly, who were the sons of William and Sarah Ann (Howard) Kelly.

My mother married Theron William McBreairty (20 August 1908 – 12 April 1992), son of Albert and Eva "Ev" (Kelly) McBreairty, on 1 November 1952. As a child, I would sit at the old Albert McBreairty Sr. homestead in Allagash, Maine, by the Empire State woodstove on long winter evenings listening to family stories told by Aunt Eva "Ev" (Kelly) McBreairty (30 March 1877 – 23 June 1974) when she babysat my sister Nola, my brother Carter and me.

When I grew older, Aunt Edith and I worked together scouring church and town records, searching for forgotten family ties. Edith, along with my mother and my Aunt Eva (McBreairty) Jackson (13 September 1917 – 2 September 2007), made at least one trip down to Fredericton and Saint John, New Brunswick, combing through archives and trying to track down anyone connected to the family.

William Kelly (15 March 1869 – 11 July 1954), Eva "Ev'" (Kelly) McBreairty's brother, had kept in contact with cousins in Upper Kingsclear, New Brunswick, for many years, but his health failed toward the end of his life, and by the time he died, we had lost complete contact.

In the 1970s, I spent a week in Saint John, New Brunswick, combing through microfilm and documents at the Archives of the New Brunswick Museum. Then again in 1977, while attending the Maritime Writers' Workshop in Fredericton, I spent as much time as I could researching the Loyalists.

After exhausting much of the documentation in official New Brunswick records and from tombstones strung out across the province, I started collecting books on the history of New Brunswick.

Once it was established that the Kellys were descendent from Loyalists, I gathered Loyalist material wherever I traveled. After an exhaustive search along 4th Avenue and through the stacks at the Strand, Argosy and Gotham bookstores in New York City and in the Brattle Book Shop in Boston, I gave up trying to locate a copy of Sabine's

Biographical Sketches of Loyalists of the American Revolution; but, one day in Francis O'Brien's bookstore in Portland, Maine, when I mentioned my Loyalist ties, Francis O'Brien disappeared into the extensive collection crammed inside the rooms of his house and reappeared with a signed copy of Sabine's double-volume set. When I expressed to Mr. O'Brien that finances prohibited me from purchasing the books, he generously offered to hold them until I could pay for them. I put down an initial payment, and after a few months the Sabine was mine.

Over the years, my cousin Timothy Hughes got involved in the Kelly genealogy. His work became invaluable. Then others took an interest: Drinda McBreairty, Mary Beth (O'Leary) Jackson, Donald "Allen" Jackson, Ethel (McBreairty) Brown Falcone and Carol (Pelletier) Pelletier. Then Ethel (McBreairty) Brown Falcone connected with our cousin Linda (Kitchen) Aitken in Upper Kingsclear, New Brunswick.

Linda spearheaded a Kelly family reunion on 20 July 2003 in Upper Kingsclear that helped re-establish a firm connection between the Kellys of the Upper St. John River Valley and members of the family in the Kingsclear-Fredericton area. Linda's assistance in tracking down information has helped immensely in rounding out the story of John Kelly and his descendants. Her familiarity with the Kingsclear area and the surrounding towns has been of tremendous help, and her hours of research at the Provincial Archives of New Brunswick have proven invaluable. Without her help, this book would definitely have been lacking.

Without Roger Mark "Mark" Smith's generosity and diligence, this work would be much less comprehensive. He was instrumental in finding, through Velma Maude (Harrison) Kelly, our cousin Jeannie Belinda (Boulter) Matthews, who has been so generous in supplying a wealth of family photographs and anecdotes gathered by her mother, Ella Rita (Kelly) Boulter (14 October 1914 – 25 May 1988). Jeannie Belinda (Boulter) Matthews was instrumental, in a telephone conversation of 29 April 2015, of obtaining from Velma Maude (Harrison) Kelly permission for me to publish photographs from her collection. This conversation is documented in a 29 April 2015 email from Jeannie.

Our cousin Kathryn (Kelly) Rioux was of immense help in gathering information on the family of James Allen and Margaret (Mauzerolle/Mazerolle/Mazerall) Kelly.

In a telephone conversation of 9 July 2015, Nora (Sturgeon) Kelley granted me permission to use the Pascal Sirois memorial card and the photograph of John Hunnewell from her collection.

Timothy Lunney, from the Howard side of the family, and Chad Pelletier contributed to a more comprehensive assessment of the Howard genealogy. Chad Pelletier also granted me permission to use his tintype of Frederick Howard and the ambrotype of Frederick Howard's mother.

Heather Lyons (DGS/MSG) at the Provincial Archives of New Brunswick (and, yet, another cousin) helped track down documentation for marriages and assisted me in acquiring publications from the PANB that proved invaluable.

John Beishlag, another cousin, has done extensive work on the Howard family. His "no nonsense" professionalism has kept me on track. I am very grateful for his permission to extrapolate from his research.

Just when we thought we had puzzled all the connections out fairly well, the Internet exploded into our lives, but, after the initial excitement subsided and obscure information was gathered, I started to notice that misinformation and much confusion got into the mix. Since Kelly is one of the most common of Irish surnames and John Kelly is nearly as ubiquitous, it is very easy to confuse one John Kelly with another. It takes a stronger individual than any I know to convince Ancestery.com that they need to correct their records.

In our family, the name Kelly has also been spelled as K-e-l-l-e-y, this was especially so with the children of Charles and Stella (Sirois) Kelly. In this instance the spelling appears to be the result of the town clerk in St. Francis, Maine, taking the liberty of adding an "e." When these Kelly men went into the American military, they were required to write their name as it was recorded. In this work, I have chosen to retain the spelling of K-e-l-l-y even though either spelling appears in all the records. I do retain the spelling exactly as it appears in quoted material.

I would like to thank Eileen Perkins and the team at Genealogical Publishing Company, Inc., Baltimore Maryland, along with the next of kin of Murtie June Clark, for granting me written permission, in an email of 7 November 2012, to quote from Murtie June Clark's *Loyalists of the Southern Campaign of the Revolutionary War*, Copyright 1981 by Genealogical Publishing Co., Inc., Baltimore, Maryland. I would also, once again, like to thank Eileen Perkins and the team at Genealogical Publishing Company, Inc., Baltimore Maryland, for granting me, in an email of 11 April 2013, written permission to quote from Harriet Stryker-Rodda's *Understanding Colonial Handwriting*, Copyright 1986 by Harriet Stryker-Rodda.

I wish to thank J.D. Lewis for granting written permission to quote from his website *The American Revolution in South Carolina* (*www.carolana.com/SC/Revolution/home.html*) in a letter dated 17 September 2013.

Anne (Sirois) Chamberland, Library Assistant II at the Acadian Archives/Archives acadiennes at the University of Maine at Fort Kent, Maine, provided digital copies of material from *Collections of the New Brunswick Historical Society*.

Running into obstacles in regard to long out-of-print books that have become too expensive to purchase and are not readily available online, Sofia Lorraine (Johnson) Birden, Associate Director at the University of Maine at Fort Kent (UMFK) Blake Library, proved invaluable in locating PDFs of some of these books. Debra A. Durkin, Library Assistant II at UMFK's Blake Library, worked diligently to facilitate inter-library loans of books that, despite the expense, I ended up purchasing because they could not be accessed except at the host libraries. Ms. Durkin's assistance in utilizing the Inter-Library Loan program for acquiring microfilm from the Provincial Archives of New Brunswick proved invaluable, and her counterpart at the Provincial Archives of New Brunswick, Robert Gilmore (DGS/MSG), who took the time to answer every question I had about confusing or illegible words and names in the many land grant peititions and land grants I transcribed, was a godsend.

Roger Drummond, as well as other members of the staff at the Provincial Archives of New Brunswick, was of immense help in assisting me in locating material in the final stages of compiling this work.

Mary-Ellen Badeau, Archivist in Cartographic Records and Aboriginal Research at the Provincial Archives of New Brunswick, was of great assistance in helping track down land grant maps and connecting me with the people at the New Brunswick Department of Natural Resources.

Permission was granted from the New Brunswick Department of Natural Resources in an email of 21 October 2013 from James Dickie, BScF, Research & Mapping Officer at the Department of Natural Resources in Fredericton, New Brunswick, to use Land Grant Map No. 125 appearing on the cover. Stella Chiasson, also at the Department of Natural Resources in Fredericton, New Brunswick, was of great assistance.

Julia Thompson, Photograph Archivist at the Provincial Archives of New Brunswick, assisted me in getting permission to use the photograph of Margery "Mysie" MacDonald (PANB Assorted Acquisitions: P37-292). Permission was granted in an email from Julia Thompson on 16 June 2015.

Dr. Leah Grandy (PhD, History) Microforms Assistant and Research Desk Assistant at the University of New Brunswick's Harriet Irving Library in Fredericton, New Brunswick, took the time to hunt down, from the vast collection of Loyalist material housed at the library, a paragraph in the Elizabeth Reed Memorial that had been poorly scanned years ago.

I would also like to thank Alexandra Fox, Microforms Assistant at the Harriet Irving Library in Fredericton, New Brunswick, who made a diligent search for information relating to the Leonard Coombes Kelly family.

Amber McAlpine-Mills at the Archives & Research Library of the New Brunswick Museum at Saint John, New Brunswick, spent endless hours researching the Kean and Coombes material housed at the museum. She is a valuable asset to anyone doing research in New Brunswick.

In an email of 26 April 2015, Margaret (Kelly) Hay, daughter of Frederick Warren "Fred" Kelly (1 April 1916 - 1 August 2012) and Mary B. Coburn (24 March 1919 – 13 December 2010), who spent many years researching the Kelly family, gave me permission to quote from her material and to publish photographs from her collection. Frederick Warren "Fred" Kelly was the son of Charles Warren "Warren" Kelly (28 May 1875 – 8 March 1953) and Susie Adelaide (2 August 1894 – 17 October 1983). Charles Warren Kelly was the son of William McKay Kelly (15 October 1849 - 27 September 1926) and Margaret "Maggie" Scott (29 May 1855 – 8 January 1931). William McKay Kelly was the son of Leonard Coombes Kelly (6 December 1810 – 17 April 1899) and Jacobina "Bina" Drummond McKaye/McKay (11 April 1819 – 23 July 1907). Margaret (Kelly) Hay also fact checked sections of the manuscript and suggested corrections.

George H. Hayward, in an email of 22 December 2013, granted me permission to quote from his *Haywards of Sunbury & Carleton Counties, N. B., and Some of Their*

Descendants. Without Mr. Hayward's help in navigating through the tangled lines of the Howard/Hayward genealogy, I would have been totally lost. His knowledge, research and documentation proved invaluable.

The quest to find the maiden name of Loyalist John Kelly's wife Mary has consumed more time than I really want to acknowledge. It included days of research by both Linda (Kitchen) Aitken and Roger Mark "Mark" Smith at the Provincial Archives of New Brunswick. Just when I had decided that Mary (Unknown) Kelly was the daughter of William Cain, Floretta (Wade) Steeves shattered that supposition in an email of 9 February 2015. Her reply to a query posted in *"Loyalist Trails" UELAC Newsletter 2015-06 Feb 8, 2015* establishes that William Cain's daughter Mary was not the wife of Loyalist John Kelly.

My friend Cynthia "Cindy" (Lupton/Gray) Hinton scoured Ancestry.com for pieces of the puzzle that led to other areas of research.

Nancy Henderson, another cousin, did an early reading of the manuscript and suggested revisions that proved invaluable. Another descendant of Loyalist John Kelly, Dr. Terry (Pelletier) Murphy, Professor of English at the University of Maine at Fort Kent, was meticulous in her proofreading of the final draft.

I would like to thank our cousin Katrina (McBreairty) Vaughn for permission to quote from an email she sent me on 12 April 2015.

For those of you not familiar with the spelling rules of the Seventeenth through the early Nineteenth century — when the letter "s" is followed by a second letter "s," the first letter was written as an "f." Names were routinely spelled phonetically, with variations that are often very dissimilar within a given document.

Dr. Amandus Johnson, in *The Records of the Swedish Lutheran Churches at Raccoon and Penns Neck, 1713-1786*, notes: "The spelling, even of proper names, was very irregular in Europe and in America until the beginning of the 19th century, when the newspapers and schools began to standardize the spelling." (p. [35])

I have used software to convert published material into usable text, which eliminates mistakes in transcription, but I had no choice but to spend countless hours transcribing wills, land grant petitions, land grants and deeds from the Provincial Archives of New Brunswick, Canada. Although I have made every attempt at accuracy, I would imagine that some mistakes have occurred. Some of these original documents are on microfilm, but a sizable number has been digitized and can be accessed at (familysearch.org).

Throughout the book, direct quotes follow the dating format as it appears, but, otherwise, I use the European format of day/month/year.

I must apologize for the lack of an index to this work, but time and financial restraints impose their own restrictions.

It should be noted that research on John Kelly and his descendants is a work in progress. If any reader can correct or add to the information contained in this material, please feel free to contact me at: dmcbreairty@yahoo.com.

INTRODUCTION

We know that our branch of the Kelly family, who settled in New Brunswick, Canada, came from West Jersey, particularly Gloucester County, but I have not been able to establish if the family emigrated directly from Ireland or migrated from another colony to West Jersey. Although John Kelly of Gloucester who fought with the British in the American Revolution is our ancestor, I have not been able to connect him to a particular Kelly family in West Jersey. Lucille Bertram and the staff at the Bergen County Historical Society Library in River Edge, New Jersey, after an extensive search through their manuscript collection, etc., could not connect the Kelly family of West Jersey to a specific place of origin in another colony or in Ireland. Neither could they connect Loyalist John Kelly to his family in West Jersey. John Kelly appears to have had brothers who also fought with the British and also came to New Brunswick, Canada, after the Revolution in 1783. At this time, there is no paper trail to connect these leads. New Jersey suffered more destruction than perhaps any colony in the Revolutionary War. Although the preservation of colonial material from this colony is impressive, much was lost in the war. Perhaps what I have assembled here will help some future researcher in establishing connections that have eluded me.

Although there are no memoirs or personal records of the Kellys, I have attempted to expand the fragmentary facts of the Kellys by including contemporary accounts of what was occurring around them. Hopefully, a reader will have a better understanding, after reading this material, of what life was like for a person or family settling in early America, living through the Revolution as Loyalists and establishing themselves in Nova Scotia and New Brunswick after the war.

Roger Mark Smith's Tribal Pages (*http://ftonsmiths.tribalpages.com*) and Linda (Kitchen) Aitken's Tribal Pages (*http://lindaai.tribalpages.com*) are valuable resources for anyone wishing to view Kelly family connections and photographs. New material is added frequently. Mark's site also contains Smith family material as well as material on other families. Both Mark and Linda are meticulous professionals when it comes to research and managing their pages. They both honor and respect privacy concerns, so there are different levels of access available. Proven family members can contribute to these sites.

The site *In Search of our Family Heritage: Roots and Branches* (*www.stoneyburn.ca*) is another source for viewing Kelly family material.

THE PHOTOGRAPHS

New Jersey American Revolution Bicentennial Medal. (Darrell McBreairty Collection.)

Gold coin passed down in the Leonard Coombes Kelly family. (Leonard C. Kelly Family Coll.)

Saint John, New Brunswick, 1791. *Cassell's Illustrated History of England*, by John Cassell (London, Paris and New York: Cassell, Petter and Galpin, 1898). (Darrell McBreairty Coll.)

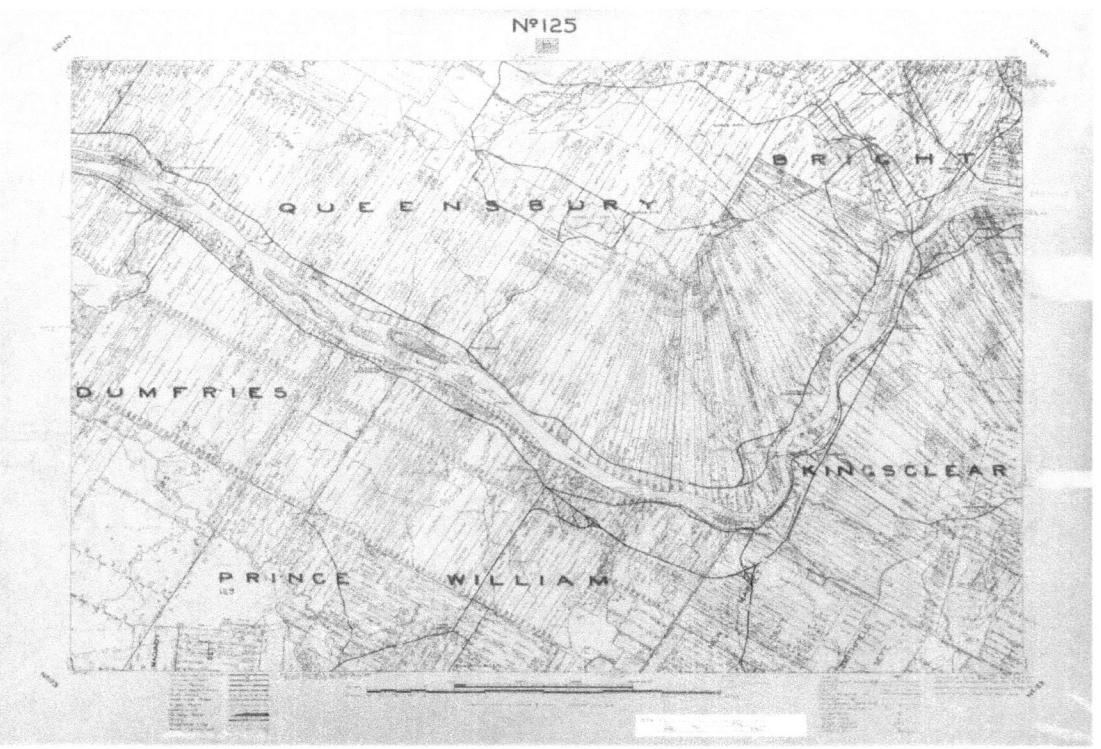

Land Grant Map (No. 125). (By Permission: New Brunswick Department of Natual Resources, Fredericton, New Brunswick, Canada.)

The Green at Fredericton. (Steel Engraving.) Artist: W. H. Bartlett; Engraver: J. C. Armytage. Published by James S. Virtue Co., London, Published for the Proprietors, by Geo: Virtue, 26 Ivy Lane, 1842. (Darrell McBreairty Collection.)

Leonard Coombes Kelly. (Leonard Coombes Kelly Family Collection.)

Jacobina (McKay) Kelly & Grandson Alan Kelly, 1902. (Ella Rita (Kelly) Boulter Coll.)

Stanley, New Brunswick, ca January, 1934. (Darrell McBreairty Collection.)

Stanley, New Brunswick, 1915. (Ella Rita (Kelly) Boulter Collection.)

Leonard Coombes Kelly tombstone, Stanley, NB. (Photo by Jeannie (Boulter) Matthews in her coll.)

Robert Kelly, Thomas "Tommy" Walton & Ella R. (Merrill) Kelly. (Ella Rita (Kelly) Boulter Coll.)

John Henry Kelly, son of Leonard C. & Jacobina (McKay) Kelly. (Ella R. (Kelly) Boulter Coll.)

William Leonard Kelly, son of Robert & Ella R. (Merrill) Kelly. (Ella R. (Kelly) Boulter Coll.)

William Leonard Kelly, 1901, son of Robert & Ella R. (Merrill) Kelly. (Ella R. (Kelly) Boulter Coll.)

Gabriel Havelock Kelly, 1901, son of Robert & Ella R. (Merrill) Kelly. (Ella R. (Kelly) Boulter Coll.)

Arthur Cleveland "Cleve" & Mabel Hilda (Jarvis) Kelly. (Ella R. (Kelly) Boulter Coll.)

William & Elizabeth (Porter) Merrill. (Ella Rita (Kelly) Boulter Collection.)

William L. Kelly, Ella R. (Kelly) Boulter, Robina (Kelly) Metcalfe & Marjorie (Hayes) Kelly. (Ella Rita (Kelly) Boulter Collection.)

William Leonard Kelly, son of Robert & Ella Rebecca (Merrill) Kelly. (Ella Rita (Kelly) Boulter Coll.)

Harold Kelly, Robert Kelly, Ella Rebecca (Merrill) Kelly, Irma (Kelly) Tucker, Arthur Cleveland Kelly and William Leonard Kelly at the Robert Kelly Farm. (Velma Maude (Harrison) Kelly Coll.)

Arthur Garfield & Irma Della (Kelly) Tucker. (Velma Maude (Harrison) Kelly Collection.)

Harold Jarvis & Velma Maude (Harrison) Kelly. (Velma M. (Harrison) Kelly Coll.)

Stanley, New Brunsiwck, Lumber Yard, January, 1934.
(Darrell McBreairty Collection.)

Margaret (Scott) Kelly.
(Margraret (Kelly) Hay Collection.)

Charles Warren & Susie (Dunphy) Kelly.
(Margaret (Kelly) Hay Collection.)

Charles Warren "Warren" Kelly.
(Margaret (Kelly) Hay Collection.)

Charles Warren Kelly Homestead, Keswick Ridge, NB, with Margaret (Kelly) Grant on porch. (Margaret (Kelly) Hay Collection.)

Susie (Dunphy) Kelly at the Charles Warren Kelly Homestead, Keswick Ridge, NB, after WWII, with horses she brought with her as part of her wedding dowry. (Margaret (Kelly) Hay Collection.)

Prince William, New Brunswick, ca 1913. The Valenzine & Sons Publishing Co. Ltd. Montreal and Toronto. Printed in Great Britain. (Darrell McBreairty Collection.)

Charles Kelly, son of William & Sarah Ann (Howard) Kelly.
(Darrell McBreairty Collection.)

Sarah Ann (Mullins) Kelly, daughter of William & Elizabeth (Diamond) Mullins.
(Darrell McBreairty Collection.)

L: Charles & R: James Kelly, sons of William & Sarah Ann (Howard) Kelly. (Kathryn (Kelly) Rioux Coll.)

Charles Kelly, son of William & Sarah Ann (Howard) Kelly. (Darrell McBreairty Collection.)

James Kelly, son of William & Sarah Ann (Howard) Kelly. (Stella (Sirois) Kelly Collection.)

James Kelly, son of William & Sarah Ann (Howard) Kelly. (Stella (Sirois) Kelly Collection.)

L: Charles Kelly, son of William & Sarah Ann (Howard) Kelly, and R: Luther Henderson, son of Luther & Ann "Annie" (Hughes) Henderson. (Flora Belle "Flo" (McBreairty) Henderson Coll.)

John Kelly, son of William & Sarah Ann (Howard) Kelly. (Arletta "Lettie" (Kelly) Gallagher Collection.)

Elizabeth (Hafford) Hunnewell, mother of Josephine (Hunnewell) Kelly, James Kelly's second wife. (Darrell McBreairty Collection.)

William Kelly house at the William Mullins/Charles Kelly farm on the St. John River in Allagash, Maine. (Lucy (Kelly) Kelly Collection.)

Benjamin & Elizabeth (Kelly) Abernathy Homestead, located on the original Barnabas Hunnewell-James Kelly property in St. Francis, Maine, with unknown child, 31 July 1941. (Darrell McBreairty Collection.)

Later photograph of the Benjamin & Elizabeth (Kelly) Abernathy Homestead, St. Francis, Maine. (Darrell McBreairty Collection

Tintype of Frederick Howard in His Union Army Uniform. (Chad Pelletier Collection.)

Ambrotype of Jane (Lunt) Howard. (Chad Pelletier Collection.)

John S. Hunnewell, also known as "John Kelly," son of Josephine (Hunnewell) Kelly. (Nora (Sturgeon) Kelley Collection.)

Memorial Card of Paschal Sirois, father of Stella (Sirois) Kelly. (Nora (Sturgeon) Kelley Collection.)

Margery "Mysie" MacDonald (PANB Assorted Acquisitioins: P37-292). Ella Rita (Kelly) Boulter caption: "Mysie McDonald at a Stanely Carnival, c. 1883." (Used with permission from PANB.)

Ella Rita (Kelly) Boulter caption: "Mysie & old Joe Whitter counting their money at the old farmers store. Old Joe sold almanacs."
(Jeannie (Boulter) Matthews Collection.)

Joe Mhitter and Margery "Mysie" MacDonald at the old farmers store, Stanley, New Brunswick. (Jeannie (Boulter) Matthews Collection.)

WEST JERSEY

John E. Pomfret in his *Province of West New Jersey 1609 – 1702: A History of the Origins of an American Colony* notes that although Giovanni da Verrazzano "skirted it as early as 1524" and that Esteuan Gomez may also have passed by in 1525, it was Henry Hudson, commanding the *Half Moon,* who finally "entered Delaware Bay on August 28, 1609" in his quest to locate a Northwest passage. Not having the necessary smaller water craft at his disposal for further exploration in such shallow waters, Hudson moved on. (p. 3)

Pomfret states that "in the spring of 1624" the Dutch West India company sent "a group of thirty families, largely Walloon refugees, . . . to America in the *Nieu Nederlant . . .* under the command of Captain May. . . . These homeseekers were the first real colonists of New Netherland." Although "[t]he majority were settled at Fort Orange (Albany), . . . others under the direction of May were employed in the planting of Fort Nassau on the South River (Delaware) at the mouth of Timber Creek."

Pomfret, citing Victor H. Paltsits in "The Founding of New Amsterdam in 1626," further states: "At Manhattan, until the coming of Peter Minuit in 1626, there were no dwellings; and Long Island was not settled until ten years later. Director Minuit, soon after his arrival, recalled the colonists from the various trading posts. . . . By 1628 there were 270 souls at New Amsterdam, while at Fort Orange only traders, fourteen in number, were permitted to remain, and on the South River a single trading vessel replaced the establishment at Fort Nassau." (pp. 6 – 7)

Pomfret continues:

> The Dutch West India Company was a poor instrument with which to fashion a colony worthy of Dutch enterprise, and unfortunately its powers and privileges were not seriously challenged until the very last. The directors and stockholders, as in all business ventures, wanted a return upon their capital. Farming was neglected in the quest for furs, and food was difficult to obtain. The company regarded the farmer as no more than an investment. His land was leased him by the Company and although each settler was advanced necessities such as livestock, wagons, and plows, these were entered upon the books of the Company as a debit to be repaid with interest. No settler held title to a single foot of land; nor could he trade on his own account. . . . The Company was soon to realize, settlers were necessary; if for no other reason, to defend the feeble establishment against . . . the English to the east, and after 1638 against the threat of the Swedes on the Delaware. (pp. 7-8)

Pomfret establishes that, although the English laid claim to the land along the Delaware River, "[n]o one bothered the Dutch . . . until the Swedes planted there in 1638. . . ." (p. 12)

Pomfret:

> About the middle of March 1638, two Swedish ships, the *Key of Calmar* and the *Griffen*, sailed into Delaware Bay and dropped anchor at Paradise Point a few miles above Cape Henlopen. This was no mere trading junket, for the Calmar carried in her hold hoes, spades, and other agricultural implements. The leader of the expedition . . . was none other than Peter Minuit, erstwhile Director of New Netherland, now in the service of Christina, "the great princess, virgin, and elected Queen of the Swedes, Goths, and Wends." Shortly after their arrival the ships moved up the river to Minquas Kill (Christina Creek) and up this creek until high ground was met. Work upon Fort Christina (Wilmington) was begun immediately. On March 29, with a Dutch trader as interpreter, Minuit purchased from five Indian chiefs lands up and down the river on both sides for "good and proper merchandise." (p. 16)

Pomfret adds

> Minuit wasted no time in commencing trading operations. . . . As soon as palisades and earthworks had been erected, Minuit went up the river to reconnoiter the position of the Dutch. At Fort Nassau he was challenged, but gave it out that his ships were in passage to the West Indies and had stopped in the river for water and wood. Peter May, however, was suspicious and sent word to Director Kiefft that the Swedes were upon the river. Kiefft ordered Jan Jansen to look into the matter on his return to the South River.
>   Kiefft solemnly warned Minuit that the whole South River "has already, for many years, been our property, occupied by our forts, and sealed with our blood; which was also done when you were a servant in New Netherland and you are, therefore, well aware of this." The Director evidently believed that Minuit was acting fraudulently, for he scoffed at the idea that the Queen of Sweden had sponsored such an expedition. He protested Minuit's occupation and warned "that we shall protect our rights in such manner as we may find most advisable." Fortunately for Minuit, Kiefft's force at Fort Nassau was too meager to carry out any threat of dispossession. (pp. 16-17)

Pomfret, citing Myers (editor) in *"Narratives of Early Pennsylvania, West New Jersey, and Delaware, 1630 – 1707*, pp. 53–893; 'Representation of New Netherland,' in *Narratives of New Netherland*, pp. 292-354, especially pp. 312-320; Johnson, *The Swedish Settlements on the Delaware* . . . [pp.] 182-196," says that by May 1638 Peter Minuit felt his little colony was secure enough for him to seek out trading options for tobacco in Virginia. At Jamestown "Governor Berkeley, however, refused to permit free trade with the

Swedes until he had corresponded with London." Pomfret explains that Minuit then headed for the West Indies, where "he hoped to trade hogsheads of wine and distilled liquor for tobacco and, perhaps, in keeping with the spirit of the age, 'take a rich Spanish prize'." Peter Minuit "lost his life in a West Indies hurricane. . . . At Christina, however, there remained twenty-three souls, founders of the first permanent white settlement along the Delaware." (p. 17)

Pomfret goes into detail about the Swedish colony and the rising tensions among the Swedes, Dutch, English and Native Americans. In 1640, Pomfret says a group of traders from the Colony of New Haven started buying from the Native Americans land along the Delaware not occupied by either the Dutch or Swedes. This move drew the Dutch and Swedes together for a time, but all three groups of European settlers pushed their own agendas with only the diplomacy of the mother countries helping to skirt outright armed conflict.

Finally, Pomfret writes, on 15 September 1655, "The Dutch flag was raised over . . . [Fort Christina] and New Sweden ceased to exist as a political entity." (p. 33)

But Pomfret points out that by the 1640s "the Dutch trader was not only being hemmed in by the English settler, but was more and more feeling the competition of the English trader. New Netherland could not erect a barrier strong enough to stem the English tide; and as the years passed the disparity in numbers grew." (p. 49)

Pomfret adds:

> Once aware of the great difference in strength between New England and New Netherland, several members of the New England Confederation, particularly Connecticut and New Haven, urged the conquest of the Dutch. By the Treaty of Hartford in 1650 the Confederation won on practically every point of dispute between the two. The Dutch agreed to accept a final boundary running ten miles east of the Hudson as soon as surveys could be made; in the meantime they pledged themselves not to build houses within four miles of that line. New Netherland was permitted to retain her small holdings about Hartford, and her claims to the Delaware were allowed to remain open. (pp. 49-50)

Pomfret writes that in 1663

> a plot was hatching in London which was to change the basic situation in the area. Many pretexts were available to justify an English descent upon New Netherland. The chief one was the conviction that New Netherland, purchasing tobacco in Maryland and Virginia and shipping via New Amsterdam, was costing the British exchequer thousands of pounds sterling annually and the English merchants unnecessary loss of trade. In July 1663, the Council for Foreign Plantations, Sir John Berkeley presiding, appointed a special committee consisting of himself, Sir George Carteret,

and William Coventry, secretary of James, Duke of York, to inquire into the feasibility of taking New Netherland. In January [1664] it reported that the seizure could be effected at small cost. The Duke was highly pleased, since as a large holder in the Royal African Company, he was interested in crippling the Dutch. He persuaded his brother, Charles II, to . . . finance the expedition. In March 1664 James also received a royal charter for large grants of land in America, chief among which was the disputed territory between the Delaware and the Connecticut Rivers. (p. 52)

Pomfret, after outlining the maneuvering of the British, cites C. M. Andrews, *The Colonial Period of American History, III* (pp. 35-69):

James appointed Colonel Richard Nicolls, a loyal follower, to be his deputy-governor, and shortly after King Charles commissioned Colonel Nicolls, Sir Robert Carr, Colonel George Carteret, and Samuel Maverick to proceed to America ostensibly to settle disputes touching New England, but with secret instructions to take New Netherland. Four frigates carrying a military force of 400 arrived in Boston harbor in July [1664] to prepare for the descent upon New Amsterdam. (p. 53)

Pomfret: "When the expedition left England in May some in Holland were suspicious even though its announced purpose was 'to settle the peace and security' of New England." With much maneuvering, overlapping land claims and intrigue, Pomfret, citing "Report of the Surrender of New Netherland, by Peter Stuyvesant, 1665" from J. Franklin Jameson's *Narratives of New Netherland, 1609-1664* (pp. 458–466), writes, "On August 29 [1664] Fort New Amsterdam surrendered without the firing of a shot." (pp. 53–54)

Pomfret reports that the British took control of the west bank of the Delaware on 30 September 1664. Pomfret, citing the *New Jersey Archives, First Series* (pp. 3-8), further adds: "On March 12, 1664, months before the seizure of New Netherland, Charles [II] . . . issued a patent bestowing upon [his brother] James title to various lands in America, including Maine, Long Island, and, disregarding prior dispositions, the territory between Connecticut and the Delaware. . . . This document is remarkable in that it ignored the Dutch occupation which, it is true, England had never formally acknowledged." (p. 57)

Pomfret, again citing *New Jersey Archives, First Series* (pp. 3-8), explains that James, Duke of York and brother of Charles II of England, presented on 24 June 1664 the portion of land that became New Jersey given to him by Charles II to John Berkeley and George Carteret. John Berkeley, during the Civil War, "had served the Duke as manager of his affairs during exile, raising funds in time of dire need. Sir George [Carteret] in 1649, as governor of the Isle of Jersey, had sheltered Charles and later defended the island against the Puritans. Both [John Berkeley and George Carteret] were members of the special committee of the Council of Foreign Plantations that in 1663 had recommended the seizure of New Netherland. The newly created province was given the name Nova Caesaria or New Jersey." (p. 57)

Citing editors W.A. Whitehead, W. Nelson and F.W. Ricord in their *New Jersey Archives*, First Series 1880-1893, Pomfret notes:

> In order to attract settlers, a planter "adventuring" to New Jersey before January 1666 was offered 150 acres of land, and additional allotments for each indentured servant over fourteen years of age. Later arrivals would receive smaller allotments. The quitrent was fixed at 1/2d. an acre. In addition, each servant, at the expiration of his term, would be given seventy-five acres of land, subject to the statutory quitrent. (58)

William Forbes Adams, in *Ireland and Irish Emigration to the New World from 1815 to the Famine*, citing Cheesman Abiah Herrick's *White Servitude in Pennsylvania: Indentured and Redemption Labor in Colony and Commonwealth*, (pp. 263-266), notes, in regard to the influx of immigrants in early Nineteenth Century America, "the increasing stream of immigrants soon flooded the country with a cheaper labor than that of the indentured servant, and although the practice lasted in Philadelphia as late as 1831, it had ceased to be significant by 1820." (p. 114)

Pomfret continues:

> Philip Carteret, a distant relative of Sir George [Carteret], was appointed governor by the proprietors and arrived at Elizabeth in August 1665, bringing with him thirty "adventurers and servants." Soon after his arrival he was plunged into a series of conflicts with the settlers already living there and could give little attention to the outlying part of his jurisdiction bordering on the Delaware. East New Jersey, as it was called, included the Dutch villages, Bergen, Hoboken, and Weehawken, which had grown up on the west bank of the Hudson, and a half dozen Puritan settlements founded by men from Long Island and New England who had been granted lands by Nicolls before he had knowledge of the grant to Berkeley and Carteret. Between the latter group and the governor there was incessant strife. (p. 58)

The Kelly family may have been Quakers when first coming into West Jersey, but documentation shows that they were members of the Church of England even in New Jersey before the Revolution.

Pomfret, citing *Collections of the Protestant Episcopal Historical Society for the year 1851*, says that George Keith reported in 1669, "There is not one Church of England as yet in either West or East Jersey...." (p. 261)

Pomfret, citing *The Journal of George Fox*, Volume II (p. 211), writes:

> In passing through New Jersey in 1672 George Fox, the Quaker leader, commented upon the sparse population on the eastern side of the Delaware. Crossing over at New Castle, "a Dutch Towne," on the way to the East Jersey settlements, he noted: "Then had we wilderness country to pass through, and wild woods where it was said it was never known before any man to ride, since called West Jersey, not then inhabited by English; so that we have travelled [the] whole day together without seeing man or woman, house or dwelling place." (pp. 60–61)

Pomfret, citing the *New Jersey Archives, First Series* (pp. 51-58), speaking of settlers in West Jersey along the Delaware in 1672, says, "The Swedes, Finns, and Dutch who lived there had recently drifted over from the New Castle district. Some were legitimate purchasers, others, squatters. However, fewer than 100 were residing there . . . in 1675 and all but a handful lived between Raccoon Creek and Salem Creek." (p.61)

Pomfret continues:

> In 1673 the war that had broken out between England and Holland was formally proclaimed on the Delaware. The inhabitants were warned that if the blockhouse at New Castle was not completed by November 1, a penalty of 1,000 guilders in wampum would be imposed. These precautions accomplished nothing, for on August 1 Dutch vessels under Evertse and Benks took New York without the firing of a shot. From that time until February 1674 New York, New Jersey and the Delaware district were under Dutch rule again. Then, by the terms of the Treaty of Westminster all were returned to Great Britain. (p.61)

Pomfret points out:

> Major Edmund Andros, commissioned governor by the Duke of York in July 1674, did not arrive in New York until October. His commission had vested him with jurisdiction over the Duke's lands from the Connecticut to the Delaware. In August, James restored to Sir George Carteret the proprietorship of the eastern half of New Jersey. The unauthorized sale by Berkeley of the western half to the Quakers, John Fenwick and Edward Byllynge, in March 1674 was ignored by the Duke, consequently Governor Andros treated the east bank of the Delaware as part of his dominion. (p. 62)

Pomfret, citing the *New Jersey Archives, First Series* (p. 209), and the *Pemberton Papers, New Jersey Estates*, Historical Society of Pennsylvania, LXII (p. 33), points out, "The joint but undivided proprietorship of Berkeley and Carteret ended on March 18, 1674, when Sir John [Berkeley] sold his interest to John Fenwick, 'gentleman,' of Binfield, County of Berks. . . . Associated with Fenwick in the transaction was Edward Byllynge, 'gentleman,' of Westminister, Middlesex County." (p. 65)

George R. Prowell, in his *History of Camden County, New Jersey*, notes that "the Concessions and Agreements published by Berkeley and Carteret, in 1664, . . . applied to the whole territory of New Jersey. . . ." Prowell writes that "The Concessions and Agreements of the proprietors, freeholders and inhabitants of the province of West New Jersey in America," made in 1676 establishes

> [t]hat no man, nor number of men upon earth, hath power or authority to rule over men's consciences in religious matters; therefore it is consented, agreed and ordained that no person or persons whatsoever within said province at any time or times hereafter, shall be any ways, upon any pretence whatever called in question, or in the least punished or hurt, either in person, estate or privilege, for the sake of his opinion, judgment, faith or worship towards God in matters of religion, but that all and every such person and persons may from time to time and at all times freely and fully have and enjoy his and their judgments, and the exercise of their consciences in matters of religious worship throughout all the said province. (p. 28)

Prowell: "Not one of the New England States, nor New York nor Virginia was quite equal to West New Jersey in its love and practice of perfect religious toleration. Under the dominant ideas of the Friends governing here, no man was asked for or about his creed when offering himself as a candidate for public office." (p. 29)

Joseph S. Sickler, writing in *The History of Salem County New Jersey* of the religious tolerance of the Quakers in Salem County, states, "It is not surprising, therefore, to find that once having established themselves in perfect freedom from all fear and religious persecutions, they were willing that other religious sects should come to their new colony and enjoy the same measure of religious toleration that they themselves had sought." (p. 65)

Sickler adds, "To this colony in West Jersey came a large number of families of varying religious faiths who had settled first in New England and who had been forced to leave that section on account of religious persecutions." (p. 66)

John E. Pomfret says, "Both Fenwick and Byllynge were members of the Society of Friends. . . . Fenwick was a courageous, though a contentious and stubborn man. . . . Pepys, the diarist, . . . referred to Byllynge as 'a cunning fellow'. . . ." (p. 65)

George R. Prowell, in his *History of Camden, County, New Jersey*, writes:

> After much controversy between John Fenwick, Edward Byllynge and Edward Byllynge's creditors, William Penn was called upon to act as

arbitrator; who, after careful examination and inquiry, decided that John Fenwick was entitled to but ten parts, and that he (Fenwick) should convey the ninety parts of said territory to such persons as should be chosen as trustees for the benefit of Edward Byllynge's creditors. The creditors, who were mostly Friends, pressed Penn into their service as one of the trustees in the sale of these lands and in the payment of Byllynge's debts, the others being Gawen Laurie and Nicholas Lucas. On February 9, 1674, John Fenwick made conveyance of the ninety parts to said trustees, reserving ten parts whereon was planted his colony. (p. 27)

Pomfret writes:

A third group of proprietors were the Quakers from Ireland. Many were men of English birth who had left England hoping to escape the persecution there. But in Ireland the irritations and the annoyances proved to be just as harsh. The Quaker movement was running strongly in Ireland, especially in the Dublin and Cork areas; first because of the missionary work of Thomas Loe, the gifted Quaker minister of Oxford, and later because of the influence of men like William Penn, Anthony Sharp, and Robert Turner. Penn, who was converted to Quakerism by Loe, was in Ireland at intervals on matters connected with his father's estates. Turner and Sharp, the most prominent of the Irish Quakers interested in colonization, had suffered as grievously as any from the persecutions. (pp. 89-90)

Pomfret:

In April 1677, another propriety was purchased by five tradesmen in the Dublin area. Four of them, Robert Turner, Robert Zane, Thomas Thackary and William Bate, settled in West Jersey. In July 1678 a propriety was sold to a group of seven which included three merchants of Cork. Only one of these men came to West Jersey. Samuel and John Dennis of Cork appointed Thomas Thackary as their agent, and later John [Dennis] settled on Timber Creek in the Irish Tenth. (p. 90)

Here Pomfret cites the *New Jersey Archives, Volume XXI* (pp. 400 & 405) before continuing:

Of the purchasers of a round dozen of the 100 shares or proprieties we know little or nothing. Moreover, because the only extant copy of Budd's *True Account* is badly defaced, the names of a half dozen of the original proprietors have not been identified. One of them was the owner of three whole shares. William Penn was not an original proprietor but after his trusteeship expired he not only purchased the shares of Daniel Waite of Middlesex and William Haige of London but also from John Fenwick, title to the Salem Tenth. (p. 90)

Once again citing the *New Jersey Archives, Volume XXI* (pp. 400 & 405), H. Clay Reed and George J. Miller (editors) in their *The Burlington Court Book, a Record of Quaker Jurisprudence in West New Jersey 1680 – 1709* (p. xxvii), state: "Two shares went to twelve Irishmen, who located in the so-called 'Irish tenth,' later Gloucester County."

The following is from *Early Church Records of Gloucester County New Jersey* compiled by Charlotte D. Meldrum and John Pitts Launey:

> The Religious Society of Friends, frequently known as the Quaker movement, began in England during the 1650s primarily due to the dedication, inspiration, and leadership of a simple, Yorkshire tailor named George Fox. The movement took its members from the ranks of the Church of England that grew dissatisfied with its corrupt and often politically motivated leaders and doctrine. The motivation to abandon land and position in England and begin again in the Jerseys was supplied by the persecution of a Puritan dominated government and an intolerant crown.
>
> Friends saw a fundamental evil in the use of repetitive ritual and ceremony and created a society carefully avoiding these practices. Rather than wedding ceremonies, public marriages were held in private homes or meeting houses. Rather than funeral services, memorial essays were carefully and lovingly composed and read to the membership at Monthly Meetings. Baptisms and sacrament known as the Lord's Supper in other denominations were not practiced. The child of two Quaker parents was accepted as a member by birthright. It was important, therefore, to keep meticulously accurate records of birth, marriages, disownments, and reinstatements.
>
> Every meeting had two copies of the *Book of Discipline*, one each, for the Men's and Women's Meetings. This volume specified in detail how Friends must conduct their daily affairs. Many forms of diversion and entertainment common in those days were forbidden, including horse racing, betting games of chance, hawking, and fox hunting. Alcohol was not forbidden, but drinking to excess or frequenting "houses of diversion" were causes for discipline. (p. vi)

George R. Prowell, in his *History of Camden, County, New Jersey*, points out:

Nearly all of the people who lived on the territory now embraced within the county of Camden and of the most part of West Jersey, for one hundred years after the first settlement was made, were members of the Society of Friends. . . .

The Society of Friends, or Quakers, arose in England about the middle of the seventeenth century, a time of considerable religious excitement, when the honest-hearted were aroused by the general prevalence of vice and immorality in which the King and court were but examples. The term Quaker (i.e., Trembler) was first used in 1650, and was given to the Friends in derision by Justice Bennet, of Derby, because George Fox, the founder of the society, bade him and his companions to tremble at the word of the Lord. Its application was further induced by the fact that some of the early preachers and others trembled violently when under strong religious exercise. They even accepted the name Quaker, so far as to style themselves "the people called Quakers" in all official documents intended for publication to the world at large. The early form of marriage certificates contained the expression "the people of God called Quakers," but in 1734 the Yearly Meeting for Pennsylvania and New Jersey agreed "that ye words 'of God' and 'called Quakers' be left out of that form for the future." In 1806 the expression was changed to the "religious society of Friends." Some of their principal characteristics, as differing from other professing Christians, was in opposition to all wars, oaths and a paid ministry, or grace of God, which is given to every man as a guide to salvation. George Fox says, moreover, "when the Lord sent me forth into the world, he forbade me to put off my hat to any one, high or low. . . ."

For refusing to pay tithes in England, the goods of Friends were taken to many times the value; for absence from the national worship twenty pounds per month was imposed, and when brought before the courts, the oath of allegiance was tendered to them as a pretext, upon their refusal to disobey the injunction "swear not at all," for the imposition of further penalties. Meetings of the Friends were broken up, and in many cases they were shamefully abused. The sober, upright lives of Friends were a constant reproach, and aroused the hatred of many around them. It is probable that fully one-half of their sufferings were due to this cause, as their persecutors certainly cared little for religion.

In 1659 a petition was presented to Parliament, signed by one hundred and sixty-four Friends, offering their own bodies, person for person, to lie in prison instead of such of their brethren as were under confinement and in danger as of their lives therefrom. More than two hundred and fifty died in prison, and while some in England were sentenced to banishment, it was only in New England that a few were hung and others had their ears cut off. . . .

> Persecutions were continued with more or less severity until the accession of William and Mary to the throne of England, when an act of toleration was passed in 1689. Prior to this, however, many Friends had sought a home for religious liberty in Massachusetts, Long Island and New Jersey, and when William Penn established his colony, in 1682, it was but natural that a large number should have been attracted thither. The first settlement of Friends in New Jersey was at Salem in 1676, and at Burlington in 1678. (pp. 24-26)

Prowell continues:

> The first settlers of these people who purchased lands in what is now Camden County, obtained shares in the proprietary right of Edward Byllynge's trustees about 1677, and a few years later they came to this county and located. The line fixed between East and West Jersey, July 1, 1676, provided that the territory of the province be laid off into ten precincts, which, however, were not so laid off until January 14, 1681, old style. At that time Daniel Leeds was surveyor-general of the Province and was ordered by the commissioners to divide the river-front of the Delaware from Assanpink to Cape May into ten equal parts, running each tenth "so far back into the woods" as to give it an area of sixty-four thousand acres. This was accomplished, and the third and fourth tenths extended from the river Crapwell, or Pensaukin Creek, on the north to the river Berkeley, or Oldmans Creek, on the south; each of the tenths laid out as above mentioned were also divided into tenths, and were each called a share of propriety. Many of the Society of Friends had fled from the persecutions to which they were subjected in England to Dublin, Ireland, and their attention was attracted to the new country by the exciting troubles between Edward Byllynge and John Fenwick, and on the 12th of April, 1677, Robert Turner, Robert Zane, Thomas Thackara, William Bates and Joseph Sleight, all of Dublin, with the exception of William Bates, who was of the county of Wickloe, Ireland, purchased one whole share of propriety of the trustees of Byllynge, which included the right to locate within the limits of West Jersey. The proprietors of West Jersey then set aside for this colony of Friends the third tenth, which was from that time called the third or Irish tenth. (pp. 29-30)

Prowell says,

> [B]efore the end of the year 1677 a colony of more than four hundred Friends found homes in West Jersey, and many more during the years immediately succeeding. When the ships bearing the Burlington

immigrants in the year 1678, arrived in the Delaware the agent of Andros, at New Castle, required them to pay duties at that point, but Sir William Jones decided this to be illegal, and the claims of the Duke of York on West Jersey were then withdrawn and the Friends were left in the full enjoyment of independence. In November, 1689, Samuel Jennings, the Deputy-Governor of West Jersey, convened the first General Assembly, and the Friends met together to make their own laws. They reaffirmed the Concessions, declared all races and religions equal, forbade imprisonment for debt and the sale of ardent spirits to the red men, demanded that lands be acquired from the Indians by purchase, and permitted that a criminal might be pardoned by the person against whom the offense was committed. (p. 29)

Pomfret cites *Documents Relative to the Colonial History of the State of New York, XII* (pp. 507-541) and Samuel Hazard's *Annals of Pennsylvania From the Discovery of the Delaware, 1609-1682* (pp. 356-418) *passim*: "At the time of the arrival of Fenwick's colonists in November [1675] only a handful of people, Swedes and Finns and a Dutchman or two, were living in West Jersey." (p. 64)

Stanley H. Craig in *Salem County New Jersey Genealogical Data Records Pertaining to Persons Residing in Salem County Prior to 1800* explains:

During the War of 1812-14 . . . records of the Philadelphia Customs House were removed to Washington for safe keeping and when the British burned the Capitol these were destroyed.

It has been said that between the years 1675 and 1700 about ninety vessels entered the Delaware, and while a number of persons are known to have come on certain vessels, it is not positively known that any complete passenger list exists. (Volume 1, p. 293)

John Camden Hotten in his *The Original Lists of Persons of Quality* documents a number of Kellys immigrating from Great Britian to the Barbados and Virginia in the 1670s. Peter Wilson Coldham in *The Complete Book of Emigrants (1607-1776)* notes Kellys shipping out from England to Barbados and Virginia from 1607 to 1660. In the volume The *Complete Book of Emigrants, 1661-1699*, Coldman lists (p. 100) a Martin Kelly, shipping out from England, as being hired as an apprentice in Virginia in 1666. In the same volume, Coldman notes (pp. 147-148) that, in Virginia, Charles Kelly took on apprentices who shipped out from England in 1668 and 1669, and, again, in Virginia, Thomas Kelly took on apprentices from England in 1668 (p. 130) and 1669 (p. 147). Coldman lists, in the same volume, other Kellys coming into Virginia as apprentices in the same period, and for the same period at Nevis in the West Indies, an Edward Kelly in 1661 (p. 12) and 1665 (p. 88) also hired apprentices who had shipped out from England.

It should be noted that Coldman writes in his introduction to *The Complete Book of Emigrants (1607-1660)*, that no Irish, Welsh or Sottish records were used as sources. (p. xii) In the introduction to *The Complete Book of Emigrants (1661-1699)*, Coldman states: "Only English sources have been used. Scotland, Wales and Ireland maintain their own records." (p. iii)

In *Salem County New Jersey Genealogical Data Records Pertaining to Persons Residing in Salem County Prior to 1800* Craig writes, "*The Welcome* from London, Robert Greenway, Master, arrived at Upland, [New Jersey], 8th mo., 1682" with Peter and William Long among the passengers. (Volume 1, pp. 305-306) The Long family later settled near the Kellys in Kingsclear, New Brunswick, Canada, and married into the Kelly family.

Thomas Cushing, M.D. and Charles E. Sheppard, Esq. in *History of the Counties of Gloucester, Salem, and Cumberland New Jersey, with Biographical Sketches of Their Prominent Citizens* point out:

> Among the pioneers seeking a better home in the then new and undeveloped country, where religious freedom would be tolerated to the furthest and fullest extent, were those brave men who faced the dangers of the storm-tossed ocean, and risked themselves in the then wilds of the miasmatic swamps in South Jersey, and finally made their homes along the tide-water creeks of Oldman and Raccoon.
>
> In what is now Logan, formerly a part of old Woolwich township, quite a number of the sturdy pioneers from Sweden and Germany pitched their tents, and made old Gloucester County their homes.
>
> Among the number of those who selected this locality we find the name of James Talman, who located at the mouth of Oldman's Creek some time previous to the Revolutionary war; also the names of Kelly, Black, Hurff, Thomas Ayres, Homan, Norton, and Dawson. Among the number who came previous to the war was Coonradt Shoemaker, who, like many others, sold himself for his passage, — that is, he bound himself to a Mr. Kelley to work a certain number of years after his arrival in this country if Kelley would pay the passage-money. After Mr. Shoemaker had served his time and earned his freedom, he located between the creeks named, about two miles from what is now Bridgeport. Here he became possessed of two hundred acres of land, and at his death, in 1790, he left his property to his five children, four sons and one daughter. (p.253)

Citing *Minutes of Burlington Monthly Meeting*, John E. Pomfret points out in *The Province of West New Jersey 1609 – 1702: A History of the Origins of an American Colony*, "The earliest centers of expansion in West Jersey were Burlington and Salem and, after the arrival of the Irish settlers, Gloucester." Pomfret extracts from the same source that "with the coming of more than a hundred Irish Friends in 1682, the Pine Point Meeting was shifted to Newton Creek, several miles further south." (p. 236)

Once again citing *Minutes of Burlington Quarterly Meeting*, Pomfret writes that "During the eighteenth century . . . both in Burlington and Gloucester counties, settlement was limited to within twenty miles of the Delaware because of the forbidding pine barrens." (p. 237)

Isaac Mickle in *Reminiscences of Old Gloucester County*, under "Extracts from the Minutes of the County Court," includes the following:

> At ye Court held at Gloucester (for ye jurisdiction thereof) on ye fourth month, anno 1686, Divers Complaints being made to ye Grand Jury of ye great loss and damage which the County suffers by reason of wolves, they, with ye concurrence of ye Bench, to encourage ye destroying of them, doe order ye severall Treasures within this county to pay ten shillings for every wolfe's head to them brought forth of ye effects of ye County tax, and ye clerk is ordered to write papers to publish ye same. (p. 44)

Making comparisons from multiple sources, Pomfret (p. 281) suggests that West Jersey had a population of "about 3,500 inhabitants" in 1702 when East and West Jersey together became the royal province of New Jersey.

George R. Prowell, in his *History of Camden, County, New Jersey*, says, "[T]his wilderness country had few inducements to cause people to break up their homes and settle here." (p.28)

Thomas Shourds in his *History and Genealogy of Fenwick's Colony* writes the following:

> John Fenwick, on his arrival to this country, found much of his territory occupied by the Swedes and Finns and Hollanders, but he settled amicably with them by confirming their title to the land they held in possession. Deeds for the Finnstown tract and the Boughtown tract and other like conveyances appears on record, and are curious documents in their way. Those settled on Raccoon Creek had made their homes on either side of the stream, and extending several miles along the same, with a Church at Swedesboro. (p. 4)

On 27 March 1749 Pahr Kalm writes in *Travels into North America* (Volume II) that he questioned ninety-one-year-old Nils Gustafson who related the following:

> On another occafion, as a fermon was preached in the Swedish church, at Raccoon, an Indian came in, looked about him; and, after hearkening a while to the preacher, he faid: *Here is a great deal of prattle and nonfenfe, but neither brandy nor cyder*; and went out again. For it is to be obferved, that

when an *Indian* makes a fpeech to his companions, in order to encourage them to war, or to anything elfe, they all drink immoderately on thofe occafions. (P.118)

Isaac Mickle in *Reminiscences of Old Gloucester, or Incidents in the History of the Counties of Gloucester, Atlantic and Camden, New Jersey* writes: "On the Racoon in Gloucester County where now Swedesborough stands, a town was built at a very early day, and became the chief post on the east of the Swedeland Stream." (p. 7)

Mickle notes, "At what time the Swedes founded the village of Racoon we are unable to tell with precision. A settlement is marked there on Lindstrom's map, as it is found in the original Swedish copy of Campanius, and this map was made in 1654. Unless preceded, therefore, by the town of Nassau, Racoon is the most ancient village in our county." (p.72)

Isaac Mickle: "The earliest inhabitants of Racoon lived in a very humble manner. They had neither tea, coffee, chocolate nor sugar, and were too poor to buy any intoxicating drinks, or vessels to distill them in. The first settlers drank at table as a substitute for tea, a decoction of sassafras; and even in 1748 they mixed the tea they then used "with all sorts of herbs," says Kalm, [*Footnote*: "Kalm,Volume I, p. 370."] "so that it no longer deserves the name of tea." (p. 73)

Kalm (Volume II) writes that during the same interview on 27 March 1749:

However, he [Nils Gustafson] thought that no cold winter came up to that which happened in the year 1697; and which is often mentioned in the almanacks of this country, and I have mentioned it in the preceding volume. For in that winter the river *Delaware* was fo ftrongly covered with ice, that the old man brought many waggons full of hay over it, near *Chriftina*; and that it was paffable in fledges even lower. No cattle, as far as he could recollect, were ftarved to death in cold winters; except, in later years, fuch cattle as were lean, and had no ftables to retire into. (pp. 119-120)

Information compiled at *Wikipedia* establishes:

Swedesboro was settled by a small group of Swedes from Pennsylvania and Delaware in the mid-1600s. The English Colonial government needed a road between the communities of Burlingtown and Salem, so they built the Kings Highway in 1691 which opened the southern portion of Gloucester County to more settlers. The area offered an abundance of fertile sandy soil, prime farmland and vast tracks of oak, birch, maple and pine trees. Originally, the town was called Raccoon. . . . Through the late 1800s, Raccoon Creek was a water route that was naturally deep enough to transport wood and farming projects to Philadelphia by the Delaware River. (*en.wikipedia.org/wiki/Swedesboro*)

Amandus Johnson, in *The Records of the Swedish Lutheran Churches at Raccoon and Penns Neck, 1713-1786*, explains (footnote 74a): "The name of Raccoon was officially changed to Swedesboro in 1763." (p. [82])

It should be noted that the distance between Salem, New Jersey, and Philadelphia is just forty-four miles and that only twenty-two miles separate Burlington, New Jersey, from Philadelphia. The distance from Salem to Burlington, New Jersey, is fifty-eight miles. More than likely the Kelly family had close ties with all the communities in the area as well as those across the river in Delaware. Although I have found Kellys in the records of Trinity Church in Wilmington, Delaware, and Christ Church in Philadelphia, further research may uncover more documentation in Pennsylvania and Delaware. Christ Church in Philadelphia was founded in 1695. (See *Christ Church-Philadelphia* under Appendix P.) Trinity Church in Wilmington, Delaware, was dedicated on 4 July 1699. (See Burr, Horace (Translator): *The Records of Holy Trinity (Old Swedes) Church, Wilmington, Delaware, from 1697-1773* in Appendix P.)

Janice (Webster) Brown at *Gloucester County, New Jersey History and Genealogy* (*www.nj.searchroots.com/Gloucesterco*) writes, "For many years the Swedes and Finns on the New Jersey side [of the Delaware River] made the trip to Ft. Christina near Wilmington[,] Delaware[,] to attend [c]hurch." In granting me written permission to use from her material in an email of 16 August 2012, Janice (Webster) Brown states: "It is well established in the history of the early Swedes that they would row across the Delaware River in all seasons to attend church there. . . . It is known that in 1699 the congregation of Holy Trinity Swedish Lutheran Church purchased a new 'canoe' from Hendrick Tussey, who lived at Verdreitige Hook (Bochten) by the Skilpot Creek for 20 shillings and was used to transport church members across the Delaware River. Penns Neck (now Pennsville, Salem Co.[,] N.J.) members went to church by boat. Prior to the building of their own churches, local Swedesboro residents followed this tradition."

In *Under Four Flags: Old Gloucester County, 1686-1964, A History of Gloucester County, New Jersey*, edited by Hazel B. Simpson, the following appears: "It was a long and hazardous journey for most of the early settlers who had to walk or ride along trails or paths newly broken through the woods, to get to meeting. In the case of the Swedes and Dutch, who were of the Lutheran denomination, they had to cross the Delaware River by shallop or skiff, to reach their place of worship in Christina (Wilmington) in Delaware, or Wicacoa (Philadelphia) parishes; to Tinicum (1642) and Crane Hook. When these church records are consulted one finds that many contributing members were "from over the river." (p. 51)

Dr. Amandus Johnson, in his introduction to *The Records of the Swedish Lutheran Churches at Raccoon and Penns Neck, 1713-1786*, writes:

> When the Swedish Lutheran Mission on the Delaware was re-established in 1697, a considerable number of Swedes and Finns had settled on the Jersey side of the River, principally at two centers, Raccoon and Penns Neck (upper and lower). . . . These colonists were accustomed to attend services in the old church at Tranhook (near present-day Wilmington) and at Tinicum Island, depending upon the location of their farms, the settlements around Penns Neck going to the southern church and those living about Raccoon Creek attending on Tinicum Island.
>
> It is likely that the worshippers would congregate near Penns Neck and about the mouth of Raccoon Creek and from there go in companies by canoes to service on Sunday mornings or on Saturday, in which case they would stay overnight with relatives or friends near the churches. The journeys across the Delaware in those days were hazardous, yes impossible at certain seasons of the year, and tragedies occurred more than once. Besides, the journeys consumed much time and kept the able-bodied men away from work during harvest and at other periods, when the farms need most attention. As a result the attendance of these far-off settlers at the churches on the east side of the river was poor and many never attended services at all. (p. [iii])

Admandus Johnson, in *The Records of the Swedish Lutheran Churches at Raccoon and Penns Neck, 1713-1786*, writes in a footnote (34) that Jöns Dylander, "dean of Wicaco," was a "remarkable linguist, he usually preached two sermons in the morning, the first one in German to the Germans, and the second in Swedish to the Swedes. In the afternoon he delivered a third sermon in English to an English congregation. His popularity with the English caused the English pastors to complain to the governor." (p. [36])

According to *The Records of the Swedish Lutheran Churches at Raccoon and Penns Neck, 1713-1786*, "Rev. Tranberg became pastor in both congregations in 1728. However, he did not confine his labors to his own parish, but extended them as far as Egg Harbor and other distant places, preaching to the Germans, English and Swedes as he was, for a while, the only Swedish pastor in America." (p. [30])

Horace Burr writes in the "Prefatory Remarks" to *The Records of Holy Trinity (Old Swedes) Church, Wilmington, Delaware, from 1697-1773* that the first European settlers "were good judges of land and located their farms frequently distant from each other whenever a good spot was found, and the few hundreds were scattered on the west side of the Delaware, from St. Georges on the south to the falls at Trenton on the north and along the inflowing water courses, and on the east side [of the Delaware] from the lower end of Penn's Neck to the region around and some distance above Raccoon creek, now Swedesburg." Speaking of settlers on both sides of the Delaware, Burr notes, "Their principal means of conveyance and travel being the log canoe rendered it necessary to locate near the river and creeks, and in their canoes they crossed the Delaware, or came down the creeks to church while navigation was open." (p. 5)

The following appears in *Under Four Flags: Old Gloucester County, 1686-1964, A History of Gloucester County New Jersey*, edited by Hazel B. Simpson: "In order to promote the transportation system in West Jersey the Gloucester County Court, in 1867, authorized the establishment of a regular ferry across the Delaware river to connect with the fast growing port of Philadelphia." (p. 71) The first license "was granted to William Royden on March 1, 1687." But it is noted that the "license was not issued until one year later 1688." (p. 74)

From *Under Four Flags: Old Gloucester County, 1686-1964, A History of Gloucester County New Jersey*: "The ferry was located near the foot of what is today Cooper Street, Camden, its boats being open flat-boats propelled by oars or sails. A few years afterwards it was purchased by William Cooper, and for more than one hundred years thereafter was everywhere known as Cooper's Ferries." (p. 74)

In speaking of the lack of regulations in regard to carriages, Mickle, citing Pierre Du Simitre's manuscript at the Philadelphia Library, notes,

> Such refinements were not introduced generally, even in Philadelphia, until the Revolution. In West Jersey most journeys were performed on horseback; and the marriage portion of the daughters of the most wealthy men generally consisted of a cow and a side-saddle. Wheeled vehicles indeed would have been of but little use in a country where roads were yet full of trees, and where streams had but few if any bridges. Funerals were frequently attended in boats, and a highly respectable gentleman [*Footnote*: "Richard M. Cooper, Esq."], late of Camden, distinctly remembered a burial of the kind which took place in his boyhood. The deceased lived upon Cooper's Creek near the head; his coffin was placed in a barge, and rowed around to the old ground upon Newton Creek, followed by several other boats containing the family and friends. (pp. 42-43)

From *Under Four Flags: Old Gloucester County, 1686-1964, A History of Gloucester County New Jersey*: "There was constant complaint about road conditions. Ruts were hub deep. In remote sections teams became stalled and could be mired for days before help arrived. During winter months it was common to find a wagon frozen fast in the ruts. It usually remained there until a thaw." (p. 71)

Continuing from *Under Four Flags: Old Gloucester County, 1686-1964, A History of Gloucester County New Jersey*: "The introduction of the stage coach in America was made during the early part of the eighteenth century, the first being between Philadelphia and New York, when a 'waggon twice a week made the trip.' In 1732 a stage took a week to travel from New York City to Boston. The wagon was nevertheless called a *flying machine*." (p. 72)

Under Four Flags: Old Gloucester County, 1686-1964, A History of Gloucester County New Jersey: "In the early conveyances seats were arranged crosswise with the entrance at front or forward. A passenger had to climb over the forward seats or benches and over passengers already seated to reach the rear benches. Naturally the ladies occupied the front benches. The early stage model accommodated seven passengers and might begin a journey as early as three or four in the morning. The only luxury was added by means of a strap of leather nailed across the back." (p. 72)

Once again from *Under Four Flags: Old Gloucester County, 1686-1964, A History of Gloucester County New Jersey*: "Just when the stage lines were established is difficult to determine. A stage line over Kings Highway to Salem from the ferry in Camden advertised as early as 1767." (p. 96)

Horace Burr says,

> After the people of other nationalities settled among the Swedes, intermarriages became frequent especially of the Swedish women, who seem to have been more numerous than the other sex.
>
> The result of these intermarriages was, that a very considerable part of the population of Wilmington and the surrounding country, except those families who have come in the last half century, are in greater or lesser degree of Swedish descent.
>
> Indeed, it is rare that among the older families one is to be found that has not more or less Swedish blood.
>
> The exceptions are found mostly among the Friends or Quakers, whose tenets forbade marrying out of their denomination, though occasionally a Quaker girl fell in love with and married a Swede. (p. 7)

It wasn't long until residents on the Jersey side of the Delaware decided to establish their own churches.

Ericus Bjork in his diary and documentation reproduced in *The Records of Holy Trinity (Old Swedes) Church, Wilmington, Delaware, from 1697-1773* states: "About May 1st [1702], particularly about Easter-tide, there was a report of irregularity and foolishness among that part of my congregation on the other side of the river, Jersey side so called, purporting that they are minded to break off from me and the Church on this side, taking a minister for themselves after their own will, and uniting with them on the other side of Rattcong Creek, who belong to Wicacoe congregation, and with whom we have had no connection since I came here in any church or congregational matters, nor they with us." (p. 88)

Horace Burr writes: "After the building of the churches at Raccoon and Penn's neck, the two mother congregations [of Christina and Wicacoe] were confined to the west side of the river. . . ." (p. 6)

But, even after churches had been established in West Jersey, some people continued to travel across the Delaware for services.

Writing in 1706, Bjork declares, "But still the Church at Rattcong Creek, established and set upon an unjust and irregular foundation, is more obstinate and spunky than ever, yet there was one and another in the meantime, in the ruinous state of things came back to his old church." (p. 111)

Dr. Amandus Johnson, in his introduction to *The Records of the Swedish Lutheran Churches at Raccoon and Penns Neck, 1713-1786*, writes:

> In spite of the fact that the settlers in this district were not very religious and many did not go to church at all, it seems that they were anxious to bury their dead in the churchyard and not in their own fields, as was done in Maryland and elsewhere at the time. They had no compunction apparently about secretly burying their dead in the graveyard, so as to avoid paying the fee to the congregation, as we find references to this fact in the church book. (p. [x])

On the other hand, Robert Gibbon Johnson says in *An Historical Account of the First Settlement of Salem, in West Jersey, by John Fenwick, Esq. Chief Proprietor of the Same* in regard to the burying practices of the early settlers of Salem County, New Jersey, "Family burying grounds were common throughout the county, and interments were continued to be made therein until long since the different religious societies had established their own." (p. 36)

According to information appearing under "Colonial Laws" in *Laws of the Royal Colony of New Jersey 1760-1769, New Jersey Archives, Third Series, Volume IV*, between 1760 and 1769, a John Kelly lived "on the Westerly Side of Raccoon Creek." (p. 412) (See Appendix A.)

The following appears in *The Records of the Swedish Lutheran Churches at Raccoon and Penns Neck, 1713-1786*, edited by Dr. Amandus Johnson:

> The financial conditions of the New Jersey colonists was usually poor and few had more than their daily needs. Although they showed considerable interest in church work, the pastors were poorly compensated for their labors, and even the small salaries allotted to them were not regularly paid, sometimes not at all. Those in poorest circumstances would pay up at least part of their subscriptions, while the members who could best afford to do so, never paid at all. When subscriptions for the pastor's salary or for expenses connected with the church were made, the members usually would be asked to give a bond for the amount, and the sums could be legally collected. In fact once or twice the law was invoked to collect the pastor's salary, but this caused so much bad feeling that it was seldom attempted. (p. [ix])

Appearing in *The Records of the Swedish Lutheran Churches at Raccoon and Penns Neck, 1713-1786*, are a John and William Kille on a "list of subscriptions for the Public Schoolhouse at Swedesborough, intended to be buildt this summer in the year of our Lord 1771. . . ." John subscribes for the sum of £1 and William for 15 shillings. (p. [164])

In *The Records of the Swedish Lutheran Churches at Raccoon and Penns Neck, 1713-1786*, a John Kelly is also listed as paying a subscription of £10 (p. [190]) "for the rebuilding of the Swedish Lutheran Evangelical Church in Swedsborough. . . ." (p. [188]) It should be noted that the articles of subscription for the rebuilding of the church were presented to the subscribers on 1 September 1783.

H. Stanley Craig in his **Gloucester County New Jersey Marriage Records** notes (p. 218) that the marriage of Malacky Kelly and Mary Hopman, of Mannenton on 15 January 1767 appears in the records of the Protestant Episcopal Church at Swedesboro. Craig also notes (p. 213) that the marriage of John Crawford and Anne Kelly on 12 July 1783 is recorded in the same church records. Craig adds (p. 9) that the marriage of John Crawford and Anne Kelly is recorded in the *New Jersey Archives*, Volume XXII, as having occurred on 13 July 1783.

Thomas Shourds, in his *History and Genealogy of Fenwick's Colony*, writes,

> In following the movements of the first English emigrants, the inquiry very naturally arises why their places of settlement were selected, as they were in this wilderness country, and the causes that contributed such action. The charts of the new world were defective, and knowledge of this particular section, in like degree limited. These people were not surrounded with prestige of any monied corporation, or backed by the royal perogative to assist them in this undertaking. The breaking up of their household was an end of all claims to an inheritance in their native land. The persecutions they had passed through, and the uncertainty of any change for the better, banished all hopes of justice and tolerance for them. Whatever may have been their attachments, or however bitter the feeling incident to separation from friends and home; no hope of return softened their grief or assuaged their sorrow. With all their earthly goods (limited among the most fortunate,) their families and such of their associates as would make the venture, left the shores of England never to return. Their departure was not surrounded with any pleasant associations, neither had their approach to the land of their adoption any anticipated welcome. Privations and dangers met them at every step, but no means were at hand whereby they could escape. They only knew that the Delaware river was the western boundary of New Jersey, but the most desirable localities whereat to make their settlement no one had given them any information. The natives, they looked upon as savages in a literal sense, and dreaded the necessity of any intercourse with them; regarding the wild beasts of the forest with less fear, and more easily

> controlled. Under these circumstances did our ancestors turn their ship from the ocean into Delaware bay and ascend the river, ignorant of where should be their abiding place.
>
> John Fenwick, with his children, his associates and servants, in the little ship *Griffin* [italics added], Captain Griffith master, sailed up the bay, about fifty miles along the eastern shore from Cape May, and anchored opposite the old Swede's fort, Elsborg, near the mouth of Assamhocking river, on the 23d of September, 1675, old style. The day following they ascended the Assamhocking river, now Salem, about three miles, and landed on the south side of the river on a point of land pleasantly located, that being, at the present computation of time, the fifth day of October, 1675. (pp. 5-6)

There are no records for John Fenwick and his family in Peter Wilson Coldman's *The Complete Book of Emigrants (1661-1699)*. An Edward Fenwick, however, is listed among the passangers from London, England, to New York in 1679. (p. 325)

John Clement in his introduction to *Sketches of the First Emigrant Settlers in Newton Township, Old Gloucester County, West New Jersey* writes,

> The influence of female example also deserves to be commended. Taken from their homes and from the circle of relatives and friends where the refinements, if not the luxuries, of life could be enjoyed, and where the strongest ties of human nature exist — the courage and the faithfulness of the wives and daughters of the first comers to the soil of New Jersey must excite the admiration of every reader. The trials and exposures through which they passed cannot, in our day, be fully appreciated. In the midst of a wilderness where even shelter was an object, these women are found, showing by word and deed that no complaint of theirs should bring despondency upon the little company. Resolute in the discharge of every duty, and unceasing in their efforts to contribute to the comfort and encouragement of their companions, they displayed those traits of character which belong to the sex alone, and which always accomplish so much when brought into action. Having shared every sacrifice and met every requirement, their position in the first endeavor to settle our State with English colonists should be made a prominent one and must ever command respect. (p. 9)

Joseph S. Sickler in *The History of Salem County New Jersey* writes (p. 17) that John Fenwick and his family and crew landed in the ship *Griffin* at the mouth of the Salem River on 23 November 1675 and that (p. 25) "[t]he *Griffin* returned to England and arrived again at Salem with emigrants within the next year." Among a list of ships coming to West Jersey from 1677 through 1705, Sickler notes (p. 26), "On 12th of twelfth month, 1677, arrived the ship *Mary* with emigrants, commanded by Capt. John Wall. The *Mary* made a second voyage from Ireland, with emigrants, and landed there at Elsinborough the same year."

Sickler writes, "Fenwick exercised excellent judgment in laying out his town of Salem, which he called New Salem. . . . Fenwick also had in mind several other settlements, but his attention at first was focused on New Salem, the capital of his colony, and his proposed town of Cohanzick, the present Greenwich." (p. 27)

Sickler states that the water ways were the only means of travel until

> [i]n 1682 the original King's road was constructed between Salem and Burlington. A Little later the King's road to Greenwich through Jericho was built. . . . The favorable location of Salem is readily seen by the fact that it was the terminal of the road from Burlington which was the main colonial town of Central New Jersey. . . . Salem was also the starting place of other roads no less important in West Jersey. From here led a road to Greenwich and another which eventually led to Cape May and the ocean. . . . Salem, Alloway and Oldman's Creeks were the chief arteries of travel until the first roads were pushed into the wilderness. . . . The Farmers had to take grain to the mills and return home with the product so that early in the colonization of the county, roads were built to enable the setters to reach the various mills. . . . The early roads of Salem were on the ridges. There was not money enough to erect bridges and to fill in causeways for approaches. The early surveyors avoided the swamps. It was their job to build without undue expense so they avoided the streams and the marshes to seek high ground whenever possible. For this reason, the early King's roads followed winding courses rather than straight lines. (pp. 52-53)

Sickler writes, "Until 1706 no court records were preserved in Salem County. This fact has led many to believe that there were no courts prior to 1706. This is not true. There were courts of some variety beginning with Fenwick. . . . It is true that the records, except a few fragments, have been lost. The reason for this may be taken from a grand jury record of 1712 . . . 'The Grand Jury of Salem, sat at December term, 1712. Whereas some years ago, the Grand Jury of the County of Salem, made application that the records should be delivered to Mr. Basse, to be bound and put in order, and then returned to the County again; but we understanding, that the records are not bound, nor returned to our County.' . . ." (pp. 56-57)

Sickler quotes (pp. 57-59) directly from records preserved at the Pennsylvania Historical Society of a criminal case in Salem in the year 1691. The murder victim "John Clark, late of Philadelphia was trading at Salem with goods according to his usual manner." (p. 58) The murderer, Thomas Lutherland, strangled Clark with a rope in the night on Clark's boat and stole Clark's goods. Lutherland escaped from prison where he had been confined after the first trial. At the final trial after Lutherland's apprehension and confession, as was the custom in English trial procedures of the day, "[t]he jury went out and were kept without meat and drink till they agreed and the next day they brought him guilty." (p. 58)

In 1682, Sickler writes,

> [A] law was passed by the Assembly of West Jersey providing for a weekly market, to be held on Tuesdays, at the wharf [in Salem]. The provisions were that no sale should take place before eleven o'clock in the morning; anyone buying goods before that time should be subject to a fine. The informer, no stranger to British law, would receive half of the fine.
>
> Fairs were established about the same time, to be held in Salem in May and October of each year, at which time all persons might buy and sell goods, wares and merchandise. The law governing these fairs gave the added inducement that all persons were exempt from arrest during the fair days and two days before and after. This respite from jail was much abused and by 1698 the town fathers, declaring "it being then taken into consideration, that since fairs have been held in this town, that foreigners do flock from other parts, not only of this county, but of the neighboring province, do sell liquor by retail during the time of such fairs, thereby encroaching upon the privilege of the inhabitants of this town, who only are authorized, and none else, to sell by retail as aforesaid," enacted an ordinance which provided that only inhabitants of Salem might sell liquor on the days in question, and if any foreigner should dare to compete with the inhabitants of Salem in the liquor selling business their stock of wet goods would be seized. In this case the informer received one half of the bootleg liquor. (p. 62)

In his *An Historical Account of the First Settlement of Salem, in West Jersey, by John Fenwick, Esq. Chief Proprietor of the Same* Robert Gibbon Johnson writes,

> As the demand for horses and other cattle increased with the rapid increase of the population, the farmers soon found that the rearing of the domestic animals would probably be to them more lucrative than almost any other business they could be engaged in; they therefore procured a law to be passed, which was to empower a person with the title of Chief Ranger of the county, who was also authorized to appoint deputies, if he thought proper, whose duties were, to look through the woods and waste lands, and take up all horses and other cattle over two years of age, not having a brand or ear-mark; for such were to be accounted strays, and forfeited to the lord proprietor of the province, unless the person claiming

> could establish his right of property therein before two justices of the peace. It was also the law, that no person whatsoever should mark any of his beasts, unless in the presence of some justice of the peace, constable, or chief ranger, under the penalty of £20. All these precautions were taken that the rightful owners in this kind of property might have it protected in safety; for in those early days, vast numbers of horses and cattle were raised in the woods and marshes, and they were only brought into the enclosures for two or three months during the inclemency of winter. This ordinance of marking was designed to prevent dishonest people of the county, horse coursers and drovers, from taking them away by stealth, and converting them to their own use. And no horse dealer or drover could pass his drove of beasts out of the province, without a certificate from the ranger, or his deputy, or some justice of the peace, under a penalty of the forfeiture of the whole of them. (pp. 74-75)

The following appears in *Under Four Flags: Old Gloucester County, 1686-1964, A History of Gloucester County New Jersey*, edited by Hazel B. Simpson: "It was the custom, in order to identify cattle, to 'mark' their ears, and in 1686 the Court ordered that all owners of stock should have their ear mark registered. At that time there were 306 registrations which show the design of each ear mark up to 1728.

"Ten years before the Court Ordered the ear marks, the Legislature in 1676 ordered that all cultivated fields be fenced to a height of 4 feet and 3 inches, which led to the erection of the snake or worm fences that continued well into the 20th century." (p. 86)

Johnson continues:

> From the increase of population, and the quantity of merchantable commodities ready for the market, store-keepers or merchants established themselves at Salem, and Cohansey or Greenwich, and carried on considerable business in the way of trade. The articles for exportation from Cohansey and Salem were deer-skins, dressed and undressed — peltry of every kind, of which the woods, swamps and marshes afforded an Abundance — besides cedar posts, shingles and bolts, staves, wheat, corn, some beef, pork and tallow. A partner of these trading firms was located in New York, to whom the cargoes were consigned, and on the return trips of their vessels brought out with them such goods as would be most saleable to the country people. The only market price for any of these agricultural productions, that I can find, was *3s. 9d.* per bushel for wheat, and *2s. 2d.* for corn.
>
> The commerce from the port of Salem, I am inclined to believe, was much greater to New York, Boston, and the West Indies, than from Cohansey. The persons to whom I stand remotely connected, traded a good deal to Boston. (pp. 75-76)

Sickler notes (p. 80) that the first newspaper published in the United States was in 1704. These first newspapers were full of shipping news, rewards being offered for the return of runaway slaves and indentured servants and notices of prisoners on the loose.

Sickler writes, "Smallpox raged throughout the colony, and in 1730 the justices and freeholders of Salem county decided that in view of the prevalence of this disease and the mortality caused thereby, that the annual fair should be postponed. Again in 1737 the officials of the county cancelled the annual fair, which would have been held at Cohansey and Salem that spring, because of another outbreak of small pox in Philadelphia." (p. 84)

Sickler: "The first notice of a stage line to Salem appears in December of 1767, in which one Aaron Silver advertises himself as a common carrier between Salem and William Cooper's ferry, now the city of Camden. . . . The line ran from Salem to Cooper's ferry in one day. The driver rested a day, then returned to Salem the third day." (p. 125)

John E. Pomfret, in his *Province of West New Jersey 1609 – 1702: A History of the Origins of an American Colony*, citing Evarts B. Greene and Virginia D. Harrington in *American Population before the Federal Census of 1790*, writes that "as late as 1708 . . . Gloucester, [had a population of] about 400. . . ." (p. 282)

In the West New Jersey section, entitled *An Hiftorical Defcription of the Province and Country of Weft-New-Jerfey in America*, of Gabriel Thomas' *An Hiftorical and Geographical Account of the Province and Country of Pennsylvania and of Weft-New-Jerfey in America*, Thomas writes:

> Befides there is *Glocester-Town*, which is a very Fine and Pleafant Place, being well ftor'd with Summer Fruits, as *Cherries*, *Mulberries*, and *Strawberries*, whither Young People come from *Philadelphia* in the Wherries to eat *Stra[w]berries* and *Cream*, within fight of which City it is fweetly Situated, being . . . but about three Miles diftance from thence. (pp. 19-20)

Thomas (*An Hiftorical Defcription of the Province and Country of Weft-New-Jerfey in America*) continues

> Now I fhall give thee an Account of the *English* Manufactory, that each County in *Weft-Nev-Jersey* affords. In the firft Place I fhall begin with *Burlington-County*, as for *Peltage*, or *Beavers Skins, Otter-Skins, Minks Skins, Musk-rats Skins, Rackcoon, Wild Cats, Martin*, and *Deer-Skins*, &c. The Trade in *Glocester-County* confifts chiefly in *Pitch, Tar*, and *Rosin*; the latter of which . . . is made by *Robert Styles*, an excellent Artift in that fort of Work, for he delivers it as clear as any *Gum-Arabick*. The Commerce carried on in *Salam-County*, is chiefly *Rice*, of which they have wonderful Produce every

Year; as alfo of *Cranberries* which grow there in great plenty, and which in Picle might be brought to Europe. (pp. 32-33)

The Journal of the American Irish Historical Society, Volume XXVI states: "William Kelly owned a house and lot in Salem township prior to 1685, as shown in "Salem Surveys" (No. 2, p. 36). A 'lot' at that time usually meant twenty acres. On April 2 1691, William Kelly gave a deed for twenty-two acres in the town of Salem. He was a weaver by trade." (p. 244)

It should be noted that George R. Prowell, in his *History of Camden, County, New Jersey,* points out that in Gloucester County, "The first birth recorded was that of the child of John and Jane Burroughs, of Gloucester River, March 14, 1687." (p. 32)

Prowell adds: "A jail was built at Gloucester in 1689. (See history of Gloucester City) [*sic*]. Courts were held in taverns and private houses until 1696, when a court-house and jail as one building was erected, which, with additions and repairs, was used until 1786, when it was destroyed by fire. . . ." (p. 33)

Isaac Mickle writes in *Reminiscences of Old Gloucester, or Incidents in the History of the Counties of Gloucester, Atlantic and Camden, New Jersey,* "After the *public buildings* at Gloucester were burnt in 1787, Woodbury was made the shire-town of the county, by a vote of the people." (p. 66)

According to documentation appearing in *West Jersey New Jersey Deed Records 1676-1721* compiled by John David Davis, in 1701, Nicholas Kelly is listed as "power of attorney to Edward Rush." (p. 156) Also on the same page, in 1701 Henry Johnson of Talbot County, Maryland, sold land to Nicholas Kelly.

Among the compilations presented by Elmer Garfield Van Name in *Old Deeds Belonging to the Salem County Historical Society with an Index of Unrecorded Deeds,* under D-137, it is noted that Thomas Kelly "of Allway's Creek in Salem [County conveyed] [t]o James Wiggins . . . of Salem 300 acres of land on a branch of Salem Creek." The "original deed" of 8 September 1724 was "unrecorded" and "[a]ssigned" on 19 October 1727 "to David Loper. . . ." It is recorded that David Loper was called Arthur Loper and that this assignation was also unrecorded.

H. Stanley Craig in *Genealogical Data: the Salem Tenth in West New Jersey,* citing *West Jersey Wills* as his source, includes documentation on the will of Thomas Kelley which was made on the 12 March 1728/9 and proven on 29 March 1729. Rachel is listed as Thomas Kelley's wife, and his children are listed as "John, Thomas, Mary, Martha and James." (p. 45) (See Appendix P, under Nelson, William (editor): *Documents Relating to the Colonial History State of New Jersey, Volume XXIII, Calendar of New Jersey Wills, Vol. I, 1670-1730.*)

According to documentation by Ronald Vern Jackson in *New Jersey Tax Lists, 1772-1822, Volume IV,* there was a John Kelley on Lower Alloways Creek in Salem County, New Jersey, in 1774 and a John Kelley in Woolwich Township, Gloucester County, New Jersey, in 1780.

Charlotte D. Meldrum and John Pitts Launey in their *Early Church Records of Gloucester County New Jersey* cite the Haddonfield Monthly Meeting records when noting that on 14 March 1747/8 (Documentation, taking into consideration the Quaker style of numbering months and the differences between the Julian and Gregorian calendars, suggests that the year for the following entry could also have been 1748, but the documentation for June 1747 seems to indicate that the following information must be from 1747.) "Abraham Kelly requests [a] certificate in order to remove himself and [his] wife Rachel to Burlington Monthly Meeting." (p. 107)

It is further noted that on 8 June 1747 "Abraham Kelly produced [a] certificate for himself, and [his] wife from [the] monthly meeting of Burlington." (p. 107)

Nelson R. Burr, in *The Anglican Church in New Jersey*, citing David Humphreys' bewailing the state of the Anglican community, which included the Kelly family, in *An Historical Account of the Incorporated Society for the Propagation of the Gospel in Foreign Parts, to the year 1728* (pp. 3-4), writes,

> Another obstacle was the religious illiteracy of the American-born, whose parents had brought at least a nominal attachment to some church. Weeks and months separated newcomers from old associations, and it was most difficult to establish parochial schools and obtain religious books. Overworked parents often became careless about imparting traditional religious instruction, and as in all frontier communities, the sense of divine things began to grow dim. Literally tens of thousands of Anglicans drifted away into the babel of sectarians. A saving remnant read the Prayer Book services at home, and they were the cornerstone of the Church's rebuilding, when the Society's missionaries came at last. (p. 22)

Sickler notes: "In later years the Episcopal Church under the Society for the Propagation of the Gospel took over the members of the Swedish congregations who had remained in this section from the settlements which antedated the English occupation. St. George's Episcopal Church at Churchtown in Lower Penns Neck township is a direct outgrowth of these first families of Swedes." (p. 65)

Joseph S. Sickler in *The History of Salem County New Jersey* writes, "The Swedish Lutheran church is to all intents and purposes, despite its name, the same as the Church of England. The organization is very similar, and bishops rule over it as in the Anglican Church. But until after the American Revolution the ministers of this church came from Sweden, and were responsible to the bishops there. The church at Raccoon, now Swedesboro, was closely connected with the parish at Penns Neck and in 1720 the joint congregations purchased a farm or glebe for the use of their minister. This farm is situated in Pilesgrove, Salem county...." (p. 106)

Nelson R. Burr in *The Anglican Church in New Jersey* relates the following in regard to the founding in 1702 of Saint Mary's Church in Burlington, New Jersey:

> At the opening of the eighteenth century, [Burlington] contained around two hundred families, living mostly in neat brick houses. It was the capital of West Jersey, the meeting-place of the courts, and a center of considerable trade, with a well-stocked market. The Churchmen began to become active in 1695, and on July 13 several bought a piece of land on Wood Street near Broad, for a cemetery, which they later enlarged and fenced. On March 6, 1702, Nathaniel Westland, Robert Wheeler, and Hugh Huddy bought the adjoining lot at the corner of Broad Street, as the site for a church.
>
> Plans were far advanced when [George] Keith and [John] Talbot appeared on October 29, 1702, and preached in the town hall on All Saints' Day. They were delighted to find many persons eager for services and willing to give about £200 to build a church at once. The faithful proceeded with a speed that pleased the Society and thoroughly alarmed the Church's opponents. . . . On August 22, 1703, the church was sufficiently ready for use, and Keith and Talbot preached the first sermons to a congregation from New York and various parts of New Jersey, including Governor Cornbury. . . . The Holy Communion was not administered, however, until Whitsunday, June 4, 1704.
>
> The parishioners joyfully left the court house and moved into the church, even though it was without floor, plaster, or glass. They still had a long way to go, and in 1703 the wardens begged the Society for a staggering list of necessities: chests of window glass, lead and solder, nails, linseed oil, "a Bell to be heard at some distance," Prayer Books, catechisms, and furnishings for the Communion table and pulpit. It took years to complete the church in the handsome style observed in 1728 by the recently arrived missionary, the Rev. Nathaniel Horwood. He described it as "a fair fabric erected of Brick, the dimensions 40 foot in Length, in Breadth 22 . . . very decently seated, with regular Pews, below, and a fair Gallery above at the West end." It was dedicated to Saint Mary the Virgin when the cornerstone was laid on March 25, 1703, the Feast of the Annunciation. (pp. 493-494)

Citing *S.P.G. Proceedings*, 1723 (pp 41-43) and David Humphreys (pp. 58-60, 187), Burr states: "Although Salem had been settled since 1675, nearly fifty years passed before the Church began to flourish there. In 1722, some Anglicans in the town and neighborhood earnestly entreated the Society [for the Propagation of the Gospel in Foreign Parts] to send them a missionary, because even the name of religion had been almost lost there." (p. 52)

Burr, citing Humphreys (pp. 187-88) and *S.P.G. Proceedings*, 1725 (pp. 37-38); 1726 (p. 40); 1727 (p.41); 1729 (p. 43), continues: "The Society . . . that very year sent John Holbrooke. . . . With the help of many Churchmen in Philadelphia and other places in Pennsylvania and New Jersey, the people built a neat little brick church. The mission prospered modestly from the start, with many adult baptisms, including conversions of Quakers and unchurched persons. There was evidence that many persons were trying to lead more Christian lives, and the increasing congregations manifested serious behavior in church. By 1726 the church was almost completed, and after June 24, 1728, the growing flock met regularly in 'Saint John's'. The only serious obstacle was a general reluctance to receive Communion, which Holbrooke attributed to deeply ingrained Quaker prejudice against the sacraments." (pp. 52-53)

Burr goes into greater detail on the history of Saint John's Church (founded in 1722) in Salem, New Jersey:

> The Church of England probably came to Salem in 1675, with a few members of John Fenwick's predominantly Quaker company. More Anglicans arrived later, and there is record of a Church of England marriage in 1691. [Footnote (p. 529): "Minute Book No. 2, Court at Salem, Office of the Secretary of State, Trenton, N.J."] The name of the minister is unknown, but it is recorded that the rector of Immanuel Church in Newcastle, Delaware, held occasional services, probably in the Salem Court House. After Saint Mary's was founded at Burlington in 1702, John Talbot used to visit Salem at irregular intervals. He mentions an unfinished church which had been generously aided by Colonel Francis Nicholson, a well-known benefactor of colonial parishes.
>
> In 1722 the Episcopalians made a determined effort to secure a missionary from the Society [for the Propagation of the Gospel in Foreign Parts], declaring that they had
>
>> never been so blessed, as to have a person settled among us to dispense the august ordinances of religion: inasmuch that even the name of it is almost lost among us; the virtue and energy of it over men's lives expiring, we won't say forgotten, for that implies previous knowledge of it ... [*sic*] The Lord in mercy look upon us, and incite you, according to your wonted piety, to have compassionate regard to our case.
>
> The Society could hardly overlook such an appeal, and in 1722 constituted Salem as a mission, under the care of the Rev. John Holbrooke. Before he arrived, the Rev. Messrs. Hesselius and Lidenius, ministers to the Swedish Lutheran churches in West Jersey, read prayers and preached at Salem. The Society voted £10 to each of them for the

favor, and even gave Hesselius £30 to help him return with his family to Sweden.

Holbrooke arrived in 1724, and ministered to the parish and neighboring places for about seven years, probably the toughest period of his life. The first difficulty was to persuade his flock to finish their church. A parish already had been organized, with Benjamin Vining and John Coleman as the first wardens. But little or nothing had been done to provide a place of worship, except in a room in the Salem County Court House. Some accounts allude to a "frame chapel" as having existed before the brick church, but Holbrook does not mention it, and an old picture of the brick church does not show a chapel beside it, as is sometimes stated.

Urged by Holbrooke, the people (although generally poor) contributed generously to erect a neat, brick church, which was begun on May 7, 1725, even though the land, including the present site, was not deeded until 1727. By February of that year the building was "almost completed," with a bell but without glass. It was formally opened for services on June 24, 1728, and accordingly was named "Saint John's." The parish was incorporated with that name in 1847.

The parish was most grateful to Samuel Hedge for giving the land, and Holbrooke was equally grateful to the people for his church, which he delightedly described to the Society:

> It is built of good brick and for ye materials and workmanship is reckoned a very neat church. It is forty feet long and twenty-eight broad. It was built by the contributions of the people of my congregations and of certain of ye adjacent inhabitants, among whom the people of Philadelphia were the most eminent contributors. His excellency, William Burnett, our Governor, gave ten pounds toward it.

The first Saint John's was a chapel-like edifice, with a high-peaked roof and a small square belfry topped by a short spire with a weather vane. The double-leaf front door had a narrow window on each side and a large fanlight several feet above it. There were side porches opening into the cemetery, separated from the street by a wall, with a double gate in front of the church. The building served until 1836, when the parish erected the present stone Gothic church. In 1884 the old brick church was torn down, and on its site rose a chapel, connected with the church by a cloister in 1911.

The erection of a church attracted a larger congregation, but Holbrooke was not happy. He got only £20 a year, aside from his £60 from the Society, and the low and marshy country began to play havoc with his health. The parish consisted mainly of poor farmers, and as Quakerism had "over-run" the country, he had only about seventy families and fourteen communicants in 1724-27. He had to travel a great deal, visiting a few families at Cohansey (Greenwich) and a larger congregation at Maurice River about forty miles away. There was no rectory or glebe, and he was forced to pay £15 a year in rent.

Soon after the parson arrived, he hinted that he would like to move to Trenton, where he heard the people wanted a missionary. Later he thought of going to Burlington, even though he hated to leave his poor congregation in the lurch, as some were "kind people, and seem to be well disposed." When the Society nodded approval in 1725, he declined to go, and then repented his decision. In 1732, disappointed at not receiving more help from the Society, he accepted a parish in Northampton County on the Eastern Shore of Virginia.

The Society could not let the mission fail, as it was the only one in the 140 miles between Burlington and Cape May, and had about 250 members. They therefore appointed the Rev. John Pierson, who arrived on January 30, 1734, and found the people delighted to see him. The congregation had held together fairly well during the vacancy, through the efforts of the Rev. Peter Tranberg, pastor of the Swedish Lutheran church at Penns Neck.

One of the first things the new parson did was to take a parish census. It revealed 2700 people in the county, 207 professors of the Church of England, twenty-three communicants, and a Sunday congregation of over one hundred. He gave the mission a much-needed stimulant, and began preaching one Sunday in the month at Greenwich-in-Cohansey, where the people were finishing little Saint Stephen's Church, and ministered when he could to the Swedes and English at Maurice River. Although the people were still poor and did not equal their promised contributions, they came to church more regularly. He even hoped to regain some who had joined the Quakers, and to convert most of his flock to a more friendly attitude towards the sacraments.

Having little knowledge of the country at first, he was amazed to find "nearly half ye county destitute of ye Baptismal Seal, & have nothing to distinguish them from Heathens, Save a little Tincture of Enthusiasm, which ye Fathers took into ye country with them." In 1744 he was trying, with little success, to make a Christian impression upon the Negroes and servants. Two years later, he served the Swedish church at Penns Neck, where the congregation was larger than at Salem and the people were faithful, although "a Set of Travelling enthusiasts" (the Moravians) were "very Industrious in Raising disturbances & divisions in the Church." Although Greenwich was declining, the prospects for Salem looked better, but next year Pierson died and was buried in the Salem churchyard.

Again the vast region of southern New Jersey was without a missionary, until the Society appointed the Rev. Thomas Thompson, . . . in response to a subscription sent by the wardens of Saint John's. Upon his arrival he was rudely surprised and disgusted to find "no house to lodge at & no Church-people to contribute to the Missionary's support," and that the so-called "wardens" were "never elected to that office, & what they affirm so confidently in their letter, that they have provided a house for me, is notoriously false . . . As I expected a companion of life from England, & had no home to carry her to in the cold season, I knew not what to do."

What he actually did was to resign and go to Chester, Pennsylvania. Perhaps feeling that he had been too hasty, he returned a year or two later and served Saint John's so regularly that the people were satisfied with his devotion, as well as his "sound & pure" doctrine. The Society tried to help him by ordering the vestry to get him a rectory and a glebe and add £20 to his salary. The poor congregation flatly refused, and was so offended by the attempted pressure, that they even said no minister was necessary or wanted. That was more than enough for Mr. Thompson, who in 1749 left them for good.

From that time until 1792, Saint John's had no settled Anglican pastor and the services were spasmodic. The parish owed its life to the Rev. Eric Unander of Saint George's Swedish Lutheran church in Penns Neck. From 1749 until 1755, he did his utmost to help Saint John's and attended other little Anglican congregations on weekdays. Although he was married and had several children, he had "no other support than the small & uncertain subscription of the Inhabitants of those Places which in the whole amounted to but a mere Maintenance." The parishioners of Saint John's requested the Society to assist him, but as they were unable or unwilling to help, the Society declined and the parish remained destitute.

The mission lapsed, and in 1768 a Society missionary, writing for the *Pennsylvania Journal,* complained that "at Cohansey (Greenwich) stands a church, but there is not the shadow of a congregation in the County (Cumberland). At Salem the Episcopal cause is almost as low." In 1772 the church was extensively repaired. . . .

Within a few years, war clouds began to drive over the struggling parish. . . . During the war British troops commandeered Saint John's as quarters, and of course utterly ruined it in their raid on Salem in March, 1778. Their spite was inflamed by the fact that so many of the congregation were patriots. When their commander, Colonel Charles Mawhood, posted a list of Salem men proscribed as "rebels," three-quarters of them were Episcopalians. Some of their names may still be seen on gravestones in the old churchyard. (pp. 529-533)

Joseph S. Sickler in *The History of Salem County New Jersey* writes, "The missionaries of the church of England were still complaining in the *Pennsylvania Journal* [italics added] for 1768 that 'at Cohansey in West Jersey stands a church, but there is not the shadow of a congregation in the county. At Salem the Episcopal is almost as low'." (p. 126)

The convoluted quest of locating specifics in New Jersey in regard to the Kelly genealogy has not just been complicated by the destruction caused by the Revolutionary war as William Nelson in *Archives of the State of New Jersey First Series, Volume XXII* points out in his preface: "The early Dutch churches as a rule were scrupulously careful to keep and preserve in the church archives registers of baptisms and marriages. The churches of other denominations not only were not so particular, but when records were made they were often regarded as the private property of the pastors, and were carried away by them on their removal to other charges." (p. v)

Nelson R. Burr, citing David Humphreys (pp. 44-65) again, notes that about 1727 Colonel Lewis Morris reported that "in New Jersey only about 600 persons (about four per cent of the populations) attended Anglican services, and only one and seven-tenths per cent received the Holy Communion — about 250 among 15,000 people!" (p. 33)

Pehr Kalm, writing in his *Travels into North America* (Volume II) about his time in Raccoon (Swedesboro), New Jersey, in December 1748, says,

> There is a great mixture of people of all forts in thefe colonies, partly of fuch as are lately come over from *Europe*, and partly of fuch as have not yet any fettled place of abode. Hence it frequently happens that when a clergyman has married fuch a couple, . . . the bridegroom fays he has no money at prefent, but would pay the fee at the firft opportunity: however he goes off with his wife, and the clergyman never gets his due. This proceeding has given occafion to a cuftom which is now common in *Maryland*. When the clergyman marries a very poor couple, he breaks off in the middle of the Liturgy, and cries out *Where is my fee?* The man muft then give the money, and the clergyman proceeds; but if the bridegroom has no money, the clergyman defers the marriage till another time, when the man is better provided. People of fortune, of whom the clergyman is fure to get his due, need not fear this difagreeable queftion, when they are married. (pp. 27-28)

Kalm (Volume II) continues

> There is a very peculiar diverting cuftom here, in regard to marrying. When a man dies, and leaves his widow in great poverty, or fo that fhe cannot pay all the debts with what little fhe has left, and that, notwithftanding all that, there is a perfon who will marry her, fhe muft be married in no other habit than her fhift. By that means, fhe leaves to the creditors of her deceafed hufband her cloaths, and every thing which they find in the houfe. But fhe is not obliged . . . to pay them any thing more, becaufe fhe has left them all fhe was worth, even her cloaths, keeping only a fhift to cover her, which the laws of the country cannot refufe her. As foon as fhe is married, and no longer belongs to the deceafed hufband, fhe puts on the cloaths which the fecond has given her. The *Swedifh* clergymen here have often been obliged to marry a woman in a drefs which is fo little expenfive, and fo light. This appears from the regifters kept in the churches, and from the accounts given by the clergymen themfelves. I have likewife often feen accounts of fuch marriages in the *Englifh* gazettes; which are printed in thefe colonies; and I particularly remember the following relation: A woman went, with no other drefs than her fhift, out of the houfe of her deceafed hufband to that of her bridegroom, who met her half way with fine new cloaths, and faid, before all who were prefent, that he lent them his bride; and put them on her with his own hands. It feems, he faid that he lent the cloaths, left, if he had faid he gave them, the creditors of the firft hufband fhould come, and take them from her; pretending, that fhe was looked upon as the relict of her firft hufband, before fhe was married to the fecond. (pp. 29-30)

William Nelson in *Archives of the State of New Jersey First Series, Volume XXII*, citing "The Pennsylvania Journal", June 18, 1752, No. 500, quoted in *New Jersey Archives, Volume XIX* (pp.161-165), includes the following:

> Annapolis in Maryland June 4. About a Fortnight ago there happened in Frederick County in this Province, as comical a Wedding, as we remember to have heard of: A Couple, with their Guests, (having obtain'd a License) came to the House of a reverend Clergyman, late in the Evening, after he had been in Bed some time with his Wife, and desired to be married; he willing to oblige them, got up and dress'd himself in order to perform the Ceremony; but the Bridegroom having imbib'd a Notion, that if he married a Woman with any thing, he should be obliged to pay all her Debts, and not otherwise, and as she came from the Province of New Jersey, he was

doubtful about her Circumstances; the obliging Bride, to remove all incumbrances, stripped to her Buff, and two Women held a Sheet between her and the Clergyman while he performed his Office; but she having forgot her Cap at undressing, in the midst of the Ceremony it came into her Mind, and she pulled that off too, and flung it on the Bed, and was married to her Spouse (if not in a Wedding Suit) in her Birth Day Suit: After the Ceremony was over, the Bridegroom put on her one of his own Shirts to cover her — This Account the Reader may perhaps look on as improbable and untrue, but he may be assured, it is a certain and naked Truth. (pp. xcvii-xcviii)

William Nelson in *Archives of the State of New Jersey First Series, Volume XXII*, refers to Henry Reed Stiles' *Bundling: Its Origin, Progress and Decline in America* in noting that bundling, the practice of a young couple sleeping in the same bed with their clothes on before marriage, was used as part of the courting ritual in early New Jersey. Nelson writes, "[A] word may be expected regarding that singular custom known as 'Bundling,' where young people carried on their courting under circumstances calculated to hasten the wedding. The usage is an ancient one in the rural districts of England, was introduced into New England by the early settlers, was very generally practiced by the original Dutch inhabitants of New Jersey and their descendants so late as 1830, and was much in vogue among the New England settlers in West Jersey down to the Revolution, if not later." (p. xcviii)

William Nelson again in *Archives of the State of New Jersey First Series, Volume XXII*, citing *New Jersey Archives XXIV* (p.687), notes, "A license cost a man a month's wages or more. When the Stamp Act was passed, in 1765, this was regarded as so unconscionable an additional burden that by common consent it was not enforced so far as marriage licenses were concerned, in New Jersey." (p. cix)

Kenn Stryker-Rodda, writing in the preface to his *Revolutionary Census of New Jersey*, states:

Anyone who has attempted genealogical research in New Jersey is aware of the fact that the federal census returns for the years 1790, 1800, 1810, and 1820 are not extant. Moreover, only a few fragments of colonial censuses exist, and many records of the colonial period — public, private, and ecclesiastical — were destroyed, or taken away by Loyalists during the Revolutionary War.

The only records that are state-wide are the tax ratables. Of at least 50,000 such lists compiled between 1773 and 1822, some 1,845 have been preserved. For the Revolutionary period there is at least one list for each of the townships into which the thirteen counties of the colony/state were divided. Lists for Salem, Sussex, Cape May, and Cumberland counties for the years 1772–1774 are complete; for Burlington County, only Chesterfield Township is missing, and for Gloucester County, there are lists for four of the seven townships. . . . (p. v)

There are a number of Kellys listed in the tax ratables for 1773 and 1774 in the Stryker-Rodda book, including several John Kellys located in Salem County at both Lower and Upper Alloways Creek and at Lower Penns Neck, but, since the Loyalist John Kelly who settled in Kingsclear, New Brunswick, after the war is documented in several places as being from Gloucester and that John Kelly appears to have had a brother named William who also was a New Jersey Loyalist that settled near John Kelly in New Brunswick, the William Kelly listed at Gloucester in Gloucester County in the ratable seems most likely to be connected directly to him. Keeping in mind that Irish emigrants came to North America in family groups and that the Kelly family appears to have been among the original settlers of the Irish Tenth in the 1670s, it is more than likely, in the Colonial and Revolutionary War period, that any Kelly in Burlington, Gloucester and Salem Counties was related. It should also be kept in mind that the law of primogeniture, which stipulates that the oldest male heir inherited family property, was in effect in early West Jersey.

The following appears (p. 309) in *Documents Relating to the Colonial History of the State of New Jersey, Tenth Volume of Extracts From American Newspapers Relating to New Jersey 1773-1774, Archives of the State of New Jersey, First Series, Volume XXIX* "edited by the late William Nelson succeeded by A. Van Doren Honeyman":

THE NOTED HORSE
LYON,

The Property of JOHN KELLEY, *in Gloucester County*,
WILL cover the Season, till the First of August ensuing, at the Stable of AMOS HUTCH, at *Job's-Town*, in *Burlington* County, *West New Jersey* at FORTY Shillings the season. FOUR POUNDS to insure a foal, or TWENTY SHILLINGS the single Leap. He is a Chestnut Sorrel, has three white Feet, and a Blaze in his Face, near 16 Hands high, remarkably well proportioned, and strong built, paces a Travel, and trots exceedingly well; he is supposed to be equal, if not superior in Speed to any Horse of his Blood on the Continent; his Carriage is very bold and fine. - - - Attendance will be given, and Pasture provided at *Two Shillings and Six-pence per Week*, by

Isaac Kelley

March 22, 1774.

THE WAR

Avoiding a long polemical discourse on the causes, the ensuing battle descriptions and the minutia of the differences between the opposing military forces of the American Revolution, I will attempt to confine myself, in the following pages, to what is relevant to the Kelly family.

George R. Prowell, in *The History of Camden County*, discussing the causes of the conflict, points out that "the crown and then Parliament insisted upon the power to tax the colonies as they pleased, and they made the cost of the war with France [i.e., French and Indian War (1754 – 1763)] a special pretext for enforcing this claim, because, as the ministry argued, the war had been of American origin, and in its prosecution the mother-country had accumulated an enormous debt for the protection of her domains on this side of the Atlantic." (p. 37)

Joseph S. Sickler, in *The History of Salem County New Jersey*, relates the following:

> The year of 1774 saw the clouds of war definitely hover over Salem county. . . . The struggle had long been brewing. The Stamp Act, the Navigation Acts, and now the Boston Port Bill had all caused concern and unrest in the colonies. Salem was no exception. Although it had profited greatly from the English protection of its coastwise shipping and had not suffered in the colonial wars as had New England, many of its citizens were willing and anxious to throw their support in the impending struggle against the mother country. The Town Meeting was called upon for aid at this time. The first of these was held in Salem at the court house on July 15th, 1774 "to consider of some proper measures to be taken in support of American freedom at this alarming crisis."
>
> The meeting was the Declaration of Independence as far as Salem was concerned. . . .
>
> Another public meeting was held on October 13, 1774. At this meeting Grant Gibbon was named chairman and entrusted with the difficult task of raising money for the distressed, poor and starving patriots of Boston. It is said that a sum of one hundred fifty-seven pounds was raised by subscription and forwarded by Thomas Sinnickson, a member of the committee, to Boston. Three years later when Salem county was under the heel of the invader there is no record that Boston reciprocated in raising this sum for the distressed farmers of this locality. But in 1774 this charity was widespread. As yet the battles of Lexington and Concord had not been fought, but Boston was under the heel of the British army, and sympathetic patriotic feeling extended throughout the colonies on behalf of the inhabitants of Boston.

In the early winter of this same year occurred a most startling event which materially precipitated the Revolution in West Jersey. This was the Greenwich Tea Party on the night of November 22. It happened at Greenwich, in what was once Salem county, and the participants were practically all sons of men who were residents of Salem county before the division. A brig named the *Grayhound,* Captain J. Allen, with a cargo of tea headed into Cohansey creek and discharged her cargo at Greenwich. Some accounts say that the cargo was destined for Salem but that because of storm and fear the captain decided to dock at Greenwich. Emulating the Boston Tea Party, a band of young men disguised as Indians learned the whereabouts of the stored tea and seizing it, pub[l]icly burned the cargo. . . .

The destruction of the tea caused consternation in this section. Especially indignant were the owners of the tea and the Tories who sympathized with them. Attempts were made to prosecute these men for their act, but a convenient Whig grand jury in Cumberland county refused to find bills. Civil suits were also brought against the participants, but as the colonies drifted into the Revolution these suits were abandoned and the tea owners had to bear the loss.

As the Revolution became imminent frequent meetings were held throughout Salem county not only for military purposes and for raising money, but for the economic purpose of encouraging home manufacture. The colonists knew only too well that their trade from England would be shut off, and that they, only too soon, would be thrown upon their own resources. They decided to extend the production of flax by sowing more seed than formerly. The patriotic ladies of the colony were urged to work overtime on the spinning wheel and the loom. One resolution urged "that our young women, instead of trifling their time away, do prudently employ it in learning the use of the spinning wheel."

In 1775, a committee of observation chosen in the meeting by the several townships of Salem county was formed. . . .

In June, 1775, after the war had actually opened in New England, William Patterson, secretary of the provincial congress, issued a public notice calling on each county to organize a militia company. In addition a fund of ten thousand pounds was asked for, the sum to be divided proportionately between the counties. Salem's share was near the top. . . . (pp. 130-134)

Benson J. Lossing, in his *Pictorial Field-Book of the Revolution* (Volume I), points out in a footnote that the terms *Whig* and *Tory* "were copied by us from the political vocabulary of Great Britain, and were first used here, to distinguish the opposing parties in the Revolution, about 1770." (p. 71)

The following by Gilbert Burnet appears in *Burnet's History of His Own Time, Part I*:

> The south-west counties of Scotland have seldom corn enough to serve them round the year: and the northern parts producing more than they need, these of the west usually came in the summer to buy at Leith the stores that come from the north: and from a word *whiggam*, used in driving their horses, all that drove was called the *whiggamors*, and shorter the *whiggs*. Now in that year, after the news came down of duke Hamilton's defeat, the ministers animated their people to rise, and march to Edinburgh: and they came up marching on the head of the parishes, with an unheard-of fury, praying and preaching all the way as they came. The marquis of Argyll and his party came and headed them, they being about 6000. And this was called the *whiggamors'* inroad: and ever after that all that opposed the court came in contempt to be called *whiggs*: and from Scotland the word was brought into England, where it is now one of our unhappy terms of distinction. (pp. 72-73)

A footnote on page 73 of the 1897 edition of *Burnet's History of My Own Time, Part I*, states, "It seems doubtful whether the shortened term 'Whig' was in vogue before the fight at the Pentland Hills in 1666, when Burnet himself intimates (f. 234) that it was first used. There is certainly no trace that 'ever after' 1648 it was the name given to opponents of the court. Halton, Lauderdale's brother, entitles his account of the Pentland rebellion, 'The Historie off the Whiggamor Road,' *Lauderdale Papers*, i. 252."

Lossing further states, "all whose party bias was *democratic* were called Whigs. The origin of the word *Tory* is not so well attested. The Irish malcontents, half robbers and half insurgents, who harassed the English in Ireland at the time of the massacre in 1640, were the first to whom this epithet was applied. It was also applied to the court party as a term of reproach. . . ." (Volume I, p. 71)

In footnote v accompanying "Chapter Five" in R.F. Foster's *Modern Ireland 1600-1972*, Foster includes the following in regard to the word "tory": "*Toraidhe*, the Irish word for 'raider', was applied from the mid-1640s to the banditti remnants of Irish armies. It later became a satirical sobriquet for political 'outlaws'." (p. 103)

North Callahan, in *Royal Raiders: The Tories of the American Revolution*, writing of those loyal to Great Britain in the American Revolution, notes, "They were contemptuously called 'Tories' by their enemies, after their English counterparts personified by [British Prime Minister] Lord North and his associates; but they called themselves 'Loyalists' because of their adherence to Great Britain." (p. 35)

North Callahan: "For most [colonists], independence came as a last resort; so it is no wonder that many chose to remain within the maternal fold, or at least were not convinced of the urgency of leaving it." (p. 9)

Paul H. Smith, citing, in an accompanying footnote (47), "'*State of Sir William Howe's Army,*' *filed Oct. 1777, Germain Papers. See also a conflicting return of the provincials in the British army, July 7, 1777, Clinton Papers,*" in *Loyalists and Redcoats a Study in British Revolutionary Policy*, writes, in regard to British recruitment, that "significant recruiting began only after General [William] Howe captured New York, in August and September 1776. By midsummer 1777, however, well after Britain had regained the initiative in America, only slightly more than 3,000 men were in provincial corps. . . ." Smith, citing in a footnote (48), "'*State of His Majesty's Provincial Forces,*' *May 1, 1782, British Headquarters Papers,*" notes that, "six months later this figure had jumped to only about 4,400." (pp. 76-77)

The following appears in John Graves Simcoe's preface to *Simcoe's Military Journal*:

> We find in *Rivington's Royal Gazette* [italics added], printed at New York during the presence of the British army in the city, an advertisement for recruits. . . . :
>
> ALL ASPIRING HEROES
> Have now an opportunity of distinguishing themselves by
> joining
> THE QUEEN'S RANGER HUZZARS,
> Commanded by
> Lieutenant-Colonel Simcoe.
>
> Any spirited young man will receive every encouragement, be immediately mounted on an elegant horse, and furnished with clothing, accoutrements, &c., to the amount of forty guineas, by applying to Cornet Spencer, at his quarters, No. 1033 Water street, or his rendezvous, Hewitt's Tavern, near the Coffee House, and the defeat at Brandywine, on Golden Hill.
>
> Whoever brings a Recruit shall instantly receive TWO GUINEAS.
>
> Vivant Rex et Regina. (pp. vii-viii)

Paul H. Smith, in *Loyalists and Redcoats a Study in British Revolutionary Policy*, writes that at the beginning of the Revolution the British had assumed "that only a small disaffected minority was responsible for the revolt. . . ." (p. 32) Smith adds that until 1782 British officials "apparently were unable to imagine that the great majority of Americans were not passionately devoted to the restoration of British rule." (p. 62)

Once again, in *Loyalists and Redcoats a Study in British Revolutionary Policy*, Paul H. Smith notes, "Most Englishmen believed the majority of Americans to be essentially loyal, the bulk of the rebels too cowardly and poorly trained to face the British army, and Loyalists resolutely determined to prevent the overthrow of imperial authority." (p. 168)

Smith: "From their experience, the British had found provincial corps inefficient, poorly disciplined, and composed of sickly, ignorant riffraff. The provincial, equally aggrieved, thought the British arrogant, overbearing, and condescending. Officially, he was rated junior to regular officers within each grade; socially, he was assigned an even lower position. Galled at his assumed inferiority, the provincial protested his subordinate 'status' and became in time bitterly opposed to serving with the regular army on such terms." (pp. 33-34) Smith adds, "on the whole, [General William] Howe never considered Loyalists, enlisted in provincial units, a substitute for regular reinforcements." (p. 47)

Smith writes that, during the war, "British loyalist policy, which scarcely existed as a 'policy,' was unclear and vacillated dangerously." (p. 57)

Don N. Hagist writes, in *British Soldier, American War*, "The British army was a volunteer force, and most of the men who served in it did so by choice." (p. 7) Refuting the belief that the British were no match for the Patriots, who adopted the guerrilla tactics of the Native Americans, Hagist notes, "Contrary to much popular literature, the British army adapted rapidly and effectively to the conditions of the war in America." (p. 11) Hagist points out: "The British army in America laid aside the formal linear warfare techniques practiced for European battles and adopted more rapid fluid movements by lightly armed troops in open formations." (p. 300, note 32)

In *Official Register of the Officers and Men of New Jersey in the Revolutionary War*, William Scudder Stryker lists a number of Kellys and Longs in the New Jersey Militia, New Jersey State Troops and the Continental Army. (See Stryker, William S.: *Official Register of the Officers and Men of New Jersey in the Revolutionary War* in Appendix P.)

Thomas Cushing and Charles Sheppard also note in their *History of the Counties of Gloucester, Salem, and Cumberland New Jersey, with Biographical Sketches of Their Prominent Citizens*: "Early in the war many men from New Jersey enlisted in regiments of other States, or in those raised by direct authority of the Continental Congress." (p. 39)

Once again, in attempting to trace the Kelly family, who was predominately Anglican, I have included the following from Nelson R. Burr's *The Anglican Church in New Jersey*:

> Reading the signs of the times, the clergy were already leaving New Jersey in the spring of the Battle of Lexington [19 April 1775]. Isaac Browne of Newark wrote [6 April 1775] to the Society's secretary: "I am informed that some of my Rev[eren]d Brethren in these Parts have been obliged to abscond in these troublesome Times, or at least they thôt it necessary." There is more than a hint that the aged and stubborn Loyalist had some doubt of their courage and tenacity. (pp. 392-393)

Citing George Otto Trevelyan in *The American Revolution*, Vol. III, (pp. 290-291), Charles Leonard Lundin, in his *Cockpit of the Revolution: The War for Independence in New Jersey*, states,

> In sharp contrast to the activity of these denominations was the attitude of the Episcopalians. For some years there had been considerable ill-feeling between the Anglican clergy and the leaders of the dissenting sects, particularly the Presbyterians. The Episcopalian ministers had long agitated in favor of having an American bishopric established, in order to strengthen the position of the Church in the colonies. The Dissenters, however, with inherited memories of the persecutions their forbears had suffered in England at the hands of the state church, and with a disquieting object lesson in the intolerance of the Established Church in Virginia and the Carolinas, resisted by every means in their power this proposal to increase the prestige and official power of the Church of England in the new land. (p. 101)

Lundin continues,

> So violent did the controversy become that public opinion grew almost hysterical, and the Anglicans increased general irritation by their unwise tactics. Instead of attempting to conciliate hostile opinion, they emphasized their loyalty to the King and the British government, accused the Dissenters of republican principles, and exaggerated the beneficial effect which the naming of an American bishop would have on the growth of the Church in the colonies. (p. 101)

Lundin, citing *New Jersey Archives, Volume IX* (p. 504), says, "To make matters worse in a country which was strongly unclerical in its attitude, the Anglican clergy in New Jersey petitioned the governor in 1760 to deprive justices of the peace of the right to perform marriages; and, when the governor professed lack of authority for such a step, they carried their appeal to the Lords of Trade in 1765, through the Bishop of London." (p. 102)

Lundin continues

> Nothing seems to have come of the attempt; but the mere fact that it was made at such a time is an interesting revelation of the slight importance which the clergyman attached to American opinion, and of their complete dependence on British authority. A circumstance which further alienated the Anglican ministers in New Jersey from the American point of view was the fact that most of them, owing to the small size of their congregations, depended for their support chiefly on the British Society

for the Propagation of the Gospel in Foreign Parts. Their material as well as their moral sustenance came from across the sea. (p. 102)

Citing the *Society for the Propagation of the Gospel in Foreign Parts* transcripts, Ser. B, Part I, No. 245; ibid., Ser. B, Vol. 24, No. 308, Lundin writes,

> Given this background, and the fact that the ordination oath of Anglican clergymen acknowledged the supremacy of the King and promised conformity to the doctrines, discipline, and worship of the Church of England, there could be little doubt as to the stand this group would take in the Revolution. Before independence was declared, ministers frequently preached sermons "calculated as much as the Times would permit, to mitigate the general Infatuation," or to "inculcate the principle of peace, order and good government," and occasionally received unwelcome attentions from the Sons of Liberty for their pains. (p. 102)

Lundin, citing the *Society for the Propagation of the Gospel in Foreign Parts* transcripts Ser. B, Vol. 24, Nos. 148, 310 and Samuel Davies Alexander: *Princeton College in the Eighteenth Century*, states,

> After July 1776, when it became impossible to perform the liturgy with its prayers for the King, the Royal Family, and the High Court of Parliament, virtually all the Anglican clergymen preferred closing the churches to altering the form of service. In New Jersey only one minister of the denomination, Robert Blackwell, S.P.G. missionary at Gloucester, Waterford, and Greenwich, definitely joined the Americans. . . . The influence of such ministers led a great proportion of the members of the Church of England to join the Loyalists — a fact not surprising since the generally conservative atmosphere of the Church before the Revolution appealed primarily to those persons who, for temperamental or other reasons, would naturally be attracted to the Loyalist camp when hostilities began. (p. 103)

Nelson R. Burr, citing Sir Edward Colpoy Midwinter in "The S.P.G. and the Church in the American Colonies. Three Lectures. II. New Jersey" (pp. 139-140), writes,

> New Jersey suffered hideously — more, perhaps, than any other colony except South Carolina — especially from the pillaging of ill-disciplined Hessians. Farms were ravaged, libraries were robbed, churches and meeting houses were burned. The fate of many communities is illustrated by the ruin of Hopewell and Maidenhead. Homes were stripped, cattle and sheep were driven off, every bit of clothing and house linen was

stolen, and what was not portable was destroyed. Hardly a soldier was seen without a horse loaded with booty, while hundreds of families were ruined and left to wander in the woods without clothing. (p. 393)

Citing Robert Van Amburgh Hoffman's *The Revolutionary Scenes in New Jersey* (pp. 212, 220), Nelson R. Burr says,

> In reprisal for Hessian brutalities, Whig mobs sometimes took a savage glee in desecrating Anglican churches. In Newark the Patriot party decided to treat Trinity Church as the King's troops had treated the Presbyterian meeting house when they marched through town, burning and plundering. In 1778, an infuriated crowd smashed the doors and windows, hacked great holes in the roof, and stole the pulpit hangings. Later the community repaired the damage. At Perth Amboy, in 1777, several thousand Patriot troops were billeted to watch the British on Staten Island. Many of them slept in Saint Peter's Church and nearly wrecked it, and left the churchyard a shambles. (p. 393)

The following, again from Prowell, gives some idea of the complexities of the conflict in New Jersey:

> The movement of the British army, under command of General Howe, from Boston, by way of Halifax, to the vicinity of New York, the route of Washington's forces at the battle of Long Island, August 27, 1776, the evacuation of New York by the Americans and the capture of Fort Washington, on the Hudson, by the British on November 15th — these were the events which led to Washington's retreat into New Jersey. With his diminished columns he fell back to New Brunswick, where he hoped to make a stand; but the terms of the New Jersey and Maryland Brigades and the Pennsylvania Flying Camp were about expiring, and neither arguments nor threats could prevent the men from disbanding and returning to their homes. The remnant of the army, with Lord Cornwallis harassing its rear, arrived at Princeton on December 1st, and thence passed on to Trenton, where it crossed the Delaware into Pennsylvania on the 8th. Reinforced by Sullivan and Gates, Washington recrossed the Delaware on Christmas night and effected the surprise and defeat of Colonel Rahl's Hessian contingent of the British forces.
>
> Although after the Trenton victory the American commander retired to his strong position on the Delaware shore, he had by no means relinquished his ambition to repossess Western New Jersey, and at once began preparations for a second expedition. He again marched to Trenton on December 30th. General Maxwell, who on the retreat through the State

had been left at Morristown with his brigade, including the Gloucester troops, was ordered to advance through New Brunswick, as if threatening an attack, and harass all the contiguous posts of the enemy as much as possible. On the night of January 2, 1777, Washington, after the skirmish on Assanpink Creek, swung round the British flank to the rear, reached Princeton at early dawn of the 3rd, defeated and dispersed Colonel Mawhood's force of three regiments, and was safe among the hills of the Upper Raritan while Cornwallis was lumbering along in an ineffectual pursuit. He had to mourn the loss of the gallant General Mercer, who fell in the first assault at Princeton, and whose body bore the marks of sixteen British bayonet wounds.

Washington's brilliant achievements were needed to revive the patriotic spirit of New Jersey, which previously had been fast succumbing to the advance of the foe. Howe had offered pardon and protection to all who would abandon the national cause and renew their allegiance to the King. Until Washington rolled back the tide of disaster, more than two hundred people within the State were daily abjuring their loyalty to the American government. . . . The Legislature had moved from Princeton to Burlington, and thence to Pittstown and Haddonfield, where it dissolved on December 2, 1776. Samuel Tucker, chairman of the Committee of Safety, treasurer and judge of the Supreme Court, vacated his offices and swore fealty to the crown. The whole number of the people of New Jersey who took advantage of Howe's proclamation is stated at two thousand seven hundred and three. But the victories of Trenton and Princeton lightened up the gloomy horizon; citizens found that Howe's protections did not save them from the depredations of the Hessian soldiery, who overran the State and spared neither age nor sex from outrage and plunder; what the earnest recommendations of Congress, the zealous exertions of Governor Livingston and the ardent supplications of Washington could not effect, was produced by the rapine and devastations of the Royal forces. The whole country became instantly hostile to the invaders, and sufferers of all parties rose as one man to avenge their personal injuries. With his quick insight, Washington perceived that this was the moment for the recovery of New Jersey. From his headquarters at Morristown he issued, on January 25, 1777, a proclamation giving all persons who had accepted British protection thirty days in which to repair to the nearest headquarters of the Continental service, and then to surrender their papers and receive full pardon for their past offenses. The alternative offered them was to retire with their families within the British lines or be regarded as adherents of the King of Great Britain and enemies of their country. The result was most satisfactory. Hundreds of timid inhabitants renewed their allegiance to

America, the most dangerous Tories were driven out and the army was largely increased by volunteers and by the return of many of its veterans who had deserted during the dark days of the previous November and December. (pp. 45-47)

Thomas Francis Gordon, in his *The History of New Jersey from Its Discovery by Europeans to the Adoption of the Federal Constitution*, writes that after the defeat of the Americans at the Battle of Long Island on 27 August 1776,

> [s]uccessful resistance to the victorious enemy being now hopeless, and the American troops, lying in the lines without shelter from the heavy rains, becoming daily more dispirited, the resolution was taken to withdraw the army from Long Island. This difficult movement was effected on the night of the 28th, with such silence and despatch, that all the troops and military stores, with a greater part of the provisions, and all the artillery except some heavy pieces, which, in the state of the roads, could not be drawn, were carried over in safety. Early the next morning, the British outposts perceived the rear-guard crossing the East river, out of reach of their fire. (p. 211)

Gordon continues,

> In a letter from General Washington to Congress, the state of the army, after this event, was thus feelingly described. "Our situation is truly distressing. The check our detachment sustained on the 27th ultimo, has dispirited too great a proportion of our troops, and filled their minds with apprehension and despair. The militia, instead of calling forth their utmost efforts to a brave and manly opposition, in order to repair our losses, are dismayed, intractable, and impatient to return. Great numbers of them have gone off, in some instances, almost by whole regiments, in many, by half ones, and by companies at a time." (p. 211)

Gordon:

This retreat into, and through New Jersey, was attended with almost every circumstance that could embarrass and depress the spirits. It commenced immediately after the heavy loss at Fort Washington. In fourteen days after the event, the whole flying camp claimed its discharge, and other troops also, whose engagements terminated about the same time, daily departed. The two Jersey regiments which had been forwarded by General Gates, under General St. Clair, went off to a man, the moment they entered their own state. A few officers without a single private, were all of these regiments which St. Clair brought to the commander-in-chief. The troops who were with Washington, mostly of the garrison of Fort Lee, were without tents, blankets, shoes, and the necessary utensils to dress their provisions. In this situation, the general had the address to prolong a march of ninety miles, to the space of nineteen days. During his retreat, scare an inhabitant joined him, whilst numbers daily flocked to the royal army, to make their peace, and beg protection. On the one side, was a well appointed full clad army, dazzling by its brilliance, and imposing by its success; on the other, a few poor fellows whose tattered raiment but too well justified the *sobriquet* of "ragamuffins," with which the sneering tories reproached them, fleeing for their safety. The British commissioners issued a proclamation commanding all persons assembled in arms against his Majesty's government, to disband and return to their homes; and all civil officers to desist from their treasonable practices, and to relinquish their usurped authority. A full pardon was offered to all, who within sixty days would appear before an officer of the crown, claim the benefit of the proclamation, and subscribe a declaration of his submission to the royal authority. Seduced by this proclamation, not only the ordinary people shrunk from the apparent fate of the country in this its murkiest hour, but the vapouring patriots who sought office and distinction at the hands of their countrymen, when danger in their service was distant, now crawled into the British lines, humbly craving the mercy of their conquerors; and whined out, as justification, that though they had united with others, in seeking a constitutional redress of grievances, they approved not the measures lately adopted, and were at all times opposed to independence. (p. 223)

The following is from Benson John Lossing's *The Pictorial Field-Book of the Revolution* (Volume II):

In the summer of 1777, Sir William Howe, the British commander-in-chief, sailed from New York with a large land force, and with a naval armament under his brother Richard, Earl Howe, and landing at the head of Chesapeake Bay commenced a victorious march towards Philadelphia. Washington, informed of the movement, went out from Philadelphia to meet him, and had proceeded beyond the Brandywine, in the neighborhood of Wilmington, when the van of the enemy appeared at Kennet Square. The battle of Brandywine occurred soon afterward, in which the Americans were defeated and driven back towards Philadelphia. The enemy pushed steadily forward, and entered the city in triumph. In anticipation of the possibility of such an event the Americans had applied themselves diligently to the erection of obstructions in the Delaware to prevent the ascent of the British fleet, and also in rearing batteries upon the shores to cover them. Upon isolated marshes or low islands of mud, made green by reeds, a little below the mouth of the Schuylkill, they erected a strong redoubt, with quite extensive outworks, and called it Fort Mifflin. These islands were called Great and Little Mud Islands. The former, on which the redoubt and main works were erected, has been called Fort Island ever since that time. On the opposite shore of New Jersey a strong redoubt, called Fort Mercer, was also erected and well supplied with artillery. In the deep channels of the river, between and under cover of these batteries, they sunk ranges of strong frames with iron-pointed wooden spikes, called *chevaux de frise*, which formed almost invulnerable *stockadoes*. Three miles further down the river, at Billing's Point (now Billingsport), was a redoubt with extensive outworks covering strong *stockadoes*, which were sunken there in the navigable channel of the river between the main and Billing's Island. In addition to these works several armed galleys and floating batteries were stationed in the river, all forming strong barriers against the fleet of the enemy. This circumstance troubled the British general, for he foresaw the consequences of having his supplies by water cut off, and the danger to which his army would be exposed in Philadelphia if unsupported by the fleet.

Immediately after the battle at Brandywine Earl Howe sailed down the Chesapeake, and entered the lower Delaware with several light vessels, among which was the *Roebuck* [italics added], commanded by Captain Hammond. That officer represented to General Howe that if a sufficient force could be sent to reduce the fortifications at Billingsport, he would take upon himself the task of opening a passage for the vessels through the *chevaux de frise*, or *stockadoes* at that point. Howe readily consented to attempt the important measure. Two regiments, under Colonel Stirling, were dispatched from Chester, in Pennsylvania, for that purpose. They crossed the river a little below Billingsport, marched in the rear of the unfinished works, and made a furious assault upon the garrison. The Americans were dismayed at this unexpected attack, and, believing themselves incompetent to make a successful defense, they spiked their cannons, set fire to the barracks, and fled. The English remained long enough to demolish the works on the river front, when Hammond, by the great exertions of his men, made a passage way seven feet wide in the *chevaux de frise*, and with six vessels sailed through and anchored near Hog Island. Stirling returned to Chester, and with another detachment proceeded to camp as an escort of provisions, bearing to General Howe the intelligence of his success.

Howe now determined to make a general sweep of all the American works on the Delaware, and preparatory thereto he called in his outposts, and concentrated his whole army near to and within Philadelphia. Two Rhode Island regiments, belonging to General Varnum's brigade, under Colonel Christopher Greene, garrisoned the fort at Red Bank, and about the same number of the Maryland line, under Lieutenant-colonel Samuel Smith, occupied Fort Mifflin, on Mud Island. The American fleet in the river, consisting chiefly of galleys and floating batteries, was commanded by Commodore Hazelwood. It was quite as important to the Americans to maintain these forts, and defend the river obstructions, as it was to the British to destroy them. It was, therefore, determined to hold them to the last extremity, for it was evident that such continued possession would force Howe to evacuate Philadelphia.

Count Donop, with four battalions consisting of twelve hundred picked Hessians, was sent by Howe to attack Fort Mercer at Red Bank. (pp. 291-293)

In *Reminiscences of Old Gloucester, or Incidents in the History of the Counties of Gloucester, Atlantic and Camden, New Jersey*, Isaac Mickle writes,

Late in the afternoon of the twenty-first of October, 1777, Count Donop with a detachment of about twenty-five hundred Hessians crossed the Delaware at Cooper's Point to dislodge Greene and the little handful of republicans who defended this redoubt. Owing to the precaution of the Americans in destroying the lower bridges on the intervening streams, [Footnote (p. 68): "Ward's letter, Haz. Penn. Reg. Vol. III p. 181."] the Count passed through Haddonfield and down the Clement's Bridge road to the attack. He pressed several persons whom be found along the route into his service as pilots, among whom was a negro belonging to the Cooper family, called Old Mitch, who was at work by the Cooper's Creek Bridge. A negro named Dick, belonging to the gallant Col. Ellis, and an infamous white scoundrel named McIlvaine volunteered their assistance as guides. At the bar of the Haddonfield tavern, these two loyal fellows were very loud in their abuse of the American cause; but their insolence as we shall see was soon repaid.

On the morning of the twenty-second, the Hessians appeared at the edge of a forest north of the fort, almost within cannon shot thereof. Halting here to rest from the march, Donop sent an officer with a drummer to command Greene to surrender. "King George," said the officer, "directs his rebellious subjects to lay down their arms, and promises no quarter if a battle is risked." At which Greene deputized a man to mount the parapet and return the laconic reply: "We'll see King

George damned first — we want no quarter!" The interview here terminated, and the officer returned to the Hessian camp. [Footnote (p. 68): "MSS. Notes of a Septuagenarian, penes me."]

   At four o'clock in the afternoon Donop opened a heavy cannonade from a battery which he had erected to the north-eastward; and at the same time the British ships from below the *chevaux-de-frize* [italics added] began to thunder upon the little fort. Most of the balls from the latter fell too low, and entered the bluff beneath the works. After cannonading for a short time, the Hessians advanced to the first entrenchment. Finding this abandoned, they shouted Victoria! — waved their hats, and rushed into the deserted area before the redoubt; the little drummer before mentioned, heading the onslaught with a lively march. When the first of the assailants had come up to the very abattis and were endeavoring to cut away the branches, the Americans opened a terrible fire of musketry in front and flank. Death rode in every volley. So near were the Hessians to the caponiere or looped trench which flanked the enemy when they set upon the main fort, that the wads were blown entirely through their bodies. The officers leading the attack, fought bravely. Again and again they rallied their men and brought them to the charge. They were mowed down like grass, and fell in heaps among the boughs of the abattis and into the fosse. In the thickest of the fight Donop was easily distinguished by the marks of his order and his handsome figure; but even his example availed nothing. His men repulsed from the redoubt in front, made an attack upon the escarpment on the west, but the fire from the American gallies drove them back here also with great loss; and at last, they flew in much disorder to the wood, leaving among many other slain the saucy drummer and his officer.

   Another column made a simultaneous attack upon the south, and in the technical language of a soldier, "passed the abattis, traversed the fosse and mounted the berm;" [Footnote (p. 69): "Chastelux, Vol. I. p. 263."] but they were repulsed at the fraises, and all retreated save twenty, who were standing on the berm against the shelvings of the parapet, under and out of the way of the guns, whence they were afraid to move. These were captured by M. de Mauduit, who had sallied from the fort to repair some palisades. This brave Frenchman making another sortie in a few minutes afterwards to repair the southern abattis, heard a voice from among the heaps of the dead and dying, exclaim in English, "Whoever you are, draw me hence." This was Count Donop. M. de Mauduit caused him to be carried into the fort. His hip was broken, but the wound was not at first considered as mortal. The victorious Americans, remembering the insolent message which their captive had sent them a few hours before, could not withhold marks of exultation.

"Well — is it determined," they asked aloud, "to give no quarter?"

"I am in your hands," replied Donop; "you may revenge yourselves."

M. de Mauduit enjoining the men in broken English to be generous towards their bleeding and humbled prisoner, the latter said to him, "You appear to be a foreigner, sir; who are you?"

"A French officer," answered Mauduit.

"*Je suis content,*"exclaimed the Count in French, "*je meurs entre les mains de L'honneur meme.*" [Footnote (p. 69): "I am satisified — I die in the very hands of Honor!"]

Donop was taken first to the Whitall house, just below the fort, but was afterwards removed to the residence of the Lowes, south of Woodbury Creek. He died three days after the battle, saying to M. de Mauduit in his last moments, "It is finishing a noble career early; but I die the victim of my ambition and of the avarice of my sovereign." [Footnote (p. 69): "Chastelux, Vol. I. p. 263."] To Col. Clymer he made the remarkable remark: "See here Colonel, see in me the vanity of all human pride! I have shone in all the courts of Europe, and now I am dying here on the banks of the Delaware in the house of an obscure Quaker." (pp. 68-69)

Thomas Cushing and Charles E. Sheppard write the following in their *History of the Counties of Gloucester, Salem, and Cumberland New Jersey, with Biographical Sketches of Their Prominent Citizens*: "Between the fort [Fort Mercer] and the Whitall house was the grave of Count Donop, marked by a modest stone, but the crumbling of the bank exposed his remains, and in 1874 Mr. Murray, the occupant of the Whitall house, . . . removed them to another place of interment." (p. 27)

In his *The Pictorial Field-Book of the Revolution* (Volume II), Lossing writes,

The Whitalls were Quakers, and of course, though Whigs, took no part in the war. This fact made some suspect the old man of Toryism. I was informed by the present owner that when the attack was made upon the fort, and his grandmother was urged to flee from the house, she refused, saying, "God's arm is strong and will protect me. I may do good by staying." She was left alone in the house, and while the battle was raging, and cannon-balls were driving like sleet against and around her dwelling, she calmly plied her spinning-wheel in a room in the second story. At length a twelve-pound ball from a British vessel in the river, grazing the American flag-staff (the walnut-tree) at the fort, passed through the heavy brick wall on the north gable, and, with a terrible crash, perforated a partition at the head of the stairs, crossed a recess, and lodged in another partition near where the old lady was sitting. Conceiving Divine protection a little more certain elsewhere after this manifestation of the power of gunpowder, the industrious dame gathered up her implements, and . . . retreated to the cellar, where she continued her spinning until called to attend the wounded and dying who were brought into her house at the close of the battle. She did, indeed, "do good" by remaining; for, like an angel of mercy, she went among the maimed, unmindful whether they were friend or foe, and administered every relief to their sufferings in her power. She scolded the Hessians for coming to America to butcher the people. At the same time she bound up their wounds tenderly, and gave them food and water. The scar made by the passage of that iron ball is quite prominent in the gable. . . . I saw within the house where the missile cut off the wood-work in its passage, and where it lodged. (pp, 290-291)

Thomas Cushing and Charles E. Sheppard quoted from Lossing's *The Pictorial Field-Book of the Revolution* (Volume II) in their *History of the Counties of Gloucester, Salem, and Cumberland New Jersey, with Biographical Sketches of Their Prominent Citizens*, and I have included a few of their inserts where noted in Lossing's narrative continued below:

The loss of the Americans within the fort was eight men killed, twenty-nine wounded, and a captain taken prisoner while reconnoitering. The number killed by the bursting of a cannon is not known. So close was the combat at one time that several Hessians were pierced by the gun-wads of the Americans.

The conduct of Lieutenant-colonel Greene on this occasion was highly applauded, and Congress ordered the board of war to present him with an elegant sword. This tribute was given to his family at the close of the contest, when Colonel Greene was no longer living to receive it. He had been basely murdered in his quarters near Croton River, in Westchester County, in New York, by a band of Tories consisting of about one hundred and fifty dragoons, under Colonel Delancy, who surprised his post. Colonel Greene fell after his single arm had slain several of his assailants. They attempted to carry him off, but he died upon the road. Major Flagg, a meritorious officer, was killed at the same time; also two subalterns and twenty-seven men were killed or wounded.

In commemoration of the battle of Red Bank and the valor of Colonel Greene, a monument of blue-veined marble, about fifteen feet high, was erected in 1829, just within the northern line of the outworks of Fort Mercer and within a few feet of the margin of the Delaware. This tribute to the memory of valor and patriotism was made by some New Jersey and Pennsylvania volunteers. While it is a testimony of one of the noblest traits in human character, it bears another of the existence of the most detestable. In the inscription were the words NEW JERSEY AND PENNSYLVANIA in a single prominent line. Some Jersey scoundrel almost obliterated the word PENNSYLVANIA, and afterwards some Pennsylvania vandal, in the fierceness of his retaliatory zeal for the credit of his State, disgraced it so far as insignificance could do it by obliterating the words NEW JERSEY....

The firing of the first gun from the Hessian battery upon Fort Mercer was the signal for the British vessels to approach and attack Fort Mifflin. They had already made their way through the lower barrier at Billingsport, and the *Augusta* [italics added here and with the ships named below], a sixty-four-gun ship, and several smaller vessels were anchored just above it, waiting for flood tide. As soon as Fort Mercer was attacked the *Augusta*, with the *Roebuck*, of forty-four guns, two frigates, the *Merlin*, of eighteen guns, and a galley came up, but were kept at bay by the American galleys and floating batteries. These galleys did good execution, not only upon the British vessels but by flanking the assailants at Red Bank. The attack upon Fort Mifflin was deferred until next morning, when, the Hessians being driven from Fort Mercer, the whole power of the American flotilla was brought to bear upon the British fleet. A heavy cannonade was opened upon Fort Mifflin, and attempts were made to get floating batteries in the channel in the rear of Mud Island. Lieutenant-colonel Smith, the commandant at Fort Mifflin . . . thwarted every attempt thus to outflank him (if the term may be used in reference to a garrison in a fort), and by a gallant defense essentially aided the American flotilla in repulsing the enemy. The fire was so fierce and incessant that the British ships endeavored to fall down the river. A shot struck and set fire to the *Augusta*, and at noon, while lying aground on a mud-bank near the Jersey shore, she blew up. The engagement continued with the other vessels until three o'clock in the afternoon, when the *Merlin* also took fire and blew up near the mouth of Mud Creek. The conflict now ceased the *Roebuck* dropped down the river and passed below the *chevaux de frise* at Billingsport, and the Americans remained masters of the Delaware forts for a short season.

It was indeed but a short season that quiet possession of the river was vouchsafed the patriots. Although repulsed, his ships beaten back, his mercenary allies decimated, Howe was not discouraged, and he labored eagerly and hopefully to dislodge the Americans from their strong posts upon the only avenue through which his army could receive food and clothing and his magazine supplies for the winter. A timely reinforcement from New York enabled him to act with energy. He took possession of Province Island, lying between Fort Mifflin and the main, and at different points works were thrown up to strengthen his power and annoy the patriots. This was on the 1st of November, and from that time never was a garrison more harassed than that at Fort Mifflin, and never was patience and true courage more nobly exhibited than was then shown by Lieutenant-colonel Smith and his compatriots.

Old Fort Mifflin was upon the lower end of Mud (now Fort) Island, having its principal fortification in front, for the purpose of repelling ships that might come up the river. On the side toward Province Island (a low mud bank, nearly covered at high water, and separated from Mud Island by a narrow channel) the fort had only a wet ditch without ravelin or *abatis*. [Lossing, Volume I: "*Abatis* is a French word signifying trees cut down. It is a phrase used in fortifications; and an abatis which is composed of trees felled, so as to present their branches to the enemy, is frequently found in a woody country one of the most available and efficient kinds of defense." (p. 58)] This part was flanked by a block-house at each of its angles. These were not strong. When the Americans saw the enemy take possession of Province Island, and begin the planting of batteries to bruise their weakest points, they were sensible that Fort Mifflin would be untenable if the British completed their works. Such, too, was the painful conviction of Washington, and from his camp at Whitemarsh, he put forth all his energies to prevent the evil. But, weak in numbers and deficient in everything which constitutes the strength of an army, he was obliged to see the enemy, day after day rearing his battle works, without being able to interpose. He had sent anxious requests to General Gates to forward reinforcements from the north, Burgoyne's invading army being captured, and no other formidable enemy requiring a large force in that quarter; but that officer, doubtless willing to see his rival unsuccessful, gave no heed to his orders until longer non-compliance would have been positive disobedience. To break up the encampment at Whitemarsh and move the army to the west side of the Schuylkill would be to leave depositories of stores and hospitals for the sick within the reach of the enemy. It would also leave the fords of the Schuylkill in the custody of the royal troops, and render a junction of the expected northern forces with the main army difficult, if not impossible. Furthermore, it might bring on a general engagement, which, with his weakened forces, the commander-in-chief knew might be fatal. Thus situated, Washington viewed the progress of the enemy in his designs upon Fort Mifflin with intense anxiety.

The British erected five batteries on Province Island, of eighteen, twenty-four, and thirty-two pounders, within five hundred yards of Fort Mifflin. They also brought up by the new channel made between Hog Island and the main by the changing of the current by the *chevaux de frise*, a large floating battery, mounting twenty-two twenty-four-pounders, within forty yards of an angle of the fort. They also brought to bear upon the fort four sixty-four gun ships within nine hundred yards, and two forty-gun ships. Altogether the enemy had fourteen strong redoubts, and these were well manned and furnished with heavy artillery. On the 10th of November [Cushing and Sheppard (p. 26): "(1777)"], the enemy opened their batteries on land and water, and for six consecutive days poured a storm of bombs and round-shot upon the devoted fortification. With consummate skill and courage Lieutenant-colonel Smith directed the responses from the ordnance of the fort. The artillery, drawn chiefly from Colonel Lamb's regiment, were commanded by Lieutenant Treat, who was killed on the first day of the siege by the bursting of a bomb. On that day the barracks alone suffered, but on the morning of the 11th the direction of the enemy's fire was changed, a dozen of the strong palisades were demolished, and a cannon in an embrasure was disabled. The firing did not cease until midnight, and many of the garrison were killed or wounded. Colonel Smith, the commander, had a narrow escape. He had just gone into the barracks to write a letter to General Varnum, when a ball passed through a chimney. He was struck by the scattered bricks, and for a time lay senseless. He was taken across to Red Bank, and the command devolved on Lieutenant-colonel Russell, of the Connecticut line. That officer was disabled by fatigue and ill health, and Major Thayer, of the Rhode Island line, volunteered to take his place. Major Henry, who sent daily reports to Washington of the progress of the siege, was also wounded on the 11th, but he continued with the garrison. On the 12th a two-gun battery of the Americans was destroyed, the northwest block-house and laboratory were blown up, and the garrison were obliged to seek shelter within the fort. The enemy continued to throw shells at night, and fearful indeed was the scene. At sunrise on the 13th thirty armed boats made their appearance, and during that night the heavy floating battery was brought to bear on the fort. It opened with terrible effect on the morning of the 14th, yet that little garrison of only three hundred men managed to silence it before noon. Hitherto the enemy did not know the real weakness of the garrison; on that day a deserter in a boat carried information of the fact to the British, who were seriously thinking of abandoning the siege, for they had suffered much. Hope was revived, and preparations were made for a general and more vigorous assault. At daylight on the 15th the *Iris* and *Somerset* [italics added], men-of-war, passed up the east channel to attack the fort on Mud Island in front. Several frigates were brought to bear on Fort Mercer, and the *Vigilant* [italics added], an East Indiaman of twenty twenty-four-pounders, and a hulk with three twenty-four-pounders made their way through a narrow channel on the western side, and gained a position to act in concert with the batteries on Province Island in enfilading the American works. At ten o'clock, while all was silent, a signal bugle sent forth its summons to action, and instantly the land-batteries and the shipping poured forth a terrible storm of missiles upon Fort Mifflin. The little garrison sustained the shock with astonishing intrepidity, and far into the gloom of the evening an incessant cannonade was kept up. Within an hour the only two cannons in the fort that had not been dismounted shared the fate of the others. Every man who appeared upon the platform was killed by the musketeers in the tops of the ships, whose yards almost hung over the American battery. Long before night not a palisade was left, the embrasures were ruined, the whole parapet leveled, the block-houses were already destroyed. Early in the evening Major Thayer sent all the remnant of the garrison to Red Bank, excepting forty men, with whom he remained. Among these was . . . Captain (afterward Commodore) Talbot, of the Rhode Island line, who was wounded in the hip, having fought for hours with his wrist shattered by a musket-ball. At midnight, every defense and every shelter being swept away, Thayer and his men set fire to the remains of the barracks, evacuated the fort, and escaped in safety to Red Bank. Altogether it was one of the most gallant and obstinate defenses made during the war. In the course of the last day more than a thousand discharges of cannon, from twelve to thirty-two-pounders, were made against the works on Mud Island. Nearly two hundred and fifty men of the garrison were killed and wounded. The loss of the British was great, the number was not certainly known.

Fort Mercer was still in possession of the Continental troops. Howe determined to dislodge them, for while they remained the obstructions in the river could not with safety be removed. While a portion of his force was beating down Fort Mifflin, he was busy in fortifying Philadelphia. He had extended intrenchments across from the Delaware to the Schuylkill. Having received more reinforcements from New York, he sent Cornwallis to fall upon Fort Mercer in the rear. That officer, with a detachment of about two thousand men, crossed the Delaware from Chester to Billingsport [Cushing and Sheppard (p. 27): "(Nov. 18, 1777)"], where he was joined by some troops just arrived from New York. Washington had been apprised of this movement, and had detached Gen. Huntington's brigade to join that of Varnum in New Jersey. He also ordered Major-general Greene to proceed with his division to the relief of the garrison, and to oppose Cornwallis. That able officer, accompanied by Lafayette, who had not yet quite recovered from a wound received in the battle on the Brandywine, crossed the Delaware at Burlington, and marched with considerable force toward Red Bank. He expected to be reinforced by Glover's brigade, then on its march through New Jersey, but was disappointed. Ascertaining that the force of Cornwallis was greatly superior to his own in numbers, General Greene abandoned the idea of giving him battle, and filed off toward Haddonfield. Colonel Greene, deprived of all hope of succor, evacuated Fort Mercer [Cushing and Sheppard (p. 27): "(November 20th)"], leaving the artillery, with a considerable quantity of cannon-balls and stores, in the hands of the enemy. Cornwallis dismantled the fort and demolished the works. His army was augmented by reinforcements, and with about five thousand men he took post at and fortified Gloucester Point, whence he might have a supervision of affairs in Lower Jersey. Morgan's rifle corps joined General Greene, but the Americans were not strong enough to venture a regular attack on Cornwallis. A detachment of one hundred and fifty riflemen under Lieutenant-colonel Butler, and an equal number of militia under Lafayette, attacked a picket of the enemy three hundred strong, killed between twenty and thirty of them, drove the remainder into the camp at Gloucester, and returned without losing a man. General Greene soon afterward withdrew from New Jersey and joined Washington, and Cornwallis returned to Philadelphia. The American fleet, no longer supported by the forts, sought other places of safety. On a dark night [Cushing and Sheppard (p. 27): "(Nov. 21, 1777)"], the galleys, one brig, and two sloops crept cautiously along the Jersey shore, past Philadelphia, and escaped to Burlington. Seventeen other vessels, unable to escape, were abandoned by their crews and burned, at Gloucester. The American defenses on the Delaware were now scattered to the winds; the obstructions in the river were removed, the enemy had full possession of Philadelphia; Congress had fled to the interior, and the broken battalions of the patriot army sought winter quarters on the banks of the Schuylkill, at Valley Forge. (pp. 294-299)

In their *History of the Counties of Gloucester, Salem, and Cumberland New Jersey, with Biographical Sketches of Their Prominent Citizens*, Thomas Cushing and Charles E. Sheppard provide the following:

While the Americans were encamped at Valley Forge, and the British held possession of Philadelphia, the latter at various times sent out parties to raid the country, plunder the people, and break up the feeble American posts. Among the most active troops in these enterprises were the Queen's Rangers, a corps of American Loyalists, or Tories, that had been enlisted mostly in Connecticut and the vicinity of New York. They were, as their name implies, designed for active service, and at one time they numbered about four hundred men. They had become reduced in numbers, but in the autumn of 1777 Maj. Simcoe, a young and efficient officer of the British army, was placed in command of them. By his zeal and military ability he soon made this corps a model of its kind. About the 20th of February, 1778, an expedition of this kind was sent out from Philadelphia, under the command of Col. Abercrombie, of the Fifty-second Regiment. It consisted of about five hundred men, and included the Rangers. They went to Salem by water, and remained several days, reconnoitering to ascertain the position of Wayne, who was then in New Jersey collecting horses and provisions for the American army. They also helped themselves to whatever they wished without ceremony. (p. 28)

John Graves Simcoe, in *Simcoe's Military Journal*, relates the following:

An expedition was formed under the command of the late Colonel Mawhood, consisting of the 27th and 46th regiments, the Queen's Rangers, and New Jersey Volunteers: they embarked the 12th of March [1778], and fell down the Delaware. On the 17th, the Queen's Rangers landed, at three o'clock in the morning, about six miles from Salem, the Huzzars carrying their accoutrements and swords. Major Simcoe was directed to seize horses, to mount the cavalry, and the staff, and to join Colonel Mawhood at Salem; this was accordingly executed. Major Simcoe, making a circuit and passing over Lambstone's bridge, arrived at Salem, near which Colonel Mawhood landed. The Huzzars were tolerably well mounted, and sufficient horses procured for the other exigencies of the service: Colonel Mawhood had given the strictest charge against plundering; and Major Simcoe, in taking the horses, had assured the inhabitants that they should be returned, or paid for, if they did not appear in arms, in a very few days; and, none but officers entering the houses, they received no other injury. The Queen's Rangers' infantry were about two hundred and seventy, rank and file, and thirty cavalry; Colonel Mawhood gave directions for the forage to take place on the 18th. The town of Salem lies upon a creek of that name which falls into the Delaware nearly opposite Reedy island; the Aloes, or Alewas creek, runs almost parallel to the Salem creek, and falls into the Delaware to the southward of it; over this creek there were three bridges: Hancock's was the lower one, Quintin's that in the centre, and Thompson's the upper one; between these creeks the foraging was to commence; the neck, or peninsula, formed by them was at its greatest distance seven, and at its least four miles wide. The rebel militia was posted at Hancock's and Quintin's, the nearest bridges, which they had taken up, and defended by breast-works. Colonel Mawhood made detachments to mask these bridges; and foraged in their rear: the officer who commanded the detachment, consisting of seventy of the 17th infantry, at Quintin's bridge, sent information that the enemy were assembled in great numbers at the bridge, and indicated as if they meant to pass over whenever he should quit it, in which case his party would be in great danger. Colonel Mawhood marched with the Queen's Rangers to his assistance he made a circuit, so as to fall in upon the road that led from Thompson's to Quintin's bridge, to deceive any patrole which he might meet on his march, and to make them believe that he directed it to Thompson's, not Quintin's bridge. Approaching the bridge, the Rangers halted in the wood, and Colonel Mawhood and Major Simcoe went to the party of the 17th, but in such a manner as to give no suspicion that they were part of a reinforcement; the ground was high, till within two hundred yards of the bridge, where it became marshy; immediately beyond the bridge, the banks were steep, and on them the enemy had thrown up breast-works; there was a public house very near the road, at the edge of its declivity into the marsh, on the Salem side. Colonel Mawhood asked Major Simcoe, "whether he thought, if he left a party in the house, the enemy would pass by it or not?" who replied, "that he thought they would be too cowardly to do it; but at any rate the attempt could do no harm, and, if he pleased, he would try." Colonel Mawhood directed Major Simcoe to do so, who accordingly profiting by the broken ground of the orchard which was behind it, and the clothing of his men, brought Captain Stephenson and his company into the house, undiscovered: the front windows were opened, and the back ones were shut, so that no thorough light could be seen; the women of the house were put in the cellar and ordered to be silent; the door was left open, and Lieutenant McKay stood behind it, with a bayonet, ready to seize the first person whose curiosity might prompt him to enter; the Queen's Rangers were brought into the wood near to that part where it ended in clear ground, and two companies, under Captain Saunders, were advanced to the fences at the very edge of it, where they lay flat. Colonel Mawhood then gave orders for the detachment of the 17th, who were posted near the house, to call in their sentinels and retreat up the road in full view of the enemy. This party had scarcely moved, when the enemy laid the bridge and passed it; a detachment of them went immediately across the marsh to the heights on the left, but the principal party, about two hundred, in two divisions, proceeded up the road; Captain Stephenson, as they approached the house, could hear them say, "let us go into the house," &c, but they were prevented, both by words and by action, by the officer who was at their head: he was on horseback, and spurring forward, quitted the road to go into the field, on the right, through a vacancy made by the rails being taken for fires; his party still proceeded up the road, and the first division passed the house: the officer, his sight still fixed on the red clothes of the 17th, approached close up to the fence where Captain Saunders lay; he did not immediately observe the Rangers, and, it is probable, he might not, had he not heard one of the men stifling a laugh: looking down he saw them, and galloped off; he was fired at, wounded, and taken. The division that had passed the house attempted to return: Captain Stephenson sallied, drove them across the fields. Captain Saunders pursued them; the Huzzars were let loose and afterwards the battalion, Colonel Mawhood leading them; Major Simcoe directed the 17th back to the house; with the grenadiers, and Highlanders of the Rangers, ready to force the bridge, if ordered; the enemy, for a moment, quitted it. Colonel Mawhood thought it useless to pass it. Some of the division, who passed the house, were taken prisoners, but the greater part were drowned in the Aloes creek. The officer, who was taken, proved to be a Frenchman. The Rangers had one Huzzar mortally wounded; and what was unfortunate, he was wounded by a man, whom in the eagerness of the pursuit he had passed, given quarters to, and not disarmed: the villain, or coward, was killed by another Huzzar. The corps returned to Salem.

The rebels still occupying the posts at Quintin and Hancock's bridge, and probably accumulating, Colonel Mawhood determined to attack them at the latter, where, from all reports, they were assembled to near four hundred men. He entrusted the enterprise to Major Simcoe, and went with him and a patrole opposite to the place: the Major ascended a tree and made a rough sketch of the buildings, which, by conversing with the guides, he improved into a tolerable plan of the place, and formed his mode of attack accordingly. He embarked on the 20th, at night, on board the flat boats; he was to be landed at an inlet, seven miles below Aloes creek, when the boats were immediately to be returned, and by a private road he was to reach Hancock's bridge, opposite to which, Major Mitchell was detached with the 27th regiment, to co-operate with him. Major Simcoe foresaw the difficulties, and dangers, but he kept them to himself: every thing depended upon surprise. The enemy were nearly double his numbers; and his retreat, by the absolute orders to send back the boats, was cut off; but he had just confidence in the silence, attention, and spirit of the corps. By some strange error in the naval department, when the boats arrived off Aloes creek, the tide set so strong against them that, in the opinion of the officer of the navy, they could not reach the place of their destination till mid-day. Major Simcoe determined not to return, but to land on the marshes, at the mouth of the Aloes creek; there were good guides with him: they found out a landing place, and after a march of two miles through marshes, up to the knees in mud and water, labours rendered more fatiguing by the carriage of the first wooden planks they met with, to form bridges with them over the ditches, they at length arrived at a wood upon dry land. Here the corps was formed for the attack. There was no public road which led to Hancock's bridge, but that which the Rangers were now in possession of; a bank, on which there was a footway, led from Hancock's to Quintin's bridge. Hancock's house was a large brick house; there were many store-houses round it, and some few cottages. Captain Saunders was detached to ambuscade the dyke that led to Quintin's bridge, about half a mile from the quarters, and to take up a small bridge which was upon it, as the enemy would, probably, fly that way, and if not pursued too closely, would be more easily defeated. Captain Dunlop was detached to the rear of Hancock's house; in which it was presumed the rebel officers quartered; directed to force it, occupy and barricade it, as it commanded the passage of the bridge. Different detachments were allotted to the houses supposed to be the enemy's quarters, which having mastered, they were ordered to assemble at Hancock's; a party was appropriated to relay the bridge. On approaching the place, two sentries were discovered: two men of the light infantry followed them, and, as they turned about, bayoneted them; the companies rushed in, and each, with proper guides, forced the quarters allotted to it. No resistance being made, the light infantry, who were in reserve, reached Hancock's house by the road, and forced the front door, at the same time that Captain Dunlop, by a more difficult way, entered the back door; as it was very dark, these companies had nearly attacked each other. The surprise was complete, and would have been so, had the whole of the enemy's force been present, but, fortunately for them, they had quitted it the evening before, leaving a detachment of twenty or thirty men, all of whom were killed. Some very unfortunate circumstances happened here. Among the killed was a friend of Government, then a prisoner with the rebels, old Hancock, the owner of the house, and his brother: Major Simcoe had made particular enquiry, and was informed that he did not live at home, since the rebels had occupied the bridge. The information was partly true; he was not there in the day-time, but unfortunately returned home at night: events like these are the real miseries of war. The roads which led to the country were immediately ambuscaded; and Lieutenant Whitlock was detached to surprise a patrole of seven men who had been sent down the creek: this he effected completely. On their refusal to surrender, he fired on them, only one escaped. This firing gave the first notice of the success of the enterprise to the 27th regiment; with so much silence it had hitherto been conducted. The bridge was now laid; and Major Simcoe communicated to Colonel Mitchell, that the enemy were at Quintin's bridge; that he had good guides to conduct them thither by a private road, and that the possession of Hancock's house secured a retreat. Lieutenant-Colonel Mitchell said, [sic] that his regiment was much fatigued by the cold, and that he would return to Salem as soon as the troops joined. The ambuscades were of course withdrawn, and the

Queen's Rangers were forming to pass the bridge, when a rebel patrole passed where an ambuscade had been, and discovering the corps, gallopped [sic] back. Lieutenant-Colonel Mitchell, finding his men in high spirits, had returned, purposing to march to Quintin's bridge: but being informed of the enemy's patrole, it was thought best to return. Colonel Mawhood, in public orders, "returned his best thanks to Major Simcoe and his corps, for their spirited and good conduct in the surprise of the rebel posts." Two days after, the Queen's Rangers patrolled to Thompson's bridge; the enemy, who had been posted there, were alarmed at the approach of a cow the night before, fired at it, wounded it, and then fled; they also abandoned Quintin's bridge, and retired to a creek, sixteen miles from Aloes creek. Major Simcoe, making a patrole with the Huzzars, took a circuit towards the rear of one of the parties sent out to protect the foragers: a party of the enemy had been watching them the whole day, and unluckily, the forage being completed, the detachment had just left its ground and was moving off; the enemy doing the like, met the patrole; were pursued, and escaped by the passage which the foragers had just left open. One only was taken, being pursued into a bog, which the Huzzars attempted in vain to cross, and were much mortified to see above a dozen of the enemy, who had passed round it in safety, within a few yards: they consisted of all the field officers and committee-men of the district. The prisoner was their adjutant. The enemy, who were assembled at Cohansey, might easily have been surprised; but Colonel Mawhood judged, that having completed his forage with such success, his business was to return, which he effected. The troops embarked without any accident, and sailed for Philadelphia. The horses were given back to the inhabitants, or paid for. On the passage, the ships waiting for the tide, Major Simcoe had an opportunity of landing at Billing's port, where Major Vandyke's corps was stationed, and examining it, they arrived at Philadelphia, March the 31st. (pp. 46-54)

In *The History of Salem County New Jersey*, Joseph S. Sickler comments: "Thus Simcoe lightly attributes the retreat of the Americans from Aloes creek to Cohansey creek to the scare caused by one cow. The situation was more critical than Simcoe makes it appear." (p. 166)

In *An Historical Account of the First Settlement of Salem, in West Jersey, by John Fenwick, Esq. Chief Proprietor of the Same* Robert Gibbon Johnson relates the following:

Captain Andrew Sinnickson lived at that time in Penn's Neck, and being notified of the party approaching, hastily collected together as many of his men as could be mustered, came upon the guard and their foragers, (in what was then called the Long Lane,) and after a severe contest the enemy was routed, and in the meleé the commanding officer lost his hat and cloak, and was obliged to flee to Salem without them. The next day Capt. Sinnickson sent a flag into the town, with the hat and cloak, belonging to the unfortunate officer, with something like this laconic message: "That he had to regret the sudden departure of the officer, the owner of these articles, but hoped that if he intended another visit into that township he might have the pleasure of detaining him, until they became better acquainted." (pp. 146-147)

Sickler, once again, in *The History of Salem County New Jersey*, relates the following:

> There are two newspaper accounts of the Hancock's Bridge massacre which shed but little lustre on the British arms. The patriotic account was published in the famous newspaper of Isaac Collins, the *New Jersey Gazette* at Trenton. On April eighth, [1778] nineteen days after the massacre, it contained the follow account:
>
>> On Saturday the 21st ult, about break of day our guard posted at Hancock's bridge, on Alloway's Creek, in Salem county consisting of about twenty men, were surprised by those the enemy call Jersey Volunteers: They, from their acquaintance with the country, had found means to cross the creek come upon the guard from some unsuspected quarter and being undoubtedly led by some person well acquainted with the disposition of sentries, opened the guardhouse door and came in, many of the guards being, asleep, without giving the least alarm, nay, so far from it, that it is said some of them shook hands in a friendly manner with some of the guard with whom they were intimately acquainted, as indeed they were with most of them and O tempora O mores! — immediately began bayoneting of them, without our people making the least show of resistance, not only reeking their fury on the guard but also on several of the peaceful inhabitants who were slumbering in their beds. Bacon, of the people called Quakers, was inhumanly murdered in his own house and bed; old Mr. Hancock, beside his being of that society, was a cripple in both arms, was stabbed in his bed, and is since dead of his wounds. Another of that society is also since dead of his wounds; and the life of a fourth person is despaired of.

On the other hand, a Tory newspaper contained a flamboyant account of the British expedition and the massacre. (p. 164)

Francis B. Lee, in *Archives of the State of New Jersey, Second Series, Volume II, Documents Relating to the Revolutionary History of the State of New Jersey, Volume II, Extracts From American Newspapers, Volume II, 1778,* includes the following:

PHILADELPHIA

Nothing can be stronger proof of the disaffection of the inhabitants of New-Jersey, to the interest of rebellion, than their behavior to the troops, who went from this city on the eleventh ult. under [C]ol. Mawhood. When they landed at Salem none was found to oppose or impede them from collecting forage, excepting a few, who had been prevailed upon to abandon their houses, and on the third day after the landing of the troops, to show themselves in arms, but the number being insignificant, they were easily taken prisoners. Some days after, information was received that part of the rebels were collecting at a place called Hancock's Bridge, on which the Queen's Rangers [Footnote indicated here is below.] were sent off in boats, landed at the back of them and after killing and wounding a part, made prisoners of the residue. The rebels never afterwards appeared in force, so that the troops collected the forage without any interruption, and the inhabitants from all quarters flocked to them, bringing what cattle, provision, etc. they could spare, for which they received a generous price but lamented much that the army was to depart, and leave them again to the tyranny of the rebel faction. How far this may correspond with the pompous description which will be given to the world, by the immaculate Mr. Livingston, is a matter of little amount, as truth will shine with superior lustre to misrepresentation. If it is said that the king's troops evacuated the place, before the militia could be called, it will stand the test; for it is an uncontrovertable fact, that in circuit of upwards of sixty miles, three hundred men could not be mustered; the people being fully sensible of their error, and heartily tired of the petty tyrants, who have galled and broke their spirits. This needs no further elucidation than that, in the place of fourteen hundred men who heretofore appeared and voted at the election of their assemblymen, no more than eight constituted the majority of the last electors, which is an evident demonstration that it is now a matter of indifference who now takes the lead, as tyranny and oppression is only to be expected from such as are willing to be of this number, who constitute that illegal assembly. — *The Pennsylvania Evening Post, April 3, 1778.*

[*Footnote:*] Inspite of the flippant character of this description of the most famous of the various raids along the Delaware river, the entire affair was highly discreditable to the Anglo-Hessian arms. According to military records the descent upon Salem county was made by Anglo-Hessian troops from Philadelphia, assisted by detachments from New Jersey's loyalist regiments and unorganized bands of refugee robbers. A detached regiment from Philadelphia, under the command of Colonel Charles Mawhood, having come down the river and encamping at Sharptown, marched into Salem City. Failing to surprise Colonel Anthony Wayne and a small body of troops, the British, recruiting a party of Tory adherents, known by their uniform as "Greens," resolved to "chastise the insolent rebels," among whom were three hundred militia at Quinton's Bridge, three miles from Salem City. The Whig commander at this place was Colonel Benjamin Holmes. Resolving, with Spartan-like courage, to protect the people of the southern part of the county, Colonel Holmes made such preparations for his defense as the situation afforded. Early upon the morning of the 18th of March the British advanced undiscovered to within half a mile of Quinton's Bridge, secreting themselves in a swamp and in nearby timber, which lined the bank of Alloway's creek. A small party of light horsemen then advanced as if to challenge the Whigs. The ruse was successful, and from the opposite shore the militia, under the command of Captain William Smith, rushed without military order across the bridge and into the ambuscade. In spite of Captain Smith's effort to rally his men, the timely appearance of Colonel Hand with the Cumberland militia, and the personal heroism of Andrew Bacon, who cut the draw of the bridge and in the midst of a galling fire held the King's troops in check, the Whig militia was decimated.

Thus defeated by a body of raw troops, who were in a state of exultation over their success, Major Simcoe, appealing to Colonel Mawhood, was reinforced by all the troops that could, with safety, be sent from Salem City. The night had been devoted to strengthening the position of the Whig militia, which, under the direction of Colonels Holmes and Hand, controlled the front and both flanks of the advancing British regulars. So galling was the fire that the King's troops were thrown into confusion and retreated to Salem City.

Failing in his purpose of plundering, Colonel Mawhood adopted new tactics. Addressing a letter to Colonel Hand, he proposed that the militia at Quinton's Bridge lay down their arms, promising that after paying in sterling for all cattle, hay and corn, he would re-embark for Philadelphia.

Otherwise Colonel Mawhood declared he would burn and destroy the homes of the Whigs, giving over their wives and children to the tender mercies of the refugees. To this was annexed a list of those in Salem county who would be first to "feed the vengeance of the British nation." To the letter Colonel Hand made a bold and spirited reply, characterizing the communication as the "cruel order of a barbarous Attila," refusing to lay down arms and promising retaliation if property was destroyed.

Unable to cope with the Whigs of Salem county, either by open attack or by threats, Colonel Mawhood determined upon a midnight assault against a body of four hundred militia who had been stationed at Hancock's Bridge. Conveyed thence by boats, followed by a short, forced march, with orders issued from headquarters: "Go! spare no one — put all to death — give no quarter!" Major Simcoe was detailed to put into execution a fiendish plot, in which the most notorious of the local Tories participated. Fortunately, however, the main body of the militia had departed, leaving only a small guard stationed to guard the bridge, the headquarters being the Hancock mansion. Forcing the house, the owner of the premises, Judge Hancock, a party of non-combatant Quakers and the guard of about twenty-five men, were massacred as they slept or bayonetted as they fought for freedom. A few escaped or were taken prisoners by the enemy. This ended the expedition, and within a few days the Anglo-Hessian troops returned to Philadelphia, their vessels laden with plunder. It will be noticed that no reference whatever is made to the affair at Quinton's Bridge.

For an account of this expedition, and others of a similar character, see "*New Jersey as a Colony and as a State*," Vol. II., Chapter X., p. 179, *ct seq*. (pp. 144-146)

Sickler picks up the story:

Mawhood did not run out of Salem county, as the patriots charged, but remained there for a full week, after the massacre of Hancock's Bridge. Robertson, his engineer, said that they foraged in Elsinboro, Lower Alloway's Creek, Penns Neck and other places on each day of the week following the affair at Hancock's Bridge. On the twenty-fourth of March, the British again distinguished themselves by burning the house of Col. Benjamin Holme in Elsinboro and in carrying off most of his household goods including a beautiful clock, since recovered by the Holme family, and causing other damage to this patriot's property. (p. 165)

Lee, in *Archives of the State of New Jersey, Second Series, Volume II, Documents Relating to the Revolutionary History of the State of New Jersey, Volume II, Extracts From American Newspapers, Volume II, 1778,* includes this from Colonel Mawhood:

> Colonel Mawhood, commanding a detachment of the British army at Salem, induced by motives of humanity, proposes to the militia at Quinton's bridge and the neighborhood, officers as well as private men, to lay down their arms and depart, each man to his own home. On that condition, he solemnly promises to re-embark his troops without delay, doing no further damage to the country; and he will cause his commissaries to pay for the cattle, hay and corn, that have been taken, in sterling money.
>
> If, on the contrary, the militia should be so far deluded, and blind to their true interest and happiness, he will put the arms which he has brought with him into the hands of the people well affected, called Tories, and will attack all such of the militia as remain in arms, burn and destroy their houses, and other property, and reduce them, their unfortunate wives and children, to beggary and distress; and to convince them that these are not vain threats, he has subjoined a list of the names of such as will be the first objects to feel the vengeance of the British nation.
>
> *Given under my hand at Head-Quarters, at Salem, the twenty-first day of March, 1778.*
>
>   C. MAWHOOD, [1] Colonel.
>
> [1] Conspicuous in the Battles of Trenton and Princeton.
>
> Edmund Keesby, Thomas Sinnickson, Samuel Dick, Whitten Crips, Ebenezer Howell, Edward Hall, John Bowen, Thomas Thomson, George Treiiehard, Elisha, Cattle, Andrew Sinnickson, Nicholas Keen, Jacob Hufty, Benjamin Holmes, William Shute, Anthony Sharp, and Abner Penton. (pp. 168-169)

Sickler, who quoted the main body of the above letter, notes that Mawhood "added as a postscript the names of the patriots whom he proscribed as enemies of the British nation...." (p. 166)

Quoting the 22 March 1778 letter of Colonel Elijah Hand to Colonel Mawhood, Sickler notes that "Col. Elijah Hand ... shared with Benjamin Holme the command of the American militia forces...." (p. 166)

Francis B. Lee includes this letter in *Archives of the State of New Jersey, Second Series, Volume II, Documents Relating to the Revolutionary History of the State of New Jersey, Volume II, Extracts From American Newspapers, Volume II, 1778*:

SIR,

I have been favored with what you say humanity has induced you to propose. It would have given me much pleasure to have found that humanity had been the line of conduct to your troops since you came to Salem. Not only denying quarters, but butchering our men who surrendered themselves prisoners in the skirmish at Quinton's Bridge last Thursday, and bayonetting yesterday morning at Hancock's Bridge, in the most cruel manner in cold blood, men who were taken by surprise, in a situation in which they neither could nor did attempt to make any resistance, and some of whom were not fighting men; are instances too shocking for me to relate and I hope for you to hear. — The brave are very generous and humane. — After expressing your sentiments of humanity, you proceed to make a request which I think you would despise us if we complied with. Your proposal, that we should lay down our arms, we absolutely reject.

We have taken them up to maintain rights which are dearer to us than our lives, and will not lay them down, 'till either success has crowned our cause with victory, or like many ancient worthies contending for liberty, we meet with an honorable death. You mention that if we reject your proposal, you will put arms into the hands of the Tories against us; we have no objection to the measure, for it would be a very good one to fill our arsenals with arms. — Your threats to wantonly burn and destroy our houses and other property, and reduce our wives and children to beggary and distress, is a sentiment which my humanity almost forbids me only to recite, and induces me to imagine I am reading the cruel order of a barbarous Attila, and not of a Gentleman, brave, generous and polished with a genteel European education — To wantonly destroy, will injure your cause more than ours — it will increase your enemies and our army. — To destine to destruction the property of our most distinguished men, as you have done in your proposals, is, in my opinion, unworthy a generous foe; and more like a rancorous feud between two contending Barons, than a war carried on by one of the greatest powers on earth, against a people nobly struggling for Liberty — a line of honour would mark out that these men should share the fate of their country — If your arms should be crowned with victory, which God forbid, they and their property will be entirely at the disposal of your Sovereign. The loss of their property, when their persons are out of your power, will only make them desperate and, as I said before, increase your foes and our army; and retaliation upon Tories and their property is not entirely out of our power. Be assured that these are the sentiments and determined resolution, not only of myself, but of all the officers and privates under me.

My prayer is, Sir, that this answer may reach you in health and great happiness.

Given at Headquarters at Quinton's Bridge the 22nd day of March, 1778.

ELIJAH HAND, Colonel.

To C. Mawhood, Colonel. (pp. 169-170)

Sickler continues:

On Saturday night the twenty-first, the American militia, doubtless fearing an attack at Quinton, now that their flank had been turned on the west side, withdrew their headquarters to the glassworks at Thompson's Bridge, now Alloway. On that same night, Hand and Holme formulated this letter to William Livingston, governor of New Jersey, beseeching him to send aid:

> Glass Works, Salem County,
> March 21st, 1778.
>
> Worthy Sir:
> These with our respects and would earnestly inform and recommend to your Excellency's notice the suffering state of our counties, viz, on Tuesday last a large number of the enemy landed at Salem Town as near as we can learn about or between two or three thousand and are advancing into the Country and plundering very fast; we have had two or three skirmishes with them and have lost on our side as near as we can yet learn about twelve killed and near forty taken prisoners; the loss on the enemy's side we cannot as yet positively learn, however, we are well assured we have killed some of them.
> We have made our stand on Alloways Creek the lower side at Hancock's, Quinton's or Thompson's Bridges, but last night the enemy landed out of their boats below all the aforesaid bridges and surrounded our guard at

Hancock's Bridge and took and killed almost all of them which is a part of the aforesaid loss, and we fear they will advance over all these lower counties (as we find our numbers at present are not large enough to make a proper stand against them) except you, Sir, by some means can help us to some relief which we desire you to do either by sending down some Militia or if that cannot well be done we desire you to inform General Washington of our necessity of some of the continental forces to assist us at this time and desire you, Sir, to use your influence with him to send some forces to our relief — we are under a disadvantage at present for want of field pieces and should be glad if we could be furnished with four or five of them by some means as soon as possible.

We are, Sir, your most obedient Servants
Signed,

Elijah Hand, Col.

Apparently the fear of a British attack on Quinton passed the next day for on the twenty-second, Hand dated his famous reply to Mawhood as "Headquarters at Quinton's Bridge." Simcoe said that the militia at Thompson's Bridge was alarmed by a cow, fired at it and then fled. The cow story was probably a bit of imagination on the part of the triumphant British major. However, it is true that some time after the twenty-second the American militia, still fearing a flank attack, did desert the line of Alloway's Creek to fall back some twelve miles in Cumberland county behind the shelter of Cohansey creek. Simcoe states this fact and the Americans confirm it by another letter to Governor Livingston dated at Roadstown on the Cohansey one week later.

This letter, honest and frank, is a most moving document calling attention to the pitiable state of the colonists in Salem and Cumberland counties and throwing themselves without stint upon the mercy of the new state government. The letter shows only too well the same state of mind which permeated the army at Valley Forge. It is a document which every patriotic American should read to realize the low ebb of this country's fortune in March of 1778. In part, the letter says:

A large detachment of the British army a few weeks ago made an invasion into the lower counties of this state on Delaware, and plundered a few of the inhabitants. At present a larger detachment are invading a second time. The enemy in this second incursion have, as we have been creditably informed, by the express orders of Colonel Mawhood, the commanding officer, bayonetted and butchered in the most inhuman manner a number of militia who have unfortunately fallen into their hands. Colonel Mawhood immediately after the massacre in open letters sent to both officers and privates by a flag had the effrontery to insult us with a demand that we should lay down our arms and if not, threaten to burn, destroy and lay the whole country waste and more especially the property of a number of our most distinguished men whom he named. He has since actually put his threat into execution in one instance by burning one of the finest dwelling houses in Salem County, and all the other buildings on the same farm the property of Colonel Benjamin Holme. Plunder, rapine and devastation in the most fertile and populous part of these counties widely marked their footsteps wherever they go. They are spreading disaffection. They are using every possible means to corrupt the minds of the people; they are publicly vending their goods to people who within their lines have so little virtue as to purchase from them.

We are in no state of defence. We are so exposed by reason of our situation that some of our officers civil and military have moved out of these counties for safety. Our militia during the last winter have been so fatigued out by repeated calls and continual service, and disaffection is now so widely diffused, that very few can be called out, in some places none. We have no troops of light horse regularly embodied; there is a scarcity of small arms among us and no field pieces. These two want of field pieces and artillerymen. The number of us assembled is so small that though we should use the greatest conduct and bravery we could only provoke not injure our enemy.

The extent of our country is so great, that our small number of men fatigued out, indifferently armed and without field pieces cannot defend it. As Delaware runs along these counties we are liable to be attacked in numberless places. The acquisition of these counties would be of great advantage to the enemy. They could nearly maintain their whole campaign by the plunder, forage and assistance they could draw from them.

Although the United States might not need them, yet it might perhaps be advisable to defend them to prevent the advantage the enemy might receive from them. Our riches and former virtue make us a prey to an enemy whose tender mercies are cruelties. In short our situation is beyond description deplorable. The powers civil and military are daily relaxing and disaffection prevailing. We can neither plough, plant, sow, reap nor gather. We are fast falling into poverty, distress and into the hands of our enemy. Unless there can be sent to our relief and assistance a sufficient body of standing troops, we must be under the disagreeable necessity of leaving the country to the enemy and removing ourselves and family to distant places for safety. Although the present detachment may be fled and gone before the relief reach us, yet a body of troops are necessary for our protection as long as the enemy possesses Philadelphia and that these are the sentiments not only of us the subscribers but of all the rest of the officers civil and military and other good subjects of this state in these counties.

Your humble petitioners have set forth these few hints containing not the half of their distress and misery do humbly pray your Excellency to take the premises into consideration and give your humble petitioners just relief therein as to your Excellency shall seem meet — and your humble petitioners shall ever pray.

Dated at Roadstown in Cumberland March 28, 1778 and signed.

Civil Officers: Joseph Newcomb, Joel Fithian, Samuel Leake, Ephriam Mills, Nathan Leek, John Holme, Providence Ludlam, John Peck, Jonathan Bowen, A. S. Sayre, Ebenezer Howell, Jonathan Elmer.
Military Officers: Elijah Hand, Benjamin Holme, Silas Newcomb, Abijah Holme, Samuel Ogden, Thomas Ewing, Edward Hall, Daniel Maskell, Henry Sparks, Robert Patterson, Enos Seely.

The pathetic appeal of the military officers and civilians had its immediate effect upon the commander of the New Jersey Continental line, Colonel Israel Shreve, for on the same day the letter was dispatched from Roadstown, he wrote to General Washington at Valley Forge, relaying the news of the British raid at Salem and the pitiable condition of the lower counties of New Jersey which lay upon the Delaware river. . . .

Haddonfield, March 28, 1778.

The Governor desired me to join Col. Ellis and wait at this post until he could collect a body of militia; we have now one hundred and seventy foot, twenty horse and thirty-five artillery with two iron three pounders, besides my own Regiment — the last accounts from Salem by three deserters and several other persons were that four regiments commanded by Col. Mawhood, consisting of between one thousand and twelve hundred were at that place; the Militia to the number of three hundred were at Roads Town thirteen miles below Salem; all the county on the River between that post and this place, forty-five miles, is open to the ravage of the Enemy — the tories to the number of one hundred and fifty are in arms fortifying at Billingsport with the assistance of some marines; a great number of disaffected inhabitants are trading with the enemy. Yesterday, sixty tories and marines commanded by one Cox, went to Swedesboro, took Lieut. Lloyd of the fourth Regiment, Jersey, with two recruits, plundered the house of Capt. Brown in a shocking manner, stripped his wife and children, carried off or destroyed everything in the house. Several other houses shared the same fate. Every civil and military officer is forced to fly from home; many have been taken by the tories and carried off to the city. Three days ago, three of the militia took a covered wagon and three horses with baggage and stores belonging to Daniel Cozens a Tory Captain; yesterday Col. Ellis with a small party of horse took a certain David Chew one of the tory gang; he acknowledges he has borne arms against the States; they also took some marketing going to the enemy, but the owner fled; Captain Cumming has just returned from a scout, took a wagon and two horses at a landing; no person will own the wagon. I have ordered these things sold for the use of the captors.

This country is in a miserable situation, the inhabitants afraid of every person they see. If marketing is found in any house the whole family, even little children, will deny the owners, not pretend to know anything about it. If your Excellency could spare part or all of the Brigade it would enable us to quell the Tories and collect a considerable quantity of privisions [sic] which otherwise, I fear, will fall into the hands of the enemy as it is collected in places near the River for that purpose. We shall do everything in our power to protect the virtuous inhabitants and suppress the tories; we have a negro man confined as a spy, as I believe it will appear he went to Philadelphia to give intelligence of my crossing the Delaware. I desire your Excellency's directions concerning the tryal [sic] of this spy and those of the inhabitants taken in arms against the States, as some examples seem highly necessary in this place, but I am too prolix and have only to say that a general defection prevails in many places, that from the situation of Haddonfield it must be in our possession or least it be the case with the lower counties — that the force here is too small for the purpose, scarcely enough to prevent surprise when large scouts are out. I would wish to march to Cumberland as many things are there to be had if the Enemy were terrified from thence, which I hope to effect when the militia comes in to secure this post and by a junction with me make me responsible in numbers. If your Excellency has orders, I should be happy to receive them and I am your

Excellency's very Humble Servant,
Israel Shreve, Col.

N. B. As the tories have fallen in with our parties I hope I shall stop their trade of catching officers for whom they get a reward according to the rank of the prisoners. Ammunition is wanted for the Militia as they are not furnished for common duty — they cannot be supplied from the State; therefore I shall find a wagon to receive it from the stores in camp and beg your Excellency's order to obtain it.

Governor Livingston, writing from Princeton on the ninth of April, also urged Washington to send help to the Salem county militia. But Washington, with his own troubles at Valley Forge, considering his fast diminishing army, famine, starvation, and lack of supplies was unable to send the slightest bit of help to the harrassed [sic] militia of the lower counties. By the time the American commander had received the reports from Shreve and Livingston, the British army had gone from Salem, leaving in its wake the hatred and disgust of a community whose sons had been butchered in cold blood.

It is true that war came no more to Salem county but the outraged citizens cried out for retaliation against the British invaders. There was little they could do about it except take action against the persons or the estates of those who had aided the British in any way. They were not long in doing this. On September 26th of this same year the Salem County Grand Jury returned numerous indictments against those persons who had either taken arms or otherwise aided the British cause. The court appointed Thomas Sayre, father of a family which suffered so severely at the Hancock House, and Daniel Garrison as commissioners to confiscate the estates of the Tories.

Following the indictments the court of Oyer and Terminer commenced at Salem on November 30th, 1778 and lasted without adjournment until the nineteenth of December, the same year. It has passed into history as the "Long Court." It was the act of desperate men who, grieved by their serious losses, were determined to take this action against the enemies of the state. True, the war was not over and the British army no further away than New York, but these local citizens were determined that someone should pay for these wrongs.

No less than two chief justices, John Cleves Symmes and Robert Morris, separately presided over the various sessions of the long court. The foreman of the Grand Jury was William Dickison. The local associate judges were John Holme, John Mayhew, William Mecum, William Smith and Andrew Sinnickson. The justices of the peace in attendance were Robert Johnson, Edward Keasbey, Isaac Harris, Thomas Sayre, Thomas Norris, John Summerill, Jacob Taggert, William Miller and William Dickison. It should be noticed that most of these judges had rendered military service. The court appeared to roam about the town of Salem. On many occasions it met at the Quaker Meeting House. . . . Sometimes it met in Mrs. Burrows' house, exact location unknown, and naturally in the Court house.

There seem to have been two courts sitting at the same time. They divided their crimes into three classes, the first for high treason, punishable by death, the second for seditious words, the third for misdemeanors.

On the charges of high treason four of the Tories who were so unfortunate as to fall into patriot hands were found guilty and sentenced to be hanged on February 12th, 1779. Ironically enough, two of these men, Rubin Langley and Abdon Abbott, Jr., had served in the local militia before they joined the Tories. The other two were Richard Whitaker and Joseph Hilton.

However, the death sentences were never carried out. Before the twelfth of February Governor Livingston of New Jersey, listening to the appeals for pardon, gave all four convicted men a reprieve. Whitaker was forced to leave the United States in six months from the date of his pardon. The other three, Abbott, Langley and Hilton, were also pardoned on condition that they leave the state of New Jersey.

There were numerous convictions with trifling fines for seditious words and misdemeanors. Most of these loyalists feld to Nova Scotia and other parts of the British empire. From the West Jersey volunteers is taken the following list of men who enlisted in the British loyalist regiments: Abdon Abbott, Phillip Adams, John Cowman, Jerman Davis, Rubin Langley, Michael Miller, Richard Meade, James Sutton, James Dean, Israel Elwell, Joseph Hilton, Joseph Kendall, Henry Longbaugh, Jacob Sutton, Moses Sutton, John Sutton, Thomas Sutton, Robert Whitaker. This list does not include the names of Joel Daniels and John Hanks. These two men are mentioned by Johnson as the murderers of their fellow Salem countians at Hancock House. Neither does this list mention Hugh Cowperthwaite, Jonathan Ballinger and a negro named Nicholson's Frank, who were reported to have been the guides who piloted Simcoe and his men across the marshes to Hancock's Bridge on the morning of the twenty-first of March. These men seem to have escaped the vengeance of the Salem courts in person although Cowperthwaite, a fugitive, had his estate confiscated by the commissioners. (pp. 167-172)

To give a sense of the brutal temperatures endured during this period of the war, I have included the following from *New York in the American Revolution* by Wilbur C. Abbott: "There was the fierce winter of 1779 when the authorities were assured solemnly — and no doubt truthfully — that the ice on the North River was eighteen feet thick, and that the Hudson as far north as Albany — and presumably much further — was 'mere terra firma'." (p. 243)

Robert Gibbon Johnson in *An Historical Account of the First Settlement of Salem, in West Jersey, by John Fenwick, Esq. Chief Proprietor of the Same* states:

It was currently reported, and that report believed to be true, that a negro man, who went by the name of Nicholson's Frank, and a man from Gloucester county, called Jonathan Ballanger, were the two persons who attended the murdering expedition as pilots.

Ballanger came to the house of John Steward, (a farmer, near Hancock's Bridge,) armed, that very same night, some time before day. (I use the words of Steward.) Steward said, "that he soon discovered, from the looks and conversation of Ballanger, that some evil was about to be done." With some persuasion he prevailed upon him to go into the room and lie down. When he went in he said he turned the key in the door, nor did he open it until about daylight in the morning. ["]When Ballanger came out of the room he stayed but a few minutes, went away, carrying with him his musket.

"A short time after he had left the house, the report of a gun was heard, in the direction in which Ballanger had walked, and by the side of the fence along which he had gone but a few minutes before, was found Reuben Sayres, mortally wounded; being a distance of not more than one-fourth of a mile from Steward's house."

Ballanger was not seen by any person after he left Steward's, until several years afterwards. The suspicion of the murder of Sayres could be fixed upon no one but him. Immediately after the massacre of the picket and private citizens, the refugees returned to Salem over the bridge, the draw of which they laid. Ballanger and the negro, no doubt, returned by water with the boatmen. It could have been none of the refugees who were at Hancock's. The circumstantial evidence against Ballanger was most assuredly the very strongest kind; amounting pretty near to positive. Public opinion was decidedly against him, for he was known to be a rank tory, and from the very hot bed of toryism — of those who secretly traded with the British while they occupied Philadelphia.

It was but a short mile from Hancock's bridge to where Sayres was found weltering in his blood; he had escaped thus far towards the woods or marshes, in his flight from the murdering refugees. Not a single individual of the enemy was seen any where near to the field where Sayres was found. The murderer was always believed to be none other than Jonathan Ballanger. (p. 149-151)

Johnson continues

One fellow, who usually bore the name of Proud Harry, a plasterer by trade, an insolent, swaggering scoundrel, a bragadocio; another, by name Jo. Daniels; another, if possible, worse than Satan himself, his name was John Hanks. This fellow was brought up from a boy in the family of

Morris Beesley: the son of Morris, whose name was Walker, belonged to that company of militia. Hanks, with another villain, rushed upon young Beesley to kill him. He begged of Hanks, in the most pitiable manner, to protect him, and spare his life; he urged upon him their friendship and intimacy; their having grown up from boys together. All his entreaties were in vain; the murderer heard his pleas, and then very sternly told him, that for their former intimacy alone he was determined to kill him, and then stabbed him and left him.

The poor youth lived long enough to tell this tale of woe to those people who came to take care of the dead and wounded. (p. 151)

Johnson writes,

Another instance I will mention, of a militia-man whose name was Darius Dailey, who, escaping from the [Hancock] house, was pursued by two of the refugees; while running, he saw an English soldier; he made towards him as fast as he could, calling out to him at the same time to save him; crying out, "Oh, save me, save me, soldier — I am your countryman! Save me, save me; I am a Scotchman — I am your countryman!"

The very name of countryman, even coming from the mouth of an enemy, and in the midst of slaughter, struck the tender fibres of the stern soldier's heart. He immediately put himself in an attitude of defence, and stopped the pursuing refugees, and told them that he should protect the man at all hazards that he had surrendered himself to him, and that he was his prisoner.

When his flurry had in some measure subsided, Dailey gave his name to the soldier — the soldier his name to Dailey. They were both almost struck speechless with astonishment; they now found that they had been bosom friends and school-mates together, when boys, in Scotland. Dailey was conducted a prisoner, with a few others, to Salem, whose lives had been spared by the English soldiers. (p. 152)

Again, in *The History of Salem County New Jersey, Being the Story of John Fenwick's Colony, the Oldest English Speaking Settlement on the Delaware River*, Sickler writes,

The hatred towards these guides did not die down easily. As late as 1825 a man by the name of Sayer, son of one of the patriots of that name massacred at Hancock's Bridge, was captain of a small vessel plying between Salem and Philadelphia. Becoming drunk one night he fell into the river off Market street wharf at Philadelphia. A young man standing on the wharf plunged in and saved his life. Upon being rescued, Sayre discovered that he owed his life to the bravery of the son of the Jonathan

Ballinger who guided the British to the massacre at Hancock's Bridge. Perceiving this fact, Sayre said "he would be damned if he would owe his life to such a double damned scoundrel as the son of Ballinger." Thereupon, he threw himself back in the river and with some difficulty was rescued a second time from a watery grave.

As late as 1803 at a dinner in Salem someone proposed the toast of eternal damnation to Major Simcoe. In 1933 a facetious writer in a Philadelphia newspaper, after visiting the Hancock House, commented after hearing the story of the massacre "that the Salem folks were still mad about the massacre." (pp. 172-173)

John Clement, in *Revolutionary Reminiscences of Camden County*, says:

The last encampment of the Hessian troops under Count Dunop, before the battle of Red Bank, was in Haddonfield. It was across the street near the residence of John Gill (where now stands the dwelling of John Gill, Esq.,) extending some distance into the fields. In this house Dunop had his headquarters, and although the owner was an elder among Friends, yet the urbanity and politeness of the German soldier so won upon him that [h]e was kindly remembered ever after.

This body of troops moved from Philadelphia, about twelve hundred strong, on the evening of October 21st. The inhabitants suffered from the depredations of the common soldiers, who wantonly destroyed or carried off their property and endangered their lives. This conduct aroused the people, and did much to strengthen the American cause. In reply to a letter from Lord Cornwallis, inquiring if money and stores could be sent to prisoners captured at Trenton, General Washington said, no molestatation [sic] would be offered to the convoy by any part of the regular army under his command, but he would not answer for the militia, who were resorting to arms in most parts of the State, and were exceedingly exasperated at the treatment they had met with from both the Hessian and Brittish [sic] troops.

In a letter from Postmaster Hazzard to a friend, he says, "These rascals plunder all, indiscriminately. If they see anything they like, they say: 'Rebel good for Hesse-mans,' and seize upon it for their own use. They have no idea of the distinctions between the Whig and Tory."

The presence of an officer in a house was the only protection against their depreciations, and every family sought one, with the promise of good entertainment, free of charge. These troops regarded the American people as semi-barbarous, and to destroy their property was only doing the king's service. (pp. 12-13)

Again, in *An Historical Account of the First Settlement of Salem, in West Jersey, by John Fenwick, Esq. Chief Proprietor of the Same*, Robert Gibbon Johnson writes,

> Bateman Loyd, Esq., then a lieutenant, was going from our camp to communicate information to the commander of the militia in Gloucester. He stopped at Swedesborough to take some refreshment, and fed his horse; but before he alighted, he questioned the tavern keeper, whose name was James, whether it would be safe for him to tarry there for so short a time; he was assured that he might, in the most perfect safety — but while he was eating his meal, the tories rushed into the room, secured him, and carried him a prisoner to Philadelphia, then in the possession of the enemy. That part of Gloucester and along the river were many people decided tories, and who traded privately with the enemy, and communicated to Lord Howe all the necessary intelligence respecting the militia. (p. 163)

A similar series of anecdotes appear in almost all books written about the British invasion and occupation of West New Jersy. Isaac Mickle is diligent in seeking out original sources for these stories in his *Reminiscences of Old Gloucester, or Incidents in the History of the Counties of Gloucester, Atlantic and Camden, New Jersey.*

Mickle:

> The people of Waterford were in the Revolution staunch whigs, and as such was particularly obnoxious to the British. While the latter occupied Haddonfield in 1778, most of the houses north of Cooper's Creek were searched and sacked by foragers. One morning a British officer went to the dwelling of the Champions and demanded the best horse the farm could afford. A young unbroken steed was brought out and saddled — the officer mounted and drove a little piece to the pond which intercepted the land. The colt here became unruly, and the officer was thrown into the muddy pool. As a revenge for spoiling his uniform, he commanded his men to rob the house, and then took a plough horse and rode away.
>
> A worthy old gentleman near Ellis', having a good deal of specie which he was anxious to save from some Hessians, who also rendezvoused at Haddonfield, undertook to bury it. For this purpose he went out at midnight, taking with him, unfortunately, a lantern to guide him. Having deposited his treasure he returned home; but the next morning in passing the spot, lo! he beheld his gold was gone. The old man's lamp had betrayed him to the spies who were lurking about, and they had dug up his pot almost as soon as he had concealed it.
>
> All's fair, however, in war, and it was seldom that the enemy got ahead of the Yankee boys in sharp dealing. A Waterford man hearing that some

> British who were stationed at Mount Holly were in need of flour, started off with ten bags on a speculation. The officer opened each sack, took out a handful of flour, pronounced it good, and paid a handsome price. The speculator was moving off. "Stop," said the officer, "you're leaving your bags." "You need not empty them," said the countryman, "I'll throw the bags in for the sake of the cause." When the contents came to be emptied it was discovered that there was only a small portion of flour upon the top — the rest being saw dust!" (pp. 46-47)

The footnote (p. 50) accompanying the following by Mickle states, "See a communication in the *Woodbury Constitution* [italics added], by Mr. Redfield, dated Jan. 20th, 1844."

> The almost miraculous escape of Miles Sage forms the favorite theme of every Old Gloucester soldier. Miles was in the dragoon service, and a braver trooper never lived. On one occasion, while Haddonfield was occupied by Ellis' regiment, to which our hero belonged, he, in company with one Ben Haines, was ordered to reconnoitre the enemy, who lay near Gloucester Point. Sage, having lost his companion, reached the Point and learned that the British had already moved for Haddonfield, intending surprise upon the Americans. He turned his fleet and faithful mare, and dashed off through the darkness of the night, for the camp. Driving on through Newton Creek, and over ditches and hedges with the speed of the wind, he reached the village and stopped before Col. Ellis' quarters to give the alarm. It was needless, for the house was already filled with British officers. He mounted again without having been discovered and galloped off to find his retreating countrymen. Near the eastern extremity of the town the enemy were drawn up in three ranks. Through two ranks the trooper charged successfully; but at the third his mare fell, and left him at the mercy of his foes. They surrounded him, and pierced him with no less than thirteen bayonet wounds! A Scotch officer here interposed, and had him carried to the village inn, where he was put under the care of some women. [Footnote (p. 50): "One of these women was the mother of Gov. Stratton."] One of these beseeching him to remember heaven, he exclaimed, "Why Martha, I mean to give the enemy thirteen rounds yet." He lived to tell his grandchildren of his fearful adventure, and, we have no doubt, to remember heaven too. (pp. 49-50)

Mickle says of the following: "This incident is from a MS. sent us some time ago by an esteemed friend, who was well versed in all the revolutionary history of old Gloucester."

About this time the houses of several staunch Whigs in Gloucester township were burnt, and among them the mansions of the Huggs and Harrisons, the first on Timber Creek, near the bridge, and the other nearer the Point. That the Huggs shoud have been obnoxious to the British, was no more than natural, for that family gave two officers and several privates to the revolutionary armies, and its very women were unconquerable patriots. On one occasion some Englishmen coming to the residence of Col. Joseph Hugg, began to throw a hatchet at the poultry in the yard. The matron came forth, and gave the intruders a rebuke worthy of a Spartan mother. "Do you," said she, "call yourselves officers, and thus come to rob undefended premises? I have sons who are in Washington's army. They are gentlemen, and not such puppies as you." It is no wonder, we repeat, that after this, Col. Abercombie should have burnt the house with a large quantity of hay in the rick. (p. 64)

Mickle:

Towards the close of the war, some people at Egg Harbor and others further up in the interior, got to carrying on a considerable trade with the British in New York. The Refugees often came there in large bodies and committed great depredations on the people; and the troops taken at the capture of Lord Cornwallis, who were cantoned in Virginia, frequently escaped in small parties, and by concealing themselves in the woods in the day and only travelling by night, by the assistance of guides and friends whom they found on their way, got to Egg Harbor and from thence to New York. To prevent all this, Capt. John Davis was sent with a company of men to Egg Harbor. On one occasion his lieutenant, Benjamin Bates, with Richard Powell, a private, called at a house where Davis had been informed, over night, that, two Refugee officers were lodging. Bates got to the house before any of the family had risen except two girls, who were making a fire in the kitchen. He inquired if there were any persons in the house beside the family, and was answered "none, except two men from up in the country." He bade the girls show him where they were, which they did. In passing through a room separating the kitchen from the bed-room, he saw two pistols lying on a table. Knocking at the door, he was at first refused admittance; but finding him determined to enter, the two Refugees finally let him in. They refused to tell their names, but were afterwards found to be William Giberson and Henry Lane, Refugee lieutenants, the former a notorious rascal who had committed many outrages, and killed one or two Americans in cold blood. On their way to the quarters of Davis' company, Giberson called Bates' attention to something he pretended to see at a distance; and while Bates was looking in that direction Giberson started in another, and being a very fast runner, although Bates fired his musquet at him, he made his escape. Davis on being informed of what had happened, told Bates to try again the next night. Accordingly the next night he went to the same house. While in the act of opening the door he heard the click of a musket cock, behind a large tree within a few feet of him, and turning around, saw Giberson just taking aim at him. He dropped on his knees and the ball cut the rim of his hat. Giberson started to run, but before he had got many rods Bates gave him a load of buck-shot which broke his leg. He was well guarded until he could be removed with Lane to Burlington goal, from which however he soon made his escape and went to New York. [Footnote (p. 80): "MSS. Notes of a Septuagenarian, penes me."] Giberson was a large man, of almost incredible strength and activity. It is said that at a running jump he could clear the top of an ordinary Egg Harbor wagon, but since the MSS. which we are following do not mention the fact, we think it may well be doubted. (pp. 79-80)

George R. Prowell, in his *The History of Camden County*, writes,

The Hessian marauders were scouring Southern New Jersey for better food than King George's rations, and Colonel Ellis, commandant of the Gloucester militia, was authorized to remove any cattle, sheep and hogs (excepting milch cows) from any places where he thought them in danger of falling into the enemy's hands to places of greater security, and upon the owners refusing to do so, after first giving notice to the owners, who may take care of them at their expense. This measure not proving extreme enough, Colonel Ellis was directed to remove all the horned cattle, sheep, hogs and all cows which do not give milk from the vicinity of the Jersey shore, in the counties of Burlington, Gloucester and Salem, that may be within the reach of the enemy's foraging parties, except such as might be really necessary for the inhabitants (the owners refusing to do it on notice given to them for that purpose), and that the general (Washington) be informed that the powers lodged in the Council of Safety are inadequate to the requisition of having the forage removed, and that it be recommended to him to exercise his own authority in having it effected. This stripping of the country of provender in order that the enemy might not obtain it speaks eloquently of the straits to which this section of the State was reduced.

These stern Councillors were obliged to be no respectors of the sex. The wives and daughters of Tories were as inimical to the republic as their husbands and fathers, and when the men had gone into the British service the women left behind frequently became adroit and successful spies upon the movements of the patriots. Hence the Council applied to them the extreme rigors of the treason law and either sent them after their male protectors into the British lines, locked them up in jail or held them in heavy bonds for their good behavior. Those to be sent into the enemy's camp were usually assembled at Elizabeth, from whence it was an easy task to transfer them under a flag of truce to the headquarters on Staten Island. (p. 68)

Charles Leonard Lundin, in his *Cockpit of the Revolution: The War for Independence in New Jersey*, writes, "The position of New Jersey as the cockpit of the war [had a] disastrous effect upon the morale of the people. So divided in sentiment that it was impossible for one faction ever completely to root out the other, and living, in great part, in places which were exposed throughout the contest to sudden raids from either army, the inhabitants grew more bitter and more brutal as the tides and backwashes of war swept over them again and again." (p. 219)

Although I have not been able to connect the Kellys of Pennsylvania to those of West New Jersey, it is not improbable that they are related, so I have chosen to include the following anecdote from John Warner Barber and Henry Howe's *Historical Collections of the State of New Jersey*:

About the close of the action at Princeton [(2 January 1777)], Washington detached a small party to destroy the bridge over Stony Brook, at Worth's mills, on the road from Princeton to Trenton. This party had scarcely half completed their work, before the British troops from Trenton made their appearance on the hill a short distance west of the dwelling of Mr. Worth, and commenced firing upon them. The Americans, however, pushed on their work with renewed vigor, until the cannon-balls began to strike around them, — by which time they had thrown off the loose planks into the stream, — and then hastily retreated. The baggage and artillery of the British troops were detained at the bridge nearly an hour before it could be made passable. The troops, however, were ordered to dash through the stream, (then swollen and filled with running ice, and about breast high,) and press forward as rapidly as possible toward New Brunswick. The officer, who commanded the detachment ordered to destroy the bridge, is said to have been Major (afterwards Col.) John Kelly, of Pennsylvania, who died about the year 1835. After the British appeared in sight, it was necessary that some part of the bridge should be cut away, — which was an extremely hazardous service under the fire of the enemy. Maj. Kelly, disdaining to order another to do what some might say he would not do himself, bravely took the axe and commenced cutting off the logs on which the planks of the bridge were laid. Several balls struck into the last log he was chopping, and on which he stood, when it broke down sooner than he expected, and he fell with it into the swollen stream. His men, not believing it possible for him to escape, immediately fled. Maj. Kelly, by great exertion, got out of the water and followed after them; but being unarmed and encumbered with frozen clothing, he was taken prisoner by a British soldier. (pp. 273-274)

In an attempt to explain the circumstances and complexities of the shifting about of John Kelly and his possible brothers during the war, I have found it necessary to quote extensively from William O. Raymond's "Loyalists in Arms" included in *Collections of the New Brunswick Historical Society, No. 5*.

Raymond:

> The period of enlistment was short, being at first "for two years or during the continuance of the war," which many of the men were disposed to interpret as meaning that they were pledged only to two years' service, or less if the war ended sooner. Under this impression numbers claimed their discharge at the expiration of the two years, and if it was not granted "took French leave," and were reported on the muster rolls as deserters. . . . Lieut. Col. Edward Winslow, the muster-master-general . . . [, w]riting to his friend, Major Barry, November 13, 1778, . . . refers to certain objections that had been made to sending the Loyalist regiments raised in New York, New Jersey and Pennsylvania to serve in the South. The sending of the Provincial Troops to serve in that quarter had been censured as unjust, and not consistent with the original compact. Lt. Col. Winslow says: —
>
> "This assertion arises from an idea that all or most of the provincial corps were local and intended to defend particular provinces, from which they could not be removed but by their own consent. Contracted as this sentiment may at first appear, there is some reason for it. Those men who consulted their own immediate advantage and reputation more than the public good gave assurances, for which they had no authority from the Commander-in-Chief, and seduced men into the service by promises that they should not be called on any emergency from particular places. However, as I have the honor of being connected with these troops I am not puzzled to account for the policy [of sending them to the South] [*sic*] if unable to applaud the justice of the measure. Most of the recruits enlisted for the term of two years, or during the continuance of the rebellion; there is not wanting among them men of sufficient cunning to suggest that those terms imply an option in the soldier whether he will continue in service after the expiration of the first period; quibbling and dishonorable as this suggestion may seem to a European gentleman, it is a tolerable pretence for an American laborer, and the consequence of it were

more serious than you would at first imagine. Discharges have been demanded by those who enlisted early, etc. Were they to remain entirely inactive and in the vicinity of the place where they formerly lived desertions would be frequent. The pleasure of gratifying revenge for recent persecutions and injuries, or a flush of romantic military ardor were the inducements to engage. They have been in some measure disappointed in their first expectation and a two years' service as soldiers has considerably cooled 'em in the latter. It cannot therefore be impolitic to change their ground.

["]Those who are actuated by mere caprice I do not pity, but there are many who would with alacrity serve during the rebellion under the same officers who promised to lead them — but from necessity or some other cause, their commanders have been changed, men drafted [into other corps] [sic] &c., &c., Cox-combs, Fools, & Blackguards have been provided as officers in the Provincial Line. The soldiers, unaccustomed to severity have been made miserable and unhappy. I really am no advocate for indulgencies to soldiers, but I cannot think it below the dignity of an officer who wishes well to the service in general to consult the disposition of his men."

Many of the Loyalist regiments were raised about the year 1777. . . . [John Kelly enlisted into the 4th New Jersey Volunteers in March 1777 in New York City.]

[T]he 2nd battalion of the New Jersey Volunteers, [was] raised by Lieut.-Colonel John Morris about the close of 1776. At the time of the muster of May 7, 1779, the number of non-commissioned officers and men that had been enlisted was about 408; but of these 113 had died, 4 had taken their discharge, 3 had been transferred to the navy, and 78 were returned as deserters; total number of non-effectives 198. The strength of the battalion at this time was about 210 non-commissioned officers, and men, so that in the course of less than two and a half years the non-effectives were very nearly half of the total number of enlistments. . . .

Many of the men, conceiving that they had fulfilled their term of enlistment at the expiration of two years, took French leave and returned to their families; others, discouraged by the hardships and privations concerning which the death rate speaks volumes, did not remain so long; nevertheless many faithful fellows served through the whole war and at its close sought new homes under the British flag. . . .

In Pennsylvania the Loyalists were influential and wealthy and by no means inconsiderable in numbers. It was claimed that if Sir William Howe had issued an invitation when in Philadelpha, 3,500 men would have repaired to his standard. The corps raised by this colony were the Pennsylvania Loyalists, Philadelphia Light Dragoons, Buck's County

Light Dragoons and many men also enlisted under Lt. Col. Isaac Allen in the New Jersey Volunteers. (pp. 191-195)

Paul H. Smith notes, in *Loyalists and Redcoats a Study in British Revolutionary Policy*, "The Loyalist's virtues were military weaknesses. He was generally uncertain of his position, and was disinclined to commit himself boldly. He was more likely to hesitate than to volunteer, to watch on the sidelines than to fight openly." (p. 58) Smith adds, "Many refugee Loyalists, driven from their homes by irate revolutionists and believing military service their only opportunity for useful employment, joined provincial corps despite niggardly terms offered them. In such cases, repressive revolutionary programs were the decisive factor in loyalist enlistments." (p. 66)

Raymond, in "Loyalists in Arms," gives a short summary of The New Jersey Volunteers:

> This corps, sometimes termed "Skinner's Greens," was enrolled by Brigadier General Cortlandt Skinner, the last royal attorney general of New Jersey. The corps comprised six battalions, which were afterwards consolidated into three. The officers and men were natives of New Jersey, New York and Pennsylvania. Numerically the New Jersey Volunteers was the strongest of all the Loyalist regiments and it gave a good account of itself during the war. On the 22nd August, 1777, the corps was attacked on Staten Island by a large party of Americans. The battalions commanded by Lieut. Colonels Lawrence and Barton were surprised and roughly handled, but the gallant conduct of the remaining battalions under Lieut. Col. Isaac Allen and Lieut. Col. Van Buskirk retrieved the day; the Americans were beaten off with severe loss and a large number made prisoners. Lt. Col. Allen and the third battalion shared in the occupation of Philadelphia in the early part of the year 1778. [According to documentation presented later in *The Kellys of Kingsclear*, John Kelly of Gloucester, New Jersey, who later settled in the Parish of Kingsclear, New Brunswick, throughout his military service was under the command of Lieutenant Colonel Issac Allen.] About this time various excursions were made by the men of the New Jersey Volunteers into the surrounding country in the course of which they came to be cordially hated by their old neighbors. They were termed "Skinner's Cowboys" and their marauding proclivities did not win much admiration from those who had suffered at their hands. The story of the adventures of Lieut. James Moody of this corps (written by himself), possesses all the fascination of a romance. In November, 1778, a part of the corps, including Col. Isaac Allen's battalion, was sent to the southern provinces and took part in the capture of Savannah and also in the gallant and successful defence of

that city against the combined French and American forces. They also took an active part in the great battle of Eutaw Springs. Their gallant conduct in the memorable defence of Fort "Ninety-six" will be more fully detailed when we come to speak of De Lancey's battalions. At the close of the war the New Jersey Volunteers came to New Brunswick and were assigned lands in what is now the Parish of Kingsclear. . . . The New Jersey Volunteers at first consisted of six battalions, but in consequence of severe losses the first and fifth were consolidated in April, 1778. The second battalion was for a considerable time attached to the Royal Artillery and in 1781 was merged in the Van Buskirk battalion of its own brigade. The original third and sixth Battalions were consolidated into one in April, 1778. The fourth battalion had a large Dutch element, as may be seen by inspection of the muster rolls. [Joseph Kelly (February 1873 – 28 November 1961), son of Charles and Sarah Ann (Mullins) Kelly, once told someone cutting his hair that the reason he had such a profusion of hair in his ears and nostrils in addition to that composing his bushy eyebrows was because of his Dutch ancestry. So far, there has been no documentation to support his claim.] Capt. Samuel Ryerson commanded a company in this battalion. The New Jersey Volunteers were disbanded in this province and settled in the Parish of Kingsclear, York County. (pp. 207-209)

Abraham Gesner, Esq. in his *New Brunswick with Notes for Emigrants*, points out that York County's "parishes are Fredericton, St. Mary, Douglas, Kingsclear, Queensbury, Prince William, Southampton, and Dumfries." (p. 159)

J.D. Lewis posts on the website *The American Revolution in South Carolina* that the Third New Jersey Volunteers were engaged in 1780 at the Siege of Charleston, Musgrove's Mill, King's Mountain, Ninety-Six and Long Cane; in 1781 at Long Cane, Fort Galphin, Siege of Ninety-Six and Eutaw Springs. Lewis explains:

The 3rd Battalion, New Jersey Volunteers was one of six battalions raised in New Jersey by Brigadier General Cortland Skinner. Each battalion was raised in a different geographic region.

In November of 1776, a Loyalist by the name of William Luce received permission to raise a battalion. Luce was captured by the Rebels almost immediately and so command was instead given to a prominent young man by the name of Edward Vaughn Dongen. Dongen was from Essex County which bordered both Bergen County and Staten Island. His second in command was a wealthy Loyalist from Acquackanonk, named Robert Drummond.

Drummond was instrumental in helping the British in their invasion of New Jersey. When Cornwallis' army got to Second River (the modern

Passaic), it was Drummond who found them a proper place to cross, thereby enabling them to continue their pursuit of Washington's retreating army. Drummond was also adept at recruiting, enlisting over 125 men. The men were primarily from Essex County, many of them of Dutch ancestry, while some others were Huguenot.

The battalion suffered as all other battalions of NJV were at the time — they were attempting to recruit, train, and serve while being on the outposts of the army. Picture enlisting in the army and immediately being thrown on duty and perhaps even into combat.

Initially there was not even clothing to give the men, and they had to serve until April of 1777 in whatever they wore from home. However, in April they received their first uniforms, green coats faced with white. For the next year the NJV and many other Provincials would be known by their enemy simply as "The Greens."

Throughout 1777 the battalion took part in numerous raids throughout the countryside. These mostly originated from Staten Island, which became the home to the NJV for many years. In one raid, up to Bergen County, the battalion had its first officer wounded, Captain Hudnut, who the paper said had received a bayonet to the groin.

The cumulative effect of these raids led Continental General John Sullivan to propose an attack to wipe out all the NJV.

In August of 1777, with 2,000 Continentals and Militia, mostly from New Jersey, Maryland, and Delaware, Sullivan attacked Staten Island. Many officers and men of the 1st and 5th battalions were quickly captured. The 3rd and 6th Battalions had received timely intelligence from a New Jersey Refugee and were able to throw themselves in some old fortifications, thereby avoiding many losses.

Upon the Rebels falling to plunder and otherwise retreating, the NJV were ordered to attack them wherever they could be found. They found them embarking in boats back to the Jersey shore and attacked several times. In one of these attacks, Lt. Col. Dongen was shot and mortally wounded. He did not know it at the time, but his wife had been forced to flee into the swamps by the attack with their three year old son, where she was ravished. Dongen died three days later, August 24, 1777, and within three hours his son was likewise dead from exposure and fright. They were buried together at Trinity Church, New York City.

The battalion quickly had some revenge by being a part of Sir Henry Clinton's September Grand Forage into Bergen County. These two events though, as well as numerous other skirmishes, significantly reduced the number of soldiers in all the battalions.

To make them more useful and reduce the number of excess officers, the brigade was reduced from six battalions to four. The 1st and 5th were combined into one, as were the 3rd and 6th. The merger of the 3rd and 6th battalions produced a "new" 3rd battalion. The men were no longer mostly from Essex. The 6th had been raised in Hunterdon County, in the western part of the province. The command of the new 3rd was given to Lt. Col. Isaac Allen, a Trenton lawyer who had been the commander of the 6th.

Allen was no doubt the finest commander among the different battalions of NJV. For the rest of the war, the unit would maintain an excellent record of discipline. It had by far the fewest number of desertions and was involved in more large actions than any of the other battalions.

In September of 1778, they were further strengthened with two more companies of men. These came from the West Jersey Volunteers, a unit raised earlier that year while the British Army was in Philadelphia. These men came from Salem, Gloucester and Cumberland Counties, making the 3rd the most diverse battalion of NJV.

120 men of the battalion had the honor of serving under the celebrated Captain Patrick Ferguson in their last raid into New Jersey. They, along with some men of the 1st battalion and the 5th Regiment of Foot (British), caught the famous Pulaski's Legion while asleep at Egg Harbor, New Jersey. Using only bayonets, they killed and wounded as many as 50 officers and men, losing only a few men wounded, including Ensign Camp, who was himself bayoneted in the thigh.

The theater of war shifting to the South, the 3rd battalion was a part of the expedition under Lt. Col. Archibald Campbell. Campbell was the first British officer, as he put it, to tear a star and stripe from the American flag.

In *Loyalists and Redcoats a Study in British Revolutionary Policy*, Paul H. Smith writes, "On November 27, 1778, after several frustrating delays, Lieutenant Colonel Archibald Campbell's expedition for Georgia sailed from New York with a fleet commanded by Commodore Hyde Parker. Campbell's force, consisting of over three thousand rank and file — the 71st Regiment, the Wissenbach and Woellwarth Hessian regiments, and four provincial battalions from New York and New Jersey —arrived at Tybee Island a few miles below Savannah on December 23." (p. 100) Smith adds, "The expedition to Georgia was an experiment to test both the responsiveness of the southern Loyalists and Washington's reaction to an attack on the southern colonies." (p. 101)

J.D. Lewis continues:

Campbell was sent to capture Georgia, but his plan was almost ruined by a member of the 3rd battalion. One of the transport ships that carried men of the unit, the *Neptune*, got separated from the fleet and arrived off of

Savannah weeks before any others. One of the NJV deserted and told the Rebels what was coming their way. It mattered little, as Lt. Col. Campbell and the army quickly arrived and took the city after a short battle on 29 December 1778.

While short in duration, and few in casualties on the British side, the 3rd battalion lost its light infantry commander, Captain Patrick Campbell. He was replaced by Captain Peter Campbell, no close relation. This started the battalion's most exciting time. They continued serving in Georgia throughout the year 1779.

In September, a large French fleet appeared off Savannah, and was later joined by a large force of Continentals and Militia from South Carolina. The French commander demanded the surrender of the city to the King of France, but the 2,600 British, Loyalist and Hessian troops refused and withstood a siege of over three weeks.

With Hurricane season rapidly upon them and the French fleet needing to leave, the Allied army assaulted the city, where they were repulsed with massive losses. The NJV were in a redoubt all to their own, on the front left of the line, where they were attacked by South Carolina Continentals. This repulse enabled the British to turn their attention to the conquest of South Carolina.

Sir Henry Clinton arrived in February of 1780 with a large army from New York. This army, joined by troops from Georgia, would besiege Charleston. Part of the troops from Georgia included the light infantry company of the 3rd battalion. They were a witness to the fall of the city on 12 May 1780.

The rest of the battalion marched in July of 1780 to garrison Augusta, Georgia, well into the interior of the province, and on the South Carolina border. After a short stay there, they continued on to Ninety Six, South Carolina, where they would earn their greatest laurels.

Almost immediately they were thrown into action in their new locale. Colonel Alexander Innes of the South Carolina Royalists promptly led the 3rd's light company into an ambush at Musgrove's Mills. Every officer of the company was wounded, and many of the men were killed or likewise wounded.

Back at Augusta, the sick of the unit, who had been left behind under Major Drummond, were all captured, killed or wounded by an attack on that place in September. The battalion, then at Ninety Six, rushed back to assist the defenders of the town, and were able to drive the attackers off.

Lt. Col. Allen shared command at Ninety Six with Lt. Col. John Harris Cruger of the 1st Battalion, DeLancey's Brigade. Cruger himself was the finest officer in his unit, thereby giving the post two excellent officers. Numerous raids were made around the post, with some losses on both sides. Ensign Camp, who had been wounded at Egg Harbor, had been captured and murdered on Christmas Eve of 1780.

With the defeats at King's Mountain and Cowpens, the British were thrown quickly on the defensive in South Carolina. Lord Cornwallis had taken most of the British army into North Carolina and later Virginia, leaving South Carolina open to attack. One by one the British outposts fell to Rebel partisans such as Sumter, Marion, and others.

The Continental army was ably led by General Nathanael Greene, who wished to personally lead the taking of Ninety Six. Sensing what was to happen, the British ordered the post evacuated. The problem was, none of the orders ever reached the garrison. Between May and June of 1781, the post of Ninety Six was closely besieged by a large force under Greene. The garrison itself only consisted of perhaps 600 men, all Americans. These men were from the 1st DeLancey's, 3rd NJV and some South Carolina Militia.

Timely British reinforcements arriving in Charleston enabled the British commander Lord Rawdon to lead a relief force to Ninety Six. Unable to halt their advance, Greene decided to storm Ninety Six. In a desperate attack, the force was repelled by a gallant sortie from the fort by the light companies of the NJV and DeLancey's. Greene quickly raised the siege and left the area. The outpost, after this gallant defense, was evacuated in July of 1781 and all the Loyalists of the interior moved towards Charleston.

It was in this area, at Eutaw Springs, where the battalion fought its last and bloodiest battle.

In September 1781, General Greene attacked an interior British force that included the NJV. The British were further hampered by having almost a third of their men off on rooting parties, looking for food. These unarmed detachments lost scores of men captured.

Greene's force smashed into the British camp, where Isaac Allen and the NJV held the center of the line. On the point of collapse, the British and Loyalists rallied and threw back Greene's army. The battalion had lost 40% of the men they had present that day, killed, wounded or captured.

The battalion was so weakened from these major battles over the previous year that they spent most of the next year in garrison in Charleston. This was also a result of the war drawing to an end, as Lord Cornwallis and his army had been captured at Yorktown. There were eighteen men of the battalion present at that surrender, mostly escaped or exchanged POWs.

The battalion returned to New York in January of 1783, being somewhat bolstered by some men of the Volunteers of Ireland, a regiment that had been drafted at Charleston. They remained on Long Island, withering away from men starting to desert home, until the final peace was announced later that year. Most of the Loyalists were unable to return home, due to their property being confiscated or laws passed against them. . . .

Raymond, again from "Loyalists in Arms," gives a short history of De Lancey's Brigade:

Of all the Loyalist corps none attained greater distinction than did de Lancey's Brigade. The founder of the brigade was Brigadier General Oliver de Lancey, a prominent citizen of New York, who had seen service in the old French war in which he commanded some 5,000 provincial troops under General Abercombie. General de Lancey, strange to say, had not by birth a single drop of English blood in his veins, yet at the time of the Revolution he put his life and property at stake to prevent the dismemberment of the empire. His ancestors on his father's side were French, and on his mother's Dutch. Upon the submission of Long Island to the British in August, 1776, General Howe appointed Oliver de Lancey a brigadier general with orders to raise three battalions of 500 men each for the defence of the island. By virtue of his commission Oliver de Lancey became the senior Loyalist officer in America during the war. To raise his battalions the general himself contributed large sums which were supplemented by contributions from the inhabitants of every town on Long Island, amounting in the aggregate to some thousands of pounds. The Third Battalion, commanded by Col. Gabriel G. Ludlow, consisted from the colonel down to the lowest subaltern of natives of Queen's County, Long Island, and the non-commissioned officers and privates were also natives and included many of the solid yeomanry of the island. In order to stimulate the enlistment[,] orders were issued that any reputable citizen who raised a company of seventy men should have the appointment of its officers, captain, lieutenant and ensign. The three battalions were soon raised. General de Lancey was colonel of the first, and his son-in-law, John Harris Cruger, was his lieutenant colonel. Geo. Brewerton, an alderman of New York, who had rendered distinguished service in the late French war, was colonel of the second, and his lieutenant colonel was Stephen de Lancey, eldest son of the general. Gabriel Ludlow, as just stated, commanded the Third Battalion and his lieutenant colonel was Richard Hewlett, of Hampstead, Long Island.

The battalions were organized "for the defence of Long Island and other exigencies." The first winter after their formation they were stationed respectively at Oyster Bay, Huntington and Brookhaven, three considerable towns on the north shore of Long Island. The following summer the second battalion was stationed at Kings Bridge, just above the City of New York, and the First Battalion was ordered to take post and build a fort at Huntington, while the Third did the same at Brookhaven. Lieut. Colonel Cruger had command of the fort at Huntington, and Lieut. Colonel Hewlett of that at Brookhaven. Both were resolute officers, active, alert and vigilant. The consequence was perfect security, peace and safety to the whole island which provided an asylum to the persecuted Loyalists of Connecticut, hundreds of whom, driven by bitter persecution from their homes at Stamford, Norfolk, Fairfield, etc., sought and obtained protection within the British lines on Long Island.

In July, 1777, Lieut. Colonel Hewlett and his battalion, then about 300 strong, was attacked at Brookhaven by General Parsons at the head of 1,000 men. The latter took possession of a rising ground near the fort and having mounted his cannon ordered the Loyalists to surrender. Col Hewlett replied with a contemptuous refusal; whereupon General Parsons began a cannonade and the fort replied. At the end of twelve hours the Americans retired with the loss of thirty men; Hewlett had but one man killed. Though de Lancey's Brigade had been organized principally for the defence of Long Island, General Clinton, in the fall of 1778, sent the First and Second Battalions with General Campbell to Georgia, and they arrived at Savannah on the 23rd of December. A few days later General Campbell attacked and defeated the American forces under Gen. Robert Howe with the loss of 600 men, capturing Savannah with all its stores including 71 pieces of artillery and a quantity of ammunition. In the engagement Lieut. Colonel Cruger and his men gained much credit. In conjunction with the British Light Infantry they gained the rear of the enemy by means of a bye-path and then by an impetuous charge threw them into great confusion.

In the month of September, 1779, the combined French and American forces invested Savannah. The First and Second de Lancey Battalions were with the garrison that defended the town. They fought most gallantly and materially contributed to the successful defence. Lieut. Col. Cruger had charge of an important position and repulsed the enemy in three several attacks. This brave officer and his men gained additional honor at the capture of Charleston, May 12, 1780. Their conduct was highly commended at the battle of Camden, in which General Gates suffered total defeat. The First and Second de Lanceys, however, won their greatest laurels in the heroic defence of "Fort Ninety-Six" near Camden, of which an account will here be given: —

The garrison consisted of 150 men of de Lancey's Brigade, 200 men of the New Jersey Volunteers and 200 loyal militia under Colonel King, Lieut. Colonel Cruger had but few cannon and he was short of ammunition while the defences of the post were in a very unfinished state. Every effort was made to strengthen the fortifications but the work was still incomplete when the American General Greene, with 4,000 men appeared on the scene.

On the night of the 21st of May, 1781 the besiegers broke ground and threw up two works within seventy paces of the fort. Whilst they were engaged in strengthening these works the following night they were attacked by a party of the garrison and every man of them put to the bayonet, the works demolished and even the entrenching tools carried off. The besiegers now proceeded more cautiously and by incessant labor during the next ten days advanced their trenches nearly to the fort. They were meanwhile harassed by the frequent sorties of small parties of the garrison. General Greene at this juncture peremptorily called upon the garrison to surrender. Cruger answered that Ninety-Six was committed to his charge and it was his duty as well as his inclination to defend it to the last extremity. He added that the threats or promises of General Greene were alike indifferent to him. The besiegers then opened four batteries and commenced a cross fire continuing their cannonade for several days at the same time pushing a sap and erecting batteries one of which was at a distance of only thirty-five paces from the abatis of the fort. The besiegers employed African arrows to set fire to the barracks. The African arrows, so called, were fitted to the bores of the muskets the heads being armed with a dart and combustibles attached which were set on fire just before the arrows were shot at the buildings. Colonel Cruger ordered the barracks unroofed, thus saving them from destruction, but at the same time exposing his officers and men to the night air and inclemency of the weather. Meanwhile the siege went on and the garrison continued their night sallies, often with success. In spite of all their efforts their position was daily becoming more critical. By the 12th of June the enemy's trenches were advanced to the stockade and a sergeant and six men advanced to set fire to the abatis. It was a vain attempt, they were all killed by the defenders. However, by the 16th of June, the concentrated fire of the besiegers rendered this outwork untenable and it was evacuated and with it the garrison lost communication with their water supply. Their sufferings were now extreme. With great difficulty a well was dug within the fort but no water could be found. Mid-summer was drawing on and the heat of South Carolina is always at such times excessive. The only way of obtaining water was by sending out naked negroes in the night who brought in a scant supply from within pistol shot of the American pickets, their bodies not being distinguished in the night from the dead logs with which the place abounded. In this emergency Colonel Cruger continued to be the life of the garrison, encouraging them by word and example, exhorting them to die in the last ditch rather than surrender.

At last on the 17th of June in broad day light a brave Loyalist rode at full gallop through the enemy's picket line amid a storm of bullets and delivered a message to Col. Cruger that Lord Rawdon was in full march to raise the siege. A shout went up from the defenders that reached the enemy's lines. Knowing that here was no time to lose Gen. Greene stormed the fort the next day; his forlorn hope gained the ditch and were followed by strong parties with grappling hooks and other tools to pull down the parapet. At this moment a detachment of the New Jersey Volunteers, led by Capt. Campbell and another corps of de Lancey's men led by Capt. French sprang from their sally posts, entered the ditch at opposite ends, and pushed forward with the bayonet until they met one another, having cleared all before them. General Greene beheld with astonishment his design foiled by the desperate valor of a mere handful of men. He could not persuade his soldiers to make another attempt. The next day he raised the siege and shortly afterwards Lord Rawdon appeared on the scene with his army of relief.

The defence of a place so weak and ill provided as Fort Ninety-Six for upwards of thirty days with, only 350 provincial and 200 militia against an army of 4,000 is remarkable. The garrison had one lieutenant, three sergeants and twenty-three rank and file killed, and the besiegers had one colonel, three captains, five lieutenants and one hundred and fifty-seven privates killed, not counting the loss sustained by their militia. The defence of Fort Ninety-Six will always be regarded as heroic.

At the battle of Eutaw Springs Colonel Cruger commanded one wing of the British where, as the Loyalist Historian Judge Jones tells us, "his bravery, coolness, resolution, judgment and steadiness turned the fortune of the day in favor of the British."

Meanwhile the Third Battalion under Colonel Ludlow remained at Lloyd's Neck, Long Island, to cover the wood cutters for the British Army, which says Judge Jones, was "a material piece of business and well conducted." It may be noted in passing that many of the Loyalists from Norwalk and Stamford were supporting their families during the war by cutting and selling wood for the army. They lived within the British lines at Lloyd's Neck, Oyster Bay and Eaton's Neck. About the beginning of July, 1781, the Third de Lancey's were removed. The Loyalists thereupon organized a corps for their own protection, at the head of which was Major Upham. A party of some 400 Frenchmen attempted to seize the wood at Lloyds [sic] Neck, some thousands of cords being then in process of shipment to New York. Major Upham and the Loyalists, with the help of the crews of the vessels loading, beat off the invaders with loss.

At the evacuation of Charleston in February, 1782, the two de Lancey Battalions (then consolidated into one) returned to New York, whence at the peace they retired to New Brunswick. Their grant of land was almost identical with the limits of the present Parish of Woodstock. The men of the Third deLancey's [sic] settled chiefly in Queens and Sunbury Counties. Lieut. Col. Hewlett made his home at Hampstead, naming the place after his former home, and as further proof that he had not lost his affection for the land of his nativity he not only reproduced in New Brunswick the name of Hampstead, but of Queens County, Lieutenant Gabriel DeVeber, Jr., settled at Gagetown, Captain Gerhardus Clowes, at Oromocto, Captain Elijah Miles, Captain Ichabod Smith and Lieut. Zachariah Brown in Maugerville. These men all filled important positions and their descendants are many and highly respected.

Colonel Gabriel G. Ludlow was the first mayor of St. John and after the retirement of Governor Carleton to England he was appointed president and commander-in-chief of the province and continued the foremost man of the province till his death in the year 1808. (pp. 212-217)

Paul H. Smith, in *Loyalists and Redcoats a Study in British Revolutionary Policy*, writes, "By 1779, the expense of the American war plus the burden of the war with France had placed a great strain upon the King's government." (p. 115) Smith adds, "As the administration was able to command Parliamentary support for the war only because the use of southern Loyalists promised to relieve Britain of much of her military burden, British strategy increasingly became dependent upon the cooperation of the Loyalists. When that loyalist support failed to materialize in the South, the Commons voted to abandon the war in the colonies." (p. 121)

Raymond, in "Loyalists in Arms," adds,

After the surrender of Cornwallis in October, 1781, little attempt was made to maintain the strength of the Loyalist regiments, as the subjugation of the old colonies seemed to be hopeless in consequence of this disaster, combined with the fact that the mother country was now at war with France, Holland and Spain. The corps began to dwindle, and after the peace negotiations were opened in 1782, many of the rank and file deserted the regiments and returned to their friends. They appear in the muster rolls as "deserters," but it does not seem that their officers were very seriously concerned over it, in view of the

> hop[e]lessness of the situation from a military stand point. There was but a fraction of the original strength present at the last muster of the various corps. Those who chose to disband at New York were allowed to do so. The remainder sought new homes in various parts of British America, some going to the West Indies, some to Canada, some to various places in Nova Scotia, but the greatest number that came to any one place were those who arrived at St. John on the 27th of September, 1783, under command of Lieut. Colonel Richard Hewlett, of de Lancey's Brigade. It is difficult, perhaps impossible, to ascertain the exact number who landed at St. John. It was supposed before the embarkation that the number would be about 3,000, but at the last moment many decided to take their chances with their rebel countrymen rather than face the privations and perils of an unknown wilderness. (p. 222)

Paul H. Smith, in *Loyalists and Redcoats a Study in British Revolutionary Policy*, writes in a footnote (32) that "the complete failure of the southern campaign exploded the myth of the essential loyalty of the colonies." (p. 165) Early in the war, Smith writes, under the heading "The Expedition to the Southern Colonies, 1775-76," that the British had "hoped to use the Loyalists to strike a crippling blow to colonial unity by detaching the 'less hostile' southern colonies from the revolutionary movement." (p. 18)

Although the following from Thomas Francis Gordon in *The History of New Jersey From Its Discovery by Europeans to the Adoption of the Federal Constitution* may, at first, seem irrelevant to the reader in regard to the Kelly family, reading further will greatly help in understanding the complexities and motivations of the family in choosing the Loyalist side in the Revolution and of the reasons why it was virtually impossible for the Kellys, at the end of the war, to return to New Jersey.

Gordon:

> In New York and New Jersey the British were received with open arms, by the disaffected, as their deliverers from oppression. The tories were so numerous, that, as the army advanced into the country, the militia of the islands were embodied for their defence; and these states afforded corps of regulars, equal to their quotas in the American army. Upon taking possession of Long Island, General Howe assured his army, that they were among friends, and prohibited, under the severest penalties, every species of violence. [Footnote (p. 194): "For violation of these orders some soldiers were condemned and executed."] As he advanced to the White Plains, the state Convention entertained fears of a dangerous insurrection, and seemed apprehensive of an attempt to punish the disaffected, though actually engaged in enlisting men for the British service. Much dread was felt, that they would seize the important passes of the highlands; and it was

thought dangerous to march the militia from some of the neighbouring counties for their protection, lest their absence should encourage the loyalists to assemble in arms.

On entering the Jerseys, Lord Cornwallis gave orders similar to those of General Howe, on Long Island. The proclamation, offering protection to those who would come in and take the oaths of allegiance, within sixty days, also, contained assurances, that the obnoxious laws, which had occasioned the war, would be revised. The effect of these measures, with the military success of the enemy, was to extinguish, nearly, the spirit of resistance. A few militia, only, were in arms, under General Williamson; whose indisposition, compelling him to leave the service, they were afterwards commanded by General Dickenson; but the great body of the country was either with the enemy, or had too little zeal for the cause, to hazard their lives and fortunes in its support. When urged to take up arms, they answered, "that General Howe promised them peace, liberty, and safety, and more they could not require."

The articles of association of 1775, may be deemed the entering wedge of division, between the parties in New Jersey, as in other parts of America. Those who refused to sign, or having signed, disobeyed, their requisitions, were held enemies to their country, and as such, were not only denounced by the county and township committees, but were fined and imprisoned, as well by the order of such committees, as by that of the provincial Conventions and committees of safety. Notwithstanding these measures, counter associations were attempted, resolving to pay no tax levied by order of the provincial Congress, nor to purchase any goods distrained for such taxes, or for non-attendance at militia musters. These, and like demonstrations of hostility, induced the committee of safety of the province, on the fifteenth of January, 1776, earnestly to recommend to the several county and town committees, the execution of the resolve of the continental Congress, of the second of that month, recommending due moderation and prudence, and requesting all officers of militia to lend their assistance. Under this resolution several persons, from different parts of the state, were brought before the committee of safety, and the provincial Congress, which sat from the thirty-first of January to the second of March, 1776. Most of the prisoners confessed their faults, craved pardon, and were either dismissed unscathed, or subjected to a small pecuniary mulct, and to give security, in various sums, for future good conduct. But with the progress toward independence, the number of the disaffected, increasing rapidly, gave much employment to the provincial Congress, which assembled on the tenth of June; and which framed the state constitution; and their proceedings assumed a greater degree of severity. Memorials, from several counties, complaining of the hostile intentions and proceedings of the disaffected, particularly, in Monmouth, Hunterdon, Bergen, and Sussex, called forth a reiteration of previous instructions to the county committees, and formal summons to the inculpated, to appear before the Convention. On the twenty-sixth of June, that body having intelligence, that there were several insurgents in the county of Monmouth, who took every measure in their power to contravene the regulations of Congress, and to oppose the cause of American freedom, and that it was highly necessary, that an immediate check should be given to so daring a spirit of disaffection, resolved, that Colonel Charles Read should take to his aid, two companies of the militia of the county of Burlington, and proceed, without delay, to the county of Monmouth, to apprehend such insurgents as were designated to him by the president of the Convention. Authentic information was, at the same time, received, that other disaffected persons in the county of Hunterdon had confederated for the purpose of opposing the measures of Congress, and had even proceeded to acts of open and daring violence; having plundered the house of a Captain Jones, beaten, wounded, and otherwise abused the friends of freedom in the county, and publicly declared, that they would take up arms in behalf of the King of Great Britain. In order, effectually, to check a combination so hostile and dangerous, Lieutenant-colonel Abraham Ten Eick and Major Berry were directed, with the militia of the counties of Hunterdon and Somerset, to apprehend these insurgents. On the first of July the provincial Congress resolved, that the several colonels of the counties, should, without delay, proceed to disarm all persons within their district, who, from religious principles, or other causes, refused to bear arms. Two days after the last, an additional order was given to Colonel Charles Read, Lieutenant-colonel Samuel Forman, and Major Joseph Haight, with two hundred militia of Burlington, and two hundred of Monmouth county, to proceed, without delay, to quell an insurrection in Monmouth, and to disarm and take prisoners, whomsoever they should find assembled, with intent to oppose the friends of American freedom; and to take such measures as they should think necessary for this service. On the fourth of July, Congress resolved, that as divers persons, in the county of Monmouth, who had embodied themselves, in opposition to its measures, had expressed their willingness to return to their duty, upon assurances of pardon, alleging, that they have been seduced and misled, by the false and malicious reports of others; such persons as should, without delay, return peaceably to their homes, and conform to the orders of Congress, should be treated with lenity and indulgence, and upon their good behaviour, be restored to the favour of their country; providing, that such as appeared to have been the leaders and principals in these disorders, and who, to their other guilt, had added that of seducing the weak and the unwary, should yet be treated, according to their demerits.

Under these and like resolutions many persons, among whom were several of large property and great respectability, were brought before Congress. Some were imprisoned, some fined, and others suffered to go at large upon their parole; others were compelled to enter into recognizance with security, conditioned for *their good behaviour;* and others were relegated to such places within the province, as the Congress supposed could give them the least opportunity of evil. [I have elected not to include the footnote accompanying this paragraph.]

When the state government was organized, under the constitution, the Legislature enacted a law of like tenor, with the ordinance of the convention, against treason; — and further declared, that any one owing allegiance to the state, who should by speech, writing, or open deed, maintain the authority of the King and Parliament of Great Britain, should be subject, by the first offence, to fine, not exceeding three hundred pounds, and imprisonment, not exceeding one year; and for the second, to the pillory, and the like imprisonment; — that reviling, or speaking contemptuously of the government of the state, of the Congress, or United States of America, or of the measures adopted by the Congress, or by the Legislature of the state, or maliciously doing any thing whatever, which would encourage disaffection, or manifestly tend to raise tumults and disorders in the state; or spreading such false rumours, concerning the American forces, or the forces of the enemy, as would tend to alienate the affections of the people from the government, or to terrify or discourage the good subjects of this state, or to dispose them to favour the pretensions of the enemy, should, also, be punishable in the same manner. By the same act, two justices of the peace were empowered to convene by summons or warrant, any person, whom they should suspect to be dangerous or disaffected to the government; and compel him to take the oath of abjuration, and of allegiance, under penalty of being bound with sufficient sureties to his good behaviour, or imprisoned until the meeting of the Quarter Sessions; when, upon refusal, he might be fined or imprisoned, at discretion of the court. This act drew the cords around the discontented much more closely, than they had hitherto been. But it became necessary to strain them still tighter.

An act of June 5th, 1777, declaring, that divers of the subjects of the state, having, by the arts of subtile emissaries from the enemy, been seduced from their allegiance, and prevailed upon by delusive promises, to leave their families and friends, and join the army of the King of Great Britain, and had since become sensible of their error, and desirous of returning to their duty; that many of such fugitives and others, who had been guilty of treasonable practices against the state, secreted themselves to escape the punishment of their crimes — and that, in compassion to their unhappy situation, the Legislature was desirous that no means should be left unemployed, to prevent the effusion of blood, and to give those an opportunity of returning to their allegiance, who should testify their desire to be restored to the inestimable rights of freemen. To this end the act provided, That, such offender, on or before the first of August, then next ensuing, might appear before a judge or justice of the peace, and take the oaths to the state; and should, thereupon, be pardoned his offence, and restored to the privileges of a citizen; That, if he were so far lost to every sense of duty to his country, his family, and his posterity, as to decline the clemency so proffered, his personal estate should be forfeited to the state; and all alienations thereof, and of his real estate, subsequent to the act, were declared void; That commissioners should be appointed in the respective counties, to make inventories of such personal estate, to dispose of perishable parts, or where in danger of falling into the hands of the enemy, of the whole; to keep the proceeds for the owner claiming the benefit of the act, but paying the same to the treasurer for the one of the state, in case of the non-claim of the proprietor within the prescribed time.

This act was followed by another of 18th April, 1778, directing the commissioners of the several counties to make return to a justice of the peace, of the name and late place of abode of each person whose personal estate they should seize, and to obtain from the justice a precept for summoning a jury of freeholders, to inquire whether he had, since the date of act against treason, (4th October, 1776,) [sic] and before the 5th June, 1777, joined the army of the King of Great Britain, or otherwise offended against his allegiance to the state. The jury finding against the accused, their inquisition was returned by the justice to the next court of Common Pleas; where it might be traversed, either at the return, or the succeeding, term, by the party, on entering into recognisance, to prosecute with effect. But in default, judgment of forfeiture was rendered, and the commissioners empowered to sell all the personal estate of the fugitive, and to take possession of all his books of account, bonds, mortgages, &c., in whose hands soever they might be; and to collect all debts due to him. Similar provisions were made, relative to persons committing like offences, subsequent to the act of pardon, of the 5th of June, 1777. The commissioners were, also, empowered to take into their possession and management, all the real estate of the offender, and lease the same for a term not exceeding a year, and to hold possession of such estate, before inquisition found, when it had been abandoned by the owner. Tenants in possession, were required to attorn to the commissioners. All sales of real or personal estate, by any person, against whom inquisition was found, made after the offence committed, were declared void.

This severity was carried still further by the act of December llth, 1778, directing, that all the real estate of offenders at the time of the offence, or thereafter, acquired, in fee or otherwise, against whom inquisition and judgment had been, or should be, rendered, should be forfeited to the state; and that, every person, whether an inhabitant of this state, or of any other of the United States, seized or possessed of real or personal estate, who had, since the *19th day of April, 1775,* (the day of the battle of Lexington) and before the *4th day of October, 1778,* aided and assisted the enemies of the state, or of the United States, by joining their armies within the state, or elsewhere, or had voluntarily gone to, taken refuge or continued with, or endeavoured to continue with, the enemy, and aid them by council or otherwise, and who had not since returned and become a subject in allegiance to the present government, by taking the prescribed oaths or affirmations when required, to be guilty of high treason, and on inquisition and judgment, his whole estate, real and personal, was forfeited to the state; but such proceedings affected the estate only, not the person of the offender. The real estates so forfeited were sold, and title made therefor, by the commissioners, and no error in the proceedings affected the purchaser, nor did pardon relieve the forfeiture. The forfeited estates were held liable for the debts of the offender, and some efforts, unsuccessful we believe, were made, to render them responsible for such damages as the former owners might commit in their predatory excursions.

The same act declared, every inhabitant of the state who had joined the enemy by taking refuge among them, or affording them aid by counsel or otherwise, and who should be convicted of high treason, or otherwise forfeit his estate, pursuant to the act, or should be duly convicted of treason, felony, or misdemeanour, for going to, taking refuge with, or affording any aid and assistance to the enemy, incapable of holding any office of trust or profit, or of exercising the elective franchise, and deprived all persons within the state who had suffered fine or imprisonment for refusing to testify their allegiance, by taking the oaths, of the capacity to exercise any military office.

Under these acts, a large mass of property was brought into the market and sold for the benefit of the state, and also of many of the commissioners. In 1781, the market was probably glutted, and property was very greatly sacrificed; when the act of June 26th, declaring, that the continuance of the sales might prove injurious to the interests of the state, directed their suspension until further order, and the authority of the commissioners to cease. Another act of 1781, (20th December,) [*sic*] substituted a single agent, in the respective counties, for the commissioners; and the act of

December 16th, 1783, directed such agents to proceed in the sale of such estates, and to receive in payment any obligation of the state. Subsequently, various provisions were made for satisfying the claims of the creditors of the offenders.

During the greater part of the war, the tory refugees from New Jersey were embodied on Staten, Long, and York islands; and when the British were in force in the state, they collected on the eastern and south-eastern border, and occasionally appeared in other districts. Their hostility was more malignant than that of the British soldiery, and being commonly directed by revenge, was more brutally practised, and more keenly felt. Intimately acquainted with the country, they could more suddenly enter it, strike a barbarous stroke and retreat. This spirit was encountered by one almost as fierce and ruthless, in which, however, there was the redeeming quality of patriotism. Many a tale of the romantic daring of the invaders, and of the fearless devotion of the defenders, is yet told, along the eastern shores, and amid the cedar swamps, and pine forests of the state.

The enterprise of the refugee royalists was frequently directed against the persons of the distinguished patriots of the state. Among their first successful attempts, was that on Mr. Richard Stockton. On the entrance of the British army into New Jersey, after the capture of Fort Washington, that gentleman withdrew from Congress in order to protect his family and property, at his seat near Princeton. He removed his wife and younger children into the county of Monmouth, about thirty miles from the supposed route of the British army. On the 30th of November, he was, together with his friend and compatriot John Covenhoven, at whose house he resided, dragged from his bed by night, stripped and plundered, and carried by the way of Amboy to New York. At Amboy he was exposed to severe cold weather in the common jail, which, together with subsequent barbarity in New York, laid the foundation of disease, that terminated his existence in 1781. His release was probably procured by the interference of Congress, in January.

We cannot more fully, no more truly justify the measures of severity adopted against the disaffected, than by the following extract from the speech of Governor Livingston, to the Assembly, on the 29th of May, 1778.

"I have further to lay before you, gentlemen, a resolution of Congress of the 23d of April, recommending it to the Legislatures of the several states, to pass laws, or to the executive authority of each state, if invested with sufficient power, to issue proclamations offering pardon, with such exceptions and under such limitations and restrictions as they shall think expedient, to such of their inhabitants or subjects as have levied war against any of these states, or adhered to, aided or abetted the enemy, and shall surrender themselves to any civil or military officer of any of these states, and shall return to the state to which they may belong, before the tenth day of June, next; and recommending it to the good and faithful citizens of these states, to receive such returning penitents with compassion and mercy, and forgive and bury in oblivion their past failings and transgressions.

"Though I think it my duty to submit this resolution to your serious consideration, because it is recommended by Congress, I do not think it my duty to recommend it to your approbation, because it appears to me both unequal and impolitic. It may, consistently, with profoundest veneration for that august Assembly, be presumed, that they are less acquainted with the particular circumstances and internal police of some of the states, than those who have had more favourable opportunities for that purpose. There seems, it is true, something so noble and magnanimous in proclaiming an unmerited amnesty to a number of disappointed criminals, submitting themselves to the mercy of their country; and there is in reality something so divine and christian in the forgiveness of injuries, that it may appear rather invidious to offer any thing in obstruction of the intended clemency. But as to the benevolent religion to which we are under the highest obligations to conform our conduct, though it forbids at all times and in all cases the indulgence of personal hatred and malevolence, it prohibits not any treatment of national enemies or municipal offenders, necessary to self preservation, and the general weal of society. And as to humanity, I could never persuade myself that it consisted in such lenity towards our adversaries, either British or domestic, as was evidently productive of tenfold barbarity on their part, when such barbarity would probably have been prevented by our retaliating upon them the first perpetration; and consequently our apparent inhumanity in particular instances, has certainly been humane in the final result. Alas, how many lives had been saved, and what a scene of inexpressible misery prevented, had we from the beginning treated our bosom traitors with proper severity, and inflicted the law of retaliation upon an enemy, too savage to be humanized by any other argument. As both political pardon and punishment ought to be regulated by political considerations, and must derive their expedience of impropriety from their salutary or pernicious influence upon the community, I cannot conceive what advantages are proposed by inviting to the embraces of their country, a set of beings from which any country, I should imagine, would esteem it a capital part of its felicity to remain forever at the remotest distance. It is not probable that those who deserted us to aid the most matchless connoisseurs in the refinements of cruelty, (who have exhausted human ingenuity in their engines of torture,) in introducing arbitrary power, and all the horrors of slavery; and will only return from disappointment, not from remorse, will ever make good subjects to a state founded in liberty, and inflexibly determined against every inroad of lawless dominion. The thirty-one criminals lately convicted of the most flagrant treason, and who, by the gracious interposition of government, were upon very hopeful signs of *penitence,* generously pardoned, and then with hypo-critical cheerfulness enlisted in our service, have all to a man deserted to the enemy, and are again in arms against their native country, with the accumulated guilt of its being now not only the country that first gave them life, but which hath, after they had most notoriously forfeited it, mercifully rescued them from death. Whence it is probable, that a real tory is by any human means absolutely inconvertible, having so entirely extinguished all the primitive virtue and patriotism natural to man, as not to leave a single spark to rekindle the original flame. It is indeed, against all probability, that men arrived at the highest possible pitch of degeneracy, the preferring of tyranny to a free government, should, except by a miracle of omnipotence, be ever capable of one single virtuous impression. They have, by a kind of gigantic effort of villany, astonished the whole world, even that of transcending in the enormities of desolation and bloodshed, a race of murderers before unequalled, and without competitor. Were it not for these, miscreants, we should have thought, that for cool deliberate cruelty and unavailing undecisive havoc, the sons of Britain were without parallel. But considering the education of the latter, which has familiarised them to the shedding of innocent blood from the mere thirst of lucre, they have been excelled in their own peculiar and distinguished excellence by this monstrous birth and offscouring of America, who, in defiance of nature and of nurture, have not only by a reversed ambition chosen bondage before freedom, but waged an infernal war against their dearest connexions for not making the like abhorred and abominable election. By them, have numbers of our most useful and meritorious citizens been ambushed, hunted down, pillaged, unhoused, stolen, or butchered; by them has the present contest on the part of Britain been encouraged, aided and protracted. They are therefore responsible for all the additional blood that has been spilt by the addition of their weight in the scale of the enemy. Multitudes of them have superadded perjury to treason. At the commencement of our opposition, they appeared more sanguine than others, and like *the crackling of thorns under a pot*, exceeded in blaze and noise, the calm and durable flame of the steady and persevering. They have associated, subscribed, and sworn to assist in repelling the hostile attempts of our bowelless oppressors; they have, with awful solemnity, plighted their faith and honour, to stand with their lives and fortunes by the Congress, and their general, in support of that very liberty, which, upon the first opportunity, they perfidiously armed to oppose, and have since sacrilegiously sworn utterly to exterminate. This worthy citizen has lost a venerable father; that one a beloved brother; and a third, a darling son, either immediately by their hands or by their betraying him to the enemy, who, from a momentary unintentional relapse into humanity, were sometimes inclined to spare, when these pitiless wretches insisted upon slaughter, or threatened to complain of a relenting officer, merely because he was not diabolically cruel." (pp. 194-200)

The following is from *Great Britain, Public Record Office, Headquarters Papers of the British Army in America*, PRO 30/55/7623 (page 4) quoted by Esther Clark Wright in *Loyalists of New Brunswick* (pp. 54-55) and reformatted and posted on the *On-Line Institute for Advanced Loyalist Studies* by Todd Braisted, who granted permission to quote in an email of 9 September 2013:

3d May 1783.

The declaration of John Segee a soldiers son in the Loyal Am'n Reg't who lost one of his Arms by Accident when he was a Boy of about 12 y'rs old.

Says

That on the 23d April, in north Castle, he met with a Charles Ward & three other men who were strangers to him.
They asked him where he was from, he answered from Long Island. They asked him where he was going he told them to see his friends in Bedford; on hearing of which they drew their Swords, and declared with an oath, if he did not return, they would cut his head off. He says that he returned with them, & declares that they flogged him the whole way from North Castle, to the White Plains. That at the White Plains they cut his hair, & asked him whether he would retire within the British lines if he was set at Liberty; on his answering, yes, Ward gave him between twenty & thirty strokes with his cane, and told him to go about his Bussiness [sic], and let his friends on Long Island know, that every Rascal of them that attempted to come among them would meet with the like treatment.

Esther Clark Wright points out in her *Loyalists of New Brunswick*: "Loyalists without the lines had some chance of making their peace with the American authorities, but those who had taken refuge within the British lines had little hope that such a solution would be possible for them." (p. 28)

W.S. MacNutt in *New Brunswick A History: 1784-1867* notes: "As the new situation induced by the peace negotiations became more discernible, the Loyalist position became similar to that of a third power, caught between Britain, whose good intentions they doubted, and the United States, whose intentions they recognized to be vindictive." (p. 18)

EVACUATION

In *The Kings Loyal Americans, the Canadian Fact, Marriage Licenses for Sunbury County, 1788-1829, Passenger Lists and Other List, etc.,* B. Wood-Holt quotes from the *British Headquarters Papers* the 9 October 1782 letter of John Parr, acting governor of Nova Scotia, to General Guy Carleton, Commander-in-Chief of British Forces in North America, in regard to the Loyalists settling in Nova Scotia:

> I must inform you, that it will only be in my power to provide them with Lands, and that there is not any Houses or Cover to put them under shelter, this Town is already so crowded that a considerable Body of the Recruits for the Army are Hutted in the Woods for want of Houses to Convert them into Barracks. And when I add the Scarcity and difficulty of providing fuel, and Lumber for building which is still greater, the many inconveniences and great distress these people must suffer, if any of them come into this Province this Winter, will sufficiently appear unto Your Excellency; and I am to add that what I have said of this Town may be applied to any other part of the Province; therefore I hope Sir that no necessity will compel these people to further suffering and Calamities[.] (p. 179)

Esther Clark Wright (*Loyalists of New Brunswick*) notes: "From the autumn of 1776 until the autumn of 1783, New York and Long Island were occupied by the British and were the place of refuge for those who were known for their loyalty to their king." (p. 4)

During the British occupation, Wilbur C. Abbott (*New York in the American Revolution*) writes, New York City "was scarcely even a garrison town, since the soldiers for the most part were not stationed in the city proper but on Staten Island, which became the chief receiving and cantonment station of the main body of the army when it was not on active service. (p. 247)

Citing the "*St. James Chronicle*, Nov. 9, 10, 1776, and March 22, 25, 1777," North Callahan, in *Royal Raiders: The Tories of the American Revolution*, writes that when William Howe took New York in the fall of 1776, "Only about 3,000 people remained in the city...." (p. 78) Callahan, citing the same sources, notes that after Howe took New York the Tories "flocked back into this British stronghold, until by February, 1777, the city had grown again to 11,000 people." (p. 79)

Judith L. Van Buskirk in *Generous Enemies, Patriots and Loyalists in Revolutionary New York* notes that during the British occupation of the New York islands, "The Loyalist regiments of the New Jersey Volunteers . . . made their bread through plundering raids in their old neighborhoods. They also shouldered the thankless task of supplying the city with wood." (p. 27) Van

Buskirk also notes: "The Loyalist regiments were a different breed from their European counterparts. They had a long history with their enemies that had in recent years concluded with the Loyalists' flight from their communities and the confiscation of their worldly goods. Many were eager to seek revenge, to inflict damage for damage's sake, and to confiscate goods with abandon as partial compensation fot their own losses." (p. 145)

Abbott notes that at the end of the American Revolution

> the city of New York was then scarcely more than a great village, which, in its most prosperous days before the war, had numbered hardly more than twenty thousand souls, and owing to the two fires which had occurred since the British occupation, had lost a considerable number of its original dwellings. Their places were ill-supplied by the huts and tents which sheltered some thousands of the refugee loyalists, who, with the soldiers and the original inhabitants, made up the heterogeneous population of the town on the eve of its evacuation. They were in evil plight. Hemmed in by land, and accessible by sea only to British vessels or those which risked the embargo laid by the neighboring states against this British capital, the price of provisions increased, it was declared, eight hundred per cent by the blockade. The position of these people was melancholy in the extreme. Beggars and thieves vied with each other in numbers and assurance. The jails were full, but not so full, if we are to believe contemporary accounts, as they should have been had all lawbreakers been in custody. The harbor was crowded with transports and men-of-war and hulks filled with American prisoners. Churches and public buildings had been largely converted to military uses; the houses of patriot refugees occupied by British officers or loyalist fugitives. The town was under military control; and though it lacked the horrors of a regular siege, the social brilliance which had marked the earlier years of British occupation had all but disappeared under the increasing pressure and misfortunes of the long enduring war. (pp. 263-264)

Citing the *Public Records Office, London, England, War Office Papers*, Wood-Holt writes of New York City in 1783: "Two fires had ravaged the place during the occupation destroying a substantial number of its original dwellings...

"Gaps in devastated real estate had been filled with huts and tents which furnished some sort of shelter, for thousands of souls who, with the soldiers and the original inhabitants, composed the heterogeneous population of the town on the eve of the evacuation...." (p. 178)

Wood-Holt: "With all [the] movement of soldiers and civilians during the summer and fall of 1783, New York Harbour saw such activity as it had never experienced before. Fleets of transports streamed in from every Atlantic port and the West Indies, and every American port was scoured for vessels. Private owners reaped a rich harvest from the government, as well as, individuals." (p. 190)

Wilbur C. Abbott writes, once again, in *New York in the American Revolution*:

> On the twenty-third of March, 1783, there arrived at Philadelphia a French vessel, *La Triomphe,* sent out by d'Estaing to recall the French cruisers, bearing the news of a general peace....
>
> A little less than two weeks later, on April 6, a British packet, the *Prince William Henry,* from Falmouth, reached New York, bearing the royal proclamation of February 14, declaring cessation of hostilities; and three days later this proclamation was read by the Town Mayor at the City Hall. (pp. 267-268)

Abbott further notes:

> Whatever the effect on the adherents of the patriot cause who heard the proclamation of the approaching peace read from the balcony of the old City Hall, there was no doubt of its effect on those who had remained faithful to the mother-country. To them it was not merely the death-knell of their cause, but, as many of them knew only too well, of their lives in their old homes. Anticipating this result, some six hundred of them, it was reported, had sailed for Nova Scotia in the preceding autumn. It scarcely needed the letter of Washington declaring that those of them who had served the Crown in the late war could not return to their old homes without the consent of the state authorities, to make them realize the position in which they now found themselves. (pp. 269-270)

Esther Clark Wright, citing the *Public Records Office, London, England, War Office Papers* in her *Loyalists of New Brunswick,* writes,

> Sir Guy Carleton and his staff were certainly taking great pains to smooth the way for the Loyalists. On April 11, 1783 . . . Brook Watson, the Commissary-General suggested the Loyal Refugees going to Nova Scotia would stand in want of immediate shelter for the women and children, and as there were in the King's Stores a great number of halfworn tents, with a very large quantity of new camp equipment, the Commander-in-Chief might be induced to order the storekeeper to issue two of the tents to every family going to settle that province. Brook Watson, who had spent nine years in Nova Scotia, would appreciate the necessity for shelter from the inclement weather of early spring in that area. His suggestion was approved and each family received two tents, in addition to other supplies. Damaged blankets were doled out, about one and a half for each

individual. Each man received a spade, an axe, four yards of woollen cloth, seven yards of linen cloth, two pairs of shoes, two pairs of stockings, one pair of mittens, each woman three yards of woollen cloth, six yards of linen, one pair of shoes, one pair of stockings . . ., and one pair of mittens; each child over the age of ten, three yards of woollen cloth, six linen, one pair of stockings and one pair of mittens; each child under ten, one and a half yards of wool and three yards of linen. On special orders of the Commander-in-Chief, some families received extra supplies. (pp. 48-49)

Abbott (*New York in the American Revolution*):

As early as April [1783] the exodus commenced with the sailing of the spring fleet to Nova Scotia; and every dock was crowded with refugees and their belongings. The first voyage of the transports carried a number variously estimated at from five to nine thousand, Carleton's figures being midway between these two extremes, and probably approximately correct. May saw the departure of six thousand more, and June a like number. Thenceforward every week's newspaper chronicles the emigrants by hundreds and thousands. It was said in early September that eight thousand had just left, and that there were some twelve or fourteen thousand still to go. The most, it would appear, went by sea to Nova Scotia, or to what is now New Brunswick; but many went by land to Montreal or points further west along the St. Lawrence and the lakes to what is now Ontario. These latter were for the time being chiefly from the country districts and were later joined by many who had gone the longer way by water.

By November 1783 nearly all who could had left. Though Canada and Nova Scotia had received the most, many went to the West Indies; some of the more well-to-do to England. . . ." (p. 271)

In writing about New York City in 1783, Abbott notes that at the end of the war

had come many from other parts hoping for protection and some turn of the tide which might restore them to their homes and property; so that among these thousands a considerable proportion were not natives of the city or province which had sheltered them. But they increased the great confusion and the crowd; and as this busy summer of 1783 went on, to their departure was joined that of the troops. . . . In May the Guards, Cornwallis's [*sic*] and Burgoyne's men, and the Hessians, such as had not elected to remain, were reported to have begun the voyage to England. By the end of August it would appear that all the foreign troops which had not been disbanded, or who had not deserted, were on their way home. With them went the English. Ship after ship, laden with troops, officers, and material, is noted as leaving New York or arriving in England. Late in July eight hundred men were sent to Bermuda for garrison duty; and early September saw the guns and ammunition despatched, chiefly to the West Indies. . . .

With all this movement of soldiers and civilians during this summer of 1783, New York harbor rose to heights of activity which it had never experienced before and was not to see again for many years. Fleets of transports poured in from every Atlantic port. Twelve thousand tons of shipping arrived in September — and this was a great matter in a day when a vessel of four hundred tons burden was reckoned not inconsiderable. Thirty-seven transports from Jamaica preceded this armada; and every American port was scoured for vessels. Private owners reaped a rich harvest, from government as well as individuals; and though the forts still carried the British ensign, the American flag was seen on many ships. Every issue of a New York paper carried notices relating to the embarkation during the summer. . . .

It was inevitable that this sudden and forced emigration should be accompanied not only by the hurrying to and fro of the multitude seeking to escape, by the constant passing of troops, and the hundred signs of sorrow and distress which always mark such a scene; but by a transfer of property such as New York had never seen before, and few cities have ever experienced. Naturally every refugee wished to turn his possessions into their smallest portable form; and the army was forced to dispose of its surplus material in as short a time as possible. The result was a multitude of auctions. . . . Every street, almost every block, witnessed this rapid and unbusinesslike form of exchange daily. The army administration advertised and held its periodical sales of cattle and wagons, its wood, and its surplus stores. The thoroughfares were crowded with goods of every description, vehicles, horses, stocks of merchandise, furniture, even books, pictures and clothes; and this whole summer of 1783 was transformed into one vast moving-day, with all of the turmoil and upheaval which such a time implies. Meanwhile the public buildings — the churches in particular — were purged of their occupants and set in order for their proper use, to which many of them had long been unaccustomed. (pp. 272-275)

Wood-Holt, citing the *British Headquarters Papers*, notes, "The provisional articles of peace had been signed at Paris 30 November 1782, but they did not arrive at New Brunswick until 19 March 1783." (pp. 182-183)

The Treaty of Paris formally ending the war was signed on 3 Septmeber 1783.

Writing of the final evacuation of the British from New York City, Abbott notes,

The morning of the 25th [November 1783] was clear and brilliant, if cold. The streets were crowded with holiday-makers; and the troops on both sides were promptly at their respective posts. By eight o'clock the American forces, with the light infantry as the main-guard, had reached the barrier near McGowan's Pass, where they were so close to the British rear-guard that General Knox and his staff talked with the British officers with every appearance of good-feeling, even cordiality.

Thus matters stood until one o'clock. Then the British main body began their march; and, passing along the Bowery to Chatham Street, and so to Pearl, turned off to the river and embarked. Closely following them came the Americans, a corps of dragoons, and one of artillery, some battalions of light infantry, and a rear-guard under Knox. . . . Down the Bowery to Chatham, thence through Pearl Street, they followed their late antagonists; but at Wall Street their paths diverged. The Americans marched along Wall Street to Broadway and so to Cape's Tavern, where the main body halted, while a detail of infantry and artillery proceeded to Fort George, accompanied by a curious crowd, eager to see the final act in the drama.

That act, as it proved, was in the nature not of heroic episode, but of comedy. But before it was staged, General Knox, at the head of the body of mounted citizens who had been collected at Bowling Green, rode out the Bowery to meet Washington and Clinton, who, with their escort, had meanwhile ridden in from Harlem to the Bull's Head Tavern. There, after the exchange of compliments and congratulations, the civic procession formed. At its head, escorted by a body of Westchester Light Horse, rode Washington and Clinton; then came the lieutenant-governor, van Cortlandt, with the members of the Council; then Knox and his officers, followed by the citizens on horseback; then the Speaker of the Assembly, with citizens on foot. Thus the procession made its way through the shouting crowds to the Tea Water Pump. There it divided. Knox and his officers proceeded down Chatham Street past a body of British troops still drawn up in the Fields at City Hall Park; while Washington, Clinton and their followers made their way down Pearl Street to Wall, thence to Broadway, where they joined Knox; and, as the troops fired a salute, held a reception at Cape's Tavern, while the English provost and main-guards marched down to their boats and left the city at last in the hands of the Americans.

This done, the officers and citizens, forming a procession, marched to the Battery to take part in the final ceremony of the day, the raising of the American flag over Fort George; and there the comedy began. For the British, after dismantling the fort, carrying away all the material they could, and rendering the rest useless, had taken away the halyards and the blocks by which the flag was raised, and the pole climbed. To crown the injury, some humorous member of the departing troops had greased the staff. Thus when the Americans reached the scene of their final triumph, they found the soldiers drawn up, the artillery unlimbered for a salute, and everything ready — except the flagstaff. Every effort to climb it proved fruitless. At last a sailor, aided by men who brought him a ladder, cleats, hammer and nails, climbed up the ladder as far as he could go, nailed the cleats on one by one, made his way to the top of the staff, removed the British ensign which still floated there, and secured new blocks and tackle. Then, as the halyards were reeved, and the American flag was run up, the guns boomed forth the first salute to the flag of the United States in New York harbor; and the remaining British, who had rested on their oars, to watch this by-play, rowed in silence to their ships. (pp. 279-281)

The following is from Thomas R. Millman and A.R. Kelley in *Atlantic Canada to 1900 a History of the Anglican Church*:

A moving scene was enacted upon the wharves of New York on a day in November 1783 following the signing of the Treaty of Paris [3 September 1783]. The Island of Manhattan had become almost the last place of refuge for royalists of the surrounding colonies. Troops and civilians were boarding transports that were to take the majority of them to the one mainland Atlantic province that had remained faithful to Britain. "Nova Scotia is the rage" was a headline that appeared in a London paper at the time. As the last boatload pushed off, General Washington, accompanied by a mounted escort, rode into the city, and the curtain closed upon colonial days in the royal province of New York. (pp. 45-46)

Numerous accounts have been written about the Loyalists exodus to Nova Scotia, but none captures the essence of the event better than Reverend William O. Raymond in *The River St. John* (which is essential reading for anyone interested in the early history of the European experience on the St. John River). Although it would be advised by some to direct a reader to Raymond's book instead of attempting such an extensive quote, I feel that most readers will not search out Raymond's book and, thus, would not have as great an understanding of this story.

The following is from Raymond's *The River St. John*:

The war of the Revolution was practically over in October, 1781, when Lord Cornwallis was forced to surrender to the United French and American forces at York town in Virginia. Early the next year the vanguard of the Loyalists began to make its appearance in Nova Scotia. . .

. It was not without forethought and serious consideration that the Loyalists came to settle on the River St. John. Several associations were formed at New York in 1782 to further the plans of those intending to settle in Nova Scotia. One of these associations had as its president the Reverend Dr. Seabmyand and for its secretary Sampson Salter Blowers. (The former was afterwards the first Bishop of the Episcopal Church in the United States, and the latter was Chief Justice of Nova Scotia.) Under the arrangements made by this association a great many Loyalists came to the River St. John in May, 1783. "Articles of Settlement were" agreed upon at New York as follows:

ARTICLES OF SETTLEMENT IN NOVA SCOTIA.

Made with the Loyalists at New York in 1783.

"The Reverend Dr. Samuel Seabury and Lieut. Col. B. Thompson, of the Kings American Dragoons, having been appointed by the Board of Agents to wait on his Excellency Sir Guy Carleton, Commander in Chief, in behalf of the Loyalists desirous of emigrating to Nova Scotia, read the following rough proposals, as articles of supply for the settlers in Nova Scotia:

1st. That they be provided with proper vessels, and convoy, to carry them, their horses and cattle, as near as possible to the place appointed for their settlement.
2nd. That besides the provisions for the voyage, one year's provision be allowed them, or money to enable them to purchase.
3rd. That some allowance of warm clothing be made in proportion to the wants of each family.
4th. That an allowance of medicines be granted, such as shall be thought necessary.
5th. That pairs of mill-stones, necessary iron works for grist mills, and saws and other necessary articles for saw-mills be granted them.
6th. That a quantity of nails and spikes, hoes and axes, spades and shovels, plough irons, and such other farming utensils as shall appear necessary, be provided for them, and also a proportion of window glass.
7th. That such a tract or tracts of land, free from disputed titles and as conveniently situated as may be, be granted, surveyed and divided at the public cost so as to afford from 300 to 600 acres of useful land to each family.
8th. That over and above 2,000 acres in every township be allowed for the support of a clergyman, and 1,000 acres for the support of a school, and that these lands be unalienable for ever.

9th. That a sufficient number of good muskets and cannon be allowed, with a proper quantity of powder and ball for their use, to enable them to defend themselves against any hostile invasion; also a proportion of powder and lead for hunting.

The deputation which waited on Sir Guy Carleton, viz., Rev. Dr. Seabury and Lieut. Col. B. Thompson, were assured by the Commander in Chief that he approved of the proposals submitted and that the terms of settlement would be at least equivalent to them. He desired to give every encouragement to those intending to settle in Nova Scotia and would write to the Governor of the province in their behalf. He advised the association to send agents to examine the vacant lands and see where settlements could best be made.

The following agreement in connection with the matter was widely circulated in New York and on Long Island, Staten Island and the vicinity, and signed by many heads of families:

"We whose names are hereunto subscribed do agree to remove to the province of Nova Scotia, on the above encouragement with our families, in full reliance on the future support of Government, and under the patronage of the following gentlemen as our agents, they having been approved of as such by his Majesty's Commissioner for restoring Peace: Lieut. Col. B. Thompson, K. A. D., Lieut. Col. E. Winslow, Gen. Mustermaster provincial forces; Major Joshua Upham, Rev. Dr. Samuel Seabury, Rev. John Sayre, Captain Maudsley, Amos Botsford, Esq., Samuel Cummings, Esq., Judge John Wardle, James Peters, Esq., Frederick Hauser.["]

These agents were furnished with detailed instructions directing them to ascertain the quality of soil, timber, game, limestone and other natural resources; to examine the rivers, bays, harbors, lakes and streams with regard to mills, fishing and trade; also to ascertain what difficulties and obstructions might be anticipated in forming settlements; also whether the tracts desired were free from disputed titles; also what lands in the neighbourhood were granted and to whom, whether forfeited or whether they might be purchased and at what rate, etc.

In accordance with Sir Guy Carleton's advice, Amos Botsford, Samuel Cummings and Frederick Hauser were sent as agents. They arrived at Annapolis on the 19th October, 1782, along with five hundred Loyalists who had come from New York in nine transport ships. Rev. Jacob Bailey, the S. P. G. missionary, gives a graphic account of their arrival and of the transformation it wrought in the small town, which is worth quoting in this connection. He says:

"On Saturday morning early, we were all surprised with the unexpected appearance of eleven sail of shipping, coming by Goat Island and directing their course towards the town. About nine, two frigates came to anchor, and at ten the remainder, being transports, hauled close in by the King's wharf. On board this fleet were about five hundred refugees who intend to settle in this province. They are a mixture from every province on the continent except Georgia. Yesterday they landed and our royal city of Annapolis, which three days ago contained only 120 souls, has now about 600 inhabitants. You cannot realize what an amazing alteration this event has occasioned. Everything is alive, and both the townspeople and the soldiers are lost among the strangers. All the houses and barracks are crowded and many are unable to procure any lodgings. Most of these distressed people left large possessions in the rebellious colonies, and their sufferings on account of their loyalty, and their present uncertain and destitute condition render them very affecting objects of compassion. Three agents are dispatched to Halifax to solicit lands from government."

The agents were bearers of a letter from Sir Guy Carleton to the Governor of Nova Scotia commending the Loyalists to his consideration. "These persons," he writes, "are to be considered as real efficient settlers, already acquainted with all the necessary arts of culture and habituated to settlements of the like kind: and who, independent of their just claims, will bring a large accession of strength as well as of population into the province. And as they have merited much by their exertions in support of Government, so they will not only, in my judgment, be well entitled to grants now desired, but to all such advantages of every sort which have been promised by proclamation or otherwise to persons invited to settle in that province."

The agents, on their return from Halifax, where they had a very satisfactory interview with Governor Parr and the Surveyor General, explored the country in the neighborhood of Annapolis and crossed the Bay of Fundy to St. John about the end of November. In the report afterwards transmitted to their friends at New York they write: "We found our passage up the river difficult, being too late to pass in boats and not sufficiently frozen to bear. In this situation we left the river, and for a straight course steered by a compass thro' the woods, encamping out several nights and went as far as the Oromocto, about seventy miles up the river, where there is a block-house, a British post.

"The St. John is a fine river equal in magnitude to the Connecticut or Hudson. At the mouth of the river is a fine harbor, accessible at all seasons of the year, never frozen or obstructed by ice. * * * [sic]

"There are many settlers along the river upon the intervale land, who get their living easily. The intervale lies on the river and is a most fertile soil, annually matured by the overflowing of the river, and produces crops of all kinds with little labor, and vegetables in the greatest perfection. They cut down the trees, burn the tops, put in a crop of wheat or Indian corn, which yields a plentiful increase. These intervales would make the finest meadows. The uplands produce wheat, both of the summer and winter kinds, as well as Indian corn. Here are some wealthy farmers having flocks of cattle. The greater part of the people, excepting the township of Maugerville, are tenants, or seated on the bank without leave or license merely to get their living. For this reason they have not made such improvements as might otherwise have been expected or as thorough farmers would have done. * * [sic] Immense quantities of limestone are found at Fort Howe and at the mouth of the river.

"We also went up the Kennebeccasis, a large branch of St. John's River, where is a large tract of intervale and upland which has never been granted; it is under a reserve, but we can have it. Major Studholme and Capt. Baxter, who explored the country, chose this place and obtained a grant of 9,000 acres. On each side of this grant are large tracts of good land convenient for navigation. A title for these lands may be procured sooner than for such as have been already granted such as Gage, Conway, etc., which must be obtained by a regular process in the court of escheats. The lands on the River St. John are also sufficiently near the cod fishery in Fundy Bay, and perfectly secure against the Indians and Americans. The inhabitants are computed to be near one thousand men able to bear arms. Here is a county and court established and the inhabitants at peace and seem to experience no inconveniency from the war."

Reports such as the foregoing enabled the Loyalists to act intelligently in making choice of their locations in Nova Scotia and a large number decided to go to the River St. John. Transport ships were hired by Sir Guy Carleton, and those who desired passage gave in their names at the office of the adjutant general. There was a scarcity of transports and the number of Loyalists who desired to go to Nova Scotia proved very much greater than had been anticipated. It became apparent that the ships would have to make repeated voyages. Many particulars of interest in connection with the Loyalist emigration are to be found in the newspapers of the day which are preserved in the public libraries of New York and New England — some also are in the British Museum.

The following paragraph taken from an old newspaper refers to the departure of the first party of Loyalists from New York in the spring of 1783:

"New London, Conn., April 25, 1783. We hear that the Loyalists destined for Nova Scotia from New York are to depart in two Divisions; the first, consisting of about 3,000 men, women and children, are nearly ready to sail; the second to sail as soon as the vessels return which carry the first."

As the season advanced it was found necessary to supplement the above plan by additional sailings, and the final embarkation at New York was hardly completed before winter set in.

The first fleet for Saint John sailed from Sandy Hook on the 26th of April, arriving at Partridge Island about the llth day of May[.] The most authentic account of the voyage is contained in the narrative of Walter Bates, afterwards Sheriff of Kings County, N. B., who was a passenger on board the transport ship Union. He states that early in April the Loyalist refugees on Long Island, who formed little communities at Huntington, Lloyd's Neck, Eaton's Neck and Oyster Bay, were visited by the Rev. John Sayre one of the agents for settling the Loyalists in Nova Scotia. Mr. Sayre informed them that the King offered to those who did not incline to return to their former places of abode and would go to Nova Scotia, 200 acres of land to each family and two years provisions and to furnish them with a free passage to the place selected for settlement. A public meeting was held to consider the matter and it was resolved by all present to remove with their families to the St. John River and to settle together in such a situation as would enable them to enjoy the advantages of a church and school. Mr. Bates says that Providence assigned to them the best ship and by far the best captain in the fleet. The Union took her passengers on board at Huntington Bay. The embarkation began on the llth of April and occupied five days. The manifest of the ship is still in existence and is signed by Fyler Dibblee, the deputy agent in charge. There were 209 passengers all told viz., 61 men, 39 women, 59 children over ten, 48 children under ten and 2 servants. Walter Bates says the captain received them on board "as father of a family" and took care that nothing should be wanting to render them comfortable and happy during the voyage. The Union sailed from Huntington to the place of rendezvous near Staten Island. An interesting incident now occurred. This and the story of the voyage, we shall let Mr. Bates tell in his own way: —

"Having a couple on board wishing to be married, we call upon the Rev'd. Mr. Learning, who received us with much kindness and affection — most of us formerly of his congregation — who after the marriage reverently admonished us with his blessing that we pay due regard to church and school as means to obtain the blessing of God upon our families and our industry. We embarked: next day the ship joined the fleet and on the 26th day of April, upwards of twenty sail of ships under convoy left Sandy Hook for Nova Scotia, from whence, after the pleasure of leading the whole fleet fourteen days, our good ship Union arrived at Partridge Island before the fleet was come within sight. Next day the ship was safely moored by Capt. Dan'l. Leavitt, the pilot, in the most convenient situation for landing in the Harbour of St. John, all in good health where we remained comfortable on board ship (while others was sickly or precipitated on shore from other ships) which proved a providential favor, until we could explore for a place in the wilderness suitable for our purpose of settlement. A boat was procured for the purpose and David Pickett, Israel Hait, Silas Raymond and others proceeded sixty miles up the river and reported that the inhabitants were settled on Intervale lands by the river, that the high-lands had generally been burned by the Indians and that there was no church or church minister in the country. They were informed of a tract of timbered land that had not been burned on Bellisle Bay, about thirty miles from the Harbour of St. John, which they had visited and viewed the situation favorable for our purpose of settlement. Whereupon we all agreed to go there and disembarked from on board the good ship Union, with Capt. Wilson's blessing. We placed on board a small sloop all our baggage. The next morning, with all our effects, women and children, we set sail above the falls and arrived at Bellisle Bay before sunset. Nothing but wilderness before our eyes; the women and children did not refrain from tears."

It will be seen from Bates['] narrative that the fleet of transports anchored at St. John harbor about one week before the general landing on the 18th of May. Little preparation had been made for their reception. The season had been cold and backward and, anxious as were the masters of the transports to return speedily to New York, they were obliged to tarry some days. Before the Loyalists could disembark, it was necessary to clear away the brushwood around the landing place at the Upper Cove (now the Market Slip) and to erect tents, hurricane houses of sails and other kinds of shelter. Bates' narrative seems to imply that there was no uniform plan of disembarkation. The passengers were "precipitated on shore" by the less humane captains, but on the transport Union they remained until ready to proceed to their tract of land in the parish of Kingston. However, there must have been a more or less general disembarkation on the 18th of May which day has always been observed by common consent as the anniversary of the landing of the Loyalists. . . .

The Loyalists could not but feel glad when their voyage was ended. There were in their day no light houses, beacons or fog horns to aid the navigator and the best charts were imperfect. Many of the ships were overcrowded and the accomodations not of the best. To add to the general discomfort epidemics, such as measles, broke out on board some of the vessels. Yet glad as they were to be again on shore it was with heavy hearts that many of them viewed the departure of the fleet. The grand-mother of the late Sir Leonard Tilley said to one of her descendants, "I climbed to the top of Chipman's Hill and watched the sails disappear, and such a lonely feeling came over me that, although I had not shed a tear through all the war, I sat down on the damp moss with my baby in my lap and cried."

An old New York paper informs us that nine transport ships sailed from St. John on the 29th of May, on their return to New York, and that they left the new settlers there in good health and spirits.

The days that followed the arrival of the fleet were busy days for Major Studholme and his assistant Lieut. Samuel Denny Street. By their orders, boards, shingles, bricks, etc., were supplied to the newcomers. A very interesting collection of Studholme's vouchers and receipts may be seen in the provincial archives at Halifax. The first that bears the name of Parr (Parrtown) is the following:

"Parr, on the River St. John, 31st August, 1783. Rec'd from Gilfred Studholme £5.18.10 ½ for surveying 142,660 feet lumber for use of the Loyalists settled on the River St. John." JEREMIAH REGAN.

The name of Parr, or Parrtown, was not given to the new town until some months after the arrival of the Loyalists and it was applied only to that part of the present city of St. John which lies on the east side of the harbor south of Union street. Governor Parr admits that it originated "in feminine vanity," from which we may assume that his wife suggested it. The name was never very acceptable to the people. It was soon discarded and the time-honored name of St. John restored at the incorporation of the city on the 18th of May, 1785.

Every Loyalist on his arrival received 500 feet of boards and a proportion of shingles and bricks to assist him in building a house. Many of the dwellings put up were log houses, the lumber being used for floors, partitions, doors, etc. They did not have far to go for the stone needed for the chimneys and fire places. In the course of the first twelve months, Major Studholme issued 1,731,289 feet of boards, 1,553,919 shingles and 7,400 clapboards. The lumber was obtained from James Woodman, William Hazen, Nehemiah Beckwith, Patrick Rogers and others at pretty high prices (for those days) boards £4 per M. and shingles 15s. per M. The Loyalists seem to have been industrious, for when winter came more than 1,500 dwellings had been erected. Joshua Aplin wrote Chief Justice Smith that their efforts were unparalleled, and that he could scarce credit his own eyes at the sight of such industry. But the people appeared to be almost in despair at not getting on their lands. The greater part of those in the town never meant to fix themselves there, but to settle on lands up the river and apply their money to building farm houses, purchasing live stock, etc., and great loss had been incurred by their being obliged to build at the mouth of the river.

The Kingston settlers, who came in the ship Union, were among the few that were able to proceed directly to their place of settlement. They tented for some weeks on the banks of Kingston Creek, where the mothers found occupation in nursing their children through the measles. They were visited by the Indians, with whom they established friendly relations and who supplied them with moose meat. In the month of July Frederick Hauser came to lay out their farms. Before their lots were drawn, however, reservations were made for church and school purposes. They then set to with a will, working together by common consent, clearing the ground for their cabins and cutting logs, which they were obliged often to carry some little distance with their own hands, having neither horses nor oxen to draw them, and by the month of November every man in the settlement found himself ensconsed with his family beneath his own roof in the shelter of the forest where, Walter Bates tells us, they were perfectly happy, contented and comfortable through the winter. In this respect they were fortunate indeed in comparison with many at Parrtown and St. Annes who were obliged to pass their first winter in tents.

A second important contingent of the Loyalists arrived on the 29th of June. These, as in the case of the former fleet, came from New York having embarked at various places in the vicinity. There was some delay in their sailing owing to the difficulties of embarkation and getting the vessels together. The names of the transport ships have been preserved in the following advertisement in a New York paper:

"NOTICE TO REFUGEES."

"The following Transports, viz., Two Sisters, Hopewell, Symmetry, Generous Friends, Bridgewater, Thames, Amity's Production, Tartar, Duchess of Gordon, Littledale, William and Mary and Free Briton, which are to carry companies commanded by Sylvanus Whitney, Joseph Gorham, Henry Thomas, John Forrester, Thomas Elms, John Cock, Joseph Clarke, James Hoyt, Christopher Benson, Joseph Forrester, Thomas Welch, Oliver Bourdet, Asher Dunham, Abiather Camp, Peter Berton, Richard Hill and Moses Pitcher, will certainly fall down on Monday morning (to Staten Island); it will therefore be absolutely necessary for the people who are appointed to go in these companies to be all on board tomorrow evening.

New York, June 7th, 1783."

The diary of Sarah Frost, who was a passenger in the "Two Sisters," throws much light upon the circumstances attending the voyage. Sarah (Schofield) Frost was the wife of William Frost, a sturdy loyalist of Stamford, who was proscribed and banished and threatened with death if he ever returned to Connecticut. He did return, however, as guide to an armed party, on a Saturday night in July, 1781. The party placed themselves in hiding in a swamp near the meeting house and the following day captured the Rev'd. Dr. Mather and his entire congregation. Selecting forty-eight of the most ardent "patriots," including the minister, the party hastened to their boats and brought their prisoners within the British lines at Lloyd's Neck, on Long Island, where they were greeted in no complimentary fashion by those of their old neighbors whom they had driven from their homes because of their loyalty to the King. Needless to say this exploit rendered Wm. Frost exceedingly obnoxious to the "patriots" of Stamford and rendered it impossible for him to return.

The extracts from Mrs. Frost's journal that follow will give the reader an insight into the experience of those who made the voyage to St. John in the Summer Fleet. She writes on May 25, 1783, "I left Lloyd's Neck with my family and went on board the Two Sisters, commanded by Captain Brown, for a voyage to Nova Scotia with the rest of the Loyalist sufferers. This evening the captain drank tea with us. He appears to be a very agreeable gentleman. We expect to sail as soon as the wind shall favor. We have very fair accommodation in the cabin, although it contains six families besides my own. There are two hundred and fifty passengers on board."

A few days later the ship proceeded to New York where there was an uncomfortable delay. They had expected to sail on the 9th of June but were detained a week longer, and when they left Sandy Hook they had been already three weeks on ship board. While at New York the passengers spent much of their time in making purchases of things they needed and in taking leave of their relatives and friends. The parents of Mrs. Frost had espoused the side of the Revolutionary party and her's [sic] was one of the many sad instances in which families were divided by the event of the war. She had a touching interview with her father, who came in a boat from Stamford to bid her farewell. She again writes, under date, June 9th; "Our women all came on board with their children, and there is great confusion in the cabin. We bear with it pretty well through the day, but at night one child cries in one place and one in another while we are getting them to bed. I think sometimes I will go crazy. There are so many of them, if they were as still as common, there would be a great noise amongst them."

Two days later the ships weighed anchor and dropped down to Staten Island where they remained until the 15th June, under which date Mrs. Frost writes:

"Our ship is getting under way, I suppose for Nova Scotia. I hope for a good passage. About 3 o'clock we have a hard gale and a shower which drives us all below. About 5 o'clock we came to anchor six miles off the Light House at Sandy Hook. About 6 o'clock we had a terrible squall and hail-stones fell as big as ounce balls. Billy [her husband] [sic] went out and gathered a mug full of hail stones and in the evening we had a glass of punch made of it.

"Monday, June 16, we weighed anchor about half after five in the morning, with the wind north-nor'-west and it blows very fresh. We passed the Light House about half after seven. It is now half after nine and a signal has been fired for the ships to lie to for the Bridgewater, which seems to lag behind * * * * [sic] It is now two o'clock and we are again under way. We have been waiting for another ship to come from New York and she has now overhauled us. We have a very light breeze now, but have at last got all our fleet together. We have thirteen ships, two brigs and one frigate; the frigate is our commodore's. It is now three o'clock, the men have got their lines out fishing for Mackerel. Mr. Miles has caught the first. I never saw a live one before, it is the handsomest fish I ever saw."

"Tuesday, June 17th. The wind begins to blow very fresh and I am too unwell to leave my bed. At half after five in the afternoon we are sixty miles from the Light-house, the wind south-west; they say that is a fair wind for us. We are out of sight of land at half after nine."

"Thursday, June 19th. We are still steering eastward with a fine breeze. We make seven miles an hour the chief part of the day. About noon we shift our course and are steering north by east. At about two o'clock Captain says we are 250 miles from Sandy Hook. At six o'clock we saw a sail ahead. She crowded sail and put off from us, but our frigate knew how to talk to her, for at half past seven she gave her a shot which caused her to shorten sail and lie to. Our captain looked with his spy-glass. He told me she was a Rebel brig, he saw her thirteen stripes. She was steering to the westward. The wind blows so high this evening, I am afraid to go to bed for fear of rolling out."

"Friday, June 20th. This morning our frigate fired a signal to shift our course to North-Nor'-East. Mr. Emslie, the mate, tells me that we are at five in the afternoon about 500 miles from Sandy Hook. We begin to see the fog come on, for that is natural to this place. At six our commodore fired for the ships to lie to until those behind should come up. The fog comes on very thick this evening, [sic]"

["]Saturday, June 21st. Rose at 8 o'clock. It was so foggy we could not see one ship belonging to the fleet. They rang their bells and fired guns all the morning to keep company with one another. About half after ten the fog all went off, so that we saw the chief part of our fleet around us. At noon the fog came on again, but we could hear their bells all around us. This evening the captain showed Billy and me the map of the whole way we have come and the way we have yet to go. He told us we are 240 miles from Nova Scotia at this time."

"Sunday, June 22nd. It is very foggy yet. No ship in sight nor any bells to be heard. Towards noon we heard some guns fired from our fleet but could not tell where they was. The fog was so thick we could not see ten rods, and the wind is so ahead that we have not made ten miles since yesterday noon."

"Monday, June 23rd. Towards noon the fog goes off fast, and in the afternoon we could see several of our vessels, one came close along side of us. Mr. Emslie says we are an hundred and forty miles from land now. In the evening the wind becomes fair, the fog seems to leave us and the sun looks very pleasant. Mr. Whitney and his wife, Billy and I have been diverting ourselves with a few games of crib."

By this time the passengers were thoroughly tired of the voyage. For three days the ships had lain buried in a dense fog, almost becalmed. On board the Three Sisters an epidemic of measles was causing mothers trouble and anxiety, But [sic] a change for the better was at hand and Mrs. Frost continues her journal in a more cheerful strain.

"Thursday, June 26. This morning the sun appears very pleasant. We are now nigh the banks of Cape Sable. At nine o'clock we begin to see land. There is general rejoicing. At half past six we have twelve of our ships in sight. Our captain told me just now we should be in the Bay of Fundy before morning. He says it is about one day's sail after we get into the Bay to Saint John's River. How I long to see that place though a strange land. I am tired of being on board ship, though we have as clever a captain as ever need to live."

"Friday, June 27. I got up this morning very early to look out. I can see land on both sides of us. About ten o'clock we passed Annapolis. The wind died away. Our people got their lines out to catch cod fish."

"Saturday, June 28. Got up in the morning and found ourselves nigh to land on both sides. At half after nine our Captain fired a gun for a pilot, and soon after ten a pilot came on board, and a quarter after one our ship anchored off against Fort Howe in Saint John's River. Our people went on shore and brought on board pea vines with blossoms on them, gooseberries, spruce and grass. They say this is to be our city. Our land is five and twenty miles up the river. We are to have here only a building lot 40 feet wide and an hundred feet back. Billy has gone on shore in his whale boat to see how it looks. He returns soon, bringing a fine salmon."

"Sunday, June 29. This morning it looks very pleasant. I am just going on shore with my children. . . . . [sic] It is now afternoon and I have been on shore. It is, I think, the roughest land I ever saw. We are all ordered to land tomorrow and not a shelter to go under."

Such, in brief, is the simple story told by this good lady. (pp. 506-526)

Citing the "Return of the number of Loyalists gone to St. John's River in Nova Scotia, as pr. returns left in the Commissary General's office in New York," Raymond states that there were 500 men, 335 women, 743 children and 394 servants for a total of 1,972 "Loyalists enrolled in the various companies for passage in this fleet. . . ." (p. 526)

Raymond continues:

> It is not improbable that some who handed in their names to Brook Watson at the Commisary's [sic] office did not actually embark in the fleet, but making reasonable allowance on this score the number of those who came to St. John in the June fleet was not very far short of 2,000 souls. The captains of the companies in which the Loyalists were enrolled were appointed by the Commander in chief, Sir Guy Carleton, and were well known citizens of St. John in early days. Among others who came in this fleet was John Clarke of Rhode Island, who says that at the time of his arrival only two log huts had been erected by the first comers. The government gave him and every other grantee 500 feet of very ordinary boards towards covering their buildings. . . .
>
> VESSELS continued to arrive at Parrtown during the summer of 1783, each with its contingent of loyal exiles. Many of the transports, including the Cyrus, Otter, Sovereign and Bridgewater, made repeated trips during the season. In most instances the kindness and humanity of the Captains earned the grateful acknowledgments of the Loyalists. The following address will suffice for illustration:
>
> "To Capt. WM. STEWART, Ship Sovereign."
>
> "Dear Sir Your generosity, kindness and attention to us while on board your ship, and assistance lent us on landing our property from on board demand our most warm acknowledgments. Permit us therefore to return you that unfeigned thanks for all your goodness that feeling hearts can; and as you are about to leave us accept our most sincere wishes for your happiness and prosperity, and that you may have a safe and easy passage to New York is the sincere wish of, dear Sir,
> By request of the Company,

Your most obedient, humble servant,
JOHN MENZIES, Capt. 24th Company."
"St. John's River, Aug. 12, 1783."

Very different was the conduct of the Captain of the transport Martha, which will be referred to presently.

The Americans now began to urge upon Sir Guy Carleton the speedy evacuation of New York by the British forces. But Sir Guy was too good a friend of the Loyalists to allow himself to be unduly hurried in the matter. He told them plainly that the violence of the Americans, since the cessation of hostilities, had greatly increased the number of Loyalists who were obliged to look to him for escape from threatened destruction. That their fears had been augmented by the barbarous menaces of Committees formed in various towns, cities and districts, which had threatened dire vengeance to any who ventured back to their former homes. He therefore adds, "I should show an indifference to the feelings of humanity, as well as to the honor and interest of the nation whom I serve, to leave any of the Loyalists that are desirous to quit the country, a prey to the violence they conceive they have so much cause to apprehend."

Sir Guy did his best to facilitate the emigration of all who desired to leave New York, and by his instruction the following notice was published.

"City Hall, New York, August 14, 1783.

"Notice is hereby given to all Loyalists within the lines, desirous to emigrate from this place before the final Evacuation, that they must give in their Names at the Adjutant-General's Office, on or before the 21st instant, and be ready to embark by the end of this month."

Before the arrival of the date, [sic] mentioned in the notice, 6,000 names were entered at the Adjutant-General's office for passages, and the evacuation proceeded as fast as the number of transports would admit. Four weeks later another and more emphatic notice was issued to the effect that the Loyalists were expected to embark on or before the 20th of September, and that those who neglected to embrace the opportunity need not expect to be conveyed at the public expense.

There can be little doubt that many who lingered at New York would gladly have returned to their former places of abode, but the experience of those who attempted it was too discouraging. Here is an instance as described by one of the American "patriots."

"Last week there came one of the dain'd refugees from New York to a place called Wall-Kill, in order to make a tarry with his parents. He was taken into custody immediately his head and eye-brows were shaved tarred and feathered a hog yoke put on his neck, and a cow bell thereon; upon his head a very high cap of feathers was set, well plum'd with soft tar and a sheet of paper in front, with a man drawn with two faces, representing Arnold and the Devil's imps; and on the back of it a cow, with the refugee or tory driving her off."

The forced migration of the Loyalists was a source of much amusement to the whigs of that day. A parody on Hamlet's soliloquy, "To be or not to be," was printed in the New Jersey Journal, under the title, The Tory's soliloquy. It begins:

"To go or not to go; that is the question,
Whether 'tis best to trust the inclement sky,
That scowl's indignant, or the dreary bay
Of Fundy and Cape Sable's rocks and shoals,
And seek our new domain in Scotia's wilds,
Barren and bare, or stay among the rebels,
And by our stay rouse up their keenest rage." (pp. 527-531)

Wilbur C. Abbott (*New York in the American Revolution*) writes of the mistreatment of those Loyalists unfortunate enough to fall into Patroit hands, "In this new out-door sport ["Tory-riding"] then growing popular in America rails and tar-buckets and feather-beds were used extensively — and this practice became so dear to the rougher elements that even the army had trouble to repress it." (pp. 173-174)

Returning to Raymond:

The statement of Sir Guy Carleton respecting the barbarous menaces of committees and associations, formed in various towns and districts in the United States, against all Loyalists who might attempt to return to their homes is abundantly confirmed by documentary evidence even at this distant day. We quote two instances only:

"We the officers, non-commissioned officers and privates of the 5th regiment of Delaware militia, in the County of Kent, do hereby agree to expel all refugees from this and every other part of the United States; and if any of those miscreants, whom we are obliged to consider as worse than robbers or even common murderers, shall be found among us, we do pledge ourselves by the sacred ties of honour to be united, and stand by each other in expelling them from among us by those powers which nature has given us."

The town of Philadelphia adopted the following resolution: "That the people of this town will at all times, as they have ever done, to the utmost of their power oppose every enemy to the just rights and liberties of mankind: That after so wicked a conspiracy against those rights and liberties by certain ingrates, most of them natives of these States, and who have been refugees and declared traitors to their country, it is the opinion of this town that they ought never to be suffered to return, but be excluded from having lot or portion among us. And the Committee of Correspondence is hereby requested to write to the several towns in this Commonwealth and desire them to come into the same or similar resolves if they shall think fit."

We have now to consider the circumstances under which the "Fall Fleet" came to St. John.

After the cessation of hostilities, the violent temper manifested by the victorious Americans caused the officers of the Loyalist regiments to lay their case before Sir Guy Carleton in a letter dated March 14, 1783, in which they state, "That from the purest principles of loyalty and attachment to the British government they took up arms in his Majesty's service, and relying on the justice of their cause and the support of their Sovereign and the British nation, they have persevered with unabated zeal through all the vicissitudes of a calamitous and unfortunate war. * * * * [sic] That whatever stipulations may be made at the peace for the restoration of the property of the Loyalists and permission for them to return home, yet, should the American Provinces be severed from the British Empire, it will be impossible for those who have served his Majesty in arms in this war to remain in the country. The personal animosities arising from civil dissensions have been so heightened by the blood that has been shed in the contest that the parties can never be reconciled." The letter goes on to speak of personal sacrifices made; of the anxiety felt for the future of wives and children; of the fidelity of the troops, who in the course of the contest had shown a degree of patience, fortitude and bravery almost without example; and of the great number of men incapacitated by wounds, many having helpless families who had seen better days; they therefore request: —

"That grants of land may be made to them in some of his Majesty's American Provinces and that they may be assisted in making settlements, in order that they and their children may enjoy the benefit of British government.

"That some permanent provision may be made for such of the non-commissioned officers and privates as have been disabled by wounds, and for the widows and orphans of deceased officers and soldiers.

"That as a reward for their services the rank of the officers be made permanent in America, and that they be entitled to half pay upon the reduction of their regiments."

This letter was signed by the commanders of fourteen Loyalist regiments.

The application of the officers was eventually complied with although there was some opposition in parliament when the Secretary of War proposed to place the Loyalist regiments upon the British establishment. In the course of the debate that followed Secretary Townsend said that it was only fair that those who had fought the nation's battles and risked both life and property in the war should have some recompence. Sir P. F. Clarke expressed his dissatisfaction at the idea of putting the "Provincials" on the establishment to the prejudice, as he claimed, of many of the officers of the British army. "By such a measure some of the Provincial officers would soon be promoted to the staff over the heads of many of our own Colonels," said he, "and we may soon hear of a Major General Simcoe, a Major General Fanning, etc., though those gentlemen have no rank in England."

In reply the Secretary of war expressed his surprise that any opposition should be made to placing the Provincial regiments on the establishment. Those troops once put upon the establishment, the officers would of course become entitled to rank and half-pay; and as the nation would be under the necessity of making some provision for those gallant Loyalists, he thought half pay more decent and much more eligible than a pension. As to the idea of Col. Simcoe being made a Major General, he believed that when such an event should take place the army would not be displeased at it; for a better officer or a better man did not exist in the service.

General Smith did not object to half-pay, only to rank being given to the Provincials. Mr. Onslow made a motion in opposition to continuing the rank of Provincial officers on a par with those of the British line. This was seconded by Sir Cecil Wray, who expressed his surprise that such a thing should be thought of.

The House divided on the motion. Ayes 37. Noes 76. Majority for giving rank to the Loyalist officers 39. This vote caused considerable discussion in England.

On the arrival of his Majesty's instructions relative to the disposal of the troops at New York, dated the 9th of June, the principal Loyalist regiments were ordered to hold themselves in readiness to embark for Nova Scotia, where on their arrival they were to be disbanded. The corps included in the order were the King's American Regiment, Queens Rangers, British Legion, New York Volunteers, New Jersey Volunteers,

Loyal American Regiment, De Lancey's Brigade, Prince of Wales American Regiment, Pennsylvania Loyalists, Maryland Loyalists, Loyal American Legion, Kings American Dragoons and one or two others.

Before the royal orders and instructions reached America the King's American Dragoons arrived at St. John under the command of Major Daniel Murray. They encamped at Manawagonish expecting to settle in the Township of Conway. On the 6th of July, Col. Edward Winslow wrote to Major Upham of the corps (who was in New York acting as an aide-de-camp to Sir Guy Carleton): "I am gratified excessively at the situation and behaviour of your regiment. I never saw more cheerfulness and good humor than appears among the men. They are encamped on one of the pleasantest spots I ever beheld, and they are enjoying a great variety of what you New Yorkers call luxuries, such as partridges, salmon, bass, trout, pigeons, etc. The whole regiment are this day employed in cutting and clearing a road to the river, and Major Murray and I intend to ride tomorrow where man never rode before."

The day following Winslow writes to Ward Chipman, "I am at present at Murray's head quarters in a township which we shall lay out for the provincials, and we have already cut a road from his camp to the river, about three miles. We cut yesterday, with about 120 men, more than a mile through a forest hitherto deemed impenetrable. When we emerged from it there opened a prospect superior to anything in the world I believe. A magnificent view of the immense Bay of Fundy on the one side, and a very extensive view of the River St. John, with the Falls, Grand Bay and Islands, on the other: in front the Fort, which is a beautiful object on a high hill, and all the settlements about the town, with the ships, boats, etc., in the harbor — 'twas positively the most magnificent and romantic scene I ever beheld."

The stay of the King's American Dragoons at "Camp Manawaugonish" was brief, for about the end of August they were sent up the St. John river to be disbanded in what is now the Parish of Prince William....

After the preliminaries of peace were signed in 1782, no attempt was made to maintain the normal strength of the Loyalist Regiments. They were at this time considerably reduced in numbers. Many had fallen on the field of battle, more had died of wounds and exposure, many had died of disease and some were prisoners with the enemy. When it was realized that the war was over no serious effort was made to prevent the non-commissioned officers and men from taking "French leave," and a good many left the service without the formality of a discharge. Those who did so were of course marked on the roll as "deserters" and most of them no doubt returned to their former places of abode. Some of the troops were discharged in due form at New York. Consequently when the regiments sailed for St. John they were reduced to about one fourth of their original strength.

The Royal Instructions for disbanding did not reach New York until August but, in the meantime, Lieutenant Colonels Edward Winslow, Isaac Allen and Stephen de Lancey were sent to Nova Scotia to explore and locate lands for the accommodation of their comrades in arms. The general plan of settlement was suggested by Sir Guy Carleton in a letter of the 26th of April in which he expresses the opinion that the disbanded troops should be disposed like the cantonments of an army along a frontier to serve as a bulwark against any possible invasion from the United States, the allotments to be by corps and as contiguous as possible to each other and that in the allotments the officers be interspersed among the men so that the settlers may thereby be united and in case of attack the colony may be defended by those who have been accustomed to bear arms and serve together. According to Edward Winslow's statement, the River St. John was fixed upon as the only convenient situation where there was a tract of vacant land sufficiently extensive for the purpose. By Winslow's solicitations at Halifax authority was at length obtained to lay out blocks of land for the several regiments. These blocks were afterwards known as "the twelve mile tracts." They began at Fredericton and extended up the river as far, probably, as the mouth of the Tobique.

Governor Parr was not much in favor of sending the disbanded troops to the River St. John. He wrote to Sir Guy Carleton in July that Lt. Col. deLancey [sic] wished to settle them on the Saint John: "If so," he says, "they must be content to commence their settlement 140 miles from the mouth of the river, where the ungranted lands begin, otherwise they must be provided for elsewhere." He says again, "I greatly fear the soil and fertility of that part of the province is over-rated by people who have explored it partially. I wish, it may turn out otherwise, but have my fears that there is scarce good land enough for those already sent there. If all the Provincial Corps go am certain there will not, which was the reason for my recommending the eastern side of the St. Croix river to your Excellency." Probably Edward Winslow had more to do than any other man in determining the place of settlement of the Loyal Regiments, and he certainly knew more of the valley of the St. John than did Governor Parr, who never visited it.

About the time the regiments were ready to sail from New York, General Fox, who commanded in Nova Scotia, notified Governor Parr that it was necessary at once to determine the district to be assigned to each of the corps so that on their arrival they might be sent to their destinations. On the 16th September General Fox and his military secretary, Edward Winslow, left for St. John to make a personal examination of the lands and to arrange with Major Studholme for their reception. While he was up the river on this tour of exploration General Fox wrote an interesting letter to General Haldimand, the Governor of Quebec, which, with a little abbreviation, is here given:

Augh Pack, Sep'r 28, 1783.

Sir, — Being on a tour on the River St. John's and a convenient opportunity offering I avail myself of it to acquaint your Excellency that the whole of the Provincial Regiments, consisting of upwards of 3,000 men, are embarked for the River St. John's, where they are to become settlers, and a tract of land is assigned them by his Excellency the Governor of this Province extending from the Townships of Maugerville and Burton on both sides of the river on the route to Canada, so far as to accommodate the whole which will be a considerable distance. This circumstance will facilitate the communication between the provinces of Nova Scotia and Canada, an object which I am informed your Excellency is anxious to effect and which it is very evident must greatly contribute to the benefit of both provinces.

[Signed] [sic] H. E. Fox, Brig, Gen'l

The number of those who arrived at St. John in the Fall Fleet, is commonly stated to have been about three thousand souls. The returns of the Commissary general's office show that up to the 12th of October as many as 3,396 persons connected with the Loyalist regiments had sailed to the River St. John, viz., 1826 men, 563 women, 696 children and 311 servants. The following summer an enumeration was made by Thomas Knox of the disbanded troops settled on the St. John river. His return for the Loyalist regiments gives a total of 3,520 persons, viz., 1877 men, 585 women, 865 children and 193 servants. This does not differ very materially from the other return.

The official correspondence of Sir Guy Carleton contains a pretty full account of the circumstances that attended the departure of the Loyalist regiments and their subsequent arrival at St. John. During the summer months they had been encamped near Newtown, Long Island, a short distance from Brooklyn Ferry. They embarked on the 3rd of September, and Sir Guy wrote to General Fox that he hoped they would sail on the 7th, but unforseen delays prevented their departure until some days later. The command of the troops devolved on Lieut. Col. Richard Hewlett, of the 3d battalion of De Lancey's Brigade, Lieut. Col. Gabriel De Veber, of the Prince of Wales American Regiment, being second in command.

Sir Guy Carleton's instructions to Lieut. Col. Hewlett, are contained in the following letter.

"New York, September 12, 1783.

"Sir — You are to take command of the British American Troops which are to proceed to the River St. John's in the Bay of Fundy in Nova Scotia. On your arrival there you will see that the stores intended for them are duly delivered, and you will take such steps as shall be necessary for the several corps proceeding immediately to the places allotted for their settlement, where they are to be disbanded on their arrival, provided it does not exceed the 20th of October, on which day Captain Prevost, deputy inspector of British American Forces, has directions to disband them. You will give directions to the officer commanding each corps that in case of separation they will proceed on their arrival at the River St. John's in forwarding their respective troops to the place of destination. The disembarkation of the troops must not on any account be delayed, as the transports must return to this Port with all possible dispatch. Directions have been given to Mr. Colville, assistant agent of all small craft at the River St. John, to afford every assistance in his power to the corps in getting to their places of destination, and the commanding officers will make application to him for that purpose.

(Signed) [sic] GUY CARLETON.["]

The perils of navigation are seen in the disaster that befell the transport ship Martha, one of the vessels of the fleet. The ships sailed from Sandy Hook about the 15th of September and all went well until they arrived off the south-west coast of Nova Scotia. Here the Martha was wrecked on a ledge near the Seal Islands, afterwards called "Soldier's Ledge." She had on board 174 persons, including many of the Maryland Loyalists and part of Lieutenant-Colonel Hewlett's battalion; 99 souls perished and 75 were saved by fishing boats. According to the account given by Captain Kennedy of the Maryland Loyalists the accident was due to gross neglect on the part of the master of the ship. He left New York with an old set of sails and had not above twelve men and boys to work the ship. As he reported the previous evening that he had seen land, everyone imagined he would lay to during the night, the weather being tempestous. While the crew were engaged in rigging and setting up a new main-topsail, to replace one that had gone to pieces early in the night, the ship struck on the rocks. The long-boat was smashed by the fall of the mainmast. The captain gave orders to launch the jolly boat and to the surprise of everybody, he having repeatedly proclaimed that he would be one of the last to leave the ship, he jumped into her as she went over the side, rowed to the cutter which had been previously launched, got into her and inhumanly pushed off for the shore. The empty Jolly boat was turned adrift in full view of the unhappy people on board, the master turning a deaf ear to the solicitations of Captain Kennedy, who begged him to pull in toward the stern, in order to discuss some means of saving the lives of the passengers.

Another account of this tragedy is preserved in a letter of Lieut. Michael Laffan, of Colonel Hewlett's battalion, to his brother, written at St. John on the 11th of October in which he says, "Yesterday evening I had the good fortune to arrive at this place. On the 25th of September, about 4 o'clock in the morning, the "Martha" struck against a rock off the Tusket River and was in the course of a few hours wrecked in a thousand pieces. I had the good fortune to get upon a piece of the wreck with three more officers, viz., Lieut. Henley, Lieut. Sterling, Dr. Stafford, and two soldiers (all of the Maryland Loyalists) and floated on it two days and two nights up to near our waists in water, during which time Lieut. Sterling and one of the soldiers died. On the third day we drifted to an island where we lived without fire, water, victuals or clothing, except the remnants of what we had on, about one quart of water per man (which we sipped from the cavities in the rocks) and a few raspberries and snails. On the seventh day we were espied and taken up by a Frenchman, that was out a fowling, who took us to his house and treated us with every kindness. We staid with him six days and then proceeded to a place called Cape Pursue, where we met with Captain Kennedy and about fifty of both regiments, who were saved at sea by some fishing boats, about 36 hours from the time the vessel was wrecked. Capt. Doughty, Lieut. McFarlane, Mrs. McFarlane and Ensign Montgomery perished."

The fleet which carried the Loyalist Regiments to St. John arrived on the 27th of September and three days later the troops disembarked and encamped above the Falls near the Indian House from whence Col. Hewlett intended they should proceed with all possible expedition up the river. The season was already far advanced and there was no time to lose, but Hewlett in his first letter to Sir Guy Carleton expresses his fear that the want of small craft will greatly delay their progress. He writes again on the 13th of October to inform Sir Guy that the troops had been disbanded by Major Prevost and were getting up the river as fast as the scarcity of small craft for conveying them would admit.

A very serious situation now arose. Lands had been reserved for the Provincial troops, but no proper survey had been made and officers and men alike were in a state of perplexity. We get a glimpse of the situation in the following passage in one of Edward Winslow's letters to Ward Chipman.

"I saw all those Provincial Regiments, which we have so frequently mustered, landing in this inhospitable climate, in the month of October, without shelter and without knowing where to find a place to reside. The chagrin of the officers was not to me so truly affecting as the poignant distress of the men. Those respectable sergeants of Robinson's, Ludlow's, Cruger's, Fanning's — once hospitable yeoman of the Country addressed me in language which almost murdered me as I heard it.

"Sir, we have served all the war, your honor is witness how faithfully. We were promised land; we expected you had obtained it for us. We like the country only let us have a spot to call our own."

A plan of the river had been prepared by the Surveyor General of Nova Scotia in which the blocks of land reserved appear. These were numbered and drawn for by the various regiments soon after their arrival, but the lines had not been run, nor were the lots laid out for individual settlers.

The general location of the tracts marked out for the regiments was as follows:

>Maryland Loyalists, in the Parish of St. Marys.
>New Jersey Volunteers, in the Parish of Kingsclear.
>New York Volunteers, on the Keswick Stream.
>Royal Guides and Pioneers, Bright and Queensbury.
>King's American Dragoons, Parish of Prince William.
>Queen's Rangers, in the Parish of Queensbury.
>King's American Regiment, Parish of Canterbury.
>Pennsylvania Loyalists, Parish of Southampton.
>De Lancey's 1st Battalion, Parish of Woodstock.
>De Lancey's 2nd Battalion, Parish of Northampton.

Still farther up the river were the blocks drawn by Arnold's American Legion, the Prince of Wales American Regiment, the 3d New Jersey Volunteers, the Loyal American Regiment and the 1st New Jersey Volunteers. These corps considered their lands too remote to make any attempt to settle them. The northern limit of the locations seems to have been near the Tobique and Aroostook rivers.

The season was so far advanced when the troops arrived at Parr-town that the difficulty of transport, combined with uncertainty as to location, led many of the disbanded soldiers to pass the winter at the mouth of the river. Rev. John Sayre, speaks of a vast multitude at St. John whom he found unsettled, many of them unsheltered and on the brink of despair on account of the delay in alloting their lands to them. Meanwhile Parr-town had been laid out by Paul Bedell, the deputy surveyor, and many of the disbanded officers and men drew town lots in the "Lower Cove" district, upon which they spent the winter. A careful examination of the list of the grantees of Parrtown will show that the lots as drawn by the officers and soldiers of the different regiments fall into groups. . . .

The disbanded soldiers who drew lots at Parrtown [sic] spent their first winter in rude huts, some of them in canvas tents on the Barrack square. They thatched the tents with spruce boughs, brought in boats from Partridge Island, and banked them with snow. Owing to the cold weather and the coarseness of the provisions, salt meat, etc., the women and children suffered severely; and numbers died. They were buried in the old graveyard near the present deep water terminus of the Intercolonial railway.

The last of the transports from New York arrived in December and in addition to her passengers, mostly women and children, brought a supply of clothing and provisions. The officer in charge was Lieut. John Ward of the Loyal American Regiment. . . . There was not time to build even a hut, Mr. Ward was obliged to spend his first winter under canvas and his son, John Ward, jr. [sic], was born in a tent on the Barrack square in the month of December.

A good many men of the 3d New Jersey Volunteers and of the King's American Regiment pushed up the river to St. Anne's, where they passed a calamitous winter in huts or tents. Others found shelter in the houses of the "old inhabitants" at various places along the river. (pp. 531-547)

Doreen Menzies Arbuckle notes in *The North West Miramichi*:

The year 1783 saw the arrival of 3,000 United Empire Loyalists at Saint John. At this time the western half of the New Brunswick area was the Nova Scotia county of Sunbury, while the eastern half comprised part of Cumberland County.

Due to this sudden increase of population, and the remoteness of the government at Halifax, a new province was formed north of the Isthmus of Chignecto on August 16, 1784. Consideration was given to naming it "New Ireland," a companion to Nova Scotia (New Scotland), but because of friendly relations with Germany and the House of Brunswick at the time, the British government chose the name "New Brunswick." Some two years later, on October 23, 1786, Governor Thomas Carleton moved the seat of government from Saint John to Fredericton. (p. 18)

The following comes from Rev. William O. Raymond LL.D., F.R.S.C.: "Peter Fisher, the First Historian of New Brunswick" contained in *Collections of the New Brunswick Historical Society No. 10*:

> The New Jersey Volunteers never numbered more than 1,500, of all ranks. They, however, rendered essential service in New Jersey and in the defence of Staten Island. One of the battalions under Lieut.-Col. Isaac Allen, was conspicuous for its gallantry in the campaigns in Georgia and South Carolina. At the close of the war the original six battalions had been consolidated into three, under command of Lieut.-Col. Stephen deLancey, Lieut.-Col. Isaac Allen and Lieut.-Col. Abraham Van Buskirk.
>
> The war may be said to have ended with the surrender of the army under Lord Cornwallis, at Yorktown, on October 19, 1781, and little attempt at recruiting was made subsequently; consequently the regiments continued to dwindle until, at the evacuation of New-York, two years later, they were not more than one-third of their original strength. The New Jersey Volunteers, a year after their arrival in New-Brunswick, were mustered by Thomas Knox, under the supervision of Col. Edward Winslow. The return is dated at Fort Howe, September 25, 1784, and the number of those then on their lands, and for whom the Royal bounty of provisions was furnished, was as follows: —

The accompanying graph shows that the 1st New Jersey Volunteers had 158 men, 57 women, 57 children over ten, 39 children under ten and 9 servants, for a total of 320; the 2nd New Jersey Volunteers had 132 men, 45 women, 44 children over ten, 38 children under ten and 14 servants for a total of 273; the 3rd New Jersey Volunteers had 173 men, 64 women, 47 children over ten, 42 children under ten and 6 servants, for a total of 332. The total from all three was 463 men, 166 women, 148 children over ten, 119 children under ten and 29 servants for a grand total of 925.

Raymond:

> The commander of the 3rd Battalion, Lieut.-Col. VanBuskirk, did not come with his men to the River St. John but settled in Shelburne, where he was the first mayor of the town. The troops for St. John sailed in charge of Lieut.-Col. Richard Hewlett as senior officer, with Lieut.-Col. Gabriel DeVeber second in command. They left New-York on September 15, 1783, and arrived safely in St. John harbour on the 26th, with the exception of the transports "Martha" and "Esther." The former was wrecked near Yarmouth and more than half of her passengers were lost. The "Esther," in which VanBuskirk's battalion had embarked, got off her course in the fog and narrowly escaped destruction, arriving a day or two behind her sister ships. (pp. 9-10)

Rev. William O. Raymond (*The River St. John*):

> Among those who came to Portland Point with [James] Simonds and [James] White in 1764, none was destined to play a more active and useful part than Jonathan Leavitt. He was a native of New Hampshire and at the time of his arrival was in his eighteenth year. Young as he was he had some experience as a mariner, and from 1764 to 1774 was employed as master of some one or other of the [Hazen, Simonds and White] Company's vessels. . . . In the course of time Mr. Leavitt came to be one of the most trusted navigators of the Bay of Fundy and probably none knew the harbor of St. John so well as he. In his testimony in a law suit, about the year 1792, he states that in early times the places of anchorage in the harbor were the flats on the west side, between Fort Frederick and Sand Point, which was generally used by strangers, and Portland Point where the vessels of the Company lay. It was not until 1783 that vessels began to anchor at the Upper Cove (now the Market Slip) that place being until then deemed rather unsafe. Jonathan Leavitt and his brother Daniel piloted to their landing places the transport ships that carried some thousands of Loyalists to our shores during the year 1783. (pp. 297–298)

Going back to "Peter Fisher, the First Historian of New Brunswick" (*Collections of the New Brunswick Historical Society No. 10*) Raymond, after giving some particulars on Peter Fisher, continues:

> Sir Guy Carleton's orders were that the several corps should proceed at once to the places allotted for their settlement, directions having been given to Captain John Colville, assistant agent of all small craft at the St. John River, to afford every assistance in his power to the corps in getting to their destinations. Three days after their arrival the troops disembarked and encamped above the Falls, near the Indian House. Hewlett wrote Sir Guy Carleton that he feared the want of small craft would greatly delay their progress. He writes again on the 13th October, 1783, that the troops had been disbanded and were getting up the river as fast as the scarcity of small craft for conveying them would admit.
>
> I shall pause here to relate an incident, which will indicate the source from which Peter Fisher derived the information he gives us concerning the arrival of the Loyalists at St. Ann's and their subsequent hardships.
>
> About twenty-five years ago [This piece was published in 1919.] William, the youngest son of Peter Fisher, read to me in his apartments in the old Park Hotel, in St. John, a manuscript which contained the recollections of one of his sisters of her various conversations with her old

grandmother, Mary Fisher, concerning the coming to New-Brunswick and the subsequent experience of her family at St. Ann's. Mr. Fisher did not entrust the manuscript to my hands but allowed me to make full notes, and afterwards at my request re-read the whole, in order that I might make sure of my facts. The story which now follows is, of course, not quoted from the lips of the first narrator, but is based upon the notes made by her granddaughter in which are embodied the recollections of the conversations she had with her grandmother. [Esther Clark Wright in her *Loyalists of New Brunswick* notes that the grandmother in the following was "Mrs. Lewis Fisher, wife of a private in the 3rd New Jersey Volunteers...." (p. 87)] [It should be noted that Luke Kelly was on board the *Esther*.]

THE GRANDMOTHER'S STORY.

We sailed from New-York in the ship "Esther" with the fleet for Nova-Scotia. Some of our ships were bound for Halifax, some for Shelburne and some for St. John's river. Our ship going the wrong track was nearly lost. When we got to St. John we found the place all in confusion; some were living in log houses, some building huts, and many of the soldiers living in their tents at the Lower Cove. Soon after we landed we joined a party bound up the river in a schooner to St. Ann's. It was eight days before we got to Oromocto. There the Captain put us ashore being unwilling on account of the lateness of the season, or for some other reason, to go further. He charged us each four dollars for the passage. We spent the night on shore and the next day the women and children proceeded in Indian canoes to St. Ann's with some of the party; the rest came on foot.

We reached our destination on the 8th day of October, tired out with our long journey, and pitched our tents at the place now called Salamanca, near the shore. The next day we explored for a place to encamp, for the winter was near and we had no time to lose.

The season was wet and cold, and we were much discouraged at the gloomy prospect before us. Those who had arrived a little earlier had made better preparations for the winter; some had built small log huts. This we could not do because of the lateness of our arrival. Snow fell on the 2nd day of November to the depth of six inches. We pitched our tents in the shelter of the woods and tried to cover them with spruce boughs. We used stones for fireplaces. Our tent had no floor but the ground. The winter was very cold, with deep snow, which we tried to keep from drifting in by putting a large rug at the door. The snow, which lay six feet around us, helped greatly in keeping out the cold. How we lived through that awful winter I hardly know. There were mothers, that had been reared in a pleasant country enjoying all the comforts of life, with helpless children in their arms. They clasped their infants to their bosoms and tried by the warmth of their own bodies to protect them from the bitter cold. Sometimes a part of the family had to remain up during the night to keep the fires burning, so as to keep the rest from freezing. Some destitute people made use of boards, which the older ones kept heating before the fire and applied by turns to the smaller children to keep them warm.

Many women and children, and some of the men, died from cold and exposure. Graves were dug with axes and shovels near the spot where our party had landed, and there in stormy winter weather our loved ones were buried. We had no minister, so we had to bury them without any religious service, besides our own prayers. The first burial ground continued to be used for some years until it was nearly filled. We called it "The Loyalist Provincials Burial Ground." (pp. 10-12)

Peter Fisher writes the following in the introduction to his *Notitia of New Brunswick*:

Up the River Saint John, the country appeared better; and a few cultivated spots were found occupied by old settlers. At St. Ann's, where Fredericton was afterwards built, a few scattered huts of French, &c. were found — the country all around being a continued wilderness; and hardly had these wretched outcasts of their country, pitched their tents in the cold month of October, than they were enveloped in snow; nearly two feet having fallen the first night of their encampment. Nor did their difficulties end the first year: Frequently. [sic] had these settlers to go with hand-sleds or toboggans, through the woods or on the ice, from 50 to 100 miles to procure a scanty supply for their famishing families. (p. X)

Raymond, returning to "Peter Fisher, the First Historian of New Brunswick":

The site of this old grave-yard, is on the Ketchum place at Salamanca, just below Fredericton, near the shore. Some rude headstones may perhaps yet be found there. The late Adolphus G. Beckwith told me that he remembered when a boy to have seen a number of pine "head-boards," much decayed, but still standing in this old cemetery. The painted epitaphs, or inscriptions, were in some cases fairly well preserved. He remembered, he said, that many of the names seemed to be German (or Dutch), a statement which I hardly credited at the time, but which is entirely in harmony with the old grandmother's story. Continuing her narrative, she says:

> Among those who came with us to St. Ann's, or who were there when we arrived were Messrs. Swim, Burkstaff, McComesky, three named Ridner, Wooley, Bass, Paine, Ryerse, Acker, Lownsberry, Ingraham, Buchanan, Ackerman, Donley, Vanderbeck, Smith, Essington and some few others.

Here again the grandmother's story is confirmed by the Muster Rolls of the New Jersey Volunteers, lately placed by our Historical Society in the Dominion Archives at Ottawa for safe-keeping. Nearly all the names she mentions are to be found there. In Captain Waldron Blaan's Company, we find John Swim, Vincent Swim, Moses McComesky, David Burkstaff, Frederick Burkstaff. In Col. VanBuskirk's Company we find Abraham Vanderbeck, Conrad Ridner, Abraham Ackerman, Morris Ackerman and Marmaduke Ackerman. In Captain Edward Earle's Company, Lodewick Fisher, Peter Ridnor and Peter Smith. In Captain Samuel Ryerson's Company, Samuel Buchanan. In Captain Jacob Buskirk's Company, James Ackerman.

Benjamin Ingraham, mentioned above, was a sergeant in the King's American Regiment; he served in the Carolinas, where he nearly died of yellow fever, and was severely wounded in the battle of Camden. He arrived at St. Ann's in a row-boat in October, 1783, and built a small log house in the woods into which he moved on the 6th of November, at which time there was six inches of snow on the ground.

The story now continues:

> When the Loyalists arrived there were only three houses standing on the old St. Ann's plain. Two of them were old frame houses, the other a log house (which stood near the old Fisher place). There were said to have been two bodies

of people murdered here. It could not have been long before the arrival of the Loyalists that this happened.

Many of the Loyalists who came in the spring had gone further up the river, but they were little better off for provisions than we were at St. Ann's. Supplies expected before the close of navigation did not come, and at one time starvation stared us in the face. It was a dreary contrast to our former conditions. Some of our men had to go down the river with hand-sleds or toboggans to get food for their famishing families. A full supply of provisions was looked for in the Spring, but the people were betrayed by those they depended upon to supply them. All the settlers were reduced to great straits and had to live after the Indian fashion. A party of Loyalists who came before us late in the spring, had gone up the river further, but they were no better off than those at St. Ann's. The men caught fish and hunted moose when they could. In the spring we made maple sugar. We ate fiddle heads, grapes and even the leaves of trees to allay the pangs of hunger. On one occasion some poisonous weeds were eaten along with the fiddle heads; one or two died, and Dr. Earle had all he could do to save my life.

As soon as the snow was off the ground we began to build log houses, but were obliged to desist for want of food. Your grandfather went up the river to Captain McKay's for provisions, and found no one at home but an old colored slave woman, who said her master and his man had gone out to see if they could obtain some potatoes or meal, having in the house only half a box of biscuits. Some of the people at St. Ann's, who had planted a few potatoes, were obliged to dig them up and eat them.

Again a few comments will show the reliability of the old lady's narrative. The three houses she mentions on the site of Fredericton were those of Benjamin Atherton, built about 1767 at the upper end of the town, near the site of the old Government House; Philip Weade's, which stood on the river bank in front of the Cathedral, and Olivier Thibodeau's, an Acadian, whose log house was at the lower end of town. The tradition regarding the massacre of some of the first settlers at St. Ann's refers doubtless to the destruction of the French settlement there by McCurdy's New England Rangers in February, 1759, as is described at page 242 in Dr. Raymond's "St. John River History." The party of Loyalists, who had gone further up the river in the late Spring of 1783, were the King's American Dragoons, who settled in Prince William. Resuming once more the narrative, the grandmother says:

> In our distress we were gladdened by the discovery of some large patches of pure white beans, marked with a black cross. They had probably been originally planted by the French, but were now growing wild. In our joy at the discovery we called them at first the "Royal Provincials' bread," but afterwards "The staff of life and hope of the starving." I planted some of these beans with my own hands, and the seed was preserved in our family for many years. There was great rejoicing when the first schooner arrived with corn-meal and rye. In those days the best passages up and down the river took from three to five days. Sometimes the schooners were a week or ten days on the way. It was not during the first year alone that we suffered from want of food, other years were nearly as bad.
>
> The first summer after our arrival all hands united in building their log houses. Dr. Earle's was the first that was finished. Our people had but few tools and those of the rudest sort. They had neither bricks or lime, and chimneys and fireplaces were built of stone laid in yellow clay. They covered the roofs of the houses with bark bound over with small poles. The windows had only four small panes of glass.
>
> The first store was kept by a man named Cairns, who lived in an old house on the bank of the river near the gate of the first Church built in Fredericton [in front of the present Cathedral] [*sic*]. He used to sell fish at one penny each and butternuts at two for a penny. He also sold tea at $2.00 per lb. which was to us a great boon. We greatly missed our tea. Sometimes we used an article called Labrador, and sometimes steeped spruce or hemlock bark for drinking, but I despised it.
>
> There were no domestic animals in our settlement at first except one black and white cat, which was a great pet. Some wicked fellows, who came from the States, killed, roasted and ate the cat, to our great indignation. A man named Conley owned the first cow. Poor Conley afterwards hanged himself, the reason for which was never known.

For years there were no teams, and our people had to work hard to get their provisions. Potatoes were planted among the black stumps and turned out well. Pigeons used to come in great numbers and were shot or caught by the score in nets. We found in their crops some small round beans, which we planted; they grew very well and made excellent green beans, which we ate during the summer. In the winter time our people had sometimes to haul their provisions by hand fifty or a hundred miles over the ice or through the woods. In summer they came in slow sailing vessels. On one occasion Dr. Earle and others went up the river to Canada on snowshoes with hand sleds, returning with bags of flour and biscuits. It was a hard and dangerous journey, and they were gone a long time.

For several years we lived in dread of the Indians, who were sometimes very bold. I have heard that the Indians from Canada once tried to murder the people on the St. John River. Coming down the river they captured an Indian woman of the St. John tribe, and the chief said they would spare her if she would be their guide. They had eleven canoes in all, and they were tied together and the canoe of the guide attached to the hindermost. As they drew near the Grand Falls, most of the party were asleep; and the rest were deceived by the woman, who told them that the roaring they heard was caused by a fall at the mouth of the stream which here joined the main river. At the critical moment the Indian woman cut the cord which fastened her canoe to the others and escaped to the shore, while the Canada Indians went over the fall and were lost.*

* It is of interest to know that this legend was told by the Indians to the English settlers shortly after their arrival. The name of the Indian heroine is given as Malobianah, or Malabeam.

In the early days of the settlement at St. Ann's, some fellows that had come from the States used to disturb the other settlers. They procured liquor at Vanhorne's tavern and drank heavily. They lived in a log cabin which soon became a resort for bad characters. They formed a plot to go up the river and plunder the settlers — provisions being their chief object. They agreed that if any of their party were killed in the expedition they should prevent discovery of their

> identity by putting him into a hole cut in the ice. While they were endeavoring to effect an entrance into a settler's house, a shot, fired out of a window, wounded a young man in the leg. The others then desisted from their attempt, but cut a hole in the ice and thrust the poor fellow in, who had been shot, although he begged to be allowed to die in the woods, and promised, if found alive not to betray them, but they would not trust him.

Here the story of the old grandmother comes abruptly to an end. (pp. 12-16)

According to Rev. William O. Raymond in *The River St. John,* "The last of the transports from New York arrived in December....

"A good many men of the 3d New Jersey Volunteers and of the King's American Regiment pushed up the river to St. Anne's...." (pp. 546-547)

According to material posted byTodd Braisted at *The On-Line Institute for Advanced Loyalist Studies* under "Return of Officers and Men of the Second Battalion New Jersey Volunteers Going to Annapolis Royal in Nova Scotia in the Brig Ranger James Phillips Master to be Furnished with Provisions for the Passage" Lieutenant-Colonel Allen is accompanied by a private Kelly on the Ranger. Baisted cites *Great Britain Public Records Office, War Office, Class 60, Volume 43, part 1.*

A letter dated 7 August 1783 from Lt. Col. Isaac Allen to Edward Winslow posted on the *Ancestors New Brunswick Genealogy Research* site establishes that Allen was in Wilmot, Nova Scotia, on that date. Allen writes "I expect to sail for [New] [*sic*] York in a few days...."

David Graham Bell in *Early Loyalist Saint John: The Origin of New Brunswick Politics, 1783-1786* notes in the accompanying table "Loyalists evacuated from New York to New Brunswick," accessible at (www.uelac.org/Loyalist-Ships/Fleets-NY-NB.pdf), that the Ranger arrived at Parrtown (Saint John) on 27 September 1783 from New York with 217 members of the Third New York Volunteers on board.

In addition to all the other hardships endured by the early settlers of New Brunswick, the abundance of black flies and other such insects were a constant scourge. George William Featherstonhaugh (1780 – 1866) kept a journal while he was appointed commissioner for the British in their attempt to establish the border between the State of Maine and New Brunswick in 1839. Featherstonhaugh's journal appears in *In Search of the Highlands: Mapping the Canada-Maine Boundary, 1839* as edited by Alec McEwen. On 30 August 1839, Featherstonhaugh writes:

> I have suffered excessively from the black flies today; my face and neck are stung in every part, and so inflamed and swollen that I am feverish and nervous. These insects are so numerous that it is impossible to make

an observation. If you stop for an instant to look at the compass they rush into your ears, eyes and nostrils, drawing blood at ever stroke; every puncture produces an inflamed tubercle, a constant source of itching and irritation. My face presents the appearance of a person just recovering from the smallpox. The country people say they cannot live in the woods themselves when they abound as they do in this wet season. How we shall endure this torment I cannot imagine. I am afraid we shall break down under it unless a severe frost soon occurs to check these most horrible insects. (p. 27)

Abraham Gesner, Esq. includes the following in a footnote to his *New Brunswick with Notes for Emigrants*: "The black flies and mosquitoes, so numerous in the woods, cease to sting when the thermometer is at 95, and also when the mercury descends to 55. — 75 may be called the best biting point of those insects." (p. 79)

Below, I have noted things that would have been a topic of conversation and have had a direct effect on the daily lives of our ancestors.

Citing the 5 September 1835 edition of the *Courier*, W.S. MacNutt writes, in his *New Brunswick A History: 1784-1867*, "While travelling through Westmorland in August 1835 [Sir Archibald Campbell] was arrested, charged with breaking the law against travelling on Sunday, and fined £6. . . ." (p. 243)

Another reminder of the times is this from Doreen Menzies Arbuckle's *The North West Miramichi*: "Matches were invented in 1827, and the safety type in 1855. Before they were in common use, if the household fire went out, someone had to go to a neighbour's and bring back lighted coals or a candle." (p. 27)

In his *Notitia of New Brunswick*, Peter Fisher writes the following:

When the Loyalists came to this country in 1783, snow was seen on the coasts in June, and the winters for a number of consecutive years were excessively cold, and the snow very deep. The summers being likewise very warm and dry, insomuch that Indian Corn or Maize, a plant that requires much heat flourished in great perfection for a number of years, and was the staple grain then cultivated. This was succeeded by a period of which the winters proved milder, and were broken with frequent thaws — the summers abating their warmth, with crops being less abundant: for it always followed as a matter of course, that a mild winter was succeeded by a cool summer: and although snow was seldom seen in June, still it was not uncommon early in May, or late in April, in what were called late seasons. Some years again it would be earlier, and sowing would be considerably advanced in dry weather by the latter part of April. From these data we find seasons were formerly as variable as they have been of late; but to pursue these observations a little further. It must be fresh in the recollection of the inhabitants of this Province, that in 1816, there was

> a fall of snow with very cold weather on the 7th of June — that a cold rigorous air was felt during the whole of that summer, which the sun when shining in meridian splendour could not subdue. Frosts were frequent in every month of that year — crops were blighted — even the never-failing potatoe was chilled and did not yield half its usual increase. A succession of lean years followed, each improving till 1822, which was an extraordinary fruitful year. (p. 20)

Scientists now suggest that "the year without a summer," as 1816 came to be known, was caused from a number of factors, including the eruption of Mount Tambora in the Dutch East Indies in 1815, which sent a cloud of ash into the atmosphere. This cloud moved across the northern hemisphere in the summer of 1816, blocking out the sun.

Fisher:

> The year 1825 will be long remembered on account of its destructive fires — a drought commenced about the middle of July in that year, and continued with little abatement till the middle of October, which converted the whole country into a state of combustion; in consequence of which, fires burst out simultaneously in different parts of the Province on the 7th of that ill-fated month — and swept off several flourishing settlements, and destroyed property to a great amount, as well as human life. A succession of years followed in which the rust prevailed, as some supposed from the sluggish state of the atmosphere and sudden burst of scorching sun, just as the wheat was filling in ear. The year 1831 was an uncommon fine year in every sense of the word: crops were abundant — fruits excellent — nature indeed this year appeared inclined to shew to man how easy it was to clothe the fields in abundance for man and beast. The year 1832 was a lean year, remarkable for a humid atmosphere. Scarce a day passed in the summer season without dampness; even when the day commenced bright and the sun shone unobscured, it was deficient of its usual lustre, and murkiness could be seen gathering, which usually covered it before evening. The cholera prevailed this year in the United States and Canada. Since 1832, the seasons have been unfavorable for agriculture: August, particularly, which was formerly a sultry month, appears to have lost its heat, and of late years has become cool and frosty, which, indeed, is the main cause of the lean seasons — the latter heat being wanting — whereby vegetation has been checked, and the hopes of the husbandman crushed. — The winter of 1835-6 was excessively cold. In the summer of 1836, we had two severe droughts; the first commenced about the 10th of June, and continued till the middle of July, reducing the country to a fearful state of combustion — providentially, however, rains fell, and averted the much-dreaded result; the second drought

commenced in August, and nearly destroyed the pastures throughout the country. (p. 20-21)

Again, in *Notitia of New Brunswick*, Peter Fisher notes:

A singular phenomenon was exhibited by the aurora borealis in this country on the 7th of November, 1835, about 6 o'clock, P.M. The horizon, which had been loaded with light vapours, was suddenly covered with the aurora borealis, which rapidly changed from a natural white to a bright vermillion, and then to a deep red, intermixed with pale blue and green. It first appeared in the N.E. veering to the South — it then shifted to the zenith, forming arches, which diverged to every point of the horizon; its duration was about three and a half minutes, when it settled away to the westward, and finally disappeared in that quarter. It appeared again, still more brilliant, of a red colour, about daybreak the next morning. Another phenomenon similar to this occurred on the 25th of January, 1836, about eight o'clock in the evening, when the sky became of a deep scarlet colour, which continued changing to crimson, blue and yellow for nearly an hour.

There has been but one shock of an earthquake experienced since the settlement of the county; this shock took place on the 22d of May, 1827, at twenty-five minutes past three o'clock in the morning; the duration of the vibration was about forty-five seconds; it was attended with the usual rumbling noise without thunder; the weather being very serene and pleasant. (pp. 23-24)

Fisher continues:

As Fredericton from its low situation appears to be liable to inundation from high freshets in the Spring, and as there is an old tradition that the plain on which the town stands was swept by a great ice freshet a few years before the loyalists came to the country — it may be interesting to future generations to state that a partial inundation took place on the 11th of April, 1831, occasioned by an ice jamb below Mill Creek, by which all the lower part of the town and the front street was laid under water, which came up above the Baptist Chapel in King-street, leaving but a small part of the buildings dry in the front and lower streets. A small park on the margin of the river was denuded of its railings; — no serious damage, however, was sustained. The town from the adjoining heights appeared like a low island, with the buildings partly submerged, and the river in front piled with threatening masses of ice. The jamb broke while the water was rapidly gaining on the town, and in a few hours the river resumed its usual current. (p. 75)

The following appears in Thomas R. Millman and A.R. Kelley's *Atlantic Canada to 1900 a History of the Anglican Church*:

Higher up the river a settlement was formed in the winter of 1783 on the site of the old French village of St. Anne. Three years later, when the population was four hundred, the place was named Fredericton and made the capital of the province. The parish was incorporated under the name of St. Anne and received as its rector Samuel Cooke, who had served previously for a short time at Saint John. . . . In 1790 Cooke was appointed commissary for New Brunswick by Bishop Inglis. . . . In the nine years he spent as rector of St. Anne's parish, by force of example, he earned the title of Father of the Church in New Brunswick. Services were held at first in a store and then in a church built in 1790 with aid from both the imperial and provincial governments. (p. 41)

The following is from Rev. G. Herbert Lee's *An Historical Sketch of the First Fifty Years of the Church of England in New Brunswick*:

Dr. Cooke . . . received his education at the University of Cambridge, England, and after being admitted to Holy Orders, was sent out to New Jersey, U. S., by the S.P.G. [Society for the Propagation of the Gospel], in or about the year 1749. In 1774 he went to England on business and did not return to the United States. In 1785 he was appointed Missionary to New Brunswick. On 18th August of that year he landed at Halifax, N. S., where he received a hearty welcome from Governor Parr. Living in a time when there were no railways and steamboats, Mr. Cooke was obliged to come to St. John, N. B., by a circuitous route. To get there he travelled 200 miles in a fortnight, landing on 2nd September, 1785. (p. 33)

After writing about Dr. Cooke's ministry in Saint John and ministering to outlying communities, Lee relates that

Owing to the seat of Government being changed from St. John to Fredericton, Mr. Cooke removed to the latter place in 1786. To use his own words, he left "happy in the reflection that his unremitted" endeavors to establish the Church at St. John had been so far effectual that he left his successor in possession of a decent, well-furnished Church, with a very respectable and well-behaved congregation." During his period of labour in St. John, St. Andrews and elsewhere, he baptized 153 persons, (13 of whom were negroes.) Mr. Cooke arrived at Fredericton in August, 1786, and preached the first Sunday after his arrival to 60 or 70 persons in The King's Provision Store, the only place in which a congregation could he accommodated; but being afterwards glazed and fitted up with benches, a few pews, a reading desk and a couple of stoves, was thus rendered more commodious and comfortable. The King's Provision Store stood nearly opposite the Old Central Bank building on Queen Street, Fredericton. This "Store" was in early times used for almost everything. Here were many balls and dancing parties; here music was given by drum and fife; and here Mr. Cooke, Fredericton's first Rector, preached. It appears that in October, 1786, the first Church Wardens and Vestry were appointed. (pp. 36-37)

After listing the first church wardens and vestrymen, Lee continues

Fredericton was at this time very small, and the people for the most part very poor. The congregation seldom exceeded 100 persons. On Christmas Day, 1786, Mr. Cooke had only 14 Communicants. Before the conclusion of the year he had baptized 23 white, 3 black infants, and one adult; married 5 couple, and buried one person. In 1787 the Imperial Parliament made a grant of £2,000 for the purpose of building Churches in New Brunswick, a share of which was allotted to Fredericton. Mr. Cooke accordingly set about the erection of a church; £500 being given towards that object by Government, and over £150 by Governor Carleton. Little was contributed by the people as they were "very indigent." Owing to this and other causes the church was not completed until 1790. In addition to his money donation, Governor Carleton furnished the Church in a handsome manner. Mr. Cooke, who resided near the Nashwaak, opposite Fredericton, describes Fredericton as being in length upon the river about 6 miles and in breadth back into the woods about 3. Number of inhabitants (1790) 400; 100 of whom attended Church. This number did not include the officers and soldiers of the 54th Rgt., who were most regular and constant in their attendance. In 1788 Mr. Cooke baptized a family, a man and his wife and their 2 children; also another family of 7 children whose parents were formerly Presbyterians; besides these, 28 white children, 2 black adults and one black infant. He married 9 couple and buried only one person, an Officer of the 54th Regt. During this year Mr. Cooke visited St. John upon the death of Mr. Bissett, administered the Sacrament to about 40 persons, and baptized 9 children. In 1789, 31 white and 2 black children and one black adult were baptized; 13 persons married and 4 buried. In the year 1790 Mr. Cooke was appointed Ecclesiastical Commissary to the Bishop of Nova Scotia, and visited

Nashwaak twice, where he performed several baptisms. In 1791 he instituted Mr. Price of Newfoundland to the Parish of St. Mary's, Nashwaak, the largest in the County, extending 12 miles in front upon the river St. John and running back into the country upwards of 20. It was divided into four districts — one on the river Nashwaak, another on the Penneyock, a third on the river Nashwaaksis (Little Nashwaak), and the fourth on the river Madamekeswick. In 1790 Mr. Cooke, acting on behalf of the Bishop of Nova Scotia, summoned the clergy of the Province to Fredericton, and received reports from the various missions. All attended except Dr. Byles, who was ill. The meeting was highly satisfactory, it being found that the clergy were diligent and the missions in a nourishing state. In September, 1794, Dr. Cooke called them together for the second time, and reported to the S. P. G. "the respectability and regularity of all their missionaries in the Province." But the time was now approaching when this indefatigable and faithful missionary was to be removed from the scene of his labor. His death took place in the following manner. He had been making some parochial visits in Fredericton, and was returning to his home on the opposite side of the river with his son in a bark canoe. The night of Saturday, May 23rd, 1795, was dark and windy; a sudden squall upset the canoe and both father and son were drowned, in spite of the manly efforts of the latter to save his aged parent. Bishop Inglis, in writing to the S. P. G., said: — "Never was a minister of the Gospel more beloved and esteemed or more universally lamented in his death. All the respectable people, not only of his parish but of the neighboring country, went into deep mourning on this melancholy occasion." (pp. 38-41)

Rev. G Herbert Lee writes, "The following lines in memory of Mr. Cooke and his son may be seen in St. Ann's (Christ) Church, Fredericton, N. B.: — "

Sacred
to the memory of the
REV. SAMUEL COOKE, D. D.,
the first Rector of this Church,
and first Ecclesiastical Commissary of the Province,
who, in crossing the river St. John,
to his own home,
from attending the duties of his office at Fredericton,
was unfortunately drowned,
on the 23rd day of May, MDCCXCV, in the 72nd year of
his age.
His philanthropy and those virtues which had secured

to him universal esteem, respect and affection
through life
occasioned his death to be as generally and sincerely
lamented.
Erected as an affectionate tribute of esteem
by
The Wardens and Vestry of this Church.
A Tribute
to the filial affection and distinguished fortitude of
MR. MICHAEL COOKE,
son of the Rev. Samuel. Cooke, D.D., Rector of this Church,
who in his manly efforts and persevering struggles
to preserve the life of his Venerable Parent
in the moment of drowning
added to the public calamity by the loss of his own,
in the full vigor of health,
and 31st year of his age.
In him perished an example as worthy of
imitation in the various pursuits and conduct
of his life,
as in the virtuous sensibility and heroic piety
with which it closed.
MDCCXCV (1795.) (pp. 41-42)

JOHN KELLY

John Kelly (ca 1760 – between 4 September 1824 and 29 October 1825) married 1st: Unknown Unknown; 2nd: Mary Unknown (ca 1762 or ca 1772 - ca 1845). Mary Unknown's dates are calculated from her 1839 and 1843 pension petitions contained in *Records of Old Revolutionary Soldiers and Their Widows.*

We have not been able to find primary sources for the wife/wives of John Kelly. Family lore suggests that John was married twice. If there was a first wife, no one has established her name or anything about her history. An inquiry for more Kelly information placed in *"Loyalist Trails" 2012-15 April 15, 2012* was addressed by Genealogist Richard Ripley, who states in an email of 16 April 2012: "I don't have a high quality marriage record for John and Mary. I have it that they were married 1790 in St. John, where her parents resided. I was sent this information a few years ago when I was working on the Kean family for another project, but, then, the client dropped away and sources were never provided. I keep many such fragments in my archives." Richard Ripley suggests that Mary (Unknown) Kelly was the daughter of Adjutant William and Ann (Unknown) Kean. Mary (Unknown) Kelly died in New Brunswick.

After numerous hours of further research and transcription of land grant petitions, land grants and deeds for William Kean and his wife, I cannot establish any connection between William Kean and Mary (Unknown) Kelly. The 1820 will of Ann Kean, in which she leaves everything to her sister, makes no mention of Mary (Unknown) Kelly. (See Appendix V.)

In a genealogical sketch of the Kelly family by Ella Rita (Kelly) Boulter in the possession of her daughter, Jeannie Belinda (Boulter) Matthews, Ella Rita (Kelly) Boulter writes: "John Kelly Loyalist 2nd New Jersey Volunteers settled on grant at Kellys Creek in Kingsclear. Had brother Luke, who settled at Kingsclear, also. John Kelly married Mary Caine or Kain."

It appears that Mary (Unknown) Kelly is not the daughter of Adjunct William Kean. I had come to the conculsion that Mary (Unknown) Kelly was, instead, the daughter of "William Cain," who, on 15 July 1788, attempts, in a land grant petition in York County, to help his young son John retain his land grant. (See Appendix V.) But, in an email of 9 February 2015 from Floretta (Wade) Steeves in regard to a reply I had sent her in response to a query posted in *"Loyalist Trails" UELAC Newsletter 2015-06 Feb 8, 2015*, Floretta (Wade) Steeves states, "William Cain would be my 5th g[reat] grandfather . . .[, and,] according to my information[,] his daughter Mary Eva Cain[,] born about 1768[,] married Loyalist John Pond[,] my 4th great grandfather, who settled on the Nashwaak as well."

There was a strong Irish element in Colonial North America, and anyone speaking with an Irish brogue would pronounce "Kean" as "Cain" or "Kane." The name Kean became Cain or Kane when an official attempted to replicate the name phonetically. Although I believe that Mary (Unknown) Kelly was from the Cain or Kean family, I have not been able to find a primary source to support this, so Mary's maiden name will remain as "Unknown" throughout this work.

In the *Records of Old Revolutionary Soldiers and Their Widows*, a Nellie/Nelly Cain of York County, New Brunswick, applies for relief in 1839, 1840 and 1843 under *The Act for the Relief of Old Soldiers of the Revolutionary War and Their Widows*. In her 1843 application, Nellie/Nelly is listed as being eighty-four years old, which indicates that she was born circa 1759, suggesting that she is not the mother of Mary (Unknown) Kelly. In her *"Loyalist Trails" UELAC Newsletter 2015-06 Feb 8, 2015* query, Floretta (Wade) Steeves states that Nellie/Nelly Cain was the wife of William Cain, who was not, as she points out in her email of 9 February 2015, the father of Mary (Unknown) Kelly.

According to the transcriptions of George H. Hayward in his *York County, New Brunswick, Marriage Records, Volume 1, 1812-1837*, on 17 May 1824 "Hannah Kain" of St. James Parish, Dublin, Ireland, married Thomas Clarke of the 52nd Regiment stationed at Fredericton, York County, New Brunswick, with George Best, Missionary in Fredericton, officiating and John Kelly and Thomas Wilson as witnesses. (pp. 9 & 27)

The John Kelly who is a witness at this marriage cannot be Loyalist John Kelly, who was in ill health for some time before he died between 4 September 1824 and 29 October 1825. It is possible that this John is the son of William and Hannah (Unknown) Kelly.

According to Murtie June Clark in her *Loyalists in the Southern Campaign of the Revolutionary War*, William Kean (also listed as "Kane") enlisted in the First Battalion of the Pennsylvania Loyalists commanded by Lieutenant Colonel William Allen on 14 October 1777. (Volume II, p. 118) Clark writes: "Both the Maryland and Pennsylvania Loyalists were raised in Philadelphia in the fall of 1777, their numbers made up wholly from refugees. . . . These regiments served with the British Army and went to New York with them in 1778. Later, after embarking with the army for the invasion of Georgia, they were stationed at Pensacola, at which they arrived in January 1779 after a stop-over in Jamaica. When Pensacola fell to the Spanish in May 1781, they were imprisoned in Havana, and a month later they were paroled to New York." (Volume II, pp. XV-XVI) Documentation by Clark shows that William Kean started out as a sergeant serving in the Southern Campaign and was "on duty at Pensacola. . . ." on 25 February 1780. (Volume II, p. 151) Clark documents that William Kean, upon his resignation from the Pennsylvania Loyalists, is listed as Adjutant on half-pay. (Volume II, p. 196) Clark lists under "British-American Officers in North America" in the Pennsylvania Loyalists: "Adjutant William Kean, born in Ireland, formerly a Sergeant in the Regiment, served 6 years in Provincial Corps." (Volume III, p. 368) (Clark, Murtie, June: *Loyalists in the Southern Campaign of the Revolutionary War*, Copyright 1981 by Genealogical Publishing Co., Inc., Baltimore, Maryland.)

The death notice for Ann Kean appears in the *City Gazette* of Saint John, New Brunswick, on 27 September 1820: "d. Yesterday, age 64, Ann relict of Adjutant William KEAN of the Pennsylvania Loyalists."

An article regarding the Old Burying Ground in Saint John, New Brunswick, appearing in the *Daily Telegraph* of 28 October 1874, contains the following: "A stone in the south east part of the grounds marks the last resting place of Mrs. Ann KEAN widow of Adjutant William KEAN who died 26th Sept. 1820, aged 63 years. Wm KEAN was from Pennsylvania and was Adjutant of the Pennsylvania Loyalists and settled in this Province after the corps was disbanded. We do not know where he died or where he was buried."

Stephen Davidson in "New Brunswick Newspapers Remember: Part One," appearing in *"Loyalist Trails" 2011-43 October 30, 2011*, points out that Ann Kean "became the first female loyalist to have her passing noticed in the newspapers. She was one of only 11 women to be so identified over the next quarter of a century."

William Kean appears to have had brothers who fought with the First Battalion of the Pennsylvania Loyalists. Murtie June Clark in her *Loyalists in the Southern Campaign of the Revolutionary War* documents a Private Michael Kane, along with a Sergeant William Kane, serving under Lieutenant Colonel William Allen in the Muster Roll of 30 January 1779 at Pensacola. (Volume II, p. 121) Clark notes a Private John Kean in the Muster Roll of the First Battalion of Pennsylvania Loyalists, under the Command of Lieutenant Colonel William Allen in Pensacola in February 1779. (Volume II, p. 123) The Muster Roll of 23 April 1779 at Pensacola, lists a Private John Kean under the command of Lieutenant Colonel William Allen. (Volume II, p. 124) Private Michael Kane, in Clark's documentation, appears in the 1 January 1780 "MUSTER ROLL of Captain Thomas Stephen's Company of the Combined Corps of Maryland and Pennsylvania Loyalists, Commanded by Lieut[enant] William Allen. . . ." (Volume II, p. 162) In the same company, Clark notes a, Private Michael Kane, along with Sergeant William Kane, in the Muster Rolls for 25 April 1780. (Volume II, p. 163) Clark documents that as early as the Muster Roll of 23 February 1780 at John's Island that John Kean was "on command, Carolina." (Volume II, p. 262) A Private John Kean, listed as "on command, Carolina," from Clark's documentation, appears in the "MUSTER ROLL of the Detachment of Captain Francis Fraser's Company of Guides and Pioneers, Commanded by Colonel Beverly Robinson, Charles Town Neck, 24 June 1780." (Volume II, p. 263) Private John Kane and a Private Abner Kane are listed by Clark's documentation in "Pay Abstract N[umbe]r 10, Major Daniel Plummer's Regiment, Fair Forest Militia, Ninety Six Brigade, Lieutenant Alexander Chesney's Company, men who came to Orangeburgh, S[outh]C[arolina], with Lieut[enant] Colonel John H. Cruger, 162 days pay, 14 Jun[e] – 13 Dec[ember] 1780." (Volume I, p. 324) Clark notes that in the Muster Roll of August 1782, which also lists Sergeant William Kean, Private Michael Kean is listed as "on command at Sandy Hook." (Volume II, p. 124) Clark also notes that Private Michael Kean, along with Sergeant William Kean, is in the Muster Rolls under the Command of Lieutenant Colonel William Allen in August 1783. (Volume II, p.127) (Clark, Murtie, June: *Loyalists in the Southern Campaign of the Revolutionary War,* Copyright 1981 by Genealogical Publishing Co., Inc., Baltimore, Maryland.)

Both William and Michael Kean are included in the New Brunswick land grant application of Thomas Colden in 1785. (See Appendix V.)

It should be noted that the name "Keen" is not to be confused with "Kean" in relation to the possible Cain/Kean connection to Mary Unknown who married John Kelly. Gregory B. Keen writes in "The Descendants of Joran Kyn, the Founder of Upland" appearing in *The Pennsylvania Magazine of History and Biography, Volume I* that "Joran Kyn . . . one of the earliest European residents upon the river Delaware, and for more than a quarter of a century the chief proprietor of land at Upland, New Sweden, afterwards Chester, Pennsylvania, was born in Sweden about A. D. 1620." Gregory B. Keen adds in a footnote accompanying this article that Kyn "(under the Dutch form of Kijn) is the earliest spelling of the surname met with, and it dates from 1663. The older generations of the West New Jersey branches of the family employed the form of Kijhn. Other methods numbering a dozen, Dutch and English, are attempts to render in those languages the sound of the Swedish original. Keen is the first English spelling of the name recorded, occurring as early as 1665, and is the mode adopted by the family to-day [*sic*]." (p. 325)

John Kelly, who was probably born in New Jersey, died in Kingsclear, York County, New Brunswick, Canada. According to a deposition on 24 June 1821 given in regard to the Petition of Elizabeth Reed at Kingsclear, New Brunswick, John Kelly enlisted in the Fourth Battalion of the New Jersey Volunteers in March 1777 in New York City. (See Appendix N.) Judith L. Van Buskirk in *Generous Enemies, Patriots and Loyalists in Revolutionary New York* notes that "the British army withdrew its protection from . . . New Jersey in 1777. . . ." (p. 26)

John Kelly was, according to Sabine, Jones and all other written sources, from Gloucester, New Jersey. This information, gathered from official records, contradicts online genealogical information suggesting he came from Monmouth, New Jersey. In the Land Petition of the British American Corporation of 1784, John Kelly, who is listed as John K-e-l-l-e-y, is grouped with a Luke and William Kelley. (See Appendix C.) Esther Clark Wright in *The Loyalists of New Brunswick* lists the three men together. In Clark's documentation contained in *Loyalists in the Southern Campaign of the Revolutionary War*, Sergeant William Kelly is listed in the "Muster Roll, Captain Daniel Cozens' Company, Second Battalion, New Jersey Volunteers. . . ." (Volume III, p. 151) (Clark, Murtie, June: *Loyalists in the Southern Campaign of the Revolutionary War*, Copyright 1981 by Genealogical Publishing Co., Inc., Baltimore, Maryland.) Irma Della (Kelly) Tucker states in her notes (*Ella (Kelly) Boulter Scrapbook*) that when John Kelly came to Saint John in 1783, "[h]is brother Luke came with him at the same time. . . ." More research is needed to substantiate that Luke and William Kelly are brothers of John. Luke Kelly supposedly returned to the United States, but, considering the animosity towards the Loyalists by the citizens of West Jersey, as noted by Sickler in *The History of Salem County New Jersey*, it is highly doubtful that he returned to West Jersey even though Judith L. Van Buskirk in *Generous Enemies, Patriots and Loyalists in Revolutionary New York* points out that "the quiet return of those who chose to come home raised no tumults after the first months following the British evacuation." (p. 194) Luke Kelly doesn't turn up in the appendix included in *The Centennial of the Settlement of Upper Canada by the United Empire Loyalists 1784-1884;* neither does his name appear anywhere at the website *Upper Canada (Ontario) Sundries Index.* Luke Kelly is not listed in any of the counties of Nova Scotia in Marion Gilroy's *Loyalists and Land Settlement in Nova Scotia.* Kelly family lore suggests that John had two other brothers named Leonard and Henry. A Henry Kelly is listed in the 1808 land grant petition of John Barker in York County, New Brunswick. (See Appendix B.) In the land grant petition of John Wallace in York County, New Brunswick, in 1815, it is noted that Henry Kelly has abandoned the land being petitioned for. (See Appendix B.) Linda (Kitchen) Aitken, in an email of 14 November 2012, states, "When I first became interested in Kelly history, I was told that John had a brother Henry who drowned. On the land grant map, there is a small parcel of land across from Kelly Creek labeled Henry Kelly. I think that is where William and Sarah [(Howard) Kelly] lived." It should be noted that William and Hannah (Unknown) Kelly have sons named Luke and John, who are listed on the John Wallace 1815 land grant petition mentioned above, and that John, son of William and Hannah (Unknown) Kelly, names one of his sons Luke. The first son of John and Mary (Unknown) Kelly is named William.

In a diagram of the Loyalist John Kelly family tree created by Ella Rita (Kelly) Boulter, provided by her daughter Jeannie Belinda (Boulter) Matthews, Ella Rita (Kelly) Boulter lists a Henry Kelly, son of Loyalist John Kelly, as having drowned.

A James Kelly is mentioned in a 1791 New Brunswick land grant application at Madawaska included in Appendix B.

According to the "Muster Roll of Major Thomas Millidge Company of New Jersey Volunteers in the Regiment Commanded by Lieut Coll Joseph Barton Carter Neck" a William Kelly, who was enlisted by John Williams 30 July 1777 into the 1st Battalion New Jersey Volunteers, "deserted 20th augt. . . ." (Library and Archives Canada, 395 Wellington Street, Ottawa, Ontario, Canada: *Loyalists in the Maritimes – Ward Chipman Muster Master's Office, 1777-1778,* Volume 26, p. 197, Reference MG 23 D1, Series 1, Item Number 13863.)

In her *Loyalists of New Brunswick,* Esther Clark Wright lists John Kelly as being from New Jersey and a sergeant in the Second Battalion of the Second New Jersey Volunteers. Luke Kelly is listed as being a member of the Third Battalion of the Third New Jersey Volunteers. William Kelly is listed as a member of the Second Battalion of the Second New Jersey Volunteers. Clark Wright does not list either Luke or William Kelly as being from New Jersey. (p. 297)

Clark Wright points out (*Loyalists of New Brunswick*) that some disbanded "New Jersey Volunteers went over to settle near officers who had bought farms in the older settlements of the Annapolis valley. Some sixty or more whose names appear on the list of New Brunswick Loyalists are known to have crossed the Bay [of Fundy] and settled in Nova Scotia." (p. 209)

Clark Wright adds: "The largest outward movement of New Brunswick Loyalists, naturally, was back to the country from which they had come. Undoubtedly, there were among the newcomers of 1783 those who came because transportation and provisions were being handed out, and who returned when the Royal Bounty of Provisions was no longer distributed to them." (p. 210)

In *Loyalists of New Brunswick*, Clark Wright includes the following:

> From the New Brunswick list of Loyalists, some 200 are known to have returned to the United States, and probably as many more joined in the trek. Even if twice as many more returned, the proportion is only 10%. Some observers, not realizing that the majority of the Loyalists belonged to families long settled in America, have jumped to the conclusion that any Loyalist family name encountered in the United States indicated a returned Loyalist. Actually, the New Brunswick Loyalists were very often one or two members of a large connection, the majority of whom remained in their old homes. Sometimes genealogies record the names of the Loyalist members, occasionally they list their descendants, but frequently family records omit all mention of what were considered, if known to have existed, as erring members of a family which numbered many "patriots". (p. 212)

Writing of "the movement of two hundred New Brunswick Loyalists to Upper Canada [(Ontario),]" Clark Wright, once again, in her *Loyalists of New Brunswick*, explains:

> The impetus came from the appointment of John Graves Simcoe as Lieutenant-Governor of Upper Canada and his desire to have officers who had served under him in the Queen's Rangers as members of his Council. Land was promised in lavish quantities, especially to disbanded officers, and there followed during the ensuing decade a migration from New Brunswick of such proportions as to call forth the term, "Niagara Fever". Although checking with the Ontario Land Papers and local histories produced only 200 names, it seems probable that the migration was much larger than this and that many of the untraceables disappeared in the direction of Upper Canada. Especially does it seem probable that many disbanded private soldiers who had been living in New Brunswick as hired men on farms, in saw mills or grist mills, or on vessels, joined in the trek to the new province. So many sergeants and corporals, not only of the Queen's Rangers but also of all three battalions of the New Jersey Volunteers, the Loyal American Regiment, and others, can be identified, that the supposition of a large migration of privates is strengthened. In applying for land in Upper Canada, particularly in the later stages of the

movement thither, the petitioner often omitted to mention that he had lived in New Brunswick and had had possession of or been entitled to a grant there — an omission which does not help identification of applicants for land in Upper Canada. (pp. 213-214)

Esther Clark Wright (*Loyalists of New Brunswick*) observes: "The twentieth century, with its many and easy methods of travel, is wont to assume that people in the eighteenth century did not move around a great deal. Actually, they moved around very freely, and with surprising ease, in canoe, small boat, schooner or sloop, with little trouble in packing up their few and simple movable possessions. Consequently, it is very difficult to determine the numbers settling in any district, for some families were moving out and others moving in every few years." (pp. 203-204)

It should be noted that William S. Stryker in *Official Register of the Officers and Men of New Jersey in the Revolutionary War* lists as American Patriot privates a John Kelly as serving in the First Battalion of Salem County and in the New Jersey State Troops and the Continental Army; a Patrick Kelly in the Third Battalion of Gloucester County and the Continental Army; a Uriah Kelly in the Third Battalion of Gloucester County. (p. 652)

B. Wood-Holt in Appendix I of her *The Kings Loyal Americans, the Canadian Fact, Marriage Licenses for Sunbury County, 1788-1829, Passenger Lists and Other Lists, etc.* documents that John and William Kelly, both from New Jersey and members of the Second New Jersey Volunteers, arrived on the River Saint John on the *Duke of Richmond* and that Luke Kelly, also from New Jersey, but listed as being from the Third New Jersey Volunteers, arrived on the River Saint John on the *Esther*. (p. 363)

Documentation posted at the online site *United Empire Loyalists Association of Canada, Loyalist Ships* notes that the *Duke of Richmond* left New York in the fall of 1783 during the evacuation of New York and landed in New Brunswick on 27 September 1783, while the *Esther* left New York during the evacuation of 1783 and landed on the River Saint John on 10 October 1783.

Esther Clark Wright notes in her *Loyalists of New Brunswick* that the *Esther* was 384 tons, with Robert Gill serving as master. (p. 73) Wright adds: "Colonel Richard Hewlett, commanding officer of the 2nd Battalion of DeLancey's Brigade, who had been placed in charge of the British American crops sent to the St. John River, ..." on 13 October 1783, "reported" to Commander-in-Chief Sir Guy Carleton "that the *Esther* had arrived. . . ." (p. 85)

Wright documents that Richard Davis was the master of the *Duke of Richmond* (865 tons) with 342 of the First New Jersey Volunteers and 281 of the Second New Jersey Volunteers on board. Wright adds that the *Esther* carried the Third New Jersey Volunteers, but that the total number was not known. (p.86)

Esther Clark Wright, once again in *Loyalists of New Brunswick*, reminds us that "A few who had been fighting in the Loyalist regiments returned to their former homes." (p. 106)

Not all members of the Kelly family in West New Jersey joined the Loyalist cause. As an example, Thomas Cushing and Charles E. Sheppard in *History of the Counties of Gloucester, Salem, and Cumberland New Jersey, with Biographical Sketches of Their Prominent Citizens* note that on 21 February 1838 a John H. Kelly's name is included in a list of carpenters for the Methodist Episcopal Church of Salem, New Jersey, "written on what was once evidently the fly-leaf of an old account-book. . . ." (p. 398)

Paul Minotty in his transcription published in *The Records of the Moravian Church at Oldman's Creek, Gloucest County, New Jersey* lists a William Kahaly (15 April 1772 - ?), "[s]ingle man of Woolwitch Township, son of James and Rachel Kahaly," who married Elizabeth Estlack (8 October 1778 - ?), a "single woman, daughter of Joseph and Margret Estlack," on 24 October 1796. It is noted that William Kahaly was born in Salem County. "The Marriage was performed by the Reverend Frederic Moering". (p. 56)

I have made an attempt to simplify the genealogy of the following by assigning numbers to the descending generations. William Kelly is assigned number 1, his children, number 2 and the grandchildren, number 3.

1.William Kelly, who appears to be John Kelly's brother, married Hannah Unknown. William Kelly, who lived in Prince William, New Brunswick, had a will drawn up and signed on 26 November 1835. The will was registered in the *New Brunswick, County Deed Registry Books, 1780-1930, for York (1836-1837)*, Volume 21, pp. 23-25 on 26 January 1836. (See Appendix B.)

Children of William and Hannah (Unknown) Kelly:

2.Elizabeth Kelly married Thomas Thompson on 4 January 1825. Justice of the Peace Jacob Ellgood conducted the ceremoney. Both Elizabeth Kelly and Thomas Thompson are listed as residents of Prince William. Witnesses are John Nicholson and Deborah Kelly. (George H. Hayward: *York County, New Brunswick, Marriage Records, Volume 1, 1812–1837*, pp. 27 & 49.)

2.Mary Kelly married George Ballantine 15 October 1829, with William Gibson and Ruth Hollary listed as witnesses, and Justice of the Peace Jacob Ellegood conducting the ceremony. Both Mary Kelly and George Ballantine are listed as residents of Prince William. (George H. Hayward: *York County, New Brunswick, Marriage Records, Volume 1, 1812–1837*, pp. 2 & 28.)

2.Luke Kelly (ca 1794 - 15 January 1867) married Margaret Jane Nixon 28 June 1834. Rector of Fredericton George Coster performed the ceremony, with Robert Davis and Henry Kitchen as witnesses. Both Luke Kelly and Margaret Jane Nixon are listed as residents of Prince William. (George H. Hayward: *York County, New Brunswick, Marriage Records, Volume 1, 1812–1837*, pp. 28 & 38.)

2.Deborah Kelly (ca 1796 – 1874) married Alexander Lawson on 23 March 1824. The ceremony was conducted by Missionary George Best. Both Deborah Kelly and Alexander Lawson are listed as being from Prince William. Thomas Stewart

The Kellys of Kingsclear

and James Carter were witnesses. (George H. Hayward: *York County, New Brunswick, Marriage Records, Volume 1, 1812–1837*, pp. 27 & 29.)

2.John Kelly (ca 1798 - ?) married Jane Unknown (ca 1811 - ?), who entered Canada from Ireland in 1835 according to the 1851 census for the Parish of Kingsclear, New Brunswick. Since it appears that both William and Hannah (Unknown) Kelly and John and Mary (Unknown) Kelly had sons named John, it is difficult sorting out some of the information in regard to these two John Kellys, so there may be some misinformation that will have to be clarified at a later date. The list of children for John and Jane (Unknown) Kelly appears in the 1851 census noted above. In a land grant petition contained in Appendix B, John Kelly states on 4 March 1827 that he is 27 years old. An 1841 land transaction involving John and Jane (Unknown) Kelly also appears in Appendix B.

Children of John and Jane (Unknown) Kelly:

3.Luke Kelly (ca 1833 - ?)
3.Mary Kelly (ca 1836 - ?)
3.Margaret Kelly (ca 1839 - ?)
3.William Kelly (ca 1841 - ?)
3.John Kelly (ca 1843 - ?)
3.Deborah Kelly (ca 1845 - ?)
3.Matilda Kelly (ca 1849 - ?)

2.Alexander Kelly (ca 1801 - 4 January 1872) married Catherine Bell/Bill 16 January 1843.
2.Isaac Kelly (ca 1807 - 8 July 1891) married Unknown Unknown.
2.Susannah Kelly (ca 1815 - after census 1891), apparently unmarried.

Rev. W. Christopher Atkinson, A.M. in *Historical and Statistical Account of New-Brunswick, B.N.A. with Advice to Emigrants, Third Edition, Greatly Improved and Corrected*, published in 1844, writes: "About twenty miles from the seat of government [Fredericton], on the western side of the river, close to Longs, commences the parish of Prince William. The land near this place is not favourable for agriculture. Inhabited houses in Prince William, 149; families, 151; and 3329 acres of cleared land." (p. 108)

On 17 September 1845, according to documentation in the *New Brunswick, County Deed Registry Books, 1780-1930, for York (1847-1848)*, Volume 29, pp. 652-654, Luke Kelly, son of William and Hannah (Unknown) Kelly, still living on lots three and five between his brothers Alexander and Isaac in Prince William and indebted to James and John T. Taylor and their associates, agreed to pay a sixty pound debt (with interest) off within a year to the tune of one hundred and twenty pounds. (See Appendix B.) The Taylors will turn up often in the financial dealings of the whole Kelly family for several decades.

The following appears in *Records of Old Revolutionary Soldiers and Their Widows*:

> The . . . Petition of Mary Kelly widow of the late John Kelly of the Parish of Queensbury
>   Humbly Sheweth
> That your Petitioner is the widow of ~~the~~ John Kelly late of the Parish of Kings clear in the County of York — That her husband served his late Majesty King George the Third honestly and faithfully during the whole of the Revolutionary war under the late Colonel Allen — That he came to this Country when he was disbanded and settled in the Parish of Prince William where he resided until his death, That ~~previous~~ for several years previous to his death he was most severely afflicted with Cancer of which he died —
>
> That all his little property had Lapsed into other hands and Your Petitioner left . . . nearly destitute —

Mary (Unknown) Kelly signed (8 July 1838) with an "X." (See Appendix U.)

It is apparent from documents marked with an "X" by Mary (Unknown) Kelly that she was unable to write. The person writing the above petition seems confused as to John Kelly's residence and place of death. In the probate will of John Kelly (See Appendix G.) signed on 4 September 1824, filed 29 October 1825 and registered on 1 November 1825, it states clearly that he was living in Kingsclear on 4 September 1824. The numerous land grant records, deeds, etc. (included in the appendices of this work) confirm that John Kelly lived and died in Kingsclear.

While working on the Edward Winslow estate, John Kelly was in an accident and unable to work for a period of time. (See Appendix O.)

It should be noted that although there are indications that John Kelly and his assumed brothers or male relatives first served in the Salem County Militia, the New Jersey State Troops and/or the Continental Army before joining the British forces, no mention is made of this in Mary (Unknown) Kelly's petition.

John Eardley-Wilmot, quoting the "First Report, 12th August, 1784 of the Commissioners" in "Appendix, No. 1" of his *Historical View of the Commission for Enquiring into the Losses, Services, and Claims of the American Loyalists, at the Close of the War Between Great Britain and her Colonies, in 1783: with an Account of the Compensation Granted to Them by Parliament in 1785 and 1788*, includes the following:

> We have distinguished (in the remarks contained under the title of "Observations") such Claimants as we find during the existence of the Troubles to have taken the oaths of fidelity or allegiance to the American States; but who afterwards availed themselves of the benefit of Proclamations issued by his Majesty's Commissioners, Generals, and

Governors, and sustained Losses in consequence of their taking part in favour of the British Government. We have conceived ourselves bound, by the good faith of those proclamations, to consider persons of such description as Loyalists, and to receive and report their Claims for relief under the Act. (p. 122)

The Act noted above is included in the Appendix of Eardley-Wilmot's book:

An Act for appointing Commissioners to enquire into the Losses and Services of all such Persons who have suffered in their Rights, Properties, and Professions, during the late unhappy Dissentions in America, in consequence of their Loyalty to his Majesty, and attachment to the British Government. (p. 101)

It is noted in "Appendix, No. 1" accompanying John Eardley-Wilmot's documentation that this *"Act of Parliament [was] passed in the Twenty-third year of the Reign of His Present Majesty...."* (p. 109) 1783 was the twenty-third year of the Reign of King George the Third of England.

John Kelly served in the Second and Fourth Battalions of the New Jersey Volunteers as well as other battalions that formed during the course of the war. While in the Fourth New Jersey Volunteers, John Kelly, according to E. Alfred Jones in *The Loyalists of New Jersey*, witnessed the wounding of Captain Henry Marsh "at Second River, New Jersey, early in April 1777...." (p. 140-141) (See Appendix N.) Documentation contained in *Proceedings of the New Jersey Historical Society, April, 1927, Vol. XII, No. 2* establishes that John Kelly was from Gloucester County. (p. 181) Jones notes that John Kelly is "living in the parish of Kingsclear, Province of New Brunswick, in 1822." (p. 141)

In the *Journals of the Continental Congress, 1774-1778*, Volume IX, 1777, October 3–December 31, edited by Worthington Chauncey Ford, the following was resolved by the Continental Congress in November, 1777: "That it be earnestly recommended to the several states, as soon as may be, to confiscate and make sale of all the real and personal estate therein, or such of their inhabitants and other persons who have forfeited the same, and the right to the protection of their respective states, and to invest the money arising from the sales in continental loan office certificates, to be appropriated in such manner as the respective states shall hereafter direct." (p. 971)

According to a newspaper article appearing on 30 November 1778 cited in *Documents Relating to the Revolutionary History of the State of New Jersey, Volume II, Extracts From American Newspapers, Vol. II. 1778* edited by Francis B. Lee:

At an Inferior Court of Common Pleas held for the County of Gloucester, on the 13 instant, were returned inquisitions (for joining the army of the King of Great-Britain, and other offenses against the form of their allegiance) found against . . . John Kelly [among a long list of others];

proclamation was made in open Court, and information given, that if they or any on their behalf or any person interested would traverse, a trial should be awarded, and an opportunity of prevent forfeiture given; no traverse were offered: Therefore notice is hereby given, that if neither they nor any on their behalf nor any person interested shall traverse at the next Court to be held for the county of Gloucester, on the second Tuesday in December next, the inquisitions will be taken to be true, and final judgment entered thereon in favor of the State, and their personal estates will then be forfeited to the use of the State, and their land taken into the hands of the Commissioners until the Legislature shall further order therein respecting their lands. (pp. 581-582) (To view the full extract, see Appendix P, under Kellys in *New Jersey Newspaper Extracts*.)

In *Under Four Flags: Old Gloucester County, 1686-1964, A History of Gloucester County New Jersey*, edited by Hazel B. Simpson, it is noted that: "A document signed by 165 Whigs or patriots of Old Gloucester County in the fall of 1779, gives a first class account of the strife caused by the enemy army, the Tories and refugees. Few know that the horrors of the Revolution were not all caused by the foreign enemy. Many of the dastardly acts were perpetrated by the neighbors and relatives of the inhabitants. Soon after the evacuation of Philadelphia by the British army in June 1778, the patriots rounded up the remaining Tories and refugees and convicted them of high treason, crime and misdemeanors. Some were sentenced to be executed, others were fined, exiled or imprisoned. Many had their real estate and personal property confiscated by process of law. This document of 1779 pertains to the money derived from the confiscated estates which was paid over to the State." (pp. 101-102)

Clark notes that "The New Jersey Volunteers were also known as Skinner's Greens, named in honor of their regimental commander, Brigadier General Cortland Skinner. They were recruited in New York in 1776 and served in that colony. Two battalions of this regiment were sent to the South, one to East Florida and one to Georgia. Lieutenant Colonel Isaac Allen commanded the Third Battalion, which served in the Carolinas and Georgia. Later in 1782 the Third Battalion was combined with the Second Battalion before they returned to New York." (Volume III, p. XV) (Clark, Murtie, June: *Loyalists in the Southern Campaign of the Revolutionary War,* Copyright 1981 by Genealogical Publishing Co., Inc., Baltimore, Maryland.)

The *On-Line Institute for Advanced Loyalist Studies*, hosted by Todd Braisted, in a short history of the Sixth New Jersey Volunteers, establishes that the Sixth was "the smallest of all the battalions . . . but possibly the best led and disciplined." The Sixth was formed "in early December, 1776, when Sir William Howe led the British army into Trenton. The new commander of this three company unit would be a diminutive Trenton lawyer by the name of Isaac Allen. Allen was a likeable but thoroughly organized and efficient officer, as his battalion would testify by having the smallest rate of non-battle casualties and highest rate of uniformity and functioning weapons."

Braisted: "The battalion drew their recruits primarily from the Hunterdon County area, drawing from such places as Trenton and Princeton. Washington's attack on these places probably hurt none of the battalions more than the 6th...."

The second in command, Major Richard Witham Stockton, was taken prisoner with a group of his men on 18 February 1777.

Braisted: "With the evacuation of New Jersey, the 6th battalion set up headquarters on Staten Island, where they played an important part in Sullivan's raid on 22 August 1777. Lieut. Colonel Allen was one of the few officers not surprised that day, marching his men to some old earthworks and defying all demands of surrender. The battalion was foremost in the pursuit of the retreating Continentals, including a bayonet charge on their rearguard, which resulted in the loss of several men...."

Braisted writes that three weeks after Sullivan's raid, the Sixth was involved "in Sir Henry Clinton's grand forage through Bergen County. The men of the 6th were once again in the lead and took the brunt of the casualties suffered by the NJV. Although their ranks were small, no one could question their bravery."

The *On-Line Institute for Advanced Loyalist Studies* notes that when the Sixth was drafted into the Third Battalion, Isaac Allen became the lieutenant of the Third on 25 April 1778.

The following information comes from William S. Stryker in his *The New Jersey Volunteers (Loyalists) in the Revolutionary War*:

> About the time of General Howe's occupation of Trenton, in December, 1776, the family of Isaac Allen left their home in that city, accepted protection papers and were ever afterward considered subjects of King George. Isaac Allen was commissioned December 3d, 1776 in the Sixth Battalion at the siege of Savannah, Georgia, October 9th, 1779, he appears as in command of the Third Battalion, but in the later years of the war in the Second Battalion as its lieutenant-colonel. During the war all his property in Trenton was confiscated. In the year 1783 he resumed his profession as lawyer in St. John, New Brunswick, and in after years took a seat upon the supreme bench and was a member of the Council of the Province. His death occurred in the year 1806, in the sixty-fifth year of his age. (p. 28)

According to Stryker, Lieutenant-Colonel Isaac Allen served in the Second, Third, Fourth and Sixth Battalions of the New Jersey Volunteers.

Stryker further states:

> On the 27th day of November, 1778, an expedition with two thousand troops sailed from Sandy Hook for Savannah, Georgia, and six days after landing at Tybee Island, off the harbor of that city, they took part in the fight, December 29th, on Brewton Hill. A detachment of the New Jersey

Volunteers, Lieutenant-Colonel Allen commanding, went out with the party and suffered considerably in the battle just mentioned. (pp. 13-14)

Mary(Unknown) Kelly states that John Kelly fought under the command of Colonel Isaac Allen throughout the whole war in her 1838 petition under the *Act for Relief of Old Soldiers of the Revolutionary War and Their Widows*, so, the following extract from Stryker's *The New Jersey Volunteers (Loyalists) in the Revolutionary War* may explain why John Kelly is listed as having come from North Carolina in the newspaper article published at the time of his son Leonard Coombes Kelly's death in 1899 (See Appendix W.):

During the summer of 1779 a considerable detachment of the New Jersey Volunteers was sent to reinforce the British army in South Carolina, and took part in the assault on Savannah, October 9th, 1779. A battalion under command of Lieutenant-Colonel Isaac Allen formed part of the garrison of one of the large redoubts on the south side of the city, near the river. (pp. 17-18)

Details of the battle of Long Canes in South Carolina on 12 December 1780 posted at *The American Revolution in South Carolina – Long Canes IIS7* contains the following:

Brig. Gen. Robert Cunningham, the Loyalist commander in the area, sent to Col. John Harris Cruger at Ninety-Six for support. Col. Cruger dispatched Lt. Col. Isaac Allen with 200 New Jersey Volunteers, 200 Loyalist militia, and 50 dragoons. It is not clear how many Cunningham himself had prior to the reinforcement, so that his original numbers may have been negligible at that point in time.

Initially, the Loyalists were forced to retreat in the face of an attack by Col. Clarke and Maj. James McCall with about 100 Patriots. Col. Clarke, who was wounded, then called on Col. Few to support him, but Col. Few refused or was unable to do so, nor did he tell Col. Clarke he had decided to withdraw. As a result Col. Clarke and Maj. McCall were driven back by four times their number. Col. Few and Col. Clarke were subsequently pursued by Lt. Col. Allen.

The Loyalists, commanded by Lt. Col. Isaac Allen, listed casualties of 2 killed and 9 wounded.

During the battle of Eutaw Springs, South Carolina, on 8 September 1781, according to information listed on the website *The American Revolution in South Carolina Battle of Eutaw Springs*, the Third New Jersey Volunteers was "led by Lt. Col. Isaac Allen with 66 men, including Capt. John Barbarie."

Of the Battle of Eutaw Spings, Benson J. Lossing in his *Pictorial Field-Book of the Revolution* notes: "The conflict lasted four hours, and was one of the most severely contested battles of the Revolution." (Volume II, p. 703) Lossing adds: "The loss of both parties, considering the number engaged, was very heavy. The Americans had one hundred and thirty rank and file killed, three hundred and eighty-five wounded, and forty missing; in all five hundred and fifty-five. There were twenty-two officers killed, and thirty-nine wounded. The loss of the British, according to their own statement, was six hundred and ninety-three men, of whom eighty-five were killed on the field. Including seventy-two wounded, whom they left in their camp when they abandoned it the day after the battle, Greene took five hundred prisioners." (Volume II, p. 704)

Murtie June Clark in her *Loyalists in the Southern Campaign of the Revolutionary War* documents that both John and William Kelly appear as privates in "Pay Abstract N[umbe]r 2, Major Daniel Plummer's Regiment, Fair Forest Militia, Ninety Six Brigade, Captain Shadrack Lantrey's Company, men who came to Orangeburgh, S[outh] C[arolina], with Lieut[enant] Colonel John H. Cruger, 14 Jun[e] – 13 Dec[ember] 1780. . . ." (Volume I, p. 323) Clark also documents that Private John Kelley and Private William Kelly are listed in "Pay Abstarct N[umbe]r 59, Colonel Daniel Plummer's Regiment, Fair Forest Regiment, Ninety Six Brigade, 183 days pay, 13 Jun[e] – 14 Dec[ember] 1780, for men who came to Orangeburgh with Lieut[enant] Colonel John H. Cruger at the evacuation of Ninety Six, paid 14 Mar[ch] 1782 . . . ." (Volume I, p. 327) (Clark, Murtie, June: *Loyalists in the Southern Campaign of the Revolutionary War*, Copyright 1981 by Genealogical Publishing Co., Inc., Baltimore, Maryland.)

Clark writes that "Delancey's Brigade was raised by the commander, Brigadier General Oliver Delancey, for the defense of Long Island in September 1776. Colonel George Brewerton and Lieutenant Colonel John H. Cruger went with two battalions of this brigade to Georgia in December 1778 in Lieutenant Colonel Archibald Campbell's invasion fleet. Their losses in the Southern Campaign forced the two battalions to be combined into one in February 1782, and they were returned to New York before they were evacuated to New Brunswick in 1783." (Volume III, p. XV) (Clark, Murtie, June: *Loyalists in the Southern Campaign of the Revolutionary War*, Copyright 1981 by Genealogical Publishing Co., Inc., Baltimore, Maryland.)

Clark documents under "Continental Prisoners of War" that William Kelly is included in the "[l]ist of men's names on board the several prison ships and in the barracks, Feb[ruar]y 11, 1781. . . ." (Volume I, p. 476) (Clark, Murtie, June: *Loyalists in the Southern Campaign of the Revolutionary War*, Copyright 1981 by Genealogical Publishing Co., Inc., Baltimore, Maryland.)

Clark notes that Private John Kelly and Private Luke Kelly are listed in the "Muster Roll, Captain Jacob Buskirk's Company, Provincial Light Infantry, Fourth Battalion, New Jersey Volunteers, High Hills of Santee, S[outh] C[arolina], 24 February 1781 to 24 April 1781, 60 days inclusive. . . ." (Volume III, p. 257) (Clark, Murtie, June: *Loyalists in the Southern Campaign of the Revolutionary War,* Copyright 1981 by Genealogical Publishing Co., Inc., Baltimore, Maryland.)

Private John Kelly, Clark also documents, is listed in the "Pay Abstract N[umbe]r _, Colonel Robert Ballingall's Regiment, Colleton County Militia, Captain Joseph Rhem's Company, South Carolinea Light Horse, Charlestown, S[outh] C[arolina], 62 days pay, 1 May – I Jul[y] 1781. . . ." (Volume 1, p. 176) For the same company, in "Pay Abstract N[umbe]r 84, . . . 2 Jul[y] – 1 Oct[ober] 1781, to be paid 6 Feb[ruary] 1782. . . .," Clark notes that John Kelly is listed as Sergeant. (Volume I, p. 175) (Clark, Murtie, June: *Loyalists in the Southern Campaign of the Revolutionary War,* Copyright 1981 by Genealogical Publishing Co., Inc., Baltimore, Maryland.)

Both Private John and Private Luke Kelly, according to Clark, appear in the "Muster Roll, Captain Jacob Buskirk's Company, Provincial Light Infantry, Second Battalion, New Jersey Volunteers, Quarter House, S[outh] C[arolina], 25 October 1781 to 24 December 1781, 61 days inclusive. . . ." (Volume III, p. 258) (Clark, Murtie, June: *Loyalists in the Southern Campaign of the Revolutionary War,* Copyright 1981 by Genealogical Publishing Co., Inc., Baltimore, Maryland.)

Clark documents that "Major Thomas Barclay commanded the Provincial Light Infantry Battalion which was raised on Staten Island, New York and severed in the Southern Campaign." (Volume III, pp. XV-XVI) (Clark, Murtie, June: *Loyalists in the Southern Campaign of the Revolutionary War,* Copyright 1981 by Genealogical Publishing Co., Inc., Baltimore, Maryland.)

Private John Kelly, Clark documents, appears on the "Muster Roll, Captain Peter Campbell's Company, Second Battalion, New Jersey Volunteers, Charlestown, S[outh] C[arolina], 25 April 1782 to 24 June 1782, being 61 days inclusive. . . ." (Volume III, p. 144) In the same Muster Roll, Clark notes that Private Luke Kelly is listed as being "at New York. . . ." (Volume III, p. 145) (Clark, Murtie, June: *Loyalists in the Southern Campaign of the Revolutionary War,* Copyright 1981 by Genealogical Publishing Co., Inc., Baltimore, Maryland.)

In Clark, Sergeant William Kelly is listed as "on command. . . ."in the "Muster Roll, Captain Daniel Cozens' Company, Second Battalion, New Jersey Volunteers, 24 December 1782 to 25 February 1782, location not shown. . . ." (Volume III, p. 151) (Clark, Murtie, June: *Loyalists in the Southern Campaign of the Revolutionary War,* Copyright 1981 by Genealogical Publishing Co., Inc., Baltimore, Maryland.)

W.S. MacNutt in *New Brunswick A History: 1784-1867* writes: "Almost everywhere British armies had gone throughout the war, Loyalist regiments had been present, but their most immediate, vivid memories were of the south, of the passionate, plundering campaigns that had preceded the surrender of Cornwallis at Yorktown. They had taken part in the seizure of Charleston, the joyous but dubious victory at Eutaw Springs, the magnificent defence of Fort Ninety-Six." (p. 23)

In regard to the Loyalists, MacNutt emphasizes: "Nearly all came from New York, Connecticut, and the other 'middle' colonies. Because they came from the south of New England and because many had fought in the Carolinas and Georgia, numerous writers have supposed that most of them originated in the south. But only a minute ingredient, possibley five per cent, came from the colonies south of New York and New Jersey." (p. 43)

In the 1784 land grant petition contained in the Legislative Library of New Brunswick records, John Kelly, along with William Kelly and Luke Kelly, assumed to be brothers of John Kelly, are among "the Non Commissioned Officers and favorite Men of the late disbanded British American Corps. . . ." petitioning for land at St. Anne's Point (present day Fredericton) on the St. John River. Although many petitioners sign with an "X," all three Kelly names appear in full as K-e-l-l-e-y. (See Appendix C.)

The 1784 petition states in regard to the men listed on the land grant application: "In consequence of which direction from Col. Hewlett, and assurance from their Officers, they hath themselves such houses as their circumstances, together with the Advance Season of the year would admit of and employed Themselves last winter, and this Summer improving the Lands round their respective Houses." So, it is obvious that John, Luke and William Kelly were among the Loyalists who spent the winter of 1783-84 at St. Anne's Point.

In regard to the move up to St. Ann's (Fredericton) in the late fall of 1783, Esther Clark Wright, in her *Loyalists of New Brunswick*, points out: "More than four hundred, many of them with large families, unable because of the lateness of the season to wait for the government vessels, had hired passage up the river, and had been at the expense of building shelter and clearing land at St. Ann's. It would have been easier and less expensive to have remained at Parrtown. The expense had been particularly hard on the privates, most of whom had lost good livings in the country and had served faithfully all the war." (p. 185)

Esther Clark Wright, again in *Loyalists of New Brunswick*, notes: "On the Kennebecasis, there was also a nucleus of New Jersey Volunteers, placed there in the summer of 1783 by Lieutenant-Colonel Isaac Allen of the 2nd Battalion, on a tract of 3,000 acres for possession of which he had arrangements with a Halifax merchant. This nucleus attracted other New Jersey men, especially from the 1st and 3rd Battalions, whose blocks had been located so far up the river that the battalions refused them." (p. 204)

Clark Wright states: "A flood of applications poured into the Secretary's office during 1785; the flow diminished in 1786, but kept up through 1787 and 1788, slackening again in 1789, and gradually diminishing to a mere trickle. There were difficulties still over rights of Pre-Loyalist grantees and squatters, over imperfect surveys, over lots left idle while the owners worked at their trades or hired out. . . ." (p. 184)

W.S. MacNutt (*New Brunswick A History: 1784-1867*) writes in regard to Loyalist land grants, "In the three or four years following the settlement there was a good market for real estate, and much of the interval land changed hands several times. Many of the original grants became almost meaningless as settlers wandered about the country endeavouring to fix upon more desirable locations. The enthusiasm receded as two factors became apparent. One was the the amount of good arable land was limited. The second was that, owing to the scarcity of labour, a single individual could profitably manage only a comparatively small holding." (p. 67)

On 18 August 1788 John Kelly applied "to his Excellency Thomas Carleton Esquire Lieutenant governor and Commander in Chief of the Province of New Brunswick. . . . for a grant of 200 acres of land in block number 2 between lot numbers 42 and 48. In the application, John Kelly states, "that your petitioner belonged to the Third Batt'n of N.J. Volunteers. . . ." He says that he hasn't been granted any land since his arrival in New Brunswick. (See Appendix D.)

On 4 October 1799, Stephen Jarvis and seventy others, including John Kelly, John Howard, Leonard Reed Combes and Abraham Long were granted land in Kingsclear, New Brunswick, on a 6,300 acre, more or less, portion, "being part of the Tract granted under the Great Seal of Nova Scotia to Lieut. Colonel Isaac Allen and associates in common, and surrendered by the said Grantees in order to receive the present Grant. . . ." John Kelly was granted two thirds of lot 89, which contained five hundred acres, with one third going to Reynard Wheeler. John Howard, whose daughter Sarah Ann Howard married John Kelly's son William, was given lot 61, containing two hundred and eighty acres. Abraham Long, whose descendants married into the Kelly family, received lot 91, containing two hundred and fifty acres. Leonard Reed Combes was given lot 78, which contained three hundred and fifty acres. Moses Holmes, who had applied for a grant in 1792, of which John Kelly was included, received lot 88, containing two hundred acres. (As an aside: Isaac Mills, part of whose descendants settled in St. John, Maine, and, later, Allagash, Maine, was given lot 58, containing two hundred acres.) This land grant was registered on 31 December 1799. (See Appendix F.)

W.S. MacNutt in *New Brunswick A History: 1784-1867* points out that after Nova Scotia was divided and New Brunswick established in the summer of 1784 as a separate province, Thomas Carleton, who became the first governor of New Brunswick, imposed an "ordinance [which] required that all holders of lands who had received titles under the Nova Scotian authority should register in New Brunswick within a year." (p. 56)

Esther Clark Wright (*Loyalists of New Brunswick*) states that in the regrant in 1799 of Block 2 assigned the 2nd New Jersey Volunteers in Kingsclear, New Brunswick, on 14 July 1784, "only 24 of the original names were on the regrant, although three other names may indicate sons of the original grantees. It had been very easy for grantees of Block 2 to sell their lots to officials of the province who wished to have a landed estate within reach of the capital. When Lieutenant Colonel Isaac Allen came up to look for regimental lands in the early summer of 1783, he took up land on the Kennebecasis and placed ten of his 'lads' there. Others of the regiment joined them; a few went across the Bay of Fundy to Nova Scotia and a few to Upper Canada; two or three returned to the States." (p. 182)

Clark Wright notes, "The delays and obstructions caused by the shortsightedness of the officials of Nova Scotia were resulting in the departure from the province of many Loyalists. . . ." (p. 175)

Andrew Rainsford, whose name is listed among the grantees in the 1799 grant, appears to be the source of the given name Ransford that appears for generations of males in the Kelly line. When Ransford was shortened to "Ransy" in our family, it is pronounced as "Rainsy." An Andrew W. Rainsford is listed in David Facey-Crowther's *The New Brunswick Militia Commissioned Officers' Lists, 1787-1867* as a member of the Second Battalion Carleton County Militia. Facey-Crowther notes that Andrew W. Rainsford served as "Ensign 1843 – 13 October 1847[;] Lieutenant 13 October 1847 – 1849[;] Captain and Paymaster 1849 – 1850 [and] Resigned 1850[.]" (p. 27)

Although Lieutenant-Colonel Isaac Allen (who commanded John Kelly in the New Jersey Volunteers) served as "Colonel Commandant York County Regiment 1787 – 1806 [and] Brigadier-General Militia Forces 1798 – 1806[,]" and his son John Allen served as "Inspecting Field officer of Militia 1826 - (?) [and] Quartermaster-General [commissioned] 4 May 1839 - (?); mentioned 1849[,]" (p. 111) the only mention of a Kelly being a member of the militia is a James Kelly who served as "Ensign 19 February 1848 – (?); mentioned 1849" in Third Battalion Carleton County Militia. (p. 33) Since James Kelly (30 April 1835 – 4 June 1919), son of William and Sarah Ann (Howard) Kelly, would have been twelve years old on 19 February 1848, it seems highly doubtful that he is the James Kelly listed here. It appears that the James Kelly who served in the Carleton County Militia was related to the James Kelly mentioned in the 1791 land petition at Madawaska of David Higginbothom appearing in Appendix B. A William Kelly is listed as "Ensign 1860 – (?)" in the First Battalion Northumberland County Militia. (p. 196)

David Facey-Crowther notes in *The New Brunswick Militia 1787-1867* that the New Brunswick Militia Act of 1787 "required all male inhabitants of the province between the ages of 16 and 50 to enrol [sic] in the militia. The only exceptions were members of the council and the assembly, justices of the peace, high sheriffs, coroners, and all persons holding civil and military commissioners under the crown, ministers of the Gospel, physicians and surgeons, schoolmasters, one miller to each grist mill and one ferryman to every public ferry and Quakers, except in time of invasion or insurrection. . . . Those obliged to serve were to enrol under the captain or commanding officer of the area in which they resided." (pp. 6-7)

So, it would appear that any members of the Loyalist Kelly family, serving in the militia, must have been privates.

In a transcript of a recording done by Darrell McBreairty with Eva "Ev" (Kelly) McBreairty (30 March 1877 – 23 June 1974) contained in *Conversations with A'nt Ev': an Oral History of the Allagash* (p. 25), Eva "Ev" (Kelly) McBreairty revealed that her father, Charles Burton Kelly (26 June 1839 – 6 February 1912), was an Orangeman, but, after an extensive search through the Orange Lodge files for Queensbury, Kingsclear, Prince William and Dumfries, at the Provincial Archives of New Brunswick, Linda (Kitchen)

Aitken, in an email of 10 October 2013, writes that she "only found one Kelly. Victor Kelly from my community." A search by Linda (Kitchen) Aitken on 31 January 2014 of the Carleton County Orange Lodge records proved futile. As of January 2014, the records for the Carleton County Orange Order at PANB are limited to those records commencing in 1897. The Orange Order records in New Brunswick are not complete.

Although I have not discovered any documentation connecting Charles Kelly to the Orange Order this does not mean that he and other members of the Kelly family were not sympathizers.

The following is extrapolated from the antiquated legalese of the 1820s: A debt owed to James Taylor by John Kelly came due 25 September 1920. After a writ or notice of collection was given to the High Sherriff of the County of York, Edward Winslow Miller, on 28 September 1820, John Kelly's property was awarded to James Taylor with court fees and sheriff execution fees attached. When the court and sheriff fees were not paid on the due date of 10 October 1820, John Kelly's two thirds of lot 89 in Kingsclear were seized. After proper notice and advertisement was done, John Kelly's property was auctioned in Fredericton. William Taylor of Fredericton was the highest bidder.

Once all debts were settled, these proceedings were registered in the *New Brunswick, County Deed Registry Books, 1780-1930, for York (1825-1827)*, Volume 15, pp. 236-239 on 26 June 1826. It should be noted that John Kelly died between 4 September 1824 and 29 October 1825. (See Appendix I.)

On 4 June 1823, John and Mary (Unknown) Kelly sold the rear part of lot 89 to Dominic Bradley for eighty pounds. Both John Kelly and Mary (Unknown) Kelly formalized this transaction by signing with an "X" before the Justice of the Peace on 25 June 1823. This transaction was registered in the *New Brunswick, County Deed Registry Books, 1780-1930, for York (1823-1825)*, Volume 14, pp. 47-48 on 9 August 1823. (See Appendix H.)

On 4 September 1824, John Kelly made his last will and testament in which he appointed his wife Mary as sole executrix. Mary (Unknown) Kelly was given his farm and all his holdings, and his children William, Frances, Abel, Mary Ann, Ruth and Leonard Combs were granted five shillings each.

On 29 October 1825, Samuel Denny, who had been appointed delegate, and Mary (Unknown) Kelly appeared before Lieutenant-Governor Sir Howard Douglas where the will of John Kelly, who was deceased by that date, was filed and proved. The will and the accompanying material were registered in the York County Probate Court Records on 1 October 1825. (See Appendix G.)

Ironically, on 16 March 1848, John Kelly (farmer) bought one third of lot 89 in Kingsclear from Fredericton merchant James Taylor for the sum of one hundred pounds. This transaction was recorded in *New Brunswick, County Deed Registry Books, 1780-1930, for York (1847-1848)*, Volume 29, p. 222. (See Appendix M.)

In an email dated 18 October 2012, Linda (Kitchen) Aitken notes that her great great grandfather, John Kelly, son of William and Sarah Ann (Howard) Kelly, "was living on lot 89 from sometime before 1861 until after 1901. In the 1851 census, he and his wife

Elizabeth, were living with her parents, William and Sarah Long[,] but appear to have moved to lot 89 before the 1861 census. They are counted in the 1871, 1881, 1891, 1901 censuses. (Actually Elizabeth died after 1881 and he remarried.) There are a number of other deeds and land transactions mentioning John and Elizabeth. . . . [T]his is where my g[reat] grandfather, Duncan[,] and my [G]randfather Coburn were born. Sometime between 1901 and John's death in 1911, he moved away and . . . lived with another son. Eventually this property became part of the Kitchen farm, my father's family[,] until the flooding." The flooding occurred as a result of the construction of the Mactaquac Dam on the St. John River in New Brunswick in the 1960s. In a email of 15 November 2012, Linda (Kitchen) Aitken states that the flood waters reached their heights in September 1967.

The Dictionary of Canadian Biography Online, 1821-1835 (Volume VI) states that James Taylor (February 1761 – 27 January 1834), son of Captain Matthew Taylor and Elizabeth Archibald, married Margaret Bartlett, daughter of Richard Bartlett. James Taylor Senior,

> businessman, farmer, and politician . . . had at least four sons and two daughters. . . . James Taylor went to the Saint John valley sometime in the 1780s to join the Bartletts. . . . He set himself up as a lumber merchant in the parish of Maugerville, a few miles below Fredericton. In 1811, in addition to lumbering operations, he was farming . . .; two of his sons, James and Richard, were farming independently. Taylor's assessed valuation was more than twice that of any other person in the parish and he was rivaled in worth by only four or five other landowners in the county. He also accumulated a large number of mortgages on properties of his neighbours. His sons became known in the countryside for their rough, intimidating ways; each of them appeared before the magistrates one or more times on charges of assault.

The following comes from *Wikipedia* with references to *The Dictionary of Canadian Biography Online*:

> James Taylor (ca 1794 – February 4, 1856)[, son of James Taylor and Margaret Bartlett,] was a businessman and political figure in New Brunswick. He represented York in the Legislative Assembly of New Brunswick from 1833 to 1856. He was born in Fredericton. . . . With his brothers William and John F., he entered the family business in timber, ship building and construction. In 1829, he married Nancy Hatfield, whose sister had married his brother William. Taylor was a director of the Nashwaak Mill and Manufacturing Company, later serving as president of its milling operations. He also was a founder of the Central Bank of New Brunswick and a director of the Fredericton branch of the Bank of

British North America. Taylor also helped found the Fredericton Hotel and Stage Coach Company. He ran unsuccessfully for a seat in the New Brunswick assembly in 1830, but was declared elected in 1833 after he appealed the results of the by-election held in 1832 following the death of John Dow. Taylor served as paymaster and captain in the county militia. In 1840, he was named a justice of the peace and, in 1850, a customs controller. Taylor died in office in Fredericton.

From research conducted by Linda (Kitchen) Aitken in the *New Brunswick Deed Registry Books for York County* at the Provincial Archives of New Brunswick, it appears that John Kelly was able to retain a portion of the original Kelly property, which was passed on to his son William Kelly (ca 1792 – ca 1875/76), who passed it on to his son John Kelly (ca 25 November 1824 – 6 January 1912), who remained on the property until somewhere around 1900. (See Appendix L.)

The following paragraph by Ernest Hawkins from *Annals of the Colonial Church Fredericton* describes the working life of the early settlers of New Brunswick:

> At the end of autumn, gangs of men, each under a leader, ascend one of the great rivers which form the high roads of that country, and make a settlement of shanties, or log-huts, in the thick of a forest. The men rise at day-light, and divide themselves into three parties, one of which cuts down the trees, another squares them, and a third, with oxen, drags them to the nearest stream. After a day spent in this exhausting labour, they return to their shed, and, when supper is over, lay themselves to sleep upon the floor, which is covered with hay, straw, and branches. Their plan is to arrange themselves in a circle, with their feet towards a blazing pine fire, and then any one who awakes during the night throws on fresh billets of wood. . . . When the winter has been passed in this manner, and a considerable quantity of timber has accumulated, it is formed into large flat rafts, and, towards the end of April, floated down the rivers, then swollen by the melted snow, to St. John's, or Miramichi. (Chapter I)

Hawkins, citing the Society for the Propagation of the Gospel "report of 1841, p. 189," in which the Anglican Bishop documents his visit to the principal missions of New Brunswick in 1840: "Of St. John's he speaks as 'a city rapidly increasing, with a population which already exceeds thirty thousand; a number greater,' he says, 'than that of the inhabitants of New York, when my father first visited that city'." Hawkins quotes the bishop: "When I first visited New Brunswick, many years ago, the only means of conveyance between the sea-coast and Fredericton, the capital, were supplied by two small vessels, which were frequently delayed for many days by head winds and calms. There are now, daily and nightly, steam vessels from both points." (Chapter II)

The Kellys of Kingsclear

Early Anglican records are nearly impossible to locate. Linda (Kitchen) Aitken in an email of 22 May 2012 from Upper Kingsclear, New Brunswick, writes: "From what I have heard and read, these early church records were entirely dependent on the amount of documentation by the individual clergy. Some recorded and some didn't. I really feel that the early Kellys here were Church of England, at least until 1859 when the Baptist Church was built . . . in this community. . . . Henry Kelly, son of W[illia]m and Sarah was a founding member and John, my g[reat-]g[reat-]grandfather, was a member[,] as well[,] along with the Kellys from their families."

According to Rev. I.E. Bill in *Fifty Years with the Baptist Ministers and Churches of the Maritime Provinces of Canada*, "The Church at Prince William, under the pastorate for many years of Elder Lathrop Hammond, was . . . established in 1800." (p. 34)

It should be kept in mind that Henry Alline (14 June 1748 – 2 February 1784) and his New Light Movement had an enormous influence, which continues to the present day, on the Baptists of the Maritime Provinces and the State of Maine. More information on Henry Alline and the New Light Movement can be found in Paul Kimball's *The Last Lights: The New Brunswick Free Christian Baptists, 1832-1905*.

Reverend I.E. Bill, writing of the Baptist preacher Jospeh Crandall's ministry in 1800, includes the following in his *Fifty Years with the Baptist Ministers and Churches of the Maritime Provinces of Canada*:

> About this time he was filled with an anxious desire to visit the people on the River Saint John. It was the dead of winter, and how to go he could not tell; but he could find no rest. Finally, in company with a young man going in that direction, he put on showshoes, and hastened forward with God's message. Not being accustomed to this mode of journeying, he endured much fatigue, but travelled on, preaching in all the villages. He visited Norton and Bellisle, and in the latter place many were brough to know the truth. From Bellisle he passed on to Canning, where he made the acquaintance of Elijah Estabrooks. In this dirstrict he saw the work of God revive. Then he passed up the river, preaching in different places. On his way he met a Mr. Cole from Kingsclear, who was in pursuit of him to engage him to preach a funeral sermon. He preached — the word was attended with the Spirit's power, and many were converted to God.
>
> Mr. Crandall in his letters makes special reference to this visit, and says: — "A pious sister asked for baptism, and I answered that she would be immersed at ten o'clock, A.M., the next day. Accordingly, before the hour arrived, people came from all directions for many miles around, and the ice having been opened, the candidate related a clear Christian experience, and I batized her. When we came out of the water, two more told what God had done for their souls; and we could not leave the water until fourteen happy converts had been immersed in conformity of the Saviour's example. Surely this was the Lord's work. Four or five

hundred people were present, and it was a great day of God's power. The work of the Lord spread in every direction."

He remained on the river above Fredericton for some time, preaching the Gospel and immersing believers, as far up as Woodstock. (pp. 208-209)

Reverend I.E. Bill writes that the following biographical sketch of the "life and ministry" of Lathrop Hammond (10 April 1765 – 17 November 1848) "is extracted from the" 14 September 1849 edition of the "Christian Visitor."

He was baptized by Elder Elijah Estabrooks in 1807, and united with the Church of Prince William, in the County of York. He was soon afterwards ordained a deacon, and received a license from the Church to preach, and continued to exercise his gift with acceptance till the year 1810, when by request of the Church he was ordained and became pastor of the Church at Prince William. The connection continued for a period of twenty-six years. Mr. Hammond was zealous and indefatigable in his ministerial labours. During this period there were but few ministers of the gospel of any denomination in the part of the Province where he resided; and although he was not furnished with any adequate support from his people, and was obliged to labour with his hands to meet the wants of a rising family, still, in addition to his labours with his own Church, he frequently visited other settlements, preaching the gospel, visiting the sick, attending funerals, &c.

The Church at Prince William was frequently revived, and additions were made through the instrumentality of Mr. Hammond's labours. The most extensive revival that occurred was shortly after his ordination. This extended to other settlements which he occasionally visited.

In March 1832, Mr. Hammond visited the Tobique settlements, in the County of Carleton, and spent about six weeks in preaching the gospel and imparting religious instruction from house to house in the destitute section of the Province. The Lord blessed his labours, a number of persons professed faith in Christ and were baptized in obedience of the Saviour's command. During the September following, he revisited the Tobique, and organized a Church consisting of fifteen members. He continued to visit the settlement occasionally during the seven following years; when, in 1839, he removed thither with his family, having resigned the pastoral charge of the Prince William Church in 1836, where he was succeeded by Elder Thomas W. Saunders.

Mr. Hammond continued his labours with a bood degree of success at the Tobique till his death. (pp. 244-245)

I.E. Bill notes that upon his death at Tobique "[t]he remains of Mr. Hammond were taken to the Church, and a sermon preached on the occasion by Elder Gideon Eastabrooks from 2d Tim 4:7." (p. 246)

Edward Manning Saunders, under the heading "Brief Sketches of the Lives of the Departed" in his *History of the Baptists of the Maritime Provinces*, writes that Gideon Eastabrooks (17 August 1796 – 12 March 1880) was the son of Elijah Eastabrooks (16 May 1756 – 26 September 1825), who was born in Massachusetts and "came to St. John" with his parents in 1768. Saunders also notes an Alexander Estabrooks, "of New Brunswick Universty [who] studied theology at Newton Centre, Mass.[, and w]as pastor of Englishspeaking people in Maulmain, India. His wife died. He returned home with shattered health and a morbid mind. He was intensely religious." (p. 489)

The following appears in the 22 April 1896 edtion of the *Messenger and Visitor*: "d. Prudence HOVEY, age 61 years, died at her home in Ludlow (North. Co.) 10th inst. Sister Hovey is a sister to the wife of the late Alexander ESTABROOKS, at one time missionary on the F.F. when he lost his wife to the great sorrow of his heart. She leaves four sons and two daughters." (*Provincial Archives of New Brunswick: Daniel F. Johnson's New Brunswick Newspaper Vital Statistics*, Volume 104, Number 441.)

In a transcription of a taped conversation with Eva (Kelly) McBreairty (30 March 1877 – 23 June 1974) contained in *Conversations with A'nt Ev': An Oral History of the Allagash* by Darrell McBreairty, Eva (Kelly) McBreairty, who was the daughter of Charles Burton Kelly (26 June 1839 – 6 February 1912) and Sarah Ann (Mullins) Kelly (1 September 1842 – 3 March 1924), remembered a Reverend Estabrooks, who was an early minister in Allagash, Maine, visiting her parents' house when she was a young girl. (p. 109)

The following appears in "Notes on Chapter VIII" in *Conversations with A'nt Ev': An Oral History of the Allagash* by Darrell McBreairty, under note 26: "I have not been able to locate any information in relation to this Rev. Estabrooks, but there is a Rev. Alexander Estabrooks buried at the Upper Gagetown Cemetery in Gagetown, N.B.[,] Canada. The tombstone shows that he was born November 29, 1836 and died September 18, 1893. It also states that his last wish was to have the following inscribed: 'Christ in you the hope of Glory.' It is very possible that this is the Rev. Estabrooks who ministered in Allagash, but I have not been able to establish a definite link." (p. 118)

According to his death record (001688), Reverend Alexander Estabrooks died in Saint John, New Brunswick, at the age of sixty-two on 18 September 1893. He is listed as a Baptist clergyman, with York County listed as his residence. The cause of death is listed as "Exhaustion from Chronic Gastral Disease," which he had endured for "10 years." (*Provincail Archives of New Brunswick, Vital Statistics from Government Records*) (Microfilm: F14886) (RS141).

Note 26 in "Notes on Chapter VIII," in *Conversations with A'nt Ev': An Oral History of the Allagash* by Darrell McBreairty, also contains the following from notes taken by Darrell McBreairty in conversation with Eunice (Kelly) McBreairty (10 August 1886 – 15 April 1975), daughter of Charles Burton Kelly (26 June 1839 – 6 February 1912) and Sarah Ann (Mullins) Kelly (1 September 1842 – 3 March 1924), on 25 August 1974: "Rev.

Estabrooks went to Kellys' one Sunday to visit. He asked where the boys were, and Charles Kelly answered that his sons were fishing. Estabrooks said, 'They could be doing worse. They've gut their mind on the hook'." (p. 118)

W.S. MacNutt writes, in *New Brunswick A History: 1784 -1867*, "It was among the poorer settlers in wilderness communities that the Baptists made most headway. In 1814 there were eleven organized churches in New Brunswick and by 1821 they felt strong enough to form an association of their own, independent of that in Nova Scotia where they had drawn much of their strength. For a long time their 'membership' remained comparatively small. As late as 1839 the number was under 2,000, but this is no indication of the ferment their evangelistic methods created in society at large. The movement did not acquire stability until it attracted the support of a considerable number of wealthy merchants of Fredericton and Saint John." (p. 168)

It appears because there were few or no Anglican Church buildings in the early days of the province that even if a Rector kept a register or any type of record, these documents were misplaced or lost over time.

Acting rector of Christ Church at Maugerville, Raper Milner, on 28 August 1821, states in the Memorial (contained in Appendix N) in regard to the 1792 marriage record of Elizabeth (Srymesan) Marsh and Leonard Reed at Maugerville, New Brunswick, that he has "not been able to find any such Entry by reason that there is no Register remaining, as I can find, of Marriages or other parochial Duties celebrated or performed by the said former Rector at that or any other time before or after, during his Incumbency, he having as is represented, taken the Register by him kept with him when he left the said Parish."

Elizabeth S. Sewell in her preface to *Sunbury County, New Brunswick Marriages 1766-1888, Volume 1* states, "The Anglican Church records date from 1787 after the coming of the Loyalists and end abruptly in 1803 only to resume in 1847."

Ernest Hawkins B. D. in *Annals of the Colonial Church Fredericton* writes the following:

> Sir Howard Douglas, on assuming the government of New Brunswick [in 1824], very early turned his attention to the state of religion in the province; and, with a view to obtain accurate information on the subject, addressed a circular to the members of the House of Assembly, and other gentlemen of influence, begging for a return as to the number of churches, clergymen, &c. in their several districts. From the returns thus sent in, a summary was prepared by the Rev. George Best. . . .
>
> In the county of YORK but few of the parishes had either churches or resident clergymen; so that the people, though occasionally visited by an itinerant missionary, were in a measure compelled to have recourse for religious instruction to dissenting teachers of various denominations, of whom the Baptists seem to . . . have been the most numerous. Thus, for example, in the parish of *Prince William*, containing a population of between five and six hundred, one half of whom were members of our

own communion, there was no church, and divine service was very rarely performed, while there was a Baptist meeting-house and a resident preacher. In the parish of *Kent*, extending forty-seven miles on both sides of the river St. John to the Great Falls, and thence to the boundary of Lower Canada, there was no church or clergyman nearer than Woodstock, a distance of seventy-three miles from the Falls; though the population was 2,297, and one-third of them belonged to the Church of England. In short, for the whole county of YORK, which is situated on the river St. John, above Fredericton, and contained a population of 11,072, there were only *three* clergymen (including one who was attached to the college at Fredericton), and *four* churches, two of which were in an unfinished state.

In the county of SUNBURY, which was divided into four parishes, and contained 3,227 inhabitants, there were two churches and one resident clergyman. The great majority of the people were dissenters. (Chapter II.)

In his book *Canada, Nova Scotia, New Brunswick and the other British Provinces in North America, with a Plan of National Colonization*, James S. Buckingham, who traveled through North America in 1839, reports that in that year Fredericton, New Brunswick, had a population of approximately 5,000 people. (p. 418)

For clarity, I am assigning numbers to differentiate the generations in the genealogy of the John Kelly family. John Kelly is given number 1, his children, number 2, grandchildren, number 3 and greatgrandchildren, number 4. I have also elected to list John's wife Mary as Mary Unknown although there is a strong family tradition that she may, in fact, have been a Cain or Kean.

1. John Kelly (ca 1760 – between 4 September 1824 and 29 October 1825) married 1st: Unknown Unknown; 2nd: Mary Unknown (ca 1762 or ca 1772 - ca 1845). Mary Unknown's dates are calculated from her 1839 and 1843 pension petitions contained in *Records of Old Revolutionary Soldiers and Their Widows*.

Children of John and Mary (Unknown) Kelly:

2. William Kelly (ca 1792 – ca 1875/76) married Sarah Ann Howard (ca 1796 – between 1881 and 1891 census), daughter of John Howard (ca 1770/71 – 6 July 1854) and Rebekca/Rebecca Hayward (ca 1774 – ca 1856), 23 March 1813 in Kingsclear, York County, New Brunswick. According to transcriptions compiled by George H. Hayward contained in *York County, New Brunswick, Marriage Records, Volume 1, 1812-1837* (pp. 25 & 28) from microfilm at the Provincial Archives of New Brunswick (RS 160 – York County Council Records, L/4/Volume A 1812-1837, F15550 (p. 011), the ceremony was conducted by Rev. George Pidgeon, Anglican Rector (1795-1814) of Fredericton, New Brunswick, and witnessed by Amos Dow and Richard B. Taylor. (See Appendices S and T for more information on the Hayward family.) William and Sarah Ann (Howard) Kelly lived in Queensbury, New Brunswick, where they are listed as being members of the Church of England in the 1861 census. In an email of 14 January 2014, Linda (Kitchen) Aitken says, "I suspect William was buried in Queensbury and prob[ably] Sarah as well. The Kellys on this side [south side] of the river were buried in a cemetery at Longs Creek which was later relocated [as a result of the Mactaquac Dam] to Prince William . . . ." Sarah Ann (Howard) Kelly is listed in the 1881 census as living with her son Henry Kelly in Kingsclear, New Brunswick.

Children of William and Sarah Ann (Howard) Kelly:

3.Bathsheba "Basha" "Bashey" Kelly (ca 1816 – living at 1901 census) married Fabien/Duel Mauzerolle (1815 - ?), son of Pierre and Marie Anne (Godin) Mauzerolle, 31 October 1854 in Fredericton, York, Coounty, New Brunswick.

3.Henry "Deacon" Kelly (April 1818 - 28 February 1896) married Hannah Elizabeth Hayward (April 1827 – 8 February 1901), daughter of "Deacon" Daniel and Amy (Nevers) Hayward, 30 August 1849 in Lincoln Parish, Sunbury County, New Brunswick. Henry Kelly was a farmer. Hannah Elizabeth (Hayward) Kelly was born in Lincoln Parish, Sunbury County, New Brunswick. Henry "Deacon" and Hannah Elizabeth (Hayward) Kelly, who were Baptists, were buried in the Community Cemetery, Prince William, York County, New Brunswick. More detailed documentation regarding the Henry "Deacon" and Hannah Elizabeth (Hayward) Kelly family is contained in George H. Hayward's *Haywards of Sunbury & Carleton Counties, N. B., and Some of Their Descendants* (pp. 70-72).

Children of Henry "Deacon" and Hannah Elizabeth (Hayward) Kelly:

4.Clarissa M. Kelly (ca 1850/51 – 28 February 1921) married Asa Coburn Musgrove (21 August 1850 – 8 September 1939), son of Abraham and Mary (Balmaine) Musgrove, 27 June 1877. Clarissa M. (Kelly) Musgrove was born in Kingsclear, New Brunswick, and died at Vancouver, British Columbia. Asa Coburn Musgrove was born at Millstream, Kings County, New Brunswick, and died in Vancouver, British Columbia.

4. Sarah E. "Sadie" Kelly (1852/53 – 11 June 1878/79) never married. Sarah E. "Sadie" Kelly died in Kingsclear, York County, New Brunswick.

4. Georgeanne "Georgie" Kelly (26 December 1856 – 16 February 1912) married Cleveland Campbell "Clive" Patterson (ca 1861 – 14 October 1935), son of Luther and Lydia Ann (Estey) Patterson, 8 July 1885 in Upper Kingsclear, York County, New Brunswick. Cleveland Campbell "Clive" and Georgeanne "Georgie" (Kelly) Patterson both died in Vancouver, British Columbia. Cleveland Campbell "Clive" Patterson remarried after the death of Georgeanne "Georgie" (Kelly) Patterson.

4. George Arthur Kelly (5 March 1857 – 14 December 1925) married Marion Beatrice Harris (17 July 1864 – 3 January 1943) ca 1884. George Arthur Kelly was born in Upper Kingsclear, York County, New Brunswick, and died in Fredericton, York County, New Brunswick.

4. Amy Nevers Kelly (ca 1859; gravestone: 1860 – 26 January 1946) married her cousin George W. Small (1861 – 1948), son of Bartholomew and Mary Ann (Hayward) Small, 17 January 1895 in Houlton, Aroostook County, Maine. Amy Nevers (Kelly) Small was born in Kingsclear, York County, New Brunswick, and died in Houlton, Aroostook County, Maine. George W. Small was born and died in Houlton, Aroostook County, Maine. George W. and Amy Nevers (Kelly) Small had one adopted daughter.

4. C. Augusta "Gussie" Kelly (ca 1866 – 12 December 1938) married Dr. Charles Hopkins Long (4 October 1863 – ?), son of Henry M. and Annie (Perkins) Long, 30 September 1891 in Kingsclear, York County, New Brunswick. C. Augusta "Gussie" (Kelly) Long was born in Kingsclear, York County, New Brunswick. Dr. Charles (Hopkins) Long was born in Bright, York County, New Brunswick. Dr. Charles (Hopkins) and C. Augusta "Gussie" (Kelly) Long apparently had no children.

4. Alberta "Bertie" Kelly (16 October 1865 – 6 February 1958) married Edgar Percy Slipp (10 November 1861 – 25 December 1938), son of William and Sarah Ann (Elliott?) Slipp, 15 February 1888 in Kingsclear, York County, New Brunswick. Alberta "Bertie" (Kelly) Slipp died in Crow Wing County, Minnesota. Edgar Percy Slipp was born in Queensbury, York County, New Brunswick, and died in Crow Wing County, Minnesota.

3. George H. Kelly (1819/20 – 25 April 1886) married Eunice Ann Long (10 February 1830 – 9 December 1913). George H. Kelly died in Kingsclear, York County, New Brunswick.

In the *Robert Connors Ledgers* at the Robert Connors House in Connors, New Brunswick, George Kelly appears in *Ledger B* (pp. 27-28) in 1875 and again in *Ledger B* (pp. 29-30) in 1876.

Eva "Ev" (Kelly) McBreairty in a transcript done by Darrell Robert McBreairty contained in *Conversations with A'nt Ev': an Oral History of the Allagash* (p. 26) says that her Uncle George H. Kelly was a big man.

Children of George and Eunice Ann (Long) Kelly:

4. John G. Kelly (ca 1849 – 30 July 1911) married Addie M. Bartlett (ca 1856 – after 1930 United States census), daughter of Nathan and Sophia Augusta (Unknown) Bartlett, ca 1880/1881. John G. Kelly died in Big Rapids, Mecosta County, Michigan.

In the *Robert Connors Ledgers* at the Robert Connors House in Connors, New Brunswick, John G. Kelly appears in *Ledger B* (p. 82) in 1875 and again in *Ledger D* (p. 170) in 1877.

Eva "Ev" (Kelly) McBreairty relates in a transcript done by Darrell Robert McBreairty contained in *Conversations with A'nt Ev': and Oral History of the Allagash* (p. 26) that when John G. Kelly asked his grandmother, Sarah Ann (Howard) Kelly, if he and his wife could stay in her downstairs bedroom, Sarah Ann (Howard) Kelly told him that that bedroom was reserved for visiting ministers and that he would have to take a bedroom upstairs.

4. Ambrose (ca 1850 - ?).

4. Alexander Kelly (12 July 1852 – 22 October 1936) married Susan Lahey (15 November 1860 – 14 October 1924), daughter of Richard and Elizabeth (White) McAuley Lahey, according to the 1881 New Brunswick Census, of Victoria County, St. Francois, New Brunswick. Alexander Kelly, known as "Alex" or "Eck Jr.," was born in Kingsclear, York County, New Brunswick, and died in Douglas, York County, New Brunswick. Susan (Lahey) Kelly died in Kingsclear, York County, New Brunswick.

In the *Robert Connors Ledgers* at the Robert Connors House in Connors, New Brunswick, Alexander Kelly Jr. appears in *Ledger B* (p. 278) in 1876; in *Ledger D* (p. 121) in 1877 and again in *Ledger D* (pp. 122-123) in 1878.

4. Annie Martha "Annie" Kelly (25 April 1855 – 7 April 1933) married Herbert Gaynor Winter (9 November 1850 – 28 September 1925), son of Richard Pickard and Rebecca Ward Winter, 20

October 1873 in Upper Kingsclear, York County, New Brunswick. Annie Martha "Annie" (Kelly) Winter was born in Kingsclear, York County, New Brunswick, and died in Fredericton, York County, New Brunswick. Herbert (Gaynor) Winter was born in New Brunswick, and died in Fredericton, York, County, New Brunswick.

4.Ella Jane "Belle" Kelly (1860 – 21 December 1894) married Guilford/Gilford Ira Hammond (28 December 1861 – 7 May 1940), son of Judah and Lucy (Strange/Strain) Hammond, 24 August 1880. Ella Jane (Kelly) Hammond died in Kingsclear, York County, New Brunswick. Guilford/Gilford Ira Hammond was born in Kingsclear or Prince William, York County, New Brunswick, and died in Carleton County, New Brunswick. He married Ella M. Smith after the death of Ella Jane (Kelly) Hammond.

4.Carrie E. Kelly (ca 1864/65 – 26 August 1914) married Lewis A. Wooll (ca 1860 – ?), son of John O. and Lucina (Curtis) Wooll, 8 August 1888 in Big Rapids, Mecosta County, Michigan. Carrie E. (Kelly) Wooll died in Flint, Genesee County, Michigan. Lewis A. Wooll was born in Ohio.

4.Woodford Kelly (1870 - ?).

3.John L. Kelly (25 November 1824 – 6 January 1911/12) married 1st: Elizabeth Anne "Betsy Ann" Long (1827 – between census 1881 and 1891), daughter of William and Sarah E. (Reed) Long, 17 July 1850; 2nd: Jemima (Nelson) Agnew (21 May 1832 – 3 January 1903). In the 1851 census for York County, John Kelly is listed as a lodger in the home of William and Sarah (Reed) Long. John Kelly was born in Queensbury, York County, New Brunswick, and died at Kingsclear, York County, New Brunswick. Although John Kelly's death certificate, which was registered 11 January 1911, states that he died 6 January 1911 of heart failure, at least one other record states that he died 6 January 1912. He married Jemima (Nelson) Agnew sometime between the census of 1881 and 1891. Jemima (Nelson) Agnew Kelly, whose death was registered in the *County Register of Deaths York County 1888-1919, Vital Statistics, F19141*, on 18 May 1903, was first married to John Agnew, who drowned in Kingsclear, York County, New Brunswick, 9 May 1861. In the *County Register of Deaths York County 1888-1919, Vital Statistics, F19141*, Jemima (Nelson) Agnew Kelly is recorded as having died 3 January 1902 or 1903 of pneumonia. She was listed as a Baptist and a housekeeper from Kingsclear, York County, New Brunswick.

Eva "Ev" (Kelly) McBreairty in a transcript done by Darrell Robert McBreairty contained in *Conversations with A'nt Ev': an Oral History of the Allagash* (p. 26) says that her Uncle John Kelly was a big man.

From notes taken by Darrell Robert McBreairty on 21 October 1974 with Eunice (Kelly) McBreairty contained in *Conversations with A'nt Ev': an Oral History of the Allagash* (note 22, p. 39), Eunice (Kelly) McBreairty said that she remembered her Uncle John Kelly coming to visit his brother Charles. No one knew John was coming, but when the mailman dropped him off, Charles Kelly recognized his brother as he came across the field. Since John Kelly was a very religious man, during the three days he visited "there was much Bible Reading and prayer." John Kelly then traveled down to St. Francis, Maine, where he visited for a few days with his brother James Kelly before going home. In notes with Eunice (Kelly) McBreairty by Darrell Robert McBreairty in an undated entry in a spiral binder, Eunice said that her uncle, John Kelly, came up to Allagash with the mailman from St. Francis, Maine, when Eunice was ten or eleven years old. Eunice (Kelly) McBreairty was born on 10 August 1886.

Children of John L. and Elizabeth Anne "Betsy Ann" (Long) Kelly:

4.Lucy Ann Kelly (ca 1850 – ?) either married or died between census of 1881 and 1891. Lucy Ann Kelly was born in Kingsclear, York County, New Brunswick. Lucy Ann Kelly is listed as a lodger in the home of William and Sarah (Reed) Long in the 1851 census for York County, and is listed as "Annie" in the 1881 census.

4.Eliza Lydia "Lyde" Kelly (ca 23 October 1852/53 – ?) married Harvey Kitchen (10 March 1857/58 – 17 August 1913) 4 June 1884 at Fredericton, York County, New Brunswick.

4.Elisha "Lish" Kelly (23 September 1855 – 24 August 1936) married Harriet A. "Hat" (Smith) Hammond (1855 – 4 October 1924), daughter of Sidney and Jane (Unknown) Smith, 20 October 1890 in Fredericton, York County, New Brunswick. Elisha "Lish" Kelly was born in Kingsclear, York County, New Brunswick, and died in Fredericton, York County, New Brunswick. Harriet A. "Hat" (Smith) Hammond Kelly, who was born and died in Kingsclear, York County, New Brunswick, was first married to William T. Hammond.

4.Benjamin "Ben" Kelly (14 October 1856 – 1 January 1925) married (Annie) Elizabeth "Bessie" Poore (1866 – 4 September 1906) 25 July 1888 in Upper Kingsclear, York County, New Brunswick. Benjamin "Ben" Kelly died in Cambridge, Massachusetts. (Annie) Elizabeth "Bessie" (Poore) Kelly was born in Grand Bank,

Newfoundland and died of cancer in Central Kingsclear, York County, New Brunswick.

4. Duncan David Kelly (3 January 1859 – 11 April 1935) married Sarah Ann Elliot (2 May 1869 – 14 June 1930), daughter of Joseph and Phoebe (Goodine) Elliott, 12 June 1884. The Goodines were French, with the original name of Gaudin. Duncan David Kelly was born in Kelly Creek in Kingsclear, York County, New Brunswick, and died in Saint John, New Brunswick. Sarah Ann (Elliot) Kelly was born in Queensbury, York County, New Brunswick, and died in Kingsclear, York County, New Brunswick.

Although never formally married, Duncan David Kelly and Isabelle Betts were the parents of Albert Burton Kelly (25 December 1882 – ?), who married Nancy A. Curtis on 27 December 1906 in York County, New Brunswick. Albert Burton Kelly was born in Rosborough Settlement, York County, New Brunswick.

4. Frederick S. "Fred" Kelly (21 March 1861 – 11 March 1925) married Frances Scott (1868/69 – ?), daughter of George and Robena (Smith) Scott, 1 August 1892 in Fredericton, York County, New Brunswick. Frederick S. "Fred" Kelly died in Fredericton, York County, New Brunswick. Frances (Scott) Kelly was born at Heron's Lake, New Brunswick.

In the *Robert Connors Ledgers* at the Robert Connors House in Connors, New Brunswick, a "Simon F Kelly" appears in *Ledger B* (p. 89) in 1875.

4. Henry/Harry Kelly (ca 1865 – apparently between 1871 and 1881 census).

4. Frances "Frank" Kelly (ca 9 July 1865 ? – ?) married 1st: Joseph Edward Elliot (ca 1845 – 23 January 1918) 6 December 1882 in York County, New Brunswick; 2nd: David Bock (? – ?) 4 December 1918; 3rd. Andrew James Coulsey (? – 22 September 1935) 27 January 1920 in Stanley, York County, New Brunswick. Joseph Elliot was first married to Phoebe Goodine, and he is buried in Marysville, New Brunswick.

4. Bedford George Kelly (26 September 1873/74 – 18 November 1956) married Mary Agatha Goodine (25 February 1882 – 2 July 1951), daughter of Lewis Goodine and Faye Goodine. Bedford George Kelly died in Dumfries, York County, New Brunswick. Mary Agatha (Goodine) Kelly was born in Kingsclear, York County, New Brunswick, and died in Dumfries, York County, New Brunswick. Lewis and Faye (Goodine) Goodine were both born in Kingsclear, York County, New Brunswick.

3.Elizabeth Kelly (ca 1826 - between 1871 and 1881 census) married Louis Mazerolle/Mauzerolle, son of Pierre Mazerolle/Mauzerolle and Marie Ann Godin, 31 October 1854 in Fredericton, York County, New Brunswick. (Spelling of the name Mauzerolle/Mazerolle in government and church records can take various forms even within the same family.)

Children Louis and Elizabeth (Kelly) Mazerolle/Mauzerolle:

4.Barbara Mazerolle (October 1856 - ?) married Martin Burke, son of Martin Burke and Mary Ridder, 28 September 1909. Barbara (Mazerolle) Burke was born in Mazerolle Settlement, York County, New Brunswick.
4.John Louis Mazerolle (24 January 1859 – 2 July 1943) married Josephine Louise Sears (14 July 1859 – 9 June 1940), daughter of John Sears (born in French Village, York County, New Brunswick) and Rebecca Burgoyne (born in Kingsclear, York County, New Brunswick). John Louis Mazerolle was born in Mazerolle Settlement, York County, New Brunswick. Josephine Louise Sears was born in French Village, York County, New Brunswick.
4.Alice Mazerolle (1860 - ?) was born in Kingsclear, York County, New Brunswick.
4.Eliza Mazerolle (14 January 1863 - ?) was born in Kingsclear, York County, New Brunswick.
4.Barbery Mazerolle (1865 - ?) was born in Kingsclear, York County, New Brunswick.
4.Mary Ann Mazerolle/Mazerall (March 1868 - ?) married Alexander Goodine. Both Mary Ann Mazerall and Alexander Goodine were born in Kingsclear, York County, New Brunswick.

3.Frances Ann "Fanny" Kelly (ca 1829 – between 1891 and 1901 census) married John Fred "Jack" Niles (24 January 1825 – 13 May 1902) ca 1848. Frances Ann "Fanny" Kelly was born in Queensbury, York County, New Brunswick.

Children of John Fred "Jack" and Frances Ann "Fanny" (Kelly) Niles:

4.Phebe Sophia Niles (? - ?) married Unknown Yerxa.
4.Sarah Niles (? - ?) married George Kew.
4.Agnes Niles (? - ?).
4.Julia Niles (? -?) married Frank McKeen 1 October 1879.
4.Calvin "Cal" Niles (ca 1849 ?).

In the *Robert Connors Ledgers* at the Robert Connors House in Connors, New Brunswick, Calvin Niles appears in *Ledger D* (p. 374) in 1878.

4.Eliza Jane Niles (ca 1851 - ?) married James William Smith. Eliza Jane Niles was born in Queensbury, York County, New Brunswick.

4.Charles Henry Niles (ca 1861 - ?) married Lena/Lina Elizabeth McKeen 9 March 1887 in Fredericton, York County, New Brunswick. Charles Henry Niles was born in Queensbury, York County, New Brunswick.

4.George Niles (ca 1864 - ?) was born in Queensbury, York County, New Brunswick.

4.David Niles (20 March 1865 - ?) married Annie McLean (28 July 1871 - ?) 10 July 1895.

4.Andrew Niles (after 1868 - ?) was born in Queensbury, York County, New Brunswick.

4.Lavina/Alvina Niles (ca 1871 - ?) was born in Queensbury, York County, New Brunswick.

3.William "Bill" Kelly (1831 – after 1871 census). In notes taken by Darrell Robert McBreairty with Lucy (Kelly) Kelly (2 March 1906 – 21 August 1982) 11 June 1976 contained in *Conversations with A'nt Ev': an Oral History of the Allagash* (note 21, p. 26), Lucy recalled her father William Kelly (16 March 1869 – 11 July 1954) telling her of remembering his Uncle William "Bill" Kelly, who had served on the Union side in the American Civil War, coming to visit his brother Charles Kelly in Allagash, Maine. William "Bill" Kelly was wearing his military uniform. William "Bill" Kelly was born in Queensbury, York County, New Brunswick.

3.Alexander "Eck" Kelly (10 January 1835 – 7 January 1914) married Barbara Long (28 July 1825 – 18 July 1909), daughter of Abraham Long (1794 – 1863) and Catherine Good/Goode (1796 – 1835), 7 May 1879 in Kingsclear, York County, New Brunswick. Alexander "Eck" and Barbara (Long) Kelly are buried in the Prince William Community Cemetery in York County, New Brunswick. The Long house at Kings Landing was from this family.

In the *Robert Connors Ledgers* at the Robert Connors House in Connors, New Brunswick, Alexander Kelly Sr. appears in *Ledger D* (p. 268) in 1878.

Eva "Ev" (Kelly) McBreairty in a transcript done by Darrell Robert McBreairty contained in *Conversations with A'nt Ev': an Oral History of the Allagash* (p. 26) says that her Uncle Alexander "Eck" Kelly was a big man.

In an interview by Darrell Robert McBreairty with Elva Noyes (Kelly) Brewer (9 November 1929 – 21 October 2011), daughter of Lansing/Lanson Kelly (9 June 1899 – 3 May 1943) and Lucy Ann

McBreairty (2 March 1906 – 21 August 1982), 9 February 2007 in Lauderhill, Florida, Elva said her mother told her she (Lucy) was told by her father, William Kelly, that Alexander "Eck" Kelly, who had a contentious relationship with his family, would come to Allagash, Maine, to stay, as long as the Canadian laws would allow, with his brother Charles Kelly and Charles' family before going back to New Brunswick. After a short period in New Brunswick, Alexander "Eck" Kelly would return to stay with his brother in Allagash. It should be noted that Charles Burton Kelly died 6 February 1912, and Alexander "Eck" Kelly died 7 January 1914.

Linda (Kitchen) Aitken, in an email of 29 September 2013, writes that although George Peabody states in *Kings Landing: A Living History Colourguide* that Alexander "Eck" and Barbara (Long) Kelly were married after Catherine (Goode) Long died, he is mistaken because Catherine (Goode) Long died 20 February 1885 according to the notice published 7 March 1885 in the *New Brunswick Reporter and Fredericton Advertiser* (*Provincial Archives of New Brunswick: Daniel F. Johnson's New Brunswick Newspaper Vital Statistics*, Volume 64, Number 512), and the couple married 7 May 1879 according to the wedding notice appearing 14 May 1879 in *The Christian Visitor* (*Provincial Archives of New Brunswick: Daniel F. Johnson's New Brunswick Newspaper Vital Statistics*, Volume 47, Number 1453).

In the same email, Linda (Kitchen) Aitken establishes that in the 1940s, Henry Brown (1903 – 1978) and Beatrice Lillian (Kelly) Brown (20 March 1906 – 4 June 1996) lived in the Long house. Beatrice (Kelly) Brown was the daughter of Duncan David Kelly (3 January 1859 – 11 April 1935) and Sarah Ann Elliot (2 May 1869 – 14 June 1930). Duncan David Kelly was the son of John Kelly (25 November 1824 – 6 January 1911) and Elizabeth Anne "Betsy Ann" Long (1827 – between census 1881 and 1891). John Kelly was the son of William Kelly (ca 1792 – ca 1875/76) and Sarah Ann Howard (ca 1796 – between 1881 and 1891 census). Linda (Kitchen) Aitken writes, in the same 29 September 2013 email, "The last occupants before [the Long house] was moved to Kings Landing were my paternal great uncle . . ." Harry "Bert" Kitchen (9 March 1909 – 22 April 1907), son of Tyler Kitchen and Eva Courser, and Marion Violet Kelly (28 May 1912 – ?). Marion Violet (Kelly) Kitchen was the daughter of Daniel Hayward Kelly (? – 11 June 1959) and Lydia Jewett (2 December 1883 – 29 March 1936).

In an email on 4 November 2013, Linda (Kitchen) Aitken explains that Marion Violet (Kelly) Kitchen's father, Daniel Hayward Kelly, was the son of George Arthur Kelly (1 March 1857 – 14 December 1925) and Marion Beatrice Harris (17 July 1864 – 3 January 1943); George Arthur Kelly was the son of Henry "Deacon" Kelly (April 1818 - 28 February 1896) and Hannah Elizabeth Hayward (April 1827 – 8 February 1901); Henry "Deacon" Kelly was the son of William Kelly (ca 1792 – ca 1875/76) and Sarah Anne Howard (ca 1796 – between 1881 and 1891 census); William Kelly was the son of John Kelly (ca 1760 – between 4 September 1824 and 29 October 1825) and Mary (Unknown) (ca 1762 or ca 1772 - ca 1845).

Alec McEwen, in his *In Search of the Highlands: Mapping the Canada-Maine Boundary, 1839,* quotes from George William Featherstonhaugh's journal entry of 24 August 1839 that on the right bank of the St. John River "10 miles from Fredericton [is] a small village called French Village, containing a few Indian families of mixed Canadian blood, with a small church. At ½ past nine p.m. reached a place on the left bank, crossed the ferry and walked a mile to Long's public house where made a hearty supper and went to bed." On 25 August 1839, Featherstonhaugh writes: "Rose at 5 a.m. bit by the bugs. The people of the house are civil, but entertaining such people as they do we cannot expect much beyond civility. All the second-rate taverns of this continent are alike. There is always something to eat, and a bed to lie down on. Generally there is always civil treatment. But what you may always be sure of finding is dirt, bugs, fleas, and coarse familiar manners. Walked back, crossed the ferry, and at 6 a.m. started again in our boat, which we found much sweeter than the tavern." (p. 22)

Children of Alexander "Eck" and Barbara (Long) Kelly;

4. Edward/Edmund Kelly (29 May 1877 - ?).

3. James Allen "Jim" Kelly (30 April 1835 – 4 June 1919) married 1st: Margaret Mauzerolle (ca 1839/40 – ca 1862/63), daughter of Francis Louis Mauzerolle (ca 1818 - ?) and Roseanne Mauzerolle (ca 1819 - ?), ca 1857/58; 2nd: Josephine "Josie" Hunnewell (12 February 1841 – 20 October 1920), daughter of Barnabas Hunnewell (24 July 1790 – 17 October 1868) and Elizabeth Hafford (5 July 1820 – 25 May 1905), ca 1878. Margaret (Mauzerolle) Kelly died in a sledding accident. According to transcriptions compiled by George H. Hayward contained in *York County, New Brunswick, Marriage Records, Volume 1, 1812-1837* (p. 52), and on microfilm at the Provincial Archives of New Brunswick (RS 160 – York County Council Records, L/4/Volume A 1812-1837, F15550 (p. 528), "Francis Louis Muzrall" and "Rosanne Muzarall" were married 5 June 1837 in Queensbury, York County, New Brunswick. Witnesses were Michael Tonai and Jane Smith. James Allen Kelly was born in Kingsclear, York County, New Brunswick, and died in St. Francis, Aroostook County,

Maine. James Allen "Jim" Kelly left his children to be raised by their maternal grandparents after Margret (Mauzerolle) Kelly died.

In the *Robert Connors Ledgers* at the Robert Connors House in Connors, New Brunswick, James Allen Kelly appears in *Ledger D* (p.459) in 1878, then on 1 April 1879 he appears again in *Ledger D* (p. 497), only this time under the heading of "B. Hunnewell & J. A. Kelly."

Children of James Allen and Margaret (Mauzerolle) Kelly:

4.Louis Kelly (Ca 1858 - ?) was baptized 2 October 1859 at 11 months old.

4.Matilda Margaret Kelly (15 August 1860 – 5 November 1954) married Thomas Andrew "Tommy" Goodine (4 February 1857 – 8 April 1937), son of David and Mary Ann (Niles) Goodine ca 1889. Matilda Margaret (Kelly) Goodine was born and died in Kingsclear, York County, New Brunswick. Thomas Andrew "Tommy" Goodine was born in Queensbury, York County, New Brunswick, and died in Kingsclear, York County, New Brunswick.

4.Adelaide "Addie" Kelly (ca 1862 – 6 July 1894) married Augus McMullin ca 1879. Adelaide "Addie" Kelly was baptized 1 October 1865 at five years old, which contradicts the New Brunswick census records. Adelaide "Addie" (Kelly) McMullin drowned at Canterbury, York County, New Brunswick.

Children of James Allen and Josephine (Hunnewell) Kelly:

4.John S. Hunnewell "Kelly" (ca 1874 – 21 October 1945) was born out of wedlock to Josephine Hunnewell. John S. Hunnewell was also known as "John Kelly." He had a contentious relationship with his mother, who was a rather difficult woman, according to anecdotes by her grandchildren. Josephine "Josie" (Hunnewell) Kelly was cross-eyed and decidedly unattractive. John S. Hunnewell was a veteran of World War I. He had a good relationship with Stella (Sirois) Kelly, his sister-in-law, and maintained a correspondence with her. Toward the end of his life, he sent Stella (Sirois) Kelly his coin collection. Stella (Sirois) Kelly, seeing an advertisement for free appraisal of old coins in the *Grit* or a similar periodical, made the mistake of mailing John S. Hunnewell's coin collection to the address in the advertisement. Needless to say, the coins disappeared. The family always maintained that John S. Hunnewell worked for the postal department in Alaska.

In the United States Census of 1920, appearing in the *FamilySearch* database, John S. Hunnewell, who is single, is living in Seattle, Washington, with an estimated birth date of 1874. He says he and his father were born in Maine, but his mother was born in Massachusetts. (*https://familysearch.org/ark:/61903/1:1:MHNT-6DZ*) Josephine (Hunnewell) Kelly was born in Fort Kent, Maine, on 12 February 1841. Josephine (Hunnewell) Kelly's mother, Elizabeth (Hafford) Hunnewell, was born in Maine on 5 July 1820. Maine became independent from Massachusetts in the Missouri Compromise of 4 March 1820.

In the United States Census of 1930, appearing in the *FamilySearch* database, John S. Hunnewell, who is still single, is living in Los Angeles, California, but his estimated birth year is given as 1876. He is a lodger in the household of Elsworth A. Numelley. Hunnewell states he, along with his mother and father, were born in Maine. (*https://familysearch.org/ark:/61903/1:1:XCVK-D4P*)

In the United States census of 1940 (enumerated on 6 December 1939), appearing in the *FamilySearch* database, John S. Hunnewell, who has maintained his bachelorhood, is living in Fairbanks in the Alaska Territory. His estimated birth date in Maine is given as 1874. Hunnewell is listed as "Head of Household," and rents a room for $10.00 a month. He says that his "Highest grade of school completed" was the sixth. Hunnewell responds to the question "Where did this person live on October 1, 1934?" that he was in Alaska. He says that he was employed during the week of September 24-30, 1939. He is listed as a carpenter in the "House building" industry. In regard to the "Number of weeks worked for pay or profit during 12 months ending September 30, 1939," Hunnewell says he worked eight weeks and had earned $1,000.00 "during 12 months ending September 30, 1939." (*https://familysearch.org/ark:/61903/1:1:VYWJ-8TC*)

Under "Find A Grave Index," in the *FamilySearch* database, John S. Hunnewell is listed as having died in Fairbanks, Alaska, on 21 October 1945. He is buried in the Birch Hill Cemetery in Fairbanks. (*https://familysearch.org/ark:/61903/1:1:QV28-BCB4*)

4. Elizabeth "Lizzie" Kelly (19 January 1879 – 22 November 1918) married Benjamin "Ben" Abernathy (May 1860 – 11 August 1927), son of Robert and Emily (Hanson) Abernathy, 24 March 1897 in Fort Kent, Aroostook County, Maine. Elizabeth "Lizzie" (Kelly) Abernathy was born and died in St. Francis, Aroostook County, Maine. Benjamin "Ben" Abernathy was born in Nashwaak, York

County, New Brunswick. The name Abernathy (the preferred spelling by the family in Maine) appears in the records of New Brunswick and Maine as Abnethey, Abernatha and Abernathy and other variants.

4. Charles Henry "Charlie" Kelly (31 July 1881 – 16 June 1960) married Stella Marie Sirois (21 May 1888 – 29 November 1983), daughter of Paschal Sirois (16 April 1849 – 18 October 1932) and Henriette Pelletier (8 October 1852 – 7 April 1927), 20 June 1905 in St. Francois, Madawaska County, New Brunswick. Charles Henry "Charlie" Kelly was born and died in St. Francis, Aroostook County, Maine. Stella Marie (Sirois) Kelly was born in St. Francois, Madawaska County, New Brunswick, and died in Fort Kent, Aroostook County, Maine.

3. Charles Burton "Charlie" Kelly (26 June 1839 – 6 February 1912) married Sarah Ann Mullins (1 September 1842 – 3 March 1924), daughter of William Jospeh Mullins (1812 – November 1886) and Elizabeth Diamond (15 February 1816 – September 1903/4), 25 July 1866 in St. Francis, Aroostook County, Maine. Charles Burton Kelly was born in York County, New Brunswick, and died in Allagash, Maine. It should be noted that the Catholic Church records of St. Dunston in Fredericton, New Brunswick, lists (p. 56) the baptisms of three of Charles and Sarah Ann (Mullins) Kelly's children in 1873 and states that these children are "from the lawful marriage of Charles Kelly and Sarah Mullin[s]," which would suggest that the couple was married by a Catholic priest, but Eva "Ev" (Kelly) McBreairty says in a transcript of a recording done by Darrell Robert McBreairty contained in *Conversations with A'nt Ev': an Oral History of the Allagash* (p. 33) that her parents were married in a double wedding with Neal McLean (15 July 1845 – 4 November 1914) and Sarah (Mullins) Kelly's first cousin Mary Henderson (5 February 1845 – 2 November 1911). Documentation gathered by Carol (Pelletier) Pelletier shows that John Connors (25 January 1825 – 5 November 1891) and Ellen Ann Henderson (10 November 1837 – 29 November 1922) were married in St. Francis, Aroostook County, Maine, by Barnabas Hunnewell (24 July 1790 – 17 October 1868) on 30 May 1859. "Squire" Hunnewell, whose daughter Josephine "Josie" Hunnewell (12 February 1841 – 20 October 1920) married James Allen "Jim" Kelly (30 April 1835 – 4 June 1919), served as Justice of the Peace in St. Francis, Maine. Although Sarah (Mullins) Kelly was brought up Catholic, her husband was Protestant, and both Neal McLean and Mary Henderson were Protestant. In the 1871 New Brunswick census for York County at Queensbury, Charles and Sarah Ann (Mullins) Kelly and their sons George and William are listed as belonging to the Church of England. Charles Kelly and Sarah Ann Mullins met while working at the Seven Islands on the head of the St. John River where they were employed by the Cary family. Eva "Ev" (Kelly) McBreairty in a transcript of a recording done by Darrell Robert McBreairty contained in *Conversations with A'nt Ev': an Oral History of the Allagash* (p. 24) states that her mother was 13 years old when she went to work for the Cary family at Seven Islands.

Charles and Sarah Ann (Mullins) Kelly moved to New Brunswick after their son William Kelly was born in Allagash, Maine, on 15 March 1869. On 16 May 1870, when their daughter Ida May (Kelly) McBreairty was born, they were living in an apartment in Fredericton, New Brunswick. The 1871 New Brunswick census for York County in Queensbury (p. 26) lists Charles (32 years old) and Sarah Ann (Mullins) Kelly along with their children William and George. In 1871, a "Charles Kelly of the Parish of Dumfries in the County of York" petitioned for lot number 8 on the east side of Allandale. (See Appendix K.) Ida May Kelly is not listed with the rest of her family in the 1871 census. George (4 years old) is listed as having been born in New Brunswick as is his father, but William (2 years old) and his mother "Sary A" (28 years old) are not. Eva "Ev" (Kelly) McBreairty, once again from transcripts contained in *Conversations with A'nt Ev': an Oral History of the Allagash* (p. 25), remembered her mother saying that while Charles and Sarah Ann (Mullins) Kelly lived with William and Sarah Ann (Howard) Kelly, Sarah Ann (Howard) Kelly would go over to the Anglican church every afternoon to pray. Linda (Kitchen) Aitken in an email of 17 April 2011 points out that this had to be in Queensbury, York County, New Brunswick. Information provided at the website *June 2005 - The New Brunswick Anglican - Anglican Parish of Prince William, Dumbries, Queensbury and Southamton* establishes that the St. Thomas Anglican Church in Queensbury was built by Henry William Tippet in 1849. Linda suggests that William and Sarah Ann (Howard) Kelly lived just across the St. John River opposite Kelly Creek. In the same email, Linda states: "The river was very narrow there and there was a ferry so people moved back and forth freely. It would be quite likely that even Kellys from this side [south side] of the river could have crossed the river to attend church." In an email of 13 December 2013, Linda (Kitchen) Aitken states the St. Thomas Anglican Church in Queensbury "burned in the 1930s." Linda adds that the church "would have been in the Mactaquac Flood Plain." Leonard Hilton Kelly was born at Springhill, York County, New Brunswick, on 9 April 1875. It was at Springhill, William O. Raymond points out in *The River St. John* (p. 26), where "a small army of men [found] employment during the summer in gathering sorting and rafting the almost countless logs brought down the river by the stream drivers." Shortly before moving back to Allagash, Maine, Charles and Sarah Ann (Mullins) Kelly worked for lumberman Robert Connors and were staying at his house in Connors, Madawaska County, New Brunswick, when their daughter Eva "Ev" (Kelly) McBreairty was born on 30 March 1877.

The following is from the *Colonial Farmer*, 13 May 1872 (*Provincial Archives of New Brunswick: Daniel F. Johnson's New Brunswick Newspaper Vital Statistics*, Volume 32, Number 1885):

> Charles Kelly of Kingsclear (York Co.) and his wife's sister were upset out of a canoe in which they were coming down the St. John River, a little above West's Landing, about a quarter of a mile above the Grand Falls (Victoria Co.). The woman would certainly have been drowned had not Kelly, swam around to the opposite side of the canoe and supported both himself and her by reaching across the canoe. Both were exhausted when help reached them. The accident occurred Friday 3rd.

We had all heard the legend of Charles Burton "Charlie" Kelly (26 June 1839 – 6 February 1912) and Mary Josephte (Mullins) Hughes (November 1852 – 11 September 1920) nearly going over Grand Falls. Eva "Ev" (Kelly) McBreairty brings it up *In Conversations with A'nt Ev': An Oral History of the Allagash* (p. 62). I had written about it in *At Ant Ev's* (pp. 12-13), which was published in 1977, but it wasn't until Timothy Hughes found the newspaper article long after Eva "Ev" (Kelly) McBreairty and her sister Eunice (Kelly) McBreairty had died, that we could verify that it wasn't just a legend. I quoted from what I had written in *At Ant Ev's* (pp. 12-13) in Note 8, Chapter IV, *In Conversations with A'nt Ev': An Oral History of the Allagash* (pp. 66-67).

What follows is a reworking of the story from both of these books.

Sometime in the 1950s, Edith (McBreairty) Kelley had her mother, Eunice (Kelly) McBreairty, relate the story once more so she could write it down. Edith loaned me a copy of the story when I was writing *At Ant Ev's*.

As Eunice was told, Charles Burton and Sarah Ann (Mullins) Kelly were living in Kingsclear, York County, New Brunswick, when the Morrison Lumber Company requested Charles to go on business to Allagash, Maine. Sarah accompanied her husband up river, and, while they were visiting Sarah's sister, Margaret (Mullins) Sullivan (10 April 1845 – June 1852), and Margaret's husband, Thomas Sullivan (1825 - ?), at the Sullivan home in Grand Falls, New Brunswick, word came that Mary Josephte (Mullins) Hughes was on her way down the St. John River to stay with her sister Margaret in Grand Falls. Margaret (Mullins) Hughes was expecting a baby. We have not been able to verify that Margaret was indeed expecting, but, as we know from the records, Sarah (Mullins) Kelly gave birth, in Fredericton (not Kingsclear), to Joseph Herman Kelly in February 1873.

Charles and his brother-in-law Thomas Sullivan went to meet Mary.

It should be noted that the last portage above Grand Falls was hazardous and even the most skilled boatmen never used it in high water. The second portage, about one quarter mile upstream from the last, was the one customarily used, except during low water, when the last portage was deemed a better portage. It should also be noted that during high water the river was very swift at the last portage, and the pull toward the falls very strong.

Charles had a reputation of being a very capable man with a boat, and, whether the two men decided intentionally to pass the second portage above the falls or if they missed it, it is debatable, but Eunice (Kelly) McBreairty was told that they had decided to chance the last portage.

In attempting to swing the boat to shore, Charles' pole broke. In Sullivan's attempt to pass his pole to Charles, the boat capsized. It appears that Sullivan swam to shore. Charles, who knew that Mary could not swim, had caught her and was attempting to swim ashore with her. There were people on the shore readying to go up river, and they shouted, "Let her go, Charlie, let her go!"

According to another version of the story, a log would circle three times in the whirlpool above the falls before going over, and Charles and Mary were circling for the third time in the cold waters when Charles finally caught hold of a rope that was thrown out. It is said that he even bit into it with his teeth to make certain he did not lose his grip. For many years afterwards, Mary would wake in a cold sweat as voices rang out in the dark: "Let her go, Charlie, let her go!"

In notes taken with Flora Belle "Flo" (McBreairty) Henderson on 26 April 1979 in Allagash, Maine, Flora Belle "Flo" (McBreairty) Henderson said that it was Sarah Ann (Mullins) Kelly who was expecting a baby and not Margaret (Mullins) Sullivan. Mary Josephte (Mullins) Hughes told Flo the story and did not mention Thomas Sullivan at all. Mary said that she was going down to the Fredericton, New Brunswick, area to be with her sister Sarah. Mary said that after she and Charles got to shore at Grand Falls, Charles got another canoe and they continued on to Fredericton.

Eunice (Kelly) McBreairty said, in the story she related to her daughter Edith, that on a drive at the head of the St. John River, a young man slipped from the logs, falling into the water. He could not swim, and Charles dove in to save him, but a crew of men in a bateau had been alerted. Charles, later, related how he had just missed grabbing the boy's hair but was unable to locate him again because of the wake from the bateau. The boy drowned. Charles always maintained that he would have saved him if the crew with the bateau had not come to disturb the surface of the water.

In the *Robert Connors Ledgers* at the Robert Connors House in Connors, New Brunswick, Charles Kelly appears in *Ledger B* (p. 61) in 1875; again in *Ledger B* (p. 62) in 1876; in *Ledger D* (p. 313) in 1878; in *Ledger D* (p. 314) in 1879 and with a final entry in *Ledger D* (p. 314) on 15 May 1880.

Children of Charles Burton and Sarah Ann (Mullins) Kelly:

4.George C. Kelly (4 May 1867 – 1 January 1945) married 1st: Sarah Ann "Sally Ann" Gardner (4 May 1869 – 11 July 1898), daughter of Thomas C. Gardner (17 January 1838 – 22 December 1932) and Mary Sarah Hughes (February 1846 – 1917), 19 September 1892; 2nd: Frances Ellen "Nelly" Sullivan, daughter of Thomas Sullivan (1825 – ?) and Margaret Mullins (10 April 1845 – June 1924), 2 July 1906 in Drummond, New Brunswick. George C. Kelly was born and died in Allagash, Aroostook County, Maine.

4.William Henry Kelly (15 March 1869 – 11 July 1954); baptism recorded at the Catholic Church of St. Dunston in Fredericton, York County, New Brunswick (p.56) on 14 May 1873 with William Henry Kelly listed as being aged four years; married Lucy Ann McBreairty (28 March 1881 – 2 March 1906), daughter of James McBreairty (7 June 1859 – 9 December 1914) and Barbara "Abbie" Oakes (6 July 1858 – 2 May 1925), 7 June 1905 in Sr. Francis, Aroostook County, Maine. William Henry Kelly and Lucy (McBreairty) Kelly were both born and died in Allagash, Aroostook County, Maine.

4.Ida May Kelly (6 May 1870 – 6 March 1926); baptism recorded (p.56) at the Catholic Church of St. Dunston in Fredericton, New Brunswick, 14 May 1873 with "Ida May Kelly" listed as being aged two years; married George McBreairty (17 March 1870 – 5 February 1935), son of James McBreairty (12 July 1826 – 14 October 1900) and Catherine Henderson (ca 1835 – 1875), 28 July 1896 in Allagash, Aroostook County, Maine. Ida May (Kelly) McBreairty was born in Fredericton, York County, New Brunswick, and died in Allagash, Aroostook County, Maine. George McBreairty was born and died in Allagash, Aroostook County, Maine.

4. Joseph Herman Kelly (February 1873 – 28 November 1961); baptism recorded at the Catholic Church of St. Dunston in Fredericton, New Brunswick, (p.56) 25 April 1873 with "Joseph Kelly" listed as being aged two months; married Annie Henderson (11 January 1878 – 29 October 1953), daughter of Luther Vincent Henderson (14 July 1833 – 3 September 1891) and Annie Hughes (12 July 1842 – 24 April 1921), 26 June 1900 in St. Francis, Aroostook County, Maine. Joseph Herman Kelly was born in Fredericton, York County, New Brunswick, and died in Allagash, Aroostook County, Maine. Joseph Herman Kelly always insisted, as did some of his family members, that he was born 29 February 1872, but, as can be seen from the St. Dunston records, this is incorrect. Annie (Henderson) Kelly was born and died in Allagash, Aroostook County, Maine.

4. Leonard Hilton Kelly (9 April 1875 – 29 January 1934) married Caroline K. Hafford (14 July 1878 – 2 November 1961), daughter of John "Long John" Hafford ((14 November 1845 – 21 December 1929) and Sarah Walker (29 April 1847 – 28 September 1925), 26 August 1898 in Fort Kent, Aroostook County, Maine. Leonard Hilton Kelly was born in Springhill, York County, New Brunswick, and died in Allagash, Aroostook County, Maine. Caroline K. (Hafford) Kelly was born and died in Allagash, Aroostook County, Maine. In notes taken by Darrell Robert McBreairty with Eva "Ev'" (Kelly) McBreairty in December 1973, Eva "Ev'" (Kelly) McBreairty said that on 29 January 1934 (the day of his death) Leonard Hilton Kelly's daughter Ida May Kelly (26 June 1909 – 1909) was with him all morning. His sister Ida May (Kelly) McBreairty (6 May 1870 – 6 March 1926) also appeared, with her arms outstretched, calling to him. These notes appear in the first volume of Darrell Robert McBrearity's personal journal for 1974 on an unnumbered page at the beginning of the journal.

4. Eva "Ev" Kelly (30 March 1877 – 23 June 1974) married Albert McBreairty (17 September 1877 – 4 January 1950), son of James McBreairty (12 July 1826 – 14 October 1900) and Mary Margaret Walker (28 May 1854 – ca 1907), 11 January 1899 in Allagash, Aroostook County, Maine. Eva "Ev" Kelly was born in Connors, Madawaska County, New Brunswick, and died in Allagash, Aroostook Coounty, Maine. Albert McBreairty was born and died in Allagash, Aroostook County, Maine.

4. Ransford Kelly (17 February 1879 – 15 October 1960) married Mary "Main" Mullins (19 October 1884 – 8 March 1973), daughter of Joseph William Mullins (March 1844 – 28 July 1930) and Lucinda

"Lucy" Moir (6 December 1848 - 16 April 1893), 24 July 1901. Ransford Kelly was born and died in Allagash, Aroostook County, Maine.

4.Tylor Kelly (1880 - 12 January 1894) died of diphtheria. Tylor Kelly was born and died in Allagash, Aroostook County, Maine.

4.Charles H. Kelly (15 November 1883 - 7 October 1962) married Esther Bishop (3 January 1883 - 5 April 1964), daughter of Steven Bishop and Rosanna Jackson (February 1858 - 1906). Charles Kelly was born in Allagash, Aroostook County, Maine, and died in Madawaska, Aroostook County, Maine.

4.Eunice Kelly (10 August 1886 - 15 April 1975) married Thomas James McBreairty (25 July 1884 - 10 August 1968), son of James McBreairty (12 July 1826 - 14 October 1900) and Mary Margaret Walker (28 May 1854 - ca 1907), 24 March 1905 in Allagash, Aroostook County, Maine. Thomas and Eunice (Kelly) McBreairty were both born and died in Allagash, Aroostook County, Maine. Eunice (Kelly) McBreairty's baptism is recorded in Grand Falls, New Brunswick. In a 23 November 2014 email, Guy Dubay states: "In my cardex I had the following note: Euncie Kelly born Aug. 19[,] 1886[;] baptized Aug. 26, 1886 Grand Falls." Eunice (Kelly) McBreairty and her family believed her birthdate to have been 10 August 1886. There may have been a mistake in transcription that resulted in the 19 August 1886 birthdate.

In an email of 12 April 2015 from Katrina (McBreairty) Vaughn, Katrina writes about a conversation she had with her grandmother, Eunice (Kelly) McBreairty, "I remember talking to Grammie one day[,] helping her with yarn. I asked her if she worried about the men when they were gone on the drives. Her reply has been one we have used many times over the years. She said, 'Well, you can't trust God and worry too.' That was the 'holy all of it' as Grampie [Thomas James McBreairty] would say."

3.Rhoda C. "Rhody" Kelly (26 June 1844 - 16 January1907) married James W. Howard (1834 - 25 May 1896), son of Alexander Howard (ca 1807 -26 October 1885) and Rebecca Ann Currie (28 February 1810 - 9 December 1891), 11 July 1861 in Queensbury, York County, New Brunswick, with Alexander Kelly and Francis Niles as co-signers. Rhoda Kelly was born in Qeensbury, York County, New Brunswick. James W. and Rhoda C. "Rhody" (Kelly) Howard are buried in the Prince William Community Cemetery, York County, New Brunswick.

In a transcription of a December 1970 taped conversation with Eunice (Kelly) McBreairty (10 August 1886 - 15 April 1975), daughter of Charles

Burton Kelly (26 June 1839 – 6 February 1912) and Sarah Ann (Mullins) Kelly (1 September 1842 – 3 March 1924), contained in note 12 in "Notes on Chapter II" in *Converstions with A'nt Ev': An Oral History of the Allagash* by Darrell McBreairty, Euncie, speaking of members of the Kelly family visiting Allagash, Maine, said, "Oh ya. Father's brothers were up here, different ones, an' one sister, A'nt Rhody, come up." (pp.38-39)

Children of James W. and Rhoda C. "Rhody" (Kelly) Howard:

4.Rebecca Howard (? - ?).
4.Ambrose Howard (1862 - ?).
4.Blanche Howard (1864 - ?) married Bial Hanscom.
4.Netty Howard (1866 - ?).
4.Charles Howard (April 1869 – 1944) was born in Newmarket, York County, New Brunswick and is buried in Prince William Community Cemetery, York County, New Brunswick.
4.Maude Howard (1872 - ?) married Alexander Adams 3 March 1903.
4.Elizabeth Howard (1874 - ?).
4.John Howard (1876 - ?).
4.Dawson Howard (May 1881 – 1968) is buried in Prince William Community Cemetery, York County, New Brunswick. Athough he was called "Dawson," the name Tuner is part of his given name.
4.Georgia Howard (July 1883 – ?) married Rankine P. McKay (ca 1880 - ?) 30 September 1908 in York County, New Brunswick. Rankine P. McKay was born in Upper Caverhill, New Brunswick.
4.Mary Alice Howard (1886 – 1973) married John Garfield "John" Caverhill 9 September 1914. Mary Alice (Howard) Garfield is buried in the Prince William Community Cemetery, Prince William, York County, New Brunswick.

2.John Kelly (31 August 1794 - ?) John Kelly was born in Kingsclear, York County, New Brunswick. John Kelly's christening is recorded in the *Queensbury Anglican Christenings 1792-1808* on 23 August 1795. Since John is not mentioned in the will of his father (See Appendix G.) and there is scant information about him outside of the record of his christening, it is possible that he died sometime before 1825. *York County, New Brunswick, Marriage Records, Volume 1, 1812–1837* (pp. 27 & 47) states that a John Kelly married a Katherine Sowers on 22 October 1812, but, as of this date, no one has been able to establish that this John is the son of John and Mary (Unknown) Kelly, and there seems to be no trace of any children of this John Kelly. Adding to the confusion, George H. Hayward in *York County, New Brunswick, Marriage Records, Volume 1, 1812-1837* (pp. 25 & 27) also notes a John Kelly of Prince William, New Brunswick, marrying a Hannah Howard of Kingsclear on 26 October 1826.

2. Frances "Fanny" Kelly (ca 1796 – between censuses 1861 and 1871) married Robert Heustis (ca 1786 - ?), son of Lewis Heustis, 15 or 23 April 1816 in York County, New Brunswick. (George H. Hayward: *York County, New Brunswick, Marriage Records, Volume 1, 1812–1837*, pp. 25 & 27.) The couple, both residents of Kingsclear, were married by Justice of the Peace John Lawrence. Witnesses were John Barker and James Cristy. Frances "Fanny" Kelly was born in New Brunswick. Robert and Frances "Fanny" (Kelly) Huestis settled in Wickham Parish (now Jemseg), Queens County, New Brunswick.

George Peabody, in *Kings Landing: A Living History Colourguide* (p. 44), writes that John Hunt Heustis, son of New York Loyalist Lewis Heutis who had served in the Loyal American Regiment and came to Nova Scotia (New Brunswick) "with his wife and family" in the Fall Fleet of 1783, had the Heustis house, now at Kings Landing, built in the 1840s by James Mitchell, who was married to John Hunt Heustis' daughter. Peabody suggests that the Heustis house now at Kings Landing replaced the house probably built by Lewis Heustis, who had "received a grant in Queensbury and moved there in 1787."

A Timothy Heustis appears in the *Records of Old Soldiers of the Revolutionary War and Their Widows* petitions for relief beginning in January 1842. His name is eliminated from the list in 1845. In the petition of 1843, Timothy Heustis is listed as being seventy-four years old.

Children of Robert and Frances "Fanny" (Kelly) Huestis:

3. John Huestis
3. Phoebe Huestis (ca 1819 – 11 October 1883) married Thomas Cain (1812 – 1882).
3. Mary Ann Huestis (ca 1824 – 27 October 1870) married Robert Appleby (ca 1810 – 8 April 1895) 23 February 1847.
3. Samuel Huestis (1827 – 14 April 1882) married Emma M. Dennette (1834 – 14 April 1882) 5 November 1856 in Saint John, New Brunswick. Samuel Huestis died born in Peticodiac, New Brunwick.
3. Nancy Huestis (ca 1828 – 6 April 1896) married James Somerville (1 January 1820 – March 1904). Nancy Huestis was born in Hustis Landing, Queens County, New Brunswick and died of heart failure in Hatfields Point, New Brunswick. James Somerville, who was a ship's captain, was born in Swarton, Nova Scotia and is buried in Hatfields Point, New Brunswick.
3. Sarah Huestis (19 October 1828 – 25 September 1907).
3. William Leonard Huestis (ca 1835 – 9 September 1900) married Mary Odell (22 February 1844 – 9 May 1912) 11 November 1863.

The Kellys of Kingsclear

3.Deborah E. Huestis (ca 1837 - ?) married Hiram S. Quimby.
3.Emily Jane Huestis (ca 1837 – April 1907) married John Cameron (10 December 1848 – April 1907) 13 June 1876.
3.Charles Gilbert Huestis (ca 1844 - ?) married Sarah Belyea (ca 1844 – 11 January 1898) 6 July 1871.
3.Frances Ann "Annie" Huestis (7 August 1850 – 9 December 1920) married Isaac Erb (28 May 1846 – 13 May 1921). Frances Ann "Annie" (Huestis) Erb died in Saint John, New Brunswick. Isaac Erb was born in Kars, Kings County, New Brunswick and died in Saint John, New Brunswick. Isaac Erb was noted as a premier photographer in the Canadian Maritimes.

2.Abel/Ebel Kelly married Bridget Bradley 23 April 1827. Roman Catholic Missionary in Fredericton Michael McSweeney conducted the ceremony. Both Abel/Ebel Kelly and Bridget Bradley are listed as residents of Kingsclear, York County, New Brunswick. Anthony Crock and Andrew Connors are listed as witnesses. (George H. Hayward: *York County, New Brunswick, Marriage Records, Volume 1, 1812–1837*, pp. 5 & 27.)

Children of Abel/Ebel and Bridget (Bradley) Kelly:

3.Sarah "Sally" Kelly (March 1829 – 3 September 1910) married James Lawson, son of Alexander Lawson and Deborah Kelly (ca 1796 – 1874), 29 October 1850 at Lake George, York County, New Brunswick. Sarah "Sally" (Kelly) Lawson died in Shirley, Middlesex County, Massachusetts.
3.Frances Kelly, possible daughter of Abel/Ebel and Bridget (Bradley) Kelly, married Peter Kinny 13 March 1851.

2.Mary Anne Kelly (1805 - ?) married Unknown Bradley.
2.Ruth Kelly (ca 1807 - ?) married George Howard (ca 1800 - ?) 8 July 1824. The ceremony was conducted by Justice of the Peace David McGibbon, with John Howard and Unknown Neal West as co-signers. Ruth Kelly and George Howard are both listed as residents of Kingsclear. (George H. Hayward: *York County, New Brunswick, Marriage Records, Volume 1, 1812-1837*, pp. 25 & 28.) Ruth (Kelly) Howard was born in Kingsclear, York County, New Brunswick.

Children of George and Ruth (Kelly) Howard:

3.Joseph Howard (ca 1825 - ?).
3.Sarah Howard (ca 1827 - ?) married James Brockway.
3.William Howard (ca 1829 - ?) married Elizabeth Lyon.
3.George Howard (ca 1831 - ?).

3.**Mary Ann Howard** (ca 1833 - ?).

3.**Alexander Howard** (ca 1835 - 21 November 1915) died in Fredericton, York County, New Brunswick.

3.**John Howard** (ca 1837 - 11 July 1924) married Carrie Dunphy. John Howard died in Marysville, York County, New Brunswick.

3.**Henry Howard** (ca 1839 - ?).

3.**Isaac Howard** (ca 1841 - ?).

3. **Eleanor Howard** (ca 1844 - ?).

3.**Elmira Howard** (29 May 1847 - ?) married William Brown. Elmira Howard was born at Kingsclear, York County, New Brunswick.

2.**Leonard Coombes Kelly** (6 December 1810 - 17 April 1899) married Jacobina "Bina" Drummond McKaye/McKay (11 April 1819 - 23 July 1907), daughter of Captain Duncan McKaye/McKay of "the 42nd Highlanders of the Black Watch Regiment [who] settled on the Nashwaak in 1783," and Margaret (listed as Mary in *The Daily Gleaner* article of 21 August 1957) Sutherland, 29 September 1836 in Queensbury, New Brunswick. The information quoted above comes from the newspaper article "Grandson of Loyalist: Married in 1892, Couple in Stanley Rich in Memories" (Fredericton, New Brunswick: *The Daily Gleaner*, 21 August 1957). George H. Hayward's transcription from official records contained in *York County, New Brunswick, Marriage Records, Volume 1, 1812-1837* (pp. 28 & 33) has Jacobina "Bina" McKaye/McKay listed incorrectly as Lavinia McKay. Velma Kelly writes in her *The Village in the Valley - A History of Stanley* Jacobina "Bina" Drummond McKaye/McKay "once chased a bear from near her home with a flaming stick from her fireplace." (p. 9) Leonard Coombes Kelly was born at Kelly's Creek in Kingsclear, New Brunswick, and died im Stanley, York County, New Brunswick, where he is buried in the St. Thomas Anglican Church Cemetery.

In a visit by Roger Mark Smith with Velma Maude (Harrison) Kelly in Fredericton on 3 June 2014, Velma Maude (Harrison) Kelly revealed that Gabriel Havelock Kelly, who she knew well, believed that his father, Leonard Coombes Kelly, although a member of the Kelly family, was not the son of John and Mary (Unknown) Kelly even though they reared him as such. Velma Maude (Harrison) Kelly, daughter of Harold Alexander Harrison (1902 - ?) and Dorothy Hilda Scott (1906 - ?), was married to Harold Jarvis Kelly (5 August 1926 - 23 June 2012), son of Arthur Cleveland Moore Kelly (9 February 1886 - 1 May 1963) and Mabel Jarvis (17 May 1883 - 1963). Arthur Cleveland Moore Kelly was the son of Robert Kelly (22 June 1846 - 7 July 1937) and Ella Rebecca Merrill (August 1855 - 3 February 1922). Robert Kelly was the son of Leonard Coombes and Jacobina (McKaye) Kelly. (For more detailed information on the Leonard Coombes and Jacobina "Bina" Drummond (McKaye/McKay) Kelly family see Appenidix W.)

Lieutenant John Coombes (ca 1753 – 1827), who came from Perth-Amboy, New Jersey, and served in the 2nd. New Jersey Volunteers, received a land grant (Land Grant I-29) of 550 acres at Kingsclear in 1784. Research gathered by Guy Dubay establishes that John Coombe's grandson, Leonard Reed Coombes (ca 1790 – 26 March 1862), who died at St. Leonard, New Brunswick, was the son of Jonathan Coombes and Mary Reed (25 May 1776 - ?). Mary Reed was the daughter of Leonard Reed.

E. Alfred Jones in his *The Loyalists of New Jersey* states that after the death of Captain Henry Marsh "at Second River, New Jersey, early in April 1777, . . . Marsh's widow, Elizabeth [(Srymesan) Marsh], married Lieutenant Leonard Reed." (p. 141) Elizabeth (Srymesan) Marsh married Lieutenant Leonard Reed of the King's American Regiment in 1792. John Kelly witnessed the wounding of Captain Henry Marsh. (See Appendix N.)

Guy Dubay's research establishes that the Catholic Church at Parent, New Brunswick, which is part of St. Leonard, is located on property that was owned by Leonard Reed Coombes — thus, possibly contributing to the selection of St. Leonard as the name of the town.

There appears to be no genealogical connection between the Kelly and Coombes families, but the name Leonard has passed down through the Kelly family for generations. Linda (Kitchen) Aitken and Roger Mark "Mark" Smith searched diligently for a Reed or Coombes connection to the Kellys. Mark scanned a volume of Reed family records at the *New Brunswick Museum Archives & Research Library* in Saint John, New Brunswick, but, after scouring them in great detail, no Kelly connection could be established.

Joseph S. Sickler in *The History of Salem County New Jersey* notes that the Coombes family contributed to the formation of the Presbyterian Church, known as the Pittsgrove Church, at Daretown, New Jersey. This church was organized on 30 April 1741. (p. 111)

Further information on the Leonard Reed Coombes family can be found in the *Delafield Family Papers* at the New Brunswick Museum Archives and Research Library in Saint John, New Brunswick.

Children of Leonard Coombes and Jacobina "Bina" Drummond (McKaye) Kelly:

3.John Henry Kelly (20 March 1839 - 7 September 1934) married Eliza Lewis Scott (12 March 1839 – 2 January 1930), daughter of Robert John ? Scott (20 March 1819 – 2 May 1899) and Mary Smith (1818 – 6 August 1867), 12 March 1868. John Henry amd Eliza Lewis (Scott) Kelly were both born in Stanley, York County, New Brunswick, and died in Fredericton, York County, New Brunswick, and were buried in the Fredericton Rural Extension Cemetery. Robert John ? Scott was born in

Annich, Northumberland County, England, and Mary (Smith) Scott was born in Moyseth, England.

Children of John Henry and Eliza L. (Scott) Kelly:

4.Mary Kelly (22 November 1869 - ?) married John Sutherland (25 May 1863 - 4 September 1931) 10 October 1894 in Fredericton, York County, New Brunswick.
4.Allen E. Kelly (1871 - 20 May 1893). (See memorial poem in Appendix W.)
4.Margaret "Maggie" Kelly (1 September 1874 - 7 March 1964) married William Thomas "Tom" Fraser (20 January 1867 - 23 April 1950) 30 June 1897 in Fredericton, York County, New Brunswick.

3.Duncan L. Kelly (1 January 1841 - 13 October 1919) married 1st: Mary Ann Brown (5 October 1844 - 28 October 1909) 15 November 1873; 2nd: Susan A. Fowler (1852 - ?), daughter of Fraser Fowler (1814 - 11 June 1892) and Lavinia Brown (1826 - 30 December 1886), 7 March 1912 in York County, New Brunswick. Duncan L. Kelly was born in Stanley, York County, New Brunswick. Susan A. (Fowler) Kelly was born in Durham, York County, New Brunswick. Fraser Fowler was born in Gagetown, Queens County, New Brunswick, and died in Nashwaak, York County, New Brunswick. Lavinia (Brown) Fowler was bon in Nashwaak Village, York County, New Brunswick, and died in Upper Durham, York County, New Brunswick.
3.James A. Kelly (ca 1843 - 18 January 1928) married Minnie Unknown. James A. Kelly died in Vancouver, Washington, USA, and is buried in Park Hill Cemetery in Vancouver, Washington, USA.
3.Robert Kelly (22 June 1846 - 7 July 1937) married Ella Rebecca Merrill (August 1855 - 3 February 1922), daughter of William Merrill (1819 - ?) and Elizaberth Porter (1823 - ?), 16 November 1872. Robert Kelly was born in Stanley, York County, New Brunswick, and died in Nashwaak Bridge, York County, New Brunswick. Ella Rebecca (Merrill) Kelly was born in New Brunswick, and died in Stanley, York County, New Brunswick. William and Elizabeth (Porter) Merrill were both born in New Brunswick.

Children of Robert and Ella Rebecca (Merrill) Kelly:

4.Anna Kelly (1877 - ?).
4.James R. Kelly (1879 - ?).

The Kellys of Kingsclear

4.May C. Kelly (June 1880 - ?).

4.Arthur Cleveland Moore "Cleve" Kelly (9 February 1886 – 1 May 1963) married Mabel Hilda "Hilda" Jarvis (17 May 1883 – 1 May 1963), daughter of Francis Jarvis (13 October 1856 – 1893) and Mary Ann Elizabeth Jarvis, 22 December 1916. Arthur Cleveland Moore Kelly was born in Stanley, York County, New Brunswick, and died in Fredericton, York County, New Brunswick. Mabel Hilda (Jarvis) Kelly was born in Folkstone, England. Francis Jarvis was born at Lower Sandgate Road, Folkstone, Kent, England. (See "LIEUT. A.C. KELLY HOME ON LEAVE" in Appendix W.)

4.William Leonard Kelly (1888 - ?) married Marjorie Hayes (1886 - 1950), daughter of Peter and Elizabeth (Stickney) Hayes, 14 April 1908 in York County, New Brunswick. William Leonard Kelly was born in Stanley, York County, New Brunswick. Marjorie (Hayes) Kelly married Daniel Hadjamach in 1922.

4.Irma Della Kelly (26 April 1890 - 1979) married Arthur Garfield Tucker (8 October 1885 – 9 January 1961), son of Wesley Tucker and Alice Adra DeWitt, 4 September 1912. Irma Della (Kelly) Tucker was born in Stanley, York County, New Brunswick. Arthur Garfield Tucker was born in Hainsville, York County, New Brunswick.

4.Harold Kelly (10 February 1888 – 25 November 1916) was born in Stanley, New Brunswick, and was killed in the Battle of the Somme in WW I. (See "LIEUT. A.C. KELLY HOME ON LEAVE" in Appendix W.)

3.George Kelly (ca 1848 – 12 November 1920). According to notes by Irma Della (Kelly) Tucker (*Ella (Kelly) Boulter Scrapbook*), George Kelly married in the United States and lived in St. Louis, Missouri. Irma Della (Kelly) Tucker states that George Kelly had two daughters.

3.William McKay Kelly (15 October 1849 - 27 September 1926) married Margaret "Maggie" Scott (29 May 1855 – 8 January 1931), daughter of Robert John ? Scott (20 March 1819 – 2 May 1899) and Mary Smith (1818 – 6 August 1867), 15 April 1876. William McKay Kelly was born in Stanley, York County, New Brunswick, and died in Kingsclear, York County, New Brunswick. William McKay Kelly's tombstone at St. Peter's Anglican Cemetery, Springhill, York County, New Brunswick, has his birth year as 1851, and his death certificate states he was 77 years old when he died. Margaret "Maggie" Scott was born in Stanley, York County, New Brunswick, and died in Springhill, York County, New Brunswick. Robert John ? Scott was born in Annich, Northumberland County, England, and

Mary (Smith) Scott was born in Moyseth, England. (See Margaret (Kelly) Hay Material in Appendix W.)

From an unidentified and undated newspaper clipping in the Kelly family collection:

> The funeral of the late William M. Kelly took place yesterday afternoon from his late home at Fernhill, on the Woodstock Road and was largely attended. Rev. A. F. Bate conducted a short service at the house after which the remains were taken to St. Peter's Church, Springhill, where the Church of England service for the dead was conducted by Mr. Bate, who also said the committal prayers at the grave. The pall bearers were: Frank Noble, H. B. Atherton, Walter Quartermain, John Powys. The chief mourners were Warren Kelly, Ellis Kelly, John Kelly, Robert Kelly, Alonzo Kelly, Havelock Kelly. Interment was made at St. Peter's churchyard.

Children of William McKay and Margaret "Maggie" (Scott) Kelly:

4.Charles Warren "Warren" Kelly (28 May 1875 – 8 March 1953) married Susie Adelaide Dunphy (2 August 1894 – 17 October 1983), daughter of Gilford Marvin Dunphy (1 July 1866 – 21 December 1947) and Ada Elizabeth Yerxa (29 May 1863 – 15 June 1949), 22 November 1911 in Keswick, York County, New Brunswick. Charles Warren Kelly was born in Stanley, York County, New Brunswick, and died in Keswick, York County, New Brunswick, where he is buried. Gilford Marvin Dunphy was born and died in Keswick, York County, New Brunswick. (See Margaret (Kelly) Hay Material in Appendix W.)

4.Miles R. Kelly (1879 - ?).

4.Ella Kelly (1881 - ?).

4.Ellis James Kelly (24 January 1896 – 11 October 1971) married Jean Emily "Gugga" Yerxa (31 December 1901 – 21 December 1980), daughter of William Carey Yerxa (1854 – 29 February 1928) and Jennie Elizabeth "Janie" Haines (23 April 1866 – 25 September 1924), 16 August 1922 in Queensbury, York County, New Brunswick. Ellis James McKay was born in Stanley, York County, New Brunswick. Jean Emily "Gugga" (Yerxa) McKay was born in

Lower Queensbury, York County, New Brunswick, and died in York County, New Brunswick. William Carey Yerxa was born in Douglas, York County, New Brunswick, and died in Fredericton, York County, New Brunswick. Jennie Elizabeth "Janie" (Haines) Yerxa was born in Butts Corner, York County, New Brunswick, and died in Fredericton, York County, New Brunswick.

3. Elizabeth Ann "Betsy Ann" Kelly (ca 1853 - 28 May 1891) married John James Robert Scott (22 February 1851 – 12 November 1930), son of Robert John ? Scott (20 March 1819 – 2 May 1899) and Mary Smith (1818 – 6 August 1867), 6 Novermber 1875. According to notes by Irma Della (Kelly) Tucker (*Ella (Kelly) Boulter Scrapbook*), Elizabeth Ann "Betsy Ann" (Kelly) Scott died in childbirth. John James Robert Scott was born and died in Stanley, York County, New Brunswick. Robert John ? Scott was born in Annich, Northumberland County, England, and Mary (Smith) Scott was born in Moyseth, England.

Children of John James Robert and Elizabeth Ann "Betsy Ann" (Kelly) Scott:

4. Mildred "Millie" Scott
4. Ada Scott
4. Effie Scott married ? Parker.
4. Lester Scott (1885 – 1971)
4. Arthur Norman Scott
4. Percy Scott
4. John Scott

3. Moses Alonzo Kelly (6 Dec 1859 - 9 October 1929) married Martha Abigail Sansom (April 1869 – 1 January 1929), daughter of Thomas and Mary Ann (Davis) Sansom, 20 December 1880. Moses Alonzo Kelly, who was a lawyer in Campbellton, Restigouche County, New Brunswick, was born in Stanley, York County, New Brunswick, and died in Dalhousie, Restigouche County, New Brunswick; but, according to notes by Irma Della (Kelly) Tucker (*Ella (Kelly) Boulter Scrapbook*), Moses Alonzo Kelly was killed in Campbellton, Restigouche County, New Brunswick, when a train struck the car in which he was riding. Martha Abigail (Sansom) Kelly was born in New Brunswick and died in Campbellton, Restigouche County, New Brunswick.

Children of Moses Alonzo and Martha Abigail (Sansom) Kelly:

4. Franklin "Frank" Kelly

3. Gabriel Havelock "Havelock" Kelly (1 June 1865 – 8 September 1964) married Annie Mae Clark (26 May 1871 – 1967), daughter of Moses Everet Clark and Mary Ann Arnold, 18 August 1892 in York County, New Brunswick. Gabriel Havelock "Havelock" Kelly was born in Stanley, York County, New Brunswick, and died in Fredericton, York County, New Brunswick, of a cerebral thrombosis and is buried at St. Thomas Anglican Cemetery, Stanley, York County, New Brunswick. Annie Mae (Clark) Kelly was born in St. Marys, York County, New Brunswick, and died in Stanley, York County, New Brunswick. On 4 October 1930, Gabriel Havelock "Havelock" Kelly, living in Stanley, York County, New Brunswick, applied for membership in the *New Brunswick Loyalists' Society*, Fredericton, New Brunswick. He stated in his application: "My grandfather was John Kelly [who] came from Carolina (U. S.) with Col. Allen regiment — and settled on St. John river in 1784. Took a grant of land at Kelly's Creek (Kingsclear) which is recorded in York Co. Records." (*Alice T. Fairweather Fonds/Collection* (S190 – F 26) "New Brunswick Loyalists' Society Applications," New Brunswick Museum, Saint John, New Brunswick, Canada.)

The following piece written by Ella Rita (Kelly) Boulter from the *Jeannie Belinda (Boulter) Matthews Collection* has been slightly edited for paragraph adjustments, etc. The photograph of Gabriel Havelock Kelly, dated 1901, must have been selected by Ella Rita (Kelly) Boulter to accompany the article.

Uncle Havelock
(1901)

Uncle Havelock lived to be 100 years old. He was my favorite relative, & awfully good to me. He thought the world of Papa[.] Always dressed well.

On their seventieth wedding [anniversary,] he had a new black suit made for him, so when he dressed, I said, "There, Havelock[,] you look handsome."

"I'm well aware of it, but thank you anyway[,] Ma'[a]m[,]" he answered[.] He was 96 or 7 then. He never grew senile or forgetful. His mind was always sharp and keen right to the last.

Just before he died, he said to Aunt Annie, "I keep having the strangest feeling that I'm to be sent away to a strange place."

>Then[,] Aunt Annie said, "You're an old man Havelock. Could it be that you're going to die?"
>
>"It could be that," he said.

In an email of 8 July 2014, Jeannie Belinda (Boulter) Matthews relates: "Mom's recollection of Havelock is vivid in my mind. . . . I also recall her telling the story of being at the funeral parlor [at] Havelock's death. Two teenage boys came to the door[,] and they asked her, 'Is this where the 100 year old man is like we saw in the paper?'

"'It is,' responded my mother.

"'Can we see him?'

"'Well[,] of course, you can,' said my mother. As Mom would frequently say when she recounted the story, 'I heard the old biddy daughters gasping in disbelief in the background[,] and I could feel them pursing their lips.['] (And Lordy, I do remember the 'Aunties' and their frowns of disapproval.) Despite the daughters' concerns, Mom stated that the young men [were] very respectful when they viewed the coffin.

"'He looks very good,' said one of the young men.

"'We never saw anybody that old before. Thanks for letting us see,' said the other.

"Mom would say that she had no idea who the young kids were[,] but that it showed that young people could show respect. . . ."

Children of Gabriel Havelock and Annie Mae (Clark) Kelly:

4.Bessie Anne Kelly (18 September 1893 – 2 November 1984) married James Lander Ninnes (14 November 1888 – 9 November 1958). Bessie Anne (Kelly) Ninnes was born in Stanley, York County, New Brunswick, and is buried beside her husband at St. Thomas Anglican Cemetery, Stanley, York County, New Brunswick. James Lander Ninnes was born in St. Ives, Cornwall, England and died in Stanley, York County, New Brunswick.

4.Allan Melvin Kelly (29 December 1894 – 1944) was born in Stanley, York County, New Brunswick.

4.Mary Gertrude Kelly (14 June 1896 – 1997) married James Edgar Gould (16 September 1889 – 11 July 1931) 9 October 1923 in Stanley, York County, New Brunswick. Mary Gertrude (Kelly) Gould was born in Stanley, York County, New Brunswick. James Edgar Gould was born in Dalhousie, Restigouche County, New Brunswick.

4.Nellie Jean Kelly (17 July 1897 – 1967) married Reverend Nathan Noseworthy 20 September 1927 in Stanley, York County, New

Brunswick. Nellie Jean Kelly was born in Stanley, York County, New Brunswick.

4. Elsie Ernestine Kelly (24 April 1899 – 22 June 2001) married 1st: Harry Walter Boulter (28 August 1896 – 4 December 1946), son of Samuel John Boulter (14 June 1868 – 26 November 1950) and Margaret Jane Sansom (? – ?), 3 October 1929 in Stanley, York County, New Brunswick; 2nd: Arthur Alwyn Reid on 23 April 1954 in York County, New Brunswick. Velma Kelly notes in her *The Village in the Valley – A History of Stanley* that some time after "[a] Telephone office was opened in Stanley . . . in the early 1900s. . . ." Elsie Ernestine (Kelly) Boulter Reid was "[a]mong [the] early operators. . . ." (p. 143) Elsie Ernestine (Kelly) Boulter Reid was born in Stanley, York County, New Brunswick, and is buried at St. Thomas Anglican Cemetery, Stanley, York County, New Brunswick. Harry Walter Boulter was born in Stanley, York County, New Brunswick, and died in York County, New Brunswick, and is buried at St. Thomas Anglican Cemetery, Stanley, York County, New Brunswick. Samuel John Boulter was born in Stanley, York County, New Brunswick, and died in York County, New Brunswick

4. Ina Jacie Kelly (26 June 1901 – 1941) married Vigil Green Ina Jacie (Kelly) Green is buried at St. Thomas Anglican Cemetery, Stanley, York County, New Brunswick. Ella Rita (Kelly) Boulter entered "1940" as Ina Jacie Kelly's death date in a diagram of the Gabriel Havelock Kelly family tree. Bessie Anne (Kelly) Ninnes also writes, in "Bessie Anne (Kelly) Ninnes Memories" contained in Appendix W, that Ina Jacie (Kelly) Green died in 1940.

4. George Kelly (5 July 1903 – ca 1903) was born and died in Stanley, York County, New Brunswick.

4. Isabella Joyce Kelly (October 1906 – 2000) married James Crawford MacNeill 24 June 1930 in Stanley, York County, New Brunswick.

Epilogue

By September 1967, the flood waters resulting from the construction of the Mactaquac Dam on the St. John River in New Brunswick in the 1960s covered most of the area of the Parish of Kingsclear. Even though the government moved a number of buildings to Kings Landing and made an attempt to preserve cultural artifacts, the small villages where our ancestors lived and died are gone. The landscape is forever altered. The Long House at Kings Landing does contain echoes of our family, but it is the written records and photographs that bring our ancestors back to us. I was fortunate enough to record Eva "Ev'" (Kelly) McBreairty (30 March 1877 – 23 June 1974) in the final decade of her long life, and there are recordings of her sister Eunice (Kelly) McBreairty (10 August 1886 – 15 April 1975) as well as Eunice's diaries and reminiscences collected by her daughter Edith (McBreairty) Kelley (22 October 1923 – 14 April 2008). The voices of these aged women speaking of their family are haunting, full of pathos and longing for a way of life that had long disappeared. Looking over the Kelly petitions for compensation for their losses and participation in the American Revolution, their land grant applications and deeds, we are reminded of the constant struggles to which our ancestors were subjected. The numerous records contained in the *Robert Connors Ledgers* at Connors, New Brunswick, contains the names of so many of the Kelly family and their cousins. The lumber industry took them to the headwaters of most of the rivers of New Brunswick and Northern Maine as well as to parts of Minnesota and farther west.

It is hard to imagine, but there was a time when the name Kelly was known in every little town along the St. John River, from its headwaters to the Bay of Fundy. The Kelly men were fierce lumber drivers, strong and dependable, hardworking and known for their integrity. Their word alone sealed a contract. The women were God-fearing and stern disciplinarians with a dedication to family and to community that was legendary. Although none of us have achieved great fame or fortune, we are descendent of a family who helped shape two nations. There is much more to be discovered about the history our family, but this should serve as a good starting point.

BIBLIOGRAPHY

Abbott, Wilbur C.: *New York in the American Revolution* (New York, New York: Charles Scribner's Sons, 1929).

Adams, Ph.D., William Forbes: *Ireland and Irish Emigration to the New World from 1815 to the Famine* (New Haven, Connecticut: Yale University Press, 1932; copyright © renewed 1960 by Lucy Wilcox Adams; reprinted Baltimore, Maryland: Genealogical Publishing Co., Inc., 1980).

Alexander, Samuel Davies: *Princeton College in the Eighteenth Century* (New York, New York: Anson D. F. Randolph & Company, 1872).

Alice T. Fairweather Fonds/Collection "New Brunswick Loyalists' Society Applications," New Brunswick Museum, Saint John, New Brunswick, Canada.

The American Revolution in South Carolina (www.carolana.com/SC/Revolution/home.html) © 2009 - J.D. Lewis - PO Box 1188 - Little River, SC 29566 - All Rights Reserved. Written permission to quote was granted by J.D. Lewis in a letter dated September 17, 2013.

The American Revolution in South Carolina Battle of Eutaw Springs (www.carolana.com/.../revolution_battle_of_eutaw_springs.html). © 2009 - J.D. Lewis - PO Box 1188 - Little River, SC 29566 - All Rights Reserved.

The American Revolution in South Carolina - Long Canes - IIS7 (www.carolana.com/SC/Revolution/revolution_long_canes.html). © 2009 - J.D. Lewis - PO Box 1188 - Little River, SC 29566 - All Rights Reserved.

Ancestors New Brunswick Genealogy Research (ancestorsnb.com/?p=106).

Andrews, C. M.: *The Colonial Period of American History* (New Haven, Connecticut: Yale University Press, 1934-1938).

Anglican Church Burial Register (Provincial Archives of New Brunswick, Microflim F8163, Register 1e — Burials).

Anglican Chruch Marriage Register (Provincial Archives of New Brunswick).

Antliff, W. Bruce: *Loyalist Settlements 1783-1789 New Evidence of Canadian Loyalist ClaimsResearch and Transcription* (Toronto, Ontario: The Archives of Ontario, Ministry of Citizenship and Culture, 1985).

Arbuckle, Doreen Menzies: *The North West Miramichi: A History of the Locality with Genealogies and History of the Menzies, Sinclair, Curtis, and Mullin Families* (Ottawa, Ontario, Canada: Doreen Menzies Arbuckle; Printed by Westboro Printers Limited, 1978).

Atkinson, A.M., Rev. W. Christopher: *Historical and Statistical Account of New-Brunswick, B.N.A. with Advice to Emigrants, Third Edition, Greatly Improved and Corrected* (Edinburgh, Scotland: Printed by Anderson & Bryce, 1844).

Barber, John Warner and Howe, Henry: *Historical Collections of the State of New Jersey Containing a General Collection of the Most Interesting Facts, Traditions, Historical Sketches, Anecdotes, Etc. Relating to the History and Antiquities with Geological Descriptions of Every Township in the State* (New York, New York: S. Tuttle, 1846).

Baird, Rev. Frank: *History of the Parish of Stanley and its Famous Fair* (Fredericton, New Brunswick: Printed by the McMurray Book & Stationary Company, 1950).

Bardsley, M.A., George Wareing: *English Surnames Their Sources and Significations* (London, England: Chatto & Windus, 1915).

Barrow, Mandy: "Understanding old British money - pounds, shillings and pence" (www.woodlands-junior.kent.sch.uk/customs/questions/money).

Begley, Donal F. (editor): *Irish Genealogy: A Record Finder* (Dublin, Ireland: Heraldic Artist Ltd., 1981.)

Bell, David Graham: *Early Loyalist Saint John: The Origin of New Brunswick Politics, 1783-1786* (Fredericton, New Brunswick: New Ireland Press, 1983).

Bill, Rev. I.E.: *Fifty Years with the Baptist Ministers and Churches of the Maritime Provinces of Canada* (Saint John, New Brunswick: Printed by Barnes and Company, Prince William Street, 1880).

Boulter, Ella Rita (Kelly): *Ella (Kelly) Boulter Scrapbook*, Provincial Archives of New Brunswick: MC315 Nashwaak Bicentennial Association Fonds, MS17, *Ella (Kelly) Boulter Collection*. Irma Della (Kelly) Tucker, daughter of Robert and Ella (Merrill) Kelly, added notes on the Kelly family to the scrapbook.

British Headquarters Papers, New York City 1774-1783 also known as *Carleton Papers Carleton Papers*, National Archives of Canada, Ottawa, Ontario, Canada.

Brown, Janice (Webster): *Gloucester County, New Jersey History and Genealogy* (www.nj.searchroots.com/Gloucesterco).

Buckingham, James S.: *Canada, Nova Scotia, New Brunswick and the other British Provinces in North America, with a Plan of National Colonization* (London, England, and Paris, France: Fisher, Son, & Co., 1843).

Budd, Thomas: *A True Account and Good Order Established in Pennsylvania and West New Jersey* (Philadelphia, Pennsylvania: Printed by William Bradford, 1685); new edition with an introduction and notes by Edward Armstrong (New York, New York: William Gowans, 1865).

Burnet, Gilbert: *Bishop Burnet's History of His Own Time* (6 Volumes) (London, England: Printed for Thomas Ward, 1724-1734). I have quoted from Airy, M.A., Osmund (Editor): *Burnet's History of His Own Time, A New Edition Based on that of Martin Joseph Ruth, D.D.*, (2 Volumes) (Oxford, England: At the Clarendon Press, 1897).

Burr, Nelson R.: *The Anglican Church in New Jersey* (Philadelphia, Pennsylvania: The Church Historical Society, 1954).

Bush, Bernard (compiler): *Laws of the Royal Colony of New Jersey 1760-1769, New Jersey Archives, Third Series, Volume IV* (Trenton, New Jersey: New Jersey State Library Bureau of Archives and History, 1982).

Callahan, North: *Royal Raiders: The Tories of the American Revolution* (New York, New York: The Bobbs-Merrill Company, Inc, A Subsidiary of Howard W. Sams & Co., Inc., 1963).

Campey, Lucille H.: *Planters, Paupers, and Pioneers: English Settlers in Atlantic Canada* (Toronto, Ontario: Natural Heritage Books, 2010); *With Axe and Bible: The Scottish Pioneers of New Brunswick, 1784-1874* (Toronto, Ontario: Natural Heritage Books, 2007).

Carleton Papers also known as *British Headquarters Papers, New York City 1774-1783*, National Archives of Canada, Ottawa, Ontario, Canada.

The Centennial of the Settlement of Upper Canada by the United Empire Loyalists 1784-1884, the Celebrations at Adolphustown, Toronto and Niagara, with an Appendix, Containing a Copy of the U. E. List, Preserved in the Crown Lands Department at Toronto, Published by the Centennial Committee (Toronto, Ontario: Rose Publishing Company, 1885).

Chastellux, Marquis François Jean de: *Voyages de M. le Marquis de Chastellux Dans L'Amérique Septentrionale dans les années 1780, 1781 & 1782* (Paris, France: Chez Prault, Imprimeur du Roi, Qui des Anguftins, à l'Immoralité, 1786); *Travels in North America in the Years 1780, 1781, and 1782, Translated from the French, by an English Gentleman, Who Resided in America at That Period, With Notes by the Translator* (2 Volumes) (London, England: printed for G.G. J. and J. Robinson, 1787); *Travels in North-America in the Years 1780-81-82, Translated from the French, by an English Gentleman, Who Resided in America at That Period, With Notes by the Translator, and a Biographical Sketch of the Author: Letters from Gen. Washington to the Marquis de Chastellux: and Notes and Corrections by the American Editor* (New York, New York: 1828); *Travels in North America in the Years 1780, 1781 and 1782*, a Revised Translation with Introduction and Notes by Howard C. Rice, Jr. (2 Volumes) (Chapel Hill, North Carolina: the University of North Carolina Press, Published for the Institute of Early American History and Culture at Williamsburg, Virginia, 1963). The 1828 New York edition has been utilized in this work.

Christ Church – Philadelphia (www.christchurchphila.org/Historic-Christ-Church/73).

The Christian Visitor (Provincial Archives of New Brunswick: *Daniel F. Johnson's New Brunswick Newspaper Vital Statistics*, Volume 47, Number 1453).

City Gazette, 27 September 1820 (Saint John, New Brunswick: *City Gazette*, 27 September 1820). (Provincial Archives of New Brunswick: *Daniel F. Johnson's New Brunswick Newspaper Vital Statistics*, Volume 2, Number 935).

Clark, Murtie June: *Loyalists in the Southern Campaign of the Revolutionary War* (3 Volumes) (Baltimore, Maryland: Genealogical Publishing Company, Inc., 1981). Written permission to quote from *Loyalists in the Southern Campaign of the Revolutionary War* was granted by Genealogical Publishing Co., Inc., Baltimore, Maryland, and by the next of kin of Murtie June Clark in an email of 7 November 2012.

Clay, Rev. Jehu Curtis: *Annals of the Swedes on the Delaware to Which is Added the Charter of the United Swedish Churches* (Philadelphia, Pennsylvania: J.C. Pechin, 1835); second edition, corrected and enlarged: *Annals of the Swedes on the Delaware From Their First Settlement in 1636, to the Present Time* (Philadelphia, Pennsylvania: H. Hooker & Co., 1858). For the purposes of this book, the second edition has been utilized.

Clement, John: *Revolutionary Reminiscences of Camden County* (Camden, New Jersey: Sinnickson Chew, 1876); *Sketches of the First Emigrant Settlers in Newton Township, Old Gloucester County, West New Jersey* (Camden, New Jersey: printed by Sinnickson Chew, 1877).

Coke, Daniel Parker: *The Royal Commission on the Losses and Services of American Loyalists, 1783 to 1785, Being the Notes of Mr. Daniel Parker Coke, M. P., One of the Commissioners During that Period* (Edited by Hugh Edward Egerton) (Oxford, England: Printed at the University Press by Horace Hart; Printed for Presentation of the Members of the Roxburghe Club, 1915). *(RCLSAL)* (http://www.archive.org/details/lossesservicesloy00cokerich).

Coldham, Peter Wison: *Complete Book of Emigrants, 1607-1776* (4 Volumes) (Baltimore, Maryland: Genealogical Publishing Company, Inc., 1987).

Collections of the Protestant Episcopal Historical Society for the year 1851 (New York: Stanford & Swords, Publishers, 1851).

Colonial Farmer, 13 May 1872 (Fredericton, New Brunswick: *Colonial Farmer*, 13 May 1872). (Provincial Archives of New Brunswick: *Daniel F. Johnson's New Brunswick Newspaper Vital Statistics,* Volume 32, Number 1885).

Connors, Robert: The *Robert Connors Ledgers* housed at the Robert Connors House, owned and maintained by the Bernier family in Connors, New Brunswick, are a series of ledgers documenting charges at the Connors Store, monies paid to individuals and companies, etc. Susan "Susie" (Sullivan) Bernier (14 April 1914 – 29 October 2005) granted me permission years ago to publish material from these ledgers.

Craig, H. Stanley: *Genealogical Data: The Salem Tenth in West New Jersey* (Merchantville, New Jersey: H. S. Craig, Publisher, 1926); *Gloucester County New Jersey Marriage Records* (Merchantville, New Jersey: H. Stanley Craig, Publisher, 1930); *Salem County New Jersey Genealogical Data Records Pertaining to Persons Residing in Salem County Prior to 1800* (2 Volumes) (Merchantville, New Jersey: H. Stanley Craig, Publisher, 1934); reprinted (Woodbury New Jersey: Gloucester County Historical Society, 1980, 2005); *Salem County (New Jersey) Marriage Records* (Merchantville, New Jersey: H. Stanley Craig, Publisher, 1928); reprinted (Woodbury, New Jersey: Gloucester County Historical Society, 1977).

Cushing, M.D., Thomas and Sheppard, Esq., Charles E.: *History of the Counties of Gloucester, Salem, and Cumberland New Jersey, with Biographical Sketches of Their Prominent Citizens* (Philadelphia, Pennsylvania: Everts & Peck, Press of J.B. Lippincott & Co., Philadelphia, 1883).

The Daily Gleaner, 21 August 1957 "Grandson of Loyalist: Married in 1892, Couple in Stanley Rich in Memories" (Fredericton, New Brunswick: *The Daily Gleaner,* 21 August 1957); *The Daily Gleaner*, 7 April 1890 (Fredericton, New Brunswick: *The Daily Gleaner,* 7 April 1890); *The Daily Gleaner*, 22 May 1893 (Fredericton, New Brunswick: *The Daily Gleaner,* 22 May 1893); *The Daily Gleaner*, 23 May 1893 (Fredericton, New Brunswick: *The

Daily Gleaner, 23 May 1893); *The Daily Gleaner*, 20 April 1899 (p.6) (*Provincial Archives of New Brunswick*, Microfilm: F2892). *The Daily Gleaner* is also known and cited as *The Gleaner*. *Wikipedia* notes that although it "began operating in 1880 . . . the paper has its roots in the earlier paper *The Gleaner and Northumberland Schediasma*, started in 1829."

The Daily Sun, 22 May 1893 (Saint John, New Brusnswick: *The Daily Sun*, 22 May 1893).

The Daily Telegraph, 28 October 1874 (Saint John, New Brunswick, 28 October 1874) (Provincial Archives of New Brunswick: *Daniel F. Johnson's New Brunswick Newspaper Vital Statistics*, Volume 36, Number 277).

Dalhousie University Archives (Halifax, Nova Scotia, Canada).

Davidson, Stephen: "New Brunswick Newspapers Remember: Part One" *Loyalist Trails 2011-43 October 30, 2011* (www.uelac.org/Loyalist-Trails/Loyalist-Trails-index-2011.php).

Davis, David John (compiled): *West Jersey New Jersey Deed Records 1676-1721* (Westminster, Maryland: Heritage Books, 2005).

The Dictionary of Canadian Biography Online, 1821-1835 (Volume VI) (www.biographi.ca/Vol_VI_B_Eng.htm).

Documents Relative to the Colonial History of the State of New York, XII (Albany, New York: 1849-1851).

Eardley-Wilmot, John: *Historical View of the Commission for Enquiring into the Losses, Services, and Claims of the American Loyalists, at the Close of the War Between Great Britain and her Colonies, in 1783: with an Account of the Compensation Granted to Them by Parliament in 1785 and 1788* (London, England: J. Nichols, Sons and Bentley, 1815); reprinted with a new introduction and preface by George Athan Billias (Boston, Massachusetts: Gregg Press, 1972).

Egerton, Edward Hugh (editor): *The Royal Commission on the Losses and Services of American Loyalists 1783 to 1785, Being the Notes of Mr. Daniel Parker Coke, M. P., One of the Commissioners During that Period* (London, England: Oxford, printed at the University Press by Horace Hart, 1915).

Facey-Crowther, David: *The New Brunswick Militia Commissioned Officers' Lists, 1787-1867* (Fredericton, New Brunswick: New Brunswick Historical Society, Capital Free Press, 1984); *The New Brunswick Militia 1787-1867* (New Brunswick Historical Society and New Ireland Press, 1990).

FamilyCentral History Services
(http://www.familycentral.net/index/family.cfm?ref1=37072:98&ref2=37072:99).

FamilySearch.org (https://familysearch.org). Source for deeds from *New Brunswick, County Deed Registry Books, 1780 – 1930* housed at the Provincial Archives of New Brunswick transcribed in Appendices. Also the source for *York County New Brunswick Marriage Records 1812-1837* at the Provincial Archives of New Brunswick.

Fisher Ph. D., Edgar Jacob: *New Jersey as a Royal Province 1738 to 1776* (New York: Columbia University, Longmans, Green and Co., Agents London: P. S. King & Son, 1911).

Fisher, Peter: *History of New Brunswick* (Saint John, New Brunswick: Printed by Chubb & Sears, 1825); reprinted jointly by The Government of New Brunswick and William Shives Fisher (Saint John, New Brunswick: Under the Auspices of the New Brunswick Historical Society, 1921); *Notitia of New-Brunswick, for 1836, and Extending into 1837: Comprising Historical, Geographical, Statistical, and Commercial Notices of the Province* (Saint John, New Brunswick: Printed for the Author, by Henry Chubb, 1838).

Ford (Editor), Worthington Chauncey: *Journals of the Continental Congress, 1774-1778*, Volume IX, 1777, October 3–December 31 (Washington, DC: Library of Congress, Government Printing Office, 1907).

Foster, R.F.: *Modern Ireland 1600-1972* (London, England: Allen Lane, The Penguin Press, 1988).

Gesner, Esq., Abraham: *New Brunswick with Notes for Emigrants* (London, England: Simmonds & Ward, 1847).

Gilbroy, Marion: *Loyalists and Land Settlement in Nova Scotia, Public Archives of Nova Scotia Publication No. 4* (Under the direction of D.C. Harvey, Archivist.) (Halifax, Nova Scotia: Public Archives of Nova Scotia, 1937); reprinted (Baltimore, Maryland: Reprinted for Clearfield Company, Inc. by Genealogical Publishing Co., Inc., 1990, 1995, 2002).

The Gleaner. (See under *The Daily Gleaner.*)

Gordon, Thomas Francis: *The History of New Jersey From Its Discovery by Europeans to the Adoption of the Federal Constitution* (Trenton, New Jersey: Published by Daniel Fenton, John C. Clark, printer, Philadelphia, Pennsylvania, 1834).

Great Britain Public Records Office, War Office, Class 60, Volume 43, part 1.

Greene, Evarts B. and Harrington, Virginia D: *American Population before the Federal Census of 1790* (New York, New York: Columbia University Press, 1932).

Hagist, Don N.: *British Soldier, American War* (Yardley, Pennsylvania: Westholme Publishing, LLC, 2012).

Hale, R. Wallace: *Early New Brunswick Probate Records, 1785-1835* (Bowie, Maryland: Heritage Books, Inc., 1989).

Hannay D.C.L., James: "Before the Loyalists" *The Educational Review Supplementary Readings, Canadian History Readings, Volume I, Number Ten, June 1900*, edited and published by George Upham Hay (Saint John, New Brunswick: Barnes & Co., 84 Prince William Street, 1900).

Hawkins B. D., Ernest: *Annals of the Colonial Church Fredericton* (London, England: Society for Promoting Christian Knowledge, 1847). Unnumbered pages as found at: (anglicanhistory.org/canada/nb/annals1847.html).

Hayward, George H.: *Haywards of Sunbury & Carleton Counties, N. B., and Some of Their Descendants* (Fredericton, New Brunswick, Canada: George H. Hayward, C.G. (C), 2010); first published as *George & Ann Durley Hayward, and Some of Their Descendants, 1739 – 1995* (Fredericton, New Brunswick, Canada: George H. Hayward, C.G. (C), 1995). Copies can be obtained by contacting George H. Hayward, C.G. (C), 29 Leeds Drive, Fredericton, New Brunswick, Canada, E3B 4S7. In an email of 22 December 2013, George H. Hayward gave me permission to quote from his book. *York County, New Brunswick, Marriage Records, Volume 1, 1812-1837* (Fredericton, New Brunswick: Published for Private Distribution by George H. Hayward, C.G., 1986); revised and reprinted, 1991 & 1994.

Hazard, Samuel: *Annals of Pennsylvania From the Discovery of the Delaware, 1609-1682* (Philadelphia, Pennsylvania: Hazard & Mitchell, 1850).

Herrick, Cheesman Abiah: *White Servitude in Pennsylvania: Indentured and Redemption Labor in Colony and Commonwealth* (Philadelphia, Pennsylvania: John Joseph McVey, 1926; reprinted New York, New York: Negro Universities Press, 1969; reprinted Baltimore, Maryland: Genealogical Publishing Co., Inc., 1996).

Hoffman, Robert Van Amburgh: *The Revolutionary Scenes in New Jersey* (New York, New York: The American Historical Company, Inc., 1942).

Honeyman, A. Van Doren: "The Loyalists of New Jersey in the Revolution" *Proceedings of the New Jersey Historical Society, April, 1927, Vol. XII, No. 2* (Newark, New Jersey: New Jersey Historical Society, 1927); (editor) *Documents Relating to the Colonial History of the State of New Jersey, First Series, Volume XXXIII, Calendar of New Jersey Wills, Administrations, Etc., Volume IV, 1761 – 1770* (Sommerville, New Jersey: The Unionist Gazette Association Printers, 1925); (succeeded Willaim Nelson as editor): *Documents Relating to the Colonial History of the State of New Jersey, Tenth Volume of Extracts From American Newspapers Relating to New Jersey 1773-1774, Archives of the State of New Jersey, First Series, Volume XXIX* (Paterson, New Jersey: The Call Printing and Publishing Company, 1917).

Hotten (Editor), John Camden: *The Original Lists of Persons of Quality; Emigrants; Religious Exiles; Political Rebels; Serving Men Sold for a Term of Years; Apprentices; Children Stolen; Maidens Pressed; and Others; Who Went From Great Britain to the American Plantations, 1600-1700* (London, England: Chatto and Windus, Publishers, 1874).

Humphreys, David: *An Historical Account of the Incorporated Society for the Propagation of the Gospel in Foreign Parts, to the Year 1728* (London, England: Printed by Joseph Downing, 1730).

Jackson, Ronald Vern: *New Jersey Tax Lists, 1772-1822, Volume IV* (Bountiful, Utah: Accelerated Indexing Systems, 1981).

Jameson, J. Franklin (editor): *Narratives of New Netherland, 1609-1664* (New York, New York, Charles Scribner's Sons, 1909); "Report of the Surrender of New Netherland, by Peter Stuyvesant, 1665" from *Narratives of New Netherland, 1609-1664*.

Johnson, Amandus (editor): *The Records of the Swedish Lutheran Churches at Raccoon and Penns Neck, 1713-1786* (Elizabeth, New Jersey: Colby and McGowan, Inc., 1938); reprinted (Woodbury, New Jersey: Gloucester County Historical Society, 1982); (Salem, Massachusetts: Higginson Book Co., 1997 and currently available from Higginson Book Company through their print-on-demand services).

Johnson, Amandus: *The Swedish Settlements on the Delaware, 1638-1664* (Philadelphia, Pennsylvania: University of Pennsylvania, 1911).

Johnson, Daniel F.: *Daniel F. Johnson New Brunswick Newspaper Vital Statics,* Provincial Archives of New Brunswick (archives.gnb.ca/Archives/Default.aspx?culture=en-CA).

Johnson, Robert Gibbon: *An Historical Account of the First Settlement of Salem, in West Jersey, by John Fenwick, Esq. Chief Proprietor of the Same* (Philadelphia, Pennsylvania: Published by Orrin Rogers, 1839).

Jones, E. Alfred: *Collections of the New Jersey Historical Society, Volume X: The Loyalists of New Jersey* (Newark, New Jersey: New Jersey Historical Society, 1927; reprinted 1972).

The Journal of the American Irish Historical Society, Volume XXVI (New York, New York: The American Irish Historical Society, 1927).

June 2005 - The New Brunswick Anglican — Anglican Parish of Prince William, Dumbries, Queensbury and Southamton (www.parishofprincewilliam.ca/in-the-news/june-2005---the...).

Kalm, Pahr (Peter Kalm): *Travels into North America* (2 Volumes); translated by John Reinhold Forster, F.A.S. (London, England: Printed for T. Lowndes, 1773). Peter Kalm appears on the title page of the 1773 English translation.

Keen, Gregory B.: "The Descendants of Joran Kyn, the Founder of Upland" *The Pennsylvania Magazine of History and Biography, Volume II* (Philadelphia, Pennsylvania: Publication Fund of the Historical Society of Pennsylvania, 1878).

Kelly, Velma: *The Village in the Valley — A History of Stanley* (Stanley, New Brunswick: Velma Kelly, 1983; reprinted a number of times, including 1998). Velma Kelly's full name: Velma Maude (Harrison) Kelly.

Kimball, Paul: *The Last Lights: The New Brunswick Free Christian Baptists, 1832-1905* (www.scribd.com/doc/28089173/The-Last-New-Lights).

Lee, Francis B. (editor): *Archives of the State of New Jersey, Second Series, Volume II, Documents Relating to the Revolutionary History of the State of New Jersey, Volume II, Extracts From American Newspapers, Volume II, 1778* (Trenton, New Jersey: The John L. Murphy Publishing Co., Printers, 1903).

Lee, A.M., Rev. G Herbert: *An Historical Sketch of the First Fifty Years of the Church of England in New Brunswick (1783-1833)* (Saint John, New Brunswick: "Sun" Publishing, 1880).

Lender, Mark E.: *The New Jersey Soldier (New Jersey's Revolutionary Experience) Volume 5* (Newark, New Jersey: New Jersey Historical Commission, 1975).

Lewis, J.D.: (www.carolana.com/SC/Revolution/home.html) *The American Revolution in South Carolina* © 2009 - J.D. Lewis - PO Box 1188 - Little River, SC 29566 - All Rights Reserved. Written permission to quote was granted by J.D. Lewis in a letter dated September 17, 2013.

Library and Archives Canada, 395 Wellington Street, Ottawa, Ontario, Canada.

Livermore, Elizabeth (compiler): *Index to Thomas Shourds' History and Genealogy of Fenwick's Colony* (Ann Arbor, Michigan: Elizabeth Livermore, printed by University Microfilms, Inc., 1962).

Lossing, Benson John: *The Pictorial Field-Book of the Revolution; or, Illustrations, by Pen and Pencil, of the Hisotry, Biography, Scenery, Relics, and Traditions of the War for Independence* (2 Volumes) (New York, New York: Harper Brothers, Volume I: 1851; Volume II: 1852); reprinted (Feeport, New York: Books for Library Press, 1969).

Loyalists in the Maritimes – Ward Chipman Muster Master's Office, 1777-1778, Volume 26, p. 197, Reference MG 23 D1, Series 1, Item Number 13863, Library and Archives Canada, 395 Wellington Street, Ottawa, Ontario, Canada.

"Loyalist Trails" UELAC Newsletter 2011-43 October 30, 2011 (www.uelac.org/Loyalist-Trails/Loyalist-Trails-index-2011.php); "Loyalist Trails" 2012-15 April 15, 2012 (www.uelac.org/Loyalist-Trails/Loyalist-Trails-index-2012.php); "Loyalist Trails" UELAC Newsletter 2015-06 Feb 8, 2015 (www.uelac.org/Loyalist-Trails/Loyalist-Trails-index-2015.php).

Lundin, Charles Leonard: *Cockpit of the Revolution: The War for Independence in New Jersey* (*The Princeton History of New Jersey*, Volume 2) (Princeton, New Jersey: Princeton University Press; H. Milford London: Oxford University Press, 1940).

Lunney, Timothy: "Tim Lunney's blog about the Muintir Lúingh clan of Ireland and the world wide Lunney, Lunny and Lunnie families," (*https://timothylunney.wordpress.com/?s=frederick+howard&submit=Search*).

MacNutt, W.S.: *New Brunswick A History: 1784-1867* (Toronto, Canada: MacMillan of Canada, 1963).

Marianne Grey Otty Database, Fredericton, New Brunswick: the Microforms Department of the University of New Brunswick Harriet Irving Library (http://vre.lib.unb.ca/motty).

Matthews, Jeannie Belinda (Boulter): *Jeannie Belinda (Boulter) Matthews Collection*.

McBreairty, Darrell: *At Ant Ev's* (Madawaska, Maine: Valley Publishing, 1977); *Conversations with A'nt Ev': An Oral History of the Allagash* (Madawaska, Maine: Printed by Valley Publishing Company, 1982).

McEwen, Alec (editor): *In Search of the Highlands: Mapping the Canada-Maine Boundary, 1839* (Fredericton, New Brunswick: Acadiensis Press, 1988).

Meldrum, Charlotte D. and Launey, John Pitts (compiled): *Early Church Records of Gloucester County New Jersey* (Westminster, Maryland: Heritage Books, Inc., 1995).

Messenger and Visitor, 22 April 1896 (Saint John, New Brunswick: *Messenger and Visitor*, 22 April 1896).

Mickle, Isaac: *Reminiscences of Old Gloucester, or Incidents in the History of the Counties of Gloucester, Atlantic and Camden, New Jersey* (Philadelphia, Pennsylvania: Townsend Ward, 1845); reprinted (Woodbury, New Jersey: Gloucester County Historical Society, 1968). The 1845 edition was utilized for this book.

Midwinter, Sir Edward Colpoy: *Some Letters of Colonial Days*, "Address before the Society of Colonial Wars in the State of New Jersey, at its Annual Court, at Princeton, New Jersey, May 3rd 1935" (Princeton, New Jersey: Printed by the Society, 1935); "The S.P.G. and the Church in the American Colonies. Three Lectures. II. New Jersey" (*History Magazine* Vol. IV, 1935, pp. 83-99).

Millman, Thomas R. and Kelley, A.R.: *Atlantic Canada to 1900 a History of the Anglican Church* (Toronto, Canada: Anglican Book Centre, 1983).

Minotty, Paul: *The Records of the Moravian Church at Oldman's Creek, Gloucester County, New Jersey* (Woodbury, New Jersey: Gloucester County Historical Society, Published for the Society by Elmer Garfield Van Name, 1968).

Myers, Albert Cook (editor): *Narratives of Early Pennsylvania, West New Jersey, and Delaware, 1630 – 1707* (New York, New York: Charles Scribner's Sons, 1912).

Nelson, William (editor): *Archives of the State of New Jersey, First Series, Volume XXI, Documents Relating to the Colonial History of the State of New Jersey, Volume XXI, Calendar of Records in the Office of the Secretary of State, 1664-1703* (Paterson, New Jersey, The Press Printing and Publishing Co., 1899); *Archives of the State of New Jersey, First Series, Volume XXII, Documents Relating to the Colonial History of the State of New Jersey, Volume XXII, Marriage Records, 1665-1800* (Paterson, New Jersey: The Press Printing and Publishing Co., 1900); reprinted (Baltimore, MD: Genealogical Publishing Co, 1967); reissued as *New Jersey Marriage Records 1665-1800 Edited, with an Historical Introduction on the Early Marriage Laws of New Jersey, and the Precedents on Which They Were Founded* (Baltimore, MD: Genealogical Publishing Co, 1973); *Archives of the State of New Jersey, Volume XXIII, Documents Relating to the Colonial History State of New Jersey, Volume XXIII, Calendar of*

New Jersey Wills, Volume I, 1670-1730 (Paterson, New Jersey, The Press Printing and Publishing Co., 1901); reprinted (Bowie, Maryland: Heritage Books, 1994); *Archives of the State of New Jersey, Documents Relating to the Colonial History State of New Jersey, Volume XXV, Extracts from American Newspapers, relating to New Jersey, VOL. VI, 1766-1767* (Paterson, New Jersey: The Call Printing and Publishing Co., 1903); (editor, succeeded by Honeyman, A. Van Doren): *Documents Relating to the Colonial History of the State of New Jersey, Tenth Volume of Extracts From American Newspapers Relating to New Jersey 1773-1774, Archives of the State of New Jersey, First Series, Volume XXIX* (Paterson, New Jersey: The Call Printing and Publishing Company, 1917).

New Brunswick Museum Archives & Research Library, Alice T. Fairweather Fonds/Collection "New Brunswick Loyalists' Society Applications," Saint John, New Brunswick, Canada.

The New Brunswick Reader, Volume 12, No. 10 March 19, 2005 (Saint John, New Brunswick: New Brunswick Publishing Company, a division of Brunswick News, Inc., included with Saturday editions of the Telegraph-Journal, 19 March 2005).

New Brunswick Reporter and Fredericton Advertiser, 7 March 1885 (Fredericton, New Brunswick: *New Brunswick Reporter and Fredericton Advertiser*, 7 March 1885) (Provincial Archives of New Brunswick: *Daniel F. Johnson's New Brunswick Newspaper Vital Statistics*, Volume 64, Number 512); *New Brunswick Reporter and Fredericton Advertiser*, 9 April 1890 (Fredericton, New Brunswick: *New Brunswick Reporter and Fredericton Advertiser*, 9 April 1890) (Daniel F. Johnson: Provincial Archives of New Brunswick, *Daniel F. Johnson's New Brunswick Newspaper Vital Statistics*, Volume 75, Number 2203); *New Brunswick Reporter and Fredericton Advertiser*, 24 May 1893 (Fredericton, New Brunswick: *New Brunswick Reporter and Fredericton Advertiser*, 24 May 1893) (Provincial Archives of New Brunswick: *Daniel F. Johnson's New Brunswick Newspaper Vital Statistics*, Volume 85, Number 2573); *New Brunswick Reporter and Fredericton Advertiser*, 26 April 1899 (p. 4) (*Provincial Archives of New Brunswick*, Microfilm: F12182*)*.

New Jersey Archives, First Series (Newark, New Jersey, 1880-93).

O'Callaghan, E.B. (editor): *Documents relating to the Colonial History of the State of New York, 1849-1851* (Albany, New York: Weed, Parsons and Company, *1853).*

The On-Line Institute for Advanced Loyalist Studies (www.royalprovincial.com). Permission to quote from the *On-Line Institute for Advanced Loyalsit Studies* (www.royalprovincial.com) granted by Todd Braisted by email on 22 April 2012. Todd Braisted, in an email on 9 September 2013, also granted permission to quote the John Segee 3 May 1783 declaration included at *The On-Line Institute for Advanced Loyalist Studies*.

Paltsits, Victor H.: "The Founding of New Amsterdam in 1626" (Worcester, Massachusetts: Proceedings of the American Antiquarian Society, Vol. XXXIV, pp. 39-65, April 1924).

Pascoe, Charles Frederick: *Classified Digest of the Records of the Society for the Propagation of the Gospel in Foreign Parts, 1701-1892* (London, England: Published at the Society's Office, 1893); Edition of 1901 published under title: *Two Hundred Years of the S.P.G.* "Missionary Roll" (pp. 829-924).

Peabody, George: *Kings Landing: A Living History Colourguide* (Halifax, Nova Scotia: Formac Publishing Company Limted, 1997).

Penney, Norman (editor): *The Journal of George Fox* (2 vols.) (Cambridge, United Kingdom: Cambridge University Press, 1911).

Plankenhorn, Louise (transcribed and indexed): *Records from Family Bibles in the Gloucester County Historical Society* (Woodbury, New Jersey: The Gloucester County Historical Society, 2001; reprinted 2003).

Pomfret, John E.: *The Province of West New Jersey 1609 – 1702: A History of the Origins of an American Colony* (Princeton, New Jersey: Princeton University Press, 1956). Princeton Univesity Press granted Worldwide English language rights to quote from this work on 19 October 2012.

Proceedings of the New Jersey Historical Society, April, 1927, Vol. XII, No. 2 (Newark, New Jersey: New Jersey Historical Society, 1927).

Provincial Archives of New Brunswick (PANB), Fredericton, New Brunswick, Canada, (archives.gnb.ca/Archives/Default.aspx?culture=en-CA).

Prowell, George R.: *The History of Camden County* (Philadelphia, Pennsylvania: L. J. Richards & Co., 1886).

Public Records Office, War Office Papers, London, England. The *Public Records Office* merged with the *Historical Manuscripts Commission* to form *The National Archives* in 2003.

Raymond LL.D., F.R.S.C., Rev. William O.: "Peter Fisher, the First Historian of New Brunswick" *Collections of the New Brunswick Historical Society No. 10* (Saint John New Brunswick: The New Brunswick Historical Society, 1919); reprinted in the 1921 edition of *History of New Brunswick* by Peter Fisher; "Loyalists in Arms" *Collections of the New Brunswick Historical Society No. 5* (Saint John, New Brunswick: The Sun Printing, Limited, 1904); *The River St. John* (St. John, New Brunswick: Printed by the Strathmore

Press and Published by John a Bowes, 1910); second edition edited by Dr. K.C. Webster, C.M.C. (Sackville, New Brunswick: The Tribune Press, 1950).

Records of Old Revolutionary Soldiers and Their Widows, Provincial Archives of New Brunswick (archives.gnb.ca/Archives/Default.aspx?culture=en-CA).

Reed, H. Clay and Miller, George J. (editors): *The Burlington Court Book, a Record of Quaker Jurisprudence in West New Jersey, 1680 – 1709* (Washington, District of Columbia: American Historical Association, 1944); reprinted (Baltimore, Maryland, Genealogical Publishing Co., Inc., 1998).

Report of the Secretary of the York County Agricultural Society for the Year 1851 (Fredericton, New Brunswick: Printed by James Hogg, Reporter Office, 1852).

Richard Hayne House | My New Brunswick (mynewbrunswick.ca/richard-hayne-house).

Ricord, Frederick W. and Nelson, William (editors): *Archives of the State of New Jersey, Volume IX, Administrations of President John Reading, Lieutenant-Governor Thomas Pownall, Governor Francis Bernard, Governor Thomas Boone, Governor Josiah Hardy, and Part of the Administration of Governor William Franklin, 1757-1767* (Newark, New Jersey: Daily Advertiser Printing House, 1885).

Ripley, Richard UE, MA, APG, Loyalist Researcher & Genealogist. Email: (nffgfamily@hotmail.com); website: (http://www.heritageregistry.net/).

Sabine, Lorenzo: *Biographical Sketches of Loyalists of the American Revolution* (2 Volumes) (Boston, Massachusetts: University of Boston, Little Brown and Company, 1864).

Sachse, Julius Friedrich: *Augustus Evangelical Lutheran Congregation at Trappe, Pennsylvania (Perkiomen Valley) (Montgomery County)* (Bethlehem, Pennsylvania: 1895; reprinted 1908; Apollo, Pennsylvania: Clossen Press, 1993).

Saunders, Edward Manning: *History of the Baptists of the Maritime Provinces* (Halifax, Nova Scotia: Press of John Burgoyne, Granville Street, 1902).

Sewell, Elizabeth S. (compiler): *Sunbury County, New Brunswick Marriages 1766-1888, Volume 1* (Fredericton, New Brunswick: Provincial Archives of New Brunswick, 1987).

Shourds, Thomas: *History and Genealogy of Fenwick's Colony* (Bridgeton, New Jersey: George F. Nixon, Publisher, 1876).

Sickler, Joseph S.: *The History of Salem County New Jersey, Being the Story of John Fenwick's Colony, the Oldest English Speaking Settlement on the Delaware River* (Salem, New Jersey: Sunbeam Publishing Company, 1937).

Simcoe, Lieut. Col. J.G.: *Simcoe's Military Journal* (New York, New York: Bartlett and Welford, 1844).

Simpson (Editor), Hazel B.: *Under Four Flags: Old Gloucester County, 1686-1964, A History of Gloucester County, New Jersey* (Woodbury, New Jersey: Board of Chosen Freeholders, Gloucester County, New Jersey, printed by Sinnickson Chew & Sons Co., Camden, New Jersey, 1965).

Smith, Paul H.: *Loyalists and Redcoats a Study in British Revolutionary Policy* (Chapel Hill, North Carolina: Published for the Institute of Early American History and Culture at Williamsburg, Virginia by the University of North Carolina Press, 1964).

Society for the Propagation of the Gospel in Foreign Parts.

Sparks, Jared: *The Writings of George Washington, Being His Correspondence, Addresses, Messages, and other Papers, Official and Private, Selected and Published from the Original Manuscripts; With a Life of the Author* (12 Volumes) (Boston: American Stationers Company, Russell, Odiorne, and Metcalf and Hilliard, Gray and Co., 1834-1837).

Stiles, Henry Reed: *Bundling: Its Origin, Progress and Decline in America* (Albany, New York: Knickerbocker Publishing Company, 1871).

Stryker-Rodda, Harriet: *Understanding Colonial Handwriting* (Baltimore, Maryland: Genealogical Publishing Company, Inc., 1986, 1987, 1989, 1993, 1998, 2002); originally published in *New Jersey History* (Spring-Summer, 1980). Written permission to quote from *Understanding Colonial Handwriting* was granted by Genealogical Publishing Co., Inc., Baltimore, Maryland, in an email of 11 April 2013.

Stryker-Rodda, Kenn: *Revolutionary Census of New Jersey, an Index, Based on Rateables, of the Inhabitants of New Jersey During the Period of the American Revolution* (Cottonport, Louisiana: Polyanthos, Inc., 1972); revised edition (Lamberville, New Jersey: Hunterdon House, 1986).

Stryker, William Scudder: *The New Jersey Volunteers (Loyalists) in the Revolutionary War* (Trenton, New Jersey: Naar, Day and Naar, Book and Job Printers, 1887); *Official Register of the Officers and Men of New Jersey in the Revolutionary War* (Trenton, New Jersey: Wm. T. Nicholson & Co., Printers, 1872); reprinted (Baltimore, Maryland: Genealogical Publishing Company, 1967).

Thomas, Gabriel: *An Hiftorical and Geographical Account of the Province and Country of Pennsilvania and of Weft-New-Jerfey in America* (London, England: Printed for and sold by A. Baldwin, 1698). This book is divided so that the West New Jersey section, entitled *An Hiftorical Defcription of the Province and Country of Weft-New-Jerfey in America*, has a separate pagination.

Trevelyan, George Otto: *The American Revolution* (four volumes) (New York, New York, London, England, Bombay and Calcutta, India: Longmans, Green and Company, 1899-1914).

United Empire Loyalists Association of Canada, Loyalist Ships (www.uelac.org/Loyalist-Ships/Loyalist-Ships.php).

University of New Brunswick Archives and Special Collections, Winslow Papers (http://www.lib.unb.ca/winslow).

Upper Canada (Ontario) Sundries Index (www.ontariogenealogy.com/uppercanadasundries.html).

Van Buskirk, Judith L.: *Generous Enemies, Patriots and Loyalists in Revolutionary New York* (Philadelphia, Pennsylvania: University of Pennsylvania Press, 2002; first paperback edition, 2004).

Van Doren, A. (editor): *Documents Relating to the Colonial History of The State of New Jersey, First Series, Volume XXXIII, Calendar of New Jersey Wills, Administrations, Etc., Volume IV, 1761 – 1770* (Sommerville, New Jersey: The Unionist Gazette Association Printers, 1925).

Van Name, Elmer Garfield: *Old Deeds Belonging to the Salem County Historical Society with an Index of Unrecorded Deeds* (Salem, New Jersey: Salem County Historical Society, Salem County Historical Society Publications, Volume 2, Number 1, 1961).

Wikipedia.

Winslow Papers, University of New Brunswick Archives and Special Collections, Fredericton, New Brunswick, Canada, (http://www.lib.unb.ca/winslow).

Wood-Holt, B.: *The Kings Loyal Americans, the Canadian Fact, Marriage Licenses for Sunbury County, 1788-1829, Passenger Lists and Other Lists, etc.* (Saint John, New Brunswick: Holland House, Inc., 1990; enlarged and reprinted 1991).

Wright, Esther Clark: *The Loyalists of New Brunswick* (Fredericton, New Brunswick, 1955; reprinted, Moncton, New Brunswick, 1972 and Hantsport, Nova Scotia, 1981). Quotations from Wright included in this work are from the 1972 edition.

The York County New Brunswick Marriage Records 1812-1837 can be found at *Family Search.org* (https://familysearch.org).

APPENDICES

BY WAY OF EXPLANATION

In attempting accuracy in transcribing land grant applications, deeds, wills and the like from the *Provincial Archives of New Brunswick* (PANB), I have done my best. I have tried to format the transcription to follow as closely to the original as possible with the exception of shifting page numbers from the upper corner of the page to the center. Anyone who has attempted transcribing original material from colonial times will attest to the tediousness and utter frustration of such a task.

Harriet Stryker-Rodda, in her *Understanding Colonial Handwriting,* notes, "Until the middle of the 16th century in Europe the ability to write was considered beneath a gentleman's dignity. Writing was left entirely to scribes, secretaries, or cloistered priests who studied to perfect themselves in the *art* which then closely followed precise, hand-printed forms." (p. 8)

In the Colonial period, Stryker-Rodda writes, "There were no graphite pencils." She adds that in this period, "Pens were simple tools made from feathers. Quill pens were first introduced in the Middle Ages. Goose feathers were most popular, but swans, hens and turkeys contributed their share. The good feathers that were to be used for the best pens were plucked from live birds. Excrescences were removed and the quill was heated or soaked in hot water before shaping with a penknife. In the early schools a very important part of the work of the teacher was sharpening quill pens for the day's use by students." (p. 11)

Stryker-Rodda: "Before the invention of printing, the quill was cut with a chisel-shaped edge. This produced a variation in the width of the stroke depending on the direction in which the pen was moved. Various chisel shapes were developed. They produced a variation in widths and in the amount of pressure that could be applied without breaking the quill."

Stryker-Rodda adds, "No one knows now who was responsible, or when the great discovery was made that gradually changed handwriting. It was found that a small hole in the nib would permit a longer writing span form one dip into the inkpot, because the hole would act as a minute reservoir." (pp. 11-12)

Going into further detail, Stryker-Rodda writes, "The pointed quill remained in common use in the colonies and states until 1830 when the modern steel pen nib was introduced. It was not flexible like the quill. . . . The steel nib, however, increased writing speed and produced more rhythmic and flowing letters. . . ." (p. 14)

Stryker-Rodda continues:

> Early inks were made from oak apples or galls, those swellings on trees caused by the parasitic gall fly. Copper sulfate, then called copperas or vitriol, and the sap or gum from trees, were mixed with the galls in large wooden tubs and stirred frequently for two or three weeks. The resulting thick, sticky, odorous mass was diluted with water and used as ink. Galls contain tannic acid, and if combined with iron salt, produce a purplish-

black compound. When used for writing, this ink appeared as a dark purple that grew darker with age. We see it today on surviving documents as brown.

Some inks were made with lamp black, but unlike so-called iron ink, they did not combine with the paper, but tended to crack or wear off. Iron ink bites into the surface of the paper and becomes a part of it. (p. 14)

Stryker-Rodda: "If a document was written before 1750 in this country [United States] you may be sure the paper was an immigrant. Paper-making in the colonies had its start late in the 17th century, but even after its feeble beginnings it was cheaper to import than to use domestic papers." (p. 15)

ISSUES OF CURRENCY

The following is from Abraham Gesner's *New Brunswick with Notes for Emigrants*, published in 1847:

Note D.

Currency.

The pound sterling is twenty-four shillings and fourpence currency. The pound currency contains 4 dollars; 1 dollar contains 5 shillings; 1 shilling, 2 sixpences; 1 sixpence, 6 pennies; 1 penny, 2 coppers. The value of the pound currency is about 16s. 5¼d.; the dollar, 4s. 1¼d.; the shilling, 9¾d.; the sixpence nearly 5d. sterling. In ordinary dealing in New Brunswick, the current coins of Great Britain are usually paid away at the following rates: — sovereign, 24s. 6d.; crown, 6s. 1d.; half-crown, 3s. 0½d.; shilling, 1s. 2d.; sixpence, 7½d. These rates are liable to some variation. (p. 388)

Mandy Barrow writes at "Understanding old British money - pounds, shillings and pence" (www.woodlands-junior.kent.sch.uk/customs/questions/money), "After the Norman Conquest in 1066, the pound was divided into twenty shillings or 240 pennies. It remained so until decimalization on 15 February 1971." Barrow explains that "Old money was divided into: pounds (£ or l); shillings (s. or /-) and pennies (d.)".

Peter Fisher in *Notitia of New Brunswick*, writes, "Lands in New-Brunswick are held in fee-simple: The mode formerly adopted by Government in granting land was by memorial to the Governmor and Council. This, if approved of, was entered in the Council books, and a patent was made out on the applicant's paying the stipulated fees, which on a single grant of from one to two hundred acres, amounted to £12 11S. This was the total cost, as no other charge was made for the land. A Quit Rent was reserved in most of the Grants. This mode was followd for a long time." (p.17)

APPENDIX A

Bush, Bernard (compiler): *Laws of the Royal Colony of New Jersey 1760-1769, New Jersey Archives, Third Series, Volume IV* (Trenton, New Jersey: New Jersey State Library Bureau of Archives and History, 1982).

COLONIAL LAWS

An ACT to enable the Owners and Possessors of a certain Body of Meadow and Marsh lying on the Westerly Side of Raccoon Creek, in the County of Gloucester, to keep up and maintain the Banks and other Water-works around the same, and to constitute all ten Foot Ditches therein lawful Fences.

WHEREAS the said Owners and Possessors have requested, that the following Law might be passed for the Purposes therein mentioned; and having duly advertised their intended Application, and no Objection now appearing: Therefore,

BE IT ENACTED *by the Governor, Council., and General Assembly, and it is hereby Enacted by the Authority of the same,* That the Owners and Possessors of a certain Body of Meadow and Marsh lying on the Westerly Side of *Raccoon Creek,* adjoining the River *Delaware,* within a certain Bank, beginning at the Fast Land *of John Kelly,* thence to the said River, and up the same to *Raccoon Creek's* Mouth, thence up the said Creek to the Fast Land *of Lawrence String,* and their Successors in Interest, shall at all Times hereafter, keep up and maintain the Banks upon their several and respective Meadows and Marshes in good Repair, so as effectually to prevent the Tide from overflowing the Meadow within the same; and all necessary Dams and Sluices shall be erected, supported and maintained, at the equal Expence of the Owners and Possessors thereof, in Proportion to the Quantity of Meadow they severally hold; and all Drains and Watercourses shall be kept open and clear by the Person or Persons whose Land they pass through.

AND BE IT FURTHER ENACTED *by the Authority aforesaid,* That it shall and may be lawful for the said Owners or Possessors of the said Meadows and Marshes, to meet Yearly, on the first Tuesday in *April,* at a House by them agreed upon, or from time to time adjourned unto, and there by Plurality of Voices of them so met, elect and chuse two Persons, each of whom being Owners of at least ten Acres of said Meadow or Marsh, to be Managers for the ensuing Year; until which Time, *Constantine Wilkins* and *William Key* are appointed Managers; which said Managers for the Time being, shall have Power to assess the said Owners and Possessors, in Proportion to the Meadows or Marshes they shall severally hold, in such Sum or Sums of Money as they may think necessary for the erecting, amending and repairing the necessary Dams and Sluices as aforesaid; which they shall at all Times keep in good and sufficient Repair: And if any of the said Owners or Possessors shall neglect or refuse to pay the Sum or Sums of Money so assessed, for the Space of Twenty Days after Demand made by the said Managers, or either of them; it shall and may be lawful for either of the said Managers, to commence an Action of Debt in any Court of Record, where the same may be cognizable, and recover the same, with Costs of Suit, and the said Managers may dig Mud for the Purposes aforesaid, the most convenient and least detrimental to the Owners of the Soil. (p. 412)

APPENDIX B

New Brunswick Land Grants, 1784 – 1997, Sunbury County, Volume NS-A, pp. 39-76 (RS686) (Microfilm: F16301)

[70]

Parr Town

Nova Scotia Fs.　　To all to whom these presents shall come Greeting Know ye that
J Parr　　　　　　John Parr Esquire Captain general and Governor in Chief in and over His Majesty's Province of Nova Scotia and the dependencies Vice Admiral of the same &c &c &c — Have given granted and confirmed and do by these presents give grant and confirm unto the

[Here is listed the names of the grantees and their granted lot numbers. I have included the following:]

"Col¹. Isaac Allen number fifty Six" (p. 40)
"Hendrick Day eleven hundred twenty three" (p. 60)
"John Day eleven hundred thirty five" (p. 60)
"William Day eleven hundred thirty one" (p. 60)
"John Kelly six hundred twenty five" (pp. 51-52)
"William Kelly number two hundred & thirty six" (p. 45)
"William Niles one thousand & Seventy nine" (p. 59)
"Reynard Wheeler nine hundred eighty nine" (p. 57)

[Reynard Wheeler shared part of lot 89 with John Kelly at Kingsclear, New Brunswick, and was involved in land transactions with the Kellys. Frances Ann "Fanny" Kelly (ca 1829 – between 1891 and 1901 census), daughter of William and Sarah Ann (Howard) Kelly, married John Fred Niles (24 January 1825 - ?) ca 1848. In conversations with Eva "Ev" (Kelly) McBreairty (some of which are included in my book *Conversations with A'nt Ev': an Oral History of the Allagash*), Eva "Ev" (Kelly) McBreairty stated that the Kellys were related to the Day family, so I have included them here in the event someone wants to pursue this search in the future.]

[After the listing of the lots given to each of the grantees, the specifics of the grant continue on page 66.]

& unto their several Heirs & Afsigns with all and all manner of Mines unopened excepting Mines of Gold & Silver, Lead Copper and Coals To have and to hold the said granted Premifses with all priviledges profits, commodities and appurtenances Hereunto belonging unto the said

[A list of all the grantees (pp. 66-76) is included here. The specifics of the grant continue on page 76.]

their Heirs and Afsigns forever, Yielding and paying by the said Grantees & each & every of them their Heirs & Afsigns, which by the acceptation thereof they bind & oblige themselves their Heirs Executors and Afsigns to pay to His Majesty, His Heirs & Succefsors or to any person lawfully authorised to receive the same a Free yearly Quit Rent of one farthing for each & every Lot hereby granted, the first payment of the Quit Rent to commence and become payable at the expiration of ten years from the date hereof and so to continue payable yearly thereafter forever on default thereof this Grant shall be Null and Void, Provided also that this Grant shall have been registered at the Registers Office, and a Docket thereof entered at the Auditors Office, within six months from the Date hereof, otherwise this Grant shall become null and void, In writing whereof I have signed these presents & caused the Seal of the Province to be hereunto affixed at Halifax this fourteenth day of August, in the twenty fourth year of the Reign of our Sovereign Lord George the third By the grace of God of Great Britain France and Ireland King Defender of the faith and so forth and in the year of our Lord one thousand seven hundred and Eighty four.

Nova Scotia Halifax
Regis^d. 27th August 1784
Ar. Goold Reg^r.
Ex^d.

Registered the 2. January 1785.

By His Excellencys Command
Rich Bulkeley —
Nova Scotia Halifax 14 Septr. 1784
Entered at the Auditor's Office —
Fra Shepton
Dy <u>Auditor</u>

New Brunswick Land Grants, 1784 – 1997, Sunbury County, Volume NS-1, pp. 84-86 (RS686) (Microfilm: F16300)

N° 1
N.S.

Maryland Loyalists
Block <u>N°. 1.</u>
Daniel Tukes and 57 Others
N°. 1

The Kellys of Kingsclear

Capⁿ Philip Bailey and 58 others — 29ᵗʰ. March 1785 — 1784

No. 22

NOVA SCOTIA,
GEORGE the Third by the Grace of GOD of GREAT BRITAIN, FRANCE and IRELAND, KING, Defender of the Faith, and fo forth.

To all to whom thefe Prefents fhall Come Greeting,

KNOW ye, that We, of Our fpecial Grace certain Knowledge, and mere Motion, have Given and Granted by thefe Prefents, for Us, our Heirs and Succeffors do give and grant unto

[Here is listed all the grantees, including:]

Michˡ Kelly [,] William Kelly [and] Alexander Long

Their Heirs and Afsigns a tract of land containing Ten Thousand One hundred and fifty acres in the County of Sunbury in our Province of Nova Scotia bounded situate lying and being on the River called Maguaguadairisk on the Eastern Side of the Bay of Pafsamaquady being the Lots number one, two, four, five and Six on the Eastern Side of the said River, and numbers eighteen, nineteen, twenty, twenty one and twenty two on the western side, containing in the whole of said Lots ten thousand one hundred and fifty acres being Wildernefs Lands — x

And hath Fuch Shape, Form, and Marks, as appears by a Plat thereof hereunto annexed; together with all Woods, Underwoods, Timber and Timber Trees, Lakes, Ponds, Fifhings. Waters, Water Courfes, Profits, Commodities, Appurtenances, and Hereditaments whatfoever thereunto belonging or in any Wife appertaining; together alfo with the Privileges of Hunting, Hawking and Fowling In and upon the fame, and Mines and Minerals; SAVING and referving NEVERTHELESS to us, our Heirs and Succefsors, all White Pine Trees, if any fuch shall be found growing thereon, and alfo SAVING and referving to us, our Heirs and Succefsors all Mines of Gold, Silver, Copper, Lead and Coals, TO HAVE AND TO HOLD the faid Parcel, & parcels Tract, & Tracts of Ten thousand one hundred and fifty Acres of land, and all and fingular other the Premises hereby granted unto the faid Grantees severally and, respectively and in severalty in the several & respective Shares quantities and proportions following to wit, unto the said

[The list of grantees named here includes William Kelly and Alexander Long. A sidebar contains the following:]

No. 4

The names of the following
grantees, Enumerated
above are annexed
[illegible] [illegible]:
Mich.l Kelly
Moses Burns
John M.cCarthy
W.m Masters
John Traverse

Severally One hundred Acres a piece, and in Severalty to all and every the several respective Heirs and Afsigns forever, in free and common Sociage, the said several and respective Grantees and their several and respective Heirs or Affigns YIELDING and PAYING therefor unto us, our Heirs and Succeffors, or to our Receiver General for the Time being, or to his Deputy or Deputies for the Time being yearly, that is to fay, at the Feaft of Saint Michael in every Year, at the Rate of Two Shillings for every Hundred Acres, and fo in Proportion according to the Quantities of Acres hereby granted; the fame to commence and be payable from the faid Feaft of Saint Michael which fhall firft happen after the Expiration of Ten Years from the Date hereof PROVIDED always and this prefent Grant is upon Condition that the faid several & respective Grantees & their several & respective Heirs or Affigns fhall and do within three Years after the Date hereof for every fifty Acres of Plantable Land hereby granted, clear and work three Acres at leaft, in fuch Part thereof as Respectively he or they fhall judge moft convenient and advantageous; or elfe to clear and drain three Acres of Swampy or Sunken Ground, or drain three Acres of Marfh, if any fuch contained therein. AND fhall and do within the Time aforefaid, put and keep upon every Fifty acres thereof, accounted Baren, three Neat Cattle, and continue the fame thereon, until three Acres of every Fifty be fully cleared and improved, and if there fhall be no Part of the faid Tract fit for prefent Cultivation without manuring and improving the fame respectively he or they within the Time aforefaid fhall be obliged to erect on fome Part of his or their said respective Land, one good Dwelling Houfe, to be at leaft Twenty Feet in Length and Sixteen Feet in breadth, and to put on his or their said respective Land the like Number of three Neat Cattle for every Fifty Acres; or otherwife if any Part of the faid Tract fhall be Stony or Rocky Ground, and not fit for Planting or Pafture, fhall and do within three Years as aforefaid, begin to employ thereon and continue to work for three Years then next enfusing, in digging any ftony Quary or Mine, one good and able Hand for every Fifty Acres, it fhall be accounted a fufficient Cultivation and Improvement; PROVIDED alfo, that every three Acres that fhall be cleared and worked, or cleared and drained as aforefaid, fhall be accounted fufficient Seating, Cultivation and Improvement to fave forever from Forfeiture Fifty Acres of Land in any Part of the Tract hereby granted; And the faid respective Grantees and their said respective Heirs and affigns be at Liberty to withdraw his or their Stock, or forbear working in any Quarry or Mine, in Proportion to fuch Cultivation and Improvements, as fhall be made upon the Plantable Lands, Swamps, Sunken Grounds or Marfh therein contained; AND if the faid Rent hereby referred fhall happen to be in arrear or unpaid for the Space of One Year from the Time it fhall become due, and no Diftrefs can be found on the faid Lands, Tenements and Hereditaments hereby Granded, or if this Grant fhall not be duly Regiftred in the Regifters Office of our faid Province within Six Months from the Date hereof, and a Docket alfo entered in the Auditors Office of the fame, then this Grant fhall be void, and the faid Lands, Tenements and Hereditaments hereby granted, and every Part and Parcel thereof fhall revert to us, our Heirs and Succefsors; AND PROVIDED alfo, upon this further Condition, that if the Land hereby Given and Granted to the said several grantees and their several & respective Heirs as aforefaid shall at any Time or Times hereafter come unto the Poffeffion and Tenure of any Perfon or Perfons whatever, Inhabitants of our faid Province of Nova-Scotia, either by Virture of any deed of Sale, Conveyance, Enfeoffment, or Exchange, or by Gift, Inheritance, Defcent, Devife or Marriage, fuch Perfon or Perfons being Inhabitants as aforefaid, fhall within Twelve Months after his, her or their Entry and Poffeffion of the fame, take the Oaths, prefcribed by Law, and make and fubfcribe the following Declaration, that is to fay, "I do promife and declare, that I will maintain and defend to the utmoft of my Power, the Authority of the King in his Parliament as the Supreme Legiflature of this Province," before fome one of the Magiftrates of the faid Province, and fuch Declaration and Certificate of the Magiftrate, that fuch Oaths have been taken, being recorded in the Secretary's Office of the faid Province, the Perfon or Perfons fo taking the Oaths aforefaid and making and fubfcribing the faid Declaration, fhall be deemed the lawful Poffeffor or Poffeffors of the Lands hereby granted: AND a Cafe of Default on the Part of fuch Perfon or Perfons in taking the Oaths, and making and fubfcribing the Declaration within Twelve Months as aforefaid, This prefent Grant, and every Part thereof, fhall and We do hereby declare the fame to be Null and Void to all Intents and Purpofes, and the Lands hereby Granted and every Part and Parcel thereof, fhall in like Manner revert to and become vefted in Us, our Heirs and Succeffors, any Thing herein contained to the Contrary notwithftanding.

    GIVEN under the Great Seal of our Province of Nova-Scotia: WITNESS our Trufty and Well-beloved John Parr Esquire our Captain General Governor and Commander
      in Chief, in and over our faid Province, this Twenty Ninth Day of March
        in the Year of our Lord One Thoufand Seven Hundred and Eighty four
and in the Twenty fourth Year of our Reign .

Nova Scotia Halifax   Signed in Council 29th March 1784   By His Excellency's command

Registered 4th. April 1784   R. Bulkeley   Richd. Bulkeley   Halifax 16th. April 1784
    Ar Goold Regr   Entered at the Auditors Office
    End.   Fra. Shipton

New Brunswick Registered the 9th. February 1785   Dy Audr.

New Brunswick Land Grants, 1784 – 1997, Sunbury County, Volume NS-1, pp. 112-114 (RS686) (Microfilm: F16300)

Block No. 2

Col. Isaac Allen and 143 others

No. 29

NOVA SCOTIA,
   GEORGE the Third by the Grace of GOD of GREAT BRITAIN, FRANCE and IRELAND, KING, Defender of the Faith, and fo forth.

   To all to whom thefe Prefents fhall Come Greeting,

KNOW ye, that We, of Our fpecial Grace certain Knowledge, and mere Motion, have Given and Granted by thefe Prefents, for Us, our Heirs and Succeffors do give and grant unto

[Thomas Kelly and Abraham Long are among the grantees listed here.]

in Severalty and unto their Several and respective
Their Heirs and Afsigns a Tract of Land, containing in the Whole, Thirty Eight Thousand five Hundred and fifty acres in the Township of Sunbury and County of Sunbury in Our Province of Nova Scotia bounded abutted Situated lying and being on the Southernmoft side on the River Saint John and comprehended within the Tract hereinafter described to Wit, beginning at the lower Bound of Land granted Major Lockman and thence to run South forty five degrees East Seven Hundred and Eighty five chains of four Rods each, thence North Forty five degrees <u>East</u> Six Hundred Chains, thence North forty five degrees West One Hundred and Ninety Eight, thence North Thirty four Degrees, East till it comes to the River Saint John there to be bounded by the Several courses of the said River up [illegible] Stream to the Bounds first mentioned containing on the Whole Tract Forty six Thousand and Seven Hundred and Eighty Nine Acres, Eight Thousand three Hundred and thirty Nine Acres being reserved out of said Tract for the Kings Woods for Grants heretofore

made within it, and also the Land wherein the French Trusftees tracts have made improvements not exceeding Two Hundred feet in front on the River, and to extend back that with it, as as [sic] there improvements are made and for all Such Roads as may hereafter be deemed necefsary to pafs through the Same — all [illegible] Lands and hath fuch Shape, Form, and Marks, as appears by a Plat thereof hereunto annexed; together with all Woods, Underwoods, Timber and Timber Trees, Lakes, Ponds, Fifhings. Waters, Water Courfes, Profits, Commodities, Appurtenances, and Hereditaments whatfoever thereunto belonging or in any Wife appertaining; together alfo with the Privileges of Hunting, Hawking and Fowling, In and upon the fame, and Mines and Minerals; SAVING and referving NEVERTHELESS to us, our Heirs and Succefsors, all White Pine Trees, if any fuch shall be found growing thereon, and alfo SAVING and referving to us, our Heirs and Succefsors all Mines of Gold, Silver, Copper, Lead and Coals, TO HAVE AND TO HOLD the faid Parcel, & parcels or Tract, of Thirty Eight Thousand four Hundred and Fifty Acres of land, and all and fingular other the Premises hereby granted unto the faid Several and respective Grantees Severally on the Several and respective Quantities Shares and proportions, following lotts, unto the said Lieutenant Colonel Isaac Allen Sixteen Hundred Acres . . . unto the said Abraham Long, . . . two Hundred and fifty Acres . . . unto the said Thomas Kelly, . . . Two Hundred Acres . . . to All and [illegible] of their Several Heirs and Afsigns for ever in free and common Soceage The said several and respective Grantees and Their several and respective Heirs or Affigns YIELDING and PAYING therefor unto us, our Heirs and Succeffors, or to our Receiver General for the Time being, or to his Deputy or Deputies for the Time being yearly, that is to fay, at the Feaft of Saint Michael in every Year, at the Rate of Two Shillings for every Hundred Acres, and fo in Proportion according to the Quantities of Acres hereby granted; the fame to commence and be payable from the faid Feaft of Saint Michael which fhall firft happen after the Expiration of Ten Years from the Date hereof PROVIDED always and this prefent Grant is upon Condition that the faid Several and respective Grantees their several and Respective Heirs or Affigns fhall and do within three Years after the Date hereof for every fifty Acres of Plantable Land hereby granted, clear and work three Acres at leaft, in fuch Part thereof as respectively he or they fhall judge moft convenient and advantageous; or elfe to clear and drain three Acres of Swampy or Sunken Ground, or drain three Acres of Marfh, if any fuch contained therein. AND fhall and do within the Time aforefaid, put and keep upon every Fifty acres thereof, accounted Baren, three Neat Cattle, and continue the fame thereon, until three Acres for every Fifty be fully cleared and improved, and if there fhall be no Part of the faid Tract fit for prefent Cultivation without manuring and improving the fame respectively he or they within the Time aforesaid fhall be obliged to erect on fome Part of His or their said respective Land, one good Dwelling Houfe, to be at leaft Twenty Feet in Length and Sixteen Feet in breadth, and to put on his or their said respective Land the like Number of three Neat Cattle for every Fifty Acres; or otherwife if any Part of the faid Tract fhall be Stony or Rocky Ground, and not fit for Planting on Pafture, fhall and do within three Years as aforefaid, begin to employ thereon and continue to work for three Years then next enfusing, in digging any ftony Quary or Mine, one good and able Hand for every Fifty Acres, it fhall be accounted a fufficient Cultivation and Improvement; PROVIDED alfo, that every three Acres that fhall be cleared and worked, or cleared and drained as aforefaid, fhall be accounted fufficient Seating, Cultivation and Improvement to fave forever from Forfeiture Fifty Acres of Land in any Part of the Tract hereby granted; And the faid respective Grantees and their said respective Heirs and affigns be at Liberty to withdraw his or their Stock, or forbear working in any Quarry or Mine, in Proportion to fuch Cultivation and Improvements, as fhall be made upon the Plantable Lands, Swamps, Sunken Grounds or Marfh therein contained; AND if the faid Rent hereby referred fhall happen to be in arrear or unpaid for the Space of One Year from the Time it fhall become due, and no Diftrefs can be found on the faid Lands, Tenements and Hereditaments hereby Granted, or if this Grant fhall not be duly Regiftered in the Regifters Office of our faid Province within Six Months from the Date hereof, and a Docket alfo entered in the Auditors Office of the fame, then this Grant fhall be void, and the faid Lands, Tenements and Hereditaments hereby granted, and every Part and Parcel thereof fhall revert to us, our Heirs and Succefsors; AND PROVIDED alfo, upon this further Condition, that if the Land herby Given and Granted to the said several grantees and their several & respective Heirs as aforefaid shall at any Time or Times hereafter come unto the Poffession and Tenure of any Perfon or Perfons whatever, Inhabitants of our faid Province of Nova-Scotia, either by Virture of any deed of Sale, Conveyance, or Exchange, or by Gift, Inheritance, Defcent, Devife or Marriage, fuch Perfon or Perfons being Inhabitants as aforefaid, fhall within Twelve Months after his, her or their Entry and Poffeffion of the fame, take the Oaths, prefcribed by Law, and make and fubfcribe the following Declaration, that is to fay, "I do promife and declare, that I will maintain and defend to the utmoft of my Power, the Authority of the King in his Parliament as the Supreme Legiflature of this Province," before fome one of the Magiftrates of the faid Province, and fuch Declaration and Certificate of the Magiftrate, that fuch Oaths have been taken, being recorded in the Secretary's Office of the faid Province, the Perfon or Perfons fo taking the Oaths aforefaid and making and fubfcribing the faid Declartion, fhall be deemed the lawful Poffeffor or Poffeffors of the Lands hereby granted: AND a Cafe of Default on the Part of Fuch Perfon or Perfons in taking the Oaths, and making and fubfcribing the Declaration within Twelve Months as aforefaid, This prefent Grant, and every Part thereof, fhall and We do hereby declare the fame to be Null and Void to all Intents and Purpofes, and the Lands hereby Granted and every Part and Parcel thereof, fhall in like Manner revert to and become vefted In Us, our Heirs and Succeffors, any Thing herein contained to the Contrary notwithftanding.

GIVEN under the Great Seal of our Province of Nova-Scotia: WITNESS our Trufty and Well-beloved John Parr Esquire our Captain General Governor and Commander in Chief; in and over or faid Province, this Fourteenth Day of July in the Year of our

Lord One Thoufand Seven Hundred and Eighty Four and in the Twentyfourth Year of our Reign
               J Parr

Signed in Council   En^d. [illegible], New Brunswick By His Excellencys Command
  Rich^d. Buckeley   Rich^d. Buckeley
Registered 24th. Feby 1785.
Thomas Knox
by Register

Parr Town New Brunswick
Entered at the Auditors Office
21st. April 1785.
     Thomas Knox
      Auditor

[*Sid Bar:*]

Nova Scotia
Halifax Regist^d. 15th July
1784 Ar Goold Reg^r

Nova Scotia Halifax
21 July 1784 Entered
at the Auditors Office
  Fran^s Shipton
    Dy Aud

New Brunswick Land Petitions: Original Series, York County, 1783-1918 (RS108) (Microfilm: F1024)

21

             Parr Town June 19th. 1785 —

A Memorial of com. Lotts of Land Vacant Belonging &c. The Regiment Humbly prays Your Excellency will be So good as to grant The Undersigned the grants of the Land As whe have Not Received any Land which whe have Claim in This Part of The Country As whe have Improved Some Part of the Land. & The Person not Being Present whe Humbly Begs Your Excellency will be so good As to grant Us the Land as the Time of the season Of Farming Land Is at Present & Our Intentions Of Improving the Country is att. will

So no more and Present but Remain

Your [illegible] —

{John Abell & Wife   }
{John Keilly   }
{John Blewer   }
{John Swin   }
{Luke Kelly   }
{W^m. Keilly   }
{James Fletcher & Wife }

[*verso*]

John Abell & others
Ask Land in the Pioneer
Block —

To Council 21st. June
The Land does not appear
to be Vacant —

Rec^d. 20th. June 1785

    To
His Excellency The
Governor of
Parr Town

New Brunswick Land Grants, 1784 – 1997, Sunbury County, Volume NS-A, pp. 208-210 (RS686) (Microfilm: 16302)

100

    Elias Burbidge and James Hardy
Nova Scotia fs.
               To all to whom these Presents shall come Greeting
   M. Wilmot   } Know Ye, That I Montagu Wilmot Esquire Captain General and

Regist^d. March 25th.} Governor in Chief in an over His Majesty's Province of Nova
1765 } Scotia or Acadie and its dependencies Vice Admiral of the same Colonel in His Majesty's Service and Commanding the Troops in the said Province by Virtue of the Power and Authority to me given by his present Majesty King <u>George</u> the Third under the Great Seal of Great Britain Have given granted and confirmed and do by these Presents by and with the advice and consent of His Majesty's Council for the said Province give grant and confirm unto Elias Burbidge and James Hardy their Heirs and Afsigns, a tract of Land situate, lying and being on the North side of the Bay of Fundy Bounded by Lands granted to William Best and John Burbidge Esquire on the South East, on the Northeast by the River Shepod Northwesterly by ungranted Land with all Privileges a tenances Thereunto belonging to the said

-209-

the said Granted to be equally divided by and between them as they shall agree, according to a Plan hereunto annexed containing in the whole by estimation Fifteen Hundred Acres more or lefs with all and all manner of Mines unopened excepting Mines of Gold and Silver precious Stones and Lapis Lazule, Lead, Copper and Coals in and upon the said Tract of Land situate as aforesaid saving always the previous Right of any other Person or Persons to the said Tract of Land or any part thereof. To have and to hold the said granted Premifses with all Privileges Profits Commodities and Appertenances thereunto belonging unto the said Elias Burbidge and James Hardy their Heirs and Afsigns forever Yielding and paying the said Grantees their Heirs and Afsigns which by the acceptation hereof each of the said Grantees binds and obliges himself his Heirs Executors and Afsigns to pay to his Majesty King George the Third his Heirs and Succefsors or to the Commander in Chief of the said Province for the Time being or to any person lawfully authorized to receive the same for his Majesty's use a free, yearly, Quitrent of one Shilling Sterling Money on Michaelmas day for every Fifty acres so granted and so on in proportion for a greater or lefser quantity of Land granted the first year Payment of the same to be made on, Michaelmas day next after the confirmation of Ten years for the date hereof and so to continue payable yearly hereafter for ever But in case three years Quitrent shall at any one time be behind and unpaid and no distrefs to be found on the Premifses then the Grant to the Grantee so failing shall be null and void or in case either of the said Grantees shall within Ten Years from the date hereof alienate or grant the Prmifses or any Part thereof, except by will, without Licence from the Governor Lieutenant Governor or Commander in Chief for the time being under the Seal of the said Province for which licence no Fee or Reward shall be paid then this Grant to the Grantee so alienating or granting the Premifses or any part thereof except by will shall be null and void. And moreover the Grant hereby made is upon this exprefs condition and each and every of the said Grantees binds and obliges himself his Heirs

-210-

Heirs Executors or Afsigns to plant cultivate improve or enclose, one third part of the Land hereby granted within Ten years one other Third part within Twenty years and the remaining third part within thirty years from the date of this Grant or otherwise to forfeit his Right to such Lands as shall not be under Cultivation or Improvement at the Time the forfeiture shall be incurred, And each of the said Grantees doth likewise hereby bind himself his Heirs and Afsigns to plant within Ten years from the date hereof two acres of the said Land with Hemp and to keep up the same or a like quantity of acres planted during the succefsive years. And for the more effectual accomplishment of His Majesty's Intentions for settling the Lands within this Province the Grant hereby made is upon this [illegible] further Condition that of each and every of the said Grantees shall not settle on their respective Shares one Family at least with proper Stock and Materials for the Improvement of the said Lands on or before the last day of March which will be in the Year of our Lord One thousand seven hundred and sixty seven then this Grant to each Grantee so failing shall be null and void and of none effect and the right of each Grantee so failing to settle as aforesaid shall cease and revert to the Crown and the Governor Lieutenant Governor or Commander in Chief for the time being may at his Pleasure Grant the same to any other person or Persons in the manner as if this Grant had not been made. In Witnefs whereof I have signed these Presents and caused the Seal of the Province to be Thereunto affixed at Halifax this fifteenth day of March in the fifth year of the Reign of our Sovereign Lord George the Third by the Grace of God of Great Britain France and Ireland King Defender of the faith and so forth and in the year of our Lord one thousand seven hundred and Sixty five.

By his Excellency's command with the advice and consent of His Majesty's Council.

Rich^d. Bulkeley Sec^y.

Nova Scotia Halifax.

I do hereby certify That the forgoing contains a true Copy taken from the Records this 21st. day of April 1785.

Ex^d. New Brunswick —   }   [illegible] Solomon Dy. Reg^r.
Registered 1st. Septr. 1785}

New Brunswick Land Grants, 1784 – 1997, Sunbury County, Volume NS-A, pp. 211-214 (RS686)(Microfilm: F16302)

S^t. George's — John McLeod & 152 Others

241

To all to whom these Presents Shall come Greeting Know Ye that I John Parr

Esquire our Captain General and Governor in Chief in and over His Majesty's JParr[}] Province of Nova Scotia and its dependencies Vice Admiral of the same &c &c &c have given granted and confirmed and do by These Presents give grant and confirm unto John McLeod Lot. Number one Francis Shipton Number two Thomas Storrow Number three Gillam Taylor Number four John Condon Number five John Bullock Number Six George Grant Number Seven John Odley Number Eight, William Hooper number Nine John Durney number ten Patrick Steel Number eleven Fraguar McCra number twelve John McCoy number thirteen George Kearns number fourteen William Austin number fifteen Mark Wentworth number sixteen Letter A David Loyd number one John McGibbon number two Thomas Gay number three Augustus Bailey number four William Freeman number five, Robert Bailey number six, Philip Bailey number seven Robert Hamilton number eight, Paul Bantom Junior number nine, George Bantom number Ten, Michael Dowley number eleven, Conway Bailey number Twelve John Welch number thirteen William Freeman Junior Number fourteen, William Bayley number fifteen William Hurley number sixteen Letter B William Grant number one, Daniel McMasters number Two, James Campbell number three, John Lane number four John Craig number five, Samuel Blifs number six John Gofs number seven Edmond Phelon number eight John Grant number nine, John Burns number ten James Brannon number eleven Christian Foy number twelve, Donald Glazier number thirteen Dennis Barton number fourteen Kenneth McKenzie number fifteen, William Granger number sixteen Letter C,. John Casham number one, John Eustice number two John Crew number three George Hammond number four, James Murphy number five Cornelius Ryan number six, Henry Appleton number seven, Thomas Wilkinson number eight, Donald Grant number nine, William Grant number ten, Samuel Paine nubmber eleven, Peter Mulloy number twelve William Ryan number thirteen Robert Calder number fourteen John Patrick number fifteen Dilling Ward [illegible] number Sixteen Letter E Matthew Higgins number one, Richard

-212-

Fido umber two Thomas Little number Three James Davidson number four, Michael Murphy number five, John Richards number six, William Speed number seven, Richard Hooper, number eight Henry Graham number nine, John Cundy number ten John Clark number eleven, Elizabeth Ferrol number twelve James Michael Freke Bulkeley number Thirteen, William Bottom number fourteen, David Dee number fifteen John Beck number sixteen Letter F, James Bowen number one James Riley number two, John Lidnall number three, John Nutter number four, James Hickey number five — Nicholas Wild number six, Donald McLeod number seven, Charles McAlpine number eight, James Dawley number nine, John Stronack number ten, Henry Hall number eleven William Ripley number twelve, Israel Crone number Thirteen James Troak number fourteen James Hooper number fifteen, Dennis McArty number sixteen Letter H Edward McConnogan number one, Patrick Connoly number

two John McIntosh number Three, John Corlet Cochran number four, Alexander Webster number five, John Smith number six James Andrews number seven, David N^cNamara number eight Richard Hatton number nine, William Perregine Cochran number Ten George Morris number eleven Patrick McCrystal number twelve, John Traverse number Thirteen, John Parr number fourteen, Michael Kelly number fifteen Thomas Bailey number sixteen Letter K James Morrison number one, Peter Lyons number five John McAlpine number three, William Sutherland number five, Dennis Reynolds number six, William Baxter number seven John Tutton number eight William Player number nine Gillam Butler number Ten Patrick Lawlor number eleven William Anstruther number Twelve, John Buckstaff number Thirteen Michael Shea number fourteen, John Perryman number fifteen Winkworth Allen number sixteen Letter S being all Four Lots in the Town Plot of S^t. George's Unto William Masters Lot number one Alexander Henderson number two Sarah Sinclair number three Philip Stanton number four, William Paul number five Joseph Cutler number six William Ex^d. [}] Austin number seven John Rodington number eight, Jn Shaw number nine
New [}]
Regis[}]   (Pat)

-213-

Pat McDonald number Ten William Kelly number eleven Jn Roach number Twelve Dennis McCarty number thirteen Peter White number fourteen, Hugh Conner number fifteen Edward McGuire number sixteen Jn Wallace number seventeen Patrick Donald number eighteen William Hooper number nineteen Michael Shea number Twenty Edward Traverse number Twenty one George Liester number twenty two Charles Bullock number twenty three Jn Johnson number twenty four Jn Casham number twenty five being Garden Lots at S^t. Georges with all and all manner of Mines unopened excepting mines of Gold Silver Leads Copper and Coals to Have and to Hold the said granted Premifses with all Priviledges Profits Commodities and appurtenances thereunto belonging with the said John McLeod Francis Shepton Thomas Storrow, Gillam Taylor, John Condon John Bullock George Grant, John Odley, William Hooper, John Durney, Patrick Steel, Fraguar McCra, John McCoy, George Kearns, William Austin, Mark Wentworth, David Loyd, John McGibben Thomas Gay Augustus Bailey, William Freeman, Robert Bailey Philip Bailey, Robert Hamilton, Paul Bantom Junr. George Bantom Michael Dowley Conway Bailey John Welch William Freeman Junior William Bailey William Hurly William Grant, Daniel McMasters, James Campbell, John Lane John Craig, Samuel Blifs, John Gofs, Edward Phelon, John Grant, John Burns, James Brannon, Christian Foy, Donald Glazier Dennis Barton, Kenneth McKenzie, William Granger, John Casham John Eustice, John Crew, George Hammond, James Murphey, Cornelius Ryan, Henry Appleton Thomas Wilkinson Donald Grant, William Grant, Samuel Paine, Peter Mulloy William Ryan, Robert Calder, John Patrick Dilling Ward Matthew Higgins Richard Fido, Thomas Little,

James Davidson, Michael Murphy, John Richards, William Speed, Richard Hooper, Henry Graham, John Cundy John Clark, Elizabeth Ferrol, James Michael Freke Bulkeley, William Bottom, David Dee, John Beck, James Bowen, James Riley, John Lidnall John Nutter, James Hickey Nicholas Wild, Donald McLeod, Charles McAlpine, James Dawley, John Stronack Henry Hall William

Ripley

-214-

Ripley, Israel Crone, James Troak James Hooper Dennis McArty, Edward McConnegan, Patrick Connoly, John McIntosh John Cortlet Cochran, Alexander Webster, John Smith, James Andrews David McNamara Richard Nutter W^m. Perregine Cochran George Morris Patrick McCrystal, John Traverse, John Parr, Michael Kelly, Thomas Bailey James Harrison, Peter Lyons, John McAlpine William Sutherland, Dennis Reynolds, William Baxter, John Sutton William Player, Gillam Butler Patrick Lawlor William Anstruther John Buckstaff Michael Shea, John Perryman Winchworth Allen, William Masters, Alexander Henderson, Sarah Sinclair Philip Stanton, William Paul Joⁿ. Cutler William Austin, John Rodington John Shaw Partick McDonald, William Kelly, John Roach Dennis McCarty Peter White Hugh Connor Edward McGuire, John Wallace, Patrick Donald William Hooper Michael Shea Edward Traverse, George Liester Charles Bullock John Johnson, John Casham their Heirs and Afsigns forever Yielding and paying by the said Grantees their Heirs and afsigns which by the acceptation hereof they bind and oblige themselves their Heirs Executors and Afsigns to pay to His Majesty his Heirs and Succefsers or to any person Lawfully authorized to receive the same a free yearly Quitrent of one farthing for each and every lot hereby granted the first Payment of the Quitrent to commence and become payable at the expiration of Two Years from the date hereof and so to continue payable yearly thereafter forever default thereof this Grant shall be null and void provided also that this Grant shall have been registered at the Registers office and a Docquet thereof enter'd at the Auditor's office within six months from the date hereof otherwise this Grant shall become null and void In Witnefs whereof I have signed these Presents and caused the seal of the Province to be hereunto affixed at Halifax this first day of November in the Twenty fifth year of the Reign of our Sovereign Lord George the Third by the Grace of God of Great Britain, France and Ireland King Defender of the faith and so forth and in the Year of our Lord One Thousand Seven hundred and Eighty four. — By His Excellency's Command

Nova Scotia Halifax Regis^d. 2 Novr. 1784 [}] Nova Scotia Halifax R Bulkeley
      J Solomon D Reg^r. [}] 2nd. Novr. 1784 entered at the Auditor's office
Regist^d. 26 July 1785.   Fra^l Shipton D. Auditor

New Brunswick Land Petitions: Original Series, York County, 1783-1918 (RS108) (Microfilm: F1031)

McEwen, John

Memorial of John McEwen To His Excellency Thos [illegible] [impossible to make out although somewhere in the scribbling must be the name "Carleton."]

Your Memorialist understanding your honours Had the Settling of Vacant Land, he makes bold to Trouble you, — he begs Leave to Represent that he formerly belong'd to the Corps of Guides & Pioneers, that at the [illegible] of Block No. three his Proportion of Land fell to him In Lot No. Sixteen, which is Impofsible to Cultivate or by any means to get a Living upon — through the badnefs of his Land he has been obliged to hire about for Subsiftance as he is anxious to Settle, and as there is a quantity of unimproved and Vacant Land in the block he most humbly Implores he may be Permited to occupie some Part where there may be a Pofsibility of gaining or Leasing. — he Prays he may inform that there is a grove of Vacant Land between Lots thirteen and twelve between the Farms of [illegible] and Cash containing in front about Sixteen Rods — if he Might be permited imdiately to Settle upon that Place, he as In Duty bound Must Ever Pray —

John McEwen

[*verso*]

John McEwen
asks a vacant Grove
of Land between Lots
No. 12 & 13 in Block No. 3
In Council 24th. Jany. 85.
Referred for the Surveyor
General's Return of
W. Allan's Survey

Memorial of
John McEwen

21st. May 86

New Brunswick Land Petitions: Original Series, York County, 1783-1918 (RS108) (Microfilm: F1033)

198

   Petition of John McEwen — to His Excelency Thomas Carleton Esqr. Lieu^t. Governor and Commander in Chief of the Province of New Brunswick &c &c &c

Humbly Sheweth

   That your Petitioners belong'd to the Guides & Pioneers, have Lot N°. 79. Which is given to Luke Kelly. he had not an opertunity of being in his Lot at the time of Survey, being obliged to hire out.
   As he wants to Settle imediatly, Your Petitioner humbly asks Lot N^o. Eighty five which Is Vacant. Your Petitioner Labours under a great inconvenience having saved up in produce one years Earning. he humbly hopes that your Excelency may take his Case into Consideration

                    And he as in Duty bound
                         will Ever pray

                              John McEwen

23^d April
1787

[verso]

Petition of
John McEwen

John McEwen
asks N°. 85 Block N°. 3

24th. Ap^l. 1787

New Brunswick Land Petitions: Original Series, York County, 1783-1918 (RS108) (Microfilm: F1033)

203

To his Excellency Thomas Carleton Esqr. Lieutenant Govr. and Commander in Chief of the Province of New Brunswick —

The Memorial of Luke Kelly and Ephram Van Hoozon Humbly Sheweth to Your Excellency —

that your Memorialists were both Private Soldiers in the Third Jersey Regiment Commanded by Cole Buskirk and at the Reduction of the Provincial Army, drew their allotments of land in Block N°. 12, which from its being remote from any Settlement and a variety of difficulties Made it impofsible for them to Settle, and improve there. That Your Memorialists are informed that N°s. 79 and 80 in Block N°. 3 are unoccupied the former Lott has been Thrice attempted to be Settled, the latter never —

That as it is Your Memorialists wish to Settle, if they can find an Eligible Situation; they Humbly wish your Excellency would take their Prayer in Consideration and as in duty Bound will ever Pray —

Luke Kelly

Fredericton — April 2ᵈ. 1787 — Ephram Van Hoozen

[verso]

Memorial
Luke Kelly
   &
Ephram Vanhoozen
ask lots N°.79 & 80 in Block
N°. 3 —

In Council 13ᵗʰ. Aprˡ. 1787 —

The Lot N°. 80 in Block N°. 3
is registered to Joseph Barker
Junʳ. The Petitioners may
make their Election which
of them shall be registered
for the Lot N°. 79. —

New Brunswick Land Petitions: Original Series, Madawaska County, 1783-1918 (RS108) (A1087) (Microfilm: F1037)

14

His Excelency major general Thomas Carleton Lieutenant governer and Commander in Chief in and over the province of New Brunswick &c &c &c

The memorial of David Higginbothom moſt humbly sheweth

that your Excelencys Memorialist did purchase from James Kelly a Lot of Land at Madawaska partly improve.d by the said James Kelly a lot well known to Capt.n Sproule, for which Lot your Excelencys memorialist did pay sixty pound, and has since been at Considerable expence improving said Lot, And as your Excelencys Memorialist never did receive the portion of Land granted by his Magestys instructions To Discharge.d NonComision.d officers and their familys,

Your Excelencys Memorialist moſt humbly prays that your Excelency will be pleas.d To grant him said Lot together with the donation of Land which his former service intitles him to and your Excelencys Memorialist as in Duty bound will ever pray

Fredericton
   June the 24th}
      1791}

[2]

His excelency major general
Thomas Carleton Lieutenant
Governer and Comander in
in Chief in and over the
province of New Brunswick
&c &c &c

[verso]

David Higginbothom
states that he purchased
the lot at Madawaska
alloted to James Kelly,
and asks the same to
be granted to him,
together with so much
of the adjacent lands as
he is entitled to as a

reduced Sargiant — —

---

the applicant has
purchased the lot from
Kelly which is under
great improvement —
the adjacent lands being
vacant I think he should
have an allotment there,
there being no doubt of
his extending his improvements
   G: S
   L: G

complied with
 p.ᵈ July 1791

New Brunswick Land Petitions: Original Series, York County, 1783-1918 (RS108) (A1130) (Microfilm: F4171)

724

  To the Honourable Martin Hunter Esquire President of his Majestys Council and Commander in Chief of the Province of New Brunswick &c &c &c

The Memorial of John Barker of the Parish of Kingsclear

Most humbly Sheweth that your memorialist has a large family of children eight of which are sons; the eldest at the age of twenty one, the second at the age of nineteen which sons he desires to settle near him in the adjacent neighbourhod; for which purpose your Memorialist Lodged a memorial in the Land of the late Honoruable Isaac Allen in the year 1802 for four hundred acres of Land on the south side of Land owned by your Memorialist John Barker buting on Prince William Line. your Memorialist was afterwards informed by the Honourable Isaac Allen that the Governor and Council had been graciously pleased to give their afsent to his memorial and by reason of the restriction then on Land he could not obtain a grant. He has since been informed that his memorial has mifcarried; and that Henry Kelley and Enoch Currier has made application for the same Land with an intent only of cuting what white pine timber may be found on said Land and whereas your memorialsit nor his sons never had any land by draft from government; but has paid for claims and improvements two hundred and sixty pounds, and has now under cultivation from 70 to 80 acres, therefore your

Memorialist humbly prays your Honour to consider him as the first applicant and be graciously pleased to give the above mentioned land to his two eldest sons Thomas Barker and Samuel Barker who desire to settle them selves on such land as may be obtained for them. and your Memorialist as in duty bound shall ever pray.

County of York 9th November 1808:
The application and allotm^t. — through Col. Allen — stated in this Memo^l. has never been notified in my office, consequently the Lands he describes have been considered Vacant — and several years ago Abigal Ingram & 2 others applied for a part of them, but afterwards

relinquished

[2]

relinquished their application and the Lands continued Vacant and unimproved until the recent application of Kelly and Currier within stated, to whom an allotment was made at the last meeting of Council — The applicants purchased an allotm^t. of 500 ac[res] from James [illegible] joining the Lands he now applies for, and obtained a Grant thereof in May 1799 — M^r. Barker should have taken out a Grant of the Land, by delaying their application for patents, numberlefs cases similar as this will arise throughout the Province to the detriment of many Settlers

Geo. Sproule
L. G

[verso]

John Barker

In Council 5th. Jany. 1808
Cannot be complied with.
the Land being already
allotted —

16th. Novr. 1808

New Brunswick Land Petitions: Original Series, York County, 1783-1918 (RS108) (A1137) (Microfilm: F4178)

To His Honor The President in Council —

The Memorial of John Wallace. married man — aged twenty nine years; Luke Kelly, aged twenty one and John Kelly aged seventeen years, both single men,

Most Humbly Sheweth

That Your Honor's Memorialists are of the several ages above stated, and have never received any Lands from Government. That they are desirous of forming an Establishment for themselves in the Country and there for most humbly pray that the allotments formerly minuted to Henry Kelly and Enoch Currier, (and since abandoned,) in the gore lying between the Kingsclear and Prince William Grants, and adjoining the Grant to John Barker, together with such further quantity of said vacant Gore as will make up the compliment allowed by Government to — persons of their description, may be granted to them, as they consider themselves capable of conforming to the regulations required by His Majesty's Instructions respecting the cultivation of Lands, and want it for agricultural purposes only —

And as in duty bound will ever pray —

Fredericton, 28th. July}
1815}

John Wallace —
Luke Kelley
John Kelley

referred to the Surveyor General
W<u>m</u> F. Odell

[2]

York fs.
I certify that the within Memorialists are residents in the Parish of Kingsclear capable of improving Lands — and what they have stated is [illegible]and true —

Jo<u>hn</u> All<u>an</u>
Jus<u>tice</u> Pe<u>ace</u>

29th. July 1815

The situation applied for in this
Memorial is Vacant

The Kellys of Kingsclear

Geo: Sproule

[*verso*]

John Wallace and
two others —

6th. Feb: 1816

29th July 1815
   Pd.

New Brunswick, County Deed Registry Books, 1780-1930, for York (1836-1837), Volume 21, pp. 23-25

Last Will and Testament }   (Will)
of William Kelly deceasd. }   No. 6433

{LS}   By His Excellency Major General Sir Archibald Campbell Baronett G.C.B. Lieutenant Governor and Commonwealth in Chief of the Province of New Brunswick, &c . . . &c . . . &c . . . . . To all to whom these presents shall come or may concern greetings: —

Know Ye, that at Fredericton in York County on the twenty fifth day of January in the year of our Lord one thousand and eight hundred and thirty Six before George Frederick Street Esquire, being thereunto delegated and appointed, the last Will and Testament of William Kelly late of Prince William in the County of York, deceased (a copy whereof is hereunto annexed) was proved and is now approved and allowed of by me; the said Deceased, while he lived, and at the time of his death Goods, Chattles and Credits within this Province, by means whereof the proving of the said Will, and Granting of Administration of all and Singular the said Goods, Chattles and Credits and also the auditing, allowing, and finally discharging of the account thereof unto me only doth belong. And that the Administration of all and Singular the Goods Chattles and Credits of the said

Deceased, and any way concerning his said Will is granted unto Hannah Kelly and Luke Kelly, Executors in the said Will named, having been already dully Sworn well and faithfully to administer the same, and to make and exhibit a true and perfect

Inventory of all and Singular the said Goods, Chattles and Credits, and also to render a Just and true account thereof when thereunto lawfully required. In testimony whereof I have caused the prerogative Seal of the said Province to be hereunto affixed the twenty-sixth day of January in the year of our Lord one thousand Eight hundred and thirty Six and in the Sixth year of the Reign of our Sovereign Lord William the Fourth by the Grace of God of the United Kingdom of Great Britain and Ireland King, defender of the Faith, &c. &c. &c

Registered the 26th. day of}   Geo Fred^k Street
January 1836.}   Surrogate Y.^{k} Co.^{y}

W^m· F. Odele Reg.^{r}

In the name of God, Amen, I William Kelly of the Parish of Prince William & County of York Farmer, being very weak and Sick of Body, but of perfect mind and Memory and Knowing that it is appointed for all men once to die; do make and ordain this my last Will and Testament: That is to say principally and first of all. I give and recommend my Soul into the hand of Almighty God that gave it and my Body I recommend to the Earth, to be buried in decent Christian Burial at the discretion of my Executors; nothing doubting but at the general Resurrection I shall receive the same again by the Mighty power of God. And as touching such Worldly Estate wherewith it hath pleased God to blefs me in this life, I give devise and dispose of the same in the following manner and form. First. I give and bequeat to Hannah my dearly beloved wife the third of all my Estate, as well real as personal, to be by her pofsefsed and enjoyed for her proper use and benefit during her lifetime, as the law directs, Also I give to my well beloved Son Alexander, thirty rods in Width of my farm in said Parish of Prince William, bounded by land pofsefsed or owned by W^m. Edward Wheeler, — on the upper side, the said thirty rods fronting on the River St. John and extending the whole length of the lot in a South West direction, continuing the same width to the rear; the said thirty Rods being a part of lots Number <u>Seven</u> and <u>five</u>, in the Prince William Grant. Also I give to my well beloved Son Luke, the like Number of thirty Rods of my said farm, bounded on the upper side by the said Thirty Rods bequeathed to my son Alexander, fronting and extending to the rear of my said farm in manner mentioned being a part of lots numbers <u>five</u> and <u>three</u> in said Grant. Also I give to my well beloved Son Isaac, twenty Rods, twenty Rods [sic] of my said Farm, bounded on the upper side by that lot or piece of land bequeathed to my son Luke, fronting and extending to the Rear in manner mentioned in my bequests to my Sons Luke and Alexander, being a part of lot Number <u>three</u>, and in case any remainder of my said farm on a measurement of the width thereof should occur the said remainder, together with my claim which I hold on lot number <u>One</u>, I give and bequeath to my Grandson James. Also I give to my well beloved Son John the Sum of twenty Shillings, to my Daughter Deborah the Sum of ten Shillings, to my Daughter Elizabeth fifteen Shillings, to my

Daughter Mary ten Shillings, and to my Daughter Susannah five Pounds, the said Legacies to my Son John, and Daughters above written to be paid out of my personal Estate within one year after my death, and I hereby constitute

-25-

and ordain my Wife Hannah the Executrix, and my Son Luke to be the Executor of this my last will and Testament, And I do hereby utterly disallow, revoke and disannul, all and every other former Testaments Wills Legacies, Bequests, and Executors by me in any wise before named, willed and bequeathed ratifying and Confirming this, and no other, to be my last Will and Testament. In Witnefs whereof I have hereunto set my hand and Seal this twenty Sixth day of November in the year of our Lord one thousand eight hundred and thirty five.

Signed, sealed, Published pronounced and declared
by the said William Kelly, as his last Will and Testament}
in the presence of us, who in his presence and in the   } (Signed) William Kelly {L.S.}
presence of each other, have hereunto Subscribed   }
our Names,}   {Nicholas Wheeler}
           (Signed   {George Wheeler }
                               {Israel Atherton }

New Brunswick}
York County   }   Registered this Second day of April one thousand Eight
                     hundred and thirty Six

New Brunswick Land Petitions: Original Series, York County, 1783-1918 (RS108) (A1169) (Microfilm: F4209)

Form of LAND PETITION, to be used in future.

_____

To His Excellency Major-General Howard Douglas, Baronet, Lieutenant-Governor and Commander-in-Chief of the Province of New-Brunswick, &c. &c. &c.

The Petition of John Kelly
    HUMBLY SHEWETH,

THAT he is a British Subject; was born in New Brunswick has resided all his years in this Province; aged 27 years; is very lately married, and has no Children as yet.

That he never received any Land from the Crown, and therefore prays that he may have a Grant of number seven in Lake George Settlement, also a strip of unprofitable land lying between the said lot and margin of the lake, containing in the whole about 150 acres

That the said Land is in its natural wilderness state, no improvements whatever having been made thereon, except about five acres partly cleared, three of which a crop has been raised. This improvement was made by Patrick Dougherty, who has give up his claim to it in favour of Thomas Thomson as may be seen by the accompanying document, said land being also ceded by Thomson without fee or reward to Your Petitioner

That he intends to settle and improve the same forthwith, and to comply in all respects with the Royal Instructions, being of ability so to do. That he has not directly, or indirectly, bargained or agreed for the sale or transfer of the Land applied for, to any person or persons whomsoever. — And, as in duty bound, will ever pray.

his
John X Kelly
mark

On the twenty fourth day of March 1827 before me Peter Fraser Esquire, One of His Majesty's Justices of the Peace for the County of York personally appeared the above named John Kelly and made Oath, that the several matters set forth in the above Petition are true.

P. Fraser Justice Peace

N. B. — Each Petitioner must apply separately.

[2]

{Legislative Library of N. B.}　　　　　Kelly, John　　　　　1827

March the 2 1827

This is to show that I have given up all Claim to Thomas Thomson of lot number Seven drawn by mee at lake gorge.

Patrick Dougherty

[The description of the requested land by John Kelly is repeated exactly as on the preceding page.]

[3]

SURVEYOR-GENERAL'S OFFICE,

The within lot was located to Patrick Dougherty about 7 years ago — is otherwise unapplied for & ungranted — 100 acres, The strip of land bordering the Lake marked Swamp, appears of the quantity within stated (50 acres) is vacant & unapplied for

S. P Hurd Sur Gen[l]

[verso]

John Kelley

LAND PETITION.
                132

27th April 1827

3[d] April 1827 p.[d]

New Brunswick, County Deed Registry Books, 1780-1930 for York (1839-1841), Volume 23, pp. 446-447

John Kelly & Wife}
      to   }   N[o]. 7740
   John Bell }

    This Indenture made this Twenty third day of January in the year of our Lord one thousand Eight hundred and forty one, Between John Kelly of the Parish of Kingsclear in the County of York and Province of New Brunswick Yeoman and Jane his wife of the one part and John Bell of the Parish and Province aforesaid Yeoman of the other part, Witnefseth that the [said] John Kelly and Jane his wife for and in Consideration of the Sum of one hundred pounds of lawful money of New Brunswick to them in hand well and truly paid at or before the ensealing and delivery of these presents by the said John Bell the receipt whereof is hereby Acknowledged, Have granted, bargained, sold, aliened, released, conveyed and Confirmed; and by these presents Do grant, bargain, sell, alien, release, convey and Confirm, unto the said John Bell his heirs and Afsigns All that certain piece or parcel of land Situate lying and being in the Parish of Kingslcear aforesaid, Known and distinguished as the one third part of lot Number five Granted to one Thomas Barker, beginning at a Marked ash tree on the South East side of the Prince William Reserved road, fronting on the Prince William line, measuring in front one third part of the said lot Number five — thence running to the Main Branch of a Creek distinguished by the name of Kelly's Creek and hath such Courses marks and Bounds as by reference to the Grant thereof will more fully and at large appear. Containing by Estimation, One hundred Acres be the same more or lefs the aforesaid piece or parcel of land being the upper third part of the aforesaid lot Number five. Together with all houses, out houses, Barns, Buildings, Edifices, fences, Improvements, Profits, Privileges and Appurtenances to the same belonging, or in any manner Appertaining; and the Reversion and Reversions Remainder and Remainders, Rents, ifsues, and Profits thereof — And also all the Estate, Right, title, dower Right and title of dower Interest, use, Profsefsion — property Claim and demand either at law, or in equity of them the said John Kelly and Jane his Wife of in to or out of the same, and every part, and parcel thereof with the Appurtenances. To have and to hold the said lot piece or parcel of land and Premises hereby Granted, Bargained and Sold or Meant, Mentioned or intended so to be and every apart and parcel thereof with the appurtenances unto the said John Bell his heirs and Afsigns, to the only proper use benefit and behoof of the said John Bell his heirs and Afsigns forever. In Witnefs whereof the said John Kelly and Jane his wife Have hereunto set their hands and Seals the day and year first above written.

Signed Sealed and delivered in presence }   his
of us. Read and explained before signing}   John X Kelly (LS)
Joseph Beck, John Long   }   mark
                                                               her
                                         Jane X Kelly (LS)
                                                      mark

-447-

York to wit. Be it Remembered that on this twenty third day of January one thousand Eight hundred and forty one, before me Joseph Beck Register of deeds and wills for the County of York, personally appeared John Kelly and Jane his wife Grantors in the aforegoing Indenture of bargain and sale named who Severally Acknowledged the same to be their free Act and deed Sealed and executed by them for the uses and purposes therein exprefsed — And the said Jane being by me examined Separate and apart from her said husband, declared that She Executed the same of her own free will and Accord without any fear threat or Compulsion from him her said husband.

New Brunswick}   Joseph Beck Reg.ʳ
York County.   } Registered this twenty third day of January one thousand Eight hundred and forty one.   Joseph Beck Reg.ʳ

New Brunswick Land Grants, 1784 – 1997, Sunbury County, Volume 28, p. 153 (RS686) (Microfilm: F16329)

NEW BRUNSWICK.

Wm. G. Colebrooke

Victoria, by the Grace of God, of the United Kingdom of Great Britain and Ireland, Queen, Defender of the Faith, &c. To all to whom these Presents hall come, Greeting: Know Ye that We, of our special grace, certain knowledge and mere motion have given and granted, and We do by these presents, for Us our Heirs and Successors, give and grant unto Patrick Kelly his heirs and afsigns a Tract of Land situate in the Parish of Maugerville in the County of Sunbury in our Province of New Brunswick and bounded as follows, to wit, Beginning at a Beech Tree standing in the Southeast angle of Lot number thirteen in the third Tier of Michael O'Connor's Survey of Carlow made in the year 1842, thence running by the magnet North twenty five chains (of four poles each) thence East twenty chains, thence South twenty five chains to a Birch Tree and thence West twenty chains to the place of beginning containing Fifty acres more or lefs distinguished as Lot number fourteen in the aforesaid Tier and Survey and also particularly described and marked on the Plat or Plan of Survey hereunto annexed; together with all profits, commodities, hereditaments, and appurtenances whatsoever thereunto belonging or in any wise appertaining; except and reserved, nevertheless, out of this present Grant, to Us, our Heirs and Successors, all Coals, and also all Gold and Silver, and other Mines and Minerals: TO HAVE AND TO HOLD the said Tract of Land, and all and singular the Premises hereby granted, with their appurtenances (except before excepted), unto the said Patrick Kelly his heirs and afsigns — forever. Provide always, and this present Grant is upon condition, that the same Grant be registered in the Secretary's Office of our said Province of New Brunswick, to which Registry shall be attached a duplicate of the Plan hereunto annexed.

GIVEN under the great Seal of our Province of New Brunswick,
WITNESS.

Witnefs our trusty and well beloved Sir William Macbean George Colebrooke K. H. our Lieutenant Governor and Commander in Chief of our said Province at Fredericton the twenty seventh day of December in the year of our Lord one thousand eight hundred and forty three and in the Seventh year of our Reign.

By His Excellency's Command
W^m. F. Odell

N°. 3146.

Registered the 29th. day of }
       December 1843}
            W^m. F. Odell
                 Reg^r

New Brunswick, County Deed Registry Books, 1780-1930, for York (1847-1848), Volume 29, pp. 652-654

Luke Kelly
    To   }
John Pollok Alfred }
Smithers Benjamin}   N° 10235
Wolhaupter and, }
Willm A. McLean }

    This Indenture made this Seventeenth of September in the year of our Lord one Thousand eight hundred and forty five between Luke Kelly of Prince William in the County of York farmer of the one part and John Pollok and Alfred Smithers both of the City and County of Saint John Esquire, and Benjamin Wolhaupter and William A McLean both of Fredericton in the County of York Esquires Afsefsur in law of the goods credits and effects of James Taylor and John T. Taylor both of Fredericton partners as Merchants under the Style of James Taylor Senior and Company of the Second part. Whereas the said Luke Kelly as and before the afsignment by the said James Taylor and John T. Taylor of their goods credits and effects to the said parties hereto of the Second part was and [illegible] is indebted to the Said James Taylor and John T. Taylor in the Sum of Sixty pounds of lawful Money which Said Money remains wholly unpaid by the Said Luke Kelly and is wholly due from him and whereas his Said debt so due hath pafsed by said afsignment to the Said parties hereto of the second part for good and valuable consideration and the Said parties of the Second part have consented to give time to the Said Luke Kelly for the payment of his Said debt on Security being furnished to them by Bond and Mortgage on the properties hereafter described Now this Indenture Witnefseth that the Said Luke Kelly for and in consideration of the Said debt so by him due and being as is above recited and also in consideration

consideration of the Sum of five Shillings of lawful money to him in hand well and truly paid before the ensealing of these presents by the Said John Pollok Alfred Smithers, Bejamin Wolhaupter and William A. McLean the receipt whereof is hereby acknowledged Hath granted bargained Sold aliened Released conveyed and Confirmed and by these presents Doth grant bargain sell, alien, release convey and Confirm unto the said John Pollok Alfred Smithers, Bejamin Wolhaupter and William A. McLean their Heirs and afsigns All that part of lots Number three and five in the Prince William Grant in the Parish of Prince William on which he now resides being thirty Rods fronting on the River St. John and Extending back to the Rear of said lots, bounded on the upper side by Land owned by Alexander Kelly and on the lower side by lands owned by Isaac Kelly — the said lot piece or parcels of land being devised to the said Luke Kelly by his late Father William Kelly by Will dated 25th. January 1836. Together with all houses out houses Barns buildings Edifices fences Improvements, profits privileges and appurtenances to the said lots or either of them belonging or in any manner appertaining and the Reversion and Reversions, Remainder and Remainders, Rents, issues, and profits thereof. And also all the Estate Right title Interest use pofsefsion, property Claim and demand either at law or in Equity of him the said Luke Kelly of in to or out of the same and every part and parcel of the said lots of land and premises or either of them with their and each of their appurtenances unto the said John Pollok, Alfred Smithers, Benjamin Wolhaupter and William A. McLean their heirs and afsigns forever. Provided always and these presents are upon the Exprefs Condition and it is the true intent and Meaning of the parties hereto that if the said Luke Kelly his heirs Executors or Administrators or either of them do and shall well and truly pay or Cause to be paid to the said John Pollok, Alfred Smithers, Benjamin Wolhaupter and William A McLean their heirs Executors Administrators or afsigns the just and full Sum of Sixty pounds of lawful money with interest on the Seventeenth day of September now next ensuing. Then these presents and every Clause and thing herein contained shall cease determine and become absolutely void, anything herein Contained to the Contrary notwithstanding. And whereas the said Luke Kelly Hath executed his Certain Bond or Obligation of even date herewith to the said parties of the second part herein in the penal Sum of one hundred and twenty pounds of lawful money as aforesaid. Now it is declared that the said Bond is intended and taken as Collateral Security for the payment of the said Sum of Sixty pounds and the interest thereof in manner aforesaid — and to be void on such payment. In Witnefs whereof the said Luke Kelly Hath here unto set his hand and Affixed his Seal the day and year first within Written.

Signed Sealed and delivered
In the presence of us}
Thomas Murray   }
Wm. Grigor   }

Luke Kelley {L.S.}

York County

Be it remembered that on the Seventeenth day of September 1845 personally appeared before me Asa Coy Esquire one of Her Majestys Justices of the Peace in and for the County of York at Fredericton Luke Kelly the grantor within named and acknowledged that he executed the within Indenture freely and voluntarily for the consideration, and to the uses and purposes therein stated and contained   Asa Coy JP.

New Brunswick}
York County   }   Registered the twenty Seventh day of September on thousand eight hundred and forty eight at noon.

Joseph Beck Reg^r.

APPENDIX C

New Brunswick Land Petitions: Original Series, 1783-1918 (RS108) (Microfilm: F1024)

British American Corps   1784   British American Corps

1784

{Legislative Library of N. B.}

To the Honorable Edmund Fanning Esq'ʳ Colonel of His Majesty's late King's American Regiment of Foot, Lieutt. Governor of His Majesty's Province of Nova Scotia, with the decencies Fieri Facias.
       The Memorial of the Non Commifsᵈ. Officers and favorite Men of the late disbanded British American Corps —

Most humbly sheweth,

     That Your Memorialists were Directed by Colonel Hewlett, Last Autumn, to settle at St. Ann's Point, and was also afsured by their officers, they were to hold the Lots surveyed for them on their Arrival at the Point; consisting of two Acres each. In consequence of which direction from Col. Hewlett, and afsurance from their Officers, they hath themselves such houses as their circumstances, together with the Advanced Season of the year would admit of and employed Themselves last Winter, and this Summer improving the Lands round their respective Houses.
     That Your Memorialists are under the greatest apprehension of being forced off the lands, they have improved with so much Labor & Industry, by Gentlemen that have Orders of Survey from his Excellency the Governor, which would reduce them to the most Mortifying & distrefsful Situations, as the major part of your Honor's Memorialists have large Families, and knowing not

[2]

not where His Majesty's Royal County Lands (intended for them) will fall.

Approved —   That your honor's Memorialists are sensible that
For a grant of two   nothing lays nearer your heart than an ardent desire
Acres to each of the   of settling this Infant Colony, so as to render all its
Memorialists, for the Land   Inhabitants compleatly happy, are emboldened to trouble
they are now actually upon   you with this state of their Grievances; Humbly praying

23d, Sepr, 84   you will be pleased to give such Orders for securing to your Memorialists their improved Lands as to your honor in your Wisdom shall seem most meek, and your Honor's Memorialists as in Duty bound will ever pray.

J Parr

Chars Morris Esqr.

St. Ann's on the River
St. Johns 15th Sept 1784.

[Included in the numerous signatures attached to this petition are John Kelley, Luke Kelley and William Kelley.]

[A detailed sketch of the grant is included.]

This Survey made the
3d. Novr. 1782
A. Allan Dy. Survr.
Sunbury County.

[verso]

The Memorial
    Of
Colo Fannings
    Corps
for 2 acres Lots

APPENDIX D

New Brunswick Land Petitions: Original Series, York County, 1783-1918 (RS108) (Microfilm: F1035)

To His Excellency Thomas Carleton Esquire Lieutenant Governor and Commander in Chief of the Province of New Brunswick &c &c &c

The Petition of John Kelly —

Most Humbly showeth

That your petitioner belong^d. to the Third Batt^n. of N.J. Volunteers — that he has never [illegible] any land since the Reg^{ts}. arrival — he humbly asks 200 acres in Block N°. 2 between lots 42 & 48 — joining John Leek's Line — he humbly represents that the Said land has never been occupied and is intirely unimproved. —

he has Some time Lived near the Said Land — humbly hopes your Excellency will take his Case into Consideration

and he as in Duty bound
will Ever pray
John Kelly

9th June
1788 —
313

[*verso*]

John Kelly asks 200 acres
of Land in Block, N° 2
between N°. 42 & 43.

complied with upon condition
of actual Settlement
18 Augt. 1788

20$^{th.}$ June 1788

APPENDIX E

New Brunswick Land Petitions: Original Series, York County, 1783-1918 (RS108) (Microfilm: F1038)

452

His Excellency Thomas Carleton Esqr. Lieut^t. Governor and Commander in Chief in and over the Province of New Brunswick &c &c &c

Memorial of Moses Holmes humbly Sheweth there is a Lott of Land in Lott N°. 40 Block N°. 2 Down by the 3 Battal^n New Jersey Volunteers Vakant Bounded on one Side by Wm Brothers and on the other by Henry Cole as a Pears By there Signmant on the Block if His Exelency Will be so good as to Grant it to me I will Settle it Imedatly and your Memorilist is Ever Bound to Pray

26th August 1792

[*verso*]

Wm Brothers
Abraham Long
Henry Cole
Reynard Wheeler
John Kelley

Part of Lot N°. 40 B. N°. 2

1792

Memorial of
Moses Holmes

Dismifsed

28th. August 1792

APPENDIX F

New Brunswick Land Grants, 1784 – 1997, York County, **Volume B, pp. 506–517 (RS686) (Microfilm: F16302)**

Stephen Jarvis & 70 others

New Brunswick
Nº. 355
Thoˢ. Carleton

George the Third By the Grace of God of Great Britain France and Ireland King Defender of the Faith and so forth To all to whom these presents shall come Greeting

Know Ye that we of our especial grace certain Knowledge and mere motion have given and granted and lay these presents for us our Heirs and Succefsors do give and grant unto Stephen Jarvis, John Jenkins. Andrew Rainsford, John Day, Cornelius Anderson, William Garden, Thomas Merigold, Joseph Lee Esquire, George Cyphers, John Robinson Esquire, The Honorable George Duncan Ludlow Esquire, Cornelius Thompson, The Honorable Isaac Allen Esquire, Jacob Rufsel, George Sproule Esquire, Sylvanus Plummer and Reuben Smith, Nathan Frink, David Burpe, Moses Butterworth, Daniel James, George Everett, James Bennett, David Bloomfield, Nathaniel Churchill, Thomas Everett, Peter Hantwarck, Cuff Dubois, The Heirs of the late John Biddle, John Martin, John Esty, Joseph Martin, Stephen Miller Esquire, Henry Betner, Daniel Godin, John Barbarie Esquire, George Lee, Jonathan Lawrence, Jeremiah Profser, John Nye, Isaac Mills, Hartman Freeland, John Lawrence Taylor, John Howard, John Tibbets, John Esty Junior, John Flemming, Ifsachar Currier, Edward Peters, Thomas Hollywood, David Good, George Weaver, Peter Campbell, William Whitlock, Archelaus Hammond, Leonard Reed Combes, Alexander Burgoine, Joseph Godin, Lothrop Hammond and Archelaus Hammond Junior, Thomas Costin, John Tardy, Israel West, William Brothers, Moses Holmes, John Kelley and Reynard Wheeler, William West, Abraham Long, John Barker and William Smith, in severalty unto each

-507-

each of them and in severalty unto their respective Heirs and afsigns eighty nine several lots or plantations of Land containing in the whole twenty six thousand three hundred and fifty three acres more or less with the usual allowance of ten per cent for roads and waste, the said eighty nine lots being comprehended within a Tract of Land situate lying and being on the southwesterly side of the River Saint John within the Parish of Kingsclear in the County of York, being part of the Tract granted under the Great Seal of Nova Scotia to Leiut. Colonel Isaac Allen and afsociates in common, and surrendered by the said Grantees in order to receive the present Grant in severally the said Tract which contains the abovementioned eighty nine lots being abutted and bounded as follows to wit, beginning at a dry Hemlock Tree marked C.T. standing on or near the southwesterly Bank or Shore of the River Saint John about forty nine rods, above the mouth of the Creek or Stream commonly called Phillis's Creek, being the northwesterly corner of the Glebe lot granted to the Parish of Fredericton, thence running by the magnetic needle, South thirty two degrees west by a line of blazed trees marked A.R. along the said Glebe, the deaning Lands a Tract of back land laid out and allotted in ten lots, and continuing along vacant lands until an extent of five hundred chains in the whole (of four poles each) is complete or until it meets the prolongation of the rear or southwesterly line of the Grant of the three lots in this Tract pafsed to the Honorable George Duncan Ludlow Esquire and afsociates, thence along the said prolongation, and along the said rear line of the said Grant, North twenty three degrees west one hundred and twenty two chains or to meet the upper or westerly line of the said last mentioned Grant, thence North fifty seven degrees wes[t]

-508-

west, one hundred and forty nine chains or to meet the northeasterly corner of the Tract of Land reserved for the use of the Crown in that district, thence North sixty two degrees west along the northerly line of the said Reserve two hundred and forty chains or to the southwesterly corner thereof, thence South twenty eight degrees west along the westerly line of the said Reserve, and along the prolongation thereof three hundred and seventeen chains or until it meets the upper or northwesterly line of the lot number ninety five in the Tract herein described thence along the said line of the said lot, North forty five degrees west three hundred and three chains, or until it meets the southwesterly Bank or Shore of the River Saint John aforesaid, thence along the said Bank or shore of the said River following the several courses thereof down stream until it meets the bounds first mentioned or a line running North thirty two degrees East therefrom containing in the whole of the above described Tract thirty one thousand two hundred and sixty eight acres more or less with the usual allowance of ten per cent for roads and waste, the said Tract being divided into ninety six lots or plantations numbered from number one to number ninety five both inclusive with a lot described A. all of which are included in this Grant except the five lots number six, thirteen, fourteen, fifteen and eighteen which have been already granted in three separate Grants, and the two lots number twenty four and sixty six which are reserved for public uses, (the respective numbers, marks, contents fronts or breadths and division lines of each or the above described ninety six lots being exprefsed and described on the annexed plan in the said Tract being partly improved and partly wildernefs

-509-

wildernefs land, and hath such shape form and marks as appear by the actual Survey thereof made under the direction of our Surveyor General of our Province of New Brunswick of which Survey the said plan hereunto annexed is a representation; together with all woods underwoods timber and timber trees lakes ponds fishings waters watercourses, profits, commodities, appurtenances and hereditaments whatsoever, thereunto belonging or in any wise appertaining, together also with the privilege of hunting hawking and fowling in and upon the same and mines and minerals Saving and reserving neverthelefs to us our Heirs and Succefsors all white Pine Trees if any such shall be found growing thereon, and also saving and reserving to us our Heirs and succefsors all mines of Gold Silver Copper Lead and Coals To have and to hold the said several lots or plantations of Land and all and singular other the premises hereby granted unto the said several Grantees their Heirs and afsigns in the Shares Quantities and for portions following that is to say, unto the said Stephen Jarvis the lot number one containing seven hundred acres, unto the said John Jenkins the lot number two containing seven hundred acres, unto the said Andrew Rainsford the lot number three containing five hundred and twenty acres, unto the said John Day the lot number four containing three hundred acres, unto the said Cornelius Anderson the lot number five containing five hundred and thirty acres, unto the said William Garden the lot number seven containing six hundred and ninety acres, unto the said Thomas Merigold the lot number eight containing four hundred and eighty acres, with the said Joseph Lee

-510-

the lots number nine containing five hundred acres, and number ten containing two hundred and fifty acres, unto the said George Cyphers the lot number eleven containing two hundred and fifty acres, unto the said John Robinson the lot number twelve containing two hundred acres, unto the said George Duncan Ludlow the lot number sixteen containing two hundred and thirty acres, unto the said Cornelius Thompson the lot number seventeen containing seven hundred and fifty acres, unto the said Isaac Allen the lot A containing eleven hundred and twenty seven acres, and the lot number nineteen containing seven hundred and fifty acres unto the said Jacob Rufsel the lot number twenty containing six hundred and forty acres, unto the said George Sproule the lot number twenty one containing four hundred and fifty acres, unto the said Sylvanus Plummer the lower half and unto the said Reuben Smith the upper half of the lot number twenty two containing six hundred and seventy acres, unto the said Nathan Frink the lot number twenty three containing four hundred and forty acres, unto the said David Burpe the lot number twenty five containing four hundred acres, unto the said Moses Butterworth the lot number twenty six containing one hundred and seventy acres, unto the said Daniel James the lot number twenty seven containing five hundred and forty acres, unto the said George Everett the lot number twenty eight containing five hundred acres, unto the said William Garden the lot number twenty nine containing one hundred and thirty acres, unto the said James Bennett the lots number thirty containing one hundred acres and number thirty one containing one hundred and thirty acres,

unto the said David Bloomfield the lot number thirty two containing two hundred seventy five acres, unto the said Nathanial Churchill the lot number thirty three containing five hundred and fifty five acres, unto the said Thomas Everett the lots number thirty four containing four hundred and sixty eight acres and lot umber thirty five containing two hundred and thirty acres, unto the said Peter Hantwarck the lot number thirty six containing two hundred and ten acres, unto the said Cuff Dubois the lot number thirty seven containing two hundred and forty acres, unto the Heirs of the late John Biddle the lot number thirty eight containing five hundred and forty acres, unto the said John Martin the lot number thirty nine containing one hundred and forty five acres, unto the said John Esty the lot number forty containing five hundred and seventy acres, unto the said John Martin the lot number forty one containing eight acres, unto the said Henry Betner the lot number forty two containing seven acres, unto the said Joseph Martin the lot number forty three containing one hundred acres, unto the said John Martin the lot number forty four containing one hundred acres, unto the said Stephen Miller the lot number forty five containing two hundred and thirty acres, unto the said John Martin the lot number forty six containing eight acres, unto the said Henry Betner the lots number forty seven containing eight acres and number forty eight containing one hundred acres, unto the said Daniel Godin the lot number forty nine containing one hundred and fifty three acres, unto the said John Barbarie the lots number fifty containing two hundred and eighty acres, and number

number fifty one containing four hundred and seventy six acres, unto the said George Lee the lots number fifty two containing two hundred and thirty six acres, and number fifty three containing two hundred and forty acres, unto the said Jonathan Lawrence the lot number fifty four containing two hundred acres, unto the said Jeremiah Profser the lot number fifty five containing two hundred acres, unto the said John Nye the lot number fifty six containing one hundred acres, unto the said Jeremiah Profser the lot number fifty seven containing one hundred acres, unto the said Isaac Mills the lot number fifty eight containing two hundred acres unto the said Hartman Freeland the lot number fifty nine containing three hundred acres, unto the said John Lawrence Taylor lot number sixty containing one hundred and sixty eight acres, unto the said George Duncan Ludlow the lots number sixty two containing one hundred and forty acres, and lot number sixty three containing seventy acres, unto the said John Tibbets the lot number sixty four containing three hundred and twenty acres, unto the said John

Esty Junior the lot number sixty five containing two hundred and eighty acres, unto the said George Lee the lot number sixty seven containing two hundred and fifty acres, unto the said John Flemming the lot number sixty eight containing seventy acres, unto the said Ifsachar Currier the lot number sixty nine containing three hundred and twenty acres, unto the said Edward Peters the lot number seventy containing seventy

-513-

seventy acres, unto the said Ifsachar Currier the lot number seventy one containing seventy acres, unto the said Thomas Hollywood the lot number seventy two containing one hundred and forty acres, unto the said David Good the lot number seventy three containing one hundred and forty acres, unto the said George Weaver the lot number seventy four containing two hundred and twenty acres unto the said Peter Campbell the lot number seventy five containing five hundred acres, unto the said William Whitlock the lot number seventy six containing five hundred acres, unto the said Archelaus Hammond the lot number seventy seven containing three hundred and fifty acres, unto the said Leonard Reed Combes the lot number seventy eight containing three hundred and fifty acres, unto the said Alexander Burgoine the lot number seventy nine containing nine acres, unto the said Joseph Godin the lot number eighty containing eighty acres, unto the said Lothrop Hammond and Archelaus Hammond Junior the lot number eighty one containing seventy five acres, unto the said Archelaus Hammond the lot number eighty two containing four hundred and ten acres, unto the said Alexander Burgoine the lot number eighty three containing two hundred and twenty acres, unto the said Thomas Costin the lot number eighty four containing one hundred and sixty acres, unto the said John Tardy the lot number eighty five containing one hundred and sixty acres, unto the said Israel West the lot number eighty six containing one hundred and fifty acres, unto the said William aforesaid that is

-514-

the lot number eighty seven containing one hundred and sixty acres, unto the said Moses Holmes the lot number eighty eight containing two hundred acres unto the said John Kelley two thirds and unto the said Reynard Wheeler one third of the lot number eighty nine containing five hundred acres, unto the said William West the lot number ninety containing three hundred acres unto the said Abraham Long the lot number ninety one containing two hundred and fifty acres, unto the said John Barker the lot number ninety two containing two hundred and seventy acres, unto the said Abraham Long the lot number ninety three containing three hundred acres, unto the said John Barker the lot number ninety four containing seventy acres, unto the said William Smith the lot number ninety five containing one hundred and seventy five acres, in severalty unto each of them and in severalty unto their respective Heirs and afsigns forever — They the said several Grantees and their respective Heirs or afsigns Yielding and paying therefore unto us our Heirs and Succefsors or to our Receiver General for the time being or to his Deputy or Deputies for the time being yearly that is to say, at the Feast of Saint Michael in every year at the rate of two shillings for every hundred acres, and so in proportion according to the quantities of acres hereby granted the same to commence and be payable from the said Feast of Saint Michael which shall first happen after the expiration of two years from the date hereof provided said Edic and this present Grant is upon condition that the

-515-

the said several Grantees and their respective Heirs or afsigns shall and do within three years after the date hereof for every fifty acres of plantable land hereby granted, clear and work three acres at least in each part ~~in each part~~ thereof as respectively they shall judge most convenient and advantageous or else to clear and drain three acres of swampy or sunken ground, or drain three acres of Marsh if any such be contained therein, and shall and do within the time aforesaid, put and keep upon every fifty acres thereof accounted barren three Neat Cattle and continue the same thereon until three acres for every fifty be fully cleared and improved, and if there shall be no part of the said Tract fit for present cultivation without manuring and improving the same, they within their aforesaid shall be obliged to erect on some part of their respective lots of land one good dwelling House to be at least twenty feet in length and sixteen feet in breadth, and to put on their said respective lots of Land the like number of three Neat Cattle for every fifty acres, or otherwise if any part of the said Tract shall be Stony or Rocky ground and not fit for planting or pasture shall and do within three years as aforesaid begin to employ thereon and continue to work for three years then next ensuing in digging any stone quarry or mine one good and able hand for every fifty acres it shall be accounted a sufficient activation and improvement, provided also that every three acres that shall be cleared and worked or cleared and drained as aforesaid shall

-516-

shall be accounted a sufficient sealing, cultivation and Improvement to save forever from forfeiture fifty acres of land in any part of the Tract hereby granted, and the said several Grantees and their respective Heirs and afsigns be at liberty to withdraw their stock and forbear working in any quarry or mine in proportion to such cultivation and improvement as shall be made upon the plantable Lands Swamps, Sunken grounds or Marsh therein contained, and if the said rent hereby reserved shall happen to be in arrear or unpaid for the space of one year from the time it shall become due and no distrefs can be found on the said Lands Tenements and Hereditaments hereby granted or if the Grant shall not be duly registered in the Register's office of our said Province within six months from the date hereof and a Docket thereof entered in the auditor's office of the same, then the Grant shall be void, and the said lands tenements and hereditaments hereby granted and every part and parcel thereof shall revert to us our Heirs and Succefsors, and provided also upon this further condition that if the land hereby given and granted as aforesaid shall at any time or times hereafter come unto the pofsefsion and tenure of any person or persons whatever, Inhabitation of our Province of New Brunswick either by virtue of any deed or sale conveyance enfeoffment or exchange, or by gift Inheritance descent device or marriage, such person or persons being Inhabitants as aforesaid shall within twelve months after his her or their entry and pofsefsion of the same take the oaths provided by law before some one of the Magistrates of the said Province and

-517-

and a certificate of the Magistrate that such oaths have been taken, being recorded in the Secretary's office of the said Province the person or persons so taking the oaths as aforesaid shall be deemed the lawful pofsefsor or pofsefsors of the lands hereby granted; and in case of default on the part of each person or persons in taking the oaths within twelve months as aforesaid this present grant and every part thereof shall and we do hereby declare the same to be null and void to all intents and purposes and the lands hereby granted and every part and parcel thereof shall in like manner revert to and become reverted in us our Heirs and Succefsors any thing herein contained to the contrary notwithstanding

Given under the Great seal of our Province of New Brunswick Witness our trusty and well beloved Thomas Carleton Esquire our Lieutenant Governor and Commander in Chief of our said Province at Fredericton the fourth day of October in the year of our Lord one thousand seven hundred and ninety nine and on the thirty ninth year of our Reign

By command of His Excellency in Council

Jon[n]. Odell

N[o]. 355
Registered the 31st. day of December
in the year 1799
Jon[n]. Odell
Reg[r].

APPENDIX G

York County Probate Court Records, Kelly, John 1825, (RS75) (Microfilm: F11752)

6/6   Probate of Will   John Kelly estate

His Excellency Major-General Sir Howard Douglas, Baronet, Lieutenant-Governor and Commander-in-Chief of the Province of New Brunswick &c. &c. &c. all to whom these presents shall come or may concern,

KNOW YE, That at Fredericton in York County, on the twenty ninth of October in the Year of our Lord one thousand eight hundred and twenty five before Samuel Denny Street Esquire, being thereunto delegated and appointed, the last Will and Testament of John Kelly deceased, (a Copy whereof is hereunto annexed) was proved, and is now approved and allowed by me the said Deceased having, while he lived, and at the time of his death, Goods, Chattels and Credits within this Province, by means whereof the proving of the said Will, and the granting of Administration of all and singular the said Goods, Chattels and Credits, and also the auditing, allowing and finally discharging of the account thereof unto me only doth belong: And that the Administration of all and singular the Goods, Chattels and Credits of the said deceased, and any way concerning his said Will is granted unto Mary Kelly Sole Executrix in the said Will named, having been already duly sworn well and faithfully to administer the same, and to make and exhibit a true and perfect Inventory of all and singular the said Goods, Chattels and Credits, and also to render a just and true account thereof when thereunto lawfully required.

In Testimony whereof I have caused the Prerogative Seal of the said Province to be hereunto affixed, the thirty first day of October in the Year of our Lord one thousand eight hundred and twenty five and in the Sixth Year of the Reign of our Sovereign Lord George the Fourth by the Grace of God, of the United Kingdom of Great-Britain and Ireland, King Defender of the Faith, &c.

Registered the 1st day of}
November 1825   }

[2]

2/6

In the Name of God Amen!

I John Kelly of Kings Clear in the County of York and Province of New Brunswick Farmer being very sick and weak in body but of perfect mind and memory, thanks be given unto God calling unto mind the mortality of my body, and knowing that it is appointed for all men once to die, do make and ordain this my last will and testament, that is to say, principally and first of all, I give and recommend my soul into the hand of Almighty God that gave it, and my body I recommend to the earth, to be buried in decent Christian burial, at the discretion of my executors, nothing disturbing but at the general resurrection, I shall receive the same again by the mighty power of God, And as touching such worldly estate wherewith it has pleased God to bless me within this life, I give demise, and dispossess of the same in the following manner and form

First, I give and bequeath to my six well beloved Children Namely as follows William, Frances, Abel, Mary Ann, Ruth and Leonard Combs, five Shillings each to be raised and divested out of my Estate in two years after my decease

Also I give and bequeath to Mary my dearly beloved Wife whom I likewise constitute make, and ordain my sole executrix of this my last will and testament all and singular

[3]

3/6

my lands messuages and tenements by her and her assigns, freely to be possessed and enjoyed for ever. Also I give Mary my dearly beloved Wife, all my Cattle, Stocks, Household goods debts and moveable effects of every description whatsoever. And I do hereby utterly disallow revoke and disannul all and every other former testaments, wills, legacies, bequests and executors by me in any wise before named, willed and bequeathed; ratifying and confirming this and no other, to be my last will and testament

In witness whereof, I have hereunto set my hand and Seal this fourth day of September in the year of our Lord one thousand eight hundred and twenty four.

Signed, sealed, published }
pronounced and declared by }
the said John Kelly as his }
last will and testament in }
the presence of us, who in his }   his
presence, and in the presence }   John X Kelly {LS}
of each other have hereto Sub-}   mark
scribed our names.   }
Michael McNally
Richard E. Barker
Jas. McNally

Be it remembered that on the twenty ninth Day of October in the year of our Lord One thousand Eight hundred and twenty five personally came and appeared before me Samuel Denny Street Esquire Surrogate for the County of York Michael McNally whom herein Signed as one of the witnesses to the foregoing will who having been duly sworn Did depose that

[4]

4/6

[The first paragraph is virtually illegible and the remainder of the page is a duplicate of pages 2 and 3 in a different hand, which would indicate that pages 2 and 3 were copies of this damaged page.]

[5]

5/6

he saw John Kelly late of the parish of Kingsclear in the County of York and Province of New Brunswick deceased sign and seal the foregoing testament in writing purporting to be the will of the said John Kelly being dated this fourth Day of September in the year of our Lord One thousand Eight hundred and twenty four and that he heard him publish and declare this same to be his last will and Testament; that the said John Kelly appeared to him at that time to be of sound and disposing Mind and Memory to the best of his Knowledge and Belief and that his name subscribed to the said Will as one of the witnesses thereto is his proper handwriting and was by him written and subscribed as one of the witnesses to the said Will in the said Testators presence, and that the Names Richard E. Barker and Ja^s. McNally to the said Will also Subscribed as two other witnesses thereto were So Subscribed by the said Richard E. Barker and Ja^s. McNally in his presence and in the presence of the Said Testator.

                                                      SD Street Surrogate York Co.

York fs. Be it remembered that on the twenty ninth Day of October in the year of our Lord One thousand Eight hundred and twenty five personally came and appeared before me Samuel Denny Street Esquire Surrogate for the County of York Mary Kelly sole Executrix named in the foregoing Will of John Kelly late of the Parish of Kingsclear in the County aforesaid deceased and was sworn to the authenticity of the Said Will and to the faithful Execution and performance of the Trust thereby in her reposed by taking the Oath of an Executrix as by Law required before me

                                                      SD Street Surrogate York Co.

[*verso*]

B (25)
Will of John Kelley
4th Sept. 1824
Filed 29th. Oct. 1825

APPENDIX H

New Brunswick, County Deed Registry Books, 1780-1930, for York (1823-1825), Volume 14, pp. 47-48

John Kelly & Wife}
     To   }   Nº 2394
Dominic Bradley }

    This Indenture made the twenty fourth day of June in the year of our Lord one Thousand Eight hundred and twenty three between John Kelly of Kings Clear in the County of York Farmer and Mary his wife of the one part and Dominic Bradley of the same place Laborer of the other part Witnefseth that the said John Kelly and Mary his wife for and in consideration of the sum of Eighty pounds lawful money of New Brunswick to them in hand paid before the delivery of these presents the receipt whereof they do hereby acknowledge have granted, bargained and sold, and by these presents for themselves their Heirs and Afsigns do grant bargain and sell unto him the said Dominic Bradley that rear part of a lott lying and being in the Parish of Kingsclear aforesaid known and distinguished as lott Nº. 89 in a Grant to John Kelly and Reynard Wheeler and as such marks and bounds as by reference to a plat annexed to the said Grant will more fully appear that is to say all the land in the rear of that part of lott Nº. 89 — granted to John Kelly adjoining the lower bounds of that part, of said Lott 89 granted to Reynard Wheeler and bounding below on the upper bounds of land at this time in possession of Joseph Burgoyne, commencing at a large Ash Tree that at this time grows out of the bank of a Creek that runs through that part of the said Lott Nº. 89 into the River Saint John and back of the Public Highway road Together with the privilege of a road two rods wide from the said Ash Tree or boundary through the front part of the said Lott owned by the said John Kelly to the River Saint John with all and singular the buildings and improvements rights hereditaments and appurtenances to the same belonging or in any wise appertaining To have and to hold the aforesaid granted and bargained premises with every part and parcel through

with the appurtenances thereunto belonging to him the said Dominic Bradley his Heirs and Afsigns forever. Provided always and it is hereby covenanted concluded declared and agreed upon by and between the said parties to these presents and the true intent and meaning of these that the said John Kelly reserve for himself his Heirs and Afsigns the privilege of firewood Timber or fencing Building or any other use that he or they may want together with a road two rods wide from the aforementioned Ash Tree or boundary to the rear of the above granted and bargained premises — In Witness whereof the parties to these presents have hereunto set their hands and affixed their seals the day and year first above written

Signed sealed and }
delivered in the presence of }
J. [illegible] Jun.ʳ Richᵈ Dibbler

John X Kelley {L.S.}
his mark
her
Mary X Kelley {L.S.}
mark

York — Personally appeared before me one of His Majestys Justice of the Peace for the County of York the twenty fifth day of June one Thousand Eight hundred and twenty three — John Kelly Grantee within mented and Acknowleged that he [illegible] executed the anuned written Instrument for the purpose within [illegible] —

Jeremiah [illegible] J.P.

York fs. — on the third day of July one Thousand and Eight hundred and twenty three personally appeared before me Jacob Ellegood, Mary Kelley the within named and being examined separate and apart from her said husband acknowledged that she executed this Deed as her voluntary act and without any fear or Dred from her husband

New Brunswick}
York County } Registered this ninth day of August one Thousand Eight hundred and Twenty Three.

Jacob Ellegood Justice Peace

APPENDIX I

New Brunswick, County Deed Registry Books, 1780-1930, for York (1825-1827), Volume 15, pp. 236-239

E W Miller High Sheriff}
    To   }   Nº. 2814   John Kellys Property
William Taylor   }

    This Indenture made the eleventh day of January in the year of our Lord One thousand Eight hundred and twenty six Between Edward Winslow Miller Esquire Sheriff of the County of York in the Province of New Brunswick of the one part and William Taylor of Fredericton in the said County of York Esquire. Whereas a writ of our Lord the King

-237-

called a Fieri Facias or execution under the seal of the Supreme Court of New Brunswick granted upon a judgment of the same court and bearing date or teste the twenty fifth day of September in the first year [1820] of the reign of His Majesty King George the Fourth hath been duly awarded and issued out of the same court against John Kelly directed to the Sheriff of the County of York (the said Edward Winslow Miller being then and ever since sheriff of the said County of York as aforesaid) whereby the said sheriff was commanded that he should cause to be made of the goods and chattels houses lands real estate and hereditaments of the said John Kelly in his Bailiwick as well as certain debt of Three hundred and thirty pounds which James Taylor lately in the Court of the said Lord the King before the King himself (that is to say in the supreme court aforesaid) at Fredericton recovered against him as also five pounds which in the same Court were awarded to the said James Taylor for his Damages which he had sustained as well by means of the detaining the said debt as for his costs and charges by him about his suit in that behalf expended whereof the said John Kelly was convicted as appears of record and that the said Sheriff should have that money before the said Lord the King (to wit in the supreme Court aforesaid) at Fredericton on the second Tuesday in October then next to render to the said James Taylor for his Debt and Damages as aforesaid and also that he should have there then that writ as by the judgment and writ aforesaid in the Supreme Court aforesaid remaining of record relation being thereunto had may more fully appear And whereas by an indorsement made on the said writ the said Sheriff was directed to levy by virtue of the said writ of Execution One hundred and seventy pounds Eight Shillings costs of recording and certifying the same besides Sheriff's Execution Fees and whereas the said judgment and writ having been severally inspected by one of the judges of the said

Court who certified that there was no error therein apparent to him were afterwards and before the delivery of the same writ to the said Sheriff to wit on the twenty eighth day of September in the year of our lord One Thousand eight hundred and twenty together with the said certificates recorded by the Clerk of the said Court in the Book for that purpose by him kept and whereas the

-238-

said Edward Winslow Miller sheriff as aforesaid in due execution of the writ before the return of the same writ to wit on the tenth day of October in the year of our Lord One Thousand eight hundred and twenty for want of goods and chattels of the said John Kelly within his bailiwick whereof to make and satisfy the Debt and damages aforesaid or any part thereof did by virtue of the writ aforesaid seize and take the lands and tenements hereinafter described of the said John Kelly in his Bailiwick that is to say All that the Lot piece or parcel of land Mefsuage curtilage and tenement then in the pofsefsion of the said John Kelly situate in the parish of Kingsclear in the County of York aforesaid being the two thirds of Lot Number Eighty nine comprehended within the grant to Stephen Jarvis and others and all and every part thereof and all houses out houses sheds barns stables yards buildings gardens and improvements on the said piece or parcel of land with all privileges and hereditaments thereunto belonging with the appurtenances and all the estate right title interest property claim and demand whatsoever of the said John Kelly of in and to the same And whereas also in the further execution of the said writ he the said Edward Winslow Miller Sheriff as aforesaid having first given due and Public Notice of the intended sale of the lands Tenements and premises aforesaid by advertising the same and the time and place thereof in the manner and form prescribed by the Law of this Province in such case made and provided did at the end and expiration of such Notice to wit on the ninth day of January Instant Between the hours of twelve and five in the afternoon of the same day at Fredericton aforesaid in the County of York set up and expose the same to sale by Public auction and did then and there by virtue of the writ aforesaid and the aforesaid law of the Province sell the said lands Tenements and premises of the said John Kelly above described and his whole estate right and title therein and thereto by Public auction as aforesaid to the said William Taylor he being the highest Bidder therefore to wit for the sum of Two hundred and eighty pounds of lawful money of New Brunswick aforesaid To have and to hold to him his

-239-

heirs and afsigns for ever Now This Indenture witnefseth that the said Edward Winslow Miller Sheriff as aforesaid by virtue of the writ aforesaid and pursuant to the aforesaid Law of the Province and for the mere executing the same and the power and authority thereby to him granted and the perfecting of the sale aforesaid and for and in consideration of the said sum of Two hundred and Eighty Pounds of lawful money of New Brunswick aforesaid to him in hand paid by the said William Taylor at the time of ensealing and delivering these presents the receipt whereof is hereby acknowledged for the use and purpose aforesaid hath granted bargained and sold and by these presents doth grant bargain and sell unto the said William Taylor his heirs and afsigns The Lands Tenements and Premises aforesaid of the said John Kelly and all his right Title Interest estate claim and demand of in and to the same with the appurtenances To have and to hold the said lands Tenements and premises with the appurtenances to the said William Taylor his heirs and afsigns to his and their only proper use and to and for no other use intent or purpose whatsoever — behoof forever In Witnefs whereof I have hereunto set my hand and seal the day and year first in these presents Written

Signed sealed and delivered}
in the presence of   }   E.W. Miller {L.S.}
Mary Miller John Benn   }
York fs
Be it Remembered that on this twenty sixth day of June One Thousand eight hundred and twenty-six before me personally appeared Edward Miller Esqr High Sheriff of York who acknowledged the foregoing deed of Bargain and sale to be his free act and deed sealed and executed by him for the purposes therein expressed

                                                                       H. G. Clapper Register

New Brunswick}
York County   } Registered this twenty Sixth day of June One Thousand eight hundred and twenty Six

APPENDIX J

New Brunswick, County Deed Registry Books, 1780-1930, for York (1810-1815), Volume 4, p. 332

Reynard Wheeler & wife}
     for   }
  William Kelly   }   Nº. 1512

    Know all men by these presents that Reynard Wheeler of Kingsclear in the County of York in the Province of New Brunswick Yeoman and Nancy his wife for and in consideration of the sum of Twelve pounds current money of the Province aforesaid to them in hand well and duly paid by William Kelly at or before the sealing and delivery of these presents the Receipt whereof they do hereby acknowledge & themselves to be therewith fully contented [illegible] & satisfied have granted bargained & sold and by these presents Do grant bargain sell unto the said William Kelly his heirs and afsignes one third part of Lot number Eighty nine situate lying and being in the Parish of Kingsclear, being the upper part of said lot and which was granted to the said Reynard Wheeler in the Grant to Stephen Jarvis and afsociates dated the fourth day of October in the year of Our Lord One thousand seven hundred & ninety nine together with all and singular the buildings fences, ways waters water courses profits privileges and appurtenances whatsoever to the said third part belonging or in any wise appertaining and also all the Estate Right Title Interest Dower right & title of Domain claim challenges & demand in Law or in Equity of themselves and Reynard Wheeler & Nancy his wife of in & to the said third of Lot number Eighty nine and Every part & parcel thereof To have and to hold the same one third part of Land Lot number Eighty nine with the appurtenances & herditaments belonging unto him the said William Kelly his heirs & afsigns forever to his & their own proper use benefit & behoof forever and to and for no other use intent or purpose whatsoever In witnefs whereof the said Reynard Wheeler & Nancy his wife have hereunto set their hands and seals the fifteenth day of November in the Year of our Lord One thousand and Eight hundred & thirteen

                                                    his
                                      Reynard X Wheeler {LS}
Sealed & delivered}   mark
in presence of   }
        his   }   her
Thoˢ X Brown   Nancy X Wheeler {LS}
    Mark   mark
Danˡ. Clapper

York fs on the fifteenth day of November One thousand Eight hundred & thirteen before me Daniel Clapper Esqr One of His Majesties Justices of the Peace in & for the County aforesaid and personally appeared Reynard Wheeler & acknowledged that he executed the foregoing Deed freely & for the uses & purposes therein exprefsed

Danl. Clapper Justice Peace

And on the Tenth day of May One thousand Eight hundred & fifteen Nancy Wheeler wife of the said Reynard Wheeler appeared before me & being examined separate & apart from her husband declared that she signed sealed & delivered the same freely & without threat or compulsion from him — —

Danl. Clapper Justice Peace

New Brunswick}
York County } Registered the Tenth day of May One thousand
Eight hundred & fifteen

New Brunswick Land Petitions: Original Series, York County, 1783-1918 (RS108) (A1144) (Microfilm: F4184)

1059

    To His Excellency Major General George Stracey Smyth Lieutenant Governor and Commander in Chief of the Province of New Brunswick &c. &c. &c.

The Petition of Michael McNally —

Humbly Sheweth —

    That your Petitioner has never had his Land allotted him in the Province of New Brunswick as a reduced officer in the Prince of Wales late American Regiment. has resided in the Parish of Queensbury for upwards of twenty years. and has labored and improved part of the time on the upper twenty Roods of Lott N°. 73 that he purchased from Jerias Yeamans. both on the North West and South East sides of Marzeralls Creek —

    That when your Petitioner first commenced Building and improving on the North West side of the above described Creek. the Land was unimproved. and entirely in the wild state of Nature, that there never was any improvement whatever made on the upper twenty Roods of lott N°. 73. on the North West side of the said Creek untill your Petitioner commended Building. and made the first improvement that ever was made, and if any Claims is presented contradicting to this it is false and can be proved twenty substantial Evidences of the oldest Settlers if your Excellency requests it. That the upper twenty Roods of lott No. 73 has been peaceably posses'd by different Propriators for upwards of thirty years —

& as there never was or cannot be any Just Claim presented upon the upper side or upper twenty Roods of lott No. 73 Excepting your Petitioners Claim —

> Your Petitioner most humbley begs that your Excellency will Grant unto him the upper twenty Roods of Lott No. 73 in Queenbury. commencing on the bank of the River Saint John, and continuing

We whose Names are here Subscribed } back to the rear line. according to the
to Certify to the Truth of this Petition }Original Grant to the late Corps of Guides
according to the best of our Knowledge} & Pioneers —

                         And he has in Duty bound will ever Pray

Abraham Long Capt   Michael McNally —
William Kelly senr.
L R Coombes
William West
       his
Alexander X Burgoyne
       mark
John Cliff Senr.

[2]

York fs.   Michael McNally, maketh Oath, and Saith
             that, the several matters, set forth in the
             within written petition are true.

Sworn before me at   Michael McNally
Fredericton this fifteenth
day of May 1821

        Henry Smith
           Justice of the Peace

[verso]

Michael
~~Richd.~~ McNally.

6th. March 1822

15th. May 1821 —

New Brunswick Land Petitions: Original Series, York County, 1783-1918 (RS108) (A1144) (Microfilm: F4184)

966

    To His Excellency Major General George Stracey Smyth
    Lieutenant Governor and Commander in Chief of the
    Province of New Brunswick &c. &c. &c. —

The Petition of Michael McNally, John Kelly, and Katharine Dyer
    Humbley Sheweth — That your Petitioners presented in February last. a Petition to your Excellency, showing their Claim and praying. that your Excellency. would order. that a Grant be made out for them. for their different allotments of Lott No. 73 in Queenbury
    That your Petitioners would wish to present this as a Supplement to their Former Petition, —
    That a Petition will be presented to your Excellency by Peter & Joseph Mazerall, shewing their Claims to their different a Lottments of Lott No. 73 in Queenbury, claiming some part of the Lands, which we trust, as already appear'd, and by this be more fully explained to your Excellency, to be the lawfull property of your Petitioners Michael McNally, John Kelly, and Katherine Dyer
    In the year 1783, when your Petitioners, arrived in the Province, with others of the disbanded Loyalists, lott No. 73 was occupied by four French men, more particular stated in our former Petition, whose improvements at that period could have been but small, as they had been settled on Lott No. 73 but a short time before the arrival of the loyalists in New Brunswick, That lott No. 73, in block No. 3 was originally granted to the late Corps of Guides & Pioneers, and we think in that very year 1783 every mans alotments was laid out. and no doubt the course of the lines established, if Joseph Marzirall Senior or any of his Family, had of made any improvement on Lott No. 73 except what he or they did make on the alotment divided to Joseph Marzirall Jr. Grant agreement, and on the part that Joseph Marzerall Senior purchased from the Alexander Carree, it would certainly have been a breach of Trespass, they certainly knowing, 36 years ago the exact course of the lines. — but in reality they have made no improvements

[2]

on the upper half of lott. N°. 73, that there is improvements on such a part of Lott N°. 73 Claimed by your Petitioners Mich^l. McNally, John Kelly, and Katherine Dyer, is true, but these improvements were made some by Song fa Song, and Oliver Crock. and some by other proporiators into whose Possession such alotments, became, by differant transferments but the principal improvements as been made by your Petitioners whom now hold possession. which can be made appear by. enquiry by more Senior evidences both French and English then your Petitioners have already produced, and will at the same time evidence to the unlawful Claimes of Peter & Joseph Marzerall — That Joseph Marzerall Senior has not been disceased. more then one year and neve[r] did in life pretend to have any Claim, but that of his own twenty Rods and what he purchased from Alexander Carree, nor would he if now in existence presume to Claim any more, for in reality it was all he had, he well knowing the course the lines run in 1783. he but a short time before that, took possession with the three other french men before mentioned, he no doubt would be very cautious, of clearing Lands that he knew did not belong to him and was he now living he would not suffer his sons to conduct in the way and maner they now do, That Joseph Marzerall Senior did request of your Petitioner, Michael McNally in 1818 to Petition your Excellency for a Grant of Lott N°. 73, each and every of the Propriators holding what they had in possession, and had held in peace for so many years. continuing back to the rear line. agreeable to the original Grant. which plainly evidences, that Joseph Marzerall Senior had no other Claim in view, without which back Land annext to the small peice [sic] on the bank of the river it would be of no manner of object for your Petitioner could neither have Fire wood or fenceing stuff

That M^r. George West by ordering of the Honourable Attorney General as measured the front of Lott N°. 73 and finds a sufficeancy of Land for every Propriators alotment, that they have had in peaceable possession for twenty five Years, —

[3]

That your Petitioner Michael McNally purchased twenty rods off the upper side of Lott N°. 73 from Jerias Yeamans. as will appear to your Excellency by his Bond, that all the Land on the said twenty Rods. on the South East side of Marzeralls Creek is principally cleared and under good fence and has been cultivated for twenty years by your Petitioner Michael McNally exclusive of the number of years improved by Jerias Yeamans and, without any molestation whatever, That there was not so much as one foot of improvement on the said twenty rods on the North West side of Marzeralls Creek when your Petitioner purchased from Jerias Yeamans —

That your Petitioner Michael McNally as [sic] brought up a large Family in New Brunswick. his Wife haveing fifteen Children, she dieing about Six years ago. left him in a trying situation, he wishing to settle his Children near him. convey'd unto a son that was married and a Son in Law, all the Land on the North West side of Marzeralls Creek belonging to Lotts N°. 74 & 5 and such a part of Lott. N°. 73 as I purchased from Jerias Yeamans, not doubting but I should get a Title from him when I paid all the Money according to agreement or obtain a Grant when shewing my honest and fair Claimes. to twenty rods off the upper side of Lott N°. 73, those Children did build each of them a comfortable house and clear[e]d ten or twelve acres of Land and put the same under good fence, it being entirely in the wild state of nature. when they went on to it. —

That your Petitioner Michael McNally. a youth. early in the beginning of the American Rebellion, entered into the British Army his father being an old Soldier in the same, did exert himself. according to the best of his ability for the Honour of his King and defence of his County, untill reduced as an Ensign in this Province. that he never had his alottment of Land Granted to him as a reduced Ensign, what small alottment he has had Granted was Land he purchased, more perticularly Know to the Honourable Secretary —

That your Petitioner Michael McNally John Kelly and Katherine Dyer most Humbley begs. that Your Excellency will take their case into consideration and order that a Grant be made out for them. for their differant alottments, each running back to the rear line. agreeable to the original Grant, and they and Familys as in duty bound will ever Pray —

[4]

              Michael McNally —
                  his
              John X Kelly
                 mark

York fs

              Michael McNally, John Kelly
              and Catherine Dyer, maketh oath
              and saith that, the several matters
              set forth, in the within Petition
              are true, to the best of their knowledge
              and belief. —

Sworn before me at   Michael McNally
Fredericton this 5th   his

day of May 1819. —
Henry Smith, J Peace

John X Kelly
mark
Katherine Dyer

[within folded area]

Supp1ʸ. Petition
M. McNally and
2 others

9 Jan — 19

5 Mar.

[5]

In Council 19ᵗʰ June 1819
Present.
His Excellency The Lieutenant Governor
&c. &c.

Read the Petitions of Joseph Marzerall, Peter Marzerall, Michael McNally, John Kelly, and Katharine Dyer joining parts of Lots Nº. 73, in Queensbury —

The Council advise that the Surveyor General should direct a — correct Survey to be made of said Lot, shewing what is in pofsefsion of the respective Claimants, at the joint expense of the parties.

Extract from the Minutes.

[6]

Know all men by thefe presents that I Jarius Yeamans of the Parifh of Queensbury County of York and Province of New Brunswick am held and firmly Bound to Michael McNally of the Parifh and County aforesaid in the Just and full Sum of Two Hundred and Forty Pounds of good and Lawful money of the Province aforesaid to be paid to the said Michael McNally or his Certain attorney. his Executors. Administrators or Afsigns. to which payment well and truly to be made, I Bind myself my Heirs. Executors and

Administrators firmly by thefe presents. sealed with my seal, Dated the fourteenth Day of August in the forty sixth year of the Reign of our Sovering Lord George the Third. By the Grace of God of the United Kingdom of Great Britain and Ireland King Defender of the Faith and so forth. and in the year of our Lord one Thousand Eight Hundred and Six

The Conditions of this Obligation is such that if the above Bounder Jarius Yeamans shall upon his receiving one Hundred and twenty pounds of good and Lawful money of the province aforesaid or the Value thereof in any kind of stock Horfes Excepted from the above Named Michael McNally, give unto the aforesaid Michael McNally his Heirs. Executors. administrators or afsigns a good and Lawful Title to and for a certain tract or Lot of Land in the Parifh of Queensbury and County aforesaid known and Discribed by lot Number twenty four and also a quit Claim with all his Right and Title to another half Lot adjoining the lower part of the above Discribed Lot Number seventy four and will be

[7]

at the Expence of gitting a Grant for the same if to be had in the aforesaid Michael McNally's name Then this Obligation to be void or otherwife to be and remain in full force and value —

Sign Sealed and Delivered
In the presence of
Jnº. Lawrence
Mary Lawrence

Jarius Yeamans,

New Brunswick
York County} Registerd in Book of noterial Records
the fifteenth day of February One thousand Eight hundred
& thirteen
                                            Paul Clapper
                                                Not Pub

[within first fold]

Michˡ McNally

[within second fold]

New Brunswick
York County   } Nº. 1737

The Kellys of Kingsclear

I Certify the foregoing Instrument — as
Recorded in Book E page N°. 305 of Records of Deeds
& Wills, the Twenty first day of June one thousand Eight
hundred & Fourteen —   Paul Clapper Register

[8]

I do humbly certify that I have been a settler and freeholder in Kingsclare in the County of York nearly opposite to Lott N°. 73. In Queensbury for thrity four years, and I do believe that what is represented in the Petition of Mich^l McNally John Kelley & Katharine Dyer to be Just & True according to the best of my recollection —

Kingsclare 4th. Feb^y.   Capt Abraham Long.
 —1819. —   John Cliff Senr. —

[9]

To His Excellency Major General George Stracey Smyth Lieutenant Governor and Commander in Chief of the Province of New Brunswick &c &c

The Petition of Michael McNally John Kelley and Katharine Dyer Humbley Sheweth —
  That your Petitioners are loyal Subjects, arrived in New Brunswick in the year 1783 and at present reside in the County of York, and each to them claiming a peice [sic] or part of a Lott of Land in Queensbury, being Lott N°. 73 in block N°. 3 Granted to the late Corps of Guides & Pioneers, but the said Lott N°. 73 was occupied by four French men, namely Joseph Marzerall Senr. Alexander Carree Song fa Song and Oliver Crock. these four men made choise of one to go to Halifax. And state their. to His Excellency Governor Parr; their situation whom returned with answer, to remain on their Lands they should not be Molested, accordingly the said Lott N°. 73 has been peaceabley possesed ever since, being about 32 years sence the above named French men made the first improvement on said Lott N°. 73 and by differant transferments such parts of said Lott N°. 73 became the Property of your Petitioners whom we trust will appear to your Excellency by our Claims, as by agreement. these four men divided the said Lott N°. 73, Joseph Marzerall Senr. the lowermost settler twenty roods. the other or upper part of said Lott divided between the other three Alex^r. Carree haveing [sic] his Lott adjoing [sic] Joseph Marzerall Senr. next to him Song fa Song, and the uppermost. Oliver Crock, three of those French men, considering. that their Possessions to small for the support of their Familys, sold their improvements and went otherways Alexander Carree sold his right and improvements unto Joseph Marzerall Senr. being about twenty roods. for 25£, that together

[10]

with twenty roods he held by agreement makes the Claim of Joseph Marzerall Sen[r]. forty Roods —

That your Petitioners, would wish to be very perticular and offer nothing before your Excellency but what shall appear with truth and Honesty. which we trust will be made appear by evidence and our lawfull Claims, That your Petitioners have cause to suspect that a Petition will be presented to your Excellency by Peter Marzerall & Joseph Marzerall Jun[r]. with a Quit Claim deed, shewing the sale of an improvement by Alex[r]. Carree purchased by Joseph Marzerall not mentioning Sen[r]. or Jun[r]. this said improvement of Alexander Carrie was certainly sold unto Joseph Marzerall Sen[r]. for 25£ Peter Marzeralls Claim is for forty Roods commencing at the lower bounds of said Lott N[o]. 73 not stateing in his Petition that any part of the forty roods applied for is a purchased improvement expecting, to hold according to his Petition, by his Fathers long Posession, and gives to his Brother Joseph Marzerall the Quit Claim of Alex[r]. Carree, to make him a Claim on said Lott N[o]. 73 which is certainly an unlawfull Claim, for the improvement sold by Alex[r]. Carree is in Posession of Peter Marzerall. the next improvement to that is that of Song fa Song, a part of which adjoining that in Posession of Peter Marzerall is the Property of your Petitioner John Kelley, or does your Petitioners Know of any lawfull Claim that Joseph Marzerall Jun[r]. has to any Part of said Lott N[o]. 73, That your Petitioners would ferther wish to state, that there was a joint agreement by all Proprietors of the said Lott N[o]. 73 that

[11]

that a Petition should be presented to your Excellency &c and that a Grant, be made out for them for Lott N[o]. 73, each and every of the Propreitors holding what they had in Possesion which they had held in peace for upwards of 23 years. And ferther it was jointly agreed by each and every of us that had a Claim on said Lott N[o]. 73, to employ John Beedle Esq[r] then Surveying in the County of York we think about 12 or 13 years ago, accordingly he was employ'd, did Survey Claim and lay out as we then held and do yet hold in peace, a return of which we have no doubt, may be found in the Surveyor Generals Office, and your Petitioners are still agreed, — That your Petitioner, Mich[l] M[c]Nallys barn is Built on the upper part of Said lot N[o]. 73 on the 20 Roods together with Lott N[o]. 74 that he purchased from Jerias Yeamans, whom has left this Province without giveing your Petitioner a Title according to Bargain. That your Petitioner John Kelley as [sic] Erected a Two Story House on the part of said Lott that he trusts he will shew lawfull Claim That your Petitioner Katharine Dyer purchased the whole of Oliver Crocks improvement, 20 Roods of which she sold unto Jerias Yeamans, and is now the property by purchase of Mich[l] M[c]Nally. she has a House on the lower part of said improvement whom lives with her a

Son whom has a Wife and four Children. which peice of Land is all their Support, Your Petitioners having endeavourd to inform Your Excellency as far as comes to our Recollection Humbley Prays that Your Excellency. will take their case into consideration, and order that a Grant be made out for them, according to

[12]

their Petition, trusting their Lawfull Claims will appear before your Excellency. —

            And they as in Duty Bound
              will ever Pray

         Mich^l McNally
           his
         John X Kelley
6th Feby 1819   mark

 The Situation herein described is Ungranted —   Katharine
It was originally settled by certain French Men   Dyer
who appear to bear a strong claim to a part of
the Lot 73 — All the Claimants to parts of this Lot —
have made their improvements directly perpendicular to the
Course of the River which consequently has thrown them into each
their Lands & which has caused great disappointment. I should recommend
a Correct Survey to be made of their improvements at the Expense of the
respective Claimants, when His Ex^y. & H. ck Council can more readily
determine upon their Claims   Geo [illegible] [illegible] [illegible]
May it Please your Excellency the correct division of Lott N°. 73 may be found by
the Survey of John Beedle Esqr. by joint agreement of the Propreitors

[below fold]

York fs: On the sixth day of February 1819 Michael McNally, John Kelly, and
    Catharine Dyer came before me and made oath. That the several matters
there in stated, are Just and true, to the best of their judgements — they hope to shew
—

              Henry Smith
             Justice of the Peace.

APPENDIX K

New Brunswick, County Deed Registry Books, 1780-1930, for York (1844-1845), Volume 26, p. 282

George A. Hammond   }
    To   }   Nº. 8830
Henry and Geo. H. Kelley}

    This Indenture made this fourteenth day of September in the year of our Lord one thousand Eight hundred and forty-four, Between George A. Hammond of Kingsclear in the County of York and Province of New Brunswick Farmer of the one part, and Henry Kelley and George H. Kelley of Queensbury in the said County and Province Farmers of the other part, Witnefseth that the said George A. Hammond for and in Consideration of the Sum of One hundred and Eighty pounds of lawful money of New Brunswick to him in hand well and truly paid at or before the ensealing and delivery of these presents by the said Henry Kelley and George H. Kelley the receipt whereof is hereby acknowledged Hath granted bargained sold aliened released conveyed and Confirmed, and by these presents Doth grant, bargain sell alien release convey and Confirm, unto the said Henry Kelley and George H. Kelley their heirs and afsigns All the Certain lot piece or farm of land Situtate lying and being in Kingsclear, aforesaid being lot Nº. Eighty four in the Kingsclear Grant, fronting the River Saint John and bounded on the upper side by lands occupied by the heirs of the late Francis Mazeroll and on the Easterly or lower side by lands occupied by the heirs of the late Alexander Burgoyne, Containing one hundred Sixty acres more or less, Together with all houses, out houses, Barns, Buildings, Edifices, fences, improvements, profits privileges and appurtenances to the same belonging, or in any manner appertaining, and the Reversion and Reversions Remainder and Remainders Rents, ifsues, and Profits thereof — And also all the Estate Right title Interest use pofsefsion, property Claim and demand either at law, or in equity of him the said George A. Hammond of in to or out of the same and every part and parcel thereof with the appurtenances, To have and to hold the said lot piece or parcel of land and premises hereby Granted bargained and Sold or Meant, Mentionied or intended so to be, and every part and parcel thereof with the appurtenances unto the said Henry Kelley and George H. Kelly their heirs and afsigns, to the only proper use benefit and behoof of the said Henry Kelley & George H. Kelley their heirs and afsigns forever, In Witnefs whereof the said George A. Hammond Hath hereunto set his hand and seal the day and year first above written

Signed, Sealed and delivered in presence}   George A. Hammond {L.S.}
of B.W. Hammond   }

York to wit. Be it Remembered that on the fourteenth day of September one thousand Eight hundred and forty four, before me Joseph Beck Registrar of deeds and wills for the County of York, personally appeared, George A. Hammond the Grantor in the foregoing Indenture of bargain and sale named who acknowledged that he Signed sealed and delivered the same for the uses and purposes therein Expressed.

New Brunswick}   Joseph Beck Reg^r
York County   }   Registered this fourteenth day of September one thousand Eight
                   hundred and forty four   Joseph Beck Reg^r.

New Brunswick Land Petitions: Original Series, York County, 1783-1918 (RS108) (A2210) (Microfilm: F9030)

3330   Allandale, Residents of   1870
<u>1 of</u>
1070
Schools
Oct 3/70

           To His Excellency the Honble Lemuel Allen Wilmot Lieutenant Governor of the Province of New Brunswick & the Honble the Executive Council of the Said Province

The petition of the under signed residents of Allen Dale in the parish of Dumfries in the County of York

                                                     Humbly sheweth
                                                     That your

petitioners have at much expense and labor erected a comfortable & Convenient School house on lot N° 12 on the North east side of the Allen dale road & East of lot 13 located to Lem Culanan which said lot N° 12 ~~of land~~ is vacant your petitioners therefore humbly pray that your Excellency and Honors should be pleased to direct that such lot of land should be reserved for

                                                          [2]

for the use of the said school and that the title should be veted in Such persons in trust for the use of said school as to your Excellency and Honors may ever trust & as in duty bound will ever pray

Thomas Simmons
John Simmons
John Simmons jr.
George Simmons
William Simmons
J S Madden
Jeremiah Connoly
Denis Connoly
Dominick Doherty
George McDowell
John McTague
Constantine O'Donnell
Edward O'Donnell
John McTague Senr
Hugh McTague
Ody McTague
Jeremiah Connelly Junr
Thomas L. Connelly
John Madden
Michel Neal
Danniel Riley
Thomas McTague
Charles Kelley

[verso]

31
Thomas Simmons
& 22 others pray that
the 100 acre lot No 12
North Allandale
may be granted in trust
for School
([illegible] vacant)
[illegible]

71

Recommendation from
County Members required

New Brunswick Land Petitions: Original Series, York County, 1783-1918 (RS108) (A2210) (Microfilm: F9030)

18
1071   Kelley, Charles   1871
Not vact sold to L W Longstaff
                              (LABOUR.)   [illegible] ADB
To His Excellency the Lieutenant Governor of the Province of New Brunswick,
                &c.   &c.   &c.

The PETITION of Charles Kelly of the Parish of Dumfries in the County of York

HUMBLY SHEWETH —

   That he is a British subject, of the age of eighteen years or upwards, and does not own any other Land in the Province;
   That he is desirous of purchasing One Hundred acres of Crown Land, situate as follows: —
              [Description to be full and particular.] [sic]

Lot N̲o̲ 8 East side Allandale road adjoining Lot No. 9. Owned by Robert Adams —

(not to interfere with the right to cut Timber, &c. under Licenses supplied for previous to this application.) under the provisions of the Act of Assembly intituled An Act to facilitate the settlement of Crown Lands;
   And he prays Your Excellency to approve this his Petition, and cause the same to be advertised in the *Royal Gazette*.
   And as in duty bound will ever pray.
                                                          his
Witnefs   Charles X Kelly
AD Brooks   [Signature of Petitioner.] [sic]   mark

County. York   Parish. Dumfries   Acres. 100   If Vacant. Vacant   If Survey. Yes   If improved by whom claimed, and value of improvements. none

Before me, AD Brooks one of Her Majesty's Justices of the Peace in and for the County of York personally appeared the above named Char Kelley and made oath that the several statements set forth in the foregoing Petition are just and true.

                                                   AD Brooks J. Peace.

If the Land has been surveyed at Government expense, three dollars must be forwarded to the Crown Land Office with this Petition. If surveyed, one dollar must be sent, when an Order of Survey will issue.

[verso]

18/1071   To

Charles Kelly
100 acres
Dumfries
York

Not vacant

Granted to L. W. Longstaff
*8/425

APPENDIX L

New Brunswick, County Deed Registry Books, 1780-1930, for York (1845-1846), Volume 27, pp. 153-154

William Kelly }
   To   }   N°. 9152
John Kelly   }

     This Indenture made this thirteenth day of October in the year of our Lord one thousand Eight hundred and forty five. Between William Kelly of Queensbury in the County of York and Province of New Brunswick Farmer of the one part, and John Kelly of the same place Farmer of the other part. Witnefseth that the said William Kelly for and in Consideration of the Sum of one hundred pounds of lawful money of New Brunswick to him in hand well and truly paid at or before the ensealing and delivery of these presents by the said John Kelly the receipt whereof is hereby acknowledged Hath granted bargained, sold, aliened, released, conveyed and Confirmed, and by these presents Doth grant, bargain, sell alien, release convey and Confirm unto the said John Kelly his heirs and afsigns. All that certain piece or parcel of land Situate lying and being in the Parish of Kingsclear in the said County of York, and Known and described as being one third of lot N°. Eighty nine Situate lying and being in the Parish of Kingsclear aforesaid being the upper part of said lot and which was granted to Reynard Wheeler in the grant

to Stephen Jarvis and associates dated the fourth of October one thousand Seven hundred and Ninety Nine. Together with all houses, out houses, Barns, Buildings, Edifices, fences improvements, Profits, privileges and appurtenances to the same belonging or in any manner appertaining, and the Reversion and Reversions, Remainder and Remainders Rents issues and Profits thereof. And also all the estate Right title Interest, use, pofsefsion property claim and demand either at law or in equity of him and the said William Kelly of in to or out of the same and every part and parcel thereof, with the Appurtenances. To have and to hold the said lot piece or parcel of land and premises hereby Granted, Bargained and Sold or meant Mentioned or intended so to be, and every part and parcel thereof with the appurtenances unto the said John Kelly his heirs and afsigns, to the only proper use benefit and — behoof of the said John Kelly his heirs and afsigns forever, And the said William Kelly for himself his heirs Executors and Administrators, do hereby covenant, promise grant and agree to and with the said John Kelly his heirs and afsigns in manner following that is to say, that he the said William Kelly is lawfully seized and pofsefsed of the aforesaid lot of land and premises hereby granted bargained and sold as a good indefeasible Estate of Inheritance in fee Simple, free and clear of and from all manner of incumbrances whatsoever, and that he has good right, full power, and lawful authority to grant Bargain and sell the same in manner and form as above set forth. And further that he the said William Kelly all and Singular the said lands tenements, herditaments and premises unto him the said John Kelly his heirs executors Administrators and Afsigns, against the said William Kelly his heirs Executors administrators and against the lawful Claim or demand of any and every person or persons whomsoever, shall and will warrant and for ever defend by these presents, In witness whereof the said William Kelly Hath — hereunto set his hand and Seal the day and year first above written

Signed, Sealed and delivered in presence}   W^m. Kelley {L.S.}
of us Charles A. Hartt B.W. Hammond }

York.   Be it Remembered that on the thirteenth day of October 1845, before me Asa Coy Esquire one of her Majesty's Justices of the Peace in and for the said County of York, personally appeared William Kelly Grantor in the foregoing Indenture named who acknowledged the same to be his free act and deed Sealed and executed by him for the use and purposes therein expressed.

New Brunswick}   Asa Coy J.P.
York County   }   Registered this thirteenth day of October one thousand Eight hundred and forty five

Joseph Beck Reg^r.

APPENDIX M

New Brunswick, County Deed Registry Books, 1780-1930, for York (1847-1848), Volume 29, pp. 219-221

                                                                               William Kelly [In different hand.]

Benjamin Wolhaupter Sheriff}
       To   }   Nº. 9997
James Taylor   }

    This Indenture made on the thirteenth day of March in the year of our Lord one thousand Eight hundred and forty eight, and in the Eleventh Year of the Reign of our Sovereign Lady Victoria by the Grace of God, of the United Kingdom of Great Britain and Ireland Queen Defender of the Faith &c &c &c Between Benjamin Wolhaupter of Fredericton in the County of York and Province of New Brunswick Esquire, High Sheriff of the said County of York of the one part, and James Taylor of the same place Merchant of the other part. Whereas a certain writ of our said Lady the Queen called Fieri Facias or Execution founded upon a Judgment of Her said Majestys Supreme Court of Judicature at Fredericton Hath been duly awarded and ifsued out of the said Court against William Kelly at the suit of James Taylor and John T. Taylor Executors of James Taylor deceased and bearing teste or date the twentieth day of June in the year of our Lord one thousand Eight hundred and forty Six and directed to the Sheriff of the County of York Edward W Miller Esquire being then Sheriff of the County of York as aforesaid Since deceased by which said writ the said Sheriff was Commanded that of the Goods and Chattels lands and tenements of the said William Kelly in his Bailiwick he should cause to be made as well a certain debt of Two hundred and fifty pounds which James Taylor lately deceased in his life time Received against him in the said Court of our said Lady the Queen at Fredericton aforesaid as also Five pounds which in the same Court were awarded to the said James Taylor in his life time for his damages which he sustained as well on occasion of detaining the said debt as for his Costs and Charges by him about his Suit in that behalf expended whereof he the said William Kelly was Convicted And whereupon it was considered

in the said Court that James Taylor and John T. Taylor Executors of the last will and Testament of the said James Taylor have execution against the said William Kelly of the debt and damages aforesaid according to the force form and effect of the said Recovery, and also twenty four pounds Seven Shillings and one penny which in the same Court were adjudged to the said James Taylor and John T. Taylor as such Executors for their Costs and Charges which they have been put to on occasion of our Writ of Scire Facias sued out against the said William Kelly at the suit of the said James Taylor and John T. Taylor as such Executors as aforesaid in that behalf whereof the said William Kelly was Convicted as by the said Writ Reference being thereunto had will amongst other things more fully and at large appear. And Whereas also in further execution of the said Writ he the said Edward W Miller the said Sheriff as aforesaid before the Return of the said Writ, to wit, on the twenty third day of October in the year of our Lord one thousand Eight hundred and forty seven for want of Goods and Chattels of the said William Kelly within his Bailiwick whereof to make and Satisfy the debt and damages aforesaid did by Virtue of the Writ Seize and take the lands and tenements of the said William Kelly hereinafter described within his Bailiwick that is to say. All the Right title interest Claim property and demand of the said William Kelly of in and to a Certain lot piece and parcel of land Situate lying and being in the Parish of Kingsclear in the said County of York Known and described as the one third part of lot Number Eighty nine Comprehended in the Grant to Stephen Jarvis and others, Containing one hundred and Sixty Six acres more or less Together with all dwelling Houses Sheds, Barns, Stables, Buildings, and improvements on the said land and premises and all privileges and Hereditaments thereunto belonging with the appurtanences and all the Right title Interest property Claim and demand whatsoever of the said William Kelly of in or to the same. And Whereas also in further Execution of the said Writ, he the said Edward W. Miller so being Sheriff as aforesaid having first given due and Sufficient public notice of the intended Sale of the lands, tenements and premises aforesaid by advertising the same and the time and place thereof in manner and form prescribed by the laws of this Province in such Case made and provided did at the end and expiration of such notice to wit, on the Eighteenth day of May in the year of our Lord one thousand Eight hundred and forty seven, Between the hours of Two and four o'clock in the aforesaid of the same day at the Market House in Fredericton aforesaid in the said County of York set up and expose the lands tenements hereditaments and premises hereinbefore described for sale by Public Auction and did then and there by Virture of the Writ aforesaid and the aforesaid laws of this Province, sell the lands tenements and premises of the said William Kelly above described and his whole estate Right and title therein and thereto by Public Auction as aforesaid to the said James Taylor being the highest bidder therefore, to wit, for the sum of Fifty one pounds lawful money of the said Province. And whereas after such sale the said purchase Money was paid to the said Edward W. Miller so being then Sheriff as aforesaid, but no Conveyance was thereupon made by the said Sheriff of the said lands and premises. And the said Edward W Miller afterwards and on or about the Twenty Second day of July in the year last aforesaid died without having made any such Conveyance and the said Benjamin Wolhaupter has since been duly appointed High Sheriff of the County of York and the said James Taylor hath applied to him for the same. Now this Indenture Witnefseth that the said Benjamin Wolhaupter Sheriff as aforesaid pursuant to the aforesaid laws of this Province and for the more fully executing the same and the Power and authority thereby to him granted for the perfecting the sale aforesaid and for and in Consideration of the said Sum of Fifty one pounds lawful money of New Brunswick as aforesaid and of five Shillings paid by the said James Taylor to the said Benjamin Wolhaupter at the time of ensealing and delivery of these presents the Receipt whereof is hereby acknowledged, Hath granted bargained and sold and by these presents Doth grant bargain and sell unto the said James Taylor his heirs and afsigns All the said lot piece and parcel of land and premises herein before described and all the Right title Interest property Claim and demand of him the said William Kelly of in or to the same with the appurtanences. To have and to hold the aforesaid lands tenements and Hereditaments and all and Singular the premises hereby granted bargained and sold with their and every of their appurtanences unto the said James Taylor his heirs and afsigns, and to his only proper use and behoof forever, and to and for no other use or purpose whatsoever, In Witness whereof the said Benjamin Wolhaupter Sheriff as aforesaid Hath hereunto set his hand and Seal of Office the day and year first above Written.

Signed Sealed and delivered in the presence
of the words "after deducting Sheriff fees"}   B. Wolhaupter {LS}
first obliterated   Joseph Beck   }   Sheriff of York

                      to Myshrall   }

York to wit   Be it Remembered that on the thirteenth day of March in the year of our Lord one thousand Eight hundred and forty eight personally appeared before me Joseph Beck Registrar of deeds & wills for the County of York Benjamin Wolhaupter High Sheriff of the County of York aforesaid and acknowledged his hand and seal set and Subscribed to the above Conveyance to be his own act and deed for the purposes therein mentioned.

                                                             Joseph Beck Reg^r.

   York to wit I Edward W. Miller Esquire late Deputy Sheriff of the County of York aforesaid being duly Sworn deposeth and saith that the property in and by the foregoing Indenture Conveyed and Regularly seized advertised, and sold in every Respect as by law directed.

Sworn to before me at my office   Edwd. W. Miller
in Fredericton this 13th. day of
March 1848 Joseph Beck, Reg^r.

New Brunswick}
York County   }   Registered this twentieth day of March one thousand Eight hundred and forty Eight at 1 o'clock PM. Joseph Beck
Reg^r

New Brunswick, County Deed Registry Books, 1780-1930, for York (1847-1848), Volume 29, p. 222

James Taylor}
   To   }   N°. 9998
John Kelly   }

    This Indenture made the Sixteenth day of March in the year of our Lord One thousand Eight hundred and forty eight Between James Taylor of Fredericton in the County of York Province of New Brunswick Merchant of the one part and John Kelly of Queensbury in the County aforesaid in the Province aforesaid Farmer of the other part Witnefseth that the said James Taylor for and in Consideration of the Sum of one hundred pounds of lawful money of New Brunswick to him in hand well and truly paid at or before the ensealing and delivery of these presents by the said John Kelly the Receipt whereof is hereby acknowledged Hath granted bargained and sold and by these presents Doth grant bargain sell, alien, release, convey and confirm unto the said John Kelly his heirs afsigns. All the Right title interest property claim and demand of the said James Taylor of in and to a Certain lot piece and parcel of land Situate lying and being in the Parish of Kingsclear in the said County of York, Known and described as the one third part of lot Number Eighty nine comprehended in the grant to Stephen Jarvis and others Containing one hundred and Sixty Acres more or less. Together with all houses out houses Barns Buildings, Edifices fences, Improvements profits privileges and appurtenances to the same belonging or in any manner appertaining and the Reversion and Reversions, Remainder and Remainders, Rents ifsue and Profits thereof. To have and to hold the said lot piece or parcel of land and premises hereby granted Bargained and Sold or meant mentioned or intended so to be, and every part and parcel thereof with the appurtenances unto the said John Kelly his heirs and afsigns to the only proper use benefit and behoof of the said John Kelly his heirs and afsigns forever. In Witnefs whereof the said James Taylor Hath hereunto set his hand and seal the day and year first above Written.

Signed Sealed and delivered in the presence}   James Taylor {L.S.}
of Mark Needham. WB Kinnear   }
York to wit   Be it Remembered that on the Sixteenth day of March 1848, before me William B. Kinnear a Member of the Legislative Council of this Province personally appeared James Taylor grantor in the foregoing Indenture named who acknowledged

the same to be his free act and deed executed by him for the use and purposes therein expressed.

WB Kinnear
M.L.C.

New Brunswick}
York County   }   Registered this twentieth day of March one thousand Eight hundred and forty Eight at One o'clock P.M.

Joseph Beck
Reg^r.

APPENDIX N

Elizabeth Reed Memorial

Harriet Irving Library, UNB
Great Britain: War Office
Pension Docs (WO42 Vols. 59-63) 1776-1881
Volume 62, pp.496-507
Reel #5
Item R3

Nº. 125159   WO 42/62

REQUIRED FOR PLACING ON THE PENSION, THE WIDOW OF AN OFFICER WHO DIED ON HALF PAY.

Elizabeth Reed came this Day before me, and made oath, that she was lawfully married on the 17th day of July, 1792 to Leonard Reed late a Lieutenant on Half Pay of the King's American Regiment of Foot who died at Queensbury in New Brunswick on the eighth day of February, 1818 and that she has no Pension, Allowance, or Provision from Government.

                                                                Elizabeth Reed

Sworn before me, at Queensbury — Queensbury Count of York this 23rd day of May 1823.
Wm Allen J. Peace}
County of York   }
New Brunswick   }

125159

John Barker of the Parish of Fredericton in the County of York and Province of New Brunswick, yeoman being of the age of Forty eight years, and duly Sworn deposeth and Saith that he was and is well acquainted with Elizabeth Reed late the Wife and now the Widow of the late Leonard Reed a Lieutenant in the half pay of the King's American Regiment that the Deponents Father Thomas Barker is also a Lieutenant on the halfpay of the same Regiment — That he the Deponent was present at the Marriage of the said Lieutenant Reed and the said Elizabeth which was solemnized at Magerville in the County of Sunbury and Province aforesaid in the Summer of the year one thousand seven hundred and ninety two by the late Reverend John Beardsley then Rector of the said Church who died some years since. And the Deponent further saith that he was acquainted with the said Elizabeth for some time before her intermarriage as aforesaid with the said Leonard Reed but that she was then called and known as the Widow Marsh and respected and deemed and taken to be the Widow of a Captain Marsh.

<blockquote>
Sworn before me at }   John Barker
Fredericton in the County of }
York & Province of New Brunswick}
the 28th. day of August 1821 }
John Saunders
Judge of the Supreme Court of
Judicature for the said Province
</blockquote>

-498-

> By His Honor Ward Chipman
> Esquire, President and Commander
> in Chief of the Province of New Brunswick
> &c. &c. &c.

Ward Chipman

These are to Certify that John Saunders, Esquire, by whom the annexed Certificate is signed, is Chief Justice of this Province, and that full Faith and Credit are due to his Acts and Attestations as such wheresoever the same may appear.

> Given under my Hand and Seal at Fredericton
> the Twelfth day of May in the Year of our
> Lord one thousand eight hundred and
> twenty three, and in the Fourth Year of
> His Majesty's Reign.
>
> By His Honor's Command
> Wm F. Odell

-499-

To all whom it may concern —

Ward Chipman President and Commander in Chief of the Province of New Brunswick do hereby Certify that I held the Office of Deputy Muster Master General of His late Majesty's late British American Forces at New York from the year 1777 to the year 1783. That it appears from the returns made into the said Office during that time and now in my position that Leonard Reed late of Queensbury in the County of York in the Province of New Brunswick aforesaid deceased was in August of the said year 1777 mustered and paid as an Ensign in the then Provincial Regiment called the Kings American Regiment Commanded by Colonel Edmund Fanning since deceased. And I further Certify that the said Regiment having been afterwards placed upon the British Establishment does not appear on the Record in my pofsefsion beyond the year 1777 —

Dated at Fredericton in the said Province of New Brunswick the twenty sixth day of May in the year one thousand eight hundred and twenty three.

Ward Chipman

[Unnumbered page.]

125159

By the Honorable John Saunders Esquire Chief Justice
of the Province of New Brunswick —

It is hereby certified that the within affidavit would be sufficient to establish in this Province the marriage of the within mentioned Elizabeth Reed widow with the said late Lieutenant Leonard Reed — Fredericton May 10th. 1823

John Saunders
Chief Justice

-500-

By His Excellency Major General George Stracey Smyth Lieutenant Governor and Commander in Chief of the Province of New Brunswick &c. &c. &c.

Be it known unto all to whom these are Presents shall come or may in anywise concern that the Honorable John Saunders before whom the annexed deposition of John Barker was made and whose name is subscribed thereto was on the day when the same deposition was made and now is one of the Judges in His Majesty's Supreme Court of Judicature for this Province and that Thomas Wetmore Esquire before whom the Deposition of Elizabeth Reed and John Kelly were made and whose name is severally subscribed thereto, was on the day where the same Depositions were severally made, and now is one of His Majesty's Justices of the Peace for the County of York in the same

Province and that full Faith and Credit are due, and ought to be given to their acts in their said several offices —

Given under my hand and seal at Fredericton the twenty eighth day of August in the year of our Lord one thousand eight hundred and twenty one, and in the second year of the Reign of His Majesty King George the Fourth of the United Kingdom of Great Britain and Ireland &c. &c. &c.

By His Excellency's command —
Wm F. Odell.

-501-

To the Right Honorable Viscount
Palmerston His Majesty's Secretary of
War &c. &c. &c.

The Petition of Elizabeth Reed of the
Parish of Queensbury in the County of York
in the Province of New Brunswick, Widow
most respectfully sheweth.

That the Petitioner was the wife of Henry Marsh Esquire who in the years 1776 and 1777 at Hackinsack in the late Province of New York raised the men required for a company in the Provincial Corps then commanded by Lieutenant Colonel Abraham Buskirk, and who ranked and performed duty as captain in that corps until the Beginning of April in the said year one thousand seven hundred and seventy seven when he was killed by a shot from the Rebels while he was advancing against them at the head of his company at a Place called Second River in the then Province of New Jersey. That her said Husband died she believes before the commissions were issued to the officers of that new Corps and for that reason she supposed no Pension was granted to her as his widow.

That she continued the widow of the said Captain Marsh until the seventeenth day of July one thousand seven hundred and ninety two when she intermarried with Lieutenant Leonard Reed of the Parish of Saint Mary in the County of York aforesaid then on the halfpay of the King's American Regiment.

That the said marriage was solemnized in Magerville in the county of Sunbury in the Province of New Brunswick aforesaid by the Reverend John Beardsley then Rector of that Parish who died a number of years since and the Register kept by him, if any, cannot as the Petitioner is informed and believes now be found.

That the said Lieutenant Reed departed this life on the eighth of February in the year one thousand eight hundred and eighteen at Queensbury aforesaid in which Parish and the Parish of Saint Mary aforesaid he with his family always resided from the time of His said marriage until his death.

That the Petitioner still remains the widow of the said Lieutenant Reed — and the Facts herein stated or the material parts of them being verified by Proofs accompanying this Petition,

The Petitioner humbly prays that your Lordship will be graciously pleased to submit her case to His Majesty's Royal consideration in the hope that it will receive His Majesty's most gracious favor and that she may be allowed a Pension either as the former widow of a brave men [sic] who fell in fighting His late Majesty's Battles or as the present widow of another Officer who served His Majesty faithfully during the Revolutionary War in America in a Regiment which so distinguished itself as at or about the close thereof to be put on the British Establishment and who continued to the hour of his death one of His Majesty's most loyal and faithful subjects —

And as in duty bound she will ever pray &c.

Queensbury Elizabeth Reed
York County
23rd. August 1821

County of York }
Province of   }   Be it remembered that on this twenty third day of August one
New Brunswick}   thousand eighty [sic] hundred and twenty one before me Thomas Wetmore one of His Majesty's Justices of the Peace for the County of York in New Brunswick personally came and appeared Elizabeth Reed the above named Petitioner being known to us as the widow of the late Lieutenant Leonard Reed on the halfpay of the late King's American Regiment, and under oath as the Holy

-502-

Holy Evangelists that the allegations on the above written Petition by her subscribed are correctly and truly stated.

Tho. Wetmore
Just. Peace

-503-

Maugerville New Brunswick
August 28th 1821

This may certify that I the subscriber acting Rector of Christ Church in the Parish of Maugerville in New Brunswick having at a request made in behalf of the widow of the late Lieutenant Leonard Read made search for the Registry of her intermarriage with the said Leonard Read which is stated as having been celebrated by the late Reverend John Beardsley deceased formerly Rector of this Parish in July one thousand seven hundred and ninety two, have not been able to find any such Entry by reason that there is no Register remaining, as I can find, of Marriages or other parochial Duties celebrated or performed by the said former Rector at that or any other time before or after, during his Incumbency, he having as is represented, taken the Register by him kept with him when he left the said Parish.

Raper Milner

-504-

Fredericton New Brunswick 13th. September 1821

I hereby certify that on the fifteenth day of February one thousand eight hundred and eighteen, I did perform the funeral service over the remains of the late lieutenant — Leonard Read at the Parish Church of — Queensbury in the county of York and Province of New Brunswick.

James Somerville

Acting mifsenary, in the service of the Society for Propragating the Gosple in Foragn Parts — for Queensbury — and the vacant Parishes adjacent to Fredericton —

-505-

John Kelly of the Parish of Kingsclear in the county of York and Province of New Brunswick, yeoman, being of the age of sixty years and duly sworn on the Holy Evangelists deposeth and saith that in the Month of March in the year one thousand seven hundred and seventy seven he enlisted as a soldier in the City of New York in the Provincial Corps called the fourth Battalion of the New Jersey Volunteers commanded by Lieutenant Colonel Abraham Buskirk and was placed in the company under the command of Captain Henry Marsh, that he the Deponent continued to serve His Majesty under that enlistment during the continuance of the American Rebellion and the Deponent further saith that the said Captain Henry Marsh was mortally wounded in action with the enemy at a place called Second River in the then Province of New Jersey and died of his wounds a few days after he was shot, which was within two or three Months after his, the Deponent's, enlistment as aforesaid. That he the Deponent was at the distance of nearly two miles from his said Captain when he was so wounded and saw him shortly after when he was brought in and observed that the wound was in the groin. And the Deponent further saith that he knew the wife and afterwards the widow of the said Captain Marsh and knows her to be the same person who was afterwards the wife and now the widow of the late Lieutenant Leonard Reed of the King's American Regiment who died in the month of February One Thousand eight hundred and eighteen and whose Funeral the Deponent attended at Queensbury in the said County of York.

his
John X Kelly
mark

[illegible]
[illegible] [illegible] Witmore
Sworn to, at Kingsclear in the
County of York the 24th day of
June 1821. — The same [illegible]
[illegible] [illegible] and explained to the Deponent
    Before me, T. Wetmore Juste. Peace Coy. York

-506-

New Brunswick.

    Peter Clements of the Parish of Saint Mary in the County of York and Province of New Brunswick Esquire maketh Oath and Saith that he is a Captain on the Half Pay of the late Regiment called the King's American Regiment of Foot. that he was appointed an Officer in the said Regiment in the year one thousand seven hundred and seventy six and continued in the same Regiment from that time to the close of the American Revolutionary War and came with it to this Province in the year one thousand seven hundred and Eighty three when and where it was disbanded: and the Deponent further Saith that he was well acquainted with the late Lieutenant Leonard Reed also on the halfpay of the same Regiment from his first joining the same to the time of his death. That he the said Leonard Reed's first Commission in the said Regiment (then a Provincial Regiment) bore date a few days after the Deponent's first Commission in the same Regiment in the said year One Thousand Seven hundred and Seventy Six — That the said Leonard Reed continued to Serve constantly in the same Regiment as an Officer From the date of his said Commission until the disbanding of the said Regiment as aforesaid — That the said Regiment was constantly on actual and sometimes on active and very Severe Service in all of which the said Leonard Reed sustained the Character of an active good and brave officer. That at or near the close of the Said War His late

[Unnumbered page.]

late Majesty was most graciously pleased to place the said Regiment on the British Establishment when new Commifsions were granted to all the Officers of the same Regiment according to the Rank which they then held, previous to which the said Leonard Reed had to the knowledge of the Deponent held a Commission and served four Years and upwards on full pay as a Lieutenant in the same Regiment.

Peter Clements

Sworn to at Fredericton in
New Brunswick the 27th
day of March 1822 before me

J Bliss Chief Justice

-507-

By His Excellency Major General George Stracey Smyth Lieutenant Governor and Commander in Chief of the Province of New Brunswick &c. &c. &c.

Be it known unto all to whom these Presents shall come or may in any wise concern that the Honorable Jonathan Bliss before whom the annexed Deposition of Captain Peter Clements was made and whose Name is Subscribed thereto is the Chief Justice of this Province and that full faith and credit are due and ought to be given to his Acts in his said Office

    Given under my Hand and Seal
    at Fredericton the thirtieth
    day of March in the year of our
    Lord one thousand Eight hundred
    and Twenty two and in the Third Year
    of the Reign of His Majesty King
    George the Fourth of the United Kingdom
    of Great Britain and Ireland.
    &c &c &c

    By his Excellencys command
      Wm F. Odell

APPENDIX O

Winslow Papers

The Winslow Papers

University of New Brunswick Archives and Special Collections (http://www.lib.unb.ca/winslow).

[In transcribing the material from the Winslow Papers, I have attempted to be as exact in duplicating the original material as possible with the exception of putting periods between the currency amounts in the transcription of the account books when the numbers are separated by column divisions instead of periods. This does not occur very often. When page numbers are not part of the header, especially in the account books, I have put them inside brackets. Otherwise, I place the numbers, when not appearing in a header, between hyphens and centered on the page. Winslow is often inconsistent in his spelling, especially of names, and he uses two pound signs when dealing with currency (example: £ or £).]

[From the cover of a letter:]

Mr Ward Chipman 21.st April 1810

To/ Mr Honoral
Judge Winslow

By Cap. Segee} Fredericton

[beneath fold in the letter:]

[Samuel] Lockes Obligation Dated
5 May 1810 Kelly D^r
5/ P^d Mrs Jennings

Edward Winslow's Diary, 1799-1810
(Volume: 26-)

[I have transcribed the material relevant to John Kelly (ca 1760 – between 4 September 1824 and 29 October 1825) and the period of his employment by Edward Winslow.]

1806. October. 90

Sunday. 12. Rain. — Col: Allen departed this Life. At ½ after 1 o clock p. m. — . . . .

[113]

6.th. Sept.r [1808] Settled & paid Kelly up to this day. All but 16/2. Yet due.

NB: This Mem Book Lost from the above date [7 November 1808] to the 1.st April 1809.

April 1809. 114

1.st. Rec.d Letter from sis J Wentworth &c. Rec.d Turnips of Rufsel & Hallet. 6 bus.ls. also 9 bus.ls Potatoes of Morrel.

3.d p.d poor tax to John Day . . . . . 6/.

4.th Dismifs.d Jane Hector — p.d in full 15/. Sent Letters to Chris: Hatch Esq.re Pafsamaquady to the care of M.r Leonard. — also — Letters to Ed Jillian & John Henderson - to the care of W.m Hazen jun.r Esq:. Peter Thomson absent – 4 days. — Jennins c.r 2 days work. — Kelly cutting & drawing Wood. Weather very mild, begins to be slumpy on the river. Open,d Cellar – Doors.

6th p.d Rufsell 15/. For Turnips[.] Rec.d 2 ½.lb Butter of Jo: Madget & 3 Cabbages. P.d[.]

Sunday 9.th Violent wind, hail & Sleet. River still pafsable. Jenkins [illegible] from recruiting.

11.th Rec.d 1£ Flour from M.r Moses Pickert. 2 ½.lb Butter Humphrey, & a rooster[.]

13. Morrel set.d with M.rs Jofselyn Rainy. Pol Smith hired Monday 10.th.

14.th Lent M: Miller 21.lb Indian Meal.

[115]

17.th M.rs Josselyn commences at 16/. P month. NB. The exact am.nt for Taxes & Commifsions from each Q.r's Salary is £21.17.6.

20.th Ice moves – water rises. Got up front fence.

From 20.th to 27.th Variable weather, Gen.l Hunter arriv.d 26.th. Kelly employ.d abo.r Willow Fence. Thornton sowing small seeds. Setting out Cabbage & Turnips, for greens, also onions. ~~Cucumbers~~

28.th Purdy set Fryke. A few fish. Cucumber seed planted.

29.th Soldier employ.d making locke. Bo't Butter &c. Cobun 4 ½.lb, Wilmot 12.lb. Old Ewe died.

Sunday. 30.th. Sunday. E Wind – water falls, but few fish.

1.st May. Put up Gate &c.

2.d Attended Court. Thomson sow.d 3 rows pease.

3.d Fine weather. Planted Cucumbers in the case.

Sunday 6.th & 7.th Water rises again. Took up Fryke. Letters from Rishtigouche.

8.th Rain. water rises a Little: Sally Winslow & Hester took their departure. Indian Exprefsment off for Rishtigouche. M.r Pickert & Family stop. In the rain.

9.th. 8 bottles Maple Syrup put down in Cellar Closet. —

10.th 11th Jennins & Kelly clearing for potatoes. Water rising. Cold. Lent M.rs Gardner Shoulder veal & bot veal for M.rs P.

$$\text{1809 May brot over —} \qquad\qquad 116$$

11th Thursday. Unpleasant weather, Men clearing for potatoes.

12.th Old Rose calved. Rec.d Letter from M.r Leonard. Hatch[.]

13.th Sow.d [1st from barn y.d 2 beds carrots.] [*sic*] 2.d. 2 d.o Beets, 3.d. 2 d.o Parsnips, 4.th. 2 Onions. Also 1 d.o Beets Last. — Bled the Count. Morrel.

Sunday. 14. Weather still continues cold. L.r M.r Leonard.

15. Working among the drift skift. H Pickert arriv.d with a raft of poles. 1 Row pease, 2 d.o potatoes.

16. Kelly helping J Day &c. planted a few potatoes. & commenc.d plowing in rear of barn. Trim.d appletrees.

17. Kelly plowing behind the barn. Day's boys drift skift.

18. Sow,d Green pease, Bush & pole beans in the garden. Morrel. Kelly sow.d 2 kinds of pease in the field. blue & white.

19. Sow,d 2 bushels oats [illegible] 1 ½ d.o wheat by Barn. Shear.d 11 Ewes 1 yearling Ram. Alter.d 3 Lambs. turn.d all out & 1 pet Ewe — Lamb.

20.th. Kelly & Jennins burning on Mount Weltden. Plowing &c. rec.d 1 Black. Jug Vinegar & 1 d.o Rum by M.r Pickard. NB. Jennins all this week.

Sunday 21.st M.rs Jofselyn's first month ends & wages p.d.

22.d Kelly sow,d 2 bushels Wheat behind the House 1 d.o Oats, (Hilman's.)

23.d. Got up 270 M.r Pickard's poles. M.r F: Rainsford is to take remainder & to return the same number to me. Sow.d peck Timothy seed.

24.th Scott (Shoemaker) began to work. Kelly moving drift skift.

25.th Moving drift skift all day. Kelly & Jennins [Text lost in fold between pages.]

[117]

Kelly planting corn. Bo't 1 Salmon, 2/6. Of J Howard. 1 Q.r Veal J Clare 7/6. Weather Cold & unpleasant. Jennins absent at Garden's. Col: Johnstone &c. here. Bot Eas. Pot & baskets 2. A dollar for the whole.

Sunday. 28.th Cool blustering Weather. Miller here.

29.th. Rec.d Letters from Bernard Cobbe Esq: Col Lutwyche 2. &c M.r Leonard. &c. Kelly in the corn field. —

30. 31. Planting Corn & potatoes — orchard. K & J in barn.

June 1st. Young Rose calv.d bot 2 pigs of Connor. 5/. Each.

2.d. 3.d Planting potatoes in orchard. finish.d 3.d (8 or 9 bus.ls) Jennins 4 days this week.

Sunday. 4.th Cold, & Wet p.d Scott 15/. M.r Hazen here.

5.th Plowing on Mount Weltden 2 yoke Oxen. bo't 5.lb butter of M.cNally & 6.th — 15.lb d.o T. Pickard.

6.th Finsh.d plowing & began harrowing Mount Weltden.

7th. Sow,d half a bushel of wheat and began planting potatoes on the mount supposed to be 12 or 13 bushels. and on Saturday the 10th finish,d[.]

Sunday 11th being ill with the gout packets from sis Jhon Wentworth on Friday[.]

16th Sow d Swedish turnips. —

18th Sunday.

19th Sow,d Bush wheat.

24.th Kelly absent all the last week.

June 25.th 1809   118

25th Sunday. Jennins sprouting potatoes 2 Last days — p.d

26.th Kelly & Jennins hoeing corn. Rec.d Boards from A. Ingram 65 boards & 3 plank, 337apland.d 1m feet 12 doll.rs

Tuesday 27. Bot 2 Cheeses & 21 ½ lb butter of T. Pickard. 1.lb Sou: Tea.

28. Began hoeing potatoes in orchard, bot Thomson,s Cow. Kill.d Calf. estimated am.nt 7 doll.rs — sent the Skin by Dan Jewett to M.r Churchill. —

From 29. June to 10th July Ingraham's boards 337apland.d 10y 6f.t 4/6, due. Burnt chimney remov.d part of wood pile. — Confine.d with Gout. 10.th & 11.th attended Chancery - Course. — Young Rose Cow —

12. Sow.d Garden. wet weather.

Thursday 19. Kelly began mowing in the rear of the house. Wet weather. M.r Blaicher here. —

20. Pickard & Joe began mowing bad weather.

22.d Mowers went to town. Rain continues. Blaicher here.

23.d Rainy weather until Wednesday night 26.th[.]

Thursday 27. Pickard & Joe came at 12 o clock. Got in some hay. 28.th 7 or 8 suppos.d to be now in barn[.]

29. 2 Large Loads went in. The rest all in Lock.

Sunday. 30th Very fine hay-day. & the fine weather continues until this day.

August. 4.th Fryday. Got in the Last of the Crop of Hay. Barn full.

5.th Rain commenc.d & continues thro' the 6.th bot 9 chickens[.]

Sunday 6.th Rain all day & all night. —

7.th Rain tap.d 10 gallon Keg of Rum – Many in to have [illegible][.]

8 & 9. Rain continues.

10. 11. Kelly absent. Nothing done. Bot 20 chickens at [illegible][.]

12. Kelly [illegible] & commenc.d working again. Fruit Brandy [illegible] Smith. [Text lost in fold between pages.]

[119]

September 3d. 4.th Kelly began reaping oats. & 6.lb [illegible] [illegible] in[.]

10. 12. Finish.d reaping & gathering in wheat.

14. Bot' 19 Chicks Blackberries [illegible].

Oct r 10.th Book Lost & not found till 9.th Oct. r 1809. Finish.d potatoes in the orchard. Pigs fortnight old Wednesday 11.th M.r Everet finish,d Wood. House & Kitchen stoop. Bot 12.lb Fish – 4 bus.ls Turnips – 1 D.o onions.

20.th Bot 12 Turkies. 1 ½ bus.l Swedish Turnips. Rec.d Butter from M.rs Griffith 19.lb 40.lb Butter Pickard.

Nov.r 15.th Kill.d Cow. Kill.d 2 last of Hallet's pigs yesterday.

Wednesday. Dec.r 27. Calf 2 weeks old. Very ill with the Gout. Wrote Col: Lutwyche & OBrien.

1810. Jan.ry. 6. J Kelly Ds. cash of 10/ order 10/ ent.d hereby mistake.

10.th Put up Entry Stove. Bayne 5/ including Teapot. & 2/ last year. —

April. 15.th Kill.d Calf. remain ill with Gout. Black Cow. [Separate entry on what appears to be the same date.] Sow pig.d – 4 Lambs. 20.th Ice went off.

May 1. — 15 Lambs, Rose calf days old.

7th. Sow.d 2. Bushels wheat behind the barn. 2 D.o oats - & ½ bus.l pease (together.) Early blue – roses in the Garden.

9.th Sow.d 2 ½ bus.ls wheat. on Mount Weltden. Lock in Garden. Black Cow will calve about the 10.th of Feb.ry Rec.d Letters from Col Lutwyche, M.t Weltden & Edward.

10.th Sow.d ½ bus.l pease – Locke in Garden. Jennins on the Mount d.s Jenkins a Bull Calf. to 339aplan a heifor.

14.th Sow.d Clover – seed on Wheat Ground, ploughing orchard.

15.th Rain, Locke & Kelly putting up front fence.

17.th Sow.d Flaxseed in orchard. [illegible] 21.st Sow.d potatoe – oats.

25.th to the end. Finish.d orchard. 62 [illegible] Corn. 26.th Shearing Sheep. 12 Ewes 2 Weathers 1 Ram 14 Lambs 5 Ewes & 9 Weathers Planting potatoes. 10 bushels. Rain — 1 Lamb died.

June 1810

1.st Settled with Kelly as p Acc.nt Book to this day.

4.th [illegible] 4 bus.ls white potatoes in New field [illegible].

8.th Finish.d front fence. Various other work.

13.th Sow.d 1 ½ oz Swedish Turnip seed.

14 Young Rose will probably calve ab.t 14.th March.

Fryday 15.th & 16.th Kelly & Locke on highway.

17.th Sunday. Bot 1 bus.l Rye of Clements 6/6.

18.th 19.th Sow.d ½ bus.l Buckwheat. Young Black Heifer.

24.th Old Rose. 22.d finish.d my 6 days on the Road. 3 Locke. 3 Kelly.
          23.d Kelly & Locke for themselves 1 day each.

25.th 26.th Locke & Kelly hoeing potatoes.

To 5.th July. Hoeing – making bridge & clearing for turnips.

24th. began mowing & ended 9th. Aug.t —

October 20.th. Found This book 20.th Oct.r Since the Last date have attended the Circuit at S.t Andrews & the Court at Fredericton, & got the whole of the Crop in. Consisting of
Hay by estimation 20 tons —
Wheat Bushels — Corn —
Pease — Beans — Oats —
           100.
Potatoes 60 in the Back Bin.} clear
D.o   40. In Long Bin — } blues
D.o   30. Scatter.d —
_____

Clear.d the island. & plow.d the potatoe field — Mount Weltden. The meadow below [Text hidden behind remaining edge of extracted page.]

[121]

October 20th Plowing with 2 Yoke Oxen Mount Weltden. Pull.d 10 or 12 bushels turnips.

21.st Sunday. —

22.d} various kinds of work.

23.d} rec.d Letters J Frazer Halifax[.]

24.th] got in Cabbage & Cutting Wood hill.

28.th Sunday. To the end. Aunt Sally here. — Men cutting wood &c.

November 3.d Kill,d Garden [illegible] [illegible] 108.lb banking cellar &c.

4th. Severe weather, Ice making fast in the river.

5.th Front fence. 6.th Lock threshing, Kelly absent 2 day Vefsels stop.d by the ice & remain in that state till Wednesday the 15.th when a thaw enables Segee to get up to Fredericton. Articles on board for me as follows. Vid: Red book. Kill.d Sow. Wentworth [illegible]. Wheat all thresh.d 17 or 18 bus.ls.

Jan.ry [1811] 6.th. 2 Q.r beef Miller small, Mutton Pickart. 5 geese [illegible], Flour & Meal from mill.

Edward Winslow's Accounts # 1, 1770-1811
(Volume: 31-1)

[I have extrapolated and transcribed the material relevant to John Kelly (ca 1760 – between 4 September 1824 and 29 October 1825).]

1809. December	74	
23.rd Kelly D.r p.d M.rs Jennins.		7.6.
1810. Jan.ry 6. J. Kelly D.r cash 10/. Order 10/.		1.0.0.
17.th J Kelly D.r Leather apron of Ring & Hart. .		.3.
[75]		
[February] 25.th J Kelly D.r Cash 1 doll.r in Town /-		0.5.0.
March 1810.	76	
16.th J Kelly D.r Cash p.d D.or Emerson Prec̱ṯ.		16/9.
26.th J Kelly D.r Cash p.d M.r Ring. . . 2/6.		
28.th To cash 5 ¼ dollars -		£1.6.3.

April 4.th To cash p.d D.or Emerson's bill   .16.9
To 7 days absent time.
N.B. 1 p.r oxen standing still}

[77]

May 6.th [Date out of sequence.] J Kelly D.r p.d M.rs Jennins 1 doll.r .   5/.

5.th S: Locke commenc.d working for me at 8 doll.rs p month. —

Monday 7.th M.rs Jocelyn began work again in my service.

June 2.d Kelly D.r p.d for Hat. To M.rs Jocelyn . . .   2/6.

19.th J Kelly D.r order on Taylor 15/. D.o Wilmot 15/ 1.10.0.

1810. July. —   78

5.th J Kelly D.r order on M.r Wilmot   £3.0.0.

[September] 12.th J Kelly D.r order on P. Frazer.   11/6.
           1.lb Tobacco. . . . . .   2/6.

[79]

[October] 12. J Kelly D.r cash p.d Bombadier Smith R.A. [Royal Artillery]
by M.r Miller — for a silver watch as p rec.r 22. Dollars £5.10.0

Oct.r 22.d D.o [account rendered from] Stephen Cameron ag.st John Kelly . . .   2.1.10

1810. November 1.st —   80

5.th John Kelly D.r order on P: Frazer for 10 dollars £2.10. — to cash 10/. . . .   3.0.0.

Dec.r 1.st John Kelly D.r order on P: Frazer 40/} to a Great coat of M.r Miller 40/ £4.0.0

[81]

27 John Kelly D.r Cash for Tobacco — 1/3.

1811 January —   82

7.th John Kelly D.r p.d Self Cash One Dollar —   5/-

               Feb.ry 11.th 1811.   84

Feb.ry 11.th John Kelly D.r 2 shirts at 10/.   £1.10.0
       1 shirt ret.d.

March 2.d J Kelly D.r Cash 1 Doll.r   5/.

                       [85]

9.th J Kelly D.r To absent days 1 whole week. Cattle idle all the time.

                       -86-

J Kelly D.r To am.nt Acc.nt
C.r
By ball.ce old acc.nt to
July 1810 . . . .   £5.6.3.
By wages to Jan.ry}   15.
P particular bill}
1811. By D.o 1.st June}
p particular bill}

                       -90-

Dec.r Absent time John Kelly since Dec.r 1808

7.th Working days . . . —   3.

25.th D.o from Sunday night to Thursday 4. Night.

Jan.ry 9.th [1809] D.o   .   .   .   .2.

Feb.ry 5.th D.o . . . . 3.

Mar 26.th from Fryday to Wednesday   5.

                       -92-

                 2/5 p day

Kelly came 3.d June Fryday 1808.

3.d plowing for corn . . . .

4.th D.o & sheering sheep . . . .

5.th Sunday.

6.th Harrowing &c. for Corn.

7.th 8.th D.o & planting corn & potatoes. Pitch pole.

9. 10. 11. D.o & ditching – by causeway.

12. Sunday. To Sunday 19. In town.

20. 21. 22. 23.} Cearing &c. . . . . . 4 – days.

Fryday. 24. Rain all day. —

25. Sowing 344apland Turnips.

Sunday 26.th — Rain. Work – 6 days this week.

Sunday July 3. Work this week 6 days getting in Hay on Sunday being consider.d equal to time spent ditching on the — highway &c.

4.th 5.th Hoeing &c.

6.th Rain — in town.

7.th absent

Wednesday. 8.th Return.d/mowing.

9.th Mowing. 3 days this week.

Sunday. 10.

11.th Rain — on the highway.

To Sunday 17.th C.r 5. Days this week. 3 mowing.

18. to 23.ᵈ inclusive. Mowing 6 days.

24.ᵗʰ Sunday.

-93-

Saturday 30. 6 days to this day — Rain.

Sunday 31.

Aug.ᵗ 1. 2. 3. Thursday ½ day rain. —

21.ˢᵗ Sunday. Kelly & Joe [Wherry] Left off for fast day[.]

1809. March 5.ᵗʰ·   94

Rec.ᵈ Edward Winslow Three pounds, seventeen shill gs & five pence in full for a debt due to me from John Kelly. Jacob D Blaicher £3.17.5.

April 8.ᵗʰ Rec.ᵈ of Ed Winslow one shilling in full of all accounts to this day. Also twenty shillings on acc.ⁿᵗ John Kelly. Joseph Wherry X Mark.

Edward Winslow's Accounts # 2, 1770-1811
(Volume: 31-2)

[I have extrapolated and transcribed the material relevant to John Kelly (ca 1760 – between 4 September 1824 and 29 October 1825).]

45. 89 [Number 89 added later.]

D.ʳ John Kelly

1809. Febr.ʸ 1.ˢᵗ To order on M.ʳ Wilmot	1.0.0.
To afsum,d to pay M.ʳ Blaicher	3.17.3.
20.ᵗʰ To 1.ˡᵇ Tobacco by Jennins	.2.
March 25.th To Cash 1 dollar	0.5.0.
April 6.th To 4 dollars p.ᵈ Joe Wherry	1.0.0.

14.th To order on M.r Wilmot for 4 dollars		1.0.0.
May 1st To absent days 4 different times estimated at . . .		0.12.2
Ball.d		£7.16.5

June 10.th To a pair of Boots of Scott 2

19.th To order on M.r Wilmot . . . . 4. —

25.th To d.o . . . . <u>1.</u>
                                                                                                                                                                                7.0.0.

18.th July To order M.r Wilmot . . . . . . 1.0.0.

Oct.r 22.d To Cash 1 p.d Gold & 6/ doll.rs . . . . . 1.10.
        To order M.r Wilmot . . . . . . 1.10.
        Cash to pay M.rs Corneilson . . . . 2.6.
        To 6 absent days in August at 3/. . . . . 18.
        To 5 D.o in October at 3/. . . . . . 15.
        To 2.lb Tobacco at different times . . . . 5.
        To 1.lb Tobacco by Jennins . . . . . .2.6.

1810. Jan.ry 6. To Cash 10/. Order 10/ . . . . . 1.0.0.
             To leather apron of Ring . . . . . .3.0.
             To Cash in town 1 doll.r . . . . . <u>.5.</u>

Feb.ry 25.th   Carried over p. . . .   £14.18.6

C.r   90 46. [sic] [Number 90 added later.]

1809. Feb.ry 1.st By ball.ce due on settlement . . . . . £1.16.5.
            By wages to 1.st March 6 doll<u>rs</u> . . . . 2.0.0.
            By d.o — to 1.st April . . . 2.0.0.
            By d.o to 1.st May . . . . <u>2.</u>
                                                                                                                                £7.16.5.

By ~~absent~~ [crossed out illegible word] ~~different times~~ }
~~estimated at~~}   4.~~12.~~5.

           Ball.d to the 1.st May —

June 1. By wages to this day . . . .   2.

July 1 By D.º to this day		2.15.
Aug.ᵗ 1. By D.º this day		2.15.
Sept.ʳ 1. By d.º this day		2.15.
Oct.ʳ 1. By d.º this day		2.15.
By 5 months to May deducting 1 for sicknefs at 2£.		10.0.0.
1810. Brot over		14.18.6.
Feb.ʳʸ 26. To p.ᵈ Ring mending shoes	0.2.6.	
To cash 5 ¼ dollars	1.6.3	
To p.ᵈ D.º Emerson's ball	0.16.9.	

carried to page 51.

51. 99 [Number 99 added later.]

D.ʳ M.ʳ John Kelly

1810 June 1.ˢᵗ To amount of my advances for you } & absent time from 1.ˢᵗ June 1809. To} 1.ˢᵗ June 1810. As p particular bill.		22.2.
To D.ᵒʳ Emerson's bill omitted by mistake		0.16.9.
		£22.18.9.
June 2.ᵈ To p.ᵈ M.ʳˢ Jocelyn for Hat	0.2.5.	
19.ᵗʰ. To order on Wilmot 15/. D.º Taylor 15/.	1.10.0.	
24.ᵗʰ To cash p.ᵈ M.ʳˢ Jennins	0.5.0.	
July 5.ᵗʰ To order on Wilmot 12.ˡᵇ Tobacco 2/6.	3.2.6.	
Sept.ʳ 12.ᵗʰ To order on M.ʳ P: Frazer 11/6. Tobacco 2/6.	0.14.0.	
Oct.ʳ 20.ᵗʰ To p.ᵈ Bombadier Smith for Watch	5.10.0.	
22.ᵈ p.ᵈ Cameron p rec.ᵗ	2.1.10.	

Nov.r 5.th To order P. Frazer 10 dollars, Cash 2 d.o . .   3.0.0.

Dec.r 1.st To order on d.o 40/. D.o M.r Miller 40/ . .   4.0.0.
                                                                                    20.9.10

To absent days during the last   }
six months in June [illegible]: 5 days –}
July 3. Sept.r 4. & 2. In Nov.r & Dec.r 8} due EW.

Absent days 23. To be accounted for.   2.17.6.

Dec.r 27 To cash for Tobacco 1/3   1811 Jany 7 Cash one Dollar   0.6.3.

1811 March 10 ap.d to pay J.D. Blaicher £2.19.0 Cash 5/.   3.4.0.
To 2 Shirts [illegible] /. 9.th March absent 7 days
mistake ~~M.r P: Fraser bill for Fraser in last June 10/6~~   ~~0.10.6.~~

March 25 To Cash one Dollar -------------------------0.5.0.

May To 2 dollars Cash & 3 days absence 7/6   0.7.6.   0.[?].6.
                                                                                    7.10.3.

           Contra   C.r   100

1810 June 1.st By wages from June 1st 1809}
            to June 1st 1810. As p bill   }   27.15.
                                                                          22.18.9.
                                                                          £4.16.3.

June 1.st Ball. Due to John Kelly   }
p adjustment this day made   }   5.6.3.

July 1.st By wages to this day paymen.t   2.0.0.
Aug.t 1.st By wages to this day p d.o   2.15.
Sept.r 1.st By D.o to d.o p d.o   2.15.
Oct.r 1.st By D.o to d.o p d.o   2.15.
Nov.r 1.st By D.o to d.o p d.o   2.15.
Dec.r 1.st By D.o to d.o   2.0   15.0.0.
                                                                                    £20.1.3

1811

Jan.y 1. By Months wages to this Date —
Feby 1   By D.º   D.º   D.º}
Mar 1   By D.º   D.º   D.º}
April 1. By D.º   D.º   D.º}at 40/.   12.
May 1. By D.º   D.º   D.º}   £32.1.3.
June 1. By D.º   D.º   D.º}
July 1.

-103-

J Kelly D.r

1811. To am.nt of acc.nt to Jan.ry   20.9.10
       To absent days to Jan.ry 23 —   2.7.6
       To p.d Sundries p bill . . . .   7.10.3.
                                                 7.
                                                                7.7.

       To 14 absent days since Jan.ry   1.15.0.
                                                 32.02.7.

Am.t Kelly's ball.ce & wages   33.1.3.

APPENDIX P

Published Sources:

Burr, Horace (Translator): *The Records of Holy Trinity (Old Swedes) Church, Wilmington, Delaware, from 1697-1773* (Papers of the Historical Society of Delaware, IX; translated from the original Swedish by Horace Burr, with an Abstract of the English records from 1773 to 1810) (Wilmington, Delaware: Historical Society of Delaware, 1890); *Catalogue and Errata of The Records of Holy Trinity (Old Swedes) Church* (Wilmington, Delaware: Historical Society of Delaware, Press of Charles L. Story, 1919).

[I have taken the liberty of putting the information from *The Records of Holy Trinity (Old Swedes) Church, Wilmington, Delaware, from 1697-1773* in order by year. As was standard practice in recording church or governmental information, everything was documented under the males. When female members of the Howard, Kelly/Kelley or Long families are mentioned, I have listed the entry under their surname instead of that of their husband. I have entered any corrections or notations gathered from information occurring in *Catalogue and Errata of The Records of Holy Trinity (Old Swedes) Church* after the entries generated from *The Records of Holy Trinity (Old Swedes) Church, Wilmington, Delaware, from 1697-1773*.]

Howard Family

1748: Margret Howard married Edward Ogle June 1748. (p. 404) *Catalogue and Errata of The Records of Holy Trinity (Old Swedes) Church*: June 1748 corrected to 20 June 1748. (p. 161)

1758: John Howard Married Rachel Evans 16 August 1758. (p. 708)

1777: Daniel Howard married Sara Porter 15 November 1777. (p. 748) *Catalogue and Errata of The Records of Holy Trinity (Old Swedes) Church*: Sara listed as Sarah. (pp. 27 & 102)

Kelly Family

1720: "William Kellam and Miss Mary Reynolds by license married" 23 August 1720. (p. 259) *Catalogue and Errata of The Records of Holy Trinity (Old Swedes) Church*: Kellam appears as Kellum (pp. 31 & 103).

1730: Maria Kelle, daughter of Martin Kelle and wife Catharina, born 2 April 1730 and baptized 12 April 1730. (p. 333) *Catalogue and Errata of The Records of Holy Trinity (Old*

Swedes) Church: birth of 2 April 1730 is corrected to "2 months old" at baptism, and Kell is printed as Kelly in the reference column. (p. 160)

1738: Sara Kelly married Bryan Culen 12 October 1738. (p. 366) *Catalogue and Errata of The Records of Holy Trinity (Old Swedes) Church*: Culen is corrected to Cullin. (p. 14 & p. 89) *Ibid.*: Sara Kelly appears as Sarah Kelley (p. 14) and as Sarah Kelly (p. 89).

1745: David Kelly married Ann Royly February 1745. (p. 392) *Catalogue and Errata of The Records of Holy Trinity (Old Swedes) Church*: David is corrected to Daniel. (p. 161)

1747: Martha Kelley married Cain Wholohan 24 November 1747. (p. 402)

1748: Agnes Kelly married Robert McGarrout 3 May 1748. (p. 404) *Catalogue and Errata of The Records of Holy Trinity (Old Swedes) Church*: Kelly corrected to Ketly. (p. 161)

1753: Matthew Kelly married Jane Stotts 12 June 1753. (p. 694)

1754: Else Kelley, daughter of Adam and Margret Kelley, born 9 March 1754 and baptized 3 June 1754. (p. 572)

1754: James Kelly married Sarah McMolland 23 December 1754. (p. 698)

1755: Marget Kelly married Isaac Adams 6 August 1755. (p. 700)

1756: Thomas Kellum & Rachel Taylor were married by license 10 May 1756. (p. 702) Kellum remains Kellum throughout *Catalogue and Errata of The Records of Holy Trinity (Old Swedes) Church*.

1757: John Kell married Agnes Pharas 15 September 1757. (p. 705) Kell remains Kell throughout *Catalogue and Errata of The Records of Holy Trinity (Old Swedes) Church*.

1757: Margreta Kelly married Solomon Springer 3 December 1757. (p. 706)

1759: Patrick Kelly married Anne Hide 3 August 1759. (p. 710)

1762: Margrete Kelly married Thomas Joanes 5 October 1762. (p. 717) *Catalogue and Errata of The Records of Holy Trinity (Old Swedes) Church*: Joanes appears as Jones (pp. 30 & 88).

1771: Mary Kelly married Lawrence Woods 2 January 1771. (p. 733)

1779: William Kiley, son of William and Ester Kiley, born 6 August 1779 and baptized 7 April 1780. (p. 645)

1782: James Kelley, son of William and Ester Kelley, born 11 February 1782 and baptized 5 May 1782. (p. 649)

1787: Samuel Kelly married Margret Gray 4 September 1787. (p. 761)

1788: Barnaby Kelly married Onore Suraney 21 October 1788. (p. 762)

1789: Charles Gelly married Ann Crosby 20 July 1789. (p. 763) Gelly remains Gelly throughout *Catalogue and Errata of The Records of Holy Trinity (Old Swedes) Church*.

1789: Neil Kelly married Magdalena McCafferty. (763) Although Neil Kelly and Magdalena McCafferty are listed in both the male and female indices as appearing on page 763 of *The Records of Holy Trinity (Old Swedes) Church, Wilmington, Delaware, from 1697-1773*, in the Errata section of *Catalogue and Errata of The Records of Holy Trinity (Old Swedes) Church*: Burr points out that their names are omitted on page 763 of *The Records of Holy Trinity (Old Swedes) Church, Wilmington, Delaware, from 1697-1773* and corrects the names to Neil Kellog and Magdaline McCassit, who were married 25 July 1789. (p. 165)

1790: Charles Kelly married Debora Cobbs 21 October 1790. (p. 764)

1793: Margaret Kelley (parents listed as Kelley) baptized 8 August 1793. (p. 670)

Long Family

1729: Thomas Long married Jean Perkins "Governor's License" 30 March 1729. (p. 310)

1735: Thomas Long married Martha Thatcher 8 September 1735. (p. 359)

1744: Mathew Long married Ellenor Burnside 1744. (p. 388)

1745: Jacob Long married Ann Yung October 1745. (p. 394) *Catalogue and Errata of The Records of Holy Trinity (Old Swedes) Church*: Yung appears as Yung (p. 33) and as Young. (p. 117).

1755: Alexander Long married Margret Morrison 9 June 1755. (p. 699)

1757: John Long married Rebecca Wallace 13 February 1757. (p. 704)

1758: John Long married Christian Paulson 9 March 1758. (p. 707)

1760: Rebecca Long married Thomas David 29 March 1760. (p. 712) *Catalogue and Errata of The Records of Holy Trinity (Old Swedes) Church*: 29 March 1760 corrected to 29 April 1760. (p. 163)

1793: Mary Long married David Logan 11 January 1793. (p. 765)

Christ Church – Philadelphia (Founded in 1695) (*www.christchurchphila.org/Historic-Christ-Church/73*):

[Despite the fact that I cannot establish direct ties to the Loyalists of our family who settled in New Brunswick, Canada, to this church, I have decided to include the following records from Christ Church in Philadelphia.]

HOWARD

10 September 1711: Burial: John Howard (Record Book Year: 1709-1785).

16 October 1711: Burial: John Howard (Record Book Year: 1709-1785).

30 August 1727: Burial: John Howard; Location: Strangers' Burial Ground; Notes: "Stranger G." — no relations listed (Record Book Year: 1726-1730).

30 March 1731: Baptism: John Howard, aged 3 years, son of Thomas and Grace Howard; Minister: Rev. Archibald Cummings (Record Book Year: 1709-1768).

28 October 1733: Burial: John Howard; Location: Unknown; Notes: no relations listed (Record Book Year: 1731-1735).

9 August 1744: Marriage: John Howard and Sarah Moet; Location: Christ Church; Notes: "Sarah Moet wid.o" (Record Book Year: 1709-1800).

6 August 1746: Burial: Joseph Howard, son of John Howard; Location: Unknown; Notes: apparently a common burial of Joseph and Richard, sons of John Howard — no mother listed (Record Book Year: 1739-1746).

6 August 1746: Burial: Richard Howard, son of John Howard; Location: Unknown; Notes: apparently a common burial of Joseph and Richard, sons of John Howard — no mother listed (Record Book Year: 1739-1746).

17 March 1751: Baptism: Grace Howard, daughter of John and Grace Howard; Born: 4 October 1750; Minister: Rev. Robert Jenney, L.L.D. (Record Book Year: 1709-1768).

7 September 1757: Burial: Unnamed Howard, son of John Howard; Location: Unknown; Notes: "John Howard's son" — no further information listed (Record Book Year: 1756-1760).

11 January 1760: Baptism: Sarah Howard, daughter of John and Sarah Howard; Born: 4 February 1758; Minister: Rev. Robert Jenney, L.L.D. (Record Book Year: 1709-1768).

25 August 1760: Baptism: Elizabeth Howard, daughter of John and Sarah Howard; Born: 30 July 1760; Minister: Rev. Robert Jenney, L.L.D. (Record Book Year: 1709-1768).

11 April 1761: Burial: Unnamed Howard, daughter of John Howard; Location: Unknown; Notes: "John Howard's Daughter" — no further information listed (Record Book Year: 1761-1764).

28 December 1764: Marriage: John Howard and Bridget Osborn; Location: Christ Church; Minister: Reverend Mr. Sturgeon; Notes: "L_marriages by License from the Governor" (Record Book Year: 1709-1800).

8 July 1773: Baptism: John Howard, son of Thomas and Jane Howard; Born: 7 January 1773; Minister: Rev. Richard Peters, D.D. (Record Book Year: 1769-1794).

Marriage: John Howard and Margaret Chew; Minister: Revd. William White (Record Book Year: 1709-1800).

KEAN/KANE

19 July 1725: Burial: William Kane, son of Abel and Ann Kane (Record Book Year: 1709-1785).

2 January 1738: Burial: Mary Kane, daughter of William Kane; Location: unknown; Notes: no mother listed (Record Book Year: 1736-1739).

KELLY

8 July 1723: Marriage: John Kelly and Eleanour Hughes; Location: Christ Church; (Record Book Year: 1709-1800).

24 April 1737: Baptism: John Kelly, son of John and Rebecca Kelly, aged 1 week; Minister: Rev. Archibald Cummings (Record Book Year: 1709-1768).

11 August 1741: Marriage John Kelly and Jane Sullivan; Location: Christ Church; Notes: "Jane ? Sullivav" (Record Book Year: 1709-1800).

14 January 1748: Baptism: William Kelly, son of William and Susannah Kelly; Born: 30 October 1747; Minister: Rev. Robert Jenney, L.L.D. (Record Book Year: 1709-1768).

11 April 1752: Marriage: John Kelly and Rebecca Sutton; Location: Christ Church; Minister: Reverend Mr. Sturgeon (Record Book Year: 1709-1800).

19 March 1763: Baptism: John Kelly, son of James and Mary Kelly; Born: 19 June 1762; Minister: Rev. Richard Peters, D.D. (Record Book Year: 1709-1768).

2 March 1766: Baptism: Ann Kelly, daughter of Michael and Eleanor Kelly; Born: 24 October 1765; Minister: Rev. Richard Peters, D.D. (Record Book Year: 1709-1768).

4 September 1767: Marriage: John Kelly and Rachel Aaron; Location: Christ Church; Minister: Revd. Mr. Duch ?; Notes: "L_marriages by License from the Governor." (Record Book Year: 1709-1800).

18 November 1773: Marriage: John Kelly and Martha Knight; Minister: Rev. Richard Peters, D.D. (Record Book Year: 1709-1800).

15 August 1774: Marriage: John Kelly and Mary Edge; Minister: Revd. Mr Duch ?; Notes: Posted. The rector at the time was Rev. Richard Peters. (Record Book Year: 1709-1800).

6 July 1775: Baptism: William Kelly, son of William and Margaret Kelly; Born: 30 April 1775; Minister: Rev. Richard Peters, D.D. (Record Book Year: 1769-1794).

24 September 1791: Marriage: John Kelly and Phoebe Packer; Minister: Revd. William White; Notes: "Bride and Bridegroom, negroes" (Record Book Year: 1709-1800).

21 May 1799: Baptism: Martha Jones Kelly, daughter of William and Martha Kelly; Born: 10 July 1798; Location: Saint Peter's Church; Minister: Revd. William White; Notes: "St. Peter's Church" (Record Book Year: 1795-1819).

12 May 1799: Baptism: Elizabeth Kelly, daughter of William and Martha Kelly; Born: 11 July 1799, Location: Saint Peter's Church; Minister: Revd. William White; Notes: "St. Peter's Church."; "Right Revd. D.r White Rector" (Record Book Year: 1795–1819).

3 June 1803: Baptism: William Kelly, son of John and Mary Kelly; Born: 17 May 1803; Location: Saint Peter's Church; Minister: Revd. William White; Notes: "(St. Peter's Church.)" (Record Book Year: 1795–1819).

19 April 1806: Baptism: Elizabeth Kelly, daughter of John and Mary Kelly; Born 1 November 1804; Location: Saint Peter's Church; Notes: "(St. Peter's Church)" (Record Book Year: 1795–1819).

19 April 1806: Baptism: John Kelly, son of John and Mary Kelly; Born: 6 September 1806; Location: Saint Peter's Church (Record Book Year: 1795–1819).

24 August 1805: Baptism: John Kelly, son of Will.m and Rachel Kelly; Born 3 June 1804; Minister: Unknown; Notes: "(Private Baptism)" (Record Book Year: 1795–1819).

24 August 1806: Burial: William Kelly, son of Edward Kelly; Location: Christ Church Burial Ground; Notes: no mother listed (Record Book Year: 1785-1900).

30 January 1807: Baptism: William Kelly, son of William and Rachel Kelly; Born: 23 January 1807; Minister: Unknown; Notes: "(Private Baptism)" (Record Book Year: 1795–1819).

Craig, H. Stanley: *Gloucester County New Jersey Marriage Records* (Merchantville, New Jersey: H. Stanley Craig, Publisher, 1930):

Citing marriage records from the county clerk's records:

    Arthur Kelly and Ann Collins 2 March 1805. (p. 118)
    Isaac Kelly and Sarah Sparks 9 April 1840. (p. 118)
    Stephen D. Kelly and Catharine Sailer 7 November 1837. (p. 118)]
    William Kelly and Sarah McEnny 1 September 1831. (p. 118)
    Benjamin Lock and Meriba Kelly 23 May 1805. (p. 125)
    Samuel Middleton, Jr. and Atlantic Kelly 16 April 1834. (p. 135)

Craig, Stanley H.: *Salem County New Jersey Genealogical Data Records Pertaining to Persons Residing in Salem County Prior to 1800* (2 Volumes) (Merchantville, New Jersey: H. Stanley Craig, Publisher, 1934); reprinted (Woodbury New Jersey: Gloucester County Historical Society, 1980, 2005):

Volume 1

(p. 141)

KELLY

[The numbers in parenthesis at the end of each entry corresponds to the key following the listing.]

Anne, dau Mallacky and Cathrin, b. 7 May 1762. (1)
Catherine, dau. Malachi and Mary, b. 3 January 1768. (1)
Isaac (Kelley), Int. 1797 File 2136 Q. (2)
James, s. Mallacky and Cathrin, b. 24 December 1765. (1)
John, Alloways Creek, will pr. 23 April 1754. Wf. Margaret. Bros. Thomas and James Kelly. Sister Martha Wallis. Nephews John Wallis, s. of Martha, and John Kelly, s. of Thomas . Lib. 8, p. 55. (2)
John (Kelley), m. Elizabeth Cashlow, 24 December 1768. (6)
John, a. [Must be "s."] Mallacky and Mary Christ., b. 19 September 1770. (1)
John (Kelley), Admitted by bap. 27 June 1773. (3)
John, Private, 1st Batt.; also State Troops; also Continental Army. (4)
John, 2d Major, 2d Batt., Salem Co. Militia, promoted from Captain, Revolutionary War. (4)
John (Kelley) Int. 1798. File 2233 Q. (2)
Joseph, s. Mallacky and Cathrin, b. 19 January 1764. (1)
Malacky, m. Mary Hopman, 5 January 1767. (20)
Mary (Killy), m. Thomas Cheesman 7 August 1787. (3)
Michael, Private, 1st Batt. Salem Co. Militia; also State Troops; also Continental Army. (4)
Peace (Killy), m. Mehitible Howell, 22 December 1778. (3)
Sarah, dau. Mallacky and Mary , b. 25 January 1773. (1)
Thomas (Kelley), will 12 March 1728/9; pr. 29 March 1729. Wf. Rachel. Chd. John, Thomas, Mary, Hannah, Martha and James. Lib. 3, p 32. (2)
Thomas (Killy), m. Jean Wallace, 28 March 1780. (3)
William, Pilesgrove, will 13 April 1761; pr. 4 December 1761. Wf. Mary. Lib. 10, p. 433. (2)
William, Private, 1st Batt; also State Troops; also Continental Army. (4)

1: Penns Neck Data from Records of Trinity P.E. Church, Swedesboro.
2: Data from Wills.
3: Pittsgrove Baptist Church Records.
4: Stryker's Official Register.
6: New Jersey Marriage Licenses.
20: Records of Trinity P.E. Church, Swedesboro.

Salem County New Jersey Genealogical Data Records Pertaining to Persons Residing in Salem County Prior to 1800:

Volume 2

Military Rolls
Colonial Militia in 1715
From New York State Historian's Report 1896. (p. 88)

South Side of Cohnasey
Capt. Rumsey's Company
Thom Kelley (p. 92)

Revolutionary War
From Cushing & Sheppard's *History of Gloucester, Salem, and Cumberland Counties*.

First Battalion
John and William Kelly are grouped together while Michael Kelly is listed separately from them. (pp. 94-95)

Data from Quarter Sessions
Court Records (p. 121)

August Term, 1752
Grand Jury
Thomas Kelly is listed under Delinquents. (p. 196)

December Term, 1767
Henry Telly [*sic*] is listed on the Grand Jury. (p. 208)
James Kelly is listed under the Defaulters on the Grand Jury. (p. 208)
Abner Long is listed on the Grand Jury. (p. 208)

September Term, 1769
Thomas Kelly is listed as being sick in the list of Defaulters on the Grand Jury. (p. 212)

March Term, 1770
John Kelly is listed under the Defaulters on the Grand Jury list. (p. 213)

June Term, 1770
Henry Jelly [*sic*] is listed on the Grand Jury. (p.214)

September Term, 1770

John Kelly is listed on the Grand Jury. (p. 215)
Malachi Long is among the defaulters on listed on the Grand Jury list. (p. 215)

June Term, 1773
Henry Jelly [sic] is listed on the Grand Jury. (p. 222)

Officers Chosen by the Court

1709 Overseers of Roads
Munmuth: Thomas Kelly. (p. 224)

1718 Constables
Alloways Creek: Thomas Kelly. (p. 229)

1718/19 Constables
Alloways Creek: Thomas Kelly. (p. 230)

1732 Overseers of Roads
North side of Cohansey: William Long. (p. 240)

1741 Overseers of Roads
Upper Alloways Creek: Thomas Kelly. (p. 245)

1745 Overseers of Roads
North side of Cohansey: Peter Long. (p. 247)

1777 Constables
Upper Alloways Creek: John Kelly. (p. 255)

Robert Howard is listed as a Justice for the following:
September Term, 1767. (p. 207)
September Term, 1768. (p. 209)
December Term, 1768. (p. 210)
March Term, 1769. (p. 211)
December Term, 1769. (p. 212)
June Term, 1770. (p. 214)
March Term, 1771. (p. 216)
June Term, 1771. (p. 216)
March Term, 1772. (p. 218)
September Term, 1772. (p. 219)
March Term, 1773. (p. 221)

Craig, H. Stanley: *Salem County (New Jersey) Marriage Records* (Merchantville, New Jersey: H. Stanley Craig, Publisher, 1928); reprinted (Woodbury, New Jersey: Gloucester County Historical Society, 1977):

Citing the *New Jersey Archives, Volume XXII*:

> Abel Smith and Rachel Kelly 17 May 1765. (p.14)
> John Kelley and Elizabeth Cashlow 24 December 1768. (p. 10)

Citing county clerk's records:

> William Casper and Jane Kelly 14 December 1864. (p.45)
> Patrick Donly and Mary Kelly 16 May 1857. (p. 63)
> Andrew Horner and Sarah Kelly, of Woolwich, Gloucester County, 10 March 1825. (p.100)
> David Long and Elizabeth Kelly 10 October 1799. (p. 118)
> Patrick Murphy and Judy Kelly 1 November 1858. (p. 132)
> Samuel String and Hannah Kelly 12 July 1827. (p. 176)
> John Wetherel (note by Craig: "also recorded as Wetheril") and Jane Kelly 22 March 1812. (p. 192)

Citing Pittsgrove Baptist Church records:

> Benjamin Smith and Mary Kelly 24 November 1783. (p. 243)

Johnson, Amandus (editor): *The Records of the Swedish Lutheran Churches at Raccoon and Penns Neck, 1713-1786* (Elizabeth, New Jersey: Colby and McGowan, Inc., 1938); reprinted (Woodbury, New Jersey: Gloucester County Historical Society, 1982); (Salem, Massachusetts: Higginson Book Co., 1997 and currently available from Higginson Book Company through their print-on-demand services).

Under "RECORDS OF BAPTISMS":

Raccoon 1741: "Surities Parents themselves for want of others. John Killy born 1734. August 25th. Maleky Killy born 1737. Septemb. 4th. George Killy born 1740 March 24." (p. [266]) It should be noted that the Killys are listed in a group that includes a number of Dickesons. As will be noted below, Anne Kelly married James Dickisson on 31 March 1776 at Pensneck.

Pensneck 15 January 1767: "Mallacky & Cathrine Kellys Anne B June the 7th 1762[;] Joseph B. Jan. the 19th 1764[.]" (p. [286])

Pensneck 21 February 1768: Malachi & Mary Kellys Catherine B. Jan: the 3d 1768[.]" (p. [288])

Pensneck 23 May 1773: "Mallacky and Mary Kelly's Sarah B. January the 23d. 1773." (p. [297])

Raccoon 1780: "Jesse b: 28th of Jan: inst: Malackia and Mary Christina Kelly." (p. [302])

Raccoon 1782: "Rebecca b. 15th of June inst. P. Malachy & Mary Christine Kelly." (p. [303])

Under "RECORDS OF MARRIAGES":

Pensneck 31 March 1766: "James Dickisson to Anne Kelly of Salem & Upper P.N." (p. [313])

Raccoon 12 July 1783: "John Crawford et Anne Kelly." (p. [323])

Johnson, Robert Gibbon: *An Historical Account of the First Settlement of Salem, in West Jersey, by John Fenwick, Esq. Chief Proprietor of the Same* (Philadelphia, Pennsylvania: Published by Orrin Rogers, 1839):

"February, 1733-4. . . . Ordered by the court, That Mary Kelly, for abusing the judge, Mr. Acton, in her misbehavior to him in the execution of his office, do receive ten lashes on her bare back, for her contempt, at the public whipping post." (pp. 111-112)

Lee, Francis B. (editor): *Documents Relating to the Revolutionary History of the State of New Jersey, Volume II, Extracts From American Newspapers, Vol. II, 1778* (Trenton, New Jersey: The John L. Murphy Publishing Co., Printers, 1903):

[HOWARDS]

WHEREAS inquisition was found the 14th day of May, 1778, against Philip Van Cortlandt, John Bowlsby, Edward Bowlsby, Charles Bowlsby, Richard Bowlsby, Jacob Hylor, Humphry Devenport, William Howard, George Beaty, Thomas Husk, Lawrance Buskirk, Jacob Demorest, Samuel Ryerson, Isaac Hornbeck and Nicholas Vreland; of which proclamation was made in Court, the 8th day of July, that they, or any person on their behalf, or any persons who should think themselves interested, might appear and traverse the inquisition. This is to give NOTICE that unless they, or some other person on their behalf, agreeable to the said proclamation, do appear at the next Court of Quarter-Sessions, and traverse the said inquisition, final judgment will be then entered against them.

AARON KITCHEL, Commissioner.

Morris county, July 22, 1778. (P. 350)

NOTICE is hereby given, that an Inquisition has been found against George Howard, late of Middlebrook, in the county of Somerset; which Inquisition was returned to Court last June, and upon proclamation being made, no person appeared to traverse the same.

FREDERICK FRELINGHUYSEN.

Commissioner.

Aug. 1, 1778.

---*New Jersey Gazette*, Vol. 1, No. 37, *August* 19, 1778. (p. 364)

THIS is to give notice, that there has been judgment entered the last court against Thomas Milliage, Stephen Skinner, Anthony Hollenhead, John Troop, John Steward, Ezekiel Beach, Joseph Conliff, Hugh Gaine, John Boyls, John Thorborn, Asher Dunham, William Deaman, Philip Van Cortland, Jacob Hilor, Humphrey Devanport, William Howard, George Beattee, Jacob Demarest, Isaac Hornbeck, John Bowlsby, Edward Bowlsby, Charles Bowlsby, Richard Bowlsby, Thomas Husk, Lawrence Buskirk, Samuel Ryerson, and Nicholas Vurlandt, as the law directs for their having joined the enemy, against their country: and all persons that have any demands against any of their estates, are desired to meet and make it appear at the house of Matthias Burnet, Esq, in Hanover, on the second Wednesday in January next, at ten o'clock A M. that it may be settled; and all persons indebted, are desired to pay the money as soon as possible, or have any of their effects, to deliver them up to the Commissioners, or they may depend upon being dealt with as the law directs.

ALEX CARMICHAEL,}

AARON KITCHEL} Commissioners.

Morris-County, Dec 7. 1778. (p. 593)

[KELLYS]

Feb. 17, 1778

TEN DOLLARS REWARD.

TAKEN out of the house of the subscriber at the New-Mills near Mountholly, the 13th inst. At night, a SILVER WATCH, with a silver face, maker's name C. Rigdel, London. As a certain John Kelly, alias John Wheeler, who said he was a light horseman and had lately deserted from the British army, lodged at the subscriber's house that night, he is *suspected* of the theft: He is about five feet eight or nine inches high, and had on a blue great coat, light coloured ditto under it, green jacket, and linen trowsers. Whoever takes up the *real* thief so that he may be brought to justice, and secures the Watch for the owner, shall have for the Watch only SIX DOLLARS, and for the thief FOUR DOLLARS, with reasonable charges paid by

THOMAS PLATT. (p. 58)

Sixty Dollars Reward.

WAS stolen out of the pasture of the subscriber, in Lower Makefield, Bucks county, in the night of the 6th of August last, a brown mare, fourteen hands and an half high, uncommonly broad and heavy, paces and trots, twelve years old, supposed to be with foal when stolen. A certain *George Kelly* is suspected to be the thief; he is about fifty years old, five feet ten inches high, a full-mouthed roughlooking fellow. Whoever secures said mare and thief, so that the owner may have his mare, and the thief brought to justice, shall have the above reward, or forty dollars for the mare only, by applying to Joshua Anderson, Esq. of Bucks county, Captain William Tucker, of Trenton, or to the subscriber.

JAMES WINDER.

July 23, 1778 (p. 327)

Return of the killed, wounded, missing, &c of the troops under the command of General Sir Henry Clinton, in an engagement with the Rebel

Army, on the heights of Freehold, county of Monmouth, New Jersey, the 28th of 1778.

TOTAL BRITISH.

1 Lieutenant-Colonel, 1 Captain, 2 Lieutenants, 4 Serjeants, 56 Rank and File, killed; 3 Serjeants, 45 Rank and File, died with fatigue; 1 Colonel, 1 Lieutenant Colonel, 1 Major, 7 Captains, 5 Lieutenants, 7 Serjeants, 137 Rank and File, wounded; 3 Serjeants, 61 Rank and File, missing.

TOTAL GERMAN.

1 Rank and File, killed ; 11 Rank and File, died with fatigue; 11 Rank and file, wounded.

GENERAL TOTAL.

1 Lieutenant Colonel, 1 Captain, 2 Lieutenants, 4 Serjeants, 57 Rank and File, killed; 3 Serjeants, 56 Rank and File, died with fatigue ; 1 Colonel, 1 Lieutenant Colonel, 1 Major, 7 Captains, 5 Lieutenants, 7 Serjeants, 148 Rank and File, wounded ; 3 Serjeants, 61 Rank and File, missing.

Names and rank of the officers returned, killed and wounded on the 28th of June, 1778.

Royal Artillery, Lieut Vaughan, killed. 1st Grenadiers. Capt Gore, of the 5th company, killed. 2d Grenadiers. Lieut. Colonel Hon. H. Monckton, of the 45th company, (commanding the battalion) Lieut. Kenedy, of the 44th company, killed. 1st Grenadiers. Capt Cathcart, of the 15th company, Capt Brereton, of the 17th company, Capt. Willis, of the 23d company, wounded. 2d Grenadiers. Major Gardner, of the 10th company, Capt. Leighton, of the 46th company. Capt. Powell, of the 52d company, Lieut. Gilchrist, of the 42d company, Lieut. Kelly, of the 44th company, Lieut. Paumier, of the 45th company.

Lieut. Grosse, of the 52 company, wounded.

Foot Guards. Colonel Trelawney, Captain Bellew, wounded.

15th Regiment Capt Ditmas (attached to the 2d Grenadiers) wounded.

Marines. Lieut Desborough (attached to the 2d Grenadiers) wounded.

Queen's American Rangers. Lieut. Colonel Simcoe, wounded.

H. CLINTON. (pp. 566-568)

AT an Inferior Court of Common Pleas held for the County of Gloucester, on the 13th instant, were returned inquisitions (for joining the army of the

King of Great-Britain, and other offences against the form of their allegiance) found against Andrew Jones, John Kelly, John Inglish, Jonathan Fisher, jun, Benjamin Carter, Joshua Couzens, John Carter, jun, Joseph Pratt, Joseph Clark, William Devanport, Harrison Wells, Jonathan Fisher, Thomas Nightingale, Job Thomas, Jacob Clement, jun, William Ingland, jun. William Watson, Daniel Wells, Jonathan Chew, Isaac Lord, David Chew, David Suran, John Franklin, Silas Long, Joseph Long, William Bocock, John Rodrow, William Fusman, Jacob Hewit, James Hanesy, Alexander Bartram, Peter Johnson, George Avis, William Wells, Gabriel DeVeher, jun, Edward Eglinton, Asa Lord, Conrad Bowman, Robert Whitacre, William Pinyard, Josiah Biddle, John Cox, Philip Stout, Daniel Couzens, John Gruff, Gabriel DeVeher, John O'Bryant, John Hinchman, Jeremiah Profser, John Robison, George Swanton, John Hatton, Northup Marpole, John Inglish, jun, Benjamin Duffil, James Duffil, Isaac Justice; proclamation was made in open Court, and information given, that if they or any on their behalf, or any person interested would traverse, a trial should be awarded, and an opportunity of preventing forfeitures given: no traverses were offered: Therefore notice is hereby given, that if neither they nor any on their behalf, nor any person interested shall traverse at the next Court, to be held for the county of Gloucester, on the second Tuesday in December next, the inquisitions will be taken to be true, and final judgment entered thereon in favor of the State, and their personal estates will then be forfeited to the use of the State, and their lands taken into the hands of the Commissioners until the Legislature shall further order therein respecting their lands.

JOHN SPARKS.}
JOSEPH HUGG} Commissioners.

Oct. 29, 1778. (pp. 581-582)

Marianne Grey Otty Database:

Phebe Howard, adult wife of William Howard, was Baptized 3 July 1786, as recorded at Gagetown/Nerepis[, New Brunswick].

Samuel Cain married Rebecca Carpenter 5 January 1794 at Long Island[, New Brunswick].

Nelson (editor), **William**: *Archives of the State of New Jersey, First Series, Volume XXI, Documents Relating to the Colonial History of the State of New Jersey, Volume XXI, Calendar of Records in the Office of the Secretary of State, 1664-1703* (Paterson, New Jersey, The Press Printing and Publishing Co., 1899):

> 1685-6 22d d. 12th m. (February). Mem. of sale. Wm. Groom to Richard Marshall, of 200 acres at Allowayes Creek, bought of Marcus Elgar of Middle Neck, Salem Tenth, who is to give deed, the land adjoins Dennis ffisher's 500 a.; purchase consideration to be delivered at Wm. Kelly's house at Salem Townlanding. New Jersey Colonial Documents. Salem Surveys, No. 2, p.36. (p. 551-552)

> 1691 April 2. Do. William Kelly of Salem Town, weaver, to William Hall, late of Pile Grove, now of Manneton Creek, W. J., yeoman, and wife Elizabeth, for 22 acres in the Town of Salem, sold by said Hall to Samuel Carpenter April 13, 1686, and assigned by said Carpenter on the same day to present grantor. New Jersey Colonial Documents. Salem Deeds, No. 5, p. 114. (p. 595)

> 1701-2 Feb. 27. Hue and Cry after Henry Johnson, servant to Vincent Helmsley of Talbot Co., Maryland, run away with a pass of Tho: Cornwell and a horse of Nicholas Kill, signed by John Guest with Philadelphia Co. seal. New Jersey Colonial Documents. West Jersey Records, Liber B, Part 2, p. 708. (p. 534)
>
>> 1701-2 Feb. 28. Power of attorney. Nicholas Kelly, on behalf of the above named Vincent Helmsley, to Edward Rush of Philadelphia Co., husbandman, to pursue and apprehend said run-away servant. New Jersey Colonial Documents. West Jersey Records, Liber B, Part 2, p. 708. (p. 534)

Nelson, William (editor): *Archives of the State of New Jersey, First Series, Volume XXII, Documents Relating to the Colonial History of the State of New Jersey, Volume XXII, Marriage Records, 1665-1800* (Paterson, New Jersey: The Press Printing and Publishing Co., 1900); reprinted (Baltimore, MD: Genealogical Publishing Co, 1967); reissued as *New Jersey Marriage Records 1665-1800 Edited, with an Historical Introduction on the Early Marriage Laws of New Jersey, and the Precedents on Which They Were Founded* (Baltimore, MD: Genealogical Publishing Co, 1973):

Marriage Licenses from the Office of the Secretary of State at Trenton, New Jersey:

Males (H):

(Page 186)

Howard, Alexander, and Elizabeth Miller..1768 Nov. 23
Howard, John, Philadelphia, and Sarah Bunting, Burlington....................1749 Oct. 16
Howard, Michael, Burlington, and Catherine Roche, Burlington..............1731 July 24
Howard, Michael, Burlington, and Lydia Bittle, Burlington......................1756 Sept. 9
Howard, Thomas, Middlesex, and Margaret Smith, Middlesex ....1754 Dec. 9

Females (H):

(Page 207)

Howard, Mary, and Richard Watson, Burlington.....................................1756 Aug. 13
Howard, Rebecca, and Joseph Soper, New Jersey...................................1779 Feb. 2

Males (K)

(Page 225)

Kain, William, Gloucester, and Mary Coles..1777 Sept. 6
Kean, Thomas, Cumberland, and Mary Mack...1777 Dec. 11

(Page 226)

Kell, James, Philadelphia, and Susannah White, Philadelphia..................1735 Aug. 9
Kelle, John, Cape May, and Susanna Steelman, Cape May.......................1764 Oct. 24
Kelley, Abraham, Burlington, and Deborah Hammell..............................1786 Mar. 22
Kelley, James, Burlington, and Ann Len, Burlington...............................1736 Nov. 5
Kelley, James, Burlington, and Lettice Fort..1777 Nov. 4
Kelley, John, Salem, and Elizabeth Cushlow, Salem................................1768 Dec. 24
Kelley, John, Burlington, and Rebecca Martin..1778 Sept. 30
Kellay, Joseph, Pennsylvania, and Phebe Buckman, Pennsylvania............1768 April 9
Kelley, Patrick, and Elizabeth Hibbs..1742 Feb. 14
Kelly, Andrew, Perth Amboy, and Elizabeth Akin, Perth Amboy..............1752 Aug. 18
Kelly, Cornelius, Burlington, and Penelope McDaniel, Burlington............1739 Aug. 1
Kelly, James, Hunterdon, and Martha Reeder, Hunterdon......................1773 Feb. 9
Kelly, Richard, Burlington, and Sarah Ivins, Burlington..........................1776 Feb. 28
Kelly, William, Burlington, and Katharine Sharoe, Burlington.................1745 Aug. 12
Kelly, William, Sussex, and Sebina Fennell, Sussex.................................1769 Feb. 20

(Page 228)

Kille, Abraham, Burlington, and Mary Powell......................................1768 Dec. 20
Killey, Aaron, Burlington, and Mercilah Harris, Burlington.....................1766 Jan. 28
Killey, David, Monmouth, and Hannah Woodmansey, Monmouth...........1730 Feb. 25
*Killey, Joseph, Monmouth, and Hannah Tillton, Monmouth....................1747 Aug. 20
Killy, Samuel, Burlington, and Bathsheba Richards................................1733 May 23

Females (K)

(Page 230)

Kane, Sarah, Somerset, and Francis Hollinshead, Somerset.....................1739 Nov. 3

(Page 231)

Kelley, Bridget, Bristol, Pa., and Joseph Bruton, Bristol, Pa.......................1767 Aug. 30
Kelley, Elizabeth, Philadelphia, and James Clarkson, Philadelphia............1727 June 19
Kelley, Rachel, and Zephaniah Taylor, Springfield................................1785 Oct. 25
Kelley, Sarah, Shrewsbury, and James Woolley, Shrewsbury....................1761 Dec. 8
Kelly, Amy, Woodbridge, and Elijah Harris, Piscataway.........................1757 June 15
Kelly, Anne, and John Crawford, Gloucester.......................................1783 July 13
Kelly, Elizabeth, Perth Amboy, and Dennis Dunn, Perth Amboy...............1753 April 28
Kelly, Elizabeth, Woolwich, and George Shinn, Woolwich......................1769 April 3
Kelly, Elizabeth, and John Hammell, Burlington...................................1778 Aug. 5
Kelly, Jane, Springfield, and Benjamin Trumis, Burlington......................1767 Feb. 24
Kelly, Jane, and Jacob Rail, Burlington...1778 Mar. 23
Kelly, Mary, Middlesex, and Elias V. Court, Jr., Middlesex......................1748 June 30
Kelly, Mary, Hunterdon, and James Berry, Hunterdon...........................1773 July 19
Kelly, Mary, and Samuel Davis, Burlington...1783 Nov. 7
Kelly, Rachel, Alloways Creek, and Abel Smith, Salem..........................1765 May 17
Kelly, Rebecca, and John Hunnywell, Sussex......................................1768 Jan. 26

(Page 232)

Kille, Catharine, and John Larkins, Burlington.....................................1780 July 31
Kille, Elizabeth, Burlington, and Thomas Gale, Burlington......................1739 Oct. 8
Kille, Mary, Burlington, and James Powell, Philadelphia........................1740 Sept. 5
Kille, Mercy, Gloucester, and Aaron Howell, Gloucester........................1760 Jan. 8
Killey, Anne, Shrewsbury, and Tunis Aumack, Shrewsbury.....................1758 Oct. 17

Chesterfield Friends' Marriage Records:

Males (K):

(Page 661)

*Killey, David, of Upper Freehold Township, Monmouth Co. (son of Joseph and Sarah (Tilton), and Hannah Middleton, at Chesterfield..................................14th 2d mo. 1771

    Witnesses—Samuel Killey, Amos, Margaret, Amos, Jr., Elizabeth, Jr., Elizabeth, Samuel, Sarah, Patience, Hannah, Mary and Jacob Middleton, Gervas Pharo, Nathan Wright, Daniel Tilton and others.

Females (K):

(Page 676)

Kelley, Miriam, to Hartshorn Tantum................................ .....10th 9th mo. 1795
Killey, Sarah, to Joseph Tantum..5th 11th mo. 1795

Nelson, William (editor): *Archives of the State of New Jersey, Volume XXIII, Documents Relating to the Colonial History State of New Jersey, Volume XXIII, Calendar of New Jersey Wills, Volume I, 1670-1730* (Paterson, New Jersey, The Press Printing and Publishing Co., 1901); reprinted (Bowie, Maryland: Heritage Books, 1994):

> 1687-8 Feb. 2. Harding, John, of Salem Co., freeholder and labourer; will of. Wife and children, but only eldest son John, "now supposed to be in England" is mentioned by name. Land on Manneton Creek and elsewhere. Personalproperty. Executors — John Swift of Bucks Co., Penna., glazier, and Wm. Penton of Salem Co. Witnesses — John Worlidge, John Maddocks, Wm. Penton junior. Recorded May 8, 1688.
>
>   1687-8 Feb. 11. Inventory of the estate: 240 acres of land at Manneton £25, 16 a. in Salem Town £6, debts due £34.18, by John Sysom, Alex'r Smith, Wm. Hughes, John Pledger, James Harrison, George Haslewood, John Maddocks, Sam'l Curtis, Charles Angelo, Wm. Kelly, Francis Bucle. Due by deceased, £12.14.11, to Marke Reeve, Nicholas Philpott, Thos. Hyde (for coffin 19s.), Wm. Penton (8 weeks' diet, lodging, tendance and funeral £5), John Worlidge, Roger Mall, Edw. Bradway, Benj. Acton and John Snookes.   Salem Wills, A, p. 7 (p. 210)
>
> 1709-1710. Account of the estate by Wm. Penton, of Salem, showing payments to Tho: Kelly, Nathaniel Broding, Wm. Willis, Alex: Grant, Wm.

Johnson, Wm. and Andrew Thompson, Mary Smith, Chas. Angello, Henry Siddon, Hugh Middleton, John Haines and George Trenchard. (p. 79)

1713 April 10. Hall, William, Salem merchant; will of. Wife Sarah. Children — Clement, William, Nathaniel, all under age. Sarah Brading, Hannah Hall, Elizabeth Tranchard. Land bought of James Baratt, farm bought of John Alexander, sawmill and land on Morris River, land at Nantucksett, house and lot in Salem, bought of Wm. Kelley, 10 acres of marsh over against the Landing, land on Pens Neck, do. at the upper end of Salem Town, bo't of Roger Hagens and Hugh Middleton, 8 acres over against Alexander Grant, Pillegrove plantation, as bought of John Hopman. Personal property. Executors — the wife and brother Clement Plumsead (Plumsted). Witnesses — Henry Warmsley, Tiberius Johnson, Joseph Gregory, John Thompson junior. Proved February 10, 1713-4. Lib. I, p. 457 (p. 202)

1714 Sept. 14. Bowne, John, of Mattawan, Middletown, Monmouth Co., merchant; will of. Wife Frances receives £400 in right of dowry. Sister Sarah Saltar, Gershom Mot, Joseph Dennis, Jeremiah White, Thomas Saltar, Jno. Saltar, Hannah Lincon and William Hartshorne's three oldest children, legacies of plate, furniture and money; the rest of the real and personal estate is left to brothers Obadiah Bowne and Richard Saltar, who are also made executors. Witnesses — James Paul, Joseph Dennes, Marget Commen, — who in proof of will April 11, 1716, is called Margaret Frazer, formerly Cummen. Lib. A, pp. 10, 27[.]

1716 April 9. Inventory of the personal estate of £16982.5.0, of which £403.7.6 are household goods, &c., incl. 143¼ oz. of plate, £57.6.0, and a negro man, £45; the rest mortgages, bonds and book debts, the mortgagors being: Daniel Applegate, Abram Covertt, Peter van Deventer, John Throckmorton, William Wilkins, Lewis and Dorothy Nissbitt, John Ruckman, Ambrose Still, Thomas Fenton, Thomas Warne, Benjamin Cooper, Albert Amerman, John Bond, William Montgomery, Jacob Compton, Cornelius Thomson, Moidecai Gibbons, Daniel Harkett, Thomas Williams, the Kearneys, James Grover, Aria Marteson, Thomas Edwards, John Job, Benjamin Coleman, James Craig, Rob't Barclay, Chas. Hubbs, Johannes Smock and Aaron Robins; [among] the bond debtors are: . . . Tho: Combs [and], Benj. Kelly. . . . (pp. 50-54)

— — Vickery, Richard, of Salem Co.; will of. Wife Elizabeth. Daughters — Rachell and Sarah. A lot of 150 acres adjoining Thomas Kelly, another of 100 a. next to Thomas Mason. Personal property. Executors — the wife and bro. Edward Vickery. Witnesses — Helener Linch and Alex'r Grant. Proved Sept. 30, 1714.   Lib. B, p. 477 (p. 482)

1715 April 4. Horner, John, of Stoney Brook, Middlesex Co.; will of. Wife Frances, sole executrix. Sons-in-law (? stepsons) — Bearfoot Brunson and Joseph Stout; daughters-in-law (? stepdaughters) — Margaret Fleet, Mary Farnsworth, Anna Brunson; brothers — Isaac and Joshua Horner and children; sister Mary Kelley; legacies to Anne, wife of old John Snowden of Bucks Co., Penna., and to the Chesterfield Monthly Meeting of Quakers for their poor, also for building a Quaker Meetinghouse on Stoney Brook. Real and personal estate (a silver drinking cup, four negro slaves and one Indian slave). Witnesses — Tho: Leonard, John Pidcock, Abraham —, John Worth. Codicill without date gives to Rachel, daughter of brother Isaac, a silver tankard. Proved August 22, 1715.   Lib. 2, p. 20 (p. 238)

1716 Aug. 21. Higbee, Edward, of Middletown, Monmouth Co.; will of. Children — Edward, Sary Jonson, Margery Looper, Mary Race, Joseph, Rebeckah; residuary legatees Obediah and George Higbe. Only personal property disposed of. Executors — Eden Burrowes and Hugh Hartshorne. Witnesses — John Simkny (Timkny), Johannes Rees (?), Johannes Smack. Proved March 25, 1717.   Lib. A, p. 68

   1717-8 Jan. 17. Inventory of the personal estate (£64.8.0, mostly debts due by Andrew Hampton, Andrew Parse, Tho: Collings, Tho. More, Peter Marie (a desprait debt), Richard Soper, John Kelley, Stephen Pillyg, Benjamin Prigmore, Peter Bulkloo and Obadiah Winter); made by William Leeds, Auken Lefferson and Thomas Harbunt (?); sworn to by Eden Burrows, executor. (p. 226)

1721-2 Jan. 1. Horner, Joshua, of Springheld, Burlington Co.; will of. Wife Mary. Children — John, Isaac, Joshua, Joseph, Bangiman, Deliverance, Contant, Goletoh (?), Mary and Sarah. Real and personal estate. The wife sole executrix. Witnesses — Tho: Wright, John Killte (Kelly in jurat), James Starkey. Proved April 20, 1723.

   1721 Feb. 13. Inventory of the personal estate of, £90.17.6, old currency at 9s.2p. per oz., incl. a Bible, "sum" old books etc. £1.7; made by Isaac De Cow and Beniam Joones. (p. 239)

1723 Oct. 12. Combs, Thomas, of Freehold, carpenter; will of. Wife Elizabeth. Children — Robert, Rachel, Thomas, Joseph, Jonathan, John, Elizabeth; the sons all underage. Real and personal estate. Executors — the wife and Jonathan Hampton of Freehold, cordwainer. Witnesses — George Walker, John Fenton, John Campbell. Proved May 27,

1724.   Lib. A, p. 298, and Monmouth Wills
   1724 May —. Inventory of the personal estate, £92.12.6; made by Thomas Williams, George Walker and John Campbell. (p. 103)

1726 April 20. Hart, John, of Salem, merchant; will of. Daughter Jeane (under age, to be sent to school in Philadelphia and then to live with the wife of David Morriss until of age); sister Jeane Hart, living in or near Glasco, Scotland, brother William Hart, cousin Robert Hart, living with testator . Real and personal estate. Executors — David Morriss, Richard Smith and John Pledger. Witnesses — Jos. Test, Simon Worner, Sam'l Hedge. Proved April 27, 1726.   Lib. 2, p. 334
   1726 May 9. Inventory of the personal estate, £1793.7.4, incl. a watch £4.5, plate £3.9.9, old silver 4s. 7p., a looking glass 12s., an 8 day clock £9, all the shop goods £138.9.4, a silver nutmeg grater £1, 3/8 of the sloop Salem £50, 1/3 of the Pheby Hoope £15, and outstanding debts £1201.4.6 1/2 ; made by Joseph Darkin and Ro: Johnson.
   1738 May 17. Account of the estate by the surviving executors, Richard Smith and Jno. Pledger, who have spent £38 more than the inventoried value by deducting £523.4.3 3/4 insolvent debts, £115.14.7 3/4 not yet recovered debts and by paying debts due to . . . [, among others,] Rachael Kelly. . . . (p. 214-215)

1728-9 March 12. Kelley, Thomas, of Salem Co; will of. Wife Rachel executrix. Children — John, Thomas, Mary, Hannah, Martha, James. Home farm called Ruff Land in Sealem [sic] Co. Personal property. Witnesses — Frances Dunlop, Michall Walker, Thomas Allen. Proved March 29, 1729.   Lib. 3, p, 32
   1728-9 March 29. Inventory of the personal estate, £134.2.6, incl. a servant £6.10, debts due £25; made by Daniel Fog and Wm. Thompson jun. (p. 271)

1730 June 9. Kelly, John, of New Hanover Township, Burlington Co., yeoman. Bond of Joseph Richards as administrator of the estate of, John Wright fellow bondsman, both of said Co., yeomen. (p. 271)

1730 June 9. Combs, Robert, of Woodbridge, Middlesex Co., yeoman; will of. Wife Eunness. Children — Dennis, Robert (under age), other children, sons and daughters spoken of, but names not given. Real and personal estate. Executors — the wife, son Dennis and Henry Potter. Witnesses — Richard Carman, Timothy Blomfield, Nugient Kelly. Proved September 11, 1730.   Lib. B, p. 166, and Middlesex Wills (P. 103)

1730 Sept. 25. Morriss, George, of Woodbridge, Middlesex Co., gent.; will of. Wife Mary. Children — George, John, Jacob, the last two under age, Mary, Elizabeth, Sarah and Rachel; legacy to Peter Napp. Homestead at the mouth of Little Creek in Rariton River, money bequests at 8 sh. per oz. Executors — the wife, son John and Ichabod Smith. Witnesses — Edward Harneed, Nugent Kelly, Jonathan Dunnin. Proved December 11, 1730. Lib. B, p. 180 (p. 330)

1734 May 27. Account of the estate by the administrators, William Allen and Joseph Turner of Philadelphia, merchants, who have increased its value by 700 barrel staves, at 37s. 6d. per 1,000, £1.6.3, and outstanding debts collected by Peter Turner, their agent, £136.9.2, and have paid debts due to . . . [, among others,] Thomas Kelly. . . . (pp. 114-115)

Plankenhorn, Louise (transcribed and indexed): *Records from Family Bibles in the Gloucester County Historical Society* (Woodbury, New Jersey: The Gloucester County Historical Society, 2001; reprinted 2003.) (p. 114):

Kelly

The Holy Bible, 1818. Kelly Family Bible record (Burlington County). Presented October 20, 1978 by anonymous donor.

Benjamin Kelly his Book. Was Bought th Seventh m. the 2 Day 1822. Price $5

Marriages
Benjamin Kelly the Son of Joseph & Phebe Kelly was maried th 30th Day of the first m. in the year of our Lord 1817

Births
Benjamin Kelly Son of Joseph & Phebe Kelly was born the 10th day of the Eleventh m. in the Year of our Lord 1787
Elisabeth Kelly Daughter of Benjamin & Phebe Kelly was born the 8th day of the Second m. in the Year of our Lord 1818
Benjamin Kelly Son of Benjamin & Phebe Kelly was born the 17th Day of the Tenth m. in the Year of our Lord 1827
Phebe Moon Daughter William & Sarah Moon was born the 16th day of the Eight m. in the Year of our Lord 1791
Sarah Kelly Daughter Benjamin & Phebe Kelly was born the 3th [sic] day of the Second m. in the Year of our Lord 1822

Deaths

William Moon was born 2nd mo. 5th 1765 — died 5th mo. 30th 1837 — Aged 72 years 3 mo. 25 Days

Elizabeth Moon, mother of Wm. Moon born 1st mo. 30th 1721 — died 3rd mo. 13th 1814 — aged 93 years 1 month and 14 days

Elizabeth Moon Daughter of Wm. Moon and Sarah Moon born 10 mo. 10th 1787 — died 9th mo. 10th 1831 — aged 43 years & 11 months

Benjamin Kelly departed this life 5th month 6th 1838 — aged 50 years 5 months and 26 days

Phebe Kelly departed this life 4th month 1st 1862 aged 71 years 7 months and 16 days

Sachse, Julius Friedrich: *Augustus Evangelical Lutheran Congregation at Trappe, Pennsylvania (Perkiomen Valley) (Montgomery County)*:

John Kelly, son of Lawrence & Jane Kelly and sponsored by John Commons, was born 2 January and baptised 27 May 1750. (p. 31)

Anna Kelly, daughter of Laurentz and Jane Kelly and sponsored by "parents," was born 10 March and baptised 16 September 1758. (p. 51)

William Kelly, son of Laurentz and Jane Kelly and sponsored by "parents," was born 17 September 1760 and baptised 25 April 1761. (p. 57)

Shourds, Thomas: *History and Genealogy of Fenwick's Colony* (Bridgeton, New Jersey: George F. Nixon, Publisher, 1876):

> Ann Thompson, daughter of Thomas and Rebecca Thompson, married John Firth. They had four children — Elizabeth, Thomas, John and Samuel Firth.
> Hannah Thompson's first husband was John Anderson. They had one daughter, Rebecca Anderson. Hannah's second husband and was Leonard Sayres, a native of Cumberland county, but at that time his home was in Cincinnati, Ohio. Hedge Thompson, Thomas' son, married Mary Ann Parrott, daughter of Richard Parrott. Hedge and Mary Ann, his wife, had five Children -- Richard P., Thomas, Joseph H., Rebecca and Mary. Richard P. married Maria Hancock; Thomas married William Johnson's daughter; Dr. Joseph H. married Rebecca Kelly, and Mary married Samuel Starr, an Episcopal minister. Rebecca, youngest daughter of Thomas and Rebecca, married John Holme of Elsinborough. She left one daughter, Rebecca Holme, who married George W. Garrison. Jane Thompson married John Smith, of Mannington, son of Hill Smith. Their children

were Ann, Hill, and Thomas T. Smith. Ann married George W. Garrison, being his second wife, and Thomas T. married Elizabeth Hancock, daughter of Joseph Hancock.

Rachel Thompson[,] the youngest daughter of Thomas and Rebecca Thompson, married Dr. Benjamin Archer; they had one son, Fenwick Archer. Mary Thompson, third daughter of Thomas and Rebecca Thompson, died single.

Within a few years there has been different opinions respecting the property in the town of Salem, held by the county. Some persons have contended the land was given for a particular purpose, while others thought it was given to the county without reservation, and held that the representatives of the people of the county had a right to sell or rent any part of the ground, as they should think would be for the interest of the county. Samuel Hedge was left to carry out the wishes and designs in the town of Salem, and also in the town of Cohansey, of his father-in-law, John Fenwick. After the death of Fenwick all the land on the south side of Bridge street, now Market street, extending from Broadway to Fenwick creek. Samuel Hedge and his wife, Anne, became the owners. The following is an order I find in Richard Tindall's book of surveys, eighteenth page. A warrant given 7th of 11th mo., 1688.

"A warrant to Richard Tindall, Surveyor-general for the county of Salem, and to John Woolidge, his deputy, to lay out one acre of land in Salem town, given by John Fenwick to erect a Court House and Prison."

Agreeable to the words of the warrant, it was certainly given for a particular use — to erect a Court House and Prison on — and if the inhabitants of the county should in some future time remove the said buildings from the said ground, it is reasonable to suppose that the property would revert back to the heirs of the donor. (pp.16-17)

Hannah, the eldest child of Jesse and Grace Carll, born 24th of 8th month, 1757, died a young woman, unmarried. Elizabeth, another daughter, born 17th of 11th month, 1758, married Abner Fitzpatrick, whose grandfather emigrated to this country from the north of Ireland; they now spell the name Patrick. Elizabeth and her husband had six children — Mary, Phineas, Abner, Jesse, Samuel and Elizabeth. Lydia, the daughter of Jesse and Grace Carll, born 14th of 12th month, 1760, married Edward Keasbey 3d, son of Bradway Keasbey. Their children were Sarah, Prudence, Grace, Joseph, Elizabeth, and Edward. Grace, the daughter of Jesse and Grace Carll, born in 1762, married Thomas Ware, of Cumberland. They had four children -- Asbury, Jacob, Hannah, and Lydia. Ephraim, the eldest son of Jesse and Grace Carll, born 17th of 11th month, 1761, married Barbara, the daughter of Joseph and Sarah Acton. (Joseph was the son of Benjamin

Acton, Jr., and grandson of Benjamin Acton, who emigrated to New Jersey from England about the year 1690.) Ephraim and his wife, Barbara, had eight children -- Edward H., Joseph A., Hannah, William, Ephraim, Grace, Jesse, and Mary. Ephraim Carll, Sr., died in 1803, and was buried in the same graveyard in which his parents were interred. Sarah, the daughter of Jesse and Grace Carll, born in 1766, died a minor.

Prudence Carll, the daughter of Jesse and Grace, born 14th of 5th month, 1768, married Bradway Stretch, and had one daughter -- Martha Stretch. Jesse, son of Jesse and Grace Carll, was born 14th of 12th month, 1760, and his wife was Mary, the daughter of Edward Hancock, Jr. He and his wife lived and owned the property that belonged to her father and grandfather, formerly part of William Hancock's allotment of 1,000 acres, bought by him of John Fenwick, and surveyed to him by Richard Hancock in 1676. At the death of William Hancock, which took place in 1679, he devised all his landed estate to his widow, Isabella Hancock. In 1681 she sold 500 acres to John Maddox, an eminent Quaker, who emigrated to this country in 1680. In the year 1700, John Maddox sold that part of the property lying next to Monmouth river, to Jeremiah Powell, of Salem, and the southern portion adjoining the Salter tract, to John Hancock, the son-in-law of Nathaniel Chambless. Jesse and his wife, Mary Carll, had five children — Rebecca, Elizabeth, Sarah, Lydia and William Carll. William, the son of Jesse and Grace Carll, born in 1773, died a minor. John, the son of Jesse and Grace Carll, born in 1775, died a young man, unmarried. Sarah, the daughter of Jesse and Grace Carll, born 15th of 7th month, 1778, married Job Sheppard; they had two sons — John and William Sheppard.

Martha, the youngest child of Jesse and Grace Carll, born 15th of 8th month, 1780, married William Waddington, the oldest son of Jonathan, Jr., and Sarah Waddington. William and his wife had six children -- Anna, Sarah, William, Martha, Hannah and Jesse Carll Waddington. Mary, the daughter of Abner and Elizabeth Patrick, married Washington Smith, the son of Captain William Smith, of Revolutionary memory. Captain Smith commanded a company of the American Militia, which led the advance when the British troops quartered at Judge Smith's house, on the north side of Quinton's Bridge, were attacked by order of Colonels Hand and Holme. He was forced to retreat however, there being a greater number of the enemy's troops in ambuscade than his commander anticipated; but he accomplished his retreat with credit, and to the satisfaction of his superior officers. His horse was shot and killed under him during; the engagement. Washington and his wife Mary Smith had ten children — Mary Ann, Peter, Elizabeth, John P., Abner, Lucetta, Phineas, Martha, Lydia and Washington Smith. Peter Smith married Elizabeth, the daughter of James Elliott; they have issue. Samuel Smith, his son, married

Priscilla, the daughter of Samuel Kelley; she died young. His second wife was Lydia, the daughter of David and Elizabeth Finley; they had issue. (pp. 51-52)

A few Baptists settled on Oldman's creek as early as 1665; they were companions of Robert Carr. It does not appear that they had any regular meetings for a number of years after they first settled in Salem county. At a subsequent period they became members of Cohansey Church, it being at the time the nucleus [sic] around which the Baptists in West Jersey centered. It appears, by the care of the mother church, those scattering members residing on Oldman's creek and in Pilesgrove were constituted a branch of the Cohansey Church, at Daretown, in 1743. At that period there were several families from New England by the name of Reed, Elwell, Cheesman, Paullin, Wallace, Champney and Mayhew. Many of their descendants are still living in Pittsgrove at the present time, and most of them, I have been told, still adhere to the religious sect of their forefathers. Robert Kelsay was their pastor soon after the branch was organized, and continued to be until 1754. According to their record, the Baptists on Oldman's creek, in 1740, purchased a piece of ground near the head of tide water, near what in after time was known as Sculltown, for a burial ground, on which they erected a log meeting house in 1771. It has gone down, and the lot is used as a common burying ground by the neighboring inhabitants. In 1771 Pittsgrove Baptist Church became a distinct Gospel Church. The following minute made at Cohansey Church 9th of 5th month, 1771, says, "We conclude that all such of our members as shall join in . . . said intended constitution are fully dismissed from us. So, . . . recommending you to God, and the words of his grace, we . . . rest your brethren in the Faith and Fellowship of the Gospel." It was signed at their monthly meeting in behalf of the whole church by David Bowen, Clerk. They further stated that the members dismissed from Cohansey Church, who become members of Pittsgrove, were John Mayhew, Sr., William Brick, Jacob Elwell, John Dickinson, Cornelius Austin, Samuel Brick, Johanna Mayhew, Eleanor Nelson, Esther Hewes, Hannah Elwell, Matthew Aarons, Pamannah Garton, Fulida Hudson, Mathias Dickinson, Phebe Nelson, Reuhama Austin, and Rachel Brick. The church was incorporated in 1786, and John Mayhew, William Brick, William Dickinson, John Kelley, Samuel Rose, David Nichols, and Jacob Wright were made Trustees. As was the custom in the first organization of the Protestant Societies in this colony, the first Baptist meeting house in Pilesgrove was built of logs. It stood in their grave yard on the same spot where, in 1743, the frame meeting House was built. This last was of moderate size, but was a substantial structure, and remained over a century. It was sold in 1844 to the colored people for a house of worship, and the present brick house was built the same year (1844) at a cost of $2,200. They have a parsonage situated about two miles from their church, near Pole Tavern, containing, at the present time, a comfortable dwelling house, thirty acres of land, and other buildings. (pp. 412-414)

Stryker-Rodda, Kenn: *Revolutionary Census of New Jersey, an Index, Based on Rateables, of the Inhabitants of New Jersey During the Period of the American Revolution* (Cottonport, Louisiana: Polyanthos, Inc., 1972); revised edition (Lamberville, New Jersey: Hunterdon House, 1986):

1773 &1774

[COOMES]

George: Upper Penns Neck, Salem County
John: Pittsgrove, Salem County (p. 43)

[HOWARD]

Alexander: New Hanover, Burlington County
Joseph: Deerfield, Cumberland County
Mathew: Oxford, Cumberland County
Robert: Upper Penns Neck, Salem
William: Hopewell, Cumberland County (p. 76)

[CILLEY, KELLEY, KELLY]

Aaron: Springfield, Burlington County
Abraham: Willingboro, Burlington County
Arthur: Greenwich, Gloucester County
Daniel: Great Egg Harbor, Gloucester County
James: Lower Penns Neck, Salem County
James: Upper Alloways Creek, Salem County
Job: Springfield, Burlington County
John: Lower Alloways Creek, Salem County
John: Lower Penns Neck, Salem County
John (+ Shoe Maker, Thomas son): Upper Alloways Creek, Salem County
Malichi, Malica: Mannington, Salem County
Patrick: Willingboro, Burlington County
Thomas: Upper Alloways Creek, Salem County

William: Gloucester, Gloucester County
William: Hardiston, Sussex County   (p. 82)

[KILLEY, KILLY, KILLIY]

George: Pilesgrove, Salem County
Isaac: Pilesgrove, Salem County
John: Newton, Sussex County   (p. 83)

Stryker, William S.: *Official Register of the Officers and Men of New Jersey in the Revolutionary War* (Trenton, New Jersey: Wm. T. Nicholson & Co., Printers, 1872), reprinted (Baltimore, Maryland: Genealogical Publishing Company, 1967):

Thomas Cushing and Charles Sheppard in *History of the Counties of Gloucester, Salem, and Cumberland New Jersey, with Biographical Sketches of Their Prominent Citizens* note that William S. Stryker's *Official Register of the Officers and Men of New Jersey in the Revolutionary War* "is the only extensive and well-authenticated 'Record' of the kind that has been published."

Stryker, writing about his research for *Official Register of the Officers and Men of New Jersey in the Revolutionary War*, notes:

> The pension lists of the government, and the minutes of the Congress of the United States, and of the Legislature and Council of Safety of New Jersey, and all the records of the War Department, so far as they were found to relate to this State at that early period, were carefully examined. Original manuscripts, rolls of companies of Continental troops, diaries of officers, paymasters' memoranda, quartermasters' reports, treasurers' receipts, "returns" to the Commander-in-Chief, lists of soldiers paid at sundry times in Continental money, other lists of men who received notes for depreciation of said currency, — all these and various other kinds of vouchers have been most faithfully compared. (p. 7)

Stryker: "IN THE following resolutions from the *Journal of Congress* [italics added], October 9th, 1775, is the first call on New Jersey for Continental troops:"

> *Resolved*, That it be recommended to the Convention of New Jersey that they immediately raise, at the expense of the continent, *two battalions*, consisting of eight companies each, and each company of sixty-eight privates, officered with one captain, one lieutenant, one ensign, four serjeants, and four corporals.

That the privates be inlisted for one year, at the rate of five dollars per calendar month, liable to be discharged at any time on allowing them one month's pay extraordinary.

That each of the privates be allowed, instead of a bounty, one felt hat, a pair of yarn stockings, and a pair of shoes: the men to find their own arms.

That the pay of the officers, for the present, be the same as that of the officers in the present Continental Army; and in case the pay of the officers in the army is augmented, the pay of the officers in these battalions shall, in like manner, be augmented from the time of their engaging in the service.

Stryker: "A copy of the above resolutions was laid before the Provincial Congress of New Jersey, October 13th, 1775, with the following official letter of transmittal:"

Philadelphia, Oct. 12th, 1775.

Gentlemen: — Some late intelligence, laid before Congress, seems to render it absolutely necessary, for the protection of our liberties and safety of our lives, to raise several new battalions, and therefore the Congress have come into the inclosed resolutions, which I am ordered to transmit to you. The Congress have the firmest confidence that, from your experienced zeal in this great cause, you will exert your utmost endeavors to carry the said resolutions into execution with all possible expedition.

The Congress have agreed to furnish the men with a hunting-shirt, not exceeding the value of one dollar and one-third of a dollar, and a blanket, provided these can be procured; but these are not to be made part of the terms of inlistment.

I am, gentlemen,
Your most obedient humble servant,

JOHN HANDCOCK., *President*.

By order of Congress, I forward you forty-eight blank commissions for the captains and subaltern officers in the New Jersey battalions.

To the members of the Convention of New Jersey.

Stryker: "To hasten the enlistment of men for the two battalions, two hundred copies of the following advertisement were ordered to be printed:"

In Provincial Congress, held at Trenton, the 26th day of October, 1775.

WHEREAS, The Honorable Continental Congress have recommended to this Congress that there be immediately raised in this Colony, at the expense of the continent, two battalions, consisting of eight companies each, and each company to consist of sixty-eight privates, and officered with one captain, one lieutenant, one ensign, four serjeants, and four corporals, on the following conditions:

That the privates be inlisted for a year, at the rate of five dollars per calendar month, liable to be discharged at any time on allowing one month's pay extraordinary; that each of the privates be allowed, instead of a bounty, a felt hat, a pair of yarn stockings, and a pair of shoes: the men to find their own arms.

That each captain and other commissioned officer, while in the recruiting service of this continent, or on their march to join the army, shall be allowed two dollars and two-thirds of a dollar per week for their subsistence; and that the men who inlist shall, each of them, whilst in quarters, be allowed one dollar per week, and one dollar and one-third of a dollar when on their march to join the army, for the same purpose.

The form of inlistment to be in the following words:

"I, ____ ____, have this day voluntarily inlisted myself as a soldier in the American Continental Army for one year, unless sooner discharged; and do bind myself to conform in all instances to such rules and regulations as are or shall be established for the government of the said army." (pp. 9-11)

Stryker: "The authority for the organization of the Third Battalion is given in the following minute from the proceedings of Continental Congress, January 10th, 1776:"

Resolved, That another battalion be raised in New Jersey, on the same terms as the other two raised in the said Colony.

Stryker: "The Provincial Congress of New Jersey, on the 6th day of February, ordered the following notice to be published:"

PROVINCE OF NEW JERSEY,}
In Congress, February 6th, 1776.}

WHEREAS, By a resolution of the Honorable Continental Congress, a third battalion is recommended immediately to be raised in this Colony, for the service and at the expense of the United Colonies, consisting of eight companies, and each company of seventy-eight privates, and officered with one captain, two lieutenants, one ensign, four serjeants, and four corporals; which recommendation this Congress being desirous fully to comply with, do therefore resolve —

That officers of the said battalion be immediately recommended for commissions, and that the captains and subalterns be appointed and warrants issued for the inlisting the aforesaid complement of men.

Resolved, That agreeable to the recommendation of the said Honorable Continental Congress, the recruiting officer inlist none but healthy, sound, and able-bodied freemen, not under sixteen years' of age; the form of the inlistment to be in the following words:

"I, _____ _____, have this day inlisted myself as a soldier in the American Continental Army for one year, unless sooner discharged; and do bind myself to conform in all instances to such rules and regulations as are or shall be established for the government of the said army."

Resolved, That no apprentice whatsoever be inlisted within this Colony, without the consent of his master or mistress first obtained in writing; and that every person under the age of twenty-one years, inlisting himself as aforesaid, may, within twenty-four hours after their parents or guardians shall have notice of such inlistment, obtain his discharge, by refunding the money received from the recruiting officer, and returning such necessaries as may have been supplied him by the officer, or the value thereof in money.

That as to the pay and subsistence of said officers and soldiers, the same is fixed and ascertained by the said Continental Congress.

That it be recommended to the officers of said battalion to pay the strictest attention to the behaviour of the troops in quarters or on their march, that they give no reasonable cause of complaint. (pp. 18-19)

Stryker: "The *second establishment* of troops from New Jersey for the Continental Army was made by the Congress of the United Colonies, September 16th, 1776.

"The original form of the following resolutions was given in a report of the Board of War, and after being amended as given below, by the Committee of the Whole, were passed by Congress:"

Resolved, That eighty-eight battalions be inlisted as soon as possible, to serve during the present war, and that the States furnish their respective quotas in the following proportions, *viz.*:

****

New Jersey……………………..……………….….. Four battalions.

****

> That twenty dollars be given as a bounty to each non-commissioned officer and private soldier who shall inlist to serve during the present war, unless sooner discharged by Congress.
>
> That Congress make provision for granting lands . . . to the officers and soldiers who shall so engage in service, and continue therein to the close of the war, or until discharged by Congress, and to the representatives of such officers and soldiers as shall be slain by the enemy, such lands, to be provided by the United States, and whatever expense shall be necessary to procure such land; the said expense shall be paid and borne by the States in the same proportions as the other expenses of the war. . . . (p. 23)

It was also resolved:

> That the money to be given for bounties be paid by the paymaster in the department where the soldier shall inlist.
>
> That each soldier receive pay and subsistence from the time of inlistment.

Stryker: "In the minutes of Congress, October 8th, a resolution is found which provides for the giving of sundry articles of clothing in lieu of the twenty dollars bounty just referred to:"

> *Resolved*, That for the farther encouragement of the noncommissioned officers and soldiers who shall engage in the service during the war, a suit of clothes be annually given each of the said officers and soldiers, to consist, for the present year, of two linen hunting-shirts, two pair of overalls, a leathern or woolen waistcoat, with sleeves, one pair of breeches, a hat or leathern cap, two shirts, two pair of hose, and two pair of shoes, amounting, in the whole, to the value of twenty dollars, or that sum to be paid to each soldier, who shall procure those articles for himself, and produce a certificate thereof from the captain of the company to which he belongs to the paymaster of the regiment. (p. 24)

Stryker: "A new arrangement of the American Army was made by Congress, May 27th, 1778. Each battalion of infantry was to consist of nine companies, one of which was to be light infantry. Each of the field officers was to command a company; the adjutant, quartermaster, and paymaster to be taken from the line; the lieutenant of the colonel's company to have the rank of captain lieutenant. One surgeon and one surgeon's mate were added to the field and staff; one serjeant major, one quartermaster serjeant, one drum major, and one fife major made the noncommissioned staff; and six captains, one captain lieutenant, eight lieutenants, nine ensigns, twenty-seven serjeants, twenty-seven corporals, eighteen drummers and fifers, and four hundred and seventy-seven privates formed the balance of each battalion.

"The following resolution was passed by Congress, March 9th, 1779:"

> *Resolved*, That the infantry of these United States for the next campaign be composed of eighty battalions, *viz.*:
> **
> Three battalions………………………………………….. New Jersey.
> **
> That each of the said battalions consist of the number of commissioned and non-commissioned officers and privates established by an act of Congress, passed on the 27th day of May last.
>
> Whereas, Congress, by an act of January 23d last, did, among other things, authorize the Commander-in-Chief to take the most effectual measures to inlist, for the continuance of the war, new recruits in the United States, to complete the battalions to their proper complement, and, for this purpose, to grant to each new recruit who should inlist in any of the Continental battalions during the war, such a bounty as the Commander-in-Chief should think fit, but not to exceed two hundred dollars; and it being apprehended that the said provision will not answer the good purposes thereby intended —
>
> *Resolved*, That the above-recited clause of the said act of Congress be repealed, and that it be earnestly recommended to the several States to make up and complete their respective battalions to their full complement, by draughts, or in any other manner they shall think proper, and that they have their quotas of deficiencies ready to take the field, and to march to such place as the Commander-in-Chief shall direct, without delay.
>
> That a bounty of two hundred dollars, out of the Continental treasury, shall be granted to each recruit who, after the 23d day of January last, hath inlisted or shall inlist during the war; or, in case the State shall have granted as great or greater bounty, the said two hundred dollars, for every such recruit, shall be passed to the credit of the State, respectively, for whose quota he shall be raised.

Stryker: "The Legislature of New Jersey, June 9th, 1779, passed the following:"

> *An Act for recruiting, by voluntary inlistment, the three regiments of this State in the service of the United States.*
>
> WHEREAS, By the resolutions of the United States, in Congress assembled, bearing date the 9th day of March last, the several States are required to complete, by inlistments, during the war, their respective

quotas of forces in the armies of the United States; *and whereas*, it is the duty of this State to take effectual measures for complying with the said requisition, as far as the embarrassed and difficult condition thereof, in respect of the seat and operations of the war, will permit —

1. Be IT ENACTED BY THE COUNCIL AND GENERAL ASSEMBLY, *and it is hereby enacted by the authority of the same*, That three hundred and sixty-five able-bodied and effective volunteers be inlisted into the three regiments of this State in the service of the United States, to continue in the said service during the present war with Great Britain.

2. *And be it enacted by the authority aforesaid*, That the Governor or Commander-in-Chief of this State, for the time being, do, as soon as may be after the passing of this act, make application to the Commander-in-Chief of the armies of the United States for such and so many officers as he, the said Governor, may think expedient to be sent into different and convenient parts of the State, for the purpose of inlisting and forwarding the recruits which may engage in the service on the terms in this act held forth.

3. *And be it enacted by the authority aforesaid*, That there shall be allowed to each and every officer who shall be so employed in the recruiting service, and to each and every officer of the militia of this State, for every able-bodied effective recruit which he shall inlist or procure to be inlisted as aforesaid, the sum of twenty dollars, to be paid by the paymaster of the militia of the county where such recruit is inlisted, on producing a certificate from any justice of the peace, setting forth that the person so said to be inlisted hath been duly sworn or affirmed before him to serve as a soldier in one of the three regiments of this State in the service of the United States, for the term hereinabove mentioned, and likewise a certificate from some one of the officers hereinafter appointed to muster such recruits, setting forth that such recruit hath been by him mustered and approved; and where the said soldier hath been inlisted by a militia, officer, a receipt from some one of the officers of the said three regiments, setting forth that he hath received such recruit into the service.

4. *And be it enacted*, That exclusive of the sum of two hundred dollars and the bounty of clothing and lands given by the resolutions of Congress, there be paid to each able-bodied recruit, or his order, by the paymaster of the militia of the county where such recruit is inlisted, on a certificate from any justice of the peace, setting forth that the claimant hath been duly sworn or affirmed before him to serve as a soldier in one of the three regiments of this State, for the term herein above mentioned, and likewise a certificate from some one of the officers hereinafter appointed to muster such recruits, setting forth that such volunteer hath been by him mustered and approved.

5. *And it is hereby further enacted*, That each and every recruit, inlisted as aforesaid, shall be entitled to the pay and emoluments allowed to such as belong to the troops of this State, from the day of his inlistment inclusively, and shall at his election, enter into any company of any of the three regiments of this State, provided such company be not already full.

6. *And be it enacted by the authority aforesaid*, That any field officer in the service of the United States, or any field officer of the militia in the county in which such recruit shall be inlisted, shall be, and they hereby are authorized and empowered to muster any recruit so as above inlisted, and to grant a certificate as above directed of his having been so by them mustered and approved.

7. *And be it enacted*, That the paymasters of the militia, respectively, who may make any payments by virtue of this act, shall, on producing separate accounts and vouchers thereof, be allowed the same in their settlement with the State.

8. *And be it further enacted by the authority aforesaid*, That if any recruiting officer or other person, from and after the date hereof, shall presume to inlist any person in any of the counties of this State to serve in any regiment, troop, or company belonging to any of the neighbouring States, or in any other troops whatever, otherwise than in the regiments belonging to this State, or in such troops or companies as have been or shall be assigned as the quota of this State, in the service of the United States, or shall detain, convey away, or refuse to release any person so inlisted, contrary to the intent and meaning hereof, such recruiting officer or other person so offending, shall, for every such offence, forfeit and pay the sum of five hundred pounds, to be recovered in any court of record where the same may be cognizable within this State, by any person that will sue for the same; one-half to the prosecutor, and the other half to and for the use of the State.

Stryker: "On the 9th day of February, 1780, Congress called upon New Jersey for sixteen hundred and twenty men to fill up the 'Jersey Line' for the campaign of that year.

"The deficiency then existing in the three regiments was ordered to be filled by the Legislature, March nth, 1780. The act passed that date 'for completing the quota of troops belonging to this State' differs but little from that of the previous year, just recited. The former act was repealed, and a substitute passed. Four hundred volunteers were called for, and the bounty was raised to one thousand dollars, exclusive of the Continental bounty and emoluments. Two hundred dollars premium was ordered paid to each officer who procured a recruit. . . ." (pp. 43-46)

Stryker: "The act of the Legislature, March 11th, not 'fully answering the purposes thereby intended,' was amended June 14th, 1780, by calling for six hundred and twenty-four men to be raised in the several counties of this State, to continue in service until the 1st day of January, 1781, they to be raised in the following proportion:

"Bergen, thirty-three men; Essex, forty-five; Middlesex, forty-seven; Monmouth, sixty; Somerset, fifty-four; Burlington, sixty-five; Gloucester, fifty- one; Salem, fifty-one; Cape May, thirteen; Hunterdon, eighty-four; Morris, fifty-one; Cumberland, thirty; Sussex, fifty.

"On the 25th day of June, 1781, it was found necessary by the Legislature to adopt still more effectual means of completing the quota of troops. The deficit at this date was four hundred and fifty men. Recruiting officers were then appointed in the several counties. . . ." (p. 47)

Stryker: "The bounty then authorized to be paid to each recruit was twelve pounds in gold or silver. One shilling in gold, silver, or copper coin was allowed him per day, in lieu of subsistence, until he was mustered and marched to join his regiment. Thirty shillings in coin were given each recruiting officer who procured a man able to pass muster. These volunteers, unlike those embodied for the Continental troops, in 1780, were engaged to serve during the war.

"In the summer of 1780, a committee of Congress was appointed to make the 'arrangement' for the officers of the First, Second, and Third Regiments of this State. It appears that many of the line officers of the second establishment, rather than be retired as supernumeraries, accepted assignment to duty in a lower grade than that theretofore held by them.

"The joint meeting of the Legislature confirmed the arrangement
September 26th, 1780." (p. 48)

Stryker: "On the 21st of September, 1781, the three regiments landed on James river, Virginia, about five miles from Williamsburgh, and were employed in all the labor of the siege, and were present at the surrender of Yorktown, on the 19th of October.

"The news of the cessation of hostilities was announced in the camp of the brigade, April 19th, 1783, and the 'Jersey Line' were discharged November 3d, 1783.

"During the summer and fall of 1776, soldiers of this State, as officers or enlisted men, began to join organizations raised directly by authority of Congress, or those of the Continental Line of other States." (pp. 55-56)

"Privates in the Official Roster of the Continental Troops"

Kelly, Bartholemew. Captain Martin's company, Fourth Battalion, Second Establishment.
Kelly, Daniel. Third Battalion, First Establishment; Captain Ross' company, Third Battalion, Second Establishment.
Kelly, David. "Spencer's Regiment," Continental Army.
Kelly, Jacob. Captain M' Mires' company. First Battalion, First Establishment; discharged January 1st, 1776.
Kelly, Jared.

The Kellys of Kingsclear

Kelly, John. Captain Sparks' company, Second Battalion, Second Establishment; also militia.
Kelly, Matthew. Discharged April 10th, 1783 — disability.
Kelly, Patrick. Captain Mitchell's company, Fourth Battalion, Second Establishment; also militia.
Kelly, Patrick. First Battalion, Second Establishment; Captain Lloyd's company, Second Regiment. (p. 225)

Kelty, Michael. Captain Anderson's company, Third Battalion, Second Establishment; also militia.
Kelty, William. Captain Anderson's company, Third Battalion, Second Establishment; also militia. (p. 226)

"Militia in Salem County"

Second Battalion (or Eastern Battalion): John Kelley Captain, Second Major. (p. 346)

"Majors in the Official Roster of the State Troops and Militia"

Kelly, John. Captain, Second Battalion, Salem; Second Major, ditto. (p. 367)

"Serjeants in the Official Roster of the State Troops and Militia"

Kelly, Carpenter. Private, Bergen; Serjeant, ditto. (p. 467)

"Privates in the Official Roster of the State Troops and Militia"

Kelly, Abraham.
Kelly, Abram. Middlesex.
Kelly, David. Captain Jacob Ten Eyck's company, First Battalion, Somerset.
Kelly, David. Burlington.
Kelly, George. Morris.
Kelly, Jeremiah[.] Essex.
Kelly, Jesse. Middlesex.
Kelly, John. Somerset.
Kelly, John. First Battalion, Salem; also State troops; also Continental Army.
Kelly, Oliver. Matross, "Captain Neil's Eastern Company, Artillery," State troops; discharged January 1st, 1777.
Kelly, Patrick. Third Battalion, Gloucester; also Continental Army.
Kelly, Samuel. Somerset.
Kelly, Uriah. Third Battalion, Gloucester.
Kelly, William. Gloucester; also Continental Army. (p. 652)

Long, Ansey. Third Battalion, Gloucester; also Colonel Somers' battalion, State troops.
Long, Cornelius. Somerset.
Long, George. Hunterdon; also State troops; also Continental Army.
Long, Henry. Captain Maxwell's company, Second Regiment, Hunterdon.
Long, John. Captain Jacob Ten Eyck's company. First Battalion, Somerset.
Long, Moses. Third Battalion, Gloucester; also Colonel Somers' battalion, State troops.
Long, Silas. Gloucester. (p. 670)

APPENDIX Q

Howard Family in the Southern Campaign

Clark, Murtie June: *Loyalists in the Southern Campaign of the Revolutionary War* (3 Volumes) (Baltimore, Maryland: Genealogical Publishing Company, Inc., 1981):

Clark documents that a Private John Howard is listed under "Pay Abstract N[umbe]r 71, Lieut[enant] Colonel Zachariah Gibbs' Regiment, Spartan Militia, Ninety Six Brigade, Soldier's Certification, for those who came with Lieut[enant John H. Cruger to Orangeburgh, S[outh] C[arolina], and were omitted from a previous abstract; these men also served with Major Ferguson. (Abs[tract] N[umbe]r 15 in books of Captain John Cunningham, late Pay Master of Militia, and was in part paid by him), six-months pay, 13 Jun[e] – 14 Dec[ember] 1780. . . ." (Volume I, p. 277) In an unnumbered abstract, a Private John Howard is listed as "now present at Dorchester . . . [and as having] served with Colonel Ferguson, Lieutenant Samuel Young's Company, six-months pay, 14 Jun[e] – 13 Dec[ember]. . . ." (Volume I, p. 281) Private John Howard is listed in "Pay Abstract N[umbe]r _, Lieut[enant] Colonel Zachariah Gibbs' Regiment, Spartan Militia, Ninety Six Brigade, for duty under the command of Lord Rawdon, for the period 1 Jun[e] – 11 Jul[y] 1781. . . ." (Volume 1, p. 282) (Clark, Murtie, June: *Loyalists in the Southern Campaign of the Revolutionary War,* Copyright 1981 by Genealogical Publishing Co., Inc., Baltimore, Maryland.)

Private Michael Howard, in Clark's work, is listed on the "Muster Roll, Captain Thomas Hunloke's Company, Third Battalion, New Jersey Volunteers, Savannah, G[eorgia], 29 November 1779. . . ." (Volume III, p. 158) Private Michael Howard also appears on the "Muster Roll, Captain Thomas Hunloke's Company, Third Battalion, New Jersey Volunteers, Ninety-Six, S[outh] C[arolina], 24 February 1781 to 24 April 1781, 60 days inclusive. . . ." (Volume III, p. 159) Private Michael Howard also is listed on the muster roll for the same company and at the same location for the period "25 April 1781 to 24 June 1781, 61 days inclusive. . . ." (Volume III, p. 160) Private Michael Howard once again appears on the "Muster Roll, Captain Thomas Hunloke's Company, Third Battalion, New Jersey Volunteers, Charlestown, S[outh] C[arolina], 25 October 1781 to 24 December 1781, 61 days inclusive. . . ." (Volume III, p. 160) Then Private Michael Howard is listed as "on command" on the "Muster Roll, Captain Thomas Hunloke's Company, Second Battalion, New Jersey Volunteers, Charlestown, S[outh] C[arolina], 25 April 1782 to 24 June 1782, 61 days inclusive. . . ." (Volume III, p. 161) (Clark, Murtie, June: *Loyalists in the Southern Campaign of the Revolutionary War,* Copyright 1981 by Genealogical Publishing Co., Inc., Baltimore, Maryland.)

Clark notes a Private Thomas Howard as a "prisoner with rebels" on the "Muster Roll, Captain James Galbreath's Company, First Battalion, Brigadier General Oliver Delancey's Brigade, Savannah, G[eorgia], 20 November 1779. . . ." (Volume III, p. 15)

(Clark, Murtie, June: *Loyalists in the Southern Campaign of the Revolutionary War,* Copyright 1981 by Genealogical Publishing Co., Inc., Baltimore, Maryland.)

APPENDIX R

Kellys Serving in the Southern Campaign

Clark, Murtie June: *Loyalists in the Southern Campaign of the Revolutionary War* (3 Volumes) (Baltimore, Maryland: Genealogical Publishing Company, Inc., 1981):

It is possible that Private Anthony Kelly appearing in the muster rolls of the Guides and Pioneers and Private Patrick Kelley and a Sergeant Benjamin Kelley appearing in the muster rolls of the Queens Rangers are related to John Kelly. Although a Private Barnabas/Barnabis/Barnabus/Barny Kelly appears in the Muster Rolls of the Queens Rangers, only Private Barnabas Kelly serving in the Pennsylvania Loyalists is a strong contender for connection to the John Kelly family.

Clark documents that in the "MUSTER ROLL of Captain (Thomas) Golden's Company in the First Battalion of Pennsylvania Loyalists Commanded by Lieutenant Colonel (William) Allen, Nov[ember] 27, 1777. . . ." Private Barnabas Kelly "deserted Nov[ember] 24, 1777. . . ." (Volume II, p. 91) (Clark, Murtie, June: *Loyalists in the Southern Campaign of the Revolutionary War,* Copyright 1981 by Genealogical Publishing Co., Inc., Baltimore, Maryland.)

Clark writes that "The Queen's Rangers were raised in New York and Connecticut and combined with the Queen's Own Loyal Virginia Regiment in 1776. They were in the 1777 campaigns in Philadelphia, Brandywine, and Germantown, and later fought at New York and Monmouth. In 1781 they were sent to Virginia and surrendered at Yorktown." (Volume II p. XVII) (Clark, Murtie, June: *Loyalists in the Southern Campaign of the Revolutionary War,* Copyright 1981 by Genealogical Publishing Co., Inc., Baltimore, Maryland.)

Private Barnabas Kelly, in Clark's documentation, is listed in the "MUSTER ROLL of Captain (Thomas) Golden's Company of the First Battalion of Pennsylvania Loyalists Commanded by Lieut[enant] Colonel William Allen, 1778. . . ." (Volume II, p. 92) (Clark, Murtie, June: *Loyalists in the Southern Campaign of the Revolutionary War,* Copyright 1981 by Genealogical Publishing Co., Inc., Baltimore, Maryland.)

Clark's research notes that Private Barnabas Kelly appears on the "MUSTER ROLL of Captain Thomas Golden's Company of the First Battalion of Pennsylvania Loyalists Commanded by Lieut[enant] Colonel William Allen, August 1778. . . ." (Volume II, p. 94) (Clark, Murtie, June: *Loyalists in the Southern Campaign of the Revolutionary War,* Copyright 1981 by Genealogical Publishing Co., Inc., Baltimore, Maryland.)

Clark lists a Private Nathaniel Kelly on the "Muster Roll, Captain Charles Harrison's Company, Third Battalion, New Jersey Volunteers, Savannah, G[eorgia], 29 November 1779. . . ." as having "died 6 Feb[ruary] 1779. . . ." (Volume III, p. 152) (Clark, Murtie, June: *Loyalists in the Southern Campaign of the Revolutionary War,* Copyright 1981 by Genealogical Publishing Co., Inc., Baltimore, Maryland.)

Private Neal Kelly is found on the "Muster Roll, Lieut[enant] Colonel John Harris Cruger's Company, First Battalion, Brigadier General Oliver Delancey's Brigade, Savannah, G[eorgia], 20 November 1779. . . ." as having "died 20 Sept[ember] 1779. . . ." (Volume III, p. 1) (Clark, Murtie, June: *Loyalists in the Southern Campaign of the Revolutionary War,* Copyright 1981 by Genealogical Publishing Co., Inc., Baltimore, Maryland.)

Clark notes that Private Dennis Kelly on the "Muster Roll, Major Thomas Bowden's Company, Second Battalion, Brigadier General Oliver Delancey's Brigade, Savannah, G[eorgia], 28 November 1779. . . [is listed as] sick, Regimental Hosp[ital]. . . ." (Volume III, p. 39) A Private Dennis Kelley, who may not be the same as the Dennis Kelly listed above, is listed in the "Muster Roll, Captain William Johnston's Company, New York Volunteers, Savannah G[eorgia], 29 November 1779. . . ." (Volume III, p. 198) (Clark, Murtie, June: *Loyalists in the Southern Campaign of the Revolutionary War,* Copyright 1981 by Genealogical Publishing Co., Inc., Baltimore, Maryland.)

Sergeant Daniel Kelly, appearing on the "Muster Roll, Captain Thomas Hunloke's Company, Third Battalion, New Jersey Volunteers, Savannah, G[eorgia], 29 November 1779. . . .[,] transferred to the light infantry, 25 Oct[ober]. . . ." (Volume III, p. 158) (Clark, Murtie, June: *Loyalists in the Southern Campaign of the Revolutionary War,* Copyright 1981 by Genealogical Publishing Co., Inc., Baltimore, Maryland.)

Clark notes that Corporal Daniel Kelly, listed on the "Muster Roll, Captain Barent Roorback's Company, First Battalion, Brigadier General Oliver Delancey's Brigade, Savannah, G[eorgia], 20 November 1779. . .[,] died 15 November 1779. . . ." (Volume III, p. 26) Sergeant Daniel Kelly appears on the "Muster Roll Peter Campbell's Company, Third Battalion, New Jersey Volunteers, Savannah, G[eorgia], 29 November 1779. . . ." (Volume III, p. 140) (Clark, Murtie, June: *Loyalists in the Southern Campaign of the Revolutionary War,* Copyright 1981 by Genealogical Publishing Co., Inc., Baltimore, Maryland.)

A Private Kuen Kelley is listed on the "Muster Roll, Captain James Raymond's Company, First Battalion, Brigadier General Oliver Delancy's Brigade, Savannah G[eorgia], 20 November 1779. . . ." (Volume III, p. 25) (Clark, Murtie, June: *Loyalists in the Southern Campaign of the Revolutionary War,* Copyright 1981 by Genealogical Publishing Co., Inc., Baltimore, Maryland.)

Private George Kelly, on the "Muster Roll, Captain Thomas William Moore's Company, Second Battalion, Brigadier General Oliver Delancey's Brigade, Savannah, G[eorgia], 29 November 1779. . . [is listed as] sick, Regimental Hosp[ital]. . . ." (Volume III, p. 58) (Clark, Murtie, June: *Loyalists in the Southern Campaign of the Revolutionary War,* Copyright 1981 by Genealogical Publishing Co., Inc., Baltimore, Maryland.)

Clark notes a Private David Kelly on the "Muster Roll, Captain Norman McLeod's Company, Provincial Light Infantry, Second Battalion, New Jersey Volunteers, High Hills of Santee, S[outh] C[arolina], 24 February 1781 to 24 April 1781, 60 days incl[usive]. . . ." (Volume III, p. 259) Clark documents that in the same company and location in the muster roll for "25 October 1781 to 24 December 1781, 60 days incl[usive]. . . . [that Private David Kelly] died, 25 Oct[ober] 1781. . . ." (Volume III, p. 260) (Clark, Murtie, June: *Loyalists in the Southern Campaign of the Revolutionary War,* Copyright 1981 by Genealogical Publishing Co., Inc., Baltimore, Maryland.)

Private Michael Kelly's name appears on the "Muster Roll, Lieut[enant] Colonel Stephen Delancey's Company, Second Battalion, Brigadier General Oliver Delancey's Brigade, Savannah, G[eorgia], 29 November 1779. . . ." (Volume III, p. 35) Clark notes that Private Michael Kelly on the "Muster Roll, Captain Joseph Lee's Company, Second Battalion, New Jersey Volunteers, Charlestown, S[outh] C[arolina]. 25 April 1782 to 24 June 1782, 61 days inclusive. . . . enlisted 30 Mar[ch]. . . ." (Volume III, p. 166) Once again Clark notes that a Private Michael Kelley appears on the "Muster Roll, Captain Joseph Lee's Company, Second Battalion, New Jersey Volunteers, Hallett's Cove, January 25, 1783. . . ." (Volume III, p. 167) (Clark, Murtie, June: *Loyalists in the Southern Campaign of the Revolutionary War,* Copyright 1981 by Genealogical Publishing Co., Inc., Baltimore, Maryland.)

Drummer Neal Kelly appears on the "Muster Roll, Captain Gilbert Willett's Company, Provincial Light Infantry, Third Battalion, Brigadier General Delancey's Brigade, 24 February 1781 to 24 April 1781, 60 days inclusive. . . ." (Volume III, p. 262) Drummer Neal Kelly's name appears on the muster roll for the same company and location for the period "25 April 1781 to 24 June 1781, 61 days inclusive. . . ." (Volume III, p. 263) Then a Bugler Neal Kelly appears on the "Muster Roll, Captain Gilbert Willett's Company, Provincial Light Infantry, First Battalion, New Jersey Volunteers, Quarter House, S[outh] C[arolina], 25 October 1781 to 24 December 1781, 61 days. . . ." (Volume III, p. 264) A Private Neal Kelly turns up "on command." on the "Muster Roll, Lieut[enant] Colonel John Harris Cruger's Company, First Battalion, Brigadier General Oliver Delancey's Brigade, Charlestown, 25 April 1782 to 24 June 1782, 61 days inclusive. . . ." (Volume III, p. 3) (Clark, Murtie, June: *Loyalists in the Southern Campaign of the Revolutionary War,* Copyright 1981 by Genealogical Publishing Co., Inc., Baltimore, Maryland.)

Clark lists a Private Patrick Kelly on the "Muster Roll, Captain Isaac Atwood's Company, King's American Regiment, Georgetown, S[outh] C[arolina], 24 February 1781 to 24 April 1781, 60 days inclusive. . . ." (Volume III, p. 82) Private Patrick Kelly appears on the "Muster Roll, Captain Isaac Atwood's Company, King's American Regiment, Savannah, G[eorgia], 25 April 1781 to 24 June 1781, 61 days inclusive. . . ." (Volume III, p. 84) Clark notes a Private Patrick Kelly on the "Muster Roll, Lieut[enant] Colonel George Campbell's Company, King's American Regiment, Savannah, G[eorgia] 25 October 1781 to 24 December 1781, 61 days inclusive. . . ." (Volume III, p. 72) Private Patrick Kelly turns up on the "Muster Roll, Lieut[enant] Colonel George Campbell's Company, King's American Regiment, Savannah, G[eorgia] 25 April 1782 to 24 June 1782, 61 days inclusive. . . ." (Volume III, p. 73) (Clark, Murtie, June: *Loyalists in the Southern Campaign of the Revolutionary War,* Copyright 1981 by Genealogical Publishing Co., Inc., Baltimore, Maryland.)

Clark: "Colonel Edmund Fanning raised the King's American Regiment in New York in 1776. After service in the North they were sent into Virginia and afterwards were transferred to Charleston and Savannah where they took part in many of the operations in the Southern theater. In 1783 they went to Canada where they were disbanded." (Volume III, p. XV) (Clark, Murtie, June: *Loyalists in the Southern Campaign of the Revolutionary War,* Copyright 1981 by Genealogical Publishing Co., Inc., Baltimore, Maryland.)

A Sergeant William Kelly appears in the Muster Rolls of the Volunteers of Ireland. Clark notes that "The Volunteers of Ireland were raised in Philadelphia in 1777 and severed with the army in New York until December 1779, when they were ordered to Charleston. They served in the South until December 1782, when they returned to New York. They were evacuated to England in 1783." (Volume III, p. xvi) (Clark, Murtie, June: *Loyalists in the Southern Campaign of the Revolutionary War,* Copyright 1981 by Genealogical Publishing Co., Inc., Baltimore, Maryland.) Since William Kelly, presumably the brother of John, came to New Brunswick with the New Jersey Volunteers, it is unlikely that he is the William who served in the Volunteers of Ireland.

APPENDIX S

Hayward Family Material

New Brunswick Land Petitions: Original Series, York County, 1783-1918 (RS108) (Microfilm: F1024)

Hayward, George

Personally appeared George Hayward inhabitant of the County of Sunbury and made Oath that he has been a settler on the River S^t. John ever since the year 1763. That he is well acquainted with the situation of the lands at aforesaid known by the name of S^t. Anne.

That from the present bound of the Town Plott at that place, southerly to Mill Creek, there has never been since that time a building of any kind erected till the reduced Army came to this Country in the year 1783. nor was there any land cleared on the before mentioned tract or bound since the year 1763. except removing for the convenience of cutting Hay such logs as have floated on the Intervale, which was before cleared, or the young growth of Alders but no Standing Timber. —

Signed Geo Hayward

Sworn before me this
5th. of July 1784.
Signed Daniel Lyman
     Justice of the Peace.

A true Copy of the Original
Monson Hoyt

[verso]

In pofsefsion of L^t. Campbell
42^d. Reg^t.

New Brunswick Land Petitions: Original Series, Sunbury County, 1783-1918 (RS108) (Microfilm: F1034)

216

To his Excellency Thos. Carleton Esqr. Lieut^t. Governor & Commander in Chief for the Province of New Brunswick &c. &c.

The Memorial of Robert Smyth
Humbly Sheweth

That your Memorialist has for valuable Consideration Sold to George Howard the Lot of Land your Excellency was pleased to Afsign him on the Oromocto. your Memorialist therefore Prays your Excellency to order that the Grant may be made out in the Name of the Said George Howard & your Memorialist as in duty bound will ever Pray

October 6th. 1787 —   Robert Smyth

[*verso*]

Robert Smyth
asks that the Lands
afsigned him on the
Oromocto may be granted
to George Howard —

/In Council 25th. October 1787

Complied with.

6th. Octr. 1787

New Brunswick Land Petitions: Original Series, Sunbury County, 1783-1918 (RS108) (Microfilm: F1035)

234

To his Excellency Thomas Carleton Esqr. Lieutenant Governor and Commander in Chief of the Province of New Brunswick &^{c}. &^{c} &^{c}

May it pleafe your Excellency
the Memorial of George Hayward
            Humbly Sheweth

That in the year 1763 your Memorialift came with his Family from Great Britain to Nova Soctia in order to Become a Settler of that province he applied to the Board of Trade; who gave him a letter of Recommendation to Receive Five Hundred Acres of land where he Should like, the Same Being Vacant and more According as he Should improve or his family want to improve your Memorialift came to the River S^t. Johns But not Being in Circumstances to go on a New farm where he Could find it Vacant he has until he was able By his care and Induftry to purchafe and never afked for any lands your Memorialift now having purchafed a piece of land on the Oromocto at the French Lake where he is Building a Houfe and Moving his family and Intends to ufe his Endevours to Make a Good Settlement, Your Memorialift having two Sons young Men; and their Being two Vacant Lotts N^o. Sixteen and Seventeen that Lays adjoining the Land your Memorialift is Now improving, your Memorialist Humbly afketh that if it May pleafe your Excellency in the Wifdom of your Counfil to Grant the two Vacant Lotts to your Memorialift or to his two Sons he will Endeavour to Improve it and as in Duty Bound will Ever pray — &c.

Lincoln aug^t. [*sic*] 20$^{\underline{th}}$. 1788

[*verso*]

George Hayward
20th. Aug. 1788
asks Lots N°. 16 & 17.
on the Oromocto.

    To His Excellency
In Council 5th. Sep^t.   Thomas Carleton Esqr.

Comply^d. with on condition   Lieut Governor and Commander in Chief
of actual Settlement.   of the Province of New Brunswick &c. &c. &c.

New Brunswick Land Petitions: Original Series, Sunbury County, 1783-1918 (RS108) (Microfilm: F1039)

To His Excellency Thomas Carleton Esquire, Lieutenant Governor and Commander in Chief in and over the Province of New Brunswick &c. &c. &c.

The Memorial of the Members of the Church of England, Inhabitants of the County of Sunbury moft humbly Sheweth,

That a part of your Memorialists having formerly Petitioned your Excellency for a Grant upon vacant Lot Nº. 15 in Fheffield as a Glibe for that Parish, to which your Excellency was pleased in Council to anfwer that the said Petition "could not be complied with" and your Memorialifts having fince been informed that a Petition has been Prefented to your Excellency on the part of a Number of Difenters claiming the said Lot as a Glibe allotted for their use by the Government of Nova Scotia prier to the eftablishment of this Province and aferting among other things that the Members of the Eftablished Church in that Parish men few in Number, and otherwise unworthy of Notice —

And as your Memorialifts are able to disprove that and many other things aferted in said Petition, and to shew some important facts refpecting the Premifes, not fet forth in their former Memorial they humbly pray that your Excellency may be pleased to direct the whole to be reconfidered and when

[2]

when your Excellency is informed that from Seventy to a hundred persons regularly or conftantly attend the Church in Fheffield, it is humbly hoped that your Excellency will not give credit to that afertion, but be entreated by the humble prayer of your Excellency's Memorialists to put the Lot out of all farther dispute by granting of it for the Support it being the only ungranted Lot in the said Parish of the Religion of the eftablished Church — And your Excellency's Memorialists as in duty bound shall ever pray —

[The following appear in a long list of names accompanying this petition:]

John Abel
Wm Kelley
John Hayward

[verso]

1793

Application on behalf
of the Parish of Sheffield
for the ungranted Lot
Nº. 15 in that Parish
and praying the whole
question to be reconsidered.

19th. June 1793

New Brunswick Land Petitions: Original Series, Sunbury County, 1783-1918 (RS108) (1798-1801) (Microfilm: F1041)

390

To his Excellency Thomas Carleton Esquire Lieutenant Governor and Commander in Chief of the Province of New Brunswick &c &c &c

The Memorial of William Car and Benin Foster both of Burton in the County of Sunbury humbly shews that your memorialist Car has received a grant from Government of about seventy acres of land in Burton and finds the same infufficient for a farm and cannot support his family upon it — your memorialist Foster has never received a grant of any land, and has a large family

your memorialists therefore humbly pray your Excellency to grant to each of them five hundred acres of Land on the South side of the Oromocto of the back lands in or near the rear of lands granted to George Hayward

on

[2]

on which, if your Excellency see fit to grant the same, your memorialists will immediately settle and improve and your memorialists as in duty bound shall ever pray

February 1st 1799

[3]

Nathanial Churchill Junr., Samuel Churchill — and Jonathan Shaw — ask lands in the same tract as within described, in the proportion of five hundred acres to each, and on the consideration of immediate settlement.

February 1st
1799.

[verso]

Car and Foster
Memorial

Car. Foster & Churchill
ask lands in the rear
of the Tract granted
to Hayward on the
Oromocto. This appears
to be the tract applied
for in 1802 by Benjn Rockwell
and afsociates in which the
Memorialists are included

12th. March 1799

New Brunswick, County Deed Registry Books, 1780-1930, for Sunbury (1786-1791), Volume B4, pp. 285 - 290

This Indenture made the tenth day of April in the year of our Lord one thousand seven hundred and eighty seven Between Arthur Goold of Halifax in the Province of Nova Scotia Esquire and Boadecia his Wife of the one part and George Howard of Lincoln in the County of Sunbury and Province of New Brunswick, Yeoman, of the other part Witnefseth that for and in consideration of the Sum of seventy Pounds lawful Money of the Province of New Brunswick a

-286-

aforesaid to the said Arthur Goold in hand paid by the faid George Howard before the ensealing and delivery of these Presents (which is hereby and by the said Arthur Goold acknowledged and declared to be in full satisfaction for the absolute purchase of the fee-simple and inheritance of the Lot of Land and Premises with the Appurtenances herein after mentioned to be bargained and fold) the Receipt whereof the faid Arthur Goold doth hereby acknowledge and thereof and of every part thereof doth clearly exonerate acquit and discharge the faid George Howad his Heirs Executors Administrators and Afsigns and every of them for ever by these Presents, He the said Arthur Goold hath granted bargained sold aliened enfeoffed released conveyed and confirmed and by these Presents Doth grant bargain sell aleine enfeoff release convey and confirm unto the said George Howard his Heirs and Afsigns for ever All that certain Lot or Tract of Land Known by Lot Number five abutted and bounded as described in a Lease thereof made by the said Arthur Goold to the faid George Howard containing five hundred Acres more or lefs being part of three thousand Acres granted by Government to the said Arthur Goold on the South-Weft Side of the River St. John now in the Township of Lincoln County of Sunbury and Province of New Brunswick aforesaid (Reference being had to the said Grand and Lease may more fully appear) with the

-287-

Buidlings Improvements Rights Members and Appurtenances whatsoever to the faid Lot or Tract of Land belonging and the Reversion and Reversions Remainder and Remainders Rents Ifsuses and Profits of all and singular the faid hereby bargained and sold Lands and Premises and every part and parcel thereof and all the Eftate Right Title Intereft Property Claim and Demand whatsoever of him the faid Arthur Goold in to or out of the faid hereby bargained and sold Lands and Premises and every or any part thereof to have and to hold the said Tract or Lot of Land and Premises herein before mentioned and hereby bargained and sold or meant mentioned or intended so to be with their and every of their Appurtenances unto the said George Howard his Heirs and Afsigns to the only proper use and Behoof ~~of the said~~ of the said George Howard his Heirs and Afsigns forever and the said Arthur Goold for himself his Heirs Executors and Administrators and for every of them Doth covenant and grant to and with the said George Howard his Heirs Executors and Administrators and to and with every of them by these Presents that he the said Arthur Goold and his Heirs the said Lot or Tract of Land and Appurtenances hereby sold unto the said George Howard his Heirs and Afsigns against him the said Arthur Goold and his Heirs and against all and

-288-

every person and persons whatsoever shall and will warrant for ever defend by these Presents and that free and clear and freely and clearly acquitted exonerated and discharged of and from all and all manner of Incumberances whatsoever, he the said George Howard his Heirs or Afsigns doing executing fulfilling and performing all and every Article Matter and Thing whatsoever respecting the said Lot of Land hereby sold and released which he the said Arthur Goold his Heirs or Afsigns for concerning or refpecting the said Lot of Land in and by the said herein before mentioned Grant is or are obliged to do execute fulfill and perform any thing herein contained to the contrary thereof in any wise Notwithstanding. And the said Boadecia Goold for the consideration aforesaid and for divers other good Causes and considerations her hereunto moving Hath remised released and for ever quit claimed and by these Presents Doth remise release and for ever quit claim unto the said George Howard his Heirs and Afsigns all and all manner of Dower and Right and Title of Dower whatsoever which the said Boadecia Goold now hath may might should or of Right ought to have of in and to the said Lot or Tract of Land with its Appurtenances hereby sold and of in or to any part or parcel thereof so that she the said Boadecia Goold nor any other for her any manner of Dower Right or Title of Dower of or in the said Lot of Land or any part or

-289-

or parcel thereof at any time hereafter shall or may have or claim or prosecute against the said George Howard his Heirs or Afsigns or any of them but of and from the fame shall be utterly barred and forever excluded by these Presents — In Witnefs whereof the said Parties to these Presents have hereunto set their hands and feals the day and year first written ./.

Signed Sealed and Delivered}   Ar. Goold {LS}
in the Presence of us   }

(the wards "of the River St. John now"}
first interviewed between the 29th & 30th   }   Boadicea Goold {LS}
Lines of the first Page) —

I's. Defchamps {LS}
Char Lyons — —

Received the Day and Year first before written of and from the within named George Howard the sum of Seventy Pounds Currency being the Consideration Money within mentioned to be paid by him to me ./.

Witnefs Present
I's. Deschamps   Ar. Goold —
Char Lyons —

Nova Scotia. Before me Isaac Deschamps Esqr. one of the Justices of his Majesty's Supreme Court for the Province of Nova Scotia appeared Arthur Goold Esqr. & Boadicia his Wife, who acknowledges

-290-

the foregoing to be their act and Deed and the said Boadicia Goold being also examined feparately did acknowledge, that she figned the fame freely and voluntarily and not thro fear or other undue influence of her said husband, and that fhe doth release all claim of Dower or Right whatsoever in the Premises thereby conveyed —

Halifax April 12th. 1787 — Is. Deschamps —

By John Parr Esqr. Lieutenant Governor & Commander in Chief of His Majesty's Province of Nova Scotia &: These are to certify that Isaac Deschamps Esqr. is one of the Justices of His Majesty's Supreme Court of this Province & that full faith & Credit is & ought be given to his Acts as fuch — —

Given under my Hand & Seal at Halifax this 14th. day of April 1787 in the twenty seventh year of his Majesty's Reign — —
No.173 —   J Parr —

Received & entered the 3d Day of March 1789 by me
                                                         Wm Hubbord, Regester

New Brunswick, County Deed Registry Books, 1780-1930, for Sunbury (1786-1791), Volume B4, pp. 426 - 429

This Indenture made the fourth day of November in the year of our Lord one thousand seven hundred and eighty nine Between James Simonds of the Town or Parish of Portland in the County of Saint John in the Province of New Brunswick Esquire of the one part and William Baker and George Hayward of the County of Sunbury of the same Province farmers of the other part Whereas the said James Simonds did by his deed bearing date the twenty fourth day of March in the year of our Lord one thousand seven hundred and seventy nine for the good and valuable Consideration therein mentioned grant bargain sell release and convey unto the said William Baker and George Hayward their Heirs and Afsigns forever all that certain tract or parcel of Land situate lying and being at a place called Marsisanies [Spelling?] on the South Weft Side of the River Saint John in the said County of Sunbury, abutted and bounded as follows that is to say beginning at the North Corner boundary of Jonathan Harts Land on the bank of the said River, thence running South Weft upon the North Weft Line of said Harts land to the rear or back line of a tract of Land of ten thousand Acres granted to Charles Morris Esquire by Letters Patent under the Great Seal of the Province of Nova Scotia thence running North Weft upon the said rear line till in includes and comprehends three twentieth parts of the said rear line of the said tract of ten thousand Acres thence North Eaft to the said River Saint John there by

by the several courses of the said River to the Bounds firft mentioned together with all his right and title to the same and every part and parcel thereof the said premises so conveyed by the said James Simonds to the said William Baker and George Hayward being part and parcel of the said tract of ten thousand Acres And whereas the said deed dated the said twenty fourth day of March in the year of our Lord one thousand seven hundred and seventy nine made from him the said James Simonds to the said William Baker and George Hayward of the said premises is loft or mislaid — Now this

Indenture Witnefseth that for the better confirming of the title of the said William Baker and George Hayward their Heirs and Afsigns forever to the aforesaid tract or parcel of Land so conveyed to them by the said James Simonds and for and in Consideration of the Money paid for the purchase of the said premises by them the said William Baker and George Hayward to the said James Simonds in Mannner as exprefsed in the said deed dated the said twenty fourth day of March in the year of our Lord one thousand seven hundred and seventy nine now loft or Mislaid and also for and in consideration of the sum of five Shillings to him the said James Simonds in hand paid by them the said William Baker and George Hayward at or before the ensealing and delivery of these presents the receipt whereof is

-428-

hereby acknowledged he the said James Simonds hath granted bargained sold aliened released ratified quit claimed and forever confirmed And by these presents for himself his Heirs and Afsigns doth grant bargain sell alien release ratify quit claim and forever confirm unto the said William Baker and George Hayward the Heirs and Afsigns in their actual pofsefsions now being all the said tract and parcel of land and all and singular other Hereditaments and premises which by the said herein before recited deed were granted released and conveyed unto and to the use of the said William Baker and George Hayward their Heirs and Afsigns forever, by him the said James Simonds with their and eny [sic] of their appurtenances to the said premises in any wise belonging and the reversion and reversions remainder and remainders rents ifsuses and profits of all and singular the premifes and every part and parcel thereof with the Appurtenances and also all the eftate right title intereft property claim and demand whatsoever in Law or Equity of him the said James Simonds his Heirs and Afsigns of in to or out of the said hereditaments and premises and every part and parcel thereof to have and to hold the said tract or parcel of Land with all and singular the premises and appurtenances to the said William Baker and George Hayward their Heirs and Afsigns forever and to and for no other use intent or purpose whatsoever — In Witnefs whereof the partys to these presents

-429-

the said James Simonds has hereunto set his hand and feal this day and year firft above written —

Sealed and Delivered)
in the presence of — —
Fran.^s M. Dixon   Ja Simonds {LS}
R Belvor [Spelling?]

City of Saint John Novr 4th 1789 personally appeared before me James Simonds Esqr and acknowledged sealed and delivered the above Indenture as his act and deed for the uses and purposes therein mentioned

Wm Campbell Justice of Peace —

N° 221 Rece.^d & entered December 21st 1789 —

New Brunswick, County Deed Registry Books, 1780-1930, for Sunbury (1786-1791), Volume B4, pp. 500 - 501

Know all Men by these Presents that I George Hayward of the Parish of ~~Burton~~ Lincoln in the County of Sunbury and Province of New Brunswick Yeoman for and in Consideration of the Love and Affection I bear unto my loving Daughter Nancy Hayward and diverse other good causes and consideration me thereunto moving have given granted released and quit claimed unto her the said Nancy Hayward her Heirs and Afsigns forever one equal third part of all that tract of Land granted to me the seventeenth Day of October one thousand seven hundred and eighty eight and one third part of Lots Number fixteen and seventeen and being on the South East Side of the Oromocto River at or near the French Lake in the Parish of Burton with all the Buildings and other improvements thereon with all advantage and privileges thereunto of right belonging or in any wise appertaining (except the quit rents & other conditions reserved to his Majesty in the aforementioned Grant) to have and to hold unto the said Nancy Hayward her Heirs and Afsigns forever and to her and their only use and behoof forever and I bind myself my Heirs Executors and Aminis

-501-

Administrators to warrant secure & defend the fame granted premises with the appurtenances to her the said Nancy Hayward her Heirs and Afsigns forever againft all manner of persons whatsoever Lawfully claiming the fame In Witnefs whereof I have hereunto set my hand and feal this tenth Day of May in the year of our Lord one thousand seven hundred and eighty six figned fealed & delivered in presence of — The wards <u>one third part of Number sixteen</u> between the lines fourteen & fifteen being interviewed before the execution hereof —

Joseph Clarke
Isaac Hubbard
George Hayward {LS}

Sunbury fs: On the 15th Day of July 1790 personally appeared before me William Hubbard Register for the County aforesaid the within named George Hayward and acknowledged the within written Deed to be his Act & Deed

Wm Hubbard

Recd & entered the 15th Day of July 1790 —

New Brunswick, County Deed Registry Books, 1780-1930, for Sunbury (1786-1791), Volume B4, pp. 502 -503

Know All Men by these Presents that I George Hayward of the Parish of Burton in the County of Sunbury and Province of New Brunswick Yeoman, for and in Confideration of the Love and affection I bear unto my loving Daughter Mary Hoit Wife of Joseph Hoit and for other good and valuable causes and Considerations me there unto moving have given granted released and quit claimed unto her the faid Mary Hoit Wife of said Joseph Hoit and to her and her Heirs and Afsigns forever one sixth part of all that tract of Land granted to me the said George Hayward the seventeenth Day of October one thousand seven hundred and eighty eight and one equal sixth part of Lots Numbers sixteen and seventeen lying and being on the South Eaft side of the River Oromocto at or near the French Lake in the Parish of Burton with all the Buildings Improvements and other privileges profits and emoluments whatsoever unto the fame in any manner of ways belonging or appertaining to have and to hold the aforesaid defcribed premises with all the appurtenances unto her the said Mary Hoit her Heirs and Afsigns forever and I bind myself my Heirs

-503-

Executors and Administrators by these Presents to warrant secure and defend the fame against all manner of Persons whatsoever, the King's quit rents & conditions only excepted, In Witnefs whereof I hereunto set my Hand & Seal this thirteenth Day of July in the year of our Lord one thousand seven hundred and ninety —

Signed Sealed & Delivered
In the presence of —
Joseph Clark   }
Isaac Hubbard}   George Hayward {LS}

Sunbury fs: On the 15 Day of July 1790 personally appeared before me William Hubbard Register for the County aforesaid the within named George Hayward Grantor and acknowledged the within written Deed to be his act & Deed

Wᵐ Hubbard

Nº 248
Rᵈ & entered the 15ᵗʰ July 1790 —

New Brunswick County Deed Registry Books, 1780-1930, for Sunbury (1786-1791), Volume B4, pp. 504 -505

Know Men by these presents that I George Hayward of the Parish of Burton in the County of Sunbury in the Province of New Brunswick, Yeoman, for and in Consideration of the Sum of fifty five Pounds good and lawful Money of the Province of New Brunswick aforesaid to me in hand well and truly paid by Joseph Hoit of the Parish County and Province aforesaid the receipt whereof I do hereby acknowledge have granted bargained and sold and by these presents do grant bargain and sell unto him the said Joseph Hoit his Heirs and Afsigns forever one sixth part of all that tract of Land granted to me the said George Hayward the seventeenth Day of October one thousand seven hundred and eighty eight and one full sixth part of Lots Numbers sixteen and seventeen — at or near the French Lake on the South Eaft side of the River Oromocto in the Parish of Burton with all Buildings Improvements Advantages Profits and Privileges whatsoever of right belonging or in any manner of ways appertaining unto the fame tracts of Land to have and to hold the said tracts of Land and Premises unto him the said Joseph ~~Clarke~~ Hoit his Heirs and Afsigns forever to him and their only use

-505-

use and behoof forever — and I the said George Hayward do bind myfelf my Heirs Executors and Administrators to warrant secure and defend the fame unto him the said Joseph Hoit his Heirs & Afsigns forever againft all Manner of persons whatsoever (the Kings quit rents & other usessations excepted) In Witnefs whereof I have hereunto set my Hand and Seal this thirteenth Day of July one thousand seven hundred and ninety —

Signed Sealed & Delivered
in presence of us —
Joseph Clarke }   George Hayward {LS}
Isaac Hubbard}

Sunbury fs: On the 15ᵗʰ Day of July 1790 personally appeared before me William Hubbard Register for the County aforesaid the within named George Hayward the Grantor who acknowledged the within written Deed to be his Act & Deed

Wm Hubbard

No 249
Recd & entered the 15th of July 1790 —

New Brunswick, County Deed Registry Books, 1780-1930, for Sunbury (1786-1791), Volume B4, pp. 560 -561

(N 275)

This Indenture made this thirteenth Day of Jan.y in the twenty fifth year of the reign of our Sovereign Lord George the third by the Grace of God King of Great Britain France and Ireland defender of the faith &c — and in the year of our Lord one thousand seven hundred and eighty five. Between Charles Skinner, Yeoman, and Sarah Skinner his Wife in the County of Sunbury and Province of New Brunswick of the one part, and John Simonson Gentleman of the County aforesaid of the other part. Witnefseth that the said Charles Skinner and Sarah Skinner for and in Consideration of the sum of two hundred and fifty pounds lawful Money of the Province af'd to them in hand paid by the said John Simonson the receipt whereof the said Charles Skinner and Sarah Skinner doth hereby confefs and acknowledge they the said Charles Skinner and Sarah Skinner hath granted, bargained and fold aliened and confirmed, and by these presents doth grant bargain and sell, aliene and confirm unto the said John Simonson his Heirs and Afsigns forever all that Mefsuage or tenement situate and lying in the Township of Maugerville together with all the after Divisions containing in the whole by eftimation one thousand acres more or lefs (an Island lot excepted) being the Lot No seventy in the front of the said township of Maugerville and also all Lands Trees, Woods, underwoods Titles, Commons, Common Pastures, profits commodities advantages, hereditaments ways waters and appurtenances whatsoever, to the said Mefsuage or tentament and premises above mentioned belonging or in any wise appertaining, and also the reversion and reversions, remainder and remainders unto and fervices of the said premises and of every part thereof and all the eftate, right title, interest, claim and demand whatsoever of them the said Charles Skinner and Sarah Skinner his Wife of in and to the said Mefsuage tenement and premises and every part thereof ~~and all and fingular~~ to have and to hold the said Mefsuage or tenement all and fingular the premises

-561-

premises above mentioned and every part and parcel thereof with the appurtenances unto the said John Simonson his Heirs and Afsigns ot the only proper use & behoof of the said John Simonson his Heirs and Afsigns forever and the said Charles Skinner and Sarah Skinner his Wife for them and their heirs and the said Mefsuage or tenement and every part thereof and against them and their heirs and against all and every person or persons whatsoever to the said John Simonson his Heirs and Afsigns shall and will warrant and forever defend by these presents In Witnefs whereof we have set our hands and feals the Day and year first written

Signed Sealed and delivered
in the presence of —

N. B: the second Day of in the first line was interviewed before signed and fealing

John Thomson	Charles Skinner {LS}
Art^r Nicholson	Sarah Skinner — no seal

Sunbury fs: On the twenty third Day of April in the Year of our Lord one thousand and seven hundred and ninety one personally appeared before me William Hubbard Register for the County of Sunbury aforesaid John Thomson Esqr one of the fubfcribing Witnefs to the within written Inftrument and he being duly fworn made Oath that he saw Charles Skinner within named Grantor fign feal and deliver the fame and that he at the fametime Infcribed his Name as a Witnefs and faw Arthur Nicholson the other Witnefs Infscribe his Name

N° 275   Wm Hubbard
Rec^d & entered the 23^d Day of April 1791

New Brunswick, County Deed Registry Books, 1780-1930, for Sunbury (1795-1799), Volume D6, pp. 352 -354

(N° 538)

Know All Men by these Presents that I George Hayward of Burton in the County of Sunbury and Province of New Brunswick for and in Consideration of the Sum of five hundred Pounds current Money of the Province aforesaid to me in hand well and truly paid by Charles Martin of Meramafhee in the county of Northumberland the Receipt whereof I do hereby acknowledge, have granted bargained sold aliened and by the Presents I do grant bargain fell alien and confirm unto the faid Charles Martin his Heirs Executors Administrators or Afsigns forever all that certain Lott or Tract of Land Known by Lott Number five lying and being on the south weft Side of the River St. Johns in the Township of Lincoln being part of three thousand granted to Arthur Goold Butted and Bounded as follows the South Eaft Boundary beginning at a Beach Tree and running up the River one hundred and twenty five Rods to a black Birch Tree marked thence South-weft two miles and a quarter thence South-Eaft one hundred and twenty five Rods thence Northeaft to the rear Boundary first mentioned Containing five hundred Acres more or lefs with all the Houses Meadows Island, Common pastures profits Commodities advantages hereditaments Ways Waters and appurtenances whatsoever to the Premises above mentioned any way belonging or appertaining as also all Remainder and Remainders and every part and parcel thereof with all the Right title intereft claims and demand of me the said George Hayward of in and to the faid Land, aforesaid and defcribed to have and to

-354-

[Page numbering system in original skips the number 353.]

hold the faid premises and every part and priviledge thereof; and thereunto belonging unto the said Charles Martin his Heirs and Afsigns forever and I the faid George Hayward for myself my Heirs and Afsigns the faid Land hereby granted and fold againft me his him or them and againft all perfons claiming or pretending to claim the fame by any means whatsoever to the faid Charles Martin will warrant and defend the quiet and peaceable pofsefsion of the Premises aforesaid— In Witnefs whereof I the faid George Hayward have hereunto fet my hand and Seal at Lincoln aforesaid this fifteenth Day of July 1790 —

Signed Sealed & Delivered
in Prefence of us —   George Hayward {LS}
Joseph Clarke
Isaac Hubbard —

Sunbury fs: On the 15th day of July 1790 — perfonally appeared before me William Hubbard Register for the County of Sunbury aforefaid the within named George Hayward Grantor who acknowledged the within written Deed to be his Act & Deed —

Wm Hubbard

Received and entered May the 27th 1799 —

Wm Hubbard Register —

New Brunswick, County Deed Registry Books, 1780-1930, for Sunbury (1795-1799), Volume D6, pp. 355 -357

(No 539)

Know All Men by these Presents that I George Hayward of Burton in the County of Sunbury and Province of New Brunswick for and in the Confideration of the Sum of four hundred pounds current Money of the Province aforesaid to me in hand well and truly paid by John Hayward of Lincoln in the County and Province aforesaid the Receipt whereof I do hereby Acknowledge have granted bargained sold aliened conveyed and confirmed and by these presents I the faid George Hayward do grant bargain sell convey and confirm unto the aforesaid John Hayward his Heirs Executors Administrators and Afsigns forever all that Lott or Tract of Land lying and being on the South Weft Side of the River St Johns in the Township of Lincoln County and Province aforesaid being part of a Grant granted to Charles Morris Esqr of Halifax Butted and Bounded as follows; Beginning at the North Eaft Corner of a Lott formerly William Bakers now James Glasiers running a due Northweft Course seventy four Rods up the River then leaving a Lott fifty seven Rods wide on a line Northweft course up the River formerly William Bakers now James Glasiers then commencing again at that North Eaft Boundary and running fifty seven Rods North Weft up the aforesaid River; thence four Miles and a half; thence Southeaft

fifty seven Rods on a due Southeaft Line to the aforesaid James Glasiers then having fifty seven Rods on the faid Line then commencing and running South eaft seventy four Rods thence Northeaft four Miles and a half to the first mentioned Bounds on the Bank of the River St. Johns containing eleven hundred and and [sic] seventy Acres more or lefs; with all the Houses Barns out Houses Buildings Meadow, Wood, Commons profits Commodities Advantages Hereditaments ways waters and <u>appurtenances appurtenances</u> [sic] whatsoever to the premises above mentioned as also all Remains and Remainders and every part and parcel thereof with all the Right Title Interft and Claim of me the faid George Haywad of in and to the Lands aforesaid and defcribed to have and to hold the faid granted Premises and every part and privilege thereof and thereto belonging unto the faid ~~George~~ John Hayward his Heirs and Afsigns forever and I the faid ~~John~~ George Hayward will forever warrant and defend the quiet and peaceable pofsefsion of the faid hereby granted and fold Premises againft me her him or them and againft all perfons whatsoever claiming or pretending to claim the fame by any means whatsoever to the faid John Hayward his Heirs and Afsigns for ever — In Witnefs whereof I have hereunto set my hand and seal this fifteenth Day of

of July 1790

Signed Sealed & Delivered
in Presence of us —
Jofeph Clarke   George Hayward — {LS}
Isaac Hubbard —

Sunbury County fs: On the 15th day of July 1790 perfonally came and appeared before me William Hubbard the within named George Hayward Senr, the Grantor, who acknowledged that he executed the foregoing Inftrument of writing freely for the uses & purposes therein mentioned before me

Wm Hubbard

Received & registered May the 27th 1799 —

Wm Hubbard Register

New Brunswick, County Deed Registry Books, 1780-1930, for Sunbury (1795-1799), Volume D6, pp. 360 -361

(N° 541)

Know All Men by these Presents that I George Hayward Senr of the Township of Burton in the county of Sunbury and Province of New Brunswick for and in Confideration of the Sum of three hundred pounds current Money of the Province aforesaid to me in hand well & duly paid by George Hayward jun^r of Burton County Province aforesaid the Receipt whereof I do hereby acknowledge have granted bargained sold aliened conveyed and confirmed and by these Presents I the said George Hayward do grant bargain sell alien convey and confirm to the aforesaid George Hayward jun^r his Heirs Executors Administrators and Afsigns forever one equal third part of all the Grant granted me the seventeenth Day of October one thousand seven hundred and eighty eight and one equal third part of Lotts Number fixteen and seventeen as the Grants will more fully fhew and defcribe lying and being on the South Eaft side of Oromocto at French Lake in the Township of Burton with all the Houses Buildings Meadows Wood, Common profits commodities advantages hereditaments ways waters and appurtenances whatsoever to the premises above mentioned and granted any way belonging or appertaining faving and referring all the white pine timber for the use of his Majesty his Heirs and Sucefsors; and every part and parcel thereof with all the Right title Intereſt claim of me the said George Hayward Senr of in and to the Land aforesaid to have and to hold the said granted Premises and every part and privilege thereof and thereto belonging unto the said George Hayward jun^r his Heirs and Aſsigns forever and I the said George [Hayward] for myself my Heirs and Aſsigns will forever warrant and defend the quiet and peaceable poſseſsion of the said hereby granted and Sold premises againſt me her him them and againſt all person claiming or pretending to clam the fame by any means whatsoever to the aforesaid George Hayward junior his Heirs and Aſsigns forever — —

In Witneſs whereof I have hereunto set my hand and seal at Burton aforesaid this fifteenth Day of July 1790 —

Signed Sealed & Delivered
In the Presence of us —
Joſeph Charles   George Hayward {LS}
Isaac Hubbard

Sunbury County fs: On the 15th day of July 1790 personally came and appeared before me William Hubbard Reg^r the within named George Hayward sen^r· the Grantor who acknowledged that he executed the above Inſtrument of writing for the uses & purposes therein mentioned before me

                                                            Wm Hubbard Register

Received & entered the 27th of May 1799.   Wm Hubbard Register

New Brunswick, County Deed Registry Books, 1780-1930, for Sunbury (1806-1810), Volume G9, pp. 182-183

(N° 805)

Know All Men by these presents, that George Hayward and Nancy his wife of the Parish of Burton and County of Sunbury and Province of New Brunswick and Joseph Hoit and Mary his wife of the Parish of Magerville and County & Province aforesaid — In consideration of the sum of one hundred and twenty pounds lawful money of the said Province paid by Joseph Clarke Esqr of the Parish of Magerville & County of Sunbury and Province of New-Brunswick — the Receipt whereof we do hereby acknowledge — do grant, bargain and sell unto the said Joseph Clarke his Heirs and Assigns all that tract of Land lying in the Parish of Magerville aforesaid and known and described as Lot Number forty six and the northwest half of Lot Number forty seven in the Grant of said Township or Parish of Magerville — to have and to hold the same to the said Joseph Clarke Esqr his Heirs and Assigns — And we the said George Hayward and Joseph Hoit do by these presents bind ourselves, our Heirs or Assigns, for ever, to warrant and defend the above granted and bargained premises to him the said Joseph Clarke Esqr and to his heirs and Assigns, against all claim and demands whatsoever — In Witness whereof we have hereunto set our hands and Seals this twenty fifth day june [sic] in the year of our Lord one thousand seven hundred and eighty nine

	George Hayward — {LS}
Sign'd Sealed and Deivered	Joseph Hoit — {LS}
	her
in presence of —	Mary X Hoit — {LS}
	mark
Dan Bliss	
Elizabeth Upham	{LS}

Sunbury fs: july [sic] [illegible] 25th A: D: 1789 George Hayward and Joseph Hoit two of the Grantors of the deed on the other side this sheet of paper

-183-

appearing before me acknowledged the same to be their act and deed —
Dan Bliss Junr Par —

Province of New Brunswick fs july [sic] [illegible] 25th A: D: 1789 Mary Hoit wife of the aforementioned Joseph Hoit being examined separate and apart from her said Husband declared that she executed the same aforementioned deed freely and voluntarily without any threat or compulsion from him her said Husband and acknowledged the same as her act and deed — before me

Dan Bliss {one of his Majestys
{Council for said Province

Received in the Register's Office on the 8th day of March 1810 & entered by me —
Wm Hubbard - Register —

New Brunswick Land Petitions: Original Series, Sunbury County, 1783-1918 (RS108) (A1148) (Microfilm: F4188)

To his Excellency Major General George Stracey Smyth, —
Lieutenant Governor & Commander in chief in and over the Province
of New Brunswick &c. &c. &c.

The Memorial of Holden Turner, ~~Nicholas Brown,~~
William Turner, and John Hayward, all of
Parish of Lincoln in the County of Sunbury.

Humbly Sheweth,

That Your Memorialist Holden Turner, is a native of — Scotland, and has been an Inhabitant of this Province for nearly thirty six years — is a married man, of the age of Fifty nine years, and never received any Lands from the Crown.

~~That Your Memorialist Nicholas Brown is a native of Ireland; that he has been Five years in this Province; and the two preceeding years in the Island of Newfoundland — is a married man, of the age of thirty two years — and has never had any land from the Crown.~~

That Your Memorialist William Turner, is a native of this Province, a single man, of the age of nineteen years, and has never had any land from the Crown.

And that Your Memorialist John Hayward is also a native of this Province; a single man, of the age of twenty one years, and has never had any Land from the Crown

And that Your Memorialists are all Subject to The — Crown of Great Britain, and of the several ages and situations in life above stated, and humbly pray that they may have allotments of three hundred acres to each of the married men, and two hundred to each of the single, in a vacant Tract of wildernefs Land, in the rear of Land minuted to George Brone in the Parish of Burton (in the Geary settlement so called,) and situate about South Easterly from the said Brone's

[2]

Brone's rear; That they are of sufficient ability and it is their intention forthwith, to cultivate and improve the said land — according to The Royal Instructions, and have not, nor hath either of them, directly or indirectly bargained or agreed for the sale or transfer thereof to any person or persons whatsoever.

And as in duty bound will ever pray

6th. May 1820

Holden Turner
~~Nicholas Brown~~
William Turner

John Hayward

York Fs.]

Fredericton May 6th. 1820

Personally appeared before me, Peter Fraser Esquire one of His Majesty's Justices of the Peace for said County. Holden Turner, Nicholas Brown, William Turner and John Hayward sen.r made oath to the several matters in the above petition being just and true

P. Fraser Justice Peace

[3]

The situation herein mentioned,
Is Vacant crown land
1820.5.6

A Lockwood
As.t Sur General

[*verso*]

Holden Turner and
three others —

31st. Aug.t 1820

Recommended

M
JP
N.B.

31st. Aug.t 1820

6th. May 1820 —

Paid —

New Brunswick Land Petitions: Original Series, Sunbury County, 1783-1918 (RS108) (A1147) (Microfilm: F4187)

479

To His Excellency Major General George Stracey Smyth, Lieut[t] Governor and Commander in Chief of the Province of New Brunswick &c. &c. &c.

The Petition of George Hayward Jun[r] and Jeremiah Dunn

Humbly sheweth

That your Petitioner George Hayward Jun[r] is a Native of this Province, that he now lives in Sunbury where he has always resided is married and has a family and has never received any Grant or allotment of Land from the Crown — Jeremiah Dunn is a Native of Ireland where he always resided previous to his Emigration to this Province where he arrived in the Summer of 1815 — that he has been in the Province since that period — is twenty five years of age, unmarried and has never received any Grant or Allotment of Land from the Crown —

Your Petitioners therefore humbly pray that your Excellency would be pleased to grant to each of them an allotment of land as follows — to George Hayward Jun[r] 300 acres, and to Jeremiah Dunn 200 acres in the Parish of Burton adjoining lands recently applied for by Holden Turner and others —

That it is the intention of your Petitioners

[2]

and they are of the ability forthwith to cultivate and improve the land herein applied for according to the Royal Instructions, it being now in its natural and uncultivated state and also that they have not directly or indirectly bargained or agreed for the sale or transfer of the same to any person, or persons whatsoever

And as in duty bound will ever pray

George Hayward Jun[r].
his
Jeremiah X Dunn
mark

The Situation herein described is vacant
Crown Land   A. Lockwood
15th May 1820   A.S.G.

[3]

On the 15th day of May 1820 Before me
Peter Fraser Esquire — one of His Majesty's

Justices of the Peace for the County of York
personally appeared the within named George
Hayward Junr. & Jeremiah Dunn and
severally made oath that the Several matters
and things set forth in the before written
petition are just and true

                                                      P. Fraser Justice Peace

[*verso*]

Geo: Hayward Junr.
and one other

31st. Augt. 1820

Recommended

M
JP
N.B.

15$^{\underline{th}}$. May 1820 —

P^d. in part 15/-

APPENDIX T

Howard Genealogical Research

George and Nehemiah Hayward were among the first settlers of Maugerville, New Brunswick, to receive land grants between 1765 and early 1783. William Raymond in his *The River St. John* says, "Nearly all the first settlers in the township of Maugerville were from Massachusetts, the majority from the single county of Essex." (p. 329) George H. Hayward establishes in his *Haywards of Sunbury & Carleton Counties, N. B., and Some of Their Descendants* (p. 2) that Rebekca/Rebecca (Hayward) Howard's supposed parents George and Ann (Derley/Durley) Hayward came from England, so it is highly doubtful that George and Nehemiah Hayward, originating from Massachusetts, were closely related to George and Ann (Derley/Durley) Hayward.

B. Wood-Holt in *The Kings Loyal Americans, the Canadian Fact, Marriage Licenses for Sunbury County, 1788-1829, Passenger Lists and Other List, etc.* writes, "[W]hen the Loyalists arrived in 1783 . . . [t]he Maugerville Colony numbered around 500 people. . . ." (p. 107)

Esther Clark Wright in *The Loyalists of New Brunswick* writes, "By 1783, the upriver settlement, known first as Peabody's and later as Maugerville, had a population between 350 and 400." (p. 116)

Clark Wright notes, "Maugerville was essentially a farming and lumbering community, but its inhabitants were not unmindful of other gifts of the river, such as fish and fur-bearing animals." (p.121)

Raymond, once again in *The River St. John*, states: "Mauger's Island and the first ten lots above the lower boundary were granted to Joshua Mauger, in recognition of his services to the settlers, we may suppose. Just above were the lots of Gervas Say, Nehemiah Hayward, John Russel, Samuel Upton, Zebulon Estey, John Estey, Richard Estey and Edward Coy." (p. 336) Raymond also points out that George Hayward (from Massachusetts) was among the witnesses for the marriage at Maugerville on 23 February 1766 between Gervas Say and Anna Russell. (p. 346)

It may seem like a digression to go into more detail about Maugerville, but the following from James Hannay, D.C.L. in his piece "Before the Loyalists" in *The Educational Review Supplementary Readings, Canadian History Readings, Volume I, Number Ten, June 1900*, although concentrating on the pre-Loyalist, paints a vivid picture of what life was like for the early pioneers of New Brunswick:

> The English settlers who made their homes in New Brunswick from 1762 onward, before the coming of the Loyalists, were mainly from Massachusetts, where their ancestors had settled more than a century before. . . .

The principal settlements were at the mouth of the St. John river and at Maugerville, the former consisting of the trading establishment of Messrs. Simonds, Hazen & White and the men in their employment. Their life was lonely enough and full of hardships, for they had no other connection with the outside world than the occasional trips of the sloops which made voyages between St. John and Newburyport, carrying lime, lumber and fish. But even in this respect they were highly favored in comparison with the settlers at Maugerville, Gagetown and other points on the river who had no other means of communication with each other or with the people at the mouth of the river but by boats. For it must be remembered that there were no roads in the province in those days. As a consequence there were no wheeled vehicles, except carts, and this state of affairs continued to the year 1781, or later, for when Jonathan Burpee, one of the wealthiest farmers in the Maugerville settlement, died in that year the inventory of his estate shows that he possessed neither wagon nor sleigh, but only the ironwork of a cart and half the woodwork. We may therefore infer that this cart was owned by Mr. Burpee jointly with a neighbor, and was used for the purpose of carrying the produce of their fields to their barns. . . .

These early settlers lived in a very primitive fashion and their lives were hard. They resided in log houses, most of them of small size and very scantily furnished. In the inventory of Deacon Jonathan Burpee's estate, the total value of his furniture is put down at £5 7s. 8d. It consisted of four bedsteads, two tables, two large chairs, ten small chairs, and a looking-glass. There were also two chests and a pair of andirons. There is here a total absence of articles of comfort, to say nothing of luxury. There do not appear to have been either carpets or rugs in this rich farmer's house. There was no such thing as a couch or sofa, and the chairs were no doubt of the old-fashioned straight-backed pattern, so as to be as uncomfortable as possible. Our ancestors seemed to have looked upon it as wrong to be comfortable. . . . [It has been said that furniture of this period was purposely not constructed for comfort so as to discourage guests from overextending their visit.]

Kitchen stoves had not been invented . . ., and all the cooking for the family had to be done at an old-fashioned fire-place. The great feature of a fire-place was its capacity for consuming fuel without giving out any heat. A quarter of a cord of wood might be burning in the fire-place while the people at the back of the room were freezing. The kitchen utensils of Deacon Burpee consisted of three iron pots, an iron kettle, two iron pans, a frying-pan, a gridiron, a toasting-iron, and a brass kettle. Cooking at a fire-place was done under the greatest difficulties, the heavy pots having to be lifted on to and off a crane which stretched across the fire-place. To keep one of these huge fire-places in fuel in cold weather took no small part of the labor of one man. Meat had to be roasted before the fire and bread was baked in a bake-kettle — a large pot with a flat bottom and cover. This was placed among the hot ashes and covered with large live coals from the fire. Wonderful results were obtained from this primitive system of cookery, yet it was wasteful as well as laborious.

The food of the people in those days was neither varied nor abundant. In the Maugerville settlement a good deal of corn was ground and it was regarded as the staple crop. We do not grow corn in New Brunswick now, because it can be produced more cheaply elsewhere, but some farmers in Maugerville grew it in large quantities about the year 1770. David Burpee, whose diary has been preserved, grew fifty bushels of corn in the year 1775. The price of corn varied from four shillings a bushel to nine shillings. Wheat was not much grown in New Brunswick at that time. Much of the grain was ground in hand mills a slow and laborious method, but the only one available where there were no grist-mills near the settler.

Wages were low in New Brunswick before the time of the Loyalists. The ordinary rate was two shillings a day, but 2s. 6d. was given where the work was more laborious than usual, such as mowing, farming, hoeing corn and raking hay. Women servants received 10s. a month, or £6 a year. As the currency used was that of Massachusetts one sixth had to be deducted to bring it to New Brunswick currency, so that £6 was only equal to $20 of the money of Canada at the present time [1900]. While wages were thus low everything that had to be purchased in the way of clothing was costly. Cotton goods cost about ten times as much then as they do now. The ordinary dress of both men and women was homespun. Sheep were kept on every farm for their wool. This was carded and spun by hand, and woven into cloth on a hand loom of which there was one in almost every home. Flax was also grown and spun on these little old-fashioned wheels which are now in such request as curiosities. Every farm was capable of producing the ordinary clothing and bedding of the people who lived and worked upon it. But the converting of wool and flax into clothing was laborious and placed a good deal of work upon the women of the farm. . . . The men might shear the sheep and heckle the flax but the carding, spinning and weaving had all to be done by the women.

Most of the men wore leather breeches, a garment which, however durable, could hardly have been comfortable. But every man who aspired to respectability aimed to have one good suit of broadcloth, which was expected to last him for twenty years. In the note of accounts of David Burpee we have the particulars of a suit which he purchased for himself in 1777. There were 3 ¾ yards of broadcloth at 20 shillings, 3 yards shalloon at 4 shillings, buttons, trimmings, etc., the whole amounting to £4 16s. 3d. After the tailor had been paid this suit probably cost David Burpee £6, or as much as he would be able to earn in ten weeks by working for others at the current rate of wages. This . . . explains the fact that the clothing of a dead man was valued and included in the inventory of his effects, and sold as part of the estate. No one in those days seems to have thought that there was anything singular in purchasing and wearing the clothes of a deceased neighbor. The clothing of Deacon Jonathan Burpee, for instance, was valued at £7 15s. 3d, and it included his best brown suit worth £4 5s. 6d, and a beaver hat valued at 10s. These clothes were all sold and worn by others, most of the purchasers being members of the family. . . .

Life in Maugerville one hundred and thirty years ago offered but little in the way of amusements. Musical instruments were unknown in the farm houses of that day. . . . There were few social meetings, and almost the only events that brought the people together were the services held by itinerant preachers. Even these were not frequent, and there was no settled minister until 1774, and he had but a brief career, for he turned rebel and fled to Maine in 1777. School privileges were few, and the teaching was usually done in the winter by one of the settlers who was fortunate enough to possess a better education than his neighbor. Thus David Burpee taught school in the winter of 1778-79, receiving 3s. 11½d. per month for each scholar. So far as his accounts show he had only seven scholars. . . . (pp. 266-271)

John Howard was also a Loyalist in the American Revolution. Murtie June Clark in her *Loyalists in the Southern Campaign of the Revolutionary War* documents that Private John Howard is listed as "prisoner with rebels" on 29 November 1779 under "Muster Roll, Lieut[enant] Colonel Stephen Delancey's Company, Second Battalion, Brigadier General Oliver Delancey's Brigade, Savannah, GA. . . ." (Volume III, p. 35) Clark documents that Howard remains a prisoner and is listed as such between 25 December 1783 to 24 February 1783 in the "Muster Roll, Captain Barent Roorback's Company, First Battalion, Brigadier General Oliver Delancey's Brigade, Little Plains. . . ." (Volume III, p. 29) (Clark, Murtie, June: *Loyalists in the Southern Campaign of the Revolutionary War,* Copyright 1981 by Genealogical Publishing Co., Inc., Baltimore, Maryland.)

More Howard information appears in Appendices P and Q.

John Hayward/Howard (ca 1770 or 1771 - 6 July 1854) married Rebecca/Rebecka Hayward (ca 1774 - ca 1856), possible daughter of George Hayward (ca 1739 - 31 March 1799) and Ann Derley/Durley (ca 1731 - December 1806), on 29 June 1795 at Maugerville, New Brunswick, and died in York County, New Brunswick. (Elizabeth S. Sewell: Sunbury County New Brunswick Marriages 1766-1888, Volume 1, D0089.)

According to Rebecca (Hayward) Howard's 1855 petition contained in the *Records of Old Revolutionary Soldiers and Their Widows,* she had resided in New Brunswick, from

The Kellys of Kingsclear

the time of her marriage to John Howard. (See Appendix U.) It should be noted that in the same land grant in Kingsclear, York County, New Brunswick, awarded to a group that included Isaac Allen and John Kelly on 31 December 1799, John Howard is granted 280 acres. (See Appendix F.)

The following is from research conducted by John Beishlag, who advises in an email of 21 October 2012 that this is a work in progress and that "the connection to the Carvells . . . and to Isabella Howard Nevers . . . is based on my inductive reasoning." I have augmented Beishlag's material by including further research done by Linda (Kitchen) Aitken and information gathered from George H. Hayward's *Haywards of Sunbury & Carleton Counties, N. B., and Some of Their Descendants*.

For clarity, I am assigning numbers to differentiate the generations in the genealogy of the John Howard family. John Kelly is given number 1, his children, number 2, grandchildren, number 3 and great-grandchildren, number 4.

1.John Howard (ca 1739 – ca 1783) married Unknown Unknown (ca late 1740s – ca late 1780s)*. John and Unknown (Unknown) Howard both died in New Brunswick

Children of John and Unknown (Unknown) Howard:

2.John Howard (ca 1770 – 6 July 1854) married Rebecca/Rebecka Hayward (ca 1774 – ca 1856), possible daughter of George Hayward (ca 1739 – 31 March 1799) and Ann Derley/Durley (ca 1731 – December 1806), on 29 June 1795 at Maugerville, New Brunswick. (*FamilyCentral History Services*.) The Maugerville Anglican Church records transcribed by Cleadie Barnett (PANB) notes that Rebecka Hayward was baptized 29 November 1787 along with Ann Hayward and three children of Joseph and Mary (Hayward) Hoyt. On the same date, Ann Hayward, daughter of George Hayward (ca 1739 – 31 March 1799) and Ann Derley/Durley (ca 1731 – December 1806), married William Boone at Maugerville. John and Rebecca/Rebecka (Hayward) Howard both died in York County, New Brunswick. George Hayward was born in England and married Ann Derley/Durley on 13 April 1761 in the Parish of Islington, Middlesex County, England. Ann Derley/Durley was born in Great Britain**. George H. Hayward in his *Haywards of Sunbury & Carleton Counties, New Brunswick and Some of Their Descendants* documents (p. 1) how the name Hayward and Howard are synonymous in early records, with the same person being listed with either surname from one recorded source to another.

Children of John and Rebekca/Rebecca (Hayward) Howard:

> **3.Sarah Ann Howard** (ca 1796 – between 1881 and 1891 census) married William Kelly (ca 1792 – ca 1875/76) 23 March 1813 at Kingsclear, York County, New Brunswick. The ceremony was conducted by Rev. George Pidgeon, Anglican Rector (1795 - 1814) of Fredericton, New Brunswick.

William and Sarah Ann (Howard) Kelly lived in Queensbury, New Brunswick, where they are listed as being members of the Church of England in the 1861 census.

3.Grace Howard (ca 1797 – late 1850s) married Joseph Bourgoin/Burgoine (June 1788 – ca 1850s). Joseph and Grace (Howard) Bourgoin were both born and died in Kingsclear Parish, York County, New Brunswick.

3.George Howard (ca 1800 - ?) married Ruth Kelly (ca 1805 - ?). George and Ruth (Kelly) Howard were both born in Kingsclear Parish, New Brunswick.

3.John Howard III (ca 1803 - ?) married Jane Lunt (ca 1813 - ?) 1 August 1830, with Leonard Combes Kelly and Alexander Howard as co-signers, and Justice of the Peace Daniel Morehouse conducting the ceremony. Both John Howard III and Jane Lunt are listed as residents of Kingsclear. (George H. Hayward: *York County, New Brunswick, Marriage Records, Volume 1, 1812–1837*, pp. 25 & 30.) John III and Jane (Lunt) Howard were both born in New Brunswick.

Children of John and Jane (Lunt) Howard:

4.Frederick Howard (5 November 1840 – 30 October 1907). According to a 12 April 2011 post by Timothy Lunney on his "Tim Lunney's blog about the Muintir Lúingh clan of Ireland and the world wide Lunney, Lunny and Lunnie families," Frederick Howard, "enlisted as a private in Company F of the 10th Maine Infantry Regiment of the Union Army, which mustered at Portland, Maine," on 4 October 1861. Throughout the war, Frederick Howard carried the ambrotype of his mother Jane (Lunt) Howard with him. (A copy of the ambrotype and a tintype of Frederick Howard in his Union Army uniform appear in the photo section of this book.)

After the Civil War, Frederick Howard returned to New Brunswick, and married Ruth Langdon. The couple had settled, "by 1865," in Grand Falls, where Frederick Howard owned and operated a hotel.

According to the New Brunswick census of 1881, Frederick and Ruth (Langdon) Howard had the following children: George (age 13), James (age 11), Alice (age 8), Marie (age 7) and Lillie (age 4).

Timothy Lunney: "By 1900, Frederick . . . was a widower. . . ." His daughters, Marie and Lillie, "who never married," served in the Red Cross all their adult lives. Marie, known to her family as "Molly" survived the Great Halifax Explosion of 6 December 1917. She "went to England during World War I, where she eventually became the long-term companion of Sir Thomas Lipton (of Lipton Tea fame)." Lord Lipton, Lunney writes, "left a large part of his immense fortune to endow a retirement home for Red Cross nurses."

Timothy Lunney notes, "Frederick's daughter Alice, or "Doll" as the family called her, married Herbert Coffin and settled in Fort Kent, Maine, where she and her husband owned and operated a successful lumber business."

3.Alexander Howard (ca 1807 - ?) married Rebecca Currie (ca 1811 - ?). Alexander and Rebecca (Currie) Howard were both born in New Brunswick.

3.James Howard (ca 1834 – 25 May 1896) married Rhoda Kelly (ca 1843 – 16 January 1907) 11 July 1861 in Queensbury, New Brunswick, with Alexander Kelly and Francis Niles as co-signers.

*Unknown (Unknown) Howard (ca late 1740s – ?) married 2nd: Jacob Carvell (ca 1749 – 1821). Jacob Carvell, who was a Loyalist, was born in Trenton, New Jersey, and died at Northampton, Carleton County, New Brunswick.

Children of Jacob and Unknown (Unknown) Howard Carvell:

George Lewis Carvell (ca 1805 - ?).
Hugh Hamilton Carvell (ca 1806 - ?).
John B. Carvell (1808 – 1808).
Sarah Emma Carvell (ca 1811 - ?).
William Bailey Carvell (1814 - ?).
Elizabeth Carvell (1816 - ?).
Edward Carvell (1818 - ?)
John Howard Carvell (1822 – 1901).

1.Isabella Howard (ca 1767 – ca 1828) married Samuel A. Nevers (ca 1761 – ca 1827) ca 1784. Isabelle (Howard) Nevers died in Carleton County, New Brunswick. Primary sources are scant in regard to Isabella Howard. The postulation of her being the sister of Loyalist John Howard has been derived at by JohnBeishlag, who presents a great argument. Remember: this is a work in progress.

Children of Samuel A. and Isabella (Howard) Nevers:

2.Hannah Nevers (1785 - 1809). Hannah Nevers was born in New Brunswick.
2.Frances Nevers (ca 1785 - ?).
2.Alexander Nevers (1787 – 1833).

2.George Phinehas Nevers (ca 1790 – 28 August 1857) married Mary Ann Hayward (ca June 1791 – 26 September 1871). George Phinehas Nevers was born in Sunbury County, New Brunswick, and died at Burton, Sunbury County, New Brunswick. Mary Ann (Hayward) Nevers died at Burton, Sunbury County, New Brunswick.
2.Samuel P Nevers (1791 – 1846).
2.John Green Nevers (1796 - ?).
2.Anna Isabella Nevers (1800 – 10 April 1858) married Charles Miles (? _ ?).
2.Eliza Nevers (1806 - ?).

** George H. Hayward in his *Haywards of Sunbury & Carleton Counties, New Brunswick and Some of Their Descendants* documents (p. 2) that the marriage of George Hayward and Ann Derley/Durley is listed as Marriage No. 240, page 75, and reads as follows:

> Banns of Marriage between George Hayward, Batchelour, and Ann Derley, Spinster, both of this Parish, were duly published in this Church on Three several Sundays, viz.: March the 22nd and 29th, and April 5th, 1761, according to the Act of Parliament, by me, John Dilton, Curate.
>
> The said George Hayward, Batchelour, and the said Ann Derley, Spinster, were married in this Church by Banns, this Thirteenth Day of April, in the Year of our Lord, One Thousand Seven Hundred and Sixty One, by me, John Dilton, Curate. This marriage was solemnized, as above, between us
> } George Hayward
>
> } The Mark of
> } Ann X Derley
>
> In the Presence of us} Thomas Harrison
> } Tho's Foster

I have reformatted George H. Hayward's above transcription as it appears on page 2 of *Haywards of Sunbury & Carleton Counties, New Brunswick and Some of Their Descendants* to more fully duplicate the original cursive entry contained in the parish records which George H. Hayward has also included a copy of on the same page.

I have taken the liberty of moving the second paragraph from page 3 of George H. Hayward's *Haywards of Sunbury & Carleton Counties, New Brunswick and Some of Their Descendants* to the beginning of this direct quote, otherwise, everything included is as it appears:

> George and Ann, with their infant daughter Mary, came to New Brunswick in 1763. In his petition for land at French Lake dated August

20, 1788, George said "in the year 1763 your Memorialist came with his family from Great Britain to Nova Scotia." Their daughter Mary was still living in 1851. The census that year listed her as 89 years old (born about 1762), blind, English, entered the colony in June, 1763. Several other references say the Haywards were English or that they came from England. Ann (Boone) Carr's obituary, in *The Daily Gleaner* (Fredericton, N.B.), April 7, 1890, said her mother, Ann Hayward (daughter of George and Ann Hayward), was "of Manchester, England." In fact, Ann is believed to have been born in New Brunswick, but her parents were from England, although perhaps not from Manchester. ***

George and Ann settled first in Maugerville, Sunbury Co., N.B., where they apparently lived about sixteen years on Lot 70, 1000 acres, before he received a grant to the property from the government of the Province of Nova Scotia in 1779. Later, probably about 1780, they moved across the St. John River to the Parish of Lincoln where he built a homestead which stood until 1953 when it was deliberately destroyed by fire to make room for a new dwelling.

In August, 1788 he petitioned for Lots 16 and 17 at French Lake, in the Parish of Burton, and said he had purchased land adjoining those lots which he was improving and on which he was building a house and moving his family. Later in 1788 he deeded one-third part of Lots 16 and 17 to his daughter Mary and her husband Joseph Hoyt. In 1825 Joseph and Mary Hoyt sold one full third part of land granted to George Hayward Sr., at French Lake, and the deed identified the land as that which George Hayward Sr. had lived and died on. So his son John Hayward may have taken over the Lincoln house about that time. John was married in 1791, and lived in the house in Lincoln all his married life.

It is evident from the records that George was involved in lumbering on the south-westerly side of the river at an early date; on the Charles Morris Jr. grant just below Fredericton with William Baker, at French Lake in the Parish of Burton where he was granted 914 acres and where he apparently lived with his family, at least for a few years and may have died there, and at other locations.

In 1927, Henry Wilmot wrote a sketch about the Hayward homestead in Lincoln. It accompanied a painting of the Hayward house that hung in the York-Sunbury Historical Society Museum in Officers Square, Fredericton, in the 1970s. In his sketch Mr. Wilmot referred to George as "George Nehemiah Hayward of Essex County, Mass., who arrived in Maugerville in 1763." There was a settler in Maugerville named Nehemiah Hayward who came from Massachusetts. He was granted ½ of Lot 29 in Sheffield July 2, 1770, but shortly thereafter removed to New Hampshire. Mr. Wilmot may have confused the two early settlers, George and Nehemiah, both of whom arrived in Maugerville about 160 years previous, and referred to them as one man.

Ann's maiden name came first from Allan Boone, of Geary, Sunbury Co., a descendant of William and Ann (Hayward) Boone, who said it came down by word of mouth in the Boone family. Hannah E. Smith, born 1837, a daughter of William and Rebecca (Boone) Smith, granddaughter of William and Ann (Hayward) Boone, and great granddaughter of George and Ann (Derley) Hayward, married Amasa Carr. She named a daughter Annie Derley Carr, after her daughter's great grandmother. Confirmation of Ann's maiden name was found on George and Ann's marriage certificate, located in 2010 by Marcia Thomas, a descendant of Benjamin Thomas and Mary Hayward.

The names of only four children for George and Ann Hayward have been located. And it seems likely there were only two sons, at least only two that grew to adulthood, because George said in his 1788 land petition, when his wife was 57 years old, that he had two sons, young men, so it is unlikely there were more. (pp. 2-3)

*** Mrs. Anna CARR died at Geary (Sunbury Co.) April 1st, age 100 years and 23 days. The deceased lady was the daughter of William BOON of Rhode Island and Anna HAYWARD of Manchester, England. She was born at French Lake March 9th, 1790 and was married in 1812 to Asa CARR. As a result of this union there were born 11 children, 58 grandchildren, 103 great grandchildren and two great-great grandchildren. Five sons and three daughters survive her. (*New Brunswick Reporter and Fredericton Advertiser*, 9 April 1890.)

The following appears in George Wareing Bardsley's *English Surnames their Sources and Significations*:

An interesting relic of primitive precaution against the straying of animals is found in the officership of the 'Hayward' (or 'Adam le Heyward,' as the Hundred Rolls have it), whose duty it was to guard the cattle that grazed on the village common. He was so styled from the Saxon 'hay' or 'hedge,' already spoken of in our previous chapter.
An old poem has it —

> In tyme of hervest mery it is ynough ;
> Peres and apples hongeth on bough.
> The hayward bloweth mery his horne ;
> In every felde ripe is corne.

— In 'Piers Plowman,' too, we have the word —

> I have an horne, and be a hayward,
> And liggen out a nyghtes
> And kepe my corne and my croft
> From pykers and theves.

It will be seen from these two references that the officership was of a somewhat general character. The cattle might be his chief care, but the common village interests were also under his supervision. The term has left many surnames to maintain its now decayed and primitive character; 'Hayward' and 'Haward' are, however, the most familiar. 'Hayman' doubtless, is of similar origin. . . . (pp. 234-235))

New Brunswick, County Deed Registry Books, 1780-1930, for York (1823-1825), Volume 14, pp. 68-69

John Howard }
    to   }   N° 2408
George Howard}

Know all Men by these presents that John Howard of the parish of Kings clear in the County of York and province of New Brunswick, and Rebecka his wife for and in consideration of the sum of Two hundred pounds current money of New Brunswick, to the said John Howard and Rebecka his wife in hand paid by George Howard of ~~of~~ the parish of Kings clear County and province aforesaid, the receipt whereof is hereby acknowledged. Have granted bargained and sold and by these presents do grant bargain Sell unto the said George Howard his heirs and afsigns. All that certain piece or parcel of land and premises, situate lying and being in the parish of Kings clear in the County of York aforesaid, known and described in the grant to Stephen Jarvis and others, known and distinguished by being called the upper half of Lot number twenty seven

-69-

containing two hundred acres more or lefs. bounded on the upper side by lands of Eusch Lieut [Spelling ?], and lower side by lands of John Howard together with all and Singular the profits commodities privileges appurtenances and hereditaments whatsoever thereunto belonging or in any wise appertaining, and all the Estate rights title Interest dower right and title of dower property claim and demand whatsoever either in Law or equity of them the said John Howard and Rebecka his wife, or either of them of into or out of the same, and every part thereof with the Appurtenances and the reversion or reversions remainder and remainders rents ifsues and profits thereof. To have and to hold the said piece or parcel of land and premises above described with their appurtenances unto the said George Howard his heirs & afsigns to the only proper use and behoof of the said George Howard, his heirs & afsigns forever In Witnefs whereof the said John Howard and Rebecka his wife have hereunto set their hands & seals the thirteenth of July in the year of our Lord one thousand eight hundred and twenty two.

Signed Sealed and delivered }   John Howard {LS.}
in the presence of John Allen}
York fs.   Be it remembered that on the 14 day of July in the year of our Lord 1822. personally appeared before me John Allen Esqr. John Howard and acknowledged the foregoing Instrument to be his voluntary act and deed, and that he executed the Same for the purposes therein exprefsed   John Allen J Peace
New Brunswick }
York County   }   Registered this twenty fourth day of September One thousand and Eight hundred and twenty three.

APPENDIX U

Records of Old Revolutionary Soldiers and Their Widows

[The original documents as well as the yearly re-applications of John and Rebecca Howard and Mary Kelly can be viewed at the *Provincial Archives of New Brunswick* (PANB) (archives.gnb.ca/Archives/Default.aspx?culture=en-CA).]

Document 1838-Petition-072

To His Excellency Major General Sir John Henry KCH & CB — Lieut Governor and Commander in Chief of the Province of New Brunswick

The Honorable The Legislative Council
 and
The Honorable The House of Afsembly in general Afsembly convened —

The [illegible crossed out word] Petition of Mary Kelly widow of the late John Kelly of the Parish of Queensbury
    Humbly Sheweth
That your Petitioner is the widow of ~~the~~ John Kelly late of the Parish of Kings clear in the County of York — That her husband served his late Majesty King George the Third honestly and faithfully during the whole of the Revolutionary war under the late Colonel Allen — That he came to this Country when he

was

[2]

disbanded and settled in the Parish of Prince William where he resided until his death, That ~~previous~~ for several years previous to his death he was most severely afflicted with Cancer of which he died —

That all his little property had Lapsed into other hands and Your Petitioner left [illegible crossed out word] nearly destitute — That she is now very old and infirm and dependent upon the bounty of others for her support — She therefore
    Humbly prays that in Consideration of the faithful Services of her late Husband and in compafsion to her destrefsed circumstances

Your

[3]

Your Excellency and Honors will be pleased to afford her such afsistance as may seem meet and as in duty bound will ever pray

Queensbury

8 July 1838

her
Mary X Kelly
mark

[*verso*]

34.   ~~34~~

Petition
Mary Kelly
widow of the
late John Kelly
a Soldier of the
Revolutionary War
praying and in
her present dis-
trefsed situation

[illegible] [illegible] [illegible] 1838 by
M^r. Taylor
Old Soldiers Com:

Document P2-13-1852d

Kingsclear June 22' 1852

George J. Dibble. Esqr
   Please pay Isaac Kilburn Ten Pounds it being my Provincial allowance as an old soldier of the Revolutionary War as passed las[t] June sessions
[illegible] John Howard

Rec^d. June 24 1852 from Geo J. Dibble Ten Pounds on this order from John Howard
Isaac Kilburn

Document 1855-Petition-150

To His Excellency The Honorable John Henry Thomas examiners Sutton Lieutenant Governor and Commander in Chief of the Province of New Brunswick &c &c &c

To the Honorable The Legislative Council and The Honorable The House of afsembly
The [illegible crossed out word] Petition of Rebecca Howard of Kings clear in the County of York

    Humbly sheweth

That your Petitioner is the widow of ~~the late~~ John Howard late of Kingsclear in the County of York who died in the month of July last. That her said late Husband had for many years pervious to his death been in the habit of receiving the usual allowance granted to old Soldiers of the Revolutionary war and their widows —

That your Petitioner was lawfully married to the said John Howard in the year 1794 and has ever since resided within this province — That she is now aged 81 years. That she is left without any property or means of support and at her advanced age is unable to labor for her maintenance —

                                          She

[2]

She therefore humbly prays that your Excellency and Honors will be pleased to commend favorably her situation and grant her the usual Provincial allowance made to the widows of old soldiers of the Revolutionary war in America — and as in duty bound will ever pray

                                          Rebecca Howard

I have examined the above named Petitioner and certify that the matters and things set forth in her Petition are correct and true

                                          Isaac Kilburn J.P.

Kingsclear Feby 8th 1855}

                              [verso]

The Petition of
Rebecca Howard
The widow of an
old soldier of the
Revolutionary War
praying that the
usual allowance

to the widows of such
old soldiers may
be granted to her

12th. Feby. 1855.
Mr. Taylor:
Pension Com

Document 1856-Petition-252

To the Honorable the Legislative Council And The Honorable the House of Assembly in General Assembly Convened

The Petition of Rebecca Hayward of Kingsclear in the County of York Widow

Humbly Sheweth

That your Petitioner is the Widow of John Hayward late of Kingsclear aforesaid an Old Soldier of the Revolutionary War that he was during the ~~time~~ Interval from the time he was disbanded up to the time of his death in receipt of a pension from the Government

That your petitioner is now eighty four years of age and has received the allowance granted to the Widows of Pensioners the last year The said John Hayward her husband departed this life the sixth day of July 1854

Your Petitioner therefore prays that the usual allowance may be granted to her

And your Petitioner will ever Pray

Rebecca Howard

[2]

252   ~~18~~

Petition of Rebecca Howard
of Kings clear praying for the
continuance of the grant as the
widow of an old Soldier

Ө

27th. Feby. 1856.
Mr. Macpherson
        Pensions

APPENDIX V

Kean/Cain/Kane Land Grant Petitions, Land Grants and Deeds

New Brunswick Land Petitions: Original Series, Sunbury County, 1783-1918 (RS108) (Microfilm: F1025)

3A   His Excellency Thomas Carleton Esquire Captain Governor in Chief in and for the Province of New Brunswick, Chancelor and Vice Admiral of the Same &c &c &c

May it please Your Excellency,
  The memorial of John Cunningham Adjutant of the late Loyal American Regiment, and William Kean Adjutant of the late Regiment of Pennsylvania Loyalists,
  Sheweth
  That your Memorialists not having yet obtained their land, and understanding that it is your Excellency's intention that those who make application shall be put in pofsesion of any unlocated land on which they wish to settle,
  Beg leave to Represent to your Excellency, that between lands granted to Samuel Peabody Esquire, and the Reverend — Brunston, on the River Oromocto, there is a lot which has not been granted to as located by any person, of which the [sic] wish to obtain two Hundred Acres, in part of the Quantity to which the [sic] are Intitled; the remaining part they Humbly request your Excellency will please to afsign them, in the Rear of the Block which is now the property of James Simonds Esquire, and to be bounded infront by said Block which Extends from the River St. John between four and five miles,
  Placing a fair reliance on your Excellency's benevolence, and confident that every Incouragement will be given to those who are Anxious to settle on Their land, Your Memorialists hope that their application will meet with your Excellency's approbation

Jn. Cunningham
Willm Kean

[2]

Rec. 29 January
Adj.^{nt} Cunningham L. A. R.
Adj.^{nt} Kean — P. L.
Praying Lands on the
Oromocto.

Read in Council

11.th Feb= 1785.

the Petitioners may adver=
tise for 200 acres, each, in
either of the tracts mentioned
in their Petition, provided
they have not hitherto had
any allotments of land in
this Province.
    P. L. N. J.

[3]

The Subscribers maketh oath that the [sic] Advertised a Tract of Land Lying on the Oromocto, Between the Rever.t Brunton and Samuel Peabody Esq r for three weeks Agreeable to the Governor Instructions

            Jn Cunningham
            Adj nt [illegible] L: A: R

New Brunswick
Sunbury County, 16th March 1785 Willm Kean Ajt.
Sworn before me   Late Pennsyl.a Loy. ts
Andrew Maxwell
 Justice of the Peace

[verso]

[within fold]

Jon. Cunningham}
  &   } Adj.ts
William Kean }
Affidavit that they have
   advertised —

In Council 6.th April,
A Warrant of Survey
to be ifsued. —

In Council 12.th April,

~~A warrant of Survey to give S. Peabody to survey the back Lands [illegible] in cultivation lying on the South Side of the Oromocto towards the [illegible] Creek, Lots explore a Road Thro the same. —~~

———
Rec.d 26.th March 1785.

[separate fold]

Johnathan Odell Esq.r
       Secretary
T: C   Parr

New Brunswick Land Petitions: Original Series, Saint John County, 1783-1918 (RS108) (Microfilm: F1024)

105   To His Excellency Tho.s Carleton Esq.r &c &c &c

The Memorial of Mich.l Ambrose Lieut. Late P. W. A. Reg.t in behalf of himself, Ens.n Brunson, the Widow of Ens.n Keating Six Serj.ts Three Corp.ls a Drummer, and Six Privates, of the P. Reg.t

Respectfully Sheweth

That the Reg.t was so unfortunate in the Drafts of the Army As to Draw N.o Eleven — and from its Great distance up the River and the Many inconveniencys which would naturally Mind Settlers in the pafsage there, he begs Your Excellency's approbation for Settling on Salmon River on the Bay of Fundy As he is Given to understand it is not Yet Located —

                                Mich.l Ambrose Lieut
                                Late P. W. A. Reg.t

Carleton   }
10.th Dec.r 1784}

[verso]

The Memorial of Lieut.
Ambrose, late P. W. Reg.t

———
request lands on
Salmon River in rear
of block N.o 11 —

———

to be enquired into

———

ordered —
The Memorialist may
advertise — on
18.th Janu.y

New Brunswick Land Petitions: Original Series, Kings County, 1783-1918 (RS108) (Microfilm: F1024)

To His Excellency Thom.s Carleton Esq.r &c &c &c

The Memorial of Mich.l Ambrose late Prince of Wales Amer.n Reg.t
   Humbly Sheweth
That [illegible] Number of [illegible] not [illegible] did in his former Memorial, are territories of Settling upon Salmon River with him and its they have made no application for Land anywhere this Mem.t Humbly Prays of [illegible] Excellency that the Whole of the Number Annexed, may be included in the order of Survey —
                              Mich.l Ambrose

Parr S.t John   }
New Brunswick}
14.th March 1785}

———

Lieu.t Ambrose
Lieu.t Place
Ens.n Brunson
Widow of Ens.n Keating
Serg.t Bergin
Serg.t Rawding

[2]

Serg.t McWay   John Curry
Serg.t Goslee   W.m Miles
Serg.t Richards   Th.s Chandler
Serg.t Byrns   Th.s Odle
Serg.t Williams   Ethel Seely
Serg.t Charles   John Scott
Serg.t Tabor   John Loghlin
Corp.l Young   Jo.n Ramsey

Corp.l Winnard
Corp.l Connor
Corp.l Bergin
Corp.l Copeland
Corp.l Bryan
Corp.l Anderson
Miles Ryon
William Scarborough
Dan.l Maher
Rich.d Murphy
Ruben Brunson
Jabes Adams
Joseph Hoyt
Solomon Whitlock
Mich.l Knap
Pat.k Weldon
Tho.s Oare

Phillip Riley
Jabes Thorp

[verso]

The Mem.l of Mich.l
Ambrose
      14.th Mar.h 1785

after to include the
inclofsed List of Persons
in a Draft with him
upon Salmon River.

In Council 19.th March 1785. —
      Complied with.

Rec.d 14.th March 1785

[3]

    A list of a number of the late P. W. A. Regiment who had prayed his Excellency the Governor's permifsion to form a Settlement upon Salmon River, [illegible] of Tuacks head, upon the Bay of Fundy,

Lieu.t Amrose,
Lieu.t Place,

Miles Ryon,
Wm Scarborough,

Ens.ⁿ Brunson,
Widow of Ens.ⁿ Keating,
Serg.ᵗ Bergin,
Serg.ᵗ Rawdling,
Serg.ᵗ McWay,
Serg.ᵗ Goslee,
Serg.ᵗ Richards,
Serg.ᵗ Byrns,
Serg.ᵗ Charles,
Serg.ᵗ Williams,
Serg.ᵗ Thomkins,
Serg.ᵗ Crowfoot,
Corp.ˡ Young,
Corp.ˡ Connor,
Corp.ˡ Harger,
Corp.ˡ Copeland,
Corp.ˡ Bryan,
Corp.ˡ Anderson,
Corp.ˡ Whitlock,
Corp.ˡ McMahon,

Dennis Mahor,
Rich.ᵈ Murphy,
Ruben Brunson,
Drummer Murphy,
Jabes Adams,
Mich.ˡ Knap,
Patt.ᵏ Weldon,
Tho.ˢ Oare,
John Curry,
W.ᵐ Miles,
Th.ˢ Chandler,
Th.ˢ Odle,
Ethel Seely,
John Loghlin,
James Murrony,
Phillip Riley,
Jabes Throp,
John Foy,
W.ᵐ Campbell,
Ch.ˢ Larman,
James Clark,
Pat.ᵏ Donnelly,
W.ᵐ Cain,
James Farren,

Turn —

[verso]

Lieu.ᵗ Amrose Return
of the P.ᵉ Wales's for lands on
Salmon River Bay of Fundy

15.ᵗʰ April 1785

[separate fold]

John Ramsey,
Mathew Sullivan
Peter Doran
Edward Sutton
Jonathan Wright
Drummer, James Jack.

[4]

I Mich.¹ Ambrose do Make oath that the Tract of Land for which I Memorial'd his Excellency the Governor, upon Salmon River Eastward of Tuacks head upon the Bay of Fundy, has been by Me advertised in the Publick Papers agreeable to his orders — and that I have sent several Copys with directions to have them put up in the Most publick places at Tuacks, the nearest Settlement —

        Mich.¹ Ambrose

Sworn before Me at
St. John New Brunswick
14.th March 1785

        [illegible] [illegible] Jus. Peace

[verso]

In Council 15.th April
L.t Ambrose. — W. Holland
be directed to advertise and
draw for the petitioners of
the P. W. with two [illegible]
for the Lots Surveyed on
Salmon River — Bay of Fundy.

[separate fold]

Rec.d 14.th March 1785.
Michael Ambrose,
affidavit that he has
   advertised. —
6.th April [illegible] [illegible]

———

In Council 6.th April
A Warrant of Survey
to be ifsued for 200 Acres,
each. —

———

In Council 12.th April
M.¹ Ambrose to make an

exact return of the names
of the persons who petitions
with him, and the Allotments
may take place. —

In Council 15.ᵗʰ April. —
~~W Karfsu on his return~~
~~to Survey the Land [illegible] for~~
~~Cutlers store from [illegible] Head~~
~~to Cape [illegible].~~

                see the other side.

New Brunswick Land Petitions: Original Series, Sunbury County, 1783-1918 (RS108) (Microfilm: F1025)

To his Excellency Thomas Carlton Esquire Captain General and Governor in Chief in and over his Majestys Province of New Brunswick &c. &c. &c.

20.
    The Memorial of Captain Thomas Colden in behalf of himself the other Officers, Non Commifsion'd Officers and Soldiers of the late Corps of Pennsylvania Loyalists —

Respectfully Sheweth —

    That Block N°. 7. On the River St. John was drawn by the said Corps; but that before it was laid out in Lotts the Season was so far advanced, and such small supplys of provision found at a time that, it was thought advisable for the men to remain in their present hutts till Spring.
    That they are very desirous to remove up the river as early as pofsible the ensuing season — Your Memorialist therefore humbly requests your Excellency will be pleased to direct a grant to be made out for said Corps, agreeable to a return given in at the Secretarys Office And your Memorialist will pray &c —
                                          Thom.ˢ Colden

[2]

[The following are among the list of names:]

Adj.ᵗ Wᵐ Kean 16.17
Mich.ˡ Kean 38

The Kellys of Kingsclear

Capt Colden № 1.2.3

[The list of names is followed by:]

[#20] [*sic*]
Pennsylvania Loyalists

[3]

State of the late Corps of Pennsylvania Loyalists

["Adjunct: William Kean" is listed as being "Present in New Brunswick" with one wife and no children. "Private Michael Kean" is also listed as being "Present in New Brunswick" with one wife and one child.]

39 Lots of 42 Rods each

[*verso*]

Capt[n]. Thomas Colden,
in behalf of himself, the
other Officers, non-commifs.
Officers & Privates of the late
       Pennsylvania Loyalists

prays a Grant of the Lands
allotted to that Corps; Block.7.

———————
———————

/Read in Council
2[d]. March

Referred to a future
day.

Reciev.[ed] 7th March 1785 —

Orders are given M.[r] Davidson
for the division & settling
said Corps.

Rec^d. 22^d. Feb.^{ry} 1785. —

New Brunswick Land Petitions: Original Series, Sunbury County, 1783-1918 (RS108) (Microfilm: F1025)

R. H'^{s} EXCELLENCY
THOMAS CARLETON, Efq:
Captain General and Governor in Chief of the Province of New Brunswick, and Territories thereon depending, Chancellor and Vice-Admiral of the fame, &c. &c. &c.

To G. Sproule Esq. Surveyor General —
You are forthwith, by yourfelf or your Deputy, to admeafure and lay out for Adjutant John Cunningham & Adjutant W^m. Kean two lots of 200 Acres each in a tract of Land being on the Oromocto, comprehended between the boundary of a grant to W^m. Hazen & Others & the Boundaries of N°. 8 in Israel Perleys Late Survey

and make a due Return into the Secretary's Office within
    from the Date hereof, with a Plate or Defcription hereunto annexed, and alfo certify for the Nature and Quality of the faid Lands, conformably to his Majefty's Inftructions; And for fo doing this fhall be your Warrant.

GIVEN under my Hand, at ~~PARR TOWN, this~~ S^t. John July 9th 1785.
                                    Signed T. C

[*verso*]

1785
Adj^n. Cunningham
& Kean.

9th July 1785

New Brunswick Land Grants, 1784 – 1997, Sunbury County, Volume 1 (RS686) (Microfilm: F16308)

12

~~NOVA SCOTIA,~~   New Brunswick
GEORGE the Third by the Grace of GOD of GREAT BRITAIN, FRANCE and IRELAND, KING, Defender of the Faith, and fo forth.

To all to whom thefe Prefents fhall Come Greeting,

KNOW ye, that We, of Our fpecial Grace certain Knowledge, and mere Motion, have Given and Granted by thefe Prefents, for Us, our Heirs and Succeffors do give and grant unto Heil Camp, Widow Esther Burlock, James Ingram, Jedediah Cook Junior, Widow Rachel Chichester, Samuel Troubridge, Jedediah Cook, Calvin Turner, Adjutant William Kean and Adjutant John Cunningham in severalty unto each and every of their several and respective Heirs and Afsigns several Lots and Plantations of Land comprehended to wit a tract of Land situate lying and being on the River Oromucto within the County of Sunbury, and abutted and bounded as follows to wit, beginning on the Northwest bank of the said river at a marker Elm Tree the upper or western boundary of a Tract of Land granted to Arthur Gould Esquire and running thence by the Magnet North forty five degrees West one hundred and thirty four Chains of four rodes each or until it meets the Southerly line of a Tract of Land granted to James Simonds Esqure, thence South thirty seven degrees west one hundred thirty six Chains or until it meets the lower or northerly line of a Grant to William Hazen Esquire and others thence along the said line of the said Grant South forty five degrees East one hundred and Sixety nine Chains to the Bank of the said River thence along the said Bank following the several courses thereof down Stream to the bounds first mentioned containing on the whole one thousand nine hundred acres more or lefs with allowance for Roads and subdivisions into ten lots containing two hundred Acres land more of lefs except the Lot number nine and number ten which contains one hundred and Seventy four acres each more of lefs all wildernefs Land and hath such shape form and marks as [illegible] [illegible] the [illegible] survey thereof [illegible] under the directions of our Surveyor general of our said Province of which [illegible] the plot hereunto annexed is a respresentation

~~And hath fuch Shape, Form, and Marks, as appears by a Plat thereof hereunto annexed;~~ together with all Woods, Underwoods, Timber and Timber Trees, Lakes, Ponds, Fifhings. Waters, Water Courfes, Profits, Commodities, Appurtenances, and Hereditaments whatfoever thereunto belonging or in any Wife appertaining; together alfo with the Privileges of Hunting, Hawking and Fowling In and upon the fame, and Mines and Minerals; SAVING and referving NEVERTHELESS to us, our Heirs and Succefsors, all White Pine Trees, if any fuch shall be found growing thereon, and alfo SAVING and referving to us, our Heirs and Succefsors all Mines of Gold, Silver, Copper, Lead and Coals, TO HAVE AND TO HOLD the faid ~~Parcel~~, Tract of one thousand nine hundred and forty Eight Acres of land, and all and fingular other the Premises hereby granted unto the faid Grantees severally and, respectively and in severalty in the several & respective Shares quantities and proportions following to wit, unto the said several and respective Grantees in the lots [illegible] [illegible] and proportions as follows, that is to say, unto the said Hiel Camp the Lot number one, unto the said Widow Esther Burlock Executor number two, unto Calvin Turner Esquire the Lot number three, unto the said Jedediah Cook Junior the lot number four, unto the said Widow Rachel Chichester the lot number five, unto the said Samuel Troubridge the Lot number Six, unto the said Jedediah Cook the Lot number Seven, unto the said Calvin Turner the Lot number eight, each and every of [illegible] [illegible] [illegible] [illegible] [illegible] lots containing two hundred Acres more or less, unto the said Adjutant William Kean the Lot number nine and unto the said Adjutant John Cunningham the Lot number ten, the said two last mentioned lots containing one hundred and Seventy four acres [illegible] respective granted and [illegible] several are respective

Heirs or Affigns YIELDING and PAYING therefor unto us, our Heirs and Succeffors, or to our Receiver General for the Time being, or to his Deputy or Deputies for the Time being yearly, that is to fay, at the Feaft of Saint Michael in every Year, at the Rate of Two Shillings for every Hundred Acres, and fo in Proportion according to the Quantities of Acres hereby granted; the fame to commence and be payable from the faid Feaft of Saint Michael which fhall firft happen after the Expiration of Ten Years from the Date hereof PROVIDED always and this prefent Grant is upon Condition that the faid several Grantees and their several & respective Heirs or Affigns fhall and do within three Years after the Date hereof for every fifty Acres of Plantable Land herby granted, clear and work three Acres at leaft, in fuch Part thereof as they fhall judge moft convenient and advantageous; or elfe to clear and drain three Acres of Swampy or Sunken Ground, or drain three Acres of Marfh, if any fuch contained therein. AND fhall and do within the Time aforefaid, put and keep upon every Fifty acres thereof, accounted Baren, three Neat Cattle, and continue the fame thereon, until three Acres of every Fifty be fully cleared and improved, and if there fhall be no Part of the faid Tract fit for prefent Cultivation without manuring and improving the fame they within the Time aforesaid fhall be obliged to erect on fome Part of the said Land, one good Dwelling Houfe, to be at leaft Twenty Feet in Length and Sixteen Feet in breadth, and to put on the said Land the like Number of three Neat Cattle for every Fifty Acres; or otherwife if any Part of the faid Tract fhall be Stony or Rocky Ground, and not fit for Planting or Pafture, fhall and do within three Years as aforefaid, begin to employ thereon and continue to work for three Years then next enfusing, in digging any ftony Quary or Mine, one good and able Hand for every Fifty Acres, it fhall be accounted a fufficient Cultivation and Improvement; PROVIDED alfo, that every three Acres that fhall be cleared and worked, or cleared and drained as aforefaid, fhall be accounted fufficient Seating, Cultivation and Improvement to fave forever from Forfeiture Fifty Acres of Land in any Part of the Tract hereby granted; And the faid respective Grantees and their said several and respective Heirs and affigns be at Liberty to withdraw their Stock, or forbear working in any Quarry or Mine, in Proportion to fuch Cultivation and Improvements, as fhall be made upon the Plantable Lands, Swamps, Sunken Grounds or Marfh therein contained; AND if the faid Rent hereby referred fhall happen to be in arrear or unpaid for the Space of One Year from the Time it fhall become due, and no Diftrefs can be found on the faid Lands, Tenements and

Hereditaments hereby Granded, or if this Grant fhall not be duly Regiftred in the Regifters Office of our faid Province within Six Months from the Date hereof, and a Docket alfo entered in the Auditors Office of the fame, then this Grant fhall be void, and the faid Lands, Tenements and Hereditaments hereby granted, and every Part and Parcel thereof fhall revert to us, our Heirs and Succefsors; AND PROVIDED alfo, upon this further Condition, that if the Land herby Given and Granted aforefaid shall at any Time or Times hereafter come unto the Poffession and Tenure of any Perfon or Perfosn whatever, Inhabitants of our faid Province of ~~Nova-Scotia~~ New Brunswick, either by Virture of any deed of Sale, Conveyance, Enfeoffment, or Exchange, or by Gift, Inheritance, Defcent, Devife or Marriage, fuch Perfon or Perfons being Inhabitants as aforefaid, fhall within Twelve Months after his, her or their Entry and Poffeffion of the fame, take the Oaths, ~~prefcribed by Law, and make and fubfcribe the following Declaration, that is to fay, "I do promife and declare, that I will maintain and defend to the utmoft of my Power, the Authority of the King in his Parliament as the Supreme Legiflature of this Province,"~~ before fome one of the Magiftrates of the faid Province, ~~and fuch Declaration~~ and Certificate of the Magiftrate, that fuch Oaths have been taken, being recorded in the Secretary's Office of the faid Province, the Perfon or Perfons fo taking the Oaths aforefaid and making ~~and fubfcrigin the faid Declartion,~~ fhall be deemed the lawful Poffeffor or Poffeffors of the Lands hereby granted: AND a Cafe of Default on the Part of fuch Perfon or Perfons in taking the Oaths, ~~and making and fubfcribing the Declaration~~ within Twelve Months as aforefaid, This prefent Grant, and every Part thereof, fhall and We do hereby declare the fame to be Null and Void to all Intents and Purpofes, and the Lands hereby Granted and every Part and Parcel thereof, fhall in like Manner revert to and become vefted in Us, our Heirs and Succeffors, any Thing herein contained to the Contrary notwithftanding.

    GIVEN under the Great Seal of our Province of ~~Nova-Scotia~~ New Brunswick: WITNESS our Trufty and Well-beloved Thomas Carleton Esquire our Captain General Governor and Commander in Chief, in and over our faid Province, this sixteenth Day of November in the Year of our Lord One Thousand Seven Hundred and Eighty five and in the Twenty fifth Year of our Reign

                                                      By Command of His Excellency
                                                                  Wm Odell

Grant of Heil Camp
and Others 1948 acres
of Land Oromucto
[illegible] [illegible] November 1785
Registered [illegible] Decr 1785

New Brunswick, County Deed Registry Books, 1780-1930, for Saint John (1804-1806), Volume J1, pp. 19-21

John Cain }
    To   } Nº 1325. Know all men by these Presents that I John Cain of Mafseys
Daniel O Nail} Bay County of Saint John and Province of New Brunswick North America, for and in Consideration of the sum of five Shillings lawful Money of the Province of New Brunswick to me paid by Daniel O Nail of the said Mafseys Bay County of Saint John and Province of New Brunswick the Receipt whereof I do hereby acknowledge, Have granted bargained and Sold and by these presents do grant bargain and sell unto the said Daniel O Nail and his heirs lawfully begotten the one half of the Lot Number Seven Containing two hundred acres more or lefs lying and Situated on Mafses Bay and joining to the Lot Number Six now the property of James Dawson, To have and to hold the said Lands and premises with the appurtenances to the said Daniel O Nail and his heirs only lawfully begotten and to his and their only use and behoof forever, And I do for myself my heirs Executors and

and administrators Covenant with the said Daniel O Nail and his heirs only that I am Seized of the Premises as a good Indefeasible Estate of Inheritance in fee simple free of and from all manner of Incumbrances whatsoever (costs dues, Conditions and reservations due and reserved to the King only excepted) and that I have a good right full power and lawful authority to grant bargain and Sell the same in manner and form as above written In Witnefs whereof I have hereunto set my hand and Seal this Eleventh day of August in the year of our Lord one thousand Eight hundred and two and in the Forty Second year of His Majestys Reign.

Signed Sealed & delivered }
in the presence of us   }   John Cain (LS)
William Linthwait
Robert Laidley

    Be it remembered that on the Eleventh day of August 1802 Personally came and appeared before me William Linthwait Esquire one of His Majestys Justices of the Peace for the City and County of Saint John the above named John Cain the Grantor and acknowledged the

the above to be his free act and Deed for the purposes therein mentioned.

William Linthwait.

Registered the foregoing Deed this Tenth day of November 1804.

John Chaloner Register

New Brunswick, County Deed Registry Books, 1780-1930, for Saint John (1809-1810), Volume L1, pp. 27-29

Daniel Hallet & Samuel Hallet }
    To   }   Nº 1510
Anne Kane & Katherine Hallet }

 Know All Men by these presents that Daniel Hallet and Samuel Hallet Executors of the last will and Testament of Captain Samuel Hallet deceased by virtue of the power & authority in them vested in and by the said Last will and Testament and for and in consideration of

-28-

the sum of sixty pounds Lawful money of New Brunswick to the said Daniel Hallet and Samuel Hallet well and truly paid by Anne Kane & Katherine Hallet both of the City of Saint John in the Province of New Brunswick at or before the ensealing and delivery of these presents the receipt whereof the said Daniel Hallet & Samuel Hallet do hereby acknowledge Have granted bargained and Sold and by these presents do grant bargain and sell to the said Anne Kane & Katherine Hallet all that lot piece, & parcel of ground situate Lying and being in Kings Ward of the said City known and distinguished in a Map or Chart of the said City by the number two hundred & nine fronting a certain Street commonly called Union Street bounded on the East by the number two hundred and nine and on the west by the number two hundred & Eight as by reference to the said Map or Chart may more fully appear with the dwelling Home and all and singular the buildings and fences thereon with the appurtenances thereunto belonging or in any wise appertaining and the revision and revisions, remainder and remainders rents ifsues

-29-

rents ifsues and profits of all and singular the premises with the appurtenances and also all the estate right title interest property claim and demand whatsoever of them the said Daniel Hallet & Samuel Hallet or any other person or persons of in and to the same and every part & parcel thereof with the appurtenances To Have and to Hold the said mefsuage tenements tract lot and all and singular the premises with the appurtenances and every part and parcel thereof unto the said Anne Kane and Katherine Hallet jointly or severally and to their heirs and afsigns forever to the only proper use benefit and behoof of the said Anne Kane and Katherine Hallet and to their heirs and afsigns forever In Witnefs whereof the said Daniel Hallet & Samuel Hallet executors aforesaid have hereunto set their hands & seals the tenth day of June in the year of our Lord one thousand Eight hundred & five

                 Samuel Hallet (LS)
Sealed & Delivered }   Daniel Hallet (LS)
In presence of   }
William Whitlock
James Bell
James Legee

New Brunswick, County Deed Registry Books, 1780-1930, for Saint John (1809-1810), Volume L1, pp. 139-142

John Sinnot   }
Catherine Sinnot } Esc^d.
   &   } N° 1548 This Indenture made the Twenty Second Day of April in
Anne Kane   } the year of our Lord one thousand eight hundred and eight —
   To   } Between John Sinnot of the City of Saint John in the province of
Nathaniel Golding } New Brunswick Gentleman Catherine his wife of the first part and Anne Kane of the same City of St John widow of the second part, and Nathaniel Golding of the same City of St John Tavernkeeper of the third part Witnefseth that the Said Parties of the first and second parts for and in consideration of the sum of one hundred pounds of Lawful money of the said province of New Brunswick to them the said parties of the first and second part paid by the party of the third part the receipt and payment whereof is hereby acknowledged

-140-

acknowledged
and the said parties of the first and second part confefs themselves to be fully satisfied contented and paid and do by these presents acquit exonerate and discharge the said party of the third part his heirs and afsigns for ever — have granted bargained and sold and by these presents do grant bargain and sell unto the said party of the third part his heirs and afsigns forever all that certain lot piece and parcel of ground mefsuage and tenements situate lying & being in Kings Ward in the said City of Saint John known and distinguished in the map or plan of the said City by the Number Two hundred and Nine fronting on the Street commonly called Union Street with the dwelling houses and all and singular the improvements

thereon and the appurtenances and the reversion and reversions remainder and remainders rents ifsues and profits to the same in any manner belonging or app[e]rtaining and all the Estate right title interest claim property and demand whatsoever in Law and equity of in and to the same and of in and to every part and parcel thereof with their and every of their appurtenances To have and to hold the said lot piece and parcel of ground mefsuage tenement premises and appurtenances above described and every part and parcel thereof with their and every of their appurtenances unto him the said party of the Third part his heirs and afsigns forever To the only sole and proper use behoof benefit and advantage of him the said party of the third part his heirs and afsigns for ever and the said parties of the first and second part do by these presents for themselves their heirs executors and administrators exonerate promise to and with the

-141-

said party of the third part are by these presents ~~for themselves~~ his heirs and afsigns that the said parties of the first and second part have good right full power and Lawful authority to grant bargain and sell unto the said party of the third part the said herein before described premises with the appurtenances in manner and form as they have herebefore granted bargained and sold the same and that they the said parties of the first and second part their heirs executors and administrators shall and will warrant and defend the same to the said party of the third part his heirs and afsigns for ever by these presents against all claims and demands of all person or persons whatsoever In Witnefs whereof the parties have to these presents set their hands and Seals the day and year above written

Sealed and Delivered	John Sinnot (LS)
in the presence of	Catherine Sinnot (LS)
John Chaloner	Ann Kean (LS)
Robert Reid	

City and County of Saint John } Be it remembered that on the twenty second day of April one thousand eight hundred and nine before me John Chaloner Esquire

Register of Deeds & for the City and County aforesaid personally appeared John Sinnot and Anne Kean grantors to the foregoing instrument or deed and acknowledged that they signed sealed and delivered the same as and for their free act for the purposes therein mentioned Als[o] on the same day appeared Catherine Sinnot wife of the said John who being examined separate and apart from her said husband acknowledged that she signed the same as and for her free act and deed for the purposes therein

Contained without and threat fear or cumpulsion from her said husband —

John Chaloner Register

Registered the foregoing Deed the 22d April 1809

John Chaloner Register

New Brunswick, County Deed Registry Books, 1780-1930, for Saint John (1816-1817), Volume Q1, pp. 181-183

Oliver Arnold }
     To   } No 3027 This may certify that Adjt William Kein is the rightful owner
William Kean } of the Lot No 231 in Guilford Street being forty feet by one hundred

having complied with the terms of receiving it.

By order of the Directors of the
Towns at the entrance of the River St John

Parr
River St John   Oliver Arnold
July 4th 1784

I do hereby make over and afsign unto W Calep McKinsey my right title in and to the above Lot of ground, Witnefs my hand and seal this 19th July 1784
Witnefs   Willm. Kean. (LS)
Isaac Cullin

Registered the foregoing Certificate this 7th
Sept. 1816   John Chaloner Register

Calep McKinsey }
     To   } No 3028 This Indenture made the 2d January in the year of our Lord
Samuel Hallett } one thousand seven hundred and Eighty six between Calep

McKinsey of the Town of St. John in the province of New Brunswick of the one part, and Samuel Hallett of the same place Capt. General De Lanceys late Brigade of the other part Witnefseth that the said Calep McKinsey for & in consideration of ten Shillings

Lawful money of the Province of New Brunswick to him in hand paid by the said Samuel Hallett, the receipt whereof the said Calep McKinsey doth hereby acknowledge, He the said Calep McKinsey hath granted bargained and sold, Aliened & confirmed, and by these presents doth grant bargain & sell alien release and confirm unto the said Samuel Hallett his Heirs and afsigns forever a certain Lot or tract of Land situated & lying in Guilford Street known

-182-

Known & distinguished by N°. 231 being forty feet in front in Guilford Street running One hundred feet back. And also all Lanes, Woods, underwoods titles Commons common of pasture profits commodities and advantages; Ways waters & appurtenances, whatsoever to the said Lot N° 231 and premises above mentioned belonging or in any wise appertaining, And also the reversion, & reversions, remainder and remainders rents & services of the said premises and of every part thereof, and all the estate, right title and property, claim and demand of him the said Calep McKinsey of in & to the said Lot or tract of Land N° 231 and premises, and every part thereof To have and to hold the said Lot or tract of Land, and all and singular the said premises above mentioned and every part & parcel thereof with the appurtenances unto the said Samuel Hallett his Heirs & afsigns, to the only proper use & behoof of the said Samuel Hallett his Heirs and afsigns forever; And the said Calep McKinsey & Wife for them & their Hieirs the said Lot 231 and premises and every part against them and their Heirs, and against all and every other person & persons whatsoever to the said Samuel Hallett his Heirs & afsigns, shall and will Warrant & forever defend by these presents. In Witnefs whereof the parties to these presents have interchangeably set their Hands and seals at the Town of S^t. John the day & year first above written and in the Twenty sixth year of the Reign of our Sovereign Lord George the third of Great Brittain, France, & Ireland, King defender of the faith &c — —

Signed seal[e]d & delivered }
in the presence of us }
William Whitlock }
Samuel Hallatt Junr. }

       his
Calep X McKenzie (LS)
     mark

       her
Glourannah X McKenzie (LS)
     mark

City

-183-

City and County } Be it remembered that on the seventh day of September one of Saint John } thousand Eight hundred and sixteen before me John Chaloner Esquire, Register of Deeds &c for the City & County aforesaid personally appered Samuel Hallett one of the subscribing witnefses to the foregoing written Instrument and made Oath upon the holy Evangelist of Almighty God that he saw Calep McKinsey and Gloranah McKinsey his Wife the grantors thereof sign seal & Execute the same as and for their free acts for the use and purposes therein Contained, and that he signed the same as a Witnefs thereto together with William Whitlock the other Witnefs at the same time and in the presence of each other

John Chaloner Register
Deeds &c for the City & County of Saint John

Registerd the foregoing }
Deed this 7th. September 1816 }

John Chaloner Register

RS71 Saint John County Probate Court Records – Kean, Ann 1820.

[A summary of this will appears in R. Wallace Hale's *Early New Brunswick Probate Records, 1785-1835* (p. 237).]

In the name of God, Amen. I Ann Kean of the City of Saint John in the Province of New Brunswick Widow being Mindful of my Mortality, do this twenty fifth day of September in the year of our Lord one thousand eight hundred and twenty, make and publish this my last Will and Testament in manner following. First; I desire to be decently buried in the Church Yard belonging to the Parish in which I shall happen to die, at the discretion of my Executor hereinafter named. Secondly. I give and bequeath All my personal Estate whatsoever and wheresoever and afterthat Nature Kind and quality soever the same may be, which I now possess or hereafter may possess, (after payment of my debts and funeral expenses) unto my Sister Catherine Sinnott wife of John Sinnott of the City above said gentleman, her executors, administrators and afsigns, to and for her and their own use and benefit absolutely.

And I do hereby Constitute and Appoint Samuel Hallett Junior of the City aforesaid Merchant Sole executor of this

[2]

this my last will and testament. In witnefs whereof I have herewith set my hand & seal the day and year first above written.   Ann Kean

Signed, Sealed, published and

declared by the said Executor as and
for his last will and testament, in
our presence, who, at her request
in her presence, and in the presence
of each other, have Inscribed our
names as witnefses thereto.

WB Kinnear
F.A. Kinnear
Hannah Moore

Received for Registry the
　　7th October 1820 by
　　　　John Chaloner J.r Register
　　　　　　Of Probates

[verso]

The Last Will &c of
Mrs. Ann Kean
Recd Registered & filed
the 7th October 1820
John Chaloner
D.y Register

Proved the 7th day
of October 1820 by the
oath of F. Kinnear
C Peters
[illegible]: G [illegible] &
[illegible] of [illegible]
& [illegible]

New Brunswick, County Deed Registry Books, 1780-1930, for York (1830-1831), Volume 18, pp. 218-219

John Kane & Wife }
　　　　to　　　　} No. 4796 Know all Men by these presents that John Kane of the
Francis E Beckwith} Parish of Kingsclear in the County of York and Province of New
Brunswick — Yeoman and Julia his Wife for and in Consideration of the Sum of

Fifty pounds of Current money of the Province aforesaid to the said John Kane in hand well and truly paid at or before the Sealing and delivery of these presents by Francis Edward Beckwith of the Parish of Fredericton in the County and Province aforesaid Merchant the Receipt whereof is hereby Acknowledged Have granted bargained and Sold and by these presents do grant bargain and sell unto

-219-

the said Francis Edward Beckwith his heirs and Afsigns all that Certain piece or parcel of land Situate in the Hanwell Settlement (So called) in the Parish of Kingsclear in the County and Province aforesaid being lot Number Twenty three on the South East side of Hanwell Road (so called) and bounded as follows; Beginning at the Northernangle of lot Number twenty Two Granted to John A Beckwith thence running Magnetically South Forty five degrees East one Hundred and ten Chains of four Poles each, thence north forty five degrees East Twenty chains, thence north Forty five degrees west one hundred and ten chains to the said Hanwell Road and thence along the said Road South westerly to the place of beginning containing Two hundred and Twenty acres be the same more of lefs, together with all ways, waters, privileges profits commodities, hereditaments, and Appurtenances thereunto belonging or appertaining, and all the estate Right title Dower, Right and title of Dower property Claim and demand either at Law or in Equity of them the said John Kane and Julia his Wife of into or out of the same — and every part thereof with the Appurtenances, To have and to hold the said piece or parcel of land and premises as described with the Appurtenances unto the said Francis E Beckwith his heirs and Afsigns forever. In Witnefs where of the said John Kane and Julia his Wife have hereunto set their hands and Seals the Twenty ninth day of December in the year of our Lord one thousand and Eight Hundred and thirty.

Signed Sealed and delivered in the }
presence of John Taylor W. Wilmot}   John Kean   {LS}
                                                        her
                                               Julia X Kean {LS}
                                                      mark

York fs Be it Remembered that on the Twenty ninth day of December one thousand Eight hundred and thirty before me W. Wilmot Esqr. One of His Majestys Justices for the County of York personally appeared John Kane and Julia his wife the Grantees above named and Acknowledged the foregoing Instrument to be their free Act and deed executed by them for the uses and purposes therein Mentioned and the said Julia being examined Separate and apart from her husband declared that she executed the Same freely and Voluntarily without any Threat fear or Compulsion of her said husband.

New Brunswick }   W. Wilmot J. Peace

York County   } Registered this fourth day of January one thousand Eight hundred and thirty one

New Brunswick, County Deed Registry Books, 1780-1930, for York (1830-1831), Volume 18, pp. 219-220

James Balloch & Wife}
            to   } Nº. 4797 This Indenture made this fourth day of January in the
Michael Cain   } year of our Lord one thousand Eight hundred and thirty one Between James Balloch of the Parish of Fredericton in the County of York and Province of New Brunswick — Merchant and Elizabeth his Wife of the one part, and Michael Cain of the Parish of Kingsclear — County and Province aforesaid Farmer of the other part. Witnefseth that the said James Balloch and Elizabeth his Wife for in Consideration of the Sum of Twenty Pounds of lawful Money of New Brunswick to them in hand well and truly paid at or before the ensealing and delivery of these presents by the said Michael Cain the receipt whereby acknowledged. Have granted bargained and sold and by these presents do grant bargain and sell unto the said Michael Cain his heirs and Afsigns all that tract or parcel of land Situate lying and being in the Parish of Kingsclear County and Province aforesaid Known and distinguished as Lot Number Eleven on the Southe[a]stern Side of the hanwell [sic] Road (so called) fronting thereon Eighty Rods and bounded Northeasterly by lot Number Twelve granted to Patrick Burke and Southwesterly by lot Number Ten Reserved for the use of the Church said lot Number Eleven containing there Hundred Acres more or lefs with the usual allowance of ten per Cent for Roads &c together with all and Singular the Rights Liberties privileges improvements

and hereditaments whatsoever to the same piece and tract of land belonging or in any wise appertaining and the Reversion and Reversions. Remainder and Remainders rents ifsues, and profits thereof and also all the estate right title dower right and title of dower interest use possession property claim and demand Whatsoever either at Law or in equity of them the said James Balloch and Elizabeth his Wife or either of them of into or out of the same and every part thereof with the appurtenances To have and to hold the said piece or parcel of land and Premises with the Appurtenances unto the said Michael Cain his heirs and Afsigns to the only proper use and behoof of the said Michael Cain his heirs and Afsigns forever. In Witnefs whereof the said James Balloch and Elizabeth his Wife have hereunto Set their hands and Seals the day and year above Written.
Signed Sealed and delivered in the presence}   Jas. Balloch   {LS}

of Benjamin Beveridge John Balloch }   Elizabeth Balloch {LS}

York to wit Be it Remembered that on this fourth of Jany. in the year of our Lord one Thousand and Eight hundred and thirty one before me personally appeared James Balloch and Elizabeth his Wife grantors in the foregoing deed and bargain and sale named who acknowledged to be their free act and deed Sealed and executed by them for the purpose therein exprefsed and the said Elizabeth being by me examined Separate and apart from her said husband declared that she executed the same of her own free will and accord without fear threat or Compulsion from him her said husband.

New Brunswick}   Geo Minchin J Peace
York County   } Registered this fifth day of January one thousand Eight hundred and thirty one

New Brunswick, County Deed Registry Books, 1780-1930, for York (1830-1831), Volume 18, pp. 220-221

Patrick Burke & Wife}
          to   } N°. 4798
Timothy Burke   } This Indenture made the tenth day of August in the year of our Lord one thousand Eight hundred and twenty nine Between Patrick Burk [sic] of Fredericton in the County of York in the Province of New Brunswick and Wineferd his Wife of the one part and Timothy Burke of Fredericton aforesaid labourer of the other part. Witnefseth that for and Consideration of the Sum of nine pounds of lawful Money of New Brunswick to the said Patrick and Wineferd his Wife in hand well and truly paid by the said Timothy at or before the sealing and Delivery of these presents the Receipt whereof is hereby Acknowledged. the said Partick and Wineferd his Wife have granted, bargained and Sold and by these presents do grant bargain and Sell to the said Timothy his heirs and Afsigns the upper half of that Certain lot piece or parcel of land Situate lying and being in the Hanwell Settlement in the County of York, aforesaid, Known and described as lot Number twelve in the second tract of the grant to Edward Doherty and five others on the south easterly side of the Road leading from Fredericton through the said Hanwell Settlement so called bounded South west by land granted to Anthony McMahon North east by land granted to John McComb and containing two hundred Acres more or lefs, the upper half of which said before described lot is the land hereby sold to the said Timothy, Containing One hundred Acres, more or lefs, together with all Buildings and improvements of what Kind soever. And Also all the right title interest Claim and Demand whatsoever in law or equity of them the said Patrick and Wineferd his Wife of in and to the same and every part thereof. To have and to hold the said one half of the before described lot Number twelve and all and Singular the premises hereby granted, bargained and Sold and every part with the appurtenances

The Kellys of Kingsclear

thereto belonging unto the said Timothy his heirs and Afsigns and to the only proper use and behoof of the said Timothy his heirs and Afsigns forever. In Witnefs whereof we have hereunto Set our hands and Seals the day and year first before Written.
Witnefs }
Geo. Minchin. John Rielly}

his
Patrick X Burke {LS}
mark
her
Wineferd X Burke {LS}
mark

-221-

York fs Be it Remembered that on the 10th. day of August in the year of our Lord one thousand eight [hundred] and twenty nine before me George Minchin Esqr one of His Majestys Justices of the Peace in and for the County of York personally Appeared the before named Patrick Burke and Acknowledged that he executed the foregoing deed freely and Voluntarily for the uses and purposes therein Mentioned. And at the same time also appeared the before named Wineferd Wife of the said Patrick and Acknowledged that She executed the same freely and Voluntarily for the uses and purposes therein Mentioned without any fear, threat or Compulsion of or from her said Husband She being first examined Separate and apart from him
New Brunswick}   Geo Minchin
York County   }   J Peace
Registered this fifth day of January one thousand Eight hundred and thirty one

New Brunswick, County Deed Registry Books, 1780-1930, for York (1845-1846), Volume 27, pp. 35-36

Michael Cain }   Hanwell Kingsclear [in pencil]
    to   } No. 9085. This Indenture made this Twelfth day of July in the year of
Timothy Burke} our Lord one thousand Eight hundred and forty five. Between Michael Cain of Kingsclear in the County of York and Province of New Brunswick farmer of the one part and Timothy Burke of the same place Farmer of the other part Witnefseth that the said Michael Cain for and in Consideration of the Sum of Fifty pounds of lawful money of New Brunswick to him in hand well and truly paid at or before the Sealing and delivery of these presents by the said Timothy Burke the receipt where of is hereby Acknowledged, Hath granted bargained sold Aliened released conveyed and confirmed, and by these presents Doth grant bargain Sell alien release convey and Confirm unto the said Timothy Burke his heirs and Afsigns, All that Certain lot piece and parcel of land and premises Situate lying and being in the Hanwell

Settlement so Called in the Parish of Kingsclear in the County and Province aforesaid and Known and distinguished as the lot Numbered Twelve on the North side of the Highway leading from Fredericton to Saint Andrews and Running through the said Hanwell Settlement so called and Containing Two hundred Acres more or lefs, Together with all houses, out houses, Barns Buildings Edifices fences improvements, Profits Privileges and appurtenances to the same belonging or in any manner appertaining and the Reversion and Reversions Remainder and Remainders, Rents ifsuses and Profits thereof. And also all the Estate Right title Interest use pofsefsion property Claim and demand either at law or in Equity of him the said Michael Cain of into or out of the same and every part and parcel thereof with the appurtenances, To have and to hold the said lot piece of parcel or land and premises hereby granted bargained and Sold or meant mentioned or intended so to be and every part and parcel thereof with the appurtenances unto the said Timothy Burke his heirs and Afsigns to the only proper use benefit and behoof of the said Timothy Burke his heirs and Afsigns forever In Witnefs whereof the said Michael Cain Hath hereunto set his hand and seal the day and year first above written.

Signed Sealed and delivered in the}
presence [illegible] Minchin   }   his
      Geo. Minchin   }   Michael X Cain {LS}
                                                mark

-36-

York fs. Be it Remembered that on the twelfth day of July in the year of our Lord one thousand Eight hundred and forty five personally appeared before me George Minchin Esquire one of Her Majestys Justices of the Peace in and for the County of York the within named Michael Cain and Acknowledged that he executed the within deed freely and Vountarily for the uses and purposes therein mentioned the same having been first read over to him in my presence.

New Brunswick}   Geo Minchin J Peace
York County   } Registered the fifteenth day of July one thousand Eight hundred and forty five

                                                                               Joseph Beck Reg^r.

New Brunswick Land Petitions: Original Series, York County, 1783-1918 (RS108) (Microfilm: F1026)

<u>York Co</u>
69

To His Excellency Thomas Carleton Esq.r Capt.n Gov.r in Chief of the Province of New Brunswick, Chancelor, & Vice Admiral of the same &c, &c, &c,

The Memorial of Alex.r Fairchild, Peter Veal, Daniel Cook, Isaac Adams, Isaac Benson, Mix Todd, George Emerson, Enoch Bard, Thomas Potter, John Cain, James Kerr, Larkin Ferrifs, and Thomas Green None Comifsioned Officers, and Soldiers, in the late Prince of Wales American Regiment,

Humbly Sheweth

That your Memorialists have Received a Proposition of Land allowed them by Government on the North Side of the River, S.t John, about four Miles above S.t Anns have setled [sic] and used their utmost endeavors as to improve the same, That without their knowledge or approbation a Grant has been obtained by some officer of that Corps. In which their Names were included for a small proportion of an Island, opposite their Lands, but as they wish to have part of the Island Equal with other Setlers, Your Memorialists Prays your Excellency will be Pleased to consider their being included in that Grant, and permit them to have an Equal Share of the Islands in the River with their late fellow Soldiers, whenever your Excellency shall think Proper to make a Distribution of the same

17.th March 1785

	George Emerson
Alex.r Fairchild	Enoch Bard
Peter Veal	Tho.s Potter
Dan.l Cook	John Cain
Isaac Dumas	John Kerr
Isaac Benson	Larkin Ferrifs
Mix Tod	Tho.s Green

[verso]

Memorial of
Alex.r Fairchild
and others
late non comifsioned
officers & Privates in the
Prince of Wales Amer.n Regim.t

―――

[illegible] one equal share of the
Islands in the River S.t John's
with their late fellow Soldiers

――

In Council 19.th March 1785.

Already anfwered

New Brunswick Land Petitions: Original Series, York County, 1783-1918 (RS108) (Microfilm: F1034)

325
 To his Excellency Thomas Carleton Esq.r Lieutenant Governor and Commander in Chief of the Province New Brunswick &c. &c. &c.
 The Memorial of Isaac Benson —
Sergeant of the late Prince of
Wa. Regiment
Humbly Sheweth
 That Your Memorialist was intitled to three hundred Acres of Land for himself and family, agreeable to his Majestys Proclamation two hundred of which he has received, and now occupies in the Block N.º 1
 Your Memorialist begs leave to inform your Excellency that the adjoining Lot contains one hundred Acres — formerly granted to John Cain of said Regiment is unoccupied and (as your Memorialist is informed) escheated, therefore most humbly prays that your Excellency will grant him the said Lot — to compleat his proportion of Land, And as in Duty bound will ever pray &c. &c.

       Isaac Benson

       [*verso*]

Isaac Benson asks
a Lot of Land joining
the Lot he now occupys
in Block N.º 1.

In Council 15. Aug.t 1788.
Comply with making
a Compensation to Cain.

20.th June 1788

New Brunswick Land Petitions: Original Series, York Couonty, 1783-1918 (RS108) (Microfilm: F1034)

              Benson, Isaac

To his Excellency Thomas Carleton Esq.ʳ — Lieutenant Governor and Commander in Chief of the Province of New Brunswick &c. &c. &c.

The Memorial of Isaac Benson

Humbly Sheweth

That your Memorialist is pofsefsed of two Acres of Land on Clingore Island by virtue of a Grant from his Excellency Governor Parr and having applied to the Trustees appointed to regulate the Island rights for an equal proportion with his Neighbours, was refused unlefs he would give up said Grant —

That agreeable to the regulations of said Trustees each Person receives four Acres and one half as his proportion, which your Memorialist is deprived of, not withstanding there are several persons who hold Lots on said Island that have not improved or taken pofsefsion of the same —

Your Memorialist therefore most humbly prays that Your Excellency will grant him the Lot N.º nine on Said Island Containing two Acres granted to Cap.ⁿ Stephen Hayt of the late Prince of Wales Reg.ᵗ as it is unimproved and not included in the regulations of the Trustees And he as in Duty Bound will ever pray &c. &c.

May 7.ᵗʰ 1788

[verso]

Memorial of Isaac
Benson —
Asks Lot Nº 9
Cleongore Island
referred

{Legislative Library of N. B.}

May the 12th 1788

New Brunswick Land Petitions: Original Series, York County, 1783-1918 (RS108) (Microfilm: F1034)

319

To his Excellency Thomas
Carleton Esquire, Governor
Commander in Chief
&c: &c: &c

The Memorial of William Cain

most humbly sheweth

That he served his Majesty Seventeen Years in Germany and other parts, — and in the Prince of Wales American Regiment; during the whole of the last war, — and that about four years before the peace, his son John was put upon the strength of the Regiment as a drummer.

That his son learned and performed his duty until regularly discharged when the Regiment was disbanded, and having been enlisted was considered entitled when disbanded to any priviledge extended to others.

That the poverty of your memorialists and the faithful services of the youth rendered him an object of compafsion and induced the officers of the Regiment to exert themselves to make some provision for the child.

That a tract of land thro' such particular recommendation was accordingly granted by His Excellency Governor Parr to the Child of your Memorialist, in the district between the Nashwaak and Madamkeswick rivers, which has been

since

[2]

since escheated.

That the age of the Child put it totally out of his power to improve land agreeable to the tenor of a grant, and Memorialist not supposing that in such instances it would be expected the condition exprefsed in the grant should be complied with, refused selling the place whereby he might have secured something for his son. —

That notwithstanding the age and poverty of your memorialist, together with his having a wife and large family to support, he has endeavoured to make a settlement on the said tract, but encumbered with that train of difficulties that are the perpetual attendants on indigence, he has not been enabled to clear more than two acres, and lay up logs for a house —

That trifling as such improvements may appear he flattered himself he had merited commendation for the exertions, when his circumstances were at the same time considered.

That Memorialist having laboured without ceasing the season past, and his son having arrived at an age that enables him to be usefull, will have it in their power to settle the said tract of land

That memorialist has been almost five years in the Country and received no land

Wherefore

[3]

Wherefore Memorialist humbly requests your Excellency will be pleased to take his poverty, his distrefs, his exertions. — the youth of his son, and his present prospects into consideration and be pleased to regrant the said little tract to the youth and as in duty bound they will ever pray. —

William X Cains mark

[verso]

Memo: William Cain
     July 15th:1788. —
prays that the lot formerly
granted to his son but since
escheated may be regranted
to him —

The Jury find ½ an acre cleared
on the lot.

cannot be complied with
15.th Aug.t 1788

July 15.th 1788

New Brunswick Land Petitions: Original Series, York County, 1783-1918 (RS108) (Microfilm: F1034)

258   To His Excellency Thomas Carleton
                                                           Esquire Captain General Governor
                                                                and Commander in Chief
                                                                        &c &c &c

    The Memorial of James Clarke and William Cain most humbly sheweth

That they lived in America previous to the late war and at a very early period inlisted in the Prince of Wales American Regiment and did their duty faithfully until they were disbanded in this Country.
    That they have both families which they find themselves unable to support upon the small tract of land they occupy upon the Common of Fredericton, and that they have neither of them received lands as was promised at the time of their inlistment.
    That they are very poor but ready and willing to settle lands if not at too great a distance from this place as they must occasionally labour for others to enable them to subsist their families.

That they are informed a procefs of Escheat has commenced against Block Number one, and as it is very probable much land in that tract will revert to and be in the [illegible] of the Crown,

>Memorialists humbly Pray
>your Excellency will [illegible]
>to

[2]

to Consider their situation and in case of land becoming vacant in the said block to Grant them permifsion to occupy the same. and as in duty bound they will ever Pray —

Novem.r 23d: 1787.

James X Clarks mark
W.m X Cains mark

[*verso*]

James Clarke and
William Cain —
ask for Land in Block No 1
if any escheated.

In Council 15 Aug. 1788.
May point out some
situation for themselves.

New Brunswick Land Petitions: Original Series, York County, 1783-1918 (RS108) (Microfilm: F1041)

606

To His Excellency in Council.
    The Memorial of D.r John Agnew>
Humbly sheweth
    That in the grant to Daniel Fukes and others there is granted to James Henly a share of Five hundred and fifty acres in the clafs Letter C: that more than that Quantity of Land is found to be actually contained in a gore in Mr Henly's pofsefsion being part of said clafs Letter C. and lying adjacent to the lower Line of the Tract granted to John Anderson, and that, in that part of the same clafs Letter C. which was laid out above the said Anerson's Grant, there is a strip of Land remaining after all the other grantees named in the said Grant to Daniel Fukes and others have had their full Quantities laid

off as specified in the said grant, which Remainder it is conceived is therefore Vacant and yet ungranted and your Memorialist, having yet received no Allotment of Land from government in this Province, excepting a small Lot which he purchased from John Cain, with approbation of your Excellency prays to have a Grant of the Remainder above described.

March 18th 1799   John Agnew

[verso]

1799.

Doct.r Agnew
asks a strip of land
in the clafs letter C —
in the tract of Maryland
Loyalists.

Filed 13.th March 1799

Dismissed —
Oct.r 24.th 1803

New Brunswick Land Petitions: Original Series, York County, 1783-1918 (RS108) (Microfilm: F4179)

[The original manuscript has significant damage and missing text. This transcription includes (with corrections) part of a transcription contained on the microfilm as well as transcription from the microfilm copy of the original manuscript.]

To his Honor Harris William Hailes Esquire, president and Commander in Chief of the province of New Brunswick &c   &c   &c

The Memorial of Stair Agnew Esquire

Humbly Sheweth

That notice of a Writ of Scrie Facias has been served on your Memorialist, returnable on the 3..d Tuesday in February next, repealling certain Letters patent, bearing Date on the 20th day of June 1809 to Revd. John Agnew, Stair Agnew Esq.r, George Agnew, and Urban Gage Agnew; and in Submifsion to said Writ your memo. begs leave to state to your Honour in Council, as follows.

That in the year 1789 the Revd. John Agnew, father of your memo. arrived in New Brunswick on his way to Canada for the purpose of settling his family there. That the polite reception he met with from the Governor Carleton., and his council, who afsured him, that if he stopped in New Brunswick, Lands would be given his family here, induced him to remain in this province and order your Memo. from England the following year.

That the Lot N..º 1 first Tract of the Grant in Question, lying on [the] southeasterly side of the Nashwaak, was originally minuted [to] Revd. Walter Prince l0th. June 1794. who sold his claim 1798. Henry White senior for the sum of £75. . . . It was by White released [part of manuscript missing] 6.th March 1799 to Revd. John Agnew. consideration that Agnew pay price; and it appears by an Extract from the minuted that [part of manuscript missing] price again relinquished this Lot to Revd. John Agnew 8th [May] 1799. and his Receipt to said John Agnew for the said sum of £75. bears Date 15.th Day of January 1800. This Lot is described in the grant as of 500 acres, and is the only grant that was ever made to said John Agnew in New Brunswick. He regarded it as his regimental allowance in part compensation for his Loyalty Lofses, suffering in American goals, guard houses, and for his long captivity and (confinement at the Instance of General Washington

[2]

he was well known) in [part of manuscript missing] french Dungeons: Having been captured with your Memo, [part of manuscript missing] the british Frigate Romulus, by a French squadron early in 1782. and detained during the remainder of the war. Those misfortunes were principally brought on your memorialist's Father, from his being the first clergy man in the colony of Virginia (where he resided) who dared to preach against the crimes of Rebellion, and read in his churches the proclamation of 7th November 1775. of Earle Dunmore then governor of that province. That your memorialist's Father cleared up part of the Front of his Lot, and since his Death 100. acres of it has been by your memo. sold to Henry and his son William White, as a settlement for the latter. They have made payment, are engaged in Clearing, and intend building a Dwelling House, the following summer. The other 400. acres your memo. has given to his sons John, Stair, Bryant, and his son-in-law William Carleton who are now (engaged, and for some time past) in clearing it for the purpose of settling it. Their further object is a saw mill on the Lot. The money to erect it is provided, and they are in Treaty with mill-wrights to build it. William Carleton now regards himself as reduced. He has two children, and your Memo. is inclined to settle him in the Country. His Father was a Captain in the artillery. He served at the siege of Charlestown, commanded the Artillery at Savannah, St. Augustine and New Providence. In these climates he lost his Health, which occasioned His Death. That on the 10th December 1790. The whole of the escheated Lands formally granted to Major William Anstruther, containing 1120 were ordered to be registered to your memo. on his paying Frederick

D'Ehrenstein (who had a Dwelling-House) thereon, a compensation for his improvements. His receipt, as well as that of X. Towel Esq for Expenses of Inquisition, your Memo. now holds. He also regards Lot N..º 2. of this Grant as his Regimental allowance, in part compensation for his loyalty, Lofses, personal Disability from a shot in the Battle of Brandy Wine, and his long suffering (with his father) while a french prisoner in Rhode Island, St. Domingo, and Old France. That in the year 1775. your Memo. returned to his native country (Virginia) from the schools in Glasgow, and was by his father immediately put into the Kings service. His first commifsion is dated first day of December 1775. He was 8. Days after in the severe action of the Great Bridge against Woodford, and continued in the service until made a french prisoner

[3]

[portion of the first sentence in manuscript missing] not granted [illegible] for 26 years upwards of [illegible] years after registry of them to your Memo. [part of manuscript missing] in the government never abated. When said Lot N..º 2. of [illegible] and this could only be given to your memo., at the time the Grant [water damage: illegible] &c. &c. &c. remaining 620. were readily granted to his minor children [part of manuscript missing] view he trusts of settling them in the country; and confirming the just expectations of your memo. That on the said lot N..º 2. first Tract of the grant, your memo. has about 6. acres more under fence, which has been planted and sown, and about 14. acres more cleared and in pasture, and he is engaged in clearing up 10. acres of Wood Land, which he expects to accomplish in the course of the next summer making 30. acres for this Lot of 500. the only Lands ever granted him. That the other part, or rear of the Anstruther Viz N..º 3. of the 1st Tract containing 620. acres, was granted to George and Urban Gage, youngest sons of your memo. That [to] improve their Lot, while they are unable to afsist would, since 1809. at the high rate of labour (if at all to be had) Viz from £5 .. .. to £6 .. .. per acre, have sacrificed the part so improved; and your memo. trusts the government never intended this should happen. That the second Tract of this grant viz of 300. acres, was also given to said George and Urban; that part of this Tract was the escheated Lot of a certain John Cain, minuted afterwards to Isaac Benson in the year [part of manuscript missing] and by him transferred to your Memorialist's Father, who paid [part of manuscript missing] consideration in money for it. From the uncommon [part of manuscript missing] and the remote situation of the rear and greatest part of this Tract [part of manuscript missing] (the front being improved) your memo. has been induced to [part of manuscript missing] of it to Individuals who now occupy it. with a view to give sons George and Urban, so soon as they can make the necefsary [part of manuscript missing] of said 300. acres, other Lands Located in Front of the To[well] line of them. Your memo. has felt anxious to shew the [part of manuscript missing] his family claims and certain arrangements by him made of [part of manuscript missing] properly, that your Honour in Council may Judge them. He is now an old half pay Captain, unable to begin the World again. He has raised nine children in the country, whom he supports, besides two grand children dependent on him: and Relying as does, on his landed pursuits to provide for them, He would remark, that if at any time, while he has been doing for the least, the Encouragement and Benevolence of the government, so justly extended to all, should suddenly be withdrawn from him his share of the public Indulgence, for the public advancement would be his private Disappointment. If your memo. has cultivated more, on one farm lying along a side of another, on account of his immediate [part of manuscript missing]

[4]

still he has constantly resided in the [part of manuscript missing] he is [part of manuscript missing] employed (certain [part of manuscript missing] Monkton Farm adjoining the Anstruther [part of manuscript missing] and improved, since he resided on it about 70 [part of manuscript missing] in addition to about 40. acres previously cult1vated [part of manuscript missing] built a barn (expense £120) out houses to the amount of £200 and a Dwelling House that cost him near £1OOO. on the lower side of the Nashwaack (part of the Monkton grant) his respected father cleared about 60.. acres. Built a barn (same size with your memorialist's) £120 Out Houses, say £50 and a dwelling house that cost him about £700.. .. and this expense of the Grant in question, besides the costs of Inquisition, and D'Ehrinstein's Improvements amounted to £26 .. 17 ½ your Honour in council will see that the above Estimate does not include the purchase money of the Monkton property nor the Expense of clearing it, nor yet the Expenditure on other Tracts in Sunbury and York. He therefore confidently trusts that the Exertions to settle itself, will fully meet with the approbation of your Honour in Council. The two eldest sons of your memo. deprecate any accident to their family Endevours; and especially to the Lands of their younger Brothers, who are yet unable to help themselves; and in conjuncture with your menorialist Pray your Honor in council will allow them further time, to Improve the grant in question, and in Duty bound your Memorialist will ever pray.

Dated this 5.th Day of December 1816

S Agnew

[verso]

Stair Agnew
6.th Decem.r 1816
Read & Referred for further
consideration
8.th March 1817

New Brunswick Land Grants, 1784 – 1997, Sunbury County, Volume NS-A, pp. 291-292 (RS686) (Microfilm: F4179)

Nova Scotia fs. 138 (Benoni Danks)

To all to whom these Presents shall come greetings —

William Campbell

Know Ye that I, Lord William Campbell Captain General and Governor in Chief in and over His Majesty's Province of Nova Scotia or Acadie and its dependencies, Vice Admiral of the same &c. &c. &c. by virture of the power and authority to me given by his present Majesty King George the Third under the Great Seal of Great Britain Have given, granted, and confirmed and Do by these Presents pursuant to His Majesty's order in Council bearing date the third day of December One Thousand seven hundred and Sixty six, give, grant and confirm unto Benoni Danks Esquire his Heirs and Afsigns a Tract of Land situate lying and being on the North side of the Bay of Fundy in this Province beginning at the west end of a sea bank or beach, two hundred and twenty Chains of four rods each to the westward of Quaque head being, a fixed bound at the mouth or emptying of a Lake into the said bay, thence to run North by the magnet four hundred and forty Chains, thence East four hundred and ten Chains, thence South two hundred and thirty five Chains or until it comes to the bay aforesaid, thence to be bounded by the several Courses of the said bay to the bounds first mentioned containing in the whole by estimation Ten Thousand Acres more or lefs, with allowance for all such roads as may hereafter be judged necefsary to pafs through the same, with all and all manner of mines unopened except Mines of God, Silver and Coals. To have and To hold the said granted premifses with all privileges, profits, commodities and appurtenances thereunto being unto the said Benoni Danks his Heirs and Afsigns forever — yielding and Paying by the said Grantee his Heirs and Afsigns which by the acceptation hereof he binds and obliges himself his Heirs, Executors and Afsigns to pay to His Majesty King George the Third, his Heirs and Sucefsors, or to any person lawfully authorized to receive the same for His Majesty's use a free yearly quit rent of one farthing per acre for every acre so

(granted)

granted on the feast of Saint Michael in every year; one half of which to commence and become payable on the feast of Saint Michael which shall first happen after the expiration of five years from the date of this Grant and to be payable on every ensuing feast of Saint Michael or within fourteen days after and the whole become payable in like manner at the expiration of Ten years from the date hereof on default thereof this Grant shall be null and void. And the said Grantee hereby binds and obliges himself his Heirs and Afsigns to settle the said Lands hereby granted with protestant Inhabitants within Ten years from the date of the Grant in the proportion of one person for every two hundred Acres in failure whereof the said Lands shall revert to His Majesty his Heirs and Succefsors, and this Grant shall be null and void.

In Witnefs wereof I have signed these Presents and caused the Seal of the Province to be hereunto affixed at Halifax this Twenty seventh day of September in the thirteenth year Reign of our Sovereign Lord George the Third by the Grace of God of Great Britain, France and Ireland King Defender of the faith and so forth, and in the year of our Lord one Thousand Seven hundred and Seventy three.

By His Exellency's command
Rich.d Bulkeley

Halifax Sept.r 27..th 1773
Registered by me
    Arthur Goold Reg.r

Halifax 27..th Sept.r 1773 —
Entered in the Auditor's office
    Jon..o Briyton Dep.y Recd.r

New Brunswick }
Registered the 22.d February 1787} Ex.d

New Brunswick Land Petitions: Original Series, Queens County, 1783-1918 (RS108) (Microfilm: F4199)

To His Excellency Major General Sir Howard Douglas, Baronet, Lieutenant-Governor and Commander-in-Chief of the Province of New-Brunswick, &c. &c. &c.

The Petition of John Cain aged Twenty five years, a Single Man, native of and constant resident in this Province

Humbly sheweth,

That he is a British Subject, has never applied for or received any Land from the Crown, and wishes to obtain an Allotment of vacant and unimproved Crown Land situate as follows: . . . .

On the Second and third Tier South East from the Nashwaak Stream on the rear of Land granted to James McDonald and Isaac Day, and Petitioner —being of ability to make considerable improvements prays an allotment of 200 Acres

He intends to settle and improve the same forthwith, and to comply in all respects with the Royal Instructions. he is of ability so to do, and has not bargained or agreed for the sale or transfer thereof to any person.

>and as in Duty
>bound will ever pray
>John Cain

York fs. —

Personally appeared before me George Minchin — Esquire, one of His Majesty's Justices of the Peace for the County of York aforesaid, the above named John Cain and made Oath to the truth of the statement set forth in the foregoing Petition.

May 14..th 1825.   George Minchin
                                                              J. Peace

[verso]

John Cain
23 May 1825
Recommended for
100 ac

16.th May 1825
            P.d

[separate fold]

May 14th 1825
The Situation herein described is Vacant
And unapplied for Crown Lands.

Thos Baillee
Sur General

New Brunswick Land Petitions: Original Series, Queens County, 1783-1918 (RS108) (Microfilm: F4204)

Foster, James 1826

{Legislative Library of N.B.}

To His Excellency Major General Sir Howard Douglas Bar.^t Lieut. Governor & Commander in Chief of the Province of New Brunswick &c &c &c

The Petition of James Foster, a British subject Born in Ireland, has resided in this Country for 4 years — aged thirty two — Married & has 2 children

Humbly Sheweth

That he never received any land from the Crown — that he is desirous of obtaining an allotment here of grant to McDonald, Washdamock petitioned for in May 1825 by John Cain who never settled on the same but who has ceded all claim to it in favour of your Petitioner — That it is his intention forthwith to cultivate & improve the same, & comply in all respects with the Royal instructions being of ability so to do & that he has not bargained or agreed for the sale or transfer of the same to any person whomsoever and as in duty bound will ever pray

James Foster

The above situation being more convenient to James Foster than to me, & intending to apply for myself nearer to where I live, I beg leave to withdraw my petition of May 1825 for said land —

John Cain

[2]

York fs — On the third day of March one thousand eight hundred and twenty six, before me George Minchin Esquire one of His Majesty's Justices of the peace in and for the county of York, personally appeared the before named James Foster and made oath that the several matters & things set forth in the before written petition are just and true

George Minchin
J. Peace

We do hereby certify that James Foster the within Petitioner is a person of [illegible] habbits and suftains a good character in the Neighbourhood where he refides and we have no doubt but he will make a useful settler. And we therefore recommend that that [sic] he may have an allotment of three Hundred acres of Land

Fredericton 4.th March 1826}   Samuel [illegible]
                                     William Peterson

The within situation is vacant & was applied for by J. Cain

Tho.ˢ Baillee

[*verso*]

James Foster
25.ᵗʰ May 1826

4.ᵗʰ March 1826
 Paid

New Brunswick Land Grants, 1784 – 1997, Charlotte County, Volume B, pp. 240-248 (RS686) (Microfilm: F16302)

New Brunswick Asha Brown and others: George the Third by the
N.ᵉ 134. Grace of God of Great Britain France and Ireland
Thomas Carleton — Defender of the faith and so forth — To all to whom these Presents shall come Greetings —. Know Ye that we of our special Grace, certain Knowledge and mere Motion have given and granted, and by these Presents for Us our heirs and succefsors do give and grant unto Asha Brown, Thomas Cook, John Cain, Samuel Woodward; Robert Woodward, Richard Lippencut, John Garrison, John Marks, Solomon Ferris, Elizabeth Pratt, John Hasin, James Pratt, Thomas Hendrick, Orange Sealye, Peter Stout, William Eldrage, John M ᶜCullum, Samuel Hand, Evan Thomas, Thomas Wood, James French, Isaac Woodward, Justus Sealye, Elisha Halsey, Eleaner Sanger, John Gill, Samuel Hart, Joseph Rufsell, Jonathan Wallace, Samuel Fairlamb, and Drummond Simpson in severalty unto each of them and unto each and every of their several and respective heirs and afsigns, several lots of land containing together in the whole two hundred and thirty eight acres more or lefs, comprehended within a tract of land known by the name of the six acre lots, the said tract situate, lying and being on the northerly and easterly sides of Beaver harbour within the Parish of Pennfield in Charlotte County and abutted and bounded as follows to wit beginning at a stake on the northerly back or shore of the Bay of Fundy about fifty seven chains of four poles each measured on a

right

-241-

right line easterly from the southwesterly extremity of Beaver Harbour aforesaid, thence running by the magnetic needle North sixty five chains of four poles each and twenty links thence East thirty nine chains and fifty links, thence North one hundred and seventy four chains and fifty links or until it meets the southerly line of the first range of farm lots or plantations in this district, thence along the said line of the said lots West one hundred and eighty four chains and fifty links, thence South forty eight chains, thence East fifty three chains and fifty links, thence South until it meets the northwesterly bank or shore of a creek bounding a part of the Town Plat of Pennfield to the northwest, thence crofsing the said creek and running along the northeasterly line of the said Town Plat South fifty one degrees East seven chains and sixty five links or to the easterly corner thereof; thence along the southeasterly line of the said Town Plat South thirty nine degrees west, until it meets the easterly bank or shore of Beaver Harbour thence following the several courses of the said bank or shore easterly and southerly to the East head of the said Harbour thence round the same and along the northerly bank or shore of the Bay of Fundy to the bounds first mentioned containing in the whole two thousand two hundred and thirty acres more of lefs with the usual allowance for roads and waste: The said tract being divided into three hundred and thirty eight lots, whose respective numbers, fronts, contents, and division lines are exprefsed and described on the annexed

Plan

-242-

Plan, partly improved and partly wildernefs land, / and hath such shape, form, and marks as appear by the actual survey thereof made under the directions of our Surveyor General of our said Province, of which survey the said claim hereunto annexed is a representation; Together with all woods, underwoods, timber, and timber trees, lakes, ponds, fishings, waters, watercourses, profits, commodities, appurtenances and hereditaments whatsoever thereunto belonging or in any wise appertaining, together also with the privilege of hunting, hawking and fowling in and upon the same and Mines and Minerals saving and reserving neverthelefs to us, our heirs and succefsors all white pine trees if any such shall be found growing thereon, and also saving and reserving to us our Heirs and Succefsors all Mines of Gold, Silver, Copper, Lead, and Coals. To have and To hold the said several lots of land and all and singular other the premises hereby granted, unto the said several and respective Grantees in the lots, shares, quantities and proportions as follows that is to say unto the said Asha Brown the lot number one, unto the said Thomas Cook the lot number two containing six acres each, unto the said John Cain the lot number three, unto the said Samuel Woodward the lot number four, containing seven acres each, unto the said Robert Woodward the lot number five containing six acres, unto the said Richard Lippencut the lot number six, containing

three

-243-

three acres, unto the said John Garrison the lot number fifteen, unto the said John Marks the lot number sixteen, containing six acres each, unto the said Solomon Ferris the lot number seventeen containing seven acres, unto the said John Marks the lot number eighteen, unto the said Elizabeth Pratt the lot number thirty seven, containing six acres each, unto the said John Hasin the lot number thirty eight containing eight acres, unto the said James Pratt the lot number thirty nine containing ten acres, / unto the said Thomas Hendrick the lot number one hundred and seven, containing eight acres, unto the said Orange Sealye the lot number one hundred and eight, unto the said Peter Stout the lot number one hundred and nine, unto the said William Eldrage the lot number one hundred and ten, containing six acres each, unto the said John McCollum the lot number one hundred and eleven, unto the said Samuel Hand, the lot number one hundred and thirteen, unto the said Evan Thomas the lot number one hundred and fourteen containing seven acres each; / unto the said Thomas Wool the lot number one hundred and fortythree containing eleven acres, unto the said James French the lot number two hundred and thirty nine, unto the said Isaac Woodward the lot number two hundred and fortytwo containing six acres each, unto the said Justus Sealye the lot number three hundred and nineteen containing thirteen acres, unto the said

Elisha

-244-

Elisha Halsey the lot number three hundred and twenty six containing ten acres, unto the said William Eldrage the lot number three hundred and twenty seven, containing eight acres, and the lot number three hundred and twentyeight containing seven acres, unto the said Eleazer Sanger the lot number three hundred and twenty nine, unto the said John Gill the lot number three hundred and thirty, unto the said Samuel Hart the lot number three hundred and thirty one, unto the said Joseph Rufsel the lot number three hundred and thirty two, unto the said Johnathan Wallace the lot number three hundred and thirty three, unto the said Samuel Fairlamb the lot number three hundred and thirty four, containing six acres ache, and unto the said Drummond Simpson the lot number three hundred and thirty eight, containing ten acres in severalty unto each of them, and unto each and every of their several and respective heirs and afsigns forever — They the said several and respective Grantees and their several and respective heirs or afsigns Yielding and Paying therefor unto us, our heirs and succefsors or to our Receiver General for the time being or to his deputy or deputies for the time being yearly that is to say at the feast of Saint Michael in every year at the rate of two shillings for every hundred acres and so in proportion according to the quanties [sic] of acres hereby granted the

same

-245-

same to commence and be payable from the feast of Saint Michael which shall first happen after the expiration of ten years from the date hereof Provided always and this present Grant is upon condition that the said several and respective Grantees and their several and respective heirs and afsigns shall and do within three years after the date hereof, for every fifty acres of plantable land hereby granted, clear and work three acres at least in such part thereof as respectively they shall judge most convenient and advantageous, or else to clear and drain three acres of swampy or sunken ground or drain three acres of marsh if any such contained therein And shall and do within the time aforesaid put and keep upon every fifty acres thereof accounted barren three neat cattle, and continue the same thereon until three acres for every fifty be fully cleared and improved, and if there shall be no part of the said tract fit for present cultivation without manuring and improving the same, they respectively within the time aforesaid shall be obliged to erect on some part of their respective lots of land one good dwelling house to be at least twenty feet in length and sixteen feet in breadth, and to put on their said respective lots of land the like number of three neat cattle for every fifty acres; or otherwise if any part of the said tract shall be stony or rocky ground and not fit for planting or pasture shall and do within three years as aforesaid begin

to

to employ thereon and continue to work for three years then next ensuing in digging any stony quarry or mine one good and able hand for every fifty acres it shall be accounted a sufficient cultivation and improvement Provided also that every three acres that shall be cleared and worked or cleared and drained as aforesaid shall be accounted a sufficient seating, cultivation and improvement to save for ever from forfeiture fifty acres of land in any part of the tract hereby granted, and the said several and their respective Grantees and their several and respective heirs and afsigns be at liberty to withdraw their stock or for bear working in any quarry or mine in proportion to such cultivation and improvements as shall be made upon the plantable lands, swamps, sunken grounds or marsh therein contained And if the said Rent hereby reserved shall happen to be in arrear or unpaid for the space of one year from the time it shall become due, and no distrefs can be found on the said lands tenements and hereditaments hereby granted or if this Grant shall not be duly registered in the Register's office of our said Province within six months from the date hereof and a docket also entered in the Auditor's office of the same, then this Grant shall be void and the said lands tenements and hereditaments hereby granted and every part and parcel thereof shall

revert

revert to us our heirs and succefsors: And Provided also upon this further condition that if the land hereby given and granted as aforesaid shall at any time or times hereafter come unto the pofsefsion and tenure of any person or persons whatever, Inhabitaants of our said Province of New Brunswick either by virtue of any deed of sale conveyance enfeoffment or exchange, or by gift, inheritance, descent, device or marriage, such person or persons being Inhabitants as aforesaid shall within twelve months after his her or their entry and pofsefsion of the same, take the oaths prescribed by law before some one of the Magistrates of the said Province, and a certificate of the magistrate that such oaths have been taken being recorded in the Secretary's office of the said Province, the person or persons so taking the oaths aforesaid shall be deemed the lawful pofsefsor or pofsefsors of the Lands hereby granted. And in case of default on the part of such person or persons in taking the oaths within twelve months as aforesaid this present Grant and every part thereof shall and we do hereby declare the same to be null and void to all intents and purposes, and the lands hereby granted

and

-248-

and every part and parcel thereof shall in like manner revert to and become vested in Us, our Heirs and Succefsors any thing herein contained to the contrary notwithstanding.

Given under the Great seal of our Province of New Brunswick Witnefs our trusty and well beloved Thomas Carleton Esquire, our Lieutenant Governor and Commander in Chief of our said Province at Fredericton the ninth day of November in the year of our Lord one thousand seven hundred and eighty seven, and on the twenty eighth year of our Reign.

By command of His Excellency in Council

Jon.n Odell

Fredericton New Brunswick }
Registered the 21:st day of January 1788} Pa.d

New Brunswick Land Grants, 1784 – 1997, Charlotte County, Volume B, pp. 291-297 (RS686) (Microfilm: F16302)

New Brunswick.   Joseph Rufsell and others George the Third by the Grace of God of
N.º 142   Great Britain, France, and Ireland, King Defender of the faith and so
Tho.s Carleton   forth — To all to whom these Presents shall come Greeting — Know Ye that we of our special Grace, certain Knowledge and mere Motion have given and granted and by these Presents for us, our Heirs and Succefsors do give and grant unto Joseph Rufsell, John Garrison, James Harris, Richard Lawrence, Samuel Pearce, Eleazer

Sanger and John Cain, in severalty unto each of them and unto each and every of their several and respective Heirs and Afsigns several lots or plantations of Land comprehended within a tract of Land situate, lying, and being on the easterly side of Mace's Bay to the northward of Point LeProe on the northerly shore of the Bay of Fundy partly within the Parish of Pennfield in Charlotte County and partly within the Parish of Lancaster in the County of Saint John and abutted and bounded as follows, to wit, beginning at a stump on a sandy beech or point which forms the Southeasterly point or entrance of a cove or inlet at the northeasterly part or corner of Mace's Bay aforesaid, thence or from the said stump running by the magnetic needle East ninety seven chains of four poles each thence South seventy eight chains or until it meets the northwesterly line of a tract of Land granted to Henry Coor and others thence along the said line of the said Grant South

forty five

-292-

forty five degrees West, eighty six Chains or until it meets the southerly line of lot number seven in this Grant thence West along the said line until it meets the easterly bank or shore of Mace's Bay aforesaid thence along the said bank or shore of the said bay following its several courses northerly to the bounds first mentioned — containing in the whole One Thousand four hundred and eighty five acres more of lefs with the usual allowance for roads and waste; The said tract being divided into seven lots or plantations whose respective numbers, fronts or breadths, contents in acres and division lines are exprefsed and described on the annexed Plan, partly improve and partly wildernefs Land, and hath such shape, form and marks as appear by the actual survey thereof made under the directions of our Surveyor General of our said Province of which survey the said Plan hereunto annexed is a representation — together with all woods, underwoods, timber and timber trees, lakes, ponds, fishings, waters water courses, profits, commodities, appurtenances and hereditaments whatsoever thereunto belonging or in any wise appertaining together also with the privilege of hunting hawking and fowling in and upon the same and Mines and Minerals Saving and reserving neverthelefs to Us, our Heirs and Succefsors all white Pine Trees if any such shall

be

-293-

be found growing thereon, and also saving and reserving to us our Heirs and Succefsors all Mines of Gold, Silver, Copper, Lead, and Coals. To have and To hold the said several lots or plantations of land and all and singular other the premises hereby granted unto the said several and respective Grantees in the lots, shares, quantities, and proportions as follows that is to say unto the said Joseph Rufsel the lot number one containing two hundred acres, unto the said John Garrison the lot number two, containing two hundred and thirty acres, unto the said James Harris the lot number three, containing two hundred and forty three acres, unto the said Richard Lawrence the lot number four, containing two hundred and fifty acres, unto the said Samuel Pearce the lot number five, containing two hundred and thirty acres, unto the said Eleazer Sanger the lot number six, containing one hundred and eighty seven acres and unto the said John Cain the lot number seven containing one hundred and forty five acres — in severalty unto each of them, and unto each and every of their several and respective heirs and afsigns for ever — they the said several and respective Grantees and their several and respective heirs or afsigns Yielding and Paying therefor unto us our Heirs and Succefsors or to our Receiver General for the time being or to his Deputy or deputies for the time being yearly that is to say at the feast of Saint Michael in every year at the rate of two shillings for every hundred acres and so in proportion according to the quan=

(=tities)

-294-

tities of acres hereby granted the same to commence and be payable from the feast of Saint Michael which shall first happen after the expiration of Ten years from the date hereof Provided always and this present Grant is upon condition that the said several and respective Grantees and their several and respective Heirs or Afsigns shall and do within three years after the date hereof for every fifty acres of plantable land hereby granted, clear and work three acres at least in such part thereof as respectively they shall judge most convenient and advantageous; or else to clear and drain three acres of swampy or sunken ground or drain three acres of marsh if any such contained therein And shall and do within the time aforesaid put and keep upon every fifty acres thereof accounted barren three neat cattle and continue the same thereon until three acres for every fifty be fully cleared and improved, and if there shall be no part of the said tract fit for present cultivation without manuring and improving the same, they respectively within the time aforesaid shall be obliged to erect on some part of their respective lots of Land one good dwelling house to be at least twenty feet in length and sixteen feet in breadth, and to put on their said respective lots of Land the like number of three neat cattle for every fifty acres or otherwise if any part of the said tract shall be stony or rocky ground and not fit for planting or pasture shall and do within

(three)

-295-

three years as aforesaid to employ thereon and continue to work for three years then next ensuing in digging any stony quarry or mine one good and able hand for every fifty acres it shall be accounted a sufficient cultivation and improvement Provided also

that every three acres that shall be cleared and worked or cleared and drained as aforesaid shall be accounted a sufficient seating, cultivation and improvement to save for ever from forfeiture fifty acres of Land in any part of the tract hereby, granted — and the said several and their respective Grantees and their several and respective heirs and afsigns be at liberty to withdraw their stock or forbear working in any quarry or mine in proportion to such cultivation and improvements as shall be made upon the plantable lands, swamps, sunken grounds, or marsh therein contained And if the said Rent hereby reserved shall happen to be in arrear or unpaid for the space of one year from the time it shall become due and no distrefs can be found on the said lands tenements and hereditaments hereby granted or if this Grant shall not be duly registered in the Register's office of our said Province, within six months from the date hereof and a docket also entered in the Auditor's office of the same, then this Grant shall be void, and the said Lands Tenements and Hereditaments hereby granted and every part and parcel thereof shall revert to Us our heirs and succefsors: And Provided
also

-296-

also upon this further condition that if the land hereby given and granted as aforesaid shall at any time or times hereafter come unto the pofsefsion and tenure of any person or persons whatever Inhabitaants of our said Province of New Brunswick either by virtue of any deed or sale conveyance enfeoffment or exchange; or by gift, inheritance, descent, devise, or marriage such person or persons being Inhabitants as aforesaid shall within twelve months after his her or their entry and pofsefsion of the same take the oaths prescribed by law before some one of the Magistrates of the said Province, and a certificate of the magistrate that such oaths have been taken being recorded in the Secretary's office of the said Province the person or persons so taking the oaths aforesaid shall be deemed the lawful pofsefsor or pofsefsors of the Lands hereby granted And in case of default on the part of such person or persons in taking the oaths within twelve months as aforesaid this present Grant and every part thereof shall and we do hereby declare the same to be null and void to all intents and purposes, and the Lands hereby granted and every part and parcel thereof shall in like manner revert to and become vested in Us, our Heirs and Succefsors any thing herein contained to the contrary notwithstanding. —
Given

-297-

Given under the Great seal of our Province of New Brunswick — witnefs our trusty and well beloved Thomas Carleton Esquire our Lieutenant Governor and Commander in Chief of our said Province at Fredericton the ninth day of November in the year of our Lord one thousand seven hundred and eighty seven and in the Twenty eighth year of our reign.

By command of His Excellency in Council

Fredericton New Brunswick }
Registered the 1st day of February 1788} En.d   Jon.n Odell

New Brunswick Land Grants, 1784 – 1997, Charlotte County, Volume B, pp. 321-328 (RS686) (Microfilm: F16302)

New Brunswick.   Pennfield, John Horner and others
No 144   George the Third by the Grace of God of Great
Tho.s Carleton   Britain, France, and Ireland, King Defender of
the faith and so forth — To all to whom these Presents shall come Greeting — Whereas a certain tract of Land situate, lying, and being at Beaver Harbour in the County of Charlotte in our Province of New Brunswick in America, hath been surveyed and laid out as a Town by the name of Pennfield abutted and bounded as follows to wit beginning at a stake on the westerly bank or shore of Beaver Harbour aforesaid thence running by the magnetic needle west, one thousand six hundred and forty feet, thence North three thousand six hundre and thirty feet, thence East two thousand seven hundred and sixty feet, thence North fifty degrees East five hundred and thirty three feet, thence South forty degees East five hundred and ten feet or to the northwesterly bank or shore of a creek thence along the said bank or shore of the said creek until four hundred and seventy feet are measured in a right line, thence crofsing the said creek (at right angles) to its Southeasterly bank or shore, thence South fifty one degrees East five hundred and four feet, thence South thirty nine degrees West one thousand five hundred and thirty four feet, or until it meets the easterly bank or shore of Beaver Harbour aforesaid thence following the several courses of the the banks or shores of

the

the said Harbour, and its different coves or Inlets westerly to the bounds first mentioned X containing in the whole One Hundred and ninety seven acres more or lefs — The said tract being divided into those divisions, described first, second, and third division — each division being subdivided and laid out into blocks distinguished and marked by the letters of the Alphabet — and each block being subdivided and laid out into lots distinguished and marked by numbers (regularly) from number one to number twenty inclusive except where the blocks are not compleated to squares — and the whole hath such shape, form and marks as appear by the actual survey thereof made under the directions of our Surveyor General of our said Province, of which Survey the Plat hereunto annexed is a representation. Now Know Ye that we of our special Grace, certain Knowledge, and mere Motion have given and granted and by these Presents for us, our Heirs and Succefsors do give and grant unto the several and respective Persons herein after named their Heirs and Afsigns the several and respective lots in the said Tract or Town to their respective names severally annexed distinguished and numbered agreeable to the said Plan thereof hereunto annexed, that is to say unto John Horner the lots number one, number two, number three, and number four, unto Thomas Paul lot number five, unto Moses Winder lot umber six, unto Amos Rook

-323-

Rook lot number seven, and unto John Garrison the lots — number nine, number ten, number eleven, and number twelve in the first division letter **A**, unto Elias Wright Senior lot umber seven, unto John Gill lot number fourteen, unto Hugh Mackay Esquire lot number fifteen, unto John Garrison lot lots number sixteen, number seventeen, number eighteen, and number nineteen, and unto Jonathan Dibble lot number twenty in the first division letter **B**, unto Samuel Hand lot number six, unto Elias Wright lot number seven, unto Ann Kingsley lot number eight, unto Andrew Brundage lot number nine, unto Ward Handy lot number eleven, unto Edward Bebe lot number thirteen, unto Eleazer Sanger lot number fifteen and unto Joseph Rufsell lot number seventeen in the first division letter **C**, unto Francis Pilgrim lot number one, unto Germain Davis lot number two, unto Nicholas Hillard lot number four, and unto Frederick Maybe lot number five in the first division letter **F**, unto Jonathan Wallice lot number fourteen, unto Joseph Rufsell lot number fifteen, and unto Peter Stout lot number sixteen in the first division letter **G**, unto George King lot number eight, unto Joseph Wentwork lot number thirteen, unto John Horner lots number fourteen and number fifteen, unto William Ward lot number eighteen and unto John Guyon the lots number nineteen and number twenty in the first division letter **H**, unto Samuel Cleveland the lots number sixteen and number eighteen in the first division

-324-

division letter **K**, unto John Shaw lot number two, unto Jonathan Wallice lot number six, and unto Samuel Dickinson lot number seven in the first division letter **M**, unto Samuel Little lot number two, unto Jospeh Rufsell lot number three, unto Samuel Hand the lot number four, unto Ahasuerus Ferris lot number six, and unto Luke Murphy lot number seven in the first division letter **N**, unto Elisha Halsey the lots number one and two in the first division letter **V**, unto Solomon Ferris lot number four, unto Samuel

Cleveland lot number five, and unto Simeon Linley lot number eight in the first division letter **U**, unto James Innis lot number one, unto John Hand lot number eight, and unto Millington Lockwood lot number ten in the first division letter **W**, — unto Samuel Woodward lot number eleven, unto Jacob Buffington Esquire lot number fifteen, unto Abner Hampton lot number sixteen, unto Evan Griffith lot number seventeen, unto Gideon Vernon lot number eighteen, unto John Hinchman lot number nineteen, and unto William Cook lot number twenty in the second division letter **L**, unto Benjamin Mead the lot number nine, unto Richard Mead the lot number ten, unto Anthony Woodward Junior lot number twelve, unto Richard Lippencut lot number thirteen, unto Joshua

Knight

-325-

Knight Junior lot number fourteen, unto Richard Lippencut lot number fifteen, unto Robert Woodward lot number sixteen, unto John Knight lot number seventeen, unto Thomas Leonard lot number eighteen, unto Joseph Wey lot number nineteen, and unto Joseph Parker lot number twenty in the second division letter **M**, unto Amos White the lots number five and number six, unto Abraham Woodward lot number eight, unto Thomas Buckley Senior lot number nine, unto John Dennis lot number ten, unto Paul Mersereau lot number eleven, unto George Bennison lot number twelve, unto Rhodes Rankin lot number thirteen, unto John McLean lot number fourteen unto James Harris lot number seventeen, unto Abraham Rankin lot number eighteen, unto Robert Robbins lot number nineteen, and unto John Burk lot number twenty in the second division letter **N**, unto Seth Squires lot number eight, unto Caleb Paul lot number fourteen unto John Cain lot number fifteen, and unto William Harrison lot number sixteen in the second division letter **O**, unto Orange Seelye lot number one, unto Samuel Hart lot number ten, unto Nathaniel Coleman lot number thirteen, and unto Thomas Parent Junior lot number sixteen in the second division letter **P**, unto Eleazer Sanger lot number three in the second division letter **Q**

unto

-326-

unto John Rankin lot number three, unto Anthony Woodward Senior lot number four, unto Elias Wright Junior lot number five, unto Elias Wright Senior lot number six, unto Evan Griffith lot number seven, and unto Joseph Thorn lot number eight in the second division letter **S**, unto Joshua Knight Senior the lot number one, unto Jefse Woodward Junior lot number two, unto Samuel Stillwill lot number three, unto Amos Strickland lot number four, unto Robert Fitz Randolph lot number five, unto Joseph Tomlinson lot number six, unto William Reynolds lot number seven, unto John Loffborough lot number eight, and unto Nimrod Woodward lot number nine in the second division letter **T**, unto John Knight lot number one, unto Amos Strickland lot number two, unto Joshua Knight Junior lot number three, unto Jacob Woodward lot number four, unto Jefse Woodward Junior lot number five, unto Isaac Woodward the lots number six and number seven, unto Gideon Vernon lot number eight, unto Robert Thompson lot number nine, unto Daniel Register lot number ten, unto Drummond Simpson lot number eleven, unto Isaac Woodward the lots number twelve and number thirteen, and unto Elias Wright Senior lot number fourteen, in the second division letter **V**, unto Thomas Cook lot number one, unto Isaac Powell lot number two, unto James Pearce lot number three, unto Elias Wright lot number five, unto Michael Dunfield lot number six, unto Benjamin Field Brown lot number eight, unto Evan Thomas lot

number

number nine, unto John Loffborough lot number ten, unto Nathaniel Loffborough lot number fourteen, unto Evan Thomas lot number fifteen, unto Calvin Turner lot number sixteen, unto John Marks lots number seventeen and number eighteen, and unto John Hustice lot number nineteen in the second division letter **U**, unto Richard Matthews lot number seven, unto John McDonald lot number thirteen, unto Ezra Sanger lot number fifteen, unto Eleazer Sanger lot number sixteen, and unto John McCullum lot number twenty in the second division letter **W**, unto Eleazer Sanger lot number eight, unto Jeremiah Dunn lot number eleven, unto Germain Davis lot number twelve, and unto Joseph Rufsell lot number sixteen in the second division letter **X**, and unto Thomas Parent Senior lot number twelve in the second division letter **Y**; together with all woods, underwoods, profits, commodities, appurtenances, and hereditaments whatsoever thereunto belonging or in any wise appertaining and Mines and Minerals — saving and reserving neverthelefs to us, our Heirs and Succefsors all Mines of Gold, Silver, Copper, Lead and Coals. To have and To hold the said several and respective lots and all and singular other the premises hereby granted unto the said several Grantees respectively, and unto each and every of their several and respective Heirs and Afsigns

for

for Ever — Yielding and Paying by the said grantees and each and every of them, their and each and every of their Heirs and Afsigns respectively which by the acceptation hereof each and every of them doth bind and oblige him and herself respectively, their and each of their Heirs, Executors, and Afsigns respectively to pay Us our Heirs and Sucefsors, or to any person lawfully authorized to receive the same for our use, a free yearly quit rent of one farthing for each and every lot hereby granted — The first payment there to commence and become payable from the feast of Saint Michael which shall first happen after the expiration of Ten years from the date hereof Provided also that this Grant shall have been duly registered in the Register's office of our said Province and a docket thereof entered in the Auditor's office within six months from the date hereof otherwise this Grant shall become null and void. Given under the Great seal of our Province of New Brunswick. Witnefs our trusty and well beloved Thomas Carleton Esquire, our Lieutenant Governor and Commander in Chief of our said Province at Fredericton the first day of February in the year of our Lord one thousand and seven hundred and eighty eight and in the twenty eight year of our Reign. —

By command of His Excellency in Council

Fredericton New Brunswick }   Jon.n Odell
Registered the 15th day of March 1788}

Appendix W

Further Information on the Leonard Coombes Kelly Family

Anglican Church Marriage Registrations (*Provincial Archives of New Brunswick, Microfilm: F15550, Volume 1, page 514*)

Marriage at   Fredericton New Brunswick

Leonard C. Kelly of the Parish of Queensbury in the County of York and Savina McKay of the Parish of St. Mary were Married in this Parish by Sicense this twenty ninth day of September in the Year 1836. By me

In the Presence of us   }   George Carter
Robert McKay of St Marys   }   Rector of Fredericton
James Howard of Kingsclear}   This Marriage was Solemnized
                                                        between us Leonard C Kelly
                                                                              Jabany McKay

Filed & Registered 2.nd December 1836.

Reverend Frank Baird, in his *History of the Parish of Stanley and its Famous Fair*, writes, "In 1832 the New Brunswick and Nova Scotia Land Company was organized (Incorporated 1834), and in 1835 obtained an immense Tract of Land in the North East part of York County." (p. 26)

Baird quotes from a piece written by Havelock Kelly "late in the year 1949 . . . :"

> In the spring of 1834 a party of Englishmen, headed by Lord Stanley, having recently acquired a huge tract of land in N.B. and Nova Scotia decided to form a colony on the upper Nashwaak a few miles above where the 42nd Regiment had previously located. They accordingly sent a company of men from England headed by one Captain Kendall to N.B. They arrived in Fredericton about the middle of June 1834. The commissioner decided to hire some native N.B. men to help them at the new work. (p. 28)

Havelock Kelly continues:

> Leonard C. Kelly, aged 23, youngest son of John Kelly (U.E. Loyalist who had taken land at Kelly's Creek, Kingsclear, N.B.[,] in 1784) hearing of this

new work went to Fredericton, and hired with the Company as canoe-man and ox-teamster. John Reid, aged 20, born in Ireland, a son of James Reid who had emigrated to N.B., a few years previously and settled at Tay Creek also hired at the same time as carpenter. Strange to say that these two men, Reid and Kelly, were the only ones of the first group that remained in Stanley the rest of their lives. They both married, raised large families, remained good friends and neighbours, died in the same year [1899], Reid at 84, Kelly at 89, and were buried in the same cemetery a few feet apart. Descendants of both Reid and Kelly are still here." (p. 30)

Velma Kelly, in *The Village in the Valley – A History of Stanley*, states that John Reid's wife, Margaret (Samson) Reid, and Leonard Coombes Kelly's wife, Jacobina (McKaye) Kelly, "sewed by hand the first bolts for the grist mill." Velma Kelly adds, "Mrs. Kelly once chased a bear from near her home with a flaming stick from her fireplace." (p. 9)

Baird writes, "Mr. Reid and Mr. Kelly are said to have met on Stanley Hill as one arrived by foot and the other by river." (p. 130)

Havelock Kelly, again quoted by Baird from Kelly's piece of 1949, writes, "In the summer of 1835 [Anglican] Bishop [John] Inglis of Nova Scotia made a trip to Stanley. He made the trip from Fredericton to Covered Bridge by horse-boat. He was met at that point by a canoe sent by the Company which was poled to Stanley and return by the Company's canoe-man, namely, Leonard C. Kelly." (p. 28)

W.S. MacNutt (*New Brunswick A History: 1784-1867*) notes that by 1848 "[t]he Royal Road, leading to Stanley from Fredericton, . . . had become a goat-trail." (p. 305)

Baird, citing the *Report of the Secretary of the York County Agricultural Society for the Year 1852*, notes that at the first Stanley Fair held in 1851 in Stanley, New Brunswick, Leonard Coombes Kelly won 5 shillings for "Best Mitts." (p. 97)

Baird notes that in the Stanley Branch of the York County Agricultural Society, Leonard Coombes Kelly is listed as a member in the *Report of the Secretary of the York County Agricultural Society for the Year 1852*. (p. 99)

In the *Robert Connors Ledgers* at the Robert Connors House in Connors, New Brunswick, a lined piece of paper with the heading "Little Falls, NB[,] May 23rd 1876" inserted in *Ledger B* documents that Charles Babin paid "Leonard Kelly" $1.50 on 18 May 1876. Little Falls, New Brunswick, is present day Edmundston.

Margaret (Kelly) Hay, who has so generously allowed me to quote from her notes on the Kelly family, writing of Jacobina "Bina" Drummond (McKaye) Kelly, points out that

> Jacobina married Leonard at 16. He at 23 claimed her for his wife after seeing her hanging clothes on the line in Stanley while he was boating up the Nashwaak. . . . She wanted her boys to be gentlemen and this is the way they became over the years.
>
> When Havelock, their youngest, brought his wife Annie to the home of Leonard and Jacobina, Jacobina made a gesture to relinquish her role as

matron of the home. Legend has it that Jacobina always kept some white sugar in a locked chest, as sugar was a valuable commodity then, but now she turned the key over to Annie, saying[,] "this is our home now." There were never any arguments between the two women, but Jacobina was always given the respect and honour she had earned.

Gertrude, Havelock's daughter, was her grandmother's favourite. She would tell her stories of Scotland; often mentioned were the "blue boys." These were the orphans in Britain.

Jacobina fell downstairs and broke her back. She remained at home in bed for three months before she died. Gertrude remembers that she and her sisters wore white dresses and hats with black sashes to the funeral.

Bessie Anne (Kelly) Ninnes Memories

Transcribed by Virginia Ann "Ginny" (Gould) Peters Gosselin, daughter of Alan and Joyce (Atkinson) Gould. Bessie Anne (Kelly) Ninnes (18 September 1893 – 2 November 1984), daughter of Gabriel Havelock (1 June 1865 – 8 September 1964) and Annie May (Clark) Kelly (26 May 1871 - 1967), was married to James Ninnes (14 November 1888 – 9 November 1958).

In a letter of 10 March 2015, Jeannie (Boulter) Matthews writes, "I think Bess wrote this around the time of my Aunt Irma's death (1979). . . ." Jeannie, who didn't attend the funeral, writes, "Probably people who got to Irma's funeral got a copy of this piece."

Record of the Family of Leonard and Jacobina Kelly.
(as my knowledge serves)

This is a record of the family of Leonard C Kelly and Jacobina Drummond MacKay, so far as my memory of events and stories told me will serve. The attached photocopy of a report relative to a wedding anniversary, and an enclosed note sent by my sister Elsie will serve to furnish some background. Although the newspaper report is in many ways mixed up and inaccurate.

Leonard Kelly — 1810-1899. —

    He arrived in Stanley in 1834. See attached notes.

    My grandfather was the youngest son of a United Empire Loyalist who came to New Brunswick after the American Revolution in 1783.

    The Kellys had been given a grant of land in the Upper Kingsclear area.

    It seems that only Leonard chose to come farther south. — The other members of the family remained in that area, or moved farther north along the Saint John river, or migrated back to U.S.A. We have some records of some families living near Presque Isle.

When Leonard arrived in Stanley, he was an employee of the New Brunswick and Nova Scotia Land Company — an English firm interested in colonizing in the Maritime provinces.

My grandfather arrived in Stanley in 1834. In 1836[,] he married Jacobina Drummond MacKay, the daughter of Duncan MacKay, a non-commissioned officer of the 42nd Highland Regiment of the Black Watch, in 1836.

Leonard received a grant of land through the company, in what we know as Cross Creek, and which was called Kelly's Hill extending towards Ward Settlement.

I do not think my grandfather was a very business like person or perhaps the lots went by chance as there were many more valuable lots being taken up by other settlers.

[Lucille H. Campey, in her *Planters, Paupers, and Pioneers: English Settlers in Atlantic Canada*, speaking of the land purchased by the New Brunswick and Nova Scotia Land Company, writes: "Most of the land was relatively poor, and the company struggled long and hard to attract settlers." (p. 144) Campey adds in note 119 accompanying this passage from "Chapter 5" of her book: "The company was never profitable . It had to sell much of its land below the original price it had paid, and, by 1872, the company finished trading." (p. 404)]

Their first home was in the Ward Settlement part of the lot. It was[,] as many others, a log house, probably extended as the family grew. I was born in that house as was my brother and two sisters.

As seemed the mode of life at the time, Leonard made his living by farming and lumbering.

As I have said, the record of the other members of Leonard's family is not very clear to me. I probably never was much interested. (Ella Kelly Boulter has made an intensive study of the family.)

I remember some vague stories told by my mother of quite well-to-do aunts and cousins coming to visit my grandparents on occasion, but those visits were not in my time.

Mother also spoke of grandmother visiting her in-laws, but not being very impressed.

There was a colony of black people who had either come with my great grandfather or who followed and settled in the same area. They worked for the Kellys, but grandmother did not like them.

Also, my grandmother apparently was not impressed with the Loyalist attitude. Her evaluation was "those American refugees." —

My grandparents continued to live on the farm in Ward Settlement until 1897-98 ?, when they accompanied my parents, who moved into Stanley Village.

My grandfather did not live too long. He died in 1899.

It seems very strange that while I remember (or think I do) many events, I have no recollection of my grandfather. I do not remember what he looked like — if he had a long illness, nor of his funeral. —

My grandmother survived him for a number of years, — dying[,] I think in 1908-09. (?) Record in the family Bible. [Jacobina "Bina" Drummond McKaye/McKay died on 23 July 1907.]

I will continue with a resume of the lives of their children. It is interesting, — if puzzling, that in the newspaper report, and from my father[']s conversation, there is mention of eleven children. The Bible records only nine, — eight sons and one daughter. We must conclude the record is mistaken or that two children died in infancy. —

Family of Leonard and Jacobina.

John — died 1934. — The eldest son, married Eliza Scott. They settled on a farm in Ward Settlement, and[,] as I can remember[,] seemed to have lived in comfort and had a pleasant house and a well stocked farm.

Uncle John[,] himself, could not do very strenuous work, as he had a withered arm, the result of erysipelas in early manhood.

They had three children: Allan was drowned on a spring drive, while a young man; Margaret married Thomas Fraser, who had[,] eventually, a successful barber business in Fredericton; Mary married John Sutherland, a painter and decorator. Mary and her husband lived with her parents[,] and I think John Sutherland looked carefully at the upkeep of the farm.

Uncle John and Aunt Eliza[,] in their older years, moved to Fredericton with Margaret. I presume they died in Fredericton and were buried in the Rural Cemetery there. They have no plot (except Allan's) in Stanley.

James. — died in 1928; — I have no record of his life except that he left while young and settled in the American west.

I have never heard of his coming home to visit[,] and there seem few records of his life.

I think that in later years, my father had some knowledge of him; — perhaps exchanged letters, as the record of his death is apparently in the family Bible.

William — died in 1926. Married to Margaret Scott, a sister to Eliza, John[']s wife.

They first settled in the Ward Settlement area, but later moved to Keswick, and then, after a family tragedy, to Kingsclear.

William and Margaret had two sons, — Warren and Ellis. They, as well as Robert Kelly, had had other children, who died in the diphtheria epidemic. Warren Kelly, married Susan Dunphy, and had quite a large family, with whom we have kept no close contact, except with Patricia, who married [Ray Wilfred] McAloon in Stanley and is still living there. Warren was a veteran of World War I. — His family lives in the Keswick area.

Ellis, the younger son, moved with his father to Kingsclear. He married Jean Dunphy, and they had two children, Vincent and Pauline.

It is quite interesting that[,] owing to the tragic deaths during the diphtheria epidemic, there is a great difference in the ages of Warren and Ellis, who was approximately the age of my sister Gertrude.

Ellis and his father had a very successful fruit and vegetable farm at Kingsclear. — The son Vincent still runs the farm. He has two sons. Vincent keeps some contact with our family through Elsie and Gertrude. Ellis's widow lives on the farm and keeps in contact with Gertrude. The daughter Pauline also lives on the farm, where her father built her a house. She has two daughters, now married, I think.

<u>Duncan</u> — died 1919. — Married Mary Ann Brown, settled on the farm adjoining his father's in Ward Settlement.

Duncan was the most financially successful of the Kelly men, it seems. He had a larger farm and carried on a successful lumber operation as well. He seems to have been important in local politics.

I can remember their very nice house and extensive orchard. It was my pleasure as a small girl to visit there, where I admired the nice house and furniture. I spent some of each vacation with Uncle Dunc and Aunt Mary Ann. — I think I enjoyed myself with grown-up people for some reason. My aunt and uncle were especially fond of me. —

They had no children, but provided for their three foster children. They had also cared for my mother from her early childhood until she returned to her father's home when she was 17 years old. Her father had then remarried. Aunt Mary Ann was a cousin of my mother's new mother, and I think they would gladly have kept her as their daughter.

Duncan's three foster children were teenaged children brought to Canada from an English hostel for unwanted children — from which the English government had a policy of sending these children to the so called "colonies" to provide cheap domestic help.

The three sent to Uncle Dunc were very fortunate and well provided for.

They were: Mattie (Currie), who remained with them until their deaths; Cecily (Pinnoch) and Thomas Chamberlain.

Cecily married Fred Pinnoch, another child sent from the home, and taken by a prosperous family in Limekiln. Her family [is] still living around the Stanley-Fredericton area and are very successful.

Tommy died in early manhood. —

Aunt Mary Ann became blind while still quite young and had to depend on Mattie and Cecily for caring for the household affairs. —

As they became too old to cope with the farm — my uncle moved into Stanley Village, where my aunt died. Mattie's husband's work took him to Fredericton, and Uncle Dunc spent the remainder of his life with her in Fredericton.*

<u>George — died in 1920</u>. — Like James, he left New Brunswick for the American west. He went farther south and finally settled in St. Louis. —

There are few records concerning his life so far as I know. I remember one picture of his wife and one picture of his daughter (family Bible). The little girl was called Lulu, which amused me.

George came back to visit Stanley in the early 1900's, while his mother was still alive. I imagine he kept contact with my father on his return, but[,] letters are easily destroyed, so I have only a vague memory of his visit.

> *I had omitted to include in the note on Duncan two facts of interest showing his generosity and thought.
>
> I had mentioned the diphtheria epidemic in which many children died. My mother, then living with Duncan and Mary Ann, became ill. There were no doctors in the village, and my uncle drove to Fredericton (the only means of transportation at the time) and brought a doctor back to care for my mother. Her life and that of many other children were spared by this gesture.
>
> The other fact of note to us was that at his death each of my father's children was left with a generous legacy. As well, he left a gift for Cleveland Kelly, then recently back from overseas — (W.W. I) to assist him in re-establishing himself.

<u>Robert — died 1937</u> Married Ella Merrill. They had four living children. Other children (2 little girls) had died in the diphtheria epidemic. I have mentioned Robert also settled on a farm in Ward Settlement. I think he was the least successful of any of the Kelly men. His farm was not very large, and he had less stock, and less lumber land than the others.

His family was[,] in a way[,] closer to us than any of the others, because his children seemed more our contemporaries.

His four children were William, Cleveland, Irma and Harold.

The oldest son, William, was not interested in farming but became a lumber surveyor. — He married Marjorie Hayes and had three daughters. After several years of living either with Robert or with Marjorie's father, they moved to British Columbia, where he had a position in the department of forestry, living in Cranbrook.

He died during the Spanish flu epidemic in 1919, leaving a widow and three small children, Robina, Ella and Jean.

[Jeannie (Boulter) Mattews, on 10 March 2015, writes in a note accompanying a photograph of her grandmother Marjorie (Hayes) Kelly's tombstone in Bowsman, Manitoba, "After leaving her daughter Jean Kelly to be cared for by Havelock Kelly and family, Marjorie Hayes Kelly moved to Bowsman to take a teaching job because it offered a 'teacherage'.... According to my cousin Sandy Ryan, Marjorie moved from Stanley to Bowsman in April 1919." Jeannie notes, "According to my mother Ella, Marjorie took her and Robina with her via train. My mother 'started school' at age 4 ½ because she could be trusted to sit still in the first row as her mother taught. Robina would have been 9 or 10.

"From my research I discovered my grandmother married Daniel Hajdamache on Nov. 30, 1922 in Swan River, Manitoba. Apparently, Daniel Hajdamache's dates are 1885-1961...."

Jeannie continues: "I never knew of Dan's existence until I was about 23 and my mother casually mentioned her 'evil stepfather' — the 'Russian' who sold her cow without her permission when she was about 23. Because she was angry at her stepfather, she wrote to Havelock Kelly, asking him to lend her train fare from Manitoba to Stanley, NB. So either [in] 1937 or 1938[,] my mother travelled across country[,] stopping to meet her younger sister in Montreal almost 20 years after their separation. Robina never saw her baby sister ever again. My cousin Sandy and I never met our Aunt Robina."]

Cleveland continued to live at home until the outbreak of World War I. He had been interested in military affairs, and had trained during summer courses in the Reserve Army, reaching the position of lieutenant. He[,] with many other young men, my brother Alan included, enlisted in what was then known as the N.B. Regiment — the 101th.

Cleve, fortunately, survived the various campaigns between 1914-18, though he was seriously wounded, but not invalided home.

While overseas, he met and married Hilda Jarvis, who followed him to Canada.

I have often thought what a shock her arrival in Ward Settlement must have been — to live on a primitive farm, with no bath or toilet facilities during the winter of her arrival, and with no better means of transportation into the village than a horse and sleigh. Must have been something to a carefully brought-up English school-teacher.

Besides the physical limitations, life for everyone must have been difficult that year as Irma was living home, teaching in the local school, — her mother being ill with cancer, — and Marjorie having arrived from the west with three small children and no money.

Hilda and Marjorie sought refuge with my parents as frequently as possible.

Marjorie eventually got a position teaching in Manitoba, in a district where a teachers residence was provided. This was helpful, but she could not take her youngest child, Jean, who was only a baby. My father and mother took Jean to care for, and she became the youngest member of our family, never joining her mother and sisters.

Cleve was lucky enough to get a position with the immigration department, with my father's help. He was posted to Vanceboro-St. Croix, where he soon had a home to bring Hilda. —

I think it speaks well of the family, that with all these involvements, there was so little friction and no family break-ups.

Cleve and Hilda had one son[,] Harold[,] and adopted another son[,] Edgar, who now lives in the home at St. Croix. Harold lives in Toronto.

Marjorie's two older daughters lived and were educated in Manitoba.

The older, Robina[,] married rather comfortably, I understand. She is now widowed and lives in or near Flin Flon.

A few years past, one son came to Fredericton to look up his relatives. He was a law student at U. of Manitoba. Except for this contact and letters between Ella and Robina, there is no close connection.

Ella also completed her education in Manitoba. In the late 1930's she came east, and never returned to her mother's home. (Her mother had remarried and was no longer teaching[.])

She [Ella] married William Boulter of Stanley, who, after serving in Canada during W.W. II, became an employee of the N.B. Civil Service in the Department of Lands and Forests.

They have two children. David, presently living in Botswana[,] Africa, as an instructor in the university, and Jeannie, still living near home and teaching High School English.

Jean, the infant daughter, left to the care of my parents, grew up as a member of our family.

She worked in Montreal as a secretary in the C.N.I.C. offices in Montreal. She met and married Fred Ryan[,] after his discharge from the army in 1945. For a time they were both employed in Montreal, but Fred, not being well, took an early retirement[,] and they are now living on the Ryan farm in Matapedia. They have one daughter, Sandra, who lives at home and is the manager of the K-mart store in Campbellton-Atholville area.

Harold, Uncle Bob's younger son, had gone west to work in Vancouver. He enlisted during W.W. I, and[,] unfortunately, was killed in action.

Irma, Uncle Bob's only daughter, became a teacher. — She married Arthur Tucker, and they lived in and around Stanley and Fredericton. They had no children.

As I remarked before, Uncle Bob's family, — at least Cleve and Irma[,] were closest to our family. While some years older, they were still of our generation, while the other cousins, excepting Ellis Kelly, were more nearly our parents' age.

We visited Uncle Bob's while they were still on the farm and went to Irma and Arthur's as a matter of course when they lived in Fredericton.

During W.W. I, my brother and Cleve kept in close contact while overseas.

In the years after W.W. II[,] while Gertrude's sons were at University, they went to Irma's or to Ella Boulter's as if their homes were a second home to the boys. —

For myself, I owe an undying debt of gratitude to Irma and Arthur for their unfailing kindness and support during my husband's stay in Fredericton hospital. It is sad that Irma's recent death, March 1979[,] has really ended this close relationship. There are no cousins left in any family.

<u>Betsy Ann — died 1891.</u> — The only daughter and the cherished sister, married John Scott, brother of Eliza and Margaret.

John also settled on a farm in Ward Settlement. From all reports, I think he was not too successful a farmer. They had six children, three daughters and three sons. Betsy Ann died, leaving John to cope with bringing up the family.

The three daughters seem not to have stayed at home very long to help their father.

The only daughter, Effie, who stayed in the vicinity[,] married Willard Parker of Doaktown.

I understand their son or his family live in Fredericton and Gertrude Gould has some knowledge of them.

One sister and two of the sons went to British Columbia[,] and we lost contact with them or the other sister[,] who went to Boston after her marriage.

Lester, the other son, settled in Ward Settlement, where he farmed successfully. His family live in or near Stanley. The two sons have successful fruit and vegetable farms. We do have contact with Lester's family through Elsie Reid and Gertrude Gould.

<u>Alonzo — died 1929</u> — married Abigail Sansom. They had one son, Franklin, my favorite cousin as he was my age and because I had lived in

my early adult life very much with this aunt and uncle. So Frank and I grew very dose to one another. He died while still a young man.

["]Uncle M.A.["], as he liked to be called, evidently, had no interest in farming or lumbering. He continued with his education and became a teacher.

Due to his wife's connections, he became manager of the Richard Lumber Co. office in Campbellton.

He continued his education, reading law[,] and[,] after having passed his law exams, he practiced in Campbellton, becoming the County Crown prosecutor.

He was killed in a car accident.

This report brings me to my father and our immediate family. —

Havelock — died 1964 — My father was a number of years younger than Alonzo, and[,] in a way[,] the other members of his family seemed unrelated as near relatives. John was so much older. I always felt he was a grandfather. Havelock married Annie Clark in 1892. A record of events in his life is in the attached photo-copy of one of the anniversaries, though it is quite mixed up as to facts and dates.

In his early years, and for some time after his marriage, my father continued to live on the family farm in Ward Settlement, caring for his parents.

Later he moved his family into Stanley Village where he carried on various activities.

In those days of Scott Act Temperance legislation, it was necessary that all alcoholic beverages were dispersed by prescription. For a time, he had the license as the disperser.

As this seemed not to be a full-time job, he carried on various other activities. He was a land surveyor, auctioneer, — dispenser of deeds, mortgages and marriage licenses, and somewhere along the line, he became a Justice of the Peace[,] with much knowledge of, and influence in administering small legal matters.

Finally, he became a Woods Inspector and Surveyor for the Department of Lands and Forests. He retired at 70 years old, but continued to advise people legally and dispense deeds, etc.

He and mother found the house in Stanley too big and expensive to manage and moved to Fredericton in 1961.

There were eight children, of whom brief accounts follow.

Bessie Anne — 1893. Married James Ninnes. Educated at Provincial Normal School. — Taught school briefly in N.B. and later in Quebec. Lives in Montreal. No noteworthy events to record.

Alan — 1894-1942. Enlisted in 1914 W.W. I. Both he and Cleve were among those sent to Val Cartier and shipped overseas from there.

Alan was wounded in [1917] at the Battle of [Vimy Ridge]. He was cited for courage and awarded the Military Medal.

The rather curious reports relative to this award. — His life was saved because he had in his breast pocket one of those metallic mirrors, which was pierced by the bullet, but which deflected the bullet from his heart. My sister Joyce still has the mirror.

The other story, which I received second-hand through Cleve. Alan had been really recommended for the Victoria Cross, but his commanding officer (British) refused the recommendation because of Alan's refusal to obey an order during the preparation for the attack.

It seemed that Alan[,] among others[,] had been AWOL[,] and those soldiers were told to serve in one unit. Alan refused, and went to his own unit. No other punishment was given except the change of recommendation.

I do not know how authentic the story is as Cleve got it through the grapevine, but I do know that Alan did not especially value his Military Medal.

He spent most of his life in and around Stanley[,] mostly in lumber activities, except for working in Montreal during W.W. II, in munitions work.

[In a diagram of the Gabriel Havelock Kelly family tree created by Ella Rita (Kelly) Boulter, provided by her daughter Jeannie Belinda (Boulter) Matthews, Ella Rita (Kelly) Boulter documents the following in regard to Alan Melvin Kelly's service records: "No. 22592[;] No. 1Co. 14th Batt.[;] 3rd Infantry Brig.[;] 1st Can. Div.[;] B.E.F. (W.W. I)[.]"]

<u>Gertrude — 1896</u> — Educated at Stanley High School and Provincial Normal School. — Taught school in Dalhousie. She married James Gould. After his death, resumed teaching, and after her retirement, returned to Stanley and Fredericton where she cared for our parents until their deaths. —

She had three sons. — Alan, Robert, Edgar (Ted).

Alan and Robert, after graduating from High school in Dalhousie, enlisted in the Canadian Navy in W.W. II. They completed their education after being discharged from the services, with the help of their war gratuities. —

Alan took a course in Industrial Arts at a Trade School and Provincial Normal School, and went on to get a degree from Peoria. — At that time Canadian Universities did not give degrees in Industrial Arts. He later received his Masters of Education degree from McGill.

Robert went to University of New Brunswick and received his degree in Forestry. [(]Changed to Engineering[.]) He went to U.S.A. to lecture in a

University in Texas and continued his education at Johns Hopkins University, — receiving a degree in Science.

Alan married Joyce Atkinson, and they had three children — Duncan, Rebecca and Virginia. Duncan is living in London, Ontario; Rebecca is teaching and lives in Kingston, Ontario, and Virginia is completing a Science course at U.N.B.

All three children continued their education and have degrees in their chosen fields.

Alan's second wife is Pamela Johanson. They have no children. They are living in Montreal, where Alan continues his teaching career.

Robert married Mildred Culkin. Robert is presently employed by [blank space.] They live in Connecticut.

They have three children, Roderick, Dawn and Kelly Ann. Roderick was interested in forestry and lumbering and went to western U.S.A. to follow those occupations.

Dawn, now married, is a musician. —

Kelly Ann is still in University. She loves horses and is probably working in animal husbandry.

Edgar (Ted) married Donna Jarvis. There is one son, Matthew, from that marriage.

Ted's second marriage was to Carolyn Hindness. They have one child, — Stephanie Ann.

Ted completed High school in Dalhousie and went to Teachers college (formerly P.N.S.). He taught a few years in N.B. and came to Quebec. He continued his education here at Sir George Williams (Concordia) University at McGill and received his Ph.D from New York University. He is presently employed as principal of D'Iberville LeMoyne High School in Longueil. He was too young to enlist.

Three boys to be proud of, as their efforts in obtaining an education depended entirely on themselves. Their mother was left widowed early in life[,] and her help had to be limited.

Jean — 1897-1967. Educated in N.B. as a teacher and later came to Montreal to train at Montreal General Hospital. After graduation[,] she worked for the Victorian Order of Nurses until after her marriage to Rev. Nathan Noseworthy.

They continued to live in Montreal, where her husband carried on his pastoral duties. During W.W. II[,] he had served overseas in the chaplaincy service. They had one daughter, Monica, who married Donald Stringer.

Monica has three sons, Kevin, a second-year university student, and two teen-aged boys, Daniel and Christopher[.]

Monica was widowed in February 1979. She has taken a course in Alcoholism and Drug Addictions and hopes to pursue a course in that field as a counselor in the area of addiction.

Elsie — 1898. — Like myself, Gertrude and Jean, Elsie attended P.N.S. and taught for a short time. —

Her first husband, Harry Boulter, died suddenly, — and she later married Arthur Reid. —

She has spent most of her life in Stanley. Her first husband was engaged in business in the Village, and her second husband worked as a farmer and lumberman until he became incapacitated with arthritis.

They are still living happily in the village.

Ina (Jacie) — 1900-1940 — A graduate of the Montreal General School of Nursing. Married Virgil Green — (New York.)

After her graduation, Jacie worked for a time in Montreal for the V.O.N. She left to work in New York, first in the Henry Street Settlement, which she found too depressing, and later as a Visiting Nurse (comparable to V.O.N.) in the Coney Island office.

She met Virgil (Bert) Green in New York.

They had no children.

Jacie died of cancer in 1940, and her husband died of a heart attack within a year after.

For years I kept close contact with Bert's brother Albert and his brother-in-law Percy Vanan, but they are now dead. The only possible contact would be Richard Vanan[,] a nephew — who has a gift shop and record shop in Brooklyn. — I still have his address.

George — 1902-03 — Died in infancy.

Joyce — 1906 — Married Crawford (Ford) MacNeill of Dalhousie. Has lived most of her adult life in and around Dalhousie.

Family could have done a more correct and interesting account.

I felt, however, that inaccurate and sketchy as it may be — with little opportunity for any real research, that this history may be of some value to the younger people who may wonder a little about their origins.

One thing I neglected to remark about, or had no way of inserting it[,] is the fact that has always interested me.

Apparently, with all the limited facilities for schools, my grandfather and grandmother were both able to read and write.

I do not remember grandfather[,] as I have said[,] and by the time I knew grandmother, she was confining most of her reading to her Bible and Prayer book.

All my father's brothers and[,] I presume[,] his sister, could read and write. Grandmother must have been a determined lady, as I have read accounts of the schools in the early days of Stanley. But, as I say, they could all read and write, subscribed for the local paper and discussed federal, provincial and local politics, intelligently, and in loud voices!

I remember being horrified in my teens when my father, making a deed for a neighbour, said he could not write and had him make his mark.

While none of our family [has] attained any great distinction or publicity, I think that the younger generation may take pride that they descend from honest, intelligent citizens who commanded the respect of their community.

After a series of notes on genealogical material, Bessie (Kelly) Ninnes writes about the wedding anniversary gatherings for her father and mother, Gabriel Havelock and Annie May (Clark) Kelly:

Anniversaries.

My father and mother were fortunate enough to be spared one to the other for over seventy years, and to celebrate four anniversaries with best wishes from their family and friends.

Fiftieth Anniversary. — The fiftieth anniversary was celebrated August 18 .. 1942, — Known as the Golden Wedding Anniversary. We were still living in the home in Stanley with lots of room for the visiting members of the family.

The attached pictures with comments will give some record of the occasion. [DM: I have not included the photographs, which are poor copies of copies.]

I remember it as a beautiful summer day, and we were able to spend much time out on the lawn.

Sunday 17th we had a family dinner, at which all the members of the family[,] as shown in one picture[,] were present.

I think Ella Boulter, who was spending some time with Mrs. Ed Lanson, was also present. She had spent much time after her return from the west with my parents and was extremely fond of them. Her husband was not home, being in the army.

My husband, Jim Ninnes, was at the dinner, but had to go back to Montreal, so was not present at the reception the following day.

After the dinner, the two youngest grandsons, Dan MacNeill and Ted Gould[,] presented the family gifts to the grandparents — A gold watch chain for an old fashioned watch to my father and a ring to Mother.

It is too bad that at that time they were not making "family rings." Mother would have so much enjoyed that.

Many friends and neighbors came to the reception, and were received by my parents. —

Many beautiful and useful gifts were presented. It is the only anniversary where many pictures were taken.

Sixtieth-Anniversary. — Aug. 18, 1952. —
This was not quite such an elaborate affair as the fiftieth had been but was a pleasant evening reception.

We were still living in Stanley at the time. I do not remember the occasion too vividly, as Joyce and I had driven from Dalhousie the day of the reception.

I have a feeling it was a rainy evening and everyone was in the house.

There were not so many relatives on this occasion.

As I said[,] Joyce and I drove from Dalhousie by ourselves. — Jeanie Ryan and my husband were both quite ill in hospital, so we made a quick trip.

For family presents[,] I remember we gave Mother an upholstered rocking chair, but I don't recall what my father received. I'm sure he was not neglected. —

Sixty-fifth anniversary, — 1958 — My parents were still living in Stanley, and my sister Gertrude Gould was caring for them.

This anniversary was only a small family party, with only the relatives who lived near. I think probably only Elsie, Gertrude, Jeanie Ryan and Ella Boulter were present, and perhaps some neighbors stopped to offer congratulations. The enclosed picture of four generations is the most interesting memento of this occasion.

Seventieth Anniversary — 1962 —
This was the special occasion. At the time it was unusual for couples to be fortunate enough to have such a celebration. Today it seems less unusual.

My parents had sold the house in Stanley and moved to an apartment in Devon in 1961. —

This reception was held at the Devon apartment and largely planned by Gertrude Gould, Jean Noseworthy and Elsie Reid.

I was working in Montreal — had taken my vacation and gone to Newfoundland. I almost missed the party as the plane at Torbay was about to take off the previous day when we reached the airport. However, I caught the flight safely, though my luggage missed and followed later.

The rather garbled report of the anniversary which is attached gives interesting facts.

Most of the family who lived at a distance had arrived the previous day or evening.

On the morning of the anniversary, a private service was held at St. Mary's Church. The Rev. Brian Campion was at that time the rector and a good family friend.

The guests began to arrive around three o'clock, and congratulations began. —

The usual telegrams (letters?) from the Queen and the Prime Minister of Canada were read. A special personal letter had been sent by Hon. Hugh John Flemming, the Premier of New Brunswick. My father appreciated this more than the others as it was really a personal handwritten letter from one friend to an older valued friend and employee.

This anniversary was the last family get-together. Those present were the children and grandchildren and their families.

Myself. — Gertrude Gould and her family.

Alan and Joyce and the three children, Duncan, Rebecca and Virginia.

Bob and Mildred and three children, — Roderick, — Dawn and Kelly Ann.

Ted and Donna Gould. —

Jean Noseworthy, — Monica and Dan Stringer and Kevin.

Elsie and Arthur Reid.

Joyce and Ford MacNeill, — Donna Jean and Ronnie McEwen. Dan MacNeill was in British Columbia.

Besides the immediate family, other close relatives were: Irma Tucker, — Ella and Bill Boulter; Ellis and Jean Kelly, Susan Kelly (Warren's widow) and many of the Scott connections, whom I did not know by name.

This was a very happy occasion[,] and I think has pleasant memories to all of those who were there. I think both the parents and the children had a feeling at any home-coming that it was a celebration of importance.

This 70th anniversary marked the end of such celebrations —

My father hoped to live to celebrate his one hundred birthday. — 1964, and had he lived[,] I expect that also would have been an occasion for a family re-union. —

Unhappily, my father died shortly after his ninety-ninth birthday, where he had only the usual birthday cake and close neighbors to wish him happiness.

Since Mother's birthday and Father's were only a week apart, Elsie & Gert usually tried to combine the celebration for them both. —

Most other members were too far away to join in at any of these. —

The following transcription of a newspaper clipping is from the Gabriel Havelock Kelly family collection. A typed draft of the original used for this article was found in the Ella Rita (Kelly) Boulter papers in the possession of her daughter, Jeannie Belinda (Boulter) Matthews, who was granted permission to publish from her mother's material. In the draft, it is noted that the gathering for Gabriel Havelock and Annie Mae (Clark) Kelly's wedding anniversary occurred on 18 August. It should be noted (unless there were sons who died in infancy or in their youth and not recorded) that neither Gabriel Havelock Kelly or Leonard Coombes Kelly were the eleventh son in their respective families. Bessie Anne (Kelly) Ninnes (18 September 1893 - 2 November 1984) notes this discrepancy in regard to the Leonard Coombes Kelly family in her memories.

Wednesday, August 21, 1957

Grandson Of Loyalist:
MARRIED IN 1892, COUPLE IN STANLEY RICH IN MEMORIES

In the village of Stanley, nestled in the hills of the beautiful Nashwaak Valley, live an elderly couple, who are rich in memories. They are Mr. and Mrs. Havelock Kelly, who celebrated their 65th wedding anniversary on Sunday.

Mrs. Kelly was the former Annie M. Clark, daughter of Mary Ann Arnold and Moses Everet Clark of Marysville.

Mr. and Mrs. Kelly were married August 18, 1892, by the Rev. Mr. Parsons of Marysville. Mr. Kelly is the grandson of a Loyalist, being the eleventh and youngest son of the late Leonard C. Kelly, who was the eleventh and youngest son of Sgt. John Kelly of the 2nd New Jersey Volunteers of the United Empire Loyalists, who was granted a tract of land in Kingsclear.

Leonard C. Kelly and John Reid were the original pioneers of Stanley, arriving in 1834. They met, so it is said, on Stanley Hill, Mr. Reid having come by way of the Royal Road and a trail through the woods, and Mr. Kelly coming by way of the river. Both men were employed by the New Brunswick and Nova Scotia Land Company. Both married and settled in Stanley. Leonard Kelly married the late Jacobina McKaye, daughter of Cpl. Duncan McKaye and Mary Sutherland. Duncan McKaye was a member of the 42nd Highlanders of the Black Watch Regiment, who settled on the Nashwaak in 1783.

FATHER'S STORIES

Mr. Havelock Kelly recalls many stories told him by his father — of the memorable occasion when Bishop Inglis made his first historic trip to Stanley in 1835. Leonard Kelly, the canoeman, brought His Grace up the river.

Another time Leonard, still employed by the company, started off with a yoke of oxen and a load of lumber to Cardigan. He had to travel through the newly formed Scotch settlement, which was made up of a group from the Isle of Skye. Living in rude log cabins, most with no roofs, their plight was desperate and many perished the first winter. As Leonard Kelly approached with the load of lumber, this grim, wordless band of men descended and in a matter of minutes removed the lumber and as silently turned the oxen and their driver homeward.

These, and many other stories are recalled by Havelock Kelly as he looks out over the valley. He is the last remaining link with a colorful era now long past.

SEVEN CHILDREN

Mr. and Mrs. Kelly had seven children: Mrs. James Ninnes, St. John's, Nfld.; Mrs. Nathan Noseworthy, Montreal; Mrs. Ford MacNeill, Dalhousie; Mrs. James Gould, Stanley; Mrs. Arthur Reid, Stanley; the late Mrs. Virgel Green and the late Alan Kelly, M.M. They also brought up a niece, Mrs. Fred Ryan, Fredericton, from infancy.

Mr. Kelly is the oldest member of the Alexandra Masonic Lodge, F. and A.M., and was presented with the 50-year jewel in 1952.

Mrs. Kelly is past-president of the Stanley Women's Institute and a life-member of the W.A. of St. Thomas Anglican Church.

The happy couple observed their 65th wedding anniversary by welcoming to their home many relatives and friends who came to offer their congratulations. They were the recipients of many cards and telegrams, including a personal letter of congratulations from Premier Hugh John Flemming. (The newspaper is unnamed, and no page number given.)

Jeannie Belinda (Boulter) Matthews has granted me permission to quote the following in regard to the seventieth wedding anniversary of Gabriel Havelock "Havelock" and Annie Mae (Clark) Kelly from her email of 12 May 2015:

I have vivid memories of the 70th even though I was a little girl. My cousins Sandy, Ginny, Rebecca and I still shudder at the memory of Aunt Bess being left in charge of all the kids at my house as all the adults — the "wet" ones, at least — went off gallivanting to a dance in Stanley, no doubt well fueled by generous servings of rye from my father Bill and his brother-in-law Fred Ryan, married to my aunt Jeanie Kelly Ryan. The kids all thought of Bess as a grim oldtime schoolmarm, but in recent years, I have come to think that she was probably kindhearted in her way and her offering to babysit was a sign of a generous spirit.

Velma Kelly writes in *The Village in the Valley: A History of Stanley*: "The Nova Scotia Land Company hired [Leonard Coombes Kelly] as a head-boatman in charge of moving supplies on the Nashwaak River. He was the man who poled the canoe from Nashwaak Bridge to Stanley carrying Bishop Inglis for his historic trip in 1835." (p. 25).

Margaret (Kelly) Hay states that Leonard Coombes Kelly "was also an oxen-teamster." She notes that "Leonard is buried in St. Thomas Anglican Cemetery, Stanley, New Brunswick," adding that he was buried in "Sect. #4, Row 8, #18. . . ."

Margaret (Kelly) Hay:

> One story worthy of telling is Leonard had been asked to christen the opening of a new mill in Stanley with a bottle of beer. He drank the fine liquid instead of wasting it. Then in his strong voice started to sing. One song was rather "off-colour" and offended the Catholic priest in attendance who, it is said, "never spoke to him again." The home Leonard first built in Stanley, NB[,] was just up Kelly Hill (past Roy MacAloons) located on the right side of the road at the top of the hill. Property extended to the river on the left side of the road (including the United Baptist Graveyard). Presently it is the Gilmour place. Their second home[,] and where he and Jacobina died[,] was across the Stanley bridge; first house on the right. Their nine children were born on the first farm on Kelly Hill as was their grandson (my grandfather) Warren, son of William. Four of Leonard's sons settled on farms adjoining the home-farm in Ward Settlement. On interviewing Gertrude (Havelock's daughter)[,] Leonard's grand-daughter[,] she describes her grandfather as a rather severe, not a gentle man[,] with very piercing eyes. She said the Kellys had nice hands. Gertrude's youngest son, Ted[,] had a dream that his great-grandfather [Leonard Coombes Kelly] told him there was a fortune buried in back of the old farm; but not to take it unless really desperate.

In an email of 28 July 2014, Jeannie (Boulter) Matthews revealed that a gold coin has "been passed down for generations" in the Leonard Coombes Kelly family. The coin, still owned by the family, is to be used "for bread only" and is passed down to a designated family member. (See photograph of coin in photo collection.)

The following piece, contained in the *Ella (Kelly) Boulter Scrapbook* at the Provincial Archives of New Brunswick, was written by Ella Rita (Kelly) Boulter:

THE "SCOTCH" SETTLEMENT STORY

> A group of Scottish immigrants, sent out probably between 1834-5, located between Cardigan and the Tay Stream a short distance from the present village of Stanley.
>
> There were several families of MacDonalds, also MacGillverays, Davidsons, MacDougals, MacKinnons and Hossacks, to name a few. Some, from the North of Scotland had been shepherds, but mostly they

were fishermen. They came under the leadership of one Norman Nicholson, whom a local village historian designated as "a 'bad man' who did not deal fairly or honestly with his people." The old New Brunswick Land Company[,] which did not properly organize until the following year, was not ready for them either. The houses were reported to have been "thrown up like log fences, no floors, no windows, no doors, and no chinks in the walls filled[.]" Without warmth, clothing, and very little food, fifty or more of these unfortunate people perished.

My great-grandfather[,] Leonard Kelly, then a young man, drove by the settlement, with a team of oxen[,] hauling a load of lumber to Cardigan. Suddenly he was surrounded by Scots. Without uttering a word, they unloaded the lumber, and . . . silently turned the oxen around, and Great-grandfather went back. After all it wasn't his lumber — it belonged to the company. He, too, that first year[,] nearly died from exposure and hardship. In those grim days it was every man for himself. The next year he became the Company's head canoe man and was in charge of supplies.

To get back to the settlers. In the spring, there were about a hundred who somehow survived. They were removed into Company houses in Stanley that summer, and as the years went by they prospered, but back in "Scotch Settlement[,]" as it was called, one refused to move. She was a MacDonald girl. She had lost her parents and her sweetheart that first winter, and she herself had been terribly ill. This illness left her handicapped the rest of her life, for her mind was permanently affected. The local people called her Mysie. She had been a governess, and had been fairly well educated, and spoke the purest Gaelic. Despite the handicap from her illness[,] she retained her fierce pride and independence, and scorned assistance. She remained on alone in the settlement which had failed. She planted seeds, and herbs and vegetables, and then sold her produce, and eked out a scanty living. Some cruel children taunted her, but mostly they were afraid of her, and ran when they saw her coming.

"Mysie" had second sight[,] so they said. On a May morning in 1844 she met two young men riding in a wagon. "I see danger[,] she screamed[.] "Do not go any farther." They laughed at her and went on, but at the top of Stanley Hill the horses bolted, the wagon overturned, and both men were thrown to the ground. Lieutenant Cardin's head struck a rock, killing him instantly. The other engineer, Lieut. Burke, was severely injured.

Mysie continued to roam in the woods, until a very old lady. She had a nephew, James MacDonald, who was kind and good to her. In her last years they moved her into Stanley, and built a house for her.

Old folks in Stanley often used to speak of "Mysie's Last Prayer":

> "Lord preserve us from the witches and warlocks which roam o'er the meadow[.]
> Be good to Hamish, Lord[,] and may the price of cornmeal be four dollars a barrel."

The old photo [Margery "Mysie" MacDonald (PANB Assorted Acquisitions P37-292)] was probably taken in the early nineteen hundreds. I believe it was taken in a Carnival tent. At that time[,] in a terrible rage, she nearly wrecked another Carnival tent, egged on by cruel boys, but that is another "Mysie" story. (pp. 11-13)

Sharon Bird Anderson, in an article entitled "Sole Survivor," published in *The New Brunswick Reader* of 19 March 2005, writes that Mysie and her family came to New Brunswick in 1836. "During the first Canadian winter, 48 out of 121 men, women and children in Scotch Settlement starved or froze to death. The dead included Mysie's father." (p. 14)

In *With Axe and Bible: The Scottish Pioneers of New Brunswick, 1784-1874*, Lucille H. Campey writes that Margery "Mysie" MacDonald (1828 – 1906), when her "brother died in 1892, . . . carried her brother's body over her shoulders and walked eleven miles to the Roman Catholic cemetery in Stanley to bury him. She, herself, was later buried in this same cemetery. Her Catholic credentials strongly suggest that her family's roots were in the predominately Roman Catholic district of Moidart (West Inverness-shire) rather than Skye." (pp. 111-113)

The following is a copy of a letter by Gabriel Havelock Kelly from the Dalhousie University Archives:

MS2 280-I
Stanley Dec. 15th /45

J. M. McKay
F'ton, N. B.

Re. your letter, would say: I don't know you but know your brothers quite well, also your Father James D. McKay who was my first cousin. Re. Duncan McKay your great-grandfather: he was the original grantee of the 42 regt, taking land at Nashwaak Bridge, later marrying Margaret Sutherland. He was about 21 or 22 years of age when he came to

Nashwaak in 1787 from Argyle[,] [added in the margin in the same hand] being born in 1765, my mother Jacobina McKay the youngest of the family born in 1819. I am the youngest of her family of eleven, being born in 1865 so you can see nothing very remarkable about me being his grandson. There is also another grandson living in this place, Nathaniel McKay age 90 son of Robert McKay who was [a] brother of William McKay your grandfather. (I remember your grandfather quite well) Re the other McKays listed in the Gleaner don't think they were related to the said Duncan McKay, at least they didn't settle on the Nashwaak. He, the said Duncan had four sons viz Duncan, James & William and Robert. William settled in Boistown[;] Robert staid at Nashwaak on the grant, the other 2 boys went to the U. S. There was was also 5 girls viz Anne married Forbes on the Nashwaak, Mary & Elspeth married Porters (brothers)[;] went to Presque Isle, Maine[.]

-2-

Margaret never married[,] a lame woman who lived with your grandfather most of the time and my mother in Stanley[.] Re. the Sutherlands, they stayed at Nashwaak for a long time, the younger generation have died, and moved away, there is one man Albert about my age living in Woodstock[,] N. B. Cameron's I know nothing about.

Hoping this garbled information will be of some benefit to you, and that I might see & talk it over personally with you[.] I remain yours truly[,]

Havelock Kelly

The following is from the *Ella (Kelly) Boulter Scrapbook* (p. 8) at the Provincial Archives of New Brunswick. Ella Rita (Kelly) Boulter had made a cursive copy of the clipping in her notebook given to Darrell McBreairty by her daughter, Jeannie Belinda (Boulter) Matthews, on 3 October 2014. In the notebook, Ella writes, "This has been copied from clipping of a scrapbook. The rest of the clipping is lost."

In an attempt to locate an original of this clipping, Roger Mark "Mark" Smith has searched through microfilm copies of several New Brunswick newspapers to no avail.

Leonard C Kelley — A Well Known Resident of Stanley Called Away

One of York County's oldest and best known residents passed away on Monday evening, in the person of Leonard C. Kelly, whose death occurred at the home of his son Councilor Havelock Kelly, at Stanley Village. Old age was the cause of his demise, and he had been ill about three weeks.

The deceased gentleman was a native of the parish of Kingsclear, and a son of John Kelley, a United Empire Loyalist who came to this province from North Carolina, at the close of the Revolutionary War, and obtained a grant of land.

Mr. Kelley completed 64 years of married life last September[,] and Mrs. Kelly[,] who survives[,] him is 81 years of age. Their family consisted of ten sons and one daughter. Eight of the sons are now living and six of them reside in the parish of Stanley.

One peculiarity about the deceased gentleman was that he never had a grey hair in his head, and up to the time of his death his hair was coal black in color.

Mr. Kelley was known as a Liberal of the old school and

The following is from the *The Daily Gleaner* of 20 April 1899:

STANLEY.

STANLEY, N.B. April 17. — The death of Mr. Leonard Kelly, an old and highly respected resident of this place, occurred this morning at eight o'clock. Mr. Kelly was born at Kingsclear, York County, on the 6th day of December, 1810, and was therefore in the 90th year of his age. He was the youngest son of Mr. John Kelly, a United Empire Loyalist who came from North Carolina in 1783. Mr. Kelly was one of the pioneers of Stanley and perhaps the first who came here with the intention of remaining and making a home. That was about the year 1834, and since that time until old age compelled him to relinquish the more active duties of life, always took a deep interest in whatever tended to the welfare of Stanley, and won from his fellow-citizens the highest feelings of respect. In 1835 he was married to a Miss McKay, of Nashwaak, who survives him. Besides Mrs. Kelly he leaves eight sons to mourn the loss of a kind husband and father. The funeral will take place tomorrow afternoon. Internment in the Church of England Cemetery. (p. 6) (*Provincial Archives of New Brunswick*, Microfilm: F2892.)

The *New Brunswick Reporter and Fredericton Advertiser* of 26 April 1899 carried the following:

Full of years. — By the death last week of Leonard C Kelly at the home of his son, Coun. Kelly, at Stanley Village, another landmark linking the past with the present has been obliterated. His wife aged 81 years, and eight sons survive him. The funeral service was conducted by Rev. A. B. Murray in the Episcopal church, and six of the deceased's sons acted as pall bearers. Mr. Kelly was a native of Kingsclear, and a descendant of the U. E. Loyalists. (p. 4) (*Provincial Archives of New Brunswick,* Microfilm: F12182*.)*

In the *Anglican Church Burial Registrations*, under the "Diocese of Fredericton, Province of New Brunswick, List of Burials in Parish or Mission of Stanley in the County of York[,] Year 1899," Leonard C Kelly, who is listed as a resident of Stanley Village, died at the age of 89 years, 4 months and 11 days on 17 April 1899 and was buried in Stanley Village, with Alexis Murray, Rector of Stanley, officiating.

In his *New Brunswick A History: 1784-1867*, W.S. MacNutt notes that Lieutenant-Colonel Richard Hayne came to New Brunswick "as an agent for the New Brunswick and Nova Scotia Land Company. . . ." (p. 376)

At the website **Richard Hayne House | My New Brunswick** displaying photographs of the Lieutenant-Colonel Richard Hayne house in Fredericton, New Brunswick, it is noted that Lieutenant-Colonel Richard Hayne and his family moved into their Fredericton house in 1841, the year "he was appointed Provincial Aide de Camp. Mr. Hayne served in that capacity under four successive Lieutenant Governors: Sir John Harvey; Sir Edmund Walker Head; His Excellency J. Henry T. Manners-Sutton; and the Hon. Arthur Gordon." It is also noted at the website that Richard Hayne was appointed "Adjutant General of the New Brunswick Militia" in 1851 and retired from that position in 1863. Richard Hayne returned to his native England after his retirement.

In the following entry from Ella (Kelly) Boulter's notebook, it is obvious that the anecdote refers to Lieutenant-Colonel Richard Hayne:

> Leonard Kelly carried Co[.] Haines across the river. Coming to a deep hole[,] he said[, "]Oh[,] I'm tired["] and dropped him in[.]
>
> Col[.] Haines had a bottle of whiskey & drank & drank while Leonard sat croaking for a drink. Finally[,] Col[.] [Haines] gave him a drop and said[, "]This whiskey is 7 years old[,"] & Leonard growled[, "]It's damn small for its age[."]

Other entries by Ella (Kelly) Boulter:

> Hen Hickey came from Miramichi with [an] anvil on his back, & [a] doz. qrts[.] of rum on his chest; By the time he got to Ty Creek[,] he had more weight on his back[.]
>
> Noreen Hickey & Mrs[.] Campbell [were] sisters[.]

> The mare is lame, the dog is lame, Kristy is lame, I'm lame. Hell of an outfit for a parish.

Peter Kaye went to Jarvis [with] a handful of religious tracts. The ram butted him. The papers scattered. Young Jarvis ran out & said[, "]Look at the ram spread the gospel.["]

Dick Merril[l] praying for the barrel of flour and his prayer [sentence leaves off] Lazy Merril[l] laid on floor & tapped on [the] flour barrel. When it was done, went to work[.] ["]The wives & wee ones do seem to be getting the upper hand[."]

Jilted Bride danced all night.

Murderer asks for Butcher knife back again[.]

Amos Jr. put 50¢ in [the] collection plate & coppers jumped out on the floor[.]

Sarah Terry from Wales married Thos Boulter. Fought with stepmother.

He saw a mop of hair. A minute later — came in view[.] Saying long grace & seeing the sheep, said[, "]Look at those god - -d sheep.["]

Bill Boulter getting kissed by Billy Reids[.]

[Lieutenant] Dugald Campbell['s] [(of the 42nd Highland Regiment)] son married jilted bridesmaid so the minister wouldn't be disappointed[.]

Mysie's Prayer. Lord preserve us from the witches & warlocks that roam about in the meadows, Be good to Jim, Lord[,] & may the price of cornmeal be $4.00 a barrel.

Ella (Kelly) Boulter has copied the following, more than likely, from a newspaper clipping:

> Drowned May 20[,] 1893
>
> In Memory of
> Allen E. Kelly
>
> In the cold arms of death my darling[']s
>   asleep
> Away on the brow of yon hill
> Yet still in my fancy I hear

    his sweet voice
And his spirit comes to me at will[.]

Oh Sad was the fate of my beautiful
    boy
The joy of a fond mother[']s heart
He was comely in life, & lovely
    in death
Naught else could
    have forced us to part[.]

The ice on the Nashwaak will
    melt in the spring
Bringing joy to heart of the swain
The trees on the banks their
    rich foliage will yield
But my darling will ne'r
    come again[.]

T'was up near the Narrows
    a twelve month ago
Since the water rolled over his
    head
Yet still those weird voices sound
    fresh in my ear
Saying Mother your darling is dead[.]

The pride of his father his
    dear sisters['] joy
Has gone to his Haven of rest
And there in the Presence of
    Jesus our King
He sings the sweet songs of the Blest[.]

No sin can molest him or
    trouble annoy
He is freed from all sorrow &
    pain
In the heaven above, there is
    nothing but love
For they sing of the Lamb
    that was slain.

Now rest lovely darling in
    thy narrow bed
While we wait till the signal
    is given
To go over there, all the glory
    to share
With our Allen in yonder bright
    Heaven.

Oh yes we shall meet him
    for Jesus will come
And take us away to His Home
Over there with the saints
    & Prophets of old
Together in Eden we'll roam.

R. A.

Ella (Kelly) Boulter has added: "Robert Ashfield — a tailor in Stanley. Ashfield or Ashford?" Robert Ashfield or Ashford doesn't appear in the Vital Statistics at the *Provincial Archives of New Brunswick*, but an Alberta May Ashfield, daughter of James and Jane (McCrae) Ashfield, is listed as being born at North Tay on 1 January 1886. (*Schedule A. York Births.*)

A diligent search through the *Provincial Archives of New Brunswick*, Daniel F. Johnson: *New Brunswick Newspaper Vital Statistics* has proven futile in turning up a copy of this poem.

The below series of articles, contained in the *Provincial Archives of New Brunswick*, Daniel F. Johnson: *New Brunswick Newspaper Vital Statistics*, appeared in the New Brunswick newspapers at the time of Allen E. Kelly's death.

The Daily Sun, 22 May 1893: "Stanley (York Co.) May 21 — Allen KELLY, eldest s/o John KELLY of Stanley was drowned yesterday at the Narrows on Alexander Gibson's drive. The body has not yet been recovered." (Volume 90, Number 266)

The Gleaner, 22 May 1893: "Allen KELLY, about 20 years of age, only s/o John KELLY of Stanley (York Co.) was drowned at the Narrows on the Nashwaak Saturday. Mr. Kelly was working on Mr. Gibson's drive. He was engaged with other men at breaking a jam of logs, When the break occurred the men ran for safety. Kelly either did not see the jam break, or for some other reason was unable to get away from danger, for when the men looked behind for him, he was not to be seen. He had evidently been struck with the swift running logs and stunned. The body was recovered last eve. Deceased was a nephew of M. KELLY of Stone Boot. The funeral takes place at Stanley tomorrow afternoon." (Volume 86, Number 334)

The Gleaner, 23 May 1893: "Nashwaak (York Co.) — The sad news reached us yesterday morn. Sunday that Allen KELLY of Ward Settlement was drowned while working on a jam at the Narrows on the Nashwaaak drive. Kelly was 22 years of age." (Volume 86, Number 336)

New Brunswick Reporter and Fredericton Advertiser, 24 May 1893: "Allan KELLY, eldest s/o John KELLY of Stanley (York Co.) was drowned Saturday at the Narrows on Alexander Gibson's drive, Naswaak." (Volume 85, Number 2573)

In a diagram of the Loyalist John Kelly family tree created by Ella Rita (Kelly) Boulter, provided by her daughter Jeannie Belinda (Boulter) Matthews, Ella Rita (Kelly) Boulter states that Allen E. Kelly "drowned at Hell's Gate on [the] Nashwaak River[.]"

Allen E. Kelly (1871 - 20 May 1893) was the son of John Henry (20 March 1839 - 7 September 1934) and Eliza Levis (Scott) Kelly (11 March 1847 - 2 January 1930).

The following is a transcription of a newspaper clipping (unidentified and undated newspaper) from the Robert Kelly family collection. Arthur Cleveland Kelly (9 February 1886 - 1 May 1963) and Harold Kelly (? - 25 November 1916) were the sons of Robert Kelly (22 June 1846 - 7 July 1937) and Ella Rebecca (Merrill) Kelly (August 1855 - 3 February 1922).

LIEUT. A. C. KELLY HOME ON LEAVE

Went Over With the Old 12th Battalion — Wounded at Battle of Vimy Ridge.

Among the guests at the Queen Hotel today is Lieut. A. C. Kelly, of Stanley, who arrived in the city this morning from Halifax, where he landed on Saturday from England.

Lieut. Kelly was a lieutenant in the old 71st Regiment, C company, and for many years was among those who attended camp at Sussex. At the outbreak of the war he was among the first to volunteer his services and he was attached to the 12th Battalion and went overseas with the old 12th under Lieut. Col. H. F. McLeod. He was through the battle of Vimy Ridge and was wounded on April 28th[, 1917]. He was taken to England and placed in the hospital of the Hon. Mrs. Rupert Beckett, at London. He speaks very highly of the treatment he received while in hospital. He is home on furlough and will leave this evening for his old home in Stanley.

Lieut. Kelly had another brother at the front with the 72nd Battalion. He made the supreme sacrifice on Nov. 25th, at the Battle of the Somme.

The following, included in Ella Rita (Kelly) Boulter's notebook given to Darrell McBreairty by her daughter, Jeannie Belinda (Boulter) Matthews, on 3 October 2014, is a sketch Ella Rita (Kelly) Boulter wrote:

As I pick up & sort my son's comic books, my mind strays to my own childhood reading. How I loved & enjoyed the fine stories. I recall the first acquaintance with "Anne of Green Gables." An English lady I knew, always saved all papers & magazines, & stored them away. . . . One day she gave me an enormous pile of papers[.] I ran home with my precious booty & there on this old *Family Herald* & *Weekly Star* began the said "Anne of Green Gables," such large pages — & I devoured them eagerly. I laughed & cried & lived with Anne. The cold prairie winds howled, & so did coyotes, but snuggled down by the stove, I read on, transported into another world. I acquired the nicely bound book later, but I'll never savor a story again with such relish as I did "Anne" on the pages of the long treasured[,] ancient *Family Herald*.

To a lonely little girl[,] on [a] prairie homestead[,] books meant so much — & my mother[']s stories told in her Irish lilting voice meant so much more. She was a strict Presbyterian & read me the Bible beginning when I was very young. "Mama read me Begats & Begats[,]" I would beg, as I snuggled in my warm covers — and across the years I hear — "Abraham begat Isaac & Isaac begat Jacob & Jacob begat Judas & his brethren["] — & on & on, and as I was caught up in fluffy clouds of sleep — the low lilting voice came to me — ["]and Jesse begat David the king, and David the king begat["] — Years ago[,] but it seems only yesterday[.]

Of course she told me stories every night — about the little people in Ireland & of the fairies who danced in rings in the forests.

Then came my day I had a son & I could hardly wait to start telling him these wonderful stories. Perhaps I did not have my mother's art in telling the magical stories or perhaps my son had a more practical turn of mind. "I searched all morning in the bushes looking for the fairies ring made by their little feet[,] & I couldn't find any[,]" he announced importantly stumping into the room. "Can I really see fairies[,] Mum?" "No dear[,"] I assured him, ["]just the people whose eyebrows meet can see fairies."

In a day or two — my husband's family came to call, & with them my husband[']s cousin[,] a blushing bride & her husband. All went well until I noticed my boy looking at the new member of the clan with a most peculiar, fixed stare. I followed his blue gaze[,] & I was transfixed! The newest relative had heavy[,] black eyebrows meeting squarely across his nose!

I fairly panicked, because my husband[']s people are good fine practical people, but who would certainly disapprove of telling any child such fanciful nonsense about fairies or one[']s ability to see such creatures. Thank heaven my boy was a shy child, but as I watched from the corner of my eye, as he maneuvered from one side to another to view the stranger, I was in mortal dread he would forget his shyness & pipe out "Can you really see fairies[?"]

Well he didn't, they finally went away, & I dropped in a chair to relax & listen to his questions. T[']was then I told him, all, & I expected him to be disappointed[,] but he merely sniffed & said[,] "I didn't believe that stuff anyway[;]" & now[,] after ~~twelve~~ years passed[,] I have a baby girl — Shall I tell her about fairies & little People? Time will only tell.

Ella Rita (Kelly) Boulter (14 October 1914 – 25 May 1988), daughter of William Leonard (6 August 1883 - ? December 1918) and Marjorie (Hayes) Kelly (5 December 1885 - 1950), was married to William Boulter (23 May 1915 – 8 November 1979); their children were David Boulter (3 November 1943 – 31 March 2009) and Jeannie Belinda (Boulter) Matthews. The visiting newlyweds were Douglas (23 October 1925 – 21 February 2004) and Mary (Douglass) Wortman.

Margaret (Kelly) Hay Material

In regard to William McKay Kelly (15 October 1849 - 27 September 1926), Margaret (Kelly) Hay writes:

Will was a tall (6') skinny man with rugged, severe features on a non-smiling face partially covered by his large handle-barred mustache. A lumberman foreman job took Will each winter into the New Brunswick woods not to return until Spring. He was a crotchety miser of a man, salting away all his money from his winter's wages. Possibly went west to harvest wheat in the fall as did his son, Warren.

In 1908, they moved to Keswick to the farm on the hill now owned by Boone White. His son, Warren, (now 33) married and moved in with them here for about five years.

William hated luxuries including the new telephone which appeared in his home. He would never use it. On one occasion when he was alone and the phone rang continuously, he finally picked it up and yelled, "there ain't nobody here," and hung-up! He yelled a lot at the children and they seemed to be afraid of him. He would never allow his picture to be taken.

Warren wanted his father's farm on his return from World War I, but William was asking his son for more money for the farm than the neighbours farmers' prices; so Warren bought elsewhere. The Kellys spent a couple of winters with Warren and his family on Keswick Ridge; then moved to Kingsclear to the home of son Ellis. Here, William died in 1926 and was buried in the Anglican Cemetery there.

Margaret (Kelly) Hay:

William said of Vincent when baby was one month old, "what is it?"

When Pauline was three years old playing with a hoop in the yard, rolling it with a stick, William[,] wordlessly, grabbed the hoop and threw it in the manure.

One day some onions [were] drying on the veranda[.] William kicked them off into the yard. His wife, Margaret[,] scolded him, so William went and stood under a drip which was pouring off the veranda from a rainstorm[.] [H]e apparently stayed there hoping someone would tell him to come in. They didn't!

Margaret (Kelly) Hay wrote the following about her great-grandmother:

Great-Grandmother Margaret (Scott) Kelly 1855-1931

Margaret, my namesake, was a tiny woman, barely 5 feet and weighing less than 100 pounds. She had long, natural curly hair. This daughter of Robert Scott of Stanley married William and became a typical, resourceful pioneer wife. She spent her winters alone in their small cabin, while William worked at a lumber camp. Many hours passed spinning and knitting the wool shorn from their sheep into socks, mitts and long underwear for William's next winter in the woods. To provide a few extras, Margaret raised a few hens and turkeys for sale. This helped to make their home the rather well furnished place it was, despite William's miserliness. She was a woman of ready wit and humor. This allowed her to laugh at William's moods and anger. Once Will came home unexpectedly in the night. She heard the noise and prepared her axe, telling the chore boy to open the door when she gave the signal. Luckily[,] William spoke before the axe fell.

One winter the black diphtheria struck (1882) and Margaret watched two of her babies die. Myles at 2, Minnie at 1. Four-year-old Warren fell to the plague too, but in desperation at losing another child, she stuck her knitting needle down this throat[,] breaking the abscess so he could breathe again[,] and this saved his life.

Her niece Gertrude recalls her as a lady full of fun. She loved children. Before Easter [she] would tell them, "If we get up early on Easter Sunday we can see the sun dance."

She believed in fairness. When her son Warren and friend Jimmie Howe got into mischief at school, Warren was punished and not Jimmie because his sister was the teacher. Margaret was definitely not pleased. Warren had his left hand severely hit[,] trying to force him to be right handed.

Her granddaughter Mary, Warren's oldest, remembered her fondly as being extremely kind, patient and tolerant with children. She loved the song "When You and I Were Young, Maggie" and said she hoped they'd play it at her funeral. Mary remembers sitting beside her at William's funeral and looking at the open coffin[,] whispering, "He can't roar at us now[,] Mary, can he?"

Margaret spent her last years with [her] son Ellis in Springhill. She died and was buried in St. Peter's Anglican Cemetery there.

Margaret (Kelly) Hay, writing about her Grandfather, Charles Warren "Warren" Kelly (28 May 1875 – 8 March 1953), quotes him as saying, "If you have a roof over your head, food on the table, a bed to sleep in; what more could you ask for?"

Margaret (Kelly) Hay:

My grandfather (Papa) Charles Warren (called Warren) was born in a cabin that no longer exists on the Irish Town Road near Stanley, NB. He worked hard as a chore boy at home especially during the winter when his father was away working in the woods. At eight, he nearly died of diphtheria (see story on his mother, Margaret). Not much has been passed on of Papa's early days, but as a young man, he did work on the log drives on the Nashwaak River[,] learning to be agile-footed, jumping from log to log on the moving river waters. He was also a good singer (shared with his niece Gertrude Gould).

He always had a yearning to travel — an itchy foot[,] which he passed on to several grandchildren, myself included. In his 20s, he made at least one trip west on the CNR to help in the prairie wheat harvest. On one occasion, he told of going through places called Medicine Hat, Crowsnest Pass, Cranbrook and on to Vancouver to visit a cousin, Mary Wade (Scott, his aunt) who was a book-keeper for a lumber company. He settled in Cranbrook for a year or so[,] working for a bachelor dairy farmer. The man wanted him to stay and if he did, his employer would have willed the farm to him, but Papa Kelly went back east and moved from Stanley to Keswick with his parents while he was in his early 30s.

Warren was not a tall man, perhaps 5' 7" and weighed about 138 pounds. He always walked very straight, had a flashing, warm smile and a ready-wit[,] which he inherited from his mother. "Unpredictable" was the word niece Gertrude used to describe him.

In 1911, he married Susie Dunphy and then rented the old Mann House (Mary was born) for a time; then he moved in with the Dunphys working for Susie's father. Here[,] two children were born, Percy and Fred (my father). Warren continued to farm for his father-in-law and father, moving his family into his parents['] home in 1917 before signing-up for World War

I. With his spirit for adventure, love of travel, it isn't surprising Papa signed up for action. His years in Europe never got him to the front because of a respiratory infection, so he served as a mess-cook in England. They could hear the guns in France, he said. He visited Ireland and Scotland and would spin yarns from his army days for the rest of his life. He loved people and was the life of the party — storytelling, dancing (early days), playing the mouth organ, and playing practical jokes.

Fred remembers a February morning in 1919 when they all bundled-up and travelled in sleds over the snow banks to Keswick Station to meet his father coming home. His love of the military life surfaced in the months to follow as he taught his boys judo-holds, army drills, and war games in the evening playtime. Fred was three, Percy — five, and Mary — seven.

Ada was born in the Kelly homestead when Papa went overseas. The grandparents lived upstairs[,] and Susie and the children lived down. On his return from the army, Papa took his family to Burton (near airport) to work for a fruit-farmer. Judge Slipp was the owner. Grandma ran the house, cooking and keeping boarders. During this experience, they had a one-roomer (a suspicious character) who lived secretly in the attic. One day he missed his footing and his leg plunged through the kitchen ceiling where Nana (my grandmother) was working. He was told to leave[,] but they found literature, radio equipment[,] which suggested he had communist leanings.

Papa intended to buy his father's place at Keswick, but it didn't work out[,] so Warren, Susie and 4 children bought the Ridge farm where their son Fred lives today. It was once owned by Millard Reid from Marysville[,] and the people renting it were Birds. They were a large family and had not been able to meet the house payments, so were burning the furniture and even the walls were being torn down for firewood. To start off his new farm, Papa bought two cows, two horses; Sam and Frank, from the Dunphy family, and hens, sheep and some farm machinery from Papa's war savings. Then came the task of eking-out a living on rocky, hilly, poor soil. Twice each year the mortgage payments came due, in the amount of $43.00. This was always a worry as no-one knew where the money was going to come from[,] especially the March payment. Usually, the money was made from selling potatoes at the train station or selling or trading butter, milk and eggs at Len Yerxa's store (now Alonzo Pickard's house).

Jack, Margaret and Annie were born here in Keswick Ridge. Now seven children in the family.

Warren's parents sold the farm at Keswick and bought the larger farm with an orchard in Springhill. Their son, Ellis, was managing the farm. When Great-Grandfather William died in 1922, Great-Grandmother gave

Warren the money from his father's savings to pay off the mortgage. Now the farm on Keswick Ridge belonged to the Kellys.

Farming was never Papa's strength. He loved the woods, meeting people, reading books. He read his Bible every night, but was never a church attender. With his free spirit for adventure, he would often take-off without telling anyone and walk through the woods to Stanley, Fredericton, etc., visit someone and then walk back home. Equally frustrating, said his wife and son Fred, would be when he and his son Percy would quit farming about 3 o'clock and go-off hunting when there was more work to be done. Papa was a "charmer," but not a "farmer."

His love for hunting was more for the hunt than the kill. His love for the forest made him say often, ["]there is where I want to die." Nana would scoff, "then all the neighbours would have to go and hunt for you." In later years, he'd go on fall hunting trips with Fred Coburn, Douglas Gordon and Gordon Grant. He didn't hunt much, would cook meals, and have them rolling with laughter at his jokes and stories.

When Fred was 23[,] he basically took over the farm and brought his wife, Mary Coburn, to live in the Kelly home. Mary recalls her days as a new bride was made much more pleasant by Warren's jokes helping to relieve the tension. Examples of this were putting pepper on the stove and then falling down dead in a sneezing-fit; putting bullets on the stove and watching the women scream; pretending he was a wild animal covering himself in an old fur coat and crawling around outside in the dark[,] making grunt-noises like a bear; tearing downstairs in his nightshirt (no pants)[,] gun in-hand[,] when raccoons raided the chicken house.

During World War II, Papa wanted to sign-up again. He lied about his age, got his immunization shots[,] which nearly killed him, but ended-up as a janitor at the ammunition storage headquarters in McGivney. It was 1943 and the coldest winter ever. All slept downstairs[,] but still the chamber-pots froze at night. Another year, he took the bid for janitor at the school for $6.00/year.

In an email of 4 May 2015, Margaret (Kelly) Hay added that during World War II when her grandfather, who "was too old for active duty[,] . . . tried to enlist at McGivney Station, with his false teeth in his pocket (he hated them), the officer said, 'You are not able to enlist. You don't even have your teeth.' Papa Warren spoke up indignantly, 'I don't want to bite the Germans. I want to fight them'!"

In the same email, Margaret (Kelly) Hay added the following anecdotes about her grandfather:

> He loved practical jokes: His wife Susie has the church ladies over for a sedate gathering in the living room. Warren puts pepper on the stove in

the kitchen. The ladies all start to sneeze. Even a border in the upstairs bedroom starts sneezing. All feel they are taking a cold.

He made a dummy and put it in his bed, even to having boots sticking out the end. Nana goes up and gets a real start seeing a man in her bed . . . perhaps a tramp!

His character was exemplified by his red stocking wool cap with a tassel. Also his rubber boots with one pant leg rolled up and the other tucked in.

Another occasion Papa pulled a bullet from his pocket, opens the lid of the stove saying "things are so bad I might as well end it all." Of course he only pretended to throw it in. But Nana yells, "God have mercy!"

From Margaret (Kelly) Hay's original notes:

As grandchildren entered the house, Papa was indispensable. As my mother Mary worked, he would rock us in the old rocking chair by the shed-door, read books to us, help dry the dishes (always leaving for a visit to the outdoor toilet when the utensils arrived).

When I (Margaret, second born to Fred and Mary) entered the world, it was in the Kelly parlour. Apparently, it was a difficult delivery, so at birth I was speedily taken to the kitchen and thrown into my grandfather's lap on the couch, while all attention turned towards my mother. From that moment on, Papa and I had a special bond which none of the other children could claim. Nana would often say, "Warren, you shouldn't have favourites." He would reply, "Yes, I know, but she seems more mine." He would swing me by the hour at the old russet apple-tree swing (halfway to the road), buy me something when he went to town (a skipping rope), coddle me when I got spanked, build kindling-stick log-cabins on the kitchen floor, whittle spool tops and willow whistles, give me his favourite candy — wintergreens and peppermints. (Carol, my sister, got the latter, I hated them.) He had that extra time and patience to teach me — tying knots, play hide-the-button, or let me read to him — making up the words long before I was able to read.

His good humour made him a great tease. Carol got the brunt of that more than I did. At a Springtime event, Papa did his annual search for the delicate pink-twin flowers — only he seemed to know where to find them.

Papa longed for a grandson to teach his skills of the wood to, but when my mother brought home Brian in March 1951, she put him in Papa's arms and said, "Here's your first grandson." He replied, "I'm afraid I won't be able to really enjoy him." He died at home in the bedroom beside the parlour with his wife nursing him to the end in March 1953. (From May to

August, 1951, he was in the Veterans' hospital in St. John, NB, after several strokes.)

www.ingramcontent.com/pod-product-compliance
Lightning Source LLC
Chambersburg PA
CBHW060307240426
43661CB00059B/2681